Scribble,
Scribble,
Scribble

Scribble, Scribble, Scribble

Writings on Ice Cream,

Obama, Churchill

and My Mother

SIMON SCHAMA

THE BODLEY HEAD
LONDON

THE BODLEY HEAD
LONDON

Published by The Bodley Head 2010

2 4 6 8 10 9 7 5 3 1

First published in Great Britain in 2010 by
The Bodley Head
Random House, 20 Vauxhall Bridge Road,
London SW1V 2SA

www.bodleyhead.co.uk
www.rbooks.co.uk

Addresses for companies within The Random House Group Limited can be found at:
www.randomhouse.co.uk/offices.htm

The Random House Group Limited Reg. No. 954009

A CIP catalogue record for this book
is available from the British Library

ISBN 9781847921314

The Random House Group Limited supports The Forest Stewardship
Council (FSC), the leading international forest certification organisation. All our titles that
are printed on Greenpeace approved FSC certified paper carry the FSC logo. Our paper
procurement policy can be found at www.rbooks.co.uk/environment

Mixed Sources
Product group from well-managed
forests and other controlled sources
www.fsc.org Cert no. TT-COC-2139
© 1996 Forest Stewardship Council
FSC

Typeset by Palimpsest Book Production Limited,
Falkirk, Stirlingshire FK2 9EG

Printed and bound in Great Britain by
Clays Ltd, St Ives PLC

To my editors, with gratitude

Another damned, thick, square book! Always scribble, scribble, scribble! Eh! Mr Gibbon?

The Duke of Gloucester to Edward Gibbon

Contents

List of Illustrations

6. Pablo Picasso, 1881–1973, *'Ecce Homo', After Rembrandt* from *Suite 156*, 1970. (Etching and aquatint; plate: 49.5 x 41 cm, sheet: 68.1 x 56.7 cm; Tate Gallery, London; © Succession Picasso/DACS 2010)

7. *Picasso At Work*, c. 1970. (Hulton Archive; © photo by Keystone/Getty Images)

8. Anselm Kiefer, b.1945, *Karfunkelfee*, 2009. (Gold paint, cloak, brambles, acrylic, oil, emulsion, ash and shellac on canvas in steel and glass frame; 382 x 576 x 35 cm; © Anselm Kiefer; © photo: Charles Duprat; Courtesy White Cube)

9. Anselm Kiefer, b.1945, *Shevirath Ha Kelim*, 2009. (Terracotta, acrylic, oil and shellac on canvas; 330 x 760 x 1300 cm; © Anselm Kiefer; © photo: Charles Duprat; Courtesy White Cube)

10. John Virtue, *Landscape No. 711*, 2003-4. (Acrylic, black ink and shellac on canvas; 350 x 732 cm; © John Virtue)

11. Donald Rumsfeld, Secretary of Defense, Washington, D.C., May 7, 1976. From *The Family*, a portfolio of 69 portraits. Photograph by Richard Avedon © The Richard Avedon Foundation

Scribble, Scribble, Scribble

Introduction

I have two styles of writing, anal and loopy, both adopted in slavish but futile imitation of models who used a fountain pen as though they had been born with one in their hands. I had not. My primary-school exercise books, an Abstract Expressionist field of blots and stains, looked as though the nib had wet itself on to the page rather than been purposefully guided over the paper to form actual words. And yet I loved – and still do – the purchase the metal makes on paper, and can't begin a chapter or a script or a newspaper piece without first reaching for a fountain pen and notebook. I scribble, therefore I am.

At university I thought my bizarre handwriting – more or less the calligraphic equivalent of Tourette's Syndrome, disfigured by ejaculatory whiplashes above the line – ought to submit itself to a sterner form that might attest to my arrival at an Age of Reason. So I strove for a version of the professor's hand when he corrected my essays. This was a backward-leaning row of indentations and projections: a Cambridge minuscule. The letters rose, as if they were unsure about the worthwhileness of the effort involved, a bare millimetre from flat-line horizontal and had a tightness that I thought conveyed densely packed critical power. In the professorial hand the little ts and ds were barbs on a high-voltage wire and they snagged you with small, piercing lunges of pain. 'This paragraph five times as long as it needs to be,' the hand said, or 'Do you *ever* tire of adjectives?' My chastening superego, such as it was, reached for mastery of an economic style, but the unmannerly slob of id lurked to foul its plans. So my version of the professor's writing resembled the secretion of a crippled ant, one leg dragging behind the body as it crept from left to right across the page.

But this is still the hand I use, involuntarily, when correcting the work of my own students, or printed drafts of my own. Sometimes, the students beg me to decode a completely illegible set of comments, but I reckon that decipherment is part of their educational challenge. Hell, it did *me* no harm.

'Do you know,' chuckled the girlfriend from the 1970s, a queen of the nib, waving a page of my fractured minuscule – written, I blush to recall, in green ink – 'I had *no* idea until you wrote me that note, that I was going out with a serial killer! Of course I could be wrong,' she added, flashing me one of her fine-boned sardonic smiles, 'you might just be a paranoid schizophrenic.' It wasn't her forensic diagnosis of my handwriting that stung, it was the merry way she laughed whenever she saw it, as if no one in their right mind could be expected to bother, except clinically. For our relationship to prosper, I realised I would have to make my hand lean in the opposite direction, with a degree of forwardness that testified to my ardour. On the other hand, it could not be a servile imitation of her own elegantly oblique manner, penned with long white fingers, for that would seem offputtingly craven, a bit like calligraphic cross-dressing. But wasn't I the yid with the id?

So I just let it out of the kennel to see what it could do, and thus was born that wowser of a hand: loopy, big, brash, vauntingly cursive, and often entirely out of control. Loopy is to my writing what fox is to hedgehog, Tigger is to Eeyore, Bugs is to Elmer, Rabelais to Montaigne, Björk to Coldplay. Loopy bounds and leaps and lurches and can't *wait* to get to the end of the line because – gee, gosh, boy oh boy – there's *another* line to fill, and omigod, a whole half-*page* waiting just for me to do my thing all over it. Loopy will not be confined. Loopy's hs snake skywards like a fly-fisher's line, the tails of Loopy's fs and gs and ys drop deep into the pond, Loopy frisks and gambols, Loopy jives, Loopy got da mojo, Loopy LIVES! And people – well, some people – tell me they can actually read it. Or so the nice ladies in the Burlington Arcade pretend when they watch me try out another antique Swan or Parker 51. Of course it could be in their interest to keep their smile of disbelief to themselves as Loopy goes for a test run on their scratch-pads, but they're usually called Heather so, what the hell, I trust them. And the queen of the nib? Oh, she was tickled.

And so it has been – well before my encounter with, let's call her Italica – that the call of Loopy moved me instinctively towards a kind of writing that was driven by the pleasure principle, or at least danced to a different drummer than Carefully Considered Academic Analysis. That beat is called journalism and I have always, unapologetically, enjoyed committing it. Most of the pieces collected in this book were written for the many newspapers and magazines generous enough to indulge my habit and actually pay me for the exercise. (My first book review was for the venerable *Saturday Evening Post* and I got paid $25.) A few of the lengthier, more spaciously considered pieces – catalogue essays, the occasional lecture, book reviews – made the cut if they retained something of the nervous tingle of the moment, even if the high-wire act was performed in front of an audience rather than exacting editors and their readers. In some ways the title of this collection could not be less apt, for the joke of the Duke of Gloucester's breezy enquiry at what Gibbon might be up to is comical only when one registers the pains and time it took the historian to produce every baroquely rolling sentence of his masterpiece. In that sense the pieces here are most unGibbonish, written on the fly (though after much thought): capers and flourishes that try to share the passion – whether enthusiasm or grief – for their subjects. If they were not always hot off the press, they were often hot from my head.

But then I got the hot-metal romance early. I wasn't even out of grey flannel short trousers and snake belt when our class got taken to Fleet Street some time in the mid-1950s. The *Daily Mirror* had it all, I thought: shrivelled trolls with the right kind of fungal pallor, chained to machines that chattered out type; trays of set pages; even the occasional green eyeshade; the whole wizard's den culminating in sheets of raw newsprint cascading into bins. Was there ever a headier bouquet – cheap cigarettes and printers' ink? They had to drag me back to the school coach.

Paradise got postponed. I signed up as soon as I could for the secondary-school magazine, but it was a prim production called *The Skylark*, bound in air-force-blue paper and featuring deadly reports on the doings of the school hockey team interspersed with juvenile odes to the Grampians. The paper signified the sky part, I supposed, but I was more interested in the lark. I got it when the school librarian, the son of a Labour MP, got busy with a subversive publication, printed clandestinely in the art rooms after school. Called *Perspective*, like all lefty broadsides which didn't really have any, it railed gloriously against British policy in Cyprus and defended EOKA bombs and ambushes as legitimate self-defence. I was but a baby gofer to the sixth-form comrade editor whose extreme unfriendliness I took as a sign of iron political discipline, but I loved every minute of the transgression, stacking copies in the inner sanctum of the library office, unbeknownst to the kindly Latin teacher whom we were getting in the hottest of water. It was a tribute to our modest powers of circulation, I suppose, that at some point, men in pork-pie hats and raincoats (I swear) paid a visit to the headmaster and invoked, so we heard, the Official Secrets Act. While we were happy not to be expelled along with our mastermind, our reverence for his steely wickedness only intensified with the glamour of his indictment.

The first pieces I got published in a newspaper appeared in *The Jewish Chronicle*, where I was working to keep myself in winkle-pickers, as a cutter and paster in the library. But the real bonus was getting dates with the editor's curvy daughter, who in turn procured for me the occasional classical music review. From the beginning, then, journalism was a pleasure, the only snag being that I knew absolutely nothing about classical music, save the occasional well-intentioned lunchbreak tutorial from a schoolfriend who would lecture me about Bruckner and Shostakovich, which would have been instructive had I not been distracted by the fragments of amateurishly assembled egg-salad sandwich that clung gothically to his front teeth. But for this girl I was willing to learn and through careful study noticed, in the reviews of those who did actually know something about the subject, the recurrence of certain key terms: 'lyrical', 'stirring', 'sensitive', 'brilliant' and so on. Off I went with the date to Annie Fischer, David Oistrakh or the Amadeus Quartet and, back home, more or less randomly assembled the adjectives in plausible order. You would be amazed how often they coincided with the professional notices.

At Cambridge my precocious knack for hackery found the perfect outlet, not in the classic *Varsity*, which seemed to me dominated by public-school oligarchs who said '*yaar*' indicating 'yes', while actually meaning 'not on your fucking life, sunshine'. 'Hey, could I have a job at *Varsity*?' 'Well, *yaar*.' So my friends and I peeled off to found a rival paper, called with unoriginal optimism: *New Cambridge*. I wrote, I edited a bit, I loved the picador thrusts at the opposition rag and chewed lustily on a pipe like Charles Foster Kane. On the side, my mate Martin Sorrell – the financial brains of our publishing duo – overran a glossy magazine that high-mindedly devoted itself to a single issue per issue: the state of British prisons in Michaelmas term, the state of British art in Lent. With authentically undergraduate lack of irony, it called itself *Cambridge Opinion*, and unsold towers of it were stashed in a mysterious cavity in the rooms of the amiable anthropologist Edmund Leach, who was even more chaotic than the editor (yours truly) and treated its unique combination of unsellability and pretentiousness as a tremendous hoot. Martin and I would get a sudden order for five copies of *British Art: The Future* from the Whitechapel Gallery, would scoot over to Leach's lair and attempt to extract them from his cupboard. One or other of us would disappear within its shadowy depths, sometimes torch in hand, but inevitably fail to find the missing numbers. Meanwhile, Leach's fireplace burned with suspicious brilliance. 'You wouldn't know where they might be, Dr Leach, would you?' we would ask. 'Oh no,' he would chortle, 'behind *Africa Today* possibly? Have another glass.'

Towards the end of our last year, another prolifically literary pal, Robert Lacey, won an essay competition orchestrated by the *Sunday Times* as an exercise in talent-scouting. Robert's prize was a job on the paper, then edited by Harold Evans in his sensational (but not sensationalist) prime. It was the moment when the paper took the daring step of inventing what was then called a 'colour supplement' that could include nifty advice on the best years for St-Emilion along with harrowing Don McCullin pictures of the war in Vietnam. The cheerful and, at that time, almost spherical Godfrey Smith presided over this minicolony of the paper where Robert had his desk. From one of their shrewd brains came the notion that a drop in summer sales might be countered by an ongoing series of Educational Value that readers might be induced to collect, week by week, and then assemble in their very own black plastic binder. It was to be called *A Thousand Makers of the Twentieth Century*, each micro-biography running to a few hundred words, whether the subject was Rasputin or Rommel, Pétain or Picasso. (Space allowances were made for the outsize monsters of history. Hitler must have got 800.) Organised alphabetically, it began naturally with Alvar Aalto and ended (I think) with Zog of Albania. Lacey was a hotshot editor and, being the good egg he was and is, sublet some of the work to his mates languishing in tutorial chores back in the Fens.

So I did Nazis and Dutch persons (though not Dutch Nazis) and would make trips down to the Gray's Inn Road, lurking ecstatically amidst the journalists' desks until they noticed me and even gave me the occasional reporter's chore. I was in hack heaven.

Thousand Makers was just crazy enough to succeed. Punters bought their black plastic binders by the crateload. We were a big hit and I learned something about conciseness, with which the Schama style had not hitherto been much associated. Communiqués of delight came down from On High, the office of Roy, the First Baron Thomson of Fleet. What also came down one day was an enquiry about who was going to be penning the item on the Queen. Somehow the royal name had gone unaccountably missing from our lengthy list of twentieth-century Makers. What, I thought, had she made? People happy? On the whole, tick, but what could be said about that? The TV monarchy? There was an idea. I wrote round the Usual Suspects, but no takers, so it fell to muggins, being the lowest on the totem pole. Off went something about the televised coronation, but with the faintest, merest hint that the royal round of Commonwealth ceremonies were not invariably a day at the beach (or gymkhana). Harrumphing sounds were heard from Above to the effect that something more entirely reverential was called for. The writers of *Makers*, including the doughty Godfrey, stood by my piece, but at the last minute an editorial courtier broke ranks and produced a piece of unexceptional flattery. Someone, though, leaked the story to *Private Eye*, which ran the pieces – Establishment and Not – side by side. I was, inadvertently, the custodian of integrity. But as Isaiah Berlin used to say, just because the honours that come one's way may be richly undeserved doesn't mean to say we won't take them.

I'd had my tiny taste of trouble and I wanted much more, especially since for most of the working week I was having to behave myself as a history don, dishing out anything from Abelard to Adlai Stevenson to my student victims. It wasn't the pay – £800 a year and all the Amontillado I could drink – that kept me down on the farm. I was hooked on history and would stay that way. But I needed my journalism jag too, so in between moonlighting in London and supervising in College I took on the editing of the weekly academic magazine, *The Cambridge Review*. This had been the closest a journal could get to sherry and still be made of paper. But it had been going for nearly eighty years, and now and then its pages would make room for the likes of Bertrand Russell or Sylvia Plath. It was, as everyone pointed out, An Institution. Which of course made it a prime target for the Furies who were very much at large in 1968. I had two colleagues in the editorial hot seat, both American, one Marxist, one an economist who would later make serious money. I was the wet liberal centrist in between, but most of all I wanted the *Review* to mix things up a bit. There was tear gas on the boulevards (I got a whiff of it one day in Montparnasse). Imagination had been declared by Jean-Louis Barrault to be *en pouvoir*, and in Cambridge Situationists were making silly buggers of themselves in the Senate House, along with more serious sitters-in who had the fantastic notion that some sort of academic democracy might be *en pouvoir* on King's Parade. It was absurd, but it made for fabulous copy and we dished it up, the covers of the magazine being black modernist designs on dark red and blue. Moody! Not exactly what the dons were expecting, but never mind, I hired pals like Clive James to do reviews and attempted to hold the sententiousness of my American co-editors somewhat at bay. Every week saw a panicky rendezvous with the composing printer round the corner and some heavy imbibing after we put it to bed.

A year or so later, the Revolution in the Fens but a heady memory, we dreamed up the idea of an anthology of some of the best writing over the life of the *Review* and, to our amazement, Jonathan Cape agreed to publish it. Out it came in 1972, bejacketed in a peculiar shade of pink (more or less my politics), grandly entitled *The Cambridge Mind*. Though we had pieces by examples of the most rarefied regions of the Cantabrigian medulla – G. E. Moore, J. J. Thompson, William Empson – I knew this was asking for trouble of the chucklesome kind, but I was outvoted by my more serious colleagues and collaborated in an introduction of numbing loftiness. The anthology was reviewed, rather kindly, by Hugh Trevor-Roper, who pointed out that *The Oxford Magazine* had published a similar anthology some time before called *The Oxford Sausage*. The difference in titles, he implied, with that thin literary smirk he assumed at moments of intense self-amusement, was all you needed to know. In private I knew he was right.

There followed the years of Rain in The Hague: gallons of it streaming down the windows of the old National Archive where I endured a lonely research vigil, thinking – a lot – about one of my best friends who had decided to do his research in Venice. Whenever I could I hightailed it to Amsterdam, then in the throes of stupendous cultural uproar, a non-stop porno-dope-anarcho-rock-and-roll madness. Major publications were called things like *Suck* and knew, it is fair to say, even by the standards of the time, no bounds. In a disused church a coagulated jam of bodies swayed (dancing was physically impossible) to violent music, while lava-lamp blobs oiled their way over a huge screen where once an altar had stood. Limbs became confused, and then the rest of us. Back in Cambridge, Lawrence Stone was contrasting the slow historical evolution of sex and marriage with the outbreak of what he called, smiling merrily (and quoting *that* line of Philip Larkin's), 'polymorphous sexuality'. In Amsterdam I knew what he meant.

As I slowly and painfully assembled the source materials for my first book, Carlyle's phantasmagoric vision of the archive as an interminable coral reef stretching away as far as could be imagined often appeared before me. The danger of drowning was real. So, more than ever, I needed to surface and get a hit of oxygenated journalism. Kindly, clever John Gross came to my aid with assignments to write about art for the *TLS*, and lots of hospitable editors followed – at *New Society*, Tony Elliott at the young *Time Out* (which was decent of him since I'd been part of the gang that tried to compete with him with a Richard Neville publication, *Ink*, a gloriously stoned and thus inevitably short-lived affair). After my first book appeared in 1977, to mostly positive reviews, editors on both sides of the Atlantic began commissioning pieces, which I turned in always on time and always overwritten, both length-wise and adjective-wise.

I have been lucky ever since; more than most, I think, in the generosity with which editors of all styles and philosophies have let me run around, not just in history, art and politics – the fields in which I graze in my book-length scholarly life – but in other departments of enthusiasm: music, film, theatre and, the writing which is simultaneously most challenging and most rewarding, words about food. Cooks – at least those who don't have to sweat it for a living – will tell you that the whole business is about the delivery of pleasure; the sampling of that lovely moment when, if one has done fairly well, even the most garrulous company will fall silent after a bite or two and get lost in delight. This salmagundi – a thing of various tastes and textures – is likewise offered to my readers in a similar hope that some of it, at least, might go down a treat.

Travelling

Sail Away: Six Days to New York on the *Queen Mary 2*

New Yorker, 31 May 2004

Overlooked — literally — by the seventeen-deck *Queen Mary 2*, as she slid into her berth at Pier 92 on 22 April 2004, was the dead white bird. Laid out on its funeral barge beside the USS *Intrepid*, as flightless and obsolete as the dodo, Concorde wasn't going anywhere. The sleek dream of supersonic speed, the princess of whoosh, which got you there before you'd started, was now, officially, a museum piece. The future — as the mayoral bloviations greeting the ship's midtown docking affirmed — belonged to 150,000 tons of steel capable of grinding through the ocean at all of thirty knots (that's around thirty-five m.p.h. to you landlubbers). The latest and most massive of the transatlantic liners takes twenty times as long to carry you from New York to England as a Boeing or an Airbus. And that's the good news — the reason, in fact, for Commodore Ronald Warwick, the master of the *Queen Mary 2*, to brag, at the quayside ceremonies, that Cunard was poised to compete with the airlines for a serious share of the transatlantic business.

Like those of us who had sailed with him through Force 10 gales and thirty-foot swells, the Commodore may have been pardonably giddy at coming through the worst that the feisty ocean could throw his way on a maiden North Atlantic voyage and still getting to the Statue of Liberty on schedule. But could this be the start of something really big and really slow? We take for granted the appeal of velocity, that there is money to be made and pleasure to be had from the gratification of the instantaneous: the three-gulp Happy Meal, the lightning download, the vital mobile phone message that I am here and are you there? And where has this culture of haste got us? Baghdad, apparently, where the delusions of the get-it-over-with war are being compounded by the unseemly rush to exit, leaving the whole gory mess for some other loser to sort out.

It has been thus, as Stephen Kern, in *The Culture of Time and Space 1880–1918*, points out, ever since the orgiasts of speed at the turn of the twentieth century made acceleration the necessary modern ecstasy. In 1909, the Italian writer and artist Filippo Marinetti declared, in his *Futurist Manifesto*, that 'the world's magnificence has been enriched by a new beauty: the beauty of speed'. On an afternoon two years later, a sixteen-frames-a-second movie of the investiture of the Prince of Wales was developed in a darkroom on a British express train and taken to London, where it was shown the same night. Translated into military strategy by the overarmed Great Powers, as the historian A. J. P. Taylor liked to note, the imperatives of railway timetables drove the logistics of pre-emptive mobilisation. A pause to ponder was already a defeat. So modernity bolted out of the starting gate in 1914: Archduke shot, millions of men in grey and khaki precipitately herded into railway carriages, carnage begun right on cue – before the Flemish mire slowed everything down and millions plodded to their doom.

For much of its history, Cunard has been part of this feverish hurry-up. In 1907 its flagship, the *Mauretania*, captured the Blue Riband for fastest transatlantic crossing, and kept it for twenty-two years, spurring jealous – and fatal – competition. A novel by Morgan Robertson, *The Wreck of the Titan; or, Futility*, appearing in 1898, had featured a liner named *Titan* that cuts another ship in two simply 'for the sake of speed'. And the captain of the *Titanic* was blamed for sailing full steam, even in an area notorious for ice floes, in deference to the White Star Line's determination to wrest the Blue Riband from Cunard.

Abraham Cunard, a Philadelphia shipwright, had settled in Nova Scotia, in the loyalist diaspora, after the American Revolution. The loyalists, severed from not only their homes but the mother country, had good reason to want their mail delivery to take less than six weeks, the time often needed for sailing ships to cross from Britain to Canada or the West Indies. Abraham and his son Samuel prospered with a small mail fleet, and in the 1830s Samuel, watching George Stephenson's locomotive the *Rocket* hurtle along the tracks at thirty m.p.h., became convinced that on the oceans, too, steam propulsion was about to replace sail.

Paddle-driven steamers had been in common use in both American and British coastal waters and rivers since the early nineteenth century, and steam-assisted masted ships had crossed the Atlantic since 1819. But it was only in 1838 that the first full steam crossing was made, by the St George Steam Packet Company's ship *Sirius*. Immediately the journey was cut to two weeks (twelve days to Halifax, fourteen to Boston). The *Sirius* was followed by Isambard Kingdom Brunel's *Great Western*, which added style to speed. It boasted 128 staterooms, bell ropes to summon stewards, a ladies' stewardess and a seventy-five-foot saloon, decorated with panels celebrating 'the arts and sciences'.

Disdaining both opulence and reckless speed, Samuel Cunard offered something else when, in 1839, he made a tender to the Admiralty for the conveyance of Her Majesty's Mail: dependability, guaranteed by the novel presence of an on-board engineer. In July 1840 the *Britannia*, the first of Cunard's packets, docked at Boston after a two-week crossing. A wooden-hulled ship with two masts and a central funnel, it was a footling 1,150 tons and about 200 feet long (compared with the *QM 2*'s 150,000 tons and quarter-mile length). In the port where the American Revolution began, *Britannia* was greeted with gun salutes, a performance of 'God Save the Queen' and the declaration of Cunard Festival Day.

The word 'historic' was much repeated over the public-address system last 16 April, as the *Queen Mary 2* moved out into the Solent from its Southampton berth under a classically grey English spring sky. The maiden North Atlantic crossing was hugely subscribed, and, despite the famous superstitiousness of sailors, no one aboard seemed to have been deterred by, or even to have spoken of, the tragedy that cast a shadow over the ship's prospects even before she had been formally launched. On 15 November 2003, while the *QM 2* was still in the shipyard at Saint-Nazaire, in Brittany, where it was being built, a gangway, bearing fifty people, collapsed, throwing some of them fifty feet to the concrete bed of the dry dock. Fifteen were killed and twenty-eight injured. Many of the dead and injured were shipyard workers and family members and friends, who were visiting the liner before its sail to Southampton.

In defiance of ill omens, the transatlantic send-off was exuberant; for those braving the raw breezes there was sparkling wine on the upper-deck terrace. But anxieties about the target of opportunity presented by a mass of slowly moving Anglo-American steel precluded all but a vigilantly screened handful from the dockside 'sailaway'. A spirited band did what it could with 'Rule Britannia' and 'Life on the Ocean Wave', but neither was able to compete with a phantom soprano hooting from the loudspeakers. Then the ship's whistle drowned out everything else, and streamers were tossed from the decks, landing beside flocks of indifferently bobbing seagulls. Waving hankies were to be seen only in blown-up photographs of Cunard's past glory days mounted on walls in the ship's interior.

And where were the cows? Samuel Cunard had made sure that each of his packets was equipped with at least one ship's cow, to provide a steady supply of fresh milk, which, to anyone faced with trays of small plastic miniatures of 'dairy-taste' creamer, seems like an idea whose time should come again. There would be risks, of course. During the fourth crossing of Brunel's immense *Great Eastern*, in 1861, the seas were so high that, according to one report, they not only tore off the paddles, but knocked over the deck-mounted cowshed, sending one of the animals through the skylight of the saloon, where it landed on an understandably surprised barfly. This might have happened early in the morning, for in the halcyon days of the packets saloons opened for business at 6 a.m. and closed at eleven at night. A decent breakfast on the *Britannia* in the 1840s was steak and Hock, which Cunard might think of adding to room service, as a more cheering way to start a day on the tossing waves than weak tea, overstewed coffee and dried-out croissants. And anyone who has waited all his life for the moment when, from a blanket-wrapped steamer chair, he could interrupt his reading of Anita Loos or Evelyn Waugh to summon a steward for a cup of piping-hot bouillon will have to wait a bit longer, for on the *QM 2*, I regret to report, bouillon was there none.

What there is on the *QM 2* is grandeur: lashings of it, Bel-Air baroque, heavy on the upholstery. The dominant style is officially described as 'Art Deco', but it is more *le grand style Ginger et Fred:* sweeping staircases (especially in the triple-decker main restaurant); long, curved bars (very handsome in the Chart Room); leopard-patterned carpets; and, in one theatre, bronze bas-reliefs that feature disporting deities, as in the pre-multiplex yesteryear, though the athletic statuary posted at the doors summons up Albert Speer and

'Honour the Komsomol', rather than Garbo and Groucho. Over the shipboard 'art' a tactful veil should be drawn, but there *is* great art on the *Queen Mary 2*: namely, the exterior of the ship itself – a thrilling scarlet-and-black tower of a funnel and four heroically scaled brushed-steel propeller screws mounted on deck seven, as mightily torqued as anything from the hand of Richard Serra.

Even though the ship is a small floating town – 2,600 passengers and 1,300 crew – it seldom feels crowded. It helps if you have a cool $27,000 to spare, for then you get a share of the Balmoral Suite: 2,249 square feet of what the brochure describes as 'sheer extravagance', including a dining area for eight; two interactive plasma-screen TVs; your own exercise equipment; and (the least they could do, really) 'a fully stocked bar'. For $18,000 less, you rate a not so fully stocked bar and about 250 square feet of elegant, if rather narrow, cabin and balcony. This would still be nearly 200 square feet bigger than Charles Dickens's stateroom aboard the *Britannia* in 1842. For his thirty-five guineas Dickens got a claustrophobic twelve by six: two stacked curtained bunks (no room to stow his trunk); two washstands, with jugs of water brought by stewards; a niggardly porthole, rather apt to leak; and a single oil lamp. But even this austerity was princely compared with steerage on such ships, where passengers slept communally in rows of swinging bunks 'tween decks' and cooked in their own utensils without much help in the way of lighting or ventilation.

For the cabin-class passengers, the centre of the *Britannia*, both socially and physically, was the grand, coal-heated saloon, which Dickens described, in *American Notes*, as

> a long narrow apartment, not unlike a gigantic hearse with windows in the sides; having at the upper end a melancholy stove, at which three or four chilly stewards were warming their hands; while on either side, extending down its whole dreary length, was a long, long table, over each of which a rack, fixed to the low roof and stuck full of drinking-glasses and cruet-stands, hinted dismally at rolling seas and heavy weather.

Dinner, taken on oilcloth-covered tables – which, predictably, aggravated the roll of crockery in heavy weather – was at one: roasted potatoes, baked apples and much pork, in the form of pig's head or cold ham (for some reason, pig was thought to lie easiest on ocean-going stomachs). At five, a cheerless supper was served, usually of boiled potatoes and mouldering fruit, washed down with brandy-and-water or wine, but then there was always the saloon to repair to. Those among the crew who could play a tune or two sometimes did, and there were a few books in the saloon. Only in the second half of the nineteenth century, when wooden hulls were replaced by steel and paddles by screw propellers, did a comprehensively stocked and magnificently panelled and furnished library become a crucial fixture. The heavily used library on the *QM 2* runs the gamut from Danielle Steel to Tom Clancy; there is a wall of less intensively visited Everyman classics, and I found, improbably lurking amid the bodice-rippers and spy thrillers, Albert Camus's *The Plague*.

Though the best thing about a week's Atlantic crossing is an eyeful and a day full of nothing other than the rhythm of the sea and the silvery curving rim of the world, and although Old Cunarder hands insisted that was the way that crossings, rather than mere vulgar cruises, should be, Cunard is now owned by the mother of all cruise companies, Carnival Corporation. And the job description of its toiling entertainment directors begins with the abhorrence of a vacuum. So the gym rumbles with massed treadmilling; the Canyon Ranch spa is packed with heavy massaging; the herbal sauna is crammed with oversized marine mammals (bipedal). In front of the two huge theatres, passengers line up by the statuary to hear a glamorous string trio of Ukrainian musicians dressed in miles of retro-ballgown satin taffeta give their all to 'Jealousy'; or watch spirited young British actors throw themselves into greatest hits from *Romeo and Juliet* and *A Midsummer Night's Dream*; or listen to lecturers like me pontificating about Atlantic history.

In the Queen's Room, a frighteningly accurate bust of the actual Queen Mary, the present Queen's grandmother – a human galleon who seemed to sail fully rigged through state ceremonies as lesser craft chugged contemptibly about her – surveys Gavin Skinner and Lydia Lim, the dance teachers, as they steer giggly novices through the samba, cha-cha or foxtrot, the 'walk-walk, side-together-side' contending with the unhelpful motion of the waves. On the parquet, middle-aged 'gentlemen hosts' hired to squire single ladies through the dances glide their partners around with courtly grace. After being screened for ballroom-dancing prowess and other credentials of respectability, the gentlemen hosts sign on for at least two voyages, and pay a token sum for the privilege. But if Gordon Russell Cave, an impeccably turned-out widower, is any guide, the hosts see their work more as vocation than as vacation: the purveying of shipboard happiness. The moments Gordon recalled with most pleasure were those befitting a *preux chevalier*. One widow told him, after he had walked her back to her seat, that it was the first time she had danced since her husband's death, four years before. 'I think it helped, that little moment,' he said.

Nothing aboard the ship, though, gets as much exercise as the jaws. Indeed, devoted chowhounds could spend the waking hours of the entire six-day voyage doing little more than grazing the vessel, bow to stern, since, as the ship proudly boasts, there is somewhere to eat something twenty-three hours out of twenty-four. Not surprisingly, things British are done best. If fish and chips with mushy peas is your idea of spa food (and why not?), you'll not be disappointed at the ship's pub. Come four o'clock, the Winter Garden is packed with tea parties gobbling cucumber sandwiches made of regulation-issue white-bread triangles, while a tristful harpist completes recollections of rainy afternoons trapped in British seaside palm courts, even though the trees here are fake.

Upmarket on the eighth deck, the Todd English restaurant pretty much lives up to the starry reputation of the chef of Boston's Olives by offering potato-and-truffle love letters, succulent braised short ribs and the inevitable fallen chocolate cake. But the best food on board is probably to be had at the Chef's Galley, where, in the style of a celebrity-chef TV programme, Sean Watier, an exuberantly wise-cracking chef, talks a dozen or so diners through the preparation of the meal. As he was about halfway through a mango-and-crab salad, things started to get exciting in a Quentin Tarantino kind of way. Sean capped his demo about the importance of really sharp knives by gashing his thumb. Later, while he was blowtorching the crème brûlée, he was asked about problems of cooking in heavy weather and was about to offer a breezy reply when the answer came from a phantom guest who had been there all along – the Atlantic Ocean, which lifted us all up in its big cat's paw and unceremoniously set us down again. It was exactly the 'heave and shudder . . . as of the breast of a man in deep sleep' that Evelyn Waugh has Charles Ryder sense in the midst of his transatlantic crossing in *Brideshead Revisited*. 'Either I am a little drunk,' Charles's wife, Celia, says as the cutlery starts to slide, 'or it's getting rough.' For me, back in the cabin, on deck twelve, with the floor at a tilt, and the bed the only safe place to be, the two conditions seemed mutually and unhappily self-reinforcing.

Though huge 'resort' ships like the *QM 2* come with acres of deck, big picture windows and balconies, they go to great lengths to allow passengers who may have mixed feelings about the ocean to ignore it. The planetarium, the casino, the umpteen watering holes, the golf simulator, the spa, the disco, the ballrooms, the unceasing frenzy of entertainment in big, dark spaces are all designed to keep the seawater well out of the way and even out of sight. But on this night old man Poseidon, evidently assisted by Tritons with serious attitude, was crashing the scene. On the Beaufort wind scale of 1 to 12, this one, howling around the ship like a marine banshee, was a 10, eventually getting up to seventy miles an hour, which is not far short of hurricane force. Likewise, the motion of the sea is measured by a range going from Moderate through Rough to High, the last being well beyond Very Rough. That night and much of the following day, our piece of the Atlantic was Very High, beyond which the only available term is Phenomenal, and by then your cabin is probably filling with water and men in tuxedos are ushering women and children to the boats.

As the mango-and-crab salad and I became unhappily reacquainted, the gale certainly seemed to be turning phenomenal. Everything that could fall in the cabin did so, including me. The *Queen Mary* seemed to be locked in a frenzied dance with the elements, the ship reaching and rising and then, on the crest of the churned water, going into a wicked shimmy, its sides shaking and jangling like a belly dancer on spliff, before sinking back voluptuously into the trough. Eventually a message came over the PA system from the Officer of the Watch, whose voice, resembling that of a firm but fair English schoolmaster, had already established itself as authoritative. It was not reassuring: 'Code Bravo, Code Bravo, Code Bravo.' And then it added, 'Control group to muster.' True, it spoke without much inflection, as if reporting a cricket score from a sticky wicket. But since the same announcement had been made earlier that day, followed by the information that this was a practice, repeat practice, fire drill, a real Code Bravo was not what anyone wanted to hear in this situation. An hour later the announcement 'Stand down' was heard, and another announcement, a bit later on, referred to a 'minor incident, now completely under control'.

The thing about a crew of 1,300 – which includes, after all, masseurs, cabaret singers and wine waiters – is that not all of them are trained, in the British merchant-marine tradition, to keep mum about trifling things like a fire at sea on a maiden voyage in the midst of a Force 10 gale. It was, I was assured, a teeny-weeny fire, just a razor socket burning up in a crew cabin. At the time, however, it certainly made an impression.

The next morning, the sea was still Very High, but Professor Schama, due to deliver a lecture at eleven-fifteen, was Very Low (and, for that matter, Very Rough). But I was billed to talk about the man who had given the very first lecture aboard a Cunarder, the *Cambria*, in August 1845: the African-American author and orator Frederick Douglass. Douglass was en route to what turned into a triumphal lecture tour of Britain and Ireland and had been befriended by the Hutchinson Family Singers (Asa, Jesse, Abby, John and Judson), from New Hampshire. Staunch abolitionists, the Hutchinsons had the inspired idea that Douglass might give a lecture on the iniquities of slavery, notwithstanding the fact that among the passengers were several slave owners from Georgia and Cuba. Douglass – with mixed feelings, one suspects – agreed, subject to permission of the captain, the famously capable Charles Judkins. Judkins, as it happened, was a former slave owner (perhaps a slave trader) who had seen the light, and was happy to oblige. Standing on the saloon deck, Douglass began to read from the brutal slave laws of the south, when, predictably, he was drowned out by heckling and threats of physical assault from the outraged slave owners. The Hutchinsons weighed in with inspirational songs but, until Captain Judkins called for the bosun and vowed to put the rioters in irons unless they desisted, the situation looked ugly. The captain's gesture amazed Douglass, who began his tour of Britain (as he would end it) with an unrealistically awestruck view of British racial tolerance. About Cunard, however, he felt less charitable on the return journey, also on the *Cambria*, in 1847, since it accepted his forty guineas and assured him that he would be accommodated in cabin class, only to demote him to steerage when he boarded, a scandal that made the correspondence columns of *The Times* and drew from Samuel Cunard himself a public guarantee that this sort of thing would not happen again.

Duty required that, unsteady or not, I offer this history to any hardy souls who managed to lurch and stagger their way to the theatre. But was there enough left of the lecturer to get the job done? A sympathetic programme assistant, Penny Folliott, had the answer: 'Try the injection.' I did, and whatever was in the nurse's potent syringe not only banished the queasiness but effected a startling transformation, whimpering academic translated into approximation of Russell Crowe in *Master and Commander*. The talk got delivered, seated, and diagonally. I slid a bit. But the audience slid with me.

The Atlantic had definitely got our attention; its illimitable breadth, the great kick of its kinetic energy registered in our groggy bodies. We offered it our sincere respects. All the seats in front of the big windows were now filled with people mesmerised by the immense opera of the deep-grey swell, the rolling waves as bulky and meaty as elephants in a temper. Every so often, beside ladies doing watercolours, a particularly angry, torn-up wall of seawater would slap and hammer against the window.

After a day of respite, the Atlantic returned – another gale, less brutal, but serious enough for deck joggers to be ushered inside by the crew. Shuffleboard was postponed again. Quoits were out of the question. But by this time most of us had got our sea legs and had learned to respect the motion of the ocean, moving with it. Foxtrot was recommenced in the Queen's Room, and disco caught a new beat. For that matter, the towering ship itself seemed to be having a ball, breezing ahead to the rough music of the wind and the swell. And as the *QM 2* forged along, so it became, for most of the passengers, no longer a floating resort hotel drifting innocuously into Caribbean harbours under postcard skies. This one, we told ourselves, appropriating some of the credit for its performance, was a liner, made for crossing, not cruising. 'Oh, the passengers would like it,' Commodore Warwick said, smiling, 'if I told them that was the worst weather I'd ever sailed in, but . . .' The smile continued; the sentence didn't. He wasn't about to wreck our newfound talent for salty yarns. At the dockside celebrations in New York, he conceded that the crossing had been 'turbulent'.

When the Verrazano Bridge came looming through the gentle fog and the first tugs and pilots began to spout red-white-and-blue jets of water in dwarfish greeting, many of us were caught off guard by a sense of proprietorial affection. Emotions doubled. There was the catch in the throat as, right on cue, the morning sun picked out the Statue of Liberty and then travelled from plinth to torch with telegenic precision; there was the flood of memory, the empathy – even among the Queen's Grill high-rollers – with the destitute millions who had come this way through their own storms and stresses; and the jolt of recognition, as we made the turn up the Hudson, that this, too, had been, and was still, America, perhaps the one that really mattered.

All that, I suppose, could have been predicted. What took us by surprise, as we were ushered by Lydia and Gavin, kitted up in smart grey disembarkation suits, to the immigration desks set up in the ball-room, was a valedictory urge to wish the ship well, and to try and find the words to tell others who might normally opt for Newark Airport and the seven-hour air tube to Heathrow that they might want to give the QM 2 a go; that, *mirabile dictu*, there are worse things than being made to sit down and fill the eyes with nothing but sky and rain and wind-whipped water as 150,000 tons of big ship does what it can to ride it at thirty-five miles an hour. In fact, there are few things better.

The Unloved American:
Two Centuries of Alienating Europe

New Yorker, 10 March 2003

On the Fourth of July in 1889, Rudyard Kipling found himself near Mammoth Hot Springs in Yellowstone with a party of tourists from New England. He winced as a 'clergyman rose up and told them they were the greatest, freest, sublimest, most chivalrous, and richest people on the face of the earth, and they all said Amen'. Kipling – who had travelled from India to California, and then across the North American continent – was bewildered by the patriotic hyperbole that seemed to come so naturally to the citizens of the United States. There were many things about America that he loved – battling with a twelve-pound Chinook salmon in Oregon; American girls ('They are clever; they can talk ... They are original and look you between the brows with unabashed eyes') – and he did go and live in Vermont for a while. But he was irritated by the relentless assurances that Americans seemed to require about their country's incomparable virtue. When a 'perfectly unknown man attacked me and asked me what I thought of American Patriotism,' Kipling wrote in *American Notes*, his account of the journey, 'I said there was nothing like it in the Old Country,' adding, 'always tell an American this. It soothes him.'

The Norwegian writer Knut Hamsun, who spent two miserable periods in the American Midwest in the 1880s – working as, among other things, farmhand, store clerk, railroad labourer, itinerant lecturer and (more congenially) church secretary – treated the street parades of veterans 'with tiny flags in their hats and brass medals on their chests marching in step to the hundreds of penny whistles they are blowing' as if the events were curiously remote tribal rituals. The fact that streetcars were forbidden to interrupt the parades and that no one could absent himself without incurring civic disgrace both interested and unsettled Hamsun. Something ominous seemed to be hatching in America: a strapping child-monster whose runaway physical growth would never be matched by moral or cultural maturity. Hamsun gave lectures about his stays in the United States at the University of Copenhagen, and then made them into a book, *The Cultural Life of Modern America*, that was largely devoted to asserting its non-existence.

Emerson? A dealer in glib generalisations. Whitman? A hot gush of misdirected fervour. For Hamsun, America was, above all, bluster wrapped up in dollar bills. 'It is incredible how naively cocksure Americans are in their belief that they can whip any enemy whatsoever,' he wrote. 'There is no end to their patriotism; it is a patriotism that never flinches, and it is just as loudmouthed as it is vehement.' It took a future Quisling to know this.

By the end of the nineteenth century the stereotype of the ugly American – voracious, preachy, mercenary and bombastically chauvinist – was firmly in place in Europe. Even the claim that the United States was built on a foundation stone of liberty was seen as a fraud. America had grown rich on slavery. In 1776, the English radical Thomas Day had written, 'If there be an object truly ridiculous in nature, it is an American patriot, signing resolutions of independency with the one hand, and with the other brandishing a whip over his affrighted slaves.' After the Civil War, European critics pointed to the unprotected labourers in mines and factories as industrial helots. Just as obnoxious as the fraud of liberty was the fraud of Christian piety, a finger-jabbing rectitude incapable of asserting a policy without invoking the Deity as a co-sponsor. This hallelujah Republic was a bedlam of hymns and hosannas, but the only true church was the church of the Dollar Almighty. And how could the cult of individualism be taken seriously when it had produced a society that set such great store by conformity?

The face of the unloved American did not, of course, come into focus all at once. Different generations of European critics added features to the sketch, depending on their own aversions and fears. In the early nineteenth century, with Enlightenment optimism soured by years of war and revolution, critics were sceptical of America's naive faith that it had reinvented politics. Later in the century American economic power was the enemy, Yankee industrialism the behemoth against which the champions of social justice needed to take up arms. A third generation, itself imperialist, grumbled about the unfairness of a nation's rising to both continental and maritime ascendancy. And in the twentieth century, though the United States came to the rescue of Britain and France in two world wars, many Europeans were suspicious of its motives. A constant refrain throughout this long literature of complaint – and what European intellectuals even now find most repugnant – is American sanctimoniousness, the habit of dressing the business of power in the garb of piety.

Too often, the moral rhetoric of American diplomacy has seemed to Europe a cover for self-interest. The French saw the Jay Treaty, of 1794, which regularised relations with Britain (with which republican France was then at war), as a cynical violation of the 1778 Treaty of Alliance with France, without which, they reasonably believed, there would have been no United States. In 1811, it was the British who felt betrayed by the Americans, when Madison gave in to Napoleon's demands for a trade embargo while the 'mother country' was fighting for survival. But the gap between principles and practices in American foreign policy was as nothing compared with the discrepancy between the ideal and the reality of a working democracy. Although nineteenth-century writers paid lip service to the benevolent intelligence of the Founding Fathers, contemporary American politics suggested that there had been a shocking fall from grace. At one end was a cult of republican simplicity, so dogmatic that John Quincy Adams's installation of a billiard table in the White House was taken as evidence of his patrician leanings; at the other was a parade of the lowest vices, featuring, according to Charles Dickens, 'despicable trickery at elections, under-handed tampering with public officers . . . shameless truckling to mercenary knaves'.

A few transatlantic pilgrims, of course, saw American democracy haloed with republican grandeur. When, in 1818, the twenty-three-year-old Scot Fanny Wright, along with her younger sister Camilla, visited the Capitol, the congressional morning prayer – 'may the rod of tyranny be broken in every nation of the earth!' – caused her to tremble with admiration. Only later did she concede that she might have mistaken the commercial bustle of the country for democratic zeal. And, indeed, for most European travellers extravagant idealism was followed by an equally unbalanced disenchantment. Nikolaus

Lenau, a German poet who told a friend he meant to stay in the United States for five years, managed only a brief period, from 1832 to 1833. He could not tolerate a country where, he claimed, there were no song-birds. (In the eighteenth century, the Dutch naturalist Cornelius de Pauw, lecturing on America to the court of Frederick the Great, had solemnly insisted that dogs in the New World never barked.)

Other characteristics of American life alienated the Romantics: the distaste for tragedy (a moral corrective to illusions of invincibility); the strong preference for practicality; the severance from history; and, above all, what the Germans called *bodenlosigkeit*, a willed rootless-ness, embodied in the flimsy-frame construction of American houses. Europeans watched, pop-eyed, while whole houses were moved down the street. This confirmed their view that Americans had no real loyalty to the local, and explained why they preferred utilitarian 'yards' to flower gardens. No delphiniums, no civility.

The British who arrived in the United States in the 1830s and '40s had imagined the young republic as a wide-eyed adolescent, socially ungainly and politically gauche, but with some hint of promise. What they found was a country experiencing an unprecedented growth spurt, both territorial and demographic, and characterised by an unnerving rudeness, in both senses of the word. Ladies and gentle-men dodged quids of tobacco juice and averted their gaze from the brimming cuspidors that greeted visitors to steamboat saloons and hotel and theatre lobbies. The hallmark of Jacksonian America seemed to be a beastly indifference to manners, the symptom of a society where considerateness to others was a poor second to the immediate satisfaction of personal wants.

The conduct of Americans at dinner said it all. They wolfed down their food, cramming corn bread into their sloppy maws during meals that were devoured in silence, punctuated only by slurps, grunts, scraping knives and hacking coughs. (All those cigars.) At the Plate House, in the business district of New York, the naval captain and travel writer Basil Hall was astonished by the speed at which the corned beef arrived and then by the even greater speed at which it was demolished: 'We were not in the house above twenty minutes, but we sat out two sets of company at least.' Only the boy waiters yelling orders at the kitchen broke the quiet. The lack of polite conversation suggested the melancholy and dispiriting monotony of American life, on which almost all the early reporters commented. Tocqueville explained the apparent paradox of anxiety amid prosperity as the result of the relentless obligation to be forever Up and Doing.

The European commentators' dismay at the tyranny of American materialism was disingenuous, since many of them had come to the United States to repair their tattered fortunes or make new ones. Frances Trollope decided to sojourn in America when a rich uncle did the Trollopes the disservice of marrying late in life and, still worse, begetting an heir. Fanny Wright, whose ardour for America had been relit by the Marquis de Lafayette's triumphal tour in 1824 and 1825, visited Mrs Trollope at her expensive rented house at Harrow Weald, outside London, in 1827 and persuaded her to join her. Wright had bought 2,000 acres of land on the Wolf River at Nashoba, Tennessee, with the aim of establishing a communal settlement where slaves would receive the education and practical skills that would fit them for freedom. Mrs Trollope planned to visit the Nashoba utopia, with three of her five children, and then proceed from Memphis, fifteen miles away, up the Mississippi and Ohio Rivers to the thriving new city of Cincinnati, where she intended to make a smart little bundle.

But Fanny Wright's settlement turned out to be a cluster of woebegone huts. Plank floors were set only a few feet above sodden mud. The chimney in the hut Mrs Trollope shared with Wright caught fire several times a day. Instead of a model farm, there were a few slaves who were barely subsisting. Of the all-important school there was no sight and no prospect. Mrs Trollope, aghast at the filth and the fever-bearing mosquitoes, fled with her children to Cincinnati, which was, alas, an 'uninteresting mass of buildings', where hogs rooted in the streets. Together with the French painter Auguste Hervieu (who had intended to teach at Nashoba), she flung herself into show business, remodelling a 'Western Museum', which had hitherto been a collection of natural curiosities and patriotic waxworks. Her son Henry became the Invisible Girl, booming prophecies in creepy darkness, and, with the help of glass transparencies, she created a vision of the Infernal Regions, featuring frozen lakes with erupting fountains of flame, and electric shocks should the customers, peering through grates, try and touch the exhibits.

Mrs Trollope's next venture, a galleried, gaslit emporium of consumer wonders, stocked with fancy goods supplied from Harrow by her husband, ended in debt practically before it began. Mrs Trollope was not quite prepared to admit defeat, but one of her children was seriously ill, and she decided that they had to return to England. She stopped in Washington, then spent five months with a hospitable friend in Stonington, Maryland. There, filling notebooks with a tart, vivid account of her experiences, Frances Trollope took a genteel revenge on the land that had betrayed her. 'As I declare the country to be fair to the eye and most richly teeming with the gifts of plenty, I am led to ask myself why it is that I do not like it,' she wrote. She was struck by the fact that servants called themselves 'help', and bewildered that so many thousands of young women would rather toil 'half-naked' in factories than seek to enter domestic service. When a Cincinnati neighbour, 'whose appearance more resembled a Covent Garden market-woman than any thing else', made the mistake of taking her arm and walking her about, 'questioning me without ceasing', Mrs Trollope noted that, while democracy was very fine in principle, 'it will be found less palatable when it presents itself in the shape of a hard greasy paw and is claimed in accents that breathe less of freedom than onions and whiskey'.

Domestic Manners of the Americans made Frances Trollope, at the age of fifty-two, a sudden literary reputation and £250 from the first edition. Her book was popular in Britain because it documented the stereotypes of cultural inferiority and boorish materialism that the Old World was avid to have confirmed about the New. Stendhal annotated a copy and concluded that there was indeed a 'smell of the shop' about the country. Baudelaire remarked that it was the Belgium of the West. But the book sold equally well in Boston and Baltimore, albeit to scandalised and infuriated readers. 'Trollope' soon became a popular shout of abuse in American theatres, and on display in New York was a waxwork of the author in the shape of a goblin.

The wounds inflicted on American self-love by Mrs Trollope were superficial compared with the deep punctures made by Charles Dickens. In 1842, when Dickens published *American Notes*, an account of a visit to the United States, he had a huge American readership. His novels were instant best-sellers there, and many of them – most notably *Nicholas Nickleby* and *Oliver Twist* – had been dramatised on the popular stage. Despite, or perhaps because of, the unhappiness *American Notes* engendered, 50,000 copies were sold in a week in the US.

Dickens's America is all Yankee repression and southern stupor. He saw Boston, New York and Philadelphia through the keyhole of the prison cell and the madhouse. The Tombs, in New York, served as a metaphor for the dark, unforgiving world in which it was situated. And the geographical heart of the country, though not a jail or an asylum, or a reeking warren like the Five Points, was a river of death. Decades before Joseph Conrad steamed his way upstream into the heart of imperial darkness, Dickens, travelling from Cincinnati down-stream to Cairo, Illinois (reversing Mrs Trollope's route), experienced the Mississippi as a septic ooze, a turbid soup of animal and vegetable muck. Cairo lay in the stinking belly of the beast: 'The hateful Missis-sippi circling and eddying before it, and turning off upon its southern course a slimy monster hideous to behold; a hotbed of disease, an ugly sepulchre, a grave uncheered by any gleam of promise: a place with-out one single quality, in earth or air or water, to commend it: such is this dismal Cairo.'

The sense of America as a sink of contamination extended to its society and its institutions. In the Capitol, where Fanny Wright had been flooded with tremulous rapture, Dickens saw 'the meanest perversion of virtuous Political Machinery that the worst tools ever wrought' – a clamorous gang of fakes, fools and tricksters. His habit-ual outrage extended to the unrepentant practice of slavery in the South, but he never took the North's support for emancipation as evidence of moral uprightness. The North, he wrote in a letter to a friend, hates the Negro quite as heartily as the South, but uses slav-ery as a pretext for domination.

Many people in the governing circles of both Britain and France were sympathetic to the South, not only because of the threatened interruption of raw-cotton supplies, but also because a Confederate victory would pre-empt the emergence of a gigantic and powerful nation. In November 1861, when an American warship stopped the British steamer *Trent* to remove two Confederate agents bound for London and Paris, the ailing Prince Albert had to intervene to restrain British calls for war. According to Philippe Roger, whose *L'Ennemi Américain* (2002) is a brilliant and exhaustive guide to the history of

French Ameriphobia, the fate of the South became a sentimental fashion in Napoleon III's Paris.

When the American republic failed to break up, the European angst about its economic transformation and territorial expansion became a neurosis. For some time the British government, worried about the growing imperial rivalry of the new Germany and the French Republic, had complacently assumed that American expansionism could be manipulated to keep its rivals at bay. If the American fleet would, for its own purposes, prevent European undesirables from straying into the Pacific at no cost to the British taxpayer, jolly good for the Stars and Stripes. The Spanish-American War of 1898, which the French treated as the unmasking of Yankee imperialism, was looked at in London with relaxed tolerance. Rudyard Kipling's lines on 'the White Man's burden' were written not in praise of some triumph of the Union Jack beneath far-flung palm and pine, but to celebrate the fall of Manila.

Much as he loved the energy of America, Kipling became progressively unhappy the farther east he went. Soot-black, fog-fouled Chicago, its scummy river speckled with rust and grease, was, he thought, an apparition of the American future. He stood on a narrow beam at the Chicago stockyards, looking down on the 'railway of death' that carried squealing hogs to an appointment with two lines of butchers. The fact that the stockyards were also a tourist attraction only heightened his stupefaction. Unforgettably, he saw 'a young woman of large mould, with brilliantly scarlet lips, and heavy eyebrows . . . dressed in flaming red and black, and her feet . . . were cased in red leather shoes. She stood in a patch of sunlight, the red blood under her shoes, the vivid carcasses tacked round her, a bullock bleeding its life away not six feet away from her, and the death factory roaring all round her.'

It is hard to know where fact ends and fiction begins in Kipling's *American Notes*, but the book's bravura passages established the *idées fixes* of Europeans about the muscular republic on the verge of its imperial awakening: awesomely carnivorous, racially mongrel and socially polarised, both ethically primitive and technologically advanced. At the turn of the century, that stereotype, along with America's cultural poverty (exceptions were always made for Mark Twain), imprinted itself in the literature of reporters from the Old World. In an age absorbed by the physiology of national types, *Homo americanus* seemed to have evolved for the maximisation of physical force. While chewing gum was preferable to chewing tobacco, its ubiquitousness mystified French observers like Jules Huret, until he decided that it was a workout for the over-evolved Yankee jaws and teeth, which needed all the power they could get to tear their way through the slabs of steak consumed at dinner.

Likewise, the appeal of American football – the Harvard–Yale game became almost as much a fixture of foreign itineraries as the stockyards – was explicable only as quasi-Spartan military training. What really startled Europeans was the blood-lust the sport seemed to provoke in spectators. At one Harvard–Yale game, Huret listened in appalled fascination as a nineteen-year-old yelled 'Kill him!' and 'Break his neck!' from the bleachers.

Modern anti-Americanism was born of the multiple insecurities of the first decade of the twentieth century. Just as the European empires were reaching their apogee, they were beset by reminders of their own mortality. At Adowa in 1896, the Ethiopians inflicted a crushing defeat on the Italians; in 1905, the Russian Empire was humiliated in war by the Japanese. Britain may have ruled a quarter of the world's population and geographical space, but it failed to impose its will decisively on the South African Boers. And Wilhelm II's Germany, though it was beginning to brandish its own imperial sword, remained fretful about 'encirclement'. The unstoppability of America's economy and its immigrant-fuelled demographic explosion worried the rulers of these empires, even as they staggered into the fratricidal slaughter that would ensure exactly that future.

It was self-evident that France and Britain should have been grateful for the mobilisation of American manpower in 1917, which tipped the balance against the Germans and Austrians. Colonel Charles E. Stanton's declaration 'Lafayette, we are here', and the subsequent sacrifice of American lives for a European cause, seemed to herald a restoration of transatlantic good feelings. But, as Philippe Roger (and others, like the historians David Strauss and Jean-Philippe Mathy) explains, if the war created a brief solidarity, the peace more decisively destroyed it. When Woodrow Wilson failed to persuade Congress to ratify the Treaty of Versailles and America withdrew into isolationist self-interest, all the old insecurities and animosities returned.

Wilson was perhaps the most detested of all American presidents by the French, for whom his self-righteousness was compounded by his failure to deliver results.

American generosity (in the French view) towards German reparation schedules fed into the conspiracy theories that seethed and bubbled in the anti-American press in the 1920s and early '30s. In *The American Cancer*, Robert Aron and Arnaud Dandieu went so far as to argue that the First World War had been a plot of American high finance to enslave Europe in a web of permanent debt, a view that was echoed in J.-L. Chastanet's *Uncle Shylock* and in Charles Pomaret's *America's Conquest of Europe*. The newspaper *France-Soir* calculated the weight of debt to the United States at 7,200 francs for every French man and woman. Nor was there much in the way of sentimental gratitude for General Pershing's doughboys. Why, it was asked, had the engagement of American troops on the western front been delayed until 1918? The answer was that the United States had waited until it could mobilise a force large enough not just to win the war, but to dominate the peace.

For French writers like Kadmi-Cohen, the author of *The American Abomination*, the threat from the United States was not just economic or military. America now posed a social and cultural danger to the civilisation of Europe. The greatest 'American peril' (a phrase that became commonplace in the literature) was the standardisation of social life (the ancestor of today's complaints against globalisation), the thinning of the richness of human habits to the point where they could be marketable not only inside America but, because of the global reach of American capitalism, to the entire world. Hollywood movies, which, according to Georges Duhamel, were 'an amusement for slaves' and 'a pastime for the illiterate, for poor creatures stupefied by work and anxiety', were the Trojan horse for the Americanisation of the world. Jean Baudrillard's belief that the defining characteristic of America is its fabrication of reality was anticipated by Duhamel's polemics against the 'shadow world' of the movies, with their reduction of audiences to somnolent zombies sitting in the dark.

The charge that the United States was imposing its cultural habits on the prostrate body of war-torn Europe returned with even more force after 1945. Americans thought of the Marshall Plan (together with the forgiveness of French debts) as an exercise in wise altruism; European leaders like de Gaulle bristled with suspicion at the patronising weight of the programme. Complaints against Coca-Colonisation, the mantra of the anti-globalisers, were already in full cry in the 1950s. But as Arthur Koestler, who bowed to no one in his loathing of 'cellophane-wrapped bread, processed towns of cement and glass ... the Organisation Man and the Reader's Digest', put it in 1951, 'Who coerced us into buying all this? The United States do not rule Europe as the British ruled India; they waged no Opium War to force their revolting "Coke" down our throats. Europe bought the whole package because Europe wanted it.'

Yet somehow, in the present crisis American democracy has let itself be represented as American despotism. Some in the European anti-war movement see the whole bundle of American values — consumer capitalism, a free market for information, an open electoral system — as having been imposed rather than chosen. Harold Pinter told peace marchers in London two weeks ago that the United States was a 'monster out of control'. And while representatives of the Iraqi exile community in Britain narrated stories of the atrocities their families had endured at the hands of Saddam Hussein, banners in Hyde Park equated the Stars and Stripes with the swastika.

These cavils are not necessarily false, just because they've been uttered by Ameriphobes. Fast-food nation was invented in the 1830s, and Captain Hall's puzzled observation that in America the word 'improvement' seemed to mean 'an augmentation in the number of houses and people and above all in the amount of cleared land' has not lost any of its validity with the passing of 170-odd years.

Early on, Europeans identified appetite and impatience as the cardinal American sins. Among the many anxieties of European friends, as well as enemies, of the United States is that Americans are not being told that what lies ahead may be much more testing than a fly-by war and a drive-through peace.

But of all the character flaws that Europeans have ascribed to Americans, nothing has contributed more to widening the Atlantic than national egocentricity (a bit rich, admittedly, coming from the French). Knut Hamsun put the emphatic celebration of separateness down to a lack of education about other places and cultures and commented, perhaps waspishly, 'It is almost incredible how hard America works at being a world of its own in the world.' Virtuous isolation, of course, wasn't a problem so long as the United States saw the exercise of its power primarily in terms of the defensive policing of its own continental space. But now that policing has gone irreversibly global, the imperious insistence on the American way, or else, has only a limited usefulness in a long-term pacification strategy. Like it or not, help will be needed, given America's notoriously short attention span, intolerance of casualties and grievously wounded prosperity. Serving the United Nations with notice of redundancy should its policies not replicate those of the United States and the United Kingdom might turn out to be shortsighted, since in Europe, even in countries whose governments have aligned themselves with America, there is almost no support for a war without UN sanction.

Perhaps Mrs Trollope put it best after all: 'If the citizens of the United States were indeed the devoted patriots they call themselves, they would surely not thus encrust themselves in the hard, dry, stubborn persuasion, that they are the first and best of the human race, that nothing is to be learnt, but what they are able to teach, and that nothing is worth having, which they do not possess.'

Amsterdam

An abridged version of this essay was published in John Julius
Norwich's, *The Great Cities in History*, 2009

The clever thing to do is to fly in at night. Down you go into the Schip-
hol, where not so long ago, a mere handful of centuries, there was the
inland sea, the Haarlemmermeer, and tubby buses and cogs, their holds
laden with herring or grain, bobbing on the grey water. Your plane takes
for ever to taxi, skimming along beside and over motorways, keeping
pace, cheek by jowl with the traffic, on and on until you wouldn't be
surprised if it were to flop into a canal and sail serenely all the rest of
the way to the haven city. You come into Amsterdam from the south-
west, through a loosely threaded knot of freeway lanes and down into
a broad open *plein*, engirdled with dimly corporate modernisms, the
usual pallid incandescence, doing no one any harm and no one much
good. But that's the last you'll see of bland uni-Europe; the interchangeable parts of a couldbeBaselcouldbeMalmöcouldbeBirmingham
kind of place. Into Amsterdam Zuid you go, welcomed by the soft
screams of the trams as they bend round the tracks. The peculiar brew
of Amsterdam aromas comes at you through the cab window: cooking
grease; tobacco smoke – *half zware shag* – the smoke that refuses to die
even when the smokers do; and hanging over everything the greenish-
briny-scummy smell of the black-water canals themselves, where
palings gently rot and swans tuck their wings for the night. It's not much
of a night walkers' city; no, not even those night walkers who prefer,
still, to sit in their windows bathed in lurid magenta; and the throngs
who sit outside on the Leidseplein street, sipping coffees as if it was Paris
or Rome, are mostly tourists. Amsterdam hubbubs are indoors; inside
the brown cafés from which people holding their *pils* spill on to the
street, tugging at their cigarettes.

On you go, past the walls of the darkened city broken by the pale
glimmer from the Showarma joints and the porno-shops and the

fuming *frites* stalls, before you rise over the humps of the canal bridges and hang a right over the cobbles. Bike riders, imperiously reckless, because also lovers – the boy pedalling hard, the girl sidesaddling behind – swoop right and left like maddened swallows of the night, daring you to get in their way, you in your squat taxi, and you'll get a laugh or a shout, one of those big thick-diphthonged Amsterdam laughs, the deep-lunged teeth-baring indecorous chuckle Rembrandt makes in the double portrait where he poses as the carousing Prodigal Son, Saskia his big-hipped whore on his lap. And the girl will dismount from the bike and stand, impossibly leggy, six feet in her thigh-high boots, bob-cut, leather-jacketed, kohl-eyed, tattooed, an alternation of black and scarlet, and it's all a bit much and never ever enough, not here, not in the city of laughing money and dangerous design. *Welkom in Amsterdam!*

And why was this the clever thing to do? Because after all the night action you go to your high bed in the little hotel by the *gracht*, and after a bit there are no more sounds of smashed bottles or drunken glee or screaming trams bearing the last waiters off home to Muiderpoort, only and always the lap of the water, and you sink into sleep as if barge-born and wake to a Miracle. There it is. Beyond the lace curtains and the table set with freshly boiled egg and brown bread and ham and cheese, *echte ontbijtstuk*. A place from another century; from 1640 to be somewhat more exact, caught in the time-net like a thrashing codfish, only much, much prettier. Nowhere else in the world that I know of – except of course the Other Canal Empire on the Adriatic lagoon – has this uncanny sense of graceful admission to its built memory. And the waters, history, have been kinder (or its magistrates wiser) to Amsterdam than to Venice. The *impoldering*, draining large tracts of the Zuider Zee, creating cultivable, habitable East Flevoland, took away the threat of deluge – only to bring a whole new set of problems, social and ecological, for although the city is not dying or descending into the sea, the balance of marine life has been badly damaged. But you're not going to worry yourself about all that, not this morning when you step outside and face a length of elegant canal houses: vertical, like the girl on the bike but not as broad-beamed, their gables sporting stucco dolphins that ride the roofline billows, the older brick step-gables or the sinuous curved ones shaped like an inverted bell, the *klokgevels*. Directly below them is the iron hook used to pulley up whatever couldn't be taken through the narrow street doors, and beneath the hook the shuttered doors to a loft space to store whatever that might have been: a tall mirror, ebony-framed; a heavy chest, from where it could descend to the room that awaited it. And below the shutters the rectangular, leaded windows, two or three abreast and then another storey of them before the main door, painted in gloss black that when opened would lead you into the front *voorhuis*, its floor chequered black and white, its walls lined at their skirting with tiles; a single low oak buffet, maps and paintings hanging, a many-armed brass chandelier, burnished to an almost golden glow, this hall opening through low doors (*such* low doors for such an elongated people), left and right into smaller *zijkamers*, a few chairs covered in watered damask or plush velvet, and at its far end into a grander receiving *saal* boasting its gold-stamped leather wall coverings, a tall armoire atop which sit Kung Hsi pots. And before you turn round to go down the flight of low stone steps to the street you could swear you caught a swish of petticoats on the tiled floor and the eager padding of a sleek hound.

It will do that to you, the city, pull you up alleys of time. Because the thing about Amstelredam is that no other city in the world rose to fortune *so* quickly and, once arrived, as if glutted with history's benevolence, decided not to push its luck and stayed put. There were 30,000 Amsterdammers around 1600; 200,000 a century later, but also 200,000 or even slightly fewer in 1900. There have been surges of fresh building beyond the late seventeenth century, each with its own architectural imprint. South Amsterdam (through which your car rushed) – *Amsterdam Zuid* – is itself a place of peculiar magic, touched by the genius of Berlage who built the most beautiful Bourse in the world, an encaustic theatre of investment. Inside his building, but also along the façades of the houses and apartments Berlage designed, bricks flow and glide, walls gently swell and dip. So, then, in the heart of the city, here are no skyscrapers, no International Style boxes; and where modernism was given space in the gaps blasted by war, say in the university buildings close to the Waterlooplein, the glass, plaster and brick and steel wear the aspect of intimate merriment, which is – in case you hadn't figured it by now – the style of the *stad*.

Amsterdam has an undeserved reputation for modest understatement. It's no Las Vegas, but it's always blown its own trumpet whenever it could, as if not quite believing its luck. The first full-on eulogy to its glories of untold wealth, fame, freedom was Johannes Pontanus's *Rerum et Urbis Amsteldodamensium*, published in 1614, when the city was, compared to what it would become, relatively small beer. Twenty-four years later the city officially received Marie de Medici, the Queen Mother of France, estranged from her son Louis XIII and his government dominated by Cardinal Richelieu. She had been the subject of the most spectacular cycle of allegorical paintings ever made by a Netherlandish artist, albeit a Catholic Fleming, Peter Paul Rubens, in which she features as omnipotent, omniscient, all-benevolent quasi-deity. But in 1638, although greeted with triumphal arches, firework displays, swaggering parades of the militia companies, masques staged on floating islands, processions and banquets, and though celebrated by the city orator, Caspar van Baerle, for the 'quality of her blood and that of her ancestors', that distinction was evidently equalled if not surpassed by 'the greatness of this city in trade . . . the good fortune and happiness of her citizens'. Since the gravamen of the accusations against the Queen Mother in her own country was that, in spite of Rubens's best efforts, she had brought none of those blessings to her own realm, the back-handed compliment could not have gone unnoticed.

But soon, Marie, like most of those who came to Amsterdam in the golden seventeenth century, was too busy shopping to care, haggling like an old hand with the merchants. And because Amsterdam had indeed become the *emporium mundi*, there was nowhere else she needed to go to buy anything her queenly heart desired: spices and ceramics from the Orient; perfumed tobacco from America; steel and leather from Iberia (for being at war with Spain was no bar to doing business with its traders); Turkey rugs, Persian silks; Russian sable; or perhaps even an exotic animal for a princely menagerie, one of the lions or elephants Rembrandt sketched.

But Amsterdam's spectacular fortunes were built on provisioning the bulky commonplace needs, not just the luxuries, of seventeenth-century Europe. Before it could become the place you went to buy Malacca cloves or Brazilian emeralds, it was the place that supplied wheat, rye, iron, cured fish, linens, salt, tar, hemp and timber for markets near and far. Why would you go there if you were, say, from

Norwich or Augsburg, rather than just have the things shipped directly from source? Because you knew they would be available and cheaper. And why was that? Because Amsterdam's merchants had understood that the key to market domination was the transformation of shipping. So they had used their accumulation of capital (the Amsterdam Exchange Bank was established in 1609, the first year of a twelve-year truce with Spain) to finance an extraordinary interlocking system of shipbuilding and bulk carrying. Whole Norwegian forests were bought in advance; harvests of Polish rye likewise, many years in advance, in return for making money immediately available to hard-pressed landowners. Timber, hemp – the wherewithal needed to build a fleet – were consigned to the satellite towns and villages in the country-side north of the city, where each specialised in a particular stage of shipbuilding; some in the yards on the Zaan, as carpenters; others as anchorsmiths, others still as canvas- and sail-makers. The makings of ships, designed to be sailed with smaller crew, and to maximise cargo space, were then brought by barges down to the shipyards on the IJ and the Amstel. Whether a venture was off to the Baltic, to the White Sea or to the Mediterranean, the voyage could be accomplished at a freight cost that made it impossible for merchant fleets to compete. And so the world came to Amsterdam to do its shopping and to take in the outrageousness of a city built to sate the appetites.

But it might also come for freedom. More than anywhere else in the world, Amsterdam and the Dutch saw that becoming a world city – providing living space for those who were confined to ghettos else-where, or who were allowed only a clandestine life – Jews, Mennonites, Muslims – was also good for business. Sefardi Jews in particular brought with them from their half-life as Marranos in the Spanish world a great chain of personal and commercial connections from the tobacco and sugar colonies of the Atlantic, to the great bazaars of the Maghreb. In Amsterdam they became (as they could not in Venice) merchant princes of the city, allowed to build spectacular synagogues and handsome dwellings in the heart of the Christian metropolis. Amsterdam became the hub of liberty in other ways, too – the centre of a free printing press and international book trade.

By the time that Jacob van Campen's great Town Hall, with its Maid of Peace holding her olive branch over the Dam, was completed in the 1660s, and the rotunda topped off, did the 'regents' of the great families who dominated Amsterdam politics – the Huydecopers, de Graaffs, Backers and Corvers – believe all this would last for ever, that somehow a great mercantile empire would be immune from the laws of hubris that had laid low others of that ilk to whom they constantly compared themselves – Carthage and Tyre and, more recently, Venice? If endurance as the unrivalled world city were just a matter of business, they could be confident of their staying power. But that was never the case. Immense riches generated envy, fear and hatred from neighbours. Even within the United Provinces and the state of Holland, there were plenty who despised Amsterdam's habit of throwing its weight around; wanted the republic to be as strong in land power as Amsterdam insisted it should be at sea; and who thought the great city's pragmatism a drag-weight on building a secure state. In 1650 the Stadholder William II had actually marched on Amsterdam to impose his will on the imperial city. But providence had, at least temporarily, smiled on Amsterdam. The Prince of Orange's soldiers got lost in a fog; the siege was barely begun and the Stadholder died shortly thereafter, precipitating an anti-dynastic coup in which the decentralised nature of 'Holland's Freedom' was institutionalised.

There was no sudden Carthaginian destruction (although the incursion of Louis XIV's armies into the republic in 1672, combined with an English naval attack, came close to it). If you went to Amsterdam in the middle of the eighteenth century, you might have noticed more beggars and street whores; the houses of correction full, and as the poor got poorer, the rich swaggered in a more international way, with stone facings, pedimented and pilastered, Frenchified double-doored buildings on the canal houses; more in the way of perruques and Italian singing masters catering to the plutocrats. But in most essentials, the lives of Amsterdammers, copiously fed, riotously entertained, went on in much the same way. Voltaire may have been churlish to the place where he could get published, calling Holland the land of *'canaux, canailles et canards'*. But there was still true grandeur, bravery and business in the printing of freedom.

It was only the long, grim wars of the French Revolution and Napoleonic periods that sent the city, for a while, into smoky obscurity and hardship. Amsterdam became something the regents of the golden age could never have imagined: a poor city, a church-mouse commonwealth; cheese and beggary. The *klokkenspel* carillons still sounded from the graceful church spires, but the clamour of the place had – temporarily – faded. For a while, during the decade of the Batavian Republic from 1795 to 1805, there was an upsurge of patriotic euphoria, a sense of the city taken back from the regents by its citizens. But as the brutal reality of Amsterdam's subjection to French military needs became apparent, that optimism disappeared in the mundane desperation of survival. The 'wonder of the world' – the Town Hall – was converted to become a palace for the younger brother of Napoleon, King Louis, who surprised the Emperor by taking to his people so enthusiastically that he became Koning Lodewijk.

Amsterdam had bent history to its purposes, but an age of mass mobilisation and munitions was rolling over Holland. The city suffered the most humiliating of all fates: quaintness. It became, in the nineteenth century, a cosy nook of Europe: tulips, clogs, skaters, pot-bellied stoves, pancakes and street organs; old boys in flat caps puffing at their pipes while barges filled with nothing anyone cared about drifted along from one more important place to another. For a long while its luck lay in not unduly inconveniencing the Big Boys; not getting in their way; doing them the occasional favour in regard to banks, diamonds, cigars, Indonesian rubber. Live and let live. But then there were some Big Boys who took offence at this very principle and who wanted, for example, Holland's Jews not to live. But what is so thrilling amidst the tragic horror of the great war memoirs – and if you've read Anne Frank then you must also read another masterpiece of resolution, Etty Hillesum's *Interrupted Life* – is the unquenchable sense of breeze-driven vitality, standing against the guns and the gas; something sweet waiting for its moment of rebirth.

That sweetness did burst forth again after the war, and how it exploded! Long delayed to shelter the pearly old city, a technological revolution happened and Holland and Amsterdam went from sleepy cuteness to explosive modernism in the wink of an eye. Quaintness disappeared and sharpness rushed in. Suddenly, Amsterdam was at the cutting edge of design, architecture, painting, writing. In the Sixties only London could rival the Dutch city for no-holds-barred creative mayhem, the old and the new hooked up on a dope-happy blind date. The club where you went to hear hard rock amidst swaying, sweating bodies was just off the Leidseplein and since it was housed in a disused church was called, naturally, the Paradiso.

Amsterdam once more revelled in a cosmopolitanism that looked out towards the world without ever forfeiting its intricate, domestic peculiarity. How was it — and the rest of the Netherlands — to know what was coming? That was: anger, hatred, murder; the unforeseen blow-back of precisely the liberal pluralism that, as a matter of principle, had kept its hands off the Muslim culture that moved into the city along with mass immigration. All of Amsterdam's traditions predisposed the city to believe that Turks and Moroccans would subscribe to the mutual toleration, the easy-going heterogeneity that had been at the centre of the city's culture since the seventeenth century. And that the habit of Amsterdammers to take ferocious satire, pungent polemics, on the chin would extend to this latest generation of citizens. Those assumptions died the death with Theo van Gogh's knife-pierced body lying in an Amsterdam street, assassinated by a Muslim zealot for making a film savagely and, in his eyes, indecently critical of the strictures of his religion. I've known the great, beautiful, raucous city for more than forty years and this is the first time that its humanism is on the defensive against competing waves of fear and fury.

But this too will pass, I believe. Amsterdam has endured fire and flood, armies sent to besiege it; an army of brutal occupation. It has always been able to sponge up trouble and wring it out again. Long after this essay is published, long after its author has been forgotten, there will still be crowds spilling out on to the evening streets, smoking, drinking and laughing while a carillon chimes and a convoy of bikes bounces along the cobbles, pedalled by the sheer elation of being an Amsterdammer.

Washington DC

An abridged version of this essay was published in John Julius Norwich's, *The Great Cities in History*, 2009

Are there any city avenues more inhumanly broad than those of Washington DC? For they are not really boulevards at all, these immense expanses at the centre of the institutional city. There are no sidewalk cafés with coffee-drinkers whiling away the time as they check out the evening strollers – and for the reason that there are no strollers. What there are, are Visitors to Our Nation's Capital, disgorged from tour buses, pointed at the Smithsonian Air and Space Museum, or the Washington Monument, and gathered up again when their business is done. Even new buildings like the East Wing of the National Gallery, perfectly beautiful on the interior, manage to have a broad, low stepped plaza in front of them, complete with massively monumental sculpture that sucks all human life out of the space. Bow your head, revere, and enter the temple; so the message goes. Mandatory solemnity at the expense of the human swarm was there right from the beginning. The engineer who drew up the first plan, Pierre Charles l'Enfant, prescribed avenues not less than 160 feet wide. That's what you get when you hire a French classicist; someone who doesn't notice that the place gets broiling in the summer and for whom narrower, densely tree-shaded streets might have been a kinder idea that might have encouraged some ease of street life. But what l'Enfant valued in his royal prospects were (in his endearingly strangled English) 'reciprocity of sight, variety of pleasant ride and being to ensure a rapide intercourse with all the part of the city which they will serve as does the main vains in the animal body to diffuse life through smaller vessels in quickening the active motion of the heart'.

Washington does have its true neighbourhoods where the beehive hums, people sit on stoops in the spring sunshine, and wander in and out of bars and jazzy cafés; where you can eat anything from

Ethiopian to Brazilian – Adams Morgan, for instance, where in season there is even a fine farmers' market, fruit and vegetables trucked in from farms in Maryland, Pennsylvania and Virginia, a reminder that there is true country out beyond the beltway. Or around U Street where African-American Washington comes alive near the Duke Ellington Theater. And the sense of a vast bureaucratic-punditocratic savannah is broken by Washington's bosky places, the parks and gardens laid out after the recommendations of the McMillan Commission at the turn of the century. In Rock Creek Park joggers jog (although muggers mug); the Zoo nearby is where Washingtonians come as families, and the gardens of Dumbarton Oaks, Harvard's institute of medieval and Byzantine studies, is shared between the philosophically contemplative and the blissfully amorous. But most of the young people who make up the clientele and who come to love the place aren't there because of the romance of the city, but because they need to live in an idea made architecturally visible: the idea of democratic government. That is at the beating heart of the place; the pulse of its body politic, but that same notion is also why 'Washington' in some quarters of American life is not so much an actual city as a byword for bureaucratic remoteness and self-importance.

Its problems and its many genuine splendours are both products of the original split personality of the American Republic. For Thomas Jefferson (who nonetheless seized the opportunity to be President with robust eagerness), the true America lay in the myriad farms where the yeomen citizens, whom he believed were the life-blood of democracy, were building a truly new society and polity. George Washington, whose own plantation farm, Mount Vernon, is just fourteen miles south of the District, was more ambiguous. On the one hand, he too was averse to empty pomp; on the other hand, it mattered deeply to him that the United States hold its head high in a world of vainglorious monarchies; that a capital city, like the Roman Republic, be the visible expression not just of the parity, but of the superiority of a democratic constitution. It helped foster those dreams of the New Rome that the eventual site had running through it a mucky creek grandly known as the Tiber. Washington, the city, is in fact very much the vision of Washington the man. Dolly Madison, the fourth President's wife, knew this when, on the approach of the British in 1814, she took a knife to Gilbert Stuart's beautiful portrait of Washington, cut it from its frame, rolled it and made haste with it to the soldiers' camp where she spent the night on the run from the invaders, watching the horizon flame with the ruins of the town.

The very characteristic of which self-designated conservatives (many established in Washington think tanks) complain – the artificiality of the city, its detachment from anything resembling a self-sustaining commercial economy – was precisely the reason why George Washington wanted such a capital in the first place. Metropolitan wens like London and Paris, were, he and Thomas Jefferson thought, the breeding places of idle fashion, vice and corruption. But a nation founded on the majesty of the people ought to have a great city custom-designed as a residence for democratic institutions. The relationship between the independent legislature and the governing executive, for example, ought to be made visible by their mile-long separation at opposite ends of Pennsylvania Avenue; the two, however, always in each other's sight. It was an American thing to ensure that it would be the legislature, not any executive residence, that would be the elevated structure, sitting on its eighty-foot hill, watching over the servants of the government beneath, keeping them accountable.

The very notion of a federal city originally came from necessity as much as ideology. Because of the moving theatre of peril during the revolutionary war, the itinerant Congress had shifted no fewer than eight times, and had sat in places as various as York Pennsylvania, Trenton New Jersey and the academic Nassau Hall at Princeton. To have a single, defensible site, perhaps no more than ten square miles, where law and governance were published and treasury accounts cleared, was obviously essential to the integrity and efficiency of government. A decision was taken almost as soon as the war was over in 1783, but a protracted debate then ensued as to where that site should be. The criteria were a location on a navigable river, but sufficiently far inland to be protected from the naval raids the founding fathers expected of the British – or, indeed, their ex-allies the French. The mid-Atlantic suggested itself as arbitrating between the already conflicting claims of the great sectional interests of the new republic – industrial, high-minded New England and the plantation slave world of the South. Two choice sites were on the Delaware in New Jersey or on the Potomac at the line separating Maryland and Virginia.

But even those choices were thought to favour, respectively, northern and southern preferences, so that for a few weeks two capitals, one on each site, were seriously contemplated, at least until Francis Wilkinson, in a burst of inspired ridicule, proposed building a gigantic trolley that could wheel the capital and its archives from one place to the other, along with an equestrian statue of Washington. Ultimately it was Washington himself – who had begun his career as a land surveyor – whose firm preference was for a city on the Potomac, surrounded by gentle hills and, as he thought, blessed with a benign climate, who decided the matter. When the land was plotted he rode it himself, charting its topography and imagining where, amidst the farmland and the river valley, would arise the grand buildings and monuments that would embody the vital social virtues of working democracy.

For a detailed plan Washington, in 1790, turned to Pierre Charles l'Enfant, a French military engineer who had been honourably wounded at the siege of Charleston (where the French lost the city) and had become a kind of official artist to the Continental Army. Not surprisingly l'Enfant's vision was formed by classical French urbanism from the reigns of the Sun King and Louis XV: central *grandes places*, each embellished with statuary, obelisks and monuments from which broad radial avenues would extend, along which the edifices of government would be aligned – Treasury, Department of War, Post Office (*very* important in the early Republic), Patent Office, etc. The Potomac and its Great Falls outside the city would provide (possibly by making more of the Tiber) a chain of watercourses, so that Washington would not just resemble classical Paris, but a little bit of Venice and Rome too, with a cascade falling down Capitol Hill and feeding handsome canals. Though l'Enfant ran foul of Congress, and the execution of a much-modified plan was carried out by the less grandiose Andrew Ellicott, much of his essential vision – the emblematic separation and connection of executive and legislature; the eminence of the latter, the gentility of the former; as well as those immense avenues – survived. It was the other great Enlightenment mind, that of Jefferson, who had the idea of calling the intersecting streets by letters and numbers and who made sure that both l'Enfant and Ellicott were supplied with plans of all the great European cities from Strasbourg to Amsterdam.

By 1800, when Jefferson moved into the President's House, there were just 3,000 inhabitants of the federal district, of whom a third were slave and free blacks. The House itself, resembling 'a country gentleman's dwelling' according to one visitor, already had its little colonnade and modest park and the East Room planned for state receptions, but most of it was unfinished. Abigail Adams, the first First Lady to attempt to run the House, complained of the expense of heating and lighting and the difficulty of finding thirty reliable servants who could be entrusted with its management. The Capitol was being built by the Boston architect Charles Bulfinch, who had created the domed Massachusetts State House and who provided for the nation's legislature another dome flanked by two pavilions. The ensemble when built was grand by American standards but, as the Republic grew, not ceremonious enough, resembling, as one wag put it, 'an upside-down sugar bowl between two tea chests'.

After the British burned Washington in the summer of 1814, it took time before rebuilding got under way, the eager and scientifically minded John Quincy Adams providing much of the impetus. But for decades Washington was jeered at in much of the country as the 'great Serbonian Bog' – a place of 'streets without buildings' – while its neighbour, the busy port of Georgetown, had 'buildings without streets'. The climate was more brutal than the First President imagined; mosquitoes devoured the population in the fetid summer; the water supply was foul and prone to delivering cholera to the city rather than the graceful torrents and limpid basins l'Enfant had envisioned. Hogs wandered the Mall, and at some distance from the grandeur, rickety taverns and disorderly houses made their contribution to the city's peculiar mix of solemnity and squalor; the emblems of liberty and the reality – in the persons of the unfree without whom the place would never have functioned – of slavery. Washington literally, but barely, held the line between two Americas rather than symbolising its unity.

And then in the early 1850s there arrived in town one of the most prodigious and still relatively unknown American heroes, the army engineer who as Quartermaster General of the Union would win the Civil War for the North quite as decisively as Lincoln, Grant and Sherman. Montgomery Meigs was first and foremost a builder. His spectacular brick Romanesque temple-like structure of the Pensions Building (created in the 1870s to provide welfare for old soldiers and memorialise the fallen), now the Buildings Museum, is one of the most extraordinary architectural achievements in the entire country. But it was Meigs who, throwing an immense masonry span over one gorge and an iron bridge over Rock Creek, created the aqueduct that carried, at last, a decent supply of fresh water (also imperative for the extinguishing of fires) from the Great Falls of the Potomac to the city. It was Meigs too, a regular tartar when it came to coming down hard on the dubious businessmen who saw in the growth of the District an opportunity for fat profits, who presided over the rebuilding of the Capitol to its present appearance and magnitude, and who replaced the Bulfinch sugar bowl with something taken instead from Brunelleschi, Michelangelo and Wren, but which had an iron fabric just in case the British decided to set fire to it again.

During the Civil War, Washington became a barracks — almost 100,000 troops camped there; bivouacs on the Mall, soldiers amidst the hogs and geese (for they had no intention of moving); beef and milk cattle grazing. In July 1864 the invalids and veterans under Meigs's command had to man forts and trenches at the advance of General Jubal Early, who, however, never made it. The wounded and mutilated were carried in carts and barges from the two battles of Bull Run, and some of those who perished were buried, on Meigs's orders, on the confiscated land of his former friend, Robert E. Lee, up on Arlington Heights. Meigs and Lincoln were always anxious that if the Confederacy took the Heights they would have a direct line of fire on both the White House and the Capitol, so that turning the proprietorial gentility of the Lee estate into the first national cemetery became, for them both, a matter of strategy as well as national symbolism.

Modern Washington, though, came to be in the years around the turn of the century. It was then that the old federal government buildings were replaced by the masonry-faced piles that house the Treasury, the Department of State and the rest. Every so often there were wonderful, eccentric exceptions like the Gothic Smithsonian 'castle' — the result of a legacy offered (and accepted by Congress in 1846) by English scientist James Smithson as an 'establishment for the increase of knowledge among men', a rubric sufficiently broad to extend, now, to fighter planes and space capsules as well as historical artefacts and treasures of American technology and invention. The Corcoran Gallery was intended as Washington's first art gallery, but the Beaux Arts building, designed by one of the city's mavericks, Renwick, stayed unrealised as its Confederate-leaning patron sat out the war from the safety of Paris. By the end of the century, the Corcoran and the Freer were home to spectacular collections, but it was only with the gifts of the Secretary of the Treasury, Andrew Mellon, and the Widener dynasty that the immense National Gallery was finally established on a scale befitting the collections in the 1930s. And the great memorial monuments that bookend the axis of the Mall – Washington, Lincoln and Jefferson – and which, for most visitors, along with the Capitol and the White House, *are* the 'Nation's Capital', took a long time coming. A Washington memorial of some sort was mooted almost as soon as the General-President was dead, at the end of 1799; and before long the idea of an equestrian statue was scrapped for a grander mausoleum, to house his remains, from which some sort of column or obelisk would sprout. The reluctance of the owner of Mount Vernon to release the sacred relics, the usual squabbling of interested parties *in situ*, and above all the cost of the structure meant that it took a century before, in 1885, the obelisk in its finished state was formally opened. Lincoln's great memorial with the seated figure sculpted by Daniel Chester French, the bare temple-like space decorated with the fallen hero's words and friezes of the emancipation of the slaves, was likewise a creation of the second half of the nineteenth century.

And now everyone wants a monument in Washington. Franklin Roosevelt, who specified he did *not* want one, got one anyway. A major memorial to the fallen of the Second World War, also on the Mall, is still being hotly debated. But sometimes a convergence of national passion and inspired design takes place and something gets built that transcends its own materials to become a place of true communing. Such of course is the profoundly eloquent Vietnam memorial created by Maya Lin: a basalt wall in a cut trench that rises and falls with the body count and the grief of the country.

Though Boston and New York have been my home towns, I feel I know this city well. I remember crossing the grilling breadth of Pennsylvania Avenue in 1964 to see an Assistant Secretary of Labor who became a friend and mentor, and who would well up in an impassioned Irish way at the thought of the slain Jack Kennedy not a year before; I remember the jazz piano bars in the tougher end of town around M Street and 14th; the rising hemispherical walls of Watergate; my first astounded sally into the glory of the Library of Congress Reading Room, as welcoming to a young student as the British Museum Reading Room (then) was chilly and difficult. I went back last year each week in November to give the Mellon Lectures at the National Gallery, beginning to make the white grandeur of Union Station and the amiably shouting directives of the taxi despatchers on the threshhold a kind of homecoming. I have friends, a daughter living there, all happily, all very much settled into the weave of the place; knowing its street corners and park benches, its dogs and ice cream. And there, when the cherry blossom is doing its shameless thing, and the streets of Adams Morgan are warming to the kids on the block, it's entirely possible to see Washington as not just DC, not just ideology made visible, but as an American community; and a good one at that.

Brazil

Financial Times, 22 November 2008

Mid-November . . . so it's spring, or it is in Brazil, which meant that that's where I had to be to get out of the way of autumn in New York: pumpkins, the dirge-like descent of leaves, a lot of suburban happy talk about crisp weather when I'm still lamenting the departure of uncrisp summer, the time of sweaty rot that's my idea of perfect climate. And it was just possible I'd said all I could ever say (for a while, at least) about Barack Obama, so time to change the subject and talk to 800 Brazilians about Picasso and Goya for a change. Well, they had asked for it.

'They' were the benevolent patrons of a university seminar in Porto Alegre, right on the southern border with Argentina and Uruguay, called 'Boundaries of Thought', across which, I assumed, one was invited to stride. Camille Paglia, a boundary-crosser if ever there was one, had been there last year talking about sex in art – for two-and-a-half hours, the sponsors said. They looked at me earnestly as they said it and winced, I thought, at that much sex from Professor Paglia. But my subject was calamity and an hour of that seemed more than enough.

I had been to Brazil ten years before to promote the translation of *Landscape and Memory* and was easily infatuated. Glimpses of heaven and hell opened up: tall women glided on the street rather than walked, as if they were tuning up their samba moves; herons and egrets nested amid sewage and detergent scum on the canal between the airport and São Paulo; the innocent intensity of journalists wanting to be told the history of a free press in Britain when they were still cagey about liberating theirs after the military dictatorship; being trapped happily in the embrace of an immense hulk of a man, glittering with sequins, who grinned and said: 'I am Roberto, king of the *favela*, now you must come and talk to us . . .'

'*Sim!*' I said, 'yes!', while my publisher, a sweet but fretful soul, swung his head from side to side while rolling his eyes (no small feat even for a Brazilian), which I gathered was a no. Despondent, Roberto planted a juicy kiss full on my mouth, which was a first for a book tour, but did nothing to alter the publisher's irrevocable ban. In Rio, at Ipanema, long-legged kids booted footballs on the beach while others demanded money when you parked the car, promising to 'look after it' – the alternative being not worth thinking about.

Oh, yes, I love Brazil, but Porto Alegre was different: less tropical; more, sigh, European. There is much talk about the Germans and the Italians who came there, and on to the plane came a pack of the former, drunk at noon; planting themselves wherever seats seemed to beckon, despising mere boarding-pass seat assignment; mighty shouts of 'Markus' and 'Thomas' roaring down the aisles for no particular reason anyone could make out except as an expression of *Kamerad-schaft* in the southern hemisphere. The plane skirted the Atlantic coast, breakers curling below while the flight attendants pretended to have run out of beer.

Porto Alegre is an instantly appealing place, foaming with blue jacaranda blossoms, merry with sidewalk cafés set between nine-teenth-century Brazilian town houses, their gables as curly as a gaucho's whiskers with snazzy touches of crimson or gold paint. It was Sunday, which meant, even in the Sheraton, that *feijoada* was on; a gamut of darkly stewed meats together with the *manioc farofa* I remember loving on that first trip and did again: it's fluffy and gritty at the same time, which doesn't sound enticing, but somehow is. In the park, a boy pulled out his guitar and sang samba to impress, while a circle of capoeira devotees went through their clambering motions to a dull drum beat.

A book fair was in swing; not the kind boasting marquee events with the usual suspects, but a pretty, shady plaza laid out with fifty or so stalls, each the size of a *bouquiniste*, displaying the wares of local publishers and booksellers. The organisers were proud of the egalitarian princi-ple, and it was astonishing in the age when the death of print is prematurely announced to find a smallish Brazilian city where little presses seemed to be around every corner. Charles Kiefer, the handsome professor with whom we had lunch, walked us over to one of the stalls and showed us the thirty-odd volumes that collected the fiction of his students. Another year, another volume, and the professor couldn't have been happier. If Brazilian fiction were ever in danger, it wouldn't be his fault. Myself, I was reading *The Adventures and Misadventures of Maqroll*, novellas by the Colombian author Alvaro Mutis so richly, spectacularly, sensually wondrous that you hate him for ever stopping. 'Ah,' said Kiefer, 'so good', as if he had filled his mouth with fine wine, and then, sighing a little, thought I might, in that case, enjoy a small exhibition over at the local bank devoted to Gilberto Freyre. Freyre! I hadn't thought about him for forty-odd years: a poet among historians; a romancer of the Brazilian difference: slavery and the Casa Grande, somehow made less brutal by miscegenation; the cradle of a mixed-blood culture. Oh sure. Samba slavery. Doesn't count. I had wised up to the fantasy a long time ago, but there was, nonetheless, something wickedly beautiful about Freyre's dreamy writing, and the show beneath the stained-glass ceiling advertising 'Prudence', 'Enterprise' and such like unerringly harvested the spell. Displays of Freyre's tropically coloured paintings were set above trays of sand; peeling cabinets with drawers were opened to reveal faded banquet menus, dog-eared photographs and diary entries. You entered the whole thing through the skirts of a giant carnival mannequin. Another Brazilian seduction; and I could feel my portion of northern scepticism draining away into the gentle afternoon.

The lecture was delivered: a generously receptive 800, most of whom seemed to want to ask questions, and most of them did. Eventually our hosts ushered us off to an upscale French restaurant where it would have been churlish to turn down the foie gras. It wasn't until our last night in São Paulo that we were taken, by Marcello Dantas, the designer of many of Brazil's most brilliant museums and exhibitions, to a place that boasted serious native cooking: Amazon fish ('neither salt nor freshwater,' said Dantas, beaming, 'just packed with big river nutrients'); fresh hearts of palm, warm and silky on the tongue; stupendously subtle banana ice cream (a contradiction in terms, but go figure). The place is called Brasil a Gosto. It's better than anywhere in London.

If you fly in to São Paulo from another Brazilian city, you'll land (if you use the local airport) in a startling place: bristling with tower blocks set close and white like the model for *Blade Runner*; a city 120 kilometres across; piled up *favela* slums; stunning fashion by designers such as Rosa Cha and Gloria Coelho, who does things with sequins that I can't begin to explain in the *Financial Times*. And yet, this wild, teeming antheap of a place has no billboards. The mayor, Gilberto Kassab, a Syrian-Paulista, decided they were 'visual pollution' and gave owners thirty days to get rid of them. The fine for failing to do so was 10,000 reals (about £2,500) a day. So the place throbs along beneath its pall of traffic fumes; just eleven million Paulistas trying to get to the end of the week. A place for heroes.

On the way back to New York, my nose in Alvaro Mutis's journeyings of *Maqroll the Lookout*, I'd look out myself to the fading shoreline of the tropic forest and feel wistful. Brazil is one of the places where your nerve-endings work overtime and you never want them to stop their dancing little hum and buzz.

Back in the Hudson Valley, everything decelerated. The farmers' market at the local train station was loaded with good stuff. People bustled autumnally, chirpy with the delight of a fine new president.

Comedy Meets Catastrophe: On the Korean DMZ

Financial Times, 25 September 2009

On a late-summer afternoon, the last frontier of the Cold War, the Military Demarcation Line dividing the two Koreas, is picture-perfect: a romantic landscape painter's dream, provided of course you block out the barbed-wire fence running along the summit of the high hills. Indifferent to history, the dragonflies that are everywhere in Korea bob and flutter around the gun nests. A hundred metres down the steep hillside, the Imjin River loops through idyllic country which, fifty-nine years ago, was cratered with mortar fire. On the south bank, woods tangled with wild grape grow to the river's edge. The north bank, though, is deforested, and the South Korean soldiers at the observation post tell you this is not just for a clearer path of fire for their communist enemies, but to deter defections by their own men.

From time to time, soldiers from the North Korean People's Army come to the river to catch fish for their supper, or hunt the wild boar roaming the few coppices left on their side. The pigs scavenge trash discarded by the South Korean outposts, so that indirectly, courtesy of the porkers, the south feeds the north. Without the self-provisioning, so the South Koreans humorously say of their enemy counterparts, it's bark and grass soup for dinner. A North Korean invasion, they imply, is held at bay less by their barbed wire than by the fear that should the People's Army ever make it to Seoul, it would head straight for Burger King and not come out for a week.

Smugness aside, it's hard not to notice a telling contrast between the eroded, barren uplands to the north and the brilliant green rice and corn fields to the south. Local farmers here who found themselves trapped in the Demilitarised Zone are subsidised by the Joint Security Agency (United Nations and South Korea), and their land swept of the millions of mines left behind by the Chinese during their advances in the grim war of 1950–53. No pesticides are allowed on these crops, so 'DMZ' rice, the military will tell you, is the most fragrant in all of Korea.

Et in Arcadia ego. An island of gourmet organic rice surrounded by landmined woodlands sums up the bizarre adjacence between prosperity and paranoia that is the Korean front line. And as the Clinton mission which last month sprung two American women journalists from twelve years' hard (not to mention the occasional nuclear underground test) reminds us, sixty years after the war that few outside the region remember, Korea still matters. It's the zombie war that won't lie down and it's still ravenous for trouble. The Korean question is both relic and omen; an ideological conflict preserved in aspic and the hottest of hot sauces for a hard-pressed US president and his overstretched military. Kim Jong-Il, the self-styled Dear Leader, is fond of reminding the world that his missiles can reach California. This should be a joke, but it isn't. Every time Pyongyang pounds its chest, Tokyo grins, but nervously.

Up at Observation Post Typhoon, a monarch butterfly, bigger than a humming bird, alights on a hemp sack dumped at the foot of the barbed wire. The good-natured soldier escorting us while we shoot footage for a documentary about Obama's foreign-policy challenges tells me the sacking contains a cluster bomb. Every two months or so, a lightning bolt from one of the big storms that roll through the mountains will set one off. 'The first time that happened I thought the war had started . . .'

On this late August day the servicemen seem more battle-ready to fight swine flu than the million soldiers of the KPA stationed the other side of the Demilitarised Zone. We pass platoons of them, sitting in trucks, their faces covered in protective sky-blue masks. They ask politely if they might take our temperature, a procedure they themselves observe four times a day. A soldier slides a thermometer under my armpit and, five minutes later, announces that I am in the best of health.

Comedy rubbing shoulders with catastrophe is on even more theatrical display fifty kilometres to the west at Panmunjom, where the United Nations Command Military Armistice Commission (UNCMAC) has had its base since the cessation of hostilities in 1953. Private First Class Anthony Hauch from Philadelphia reminds us –

easy ballpark cheer coming from his film-star looks – that, notwithstanding its official demilitarisation, we are in an Active Combat Zone.
'If you feel like getting off the bus and taking a leak at the side of the
road, don't.' Those landmines, five million of them, are waiting for
the unsuspecting. Do they, we ask, ever go off? 'Oh sure, they're Soviet
old-style, pretty unstable. The deer land on them now and again.'

Those ancient minefields are not the only thing about the fifty-
six-year armistice that's unstable. Every few years there is an 'incident'
that sobers up the absurdity. In 1976 a tree-trimming patrol, deemed
by the North Koreans to have violated the armistice, was attacked by
a military axe gang, two officers hacked to death. Though Private
Hauch won't say when the most recent 'incident' was, he hints that
they are not infrequent. The Chinooks parked on the helipad look
ready for action and the small troop of UN soldiers stay on high alert
because of a not-unfounded sense that Kim Jong-Il can't be relied on
to play by the usual rules, especially if reports of his ill health are true
and a power struggle for succession is about to ensue.

For Kim Jong-Il wears the uniform of a Maoist, but runs his office like
a gangster. Drug trafficking and counterfeiting supply revenue for the
nuclear game. In an infuriated response to the UN's denunciation of
this May's underground test (approximately the same grade as that
dropped on Hiroshima), the Dear Leader declared on 27 May that North
Korea was no longer bound by the armistice – which means, technically,
that the war between North Korea and the UN has now gone hot.

Still, it's hard to go trembly two kilometres away on the actual *Duck
Soup* character of the ritualised mutual nose-thumbing. It would need
a combo of Joseph Heller, Voltaire and Jaroslav Hašek (the author of
The Good Soldier Svejk) to do justice to its madness. Negotiations for
the original armistice and any discussion of infringements are
conducted in long low huts, painted respectively blue for the UN and
aluminium silver for the North Koreans. Two large buildings face off
in emblematic hostility. Ours, the South Korean, known as 'Freedom
House', sports granite floors, polished chrome and glass doors. Theirs
– optimistically named 'Welcome House' – is a number assembled
from the Leonid Brezhnev Album of Architectural Style. When the
Freedom House was seen to stand taller than its opposite number, the
North Koreans lodged a protest and added a glass-walled storey to
theirs. South Korean guards stand behind the blue huts, precisely half

of their helmeted heads hidden by the walls, the other half exposed to the foe, fists clenched at their side, as if auditioning for a martial-arts movie. Their opposite numbers prowl the Welcome terrace, stopping to brandish a pair of aggressive binoculars in our direction. But, from the roof of Freedom House, you can peer through much bigger binoculars at them glaring right back at us. I must regretfully report that the enemy has a definite edge in tactical glowering.

All this is so fabulously loony, a living museum of Cold War craziness, that one has to remind oneself that behind the mutually assured scowling there is, in fact, something profoundly serious at stake, the moral significance of which is not depleted by its repetition in the mouths of blow-hard politicians, namely the price to be paid for the survival of freedom.

The sentry boxes beside the motorway that runs south along the Han River to Seoul might seem peripheral to the life or death of one of the most vibrant and complicated political societies in all of Asia, but they are not. No one believes the KPA is about to pour down Route 77 to the capital. But the point of North Korean military bluster is to remind the US – and probably Russia and China too – that as a mischief-maker, the last true communist dictatorship (not counting life-support Cuba), the country can create havoc, whether through covert relationships with terrorists, insurgent forces taking on the US in west Asia or outright anti-American governments like Iran.

Remote and esoteric though the Korean story may seem, it still represents a tutorial in the purposes and legitimacy of using military power to enable, protect and stabilise fragile democracies far from the West. As he ponders his narrowing options in Iraq and Afghanistan, Barack Obama could do worse than to ponder Korea's modern history. In January 1950, Harry Truman's usually canny Secretary of State Dean Acheson neglected to include Korea in a statement about the perimeter of indispensable defence in east Asia. This was the green light that allowed Kim Il-Sung and his patrons Stalin and Mao to believe North Korea could overrun the South without serious opposition. Truman's decision to send troops and the UN commitment to resist aggression amounted to a belief that the credibility of the American shield for the democracies emerging after the Second World War, in Europe, Asia and above all in Japan, would not survive the fall of South Korea.

Was Truman wrong? The war that ground to a bitter stalemate in 1953 took 36,000 American lives, tens of thousands of other UN troops, and 353,000 Korean military on both sides, as well as 2.5 million Korean civilians. It was, as David Halberstam reminds us in *The Coldest Winter* (2007), a pitiless horror. And, after it was over, it was not at all clear that the Korea south of the thirty-eighth parallel that had survived was, in any sense worthy of Truman's rhetoric, a truly free, rather than merely non-communist, state.

Cold War paranoia drove American policy to turn a blind eye to succeeding authoritarian governments in Seoul, and the persecution of any oppositional figures who could be stigmatised as leftist. Only belatedly did the American government come to the aid of champions of civil rights like the late South Korean President Kim Dae-Jung. It took the atrocity of the Kwangju massacre in 1980, and the recoil against the brutal suppression of the democracy movement, for South Koreans to reclaim the true fruits of their liberation. Whatever decisions are taken about the places where American power might be used to shield fledgling electoral democracies in the Middle East and Asia, similar torturous complications are bound to occur there too.

Which may not mean, however, that the effort might not be worth the sacrifice. The contrast between the wretched, cruel and self-eviscerating tyranny in North Korea and the dazzling economic and cultural energy of the South could not be more instructive. Despite the recession, the South Korean economy is a marvel of modern enterprise. Unlike most Western economies, it manufactures globally marketable cars, mobile phones and electronic goods. And if these achievements are bought through depressed labour costs, there's precious little sign of that on a Saturday night in downtown Seoul. The streets are packed with a raucous crowd, mostly young, hitting the espresso bars. Street vendors do a roaring trade, but so do the retailers selling trainers and casual wear, much of it in the juvenile pastels that Koreans seem to enjoy.

The unimpeded right to consume may not exactly be up there with Franklin Roosevelt's Four Freedoms as a reason to commit arms to resist authoritarianism. But the consumption is not just of trainers and jeans: it's the choice to buy or reject religion (church spires are everywhere in South Korea); the right to free and fair elections and to read and speak as one wishes, usually (though not invariably) unthreatened by police. And the right to inject traditional culture with modern temerity.

On a dogstar night in front of the Seoul City Hall, I sat with a big crowd and listened to a thrilling 'new-wave Korean' band – Noreum Machi – deliver new power to traditional percussion. A robed man who beat on an immense hanging vertical drum and four girl drummers delivered a violent and ecstatic sound into the velvety darkness. There was something apt about this explosion of sound for borderline Korea. The drum is the voice of an army, but on that night in that place, it was the beat of jubilant liberty too.

Testing Democracy

9/11

Guardian, 14 September 2001

It came, literally, out of a clear blue sky, one of those eye-poppingly beautiful mornings when you forgive autumn for polishing off summer. All around New York the last rituals of American innocence were being enacted: huddles of mums and dads at the roadside reassuring their seven-year-olds that there was nothing frightening about the big old yellow school bus lumbering towards them. A grey heron was dabbling in the mill pond in our Hudson-valley suburb, oblivious, like the rest of us, to the fact that American history, in the shape of its most irrepressibly ebullient city, and American power, in the shape of its fortress Pentagon, was about to take the hit of its life.

Two nights before, millions had watched the Spielberg-Tom Hanks Second World War TV epic, *Band of Brothers*, based on Steven Ambrose's history of a paratroop company in the Normandy invasion. Like *Saving Private Ryan*, its selling point was supposed to be the unsparing realism of its combat scenes; its willingness to concede pain and terror. Up to a point. The tobacco tint of the images told you this was history, inspirational, consoling. And a history in which everything worked out just fine. Some, at least, of the good guys would make it. And whole nations of bad guys would bite the dust.

The media, reaching for one of their war-horse clichés (the other being sports), were quick to chorus that what happened was beyond the imaginings of the most feverish disaster movie. But the truth is that if the script of Bloody Tuesday had been offered to a studio, it would have been turned down not for the scale of the horror, but for its failure to supply identifiable villains. America's only usable analogy, Pearl Harbor, 7 December 1941, is on everyone's lips, on the streets and in the news studios. But there was no rising sun – nor for that matter a crescent moon – painted on the fuselage of the airplanes which slammed into the World Trade Center on Tuesday. Their markings belonged instead to United Airlines, whose corporate logo welcomes passengers to 'The Friendly Skies'.

Franklin Roosevelt bunched up American anguish and fury in his big meaty fist and smacked it out again as a war launched against an identifiable foe. The high-voltage energy on which American culture runs could be harnessed right away on concrete, practical work. Enlistment lines stretched round the block. Rubber and aluminium drives got under way. Trepidation surrendered to resolution. It was all very clear-cut; the way America likes it.

But this time the go-and-get-em American responses are scrambled by the terrifying diffuseness of the threat and the inconvenience of the enemy not being any sort of discernible nation state. 'Should the President and Congress make a formal declaration of war?' asked one CNN correspondent last night to another. 'Against whom, exactly?' he reasonably replied. She wasn't listening. 'But shouldn't we declare war?' she repeated, pointlessly. 'How about carpet-bombing everything between Jordan and Nepal?' one of my downtown friends who had seen the towers collapse in front of his eyes sardonically asked a belligerent comrade-in-suffering. 'Well, yes, that might take care of it,' was his reply. America, as Alexis de Tocqueville noticed in the mid-nineteenth century, was founded, and runs, on impatience.

Allied to impatience and impetuousness, de Tocqueville thought, was an uncompromising individualism, the American religion of self-sufficiency before which any sense of community would always have to yield. And you would suppose that if self-interest is a national cult on this side of the Atlantic, New York, the Look-at-me metropolis, would be its cathedral. But you'd be wrong. Foreigners – especially perhaps Britons who, on the basis of very little first-hand experience, still think of America as some sort of petulant child liable to throw a thermonuclear tantrum when denied its ice cream – always get New York, not to say the rest of the republic over which they used to fly en route to a ski-lodge in Colorado or the Golden Gate Bridge, wrong. This is a loud city all right, but decibels have nothing to do with decency, or the lack of it, and in the ten years I've been here, I've seen countless acts of spontaneous humanity that belie New York's reputation for callous narcissism.

In our first winter here, we managed to blow a tyre in the midst of a snowstorm, right under the George Washington Bridge, the neighbourhood which at that time richly merited its reputation as the crack capital of the Western world, and with the burned-out hulks of what once had been cars ominously decorating the roadside. But the cops who came to our rescue not only asked what they could do, but went ahead and changed the tyre (perhaps instantly sizing me up as someone seriously challenged in the jack-and-lugnut depart-ment). Since then I've seen ordinary New Yorkers go out of their way to help out people who were ill, lost or distressed in street, subway and park.

Don't get me wrong. It's not that this is the real city of angels. It's just that it's a city where people want to be doing, and if good is what has to be done, it gets done. So if there was any doubt that New York wouldn't be able to 'take it' on the chin like blitzed London, or that its citizens were too pampered a bunch to respond to catastrophe with anything but a panicky stampede to save their designer-label jogging shoes, it ought to have been laid to rest, first by the grieving calm which characterised the city and then by the outpouring of mass volunteerism which followed hard on the heels of the inferno. So many lined up quietly to volunteer for anything they could be called on to do that they had to be turned away. Lines formed round the block, waiting for hours to give blood; even when, to everyone's sorrow, there seemed to be precious few to give blood to.

We already have our local heroes and 300 of them are dead – the firemen, police and paramedics who were on the scene attempting to get people out of the World Trade Center when the towers fell on them. Their graves are the twisted remains of fire engines, shrouded, like everything else below 14th Street in a thick pall of grey ash, much of it dense with asbestos. Entire ladder companies disappeared in that holocaust.

Even to card-carrying liberals like me who have sometimes had misgivings about his red-hot temper, Mayor Giuliani changed overnight from Mussolini to Mother Teresa, appearing everywhere, often putting himself in harm's way, to comfort the distraught, encour-age the exhausted and, perhaps most important of all (especially at his press conferences), to tell the truth. A more inspiring example of common decency and instinctively practical humanity in public life you could not possibly imagine.

In glaring contrast, George Bush has yet to show his face on the island of Manhattan, lest a sooty cinder or two land on the smoothly shaved presidential chin. New Yorkers, who don't take kindly to being stood up, especially at times like this, are beginning to sound as though they might want to land something else, for all their initial basic instinct to rally round the flag and the man who is supposed to embody it.

Nor has the presidential performance on television been exactly Churchillian. Instead of bringing a traumatised country together as a family, united in shared grief and fortitude; instead of evoking the spirit of American trials past and how the republic has endured them, Bush (or his speechwriters, who need to get out of the East Wing and into the back yards of the bereft) has depended on warmed-up platitudes inherited, like much of the National Security cabinet, from the administration of Poppy and Reagan.

With every repetition of the fighting cliché, 'Make no mistake', the deeper the sinking feeling that neither he nor his administration has a clue about how to reboot their systems away from the comic-book obsession with 'missile defence' to actually protecting America from men with razor blades, box-cutters and Arabic flight-training manuals, much less an elementary degree in anthrax 101.

So instead of listening to cowboy pieties, or endlessly respooling video horror, or seeing in our mind's eye those twin towers as phantom, 110-storey tombstones, we turn to those who do, miraculously, know what they're supposed to say, feel and do: to Jeremy Glick who phoned his wife from the hijacked plane over Pennsylvania to tell her there had been a vote of all the men aboard to try to overpower the hijackers, even though they knew it would cost them all their lives, and who saved who-knows-how-many other lives by doing just that; to the son and daughter of one of the dead passengers letting themselves be interviewed on morning TV so they could appeal to the airlines to get their sister, marooned in London, back to the States for their father's funeral; to the handful of politicians who know when to speak and when to shut up; to all those in this suddenly, shockingly loving town who understand, especially when they hear the word 'revenge' thundered out by talk-show warriors, that the best, the only revenge, when you're fighting a cult that fetishises death, is life.

The Dead and the Guilty:
9/11 a year on

Guardian, 11 September 2002

For one afternoon, at least, it was grievously simple: Britons and Americans gathered, indivisibly, to mourn a shared massacre.

No terrorist attack in history had ever claimed more British lives: sixty-seven. So it seemed right that a dark Manchester drizzle was falling on Fifth Avenue on 20 September as mourners – and we were all mourners – climbed the steps of St Thomas's church, a piece of pure Barsetshire dropped into midtown Manhattan.

The usual suspects filed in: the Clintons, Kofi Annan, Mayor Giuliani, Governor Pataki. But before Tony and Cherie Blair arrived, a side door beside the choir opened and the British bereaved walked in to take their pews at the front of the church.

At once the brittle stylishness of the city collapsed into pathos. They were Britain: shapeless tweed jackets with leather elbow patches; reading glasses by Boots; Jermyn Street shirts for the upper crust. They looked lost in calamity; lost in New York. Bravery masked some faces; jaws set; staring straight ahead, afraid to blink.

Others bore the unmistakable marks of helpless, uncomprehending sorrow: red-rimmed eyes; cheeks pale with distraction, or bearing layers of repeatedly and hopelessly applied make-up. During the service, heads would suddenly bow as if bent with unsupportable feeling. At no point in particular, shoulders gently shook. An arm would reach round to do what it could.

Body language was everything that day and that week. Words had never seemed so redundant; so incapable of carrying the weight of trauma. Explicitly acknowledging this, knowing that simply showing up counted for more than any eloquence, the Prime Minister kept it brief.

A gaping, blackened ground zero had opened inside every New

Yorker (and everyone who had, through the catastrophe, become a New Yorker) and at the smoking core of the misery were, instead of words, images: spools of them, the ones you all know, looping mercilessly. The implausible glide into the steel; the blooming flower of flame; the slow, imploding crumple; the rolling tsunami of dust and shredded paperwork; the terrible drop of bodies, falling with heartbreaking grace like hunted birds.

Icons did the talking. The word means image, but also copy, and the iconology of 9/11, unlike the real thing which was utterly singular, drew on past images to guide instinctive response. Stored memories of the raising of the flag at Iwo Jima (itself an organised photo op) prompted the shot of firemen raising the flag on the torn steel ribs of the World Trade Center; a phoenix in the storm of dun ash.

The flags shouted, howled, roared. Tied as fluttering pennants to the radio antennae of Jeeps, they conquered the suburbs, as if drive-by patriotism could of itself make things better.

But other icons wept. In the days and weeks after 9/11 the city was papered with home-made or office-copied posters, bearing photos of missing loved ones, a format hitherto reserved for lost pets. Some of them bore heart-rending pocket attributes as if their indisputable like-ability ('she smiles a lot'; 'he has three-day stubble') would jog memories, help find them, bring them back safe and sound.

Quietness spoke volumes. Long lines of blood donors snaked round hospitals and clinics. Cartons of bottled water for rescue workers rose in charitable ziggurats outside police stations and schools.

And when words did finally return, they came back first as inspirational chorale: Irving Berlin's 'God Bless America' replacing 'Take Me Out to the Ballpark' as the anthem of the seventh-inning break when baseball fans get up and stre . . . tch.

In St Thomas's too, on the 20th, nothing was sung more fiercely than both national anthems, the Clintons singing 'God Save the Queen'; game Britons rising to the vocal and verbal challenge of 'The Star-Spangled Banner', a song composed during the 1812 war in which we burned Washington and the White House.

Speech returned, haltingly, in two guises: information from the inferno and pieties from the government. Rudolph Giuliani, often flanked by his commissioner of police and the fire department chief (who, respectively lost 80 and 343 of their men), mastered the first genre precisely because it was, for the mayor, a matter of common decency and practical necessity.

When George Bush began to vocalise again, it was with the pieties served up by his speechwriters, confident that his Manichaean declaration of war on evil also answered a deep need in the American public for moral clarity, spiritual consolation and recovered nerve.

He was not wrong about this. The homilies, not to mention the Waynesque vow to hunt the bad guys down — a promise yet to be fulfilled in the case of the al-Qaeda leadership — may have made Islington cringe, but then again Islington was not under attack.

The European press began to squirm uneasily at talk of evil, as if a wine-and-cheese party had suddenly turned into a Pentecostal revival meeting, and looked nervously round for the exit sign. Some of us, more accustomed to the religiosity of American life, had, and have, no problem whatever with using the e-word.

If the calculated mass murder of 3,000 innocent civilians, from eighty countries, many of them Muslims, just ordinary working people going about their business on a sunny September morning, was not an act of absolute evil, then I have no idea what is. The more serious problem with presidential rhetoric was that the Manichaean struggle between good and evil, freedom and terror, was not just the beginning, but apparently also the end of any sustained attempt to articulate just what, in this particular life-and-death struggle, was truly at stake.

Some weeks later Bill Clinton, both at Harvard and in the Richard Dimbleby lecture for the BBC, made exactly that effort. For obvious reasons the ex-president, now a New Yorker (in my very own neighbourhood), had been sparing with public commentary. But, struggling between prudence and thinly veiled exasperation, he emerged from silence, risking the wrath of patriotic blow-hards, to venture that a refusal to understand the roots of terrorism would be to guarantee its perpetuation.

Lest he be misunderstood, Clinton was also commendably clear on what the battle lines of the already bloody new century would be: the conflict between those who not only claimed a monopoly of wisdom, but the right to impose it on everyone else, against those who claimed neither. Put another way, the fight is between power based on revelation (and thus not open to argument) and power based on persuasion, and thus conditional on argument; militant theocracy against the tolerant Enlightenment.

Since the United States, notwithstanding the Pilgrims and the Great Awakening, was very much the child of the Enlightenment, one might have expected this case for tolerant, secular pluralism to be made in the most adamant and unapologetic fashion by the country's leadership.

But the shroud of mass reverence which enveloped everyone and everything after 9/11, and which once again is blanketing the anniversary, has succeeded in making secular debate about liberty into an act of indecency, disrespectful of the dead and disloyal to the flag.

The notion that the parliament of tongues is, in fact, our best vindication wins few hearts and minds right now. The centrepiece of Public Television's anniversary offerings was a *Frontline* documentary on how 9/11 had affected the religiosity of the nation.

The unsurprising answer is quite a lot. The steady drip of goodness and godliness (multi-faith, naturally) is a reminder of how impossible it seems, two and a half centuries later in America, for the magnitude of a calamity – in Voltaire's case, the Lisbon earthquake – to prompt awkward questions about either the competence or the benevolence of the Almighty.

More than one of the widows of 9/11, though, has been heard to say that she no longer talks to God; she talks to her dead husband. For the most part, though, to say out loud (as a few courageous souls have done) that religious revelation – Judaic and Christian as well as Muslim, not least the notion of a paradise for the pure – is the problem, is to risk immediate and irrevocable patriotic anathema.

Deist scepticism is, I'm sure, too cold a comfort to wish on the distraught, a mere year after the slaughter. As therapy for the traumatised, Bruce Springsteen's new hymnal, complete with gospel-choir backing and ringing with resurrectional themes of The Rising, will beat *Candide* every time. But the need to break clear from the suffocation of reverent togetherness is not just a matter of philosophical self-respect. The immediate future of the American Republic depends on it.

That the Bush administration would always prefer prayers to politics, avoiding at all costs debate, both within its own ranks and in the public arena, has long been apparent. Silence and secrecy, punctuated with disingenuousness, have consistently been its preferred modus operandi. (The problem with the Clintonites was something like the opposite: incontinent gabbiness.)

To this day, Dick Cheney, the most padlocked of all the senior members of the administration, refuses, even under legal pressure, to disclose to Congress the substance of what was discussed in closed meetings with energy-industry executives, leading to the formulation of a policy which corresponded precisely to the needs of business, rather than environmental lobbyists.

So we should not wonder at the aversion to debate, for the United States Inc. is currently being run by an oligarchy, conducting its affairs with a plutocratic effrontery which in comparison makes the age of the robber barons in the late nineteenth century seem a model of capitalist rectitude. The dominant managerial style of the oligarchy is golf-club chumminess; its messages exchanged along with hot stock tips by the mutual scratching and slapping of backs.

The corporations from which the government draws much of its personnel, including its chief executive, and which, on taking office, boasted of their business *savoir faire*, have not, in truth, produced very much, though some of them, like Dick Cheney's Halliburton, now under investigation by the Securities and Exchange Commission for creative accounting practices, have been past masters at converting political connections into corporate advantage and both into personal wealth.

The President himself owed his position at Harken Energy entirely to his name, and once there used it to get a stadium built from public funds for his Texas Rangers baseball team.

The Secretary of the Army, Thomas White – currently, one supposes, planning a war not a million miles away from a rich source of oil – was actually an executive of the spectacularly corrupt and incompetent Enron Corporation, whose implosion began the unravelling of scoundrel capitalism.

The administration's position on the scandals and follies of corporate America – essentially the world it comes from – is to flutter their fans in shock at the wickedness of Certain Individuals and to allow the selective distribution of scarlet letters while trumpeting ever more confidently the purity of the flock and the virtue of the Church. Nothing to do with us, heavens no. And it ploughs merrily ahead with policies expressly designed to come to the aid of distressed plutocracy.

Never mind that, thanks to the likes of the Secretary of the Army's and the Vice-President's old management practices, the stock exchange is mired in a debacle of broken confidence. Never mind that defenceless ex-employees of Enron, WorldCom and the like have seen their jobs and their stock-based pension plans evaporate, the President still thinks that privatisation of social security is the best way to ensure its future.

In a spin of breathtaking Orwellianism, the elimination of estate duties (paid only on fortunes of a quarter of a million dollars or more) is presented as the removal of a 'death tax', transforming a surrender of the public interest into a scene painted by Norman Rockwell with Mom or Pop able to breathe their last now that their legacy will safely pass to Junior unthreatened by the horny hand of bureaucratic brigands.

In the unedifying spectacle of the Sucker Economy, there is, as a mid-term election draws close, fuel for serious public contention; an argument, in fact, over the relative claims of community or corporation in post-9/11 America.

There are people to be held accountable, not least the oiligarch energy traders who, by manipulating demand, turn out to have caused the 2001 'energy crisis' in California which gave Republicans ammunition to pillory the Democratic governor of the state, Gray Davis. Though the hard-right ideologues who control Republican policy much more tenaciously than the smiley-face bonhomie of the President suggests want to identify the American Way, both at home and abroad, with the aggressive pursuit of self-interest, American history actually says otherwise.

It was Alexis de Tocqueville who, in the 1830s, first noticed the peculiar coexistence of a feverish, almost animal scramble for wealth, alongside a deep civic instinct; a feeling, in fact, for community.

The Republican rationalisation is to claim this as the exclusive territory of churches, but that is to ignore some of the most powerful urges in modern American life: the secular voluntarism and philanthropy which sustain museums, public broadcasting, libraries, conservation, even hospitals, and which flow not just from the rich but untold millions of middle-class Americans.

It is the same public spirit which drove the abolitionists of the nineteenth century and the Progressive movement of the early twentieth century. It moved Lady Bird Johnson to become an environmentalist and Jimmy Carter to build houses for the poor, and it is a social patriotism which is star-spangled Americanism at its most authentic.

And it has, already, made itself felt at Ground Zero. Plans to rebuild the site were initially subject to the New York port authority's requirement that the entirety of the thirteen million square feet of office and retail space lost to 9/11 be restored. Commercial rents and revenues were at stake.

This brief duly produced six architectural designs of such staggering banality, with mean little green spaces and walks shoehorned into spaces between bog-standard corporate towers. The public reaction was almost universal execration.

A series of town meetings made it overwhelmingly clear that the needs of civic rebirth and a memorial that would serve for lament, memory and meditation were a priority over business as usual. Starting over, the humane imagination, not a quality overvalued in oligarch America – though one which produced a deeply moving memorial at the site of the Oklahoma City bombing – has been called on to do its best.

This happened because voices were raised. The danger of the anniversary is that, out of respect for the dead and through a revisitation of shock, they will become, once again, reverently muffled. The administration is counting on just such a pious hush to bestow on its adventurism the odour of sanctity.

Apparently, the dead are owed another war. But they are not. What they are owed is a good, stand-up, bruising row over the fate of America; just who determines it and for what end?

The first and greatest weapon a democracy has for its own defence is the assumption of common equity; of shared sacrifice. That was what got us through the Blitz. It is, however, otherwise in oligarchic America. Those who are most eager to put young American lives on the line happen to be precisely those who have been greediest for the spoils.

The company run by the Vietnam draft-dodging ('I had other priorities') Cheney, Halliburton, has told the employees of one of its subsidiary companies (resold by Cheney) that the pension plans it was supposed to honour are now worth a fraction of what the workers had been counting on. On leaving the company in 2000 to run for Vice-President, however, Cheney himself was deemed to have 'retired' rather than resigned, thus walking away with a multimillion pension deal. So long, suckers.

Never have the ordinary people of America, the decent, working stiffs whose bodies lay in the hecatomb of Ground Zero, needed and deserved a great tribune more urgently. The greatest honour we could do them is to take back the voice of democracy from the plutocrats.

So it is altogether too bad that this Wednesday, Mayor Bloomberg and Governor Pataki, both liberal Republicans, both decent enough men, shrinking from the challenge to articulate such a debate, have decided instead to read from the Declaration of Independence, the Gettysburg Address and Franklin Roosevelt's 'Four Freedoms' speech. Those words – often sublime – derived their power from the urgency of the moment. To reiterate them merely to produce a moment of dependable veneration is to short-change both history and the present.

Though, in Britain, America is often ignorantly caricatured as a land of impoverished rhetoric, its public speech has often been the glory of its democracy.

And now it needs to sound off. Starting in New York, starting now, we need to do what the people of this astoundingly irrepressible city do best: stand up and make a hell of a noise.

The Civil War in the USA

Guardian, 5 November 2004

In the wee small hours of 3 November 2004, a new country appeared
on the map of the modern world: the DSA, the Divided States of
America. Oh yes, I know, the obligatory pieties about 'healing' have
begun; not least from the lips of the noble Loser. This is music to the
ears of the Victor of course, who wants nothing better than for us all
to Come Together, a position otherwise known as unconditional
surrender. Please, fellow curmudgeons and last ditchers, can someone on the losing side just for once not roll over and fall into a warm
bath of patriotic platitudes at such moments, but toot the flute of battle
instead; yell and holler and snarl just a wee bit? I don't want to heal
the wound, I want to scratch the damned thing until it hurts and bleeds
– and then maybe we'll have what it takes to get up from the mat. Do
we think the far-right Republican candidate Barry Goldwater, in the
ashy dawn of his annihilation in 1964, wanted to share? Don't think
so. He wanted to win; sometime. And now, by God, he has.

'We are one nation,' the newborn star of the Democrats, Senator-elect
Barack Obama, exclaimed, even as every salient fact of political life belied
him. Well might he invoke Lincoln, for not since the Civil War has the
fault line between its two halves been so glaringly clear, nor the chasm
between its two cultures so starkly unbridgeable. Even territorially (with
the exception of Florida, its peninsular finger pointing expectantly at
tottering Cuba), the two Americas are topographically coherent and
almost contiguous. One of those Americas is a perimeter, lying on the
oceans or athwart the fuzzy boundary with the Canadian lakes, and is
necessarily porous and outward-looking. The other America, whether
montagnard or prairie, is solidly continental and landlocked, its tap roots
of obstinate self-belief buried deep beneath the bluegrass and the high
corn. It is time we called those two Americas something other than
Republican and Democrat, for their mutual alienation and unforgiving

contempt are closer to Sunni and Shia, or (in Indian terms) Muslim and Hindu. How about, then, Godly America and Worldly America?

Worldly America, which of course John Kerry won by a massive landslide, faces, well, the world on its Pacific and Atlantic coasts and freely engages, commercially and culturally, with Asia and Europe in the easy understanding that those continents are a dynamic synthesis of ancient cultures and modern social and economic practices. This truism is unthreatening to Worldly America, not least because so many of its people, in the crowded cities, are themselves products of the old-new ways of Korea, Japan, Ireland or Italy. In Worldly America – in San Francisco, Chicago, San Diego, New York – the foreigner is not an anxiety, but rather a necessity. Its America is polycultural, not Pollyanna.

Godly America, on the other hand, rock-ribbed in Dick Cheney's Wyoming, stretched out just as far as it pleases in Dubya's deeply drilled Texas, turns its back on that dangerous, promiscuous, impure world and proclaims to high heaven the indestructible endurance of the American Difference. If Worldly America is, beyond anything else, a city, a street, and a port, Godly America is, at its heart (the organ whose bidding invariably determines its votes over the cooler instructions of the head), a church, a farm and a barracks; places that are walled, fenced and consecrated. Worldly America is about finding civil ways to share crowded space, from a metro-bus to the planet; Godly America is about making over space in its image. One America makes room, the other America muscles in.

Worldly America is pragmatic, practical, rational and sceptical. In California it passed Proposition 71, funding embryonic stem-cell research beyond the restrictions imposed by Bush's federal policy. Godly America is mythic, messianic, conversionary, given to acts of public witness, hence the need – in Utah and Montana and a handful of other states – to poll the voters on amendments to their state constitution defining marriage as a union between the opposite sexes. But then Worldly America is said to feed the carnal vanities; Godly America banishes and punishes them. From time to time Godly America will descend on the fleshpots of Worldly America, from Gotham (it had its citadel-like Convention there after all) to Californication, will shop for T-shirts, take a sniff at the local pagans and then return to base-camp more convinced than ever that a time of Redemption and Repentance must be at hand. But if the stiff-necked transgressors cannot be persuaded, they can be cowed and conquered.

No wonder so many of us got the election so fabulously wrong even into the early hours of Tuesday evening, when the exit polls were apparently giving John Kerry a two- or three-point lead in both Florida and Ohio. For most of us purblind writers spend our days in Worldly America and think that Godly America is some sort of quaint anachronism, doomed to atrophy and disappear as the hypermodernity of the cyber age overtakes it, in whatever fastness of Kentucky or Montana it might still circle its wagons. The shock for the Worldlies is to discover that Godly America is its modernity; that so far from it withering before the advance of the blog and the zip drive, it is actually empowered by them. The tenacity with which Godly America insists the theory of evolution is just that – a theory – with no more validity than Creationism, or that Iraqis did, in fact, bring down the twin towers, is not in any way challenged by the digital pathways of the information age. In fact, such articles of faith are expedited and reinforced by them. Holy bloggers bloviate, Pentecostalists ornament their website with a nimbus of trembling electronic radiance and, for all I know, you can download Pastor John Ashcroft singing the Praises of the Lord right to your Godpod.

Nor, it transpires, is the exercise of the franchise a sure-fire way for the Democrats to prevail. The received wisdom in these Worldly parts (subscribed to by yours truly; mea culpa) was that a massively higher turnout would necessarily favour Kerry. P. Diddy's 'Vote or Die' campaign was credited with getting out young voters en masse who ignored the polls in 2000. We saw a lot of Springsteen and Bon Jovi and ecstatic upturned faces. Who could possibly match their mobilisation, we thought? Answer: Jehovah and his Faithful Servant St Karl the Rove. The biggest story of all in 2004 is the astounding success of the Republicans in shipping millions of white evangelicals to the polls who had also stayed at home four years earlier. We thought we were fired up with righteous indignation – against the deceits of the propaganda campaign for the Iraq war, against the gross inequities of the tax cuts – but our fire was just hot air compared to the jihad launched by the Godlies against the infamy of a tax rollback, of merely presuming to diss the Dear Leader in a time of war. And the battalions of Christian soldiers made the telling difference in the few critical places where

Godly and Worldly America do actually rub shoulders (or at least share a state), Ohio above all.

By the lights of the psephology manuals, Ohio ought to have been a natural for the Democrats: ageing industrial cities such as Akron and Dayton, with big concentrations of minorities, suffering prolonged economic pain from outsourced industries. Cleveland and Cincinnati are classic cities of the Worldly plain: half-decayed, incompletely revived; great art museums, a rock'n'roll hall of fame, a terrific symphony orchestra. But drive a bit and you're in deep Zion, where the Holsteins graze by billboards urging the sinful to return to the bosom of the Almighty, the church of Friday-night high-school football shouts its hosannas at the touchdowns, and Support Our Troops signs grow as thick as the rutabaga. At first sight there's not much distance between this world and western Pennsylvania, but were the state line to be marked in twenty-foot-high electrified fences, the frontier between the two Americas couldn't be sharper. The voters of the 'Buckeye State' cities did care about their jobs; they did listen when Kerry told them the rich had done disproportionately nicely from Bush's tax cut. But they were also listening when their preachers (both black and white) fulminated against the uncleanliness of Sodom and the murder of the unborn. In the end, those whose most serious anxieties were the state of the economy and the Mess-o-potamia were outvoted by those who told exit pollers their greatest concern in 2004 was 'moral values'.

Faith-driven politics may even have had a hand in delivering Florida to Bush by a surprising margin, since it seems possible that Jewish voters there who voted for 'my son the Vice-President' Joe Lieberman (not to mention Hadassah, oy what nachas) in 2000, actually switched sides as a result of the President's support for Ariel Sharon. It wasn't that the Kerry campaign didn't notice the confessional effect. It was just that they didn't know what to do about it. Making the candidate over as some sort of altar boy (notwithstanding directives from Rome instructing the faithful on the abhorrence of his position on abortion) would have been about as persuasive as kitting him out with gun, camouflage and dead Canada geese; a laboriously transparent exercise in damning insincerity.

In Godly America the politics of impassioned conviction inevitably trumped the politics of logical argument. On CNN a fuming James

Carville wondered out loud how a candidate declared by the voting public to have decisively won at least two of the three televised debates could have still been defeated. But the 'victory' in those debates was one of body language rather than reasoned discourse. It registered more deeply with the public that the President looked hunched and peevish than that he had been called by Kerry on the irrelevance of the war in Iraq to the threat of terror. And since the insight was one of appearance, not essence, it could just as easily be replaced by countless photo-ops of the President restored to soundbite affability. The charge that Bush and his second war had actually made America less, not more, safe, and had created, not flushed out, nests of terror, simply failed to register with the majority of those who put that issue at the top of their concerns.

Why? Because, the President had 'acted', meaning he had killed at least some Middle Eastern bad dudes in response to 9/11. That they might be the wrong ones, in the wrong place – as Kerry said over and over – was simply too complicated a truth to master. Forget the quiz in political geography, the electorate was saying (for the popular commitment to altruistic democratic reconstruction on the Tigris is, whatever the White House orthodoxy, less than Wolfowitzian), it's all sand and towel-heads anyway, right? Just smash 'them' (as one ardent Bush supporter put it on talk radio the other morning) 'like a ripe cantaloupe'. Who them? Who gives a shit? Just make the testosterone tingle all the way to the polls. Thus it was that the war veteran found himself demonised as vacillating compromiser, the Osama Candidate, while a pair of draft-dodgers who had sacrificed more than 1,100 young men and women to a quixotic levantine makeover, and one which I prophesy will be ignominiously wound up by next summer (the isolationists in the administration having routed the neocons), got off scot-free, lionised as the Fathers of Our Troops.

Well, the autumn leaves have, just this week, fallen from the trees up here in the Hudson Valley and the scales from the eyes of us deluded Worldlies. If there is to be any sort of serious political future for the Democrats, they have to do far more than merely trade on the shortcomings of the incumbents – and there will be opportunities galore in the witching years ahead (a military mire, a fiscal China syndrome and, hello, right before inauguration, a visit from al-Qaeda). The real challenge is to voice an alternative social gospel to the political liturgy of the Godlies; one that redefines patriotism as an American community, not just a collection of wealth-seeking individuals; one that refuses to play a zero-sum game between freedom and justice; one in which, as the last populist president put it just a week ago, thought and hope are not mutually exclusive. You want moral values? So do we, but let them come from the street, not the pulpit. And if a fresh beginning must be made — and it must — let it not begin with a healing, but with a fight.

Katrina and George Bush

Guardian, 12 September 2005

Slipstreaming behind the annual rituals of sorrow and reverence for 9/11, George W. Bush has decreed that, five days later, on the 16th, there is to be a further day of solemnities on which the nation will pray for the unnumbered victims of Hurricane Katrina. Prayers (like vacations) are the default mode for this president, who knows how to chuckle and bow the head in the midst of disaster but not, when it counts, how to govern or to command. If you feel the prickly heat of politics, summon a hymn to make it go away; make accountability seem a blasphemy. Thus has George Bush become the Archbishop of Washington even as his aura as lord protector slides into the putrid black lagoon, bobbing with cadavers and slick with oil, that has swallowed New Orleans. No doubt the born-again President is himself sincere about invoking the Almighty. But you can hear the muttered advice in the White House: Mr President, we were in trouble after 9/11; the unfortunate episode of the schoolroom, My Little Goat and all that. But do what you did then; set yourself once more at the centre of the nation; go to the epicentre of the horror and embrace its heroes; make yourself the country's patriotic invigorator and all may yet be well.

So this weekend it was predictable that the president would shamelessly invoke the spirit of 9/11 to cover his shamefully exposed rear end – 'resolve of nation . . . defend freedom . . . rebuild wounded city . . . care for our neighbours'. But comparisons with 9/11 – the fourth anniversary of which was marked in New York yesterday – will only serve now to reinforce the differences between what the two calamities said about America, and especially about those entrusted with its government. The carnage of 9/11 generated an intense surge of patriotic solidarity, even with America's Babylon, a city scandalously and notoriously indifferent to Heartland values. This was because the mass murders had been committed by people who defined foreignness: theocratic nihilists who equated pluralist democracy with depravity. A hard-ass city supposedly abandoned to the most brutal forms of aggressive individualism (a fiction it liked to cultivate) showed instead the face of American mutualism as volunteers poured into the smouldering toxic crater. Blood and food donations piled up and a mayor disregarded his personal safety to be where he had to be, in the thick of the inferno; his daily press conferences astoundingly bullshit-free, unafraid of bearing bad news; treating his fellow citizens, *mirabile dictu*, like grown-ups.

The rest of the country looked at Zoo York and, astoundingly, saw images and heard stories that made themselves feel good about being American: the flag of defiance flown by firemen amid the Gothic ruins; the countless tales of bravery and sacrifice among those trapped inside the towers. For all the horror, this could be made into a good epic of the American character. It was this redeeming sense of national community that protected the President from any kind of serious political scrutiny whenever he invoked 9/11 as the overwhelming reason for launching the invasion of Iraq. As John Kerry found to his cost, unexamined passion triumphed over reasoned argument. Bush won re-election simply by making debate a kind of treason; an offence against the entombed.

Out of the genuinely noble response to 9/11, then, came an unconscionable deceit. Out of the ignoble response to Katrina will come a salutary truth. For along with much of New Orleans, the hurricane has swept away, at last, the shameful American era of the fearfully buttoned lip. Television networks that have self-censored themselves into abject deference have not flinched from their responsibility to show corpses drifting in the water; lines of the forlorn and the abandoned sitting amid piles of garbage outside the Convention Centre; patients from Charity Hospital waiting in the broiling sun in vain for water and medical supplies; helicopters too frightened of armed looters to actually land, but throwing bottles of water down from their twenty-foot hover. Embarrassed by their ignorance of the cesspool that was the Convention Centre, members of the government protested that it was hard to know what was really going on 'on the ground'. All they had to do was to turn on the TV to find out.

Millions of ordinary Americans did. And what they saw, as so many of them have said, was the brutality, destitution, desperation and chaos of the Third World. Instead of instinctive solidarity and compassion, they have witnessed a descent into a Hobbesian state of nature; with Leviathan offering fly-by compassion, 30,000 feet up, and then, once returned to the White House, broadcasting a defensive laundry list of deliveries, few of which showed up when and where they were needed. Instead of acts of mutual succour, there was the police force of Gretna, south of New Orleans, sealing off a bridge against incoming evacuees, and turning them back under threats of gunfire. Instead of a ubiquitous mayor with his finger on the pulse, and the guts to tell the truth, enter Michael Brown, a pathetically inadequate director of the Federal Emergency Management Agency, Fema, hounded from his eleven-year tenure as supervisor of commissioners and stewards of the International Arabian Horse Association by legal proceedings. Instead of summarily firing 'Brownie', the President ostentatiously congratulated him on camera for doing 'a heck of a job'.

Only on Friday, in an attempt at damage control, was the hapless Brown 'recalled' to Washington, his position as Fema director intact.

And instead of an urban community of every conceivable race, religion and even class brought together by trauma, another kind of city, startlingly divided by race and fortune, has symbolised everything about America that makes its people uneasy, ashamed and, finally, perhaps lethally for the conservative ascendancy and its myths, angry. A faint but detectable whiff of mortality is steaming up, not just from the Louisiana mire, but from this Republican administration. Call me a cynic, but is it entirely a coincidence that suddenly the great black hope of moderate Republicanism, Colin Powell, is everywhere, publicly repenting of his speech to the UN (and by implication damning those who supplied him with unreliable intelligence), and offering, unbidden, his own lament for the institutional meltdown that followed the breach of the levee? The administration is already thought of as a turkey and the turkey vultures are starting to wheel.

Historians ought not to be in the prophecy business, but I'll venture this one: Katrina will be seen as a watershed in the public and political life of the US, because it has put back into play the profound question of American government. Ever since Ronald Reagan proclaimed that government was not the answer but the problem, conservatism has stigmatised public service as parasitically unpatriotic, an anomaly in the robust self-sufficiency of American life. For the most part, Democrats have been too supine, too embarrassed and too inarticulate to fight back with a coherent defence of the legiti-macy of democratic government. Now, if ever, is their moment; not to revive the New Deal or the Great Society (though unapologetically preserving social security might be a start), but to stake a claim to being the party that delivers competent, humane, responsive govern-ment, the party of public trust.

For the most shocking difference between 9/11 and Katrina was in what might have been expected in the aftermath of disaster. For all the intelligence soundings, it was impossible to predict the ferocity, much less the timing, of the 9/11 attacks. But Katrina was the most anticipated catastrophe in modern American history. Perhaps the lowest point in Bush's abject performance last week was when he claimed that no one could have predicted the breach in the New Orleans levees, when report after report commissioned by him, not to mention a simulation just last year, had done precisely that. But he had cut the budget appropriation for maintaining flood defences by nearly 50 per cent, so that for the first time in thirty-seven years Louisiana was unable to supply the protection it knew it would need in the event of catastrophe. Likewise Fema, which under Bill Clinton had been a cabinet-level agency reporting directly to the President, had under his successor been turned into a hiring opportunity for polit-ical hacks and cronies and disappeared into the lumbering behemoth of Homeland Security. It was Fema that failed the Gulf; Fema which failed to secure the delivery of food, water, ice and medical supplies desperately asked for by the Mayor of New Orleans; and it was the President and his government-averse administration that had made Fema a bad joke.

In the last election campaign George W. Bush asked Americans to vote for him as the man who would best fulfil the most essential obligation of government: the impartial and vigilant protection of its citizens. Now the fraudulence of the claim has come back to haunt him, not in Baghdad, but in the drowned counties of Louisiana. In the recoil, disgust and fury felt by millions of Americans at this abdi-cation of responsibility, the President – notwithstanding his comically self-serving promise to lead an inquiry into the fiasco – will assuredly reap the whirlwind.

Obama Rising: The Denver Speech

Guardian, 30 August 2008

Oh, how the McCain campaign must have chuckled when they got an inkling of what the Obama strategists had in mind as the backdrop for his acceptance speech in the stadium of the Denver Broncos, surmounted by an apparently neutered plaster stallion. Architrave alert! Fluted columns! Cecil B. DeMille Doric! What a gift to satirists who could lampoon Obama as a wannabe Demosthenes, so self-monumentalised that he seemed to be presumptuously rehearsing the inaugural oath on the Capitol steps. It's possible that, even after one of the most memorably dramatic speeches in modern American history, they may still be betting on what they think is an eloquence aversion out there in the heartland; the ingrained suspicion that fancy phrase-making is a fig leaf for lack of substance. Early in the primary season Hillary Clinton made much of the difference between words and deeds, as if high rhetoric was a tip-off to political inadequacy. Beware fine words, that unsubtle message ran, for they are gossamer, the pretty fabric you spin when you can't hack the hard stuff of power. By this reasoning, McCain is a shoo-in, not in spite of his shortcomings in the eloquence department, but because of them. The Hanoi Hilton, after all, was a place of terrifying silence, and aw shucks will beat silver tongue every time with the regular Joes and Janes.

But this year, the year of primal national scream in the US, is this smart politics? In the end the Republican posture of laconic authenticity, of Quiet Americans, may backfire. For what Obama delivered on Thursday night deliberately left pyrotechnics to the literal fireworks that brought the convention to an end. Instead he delivered severity; combative polemic over the hurting body of the republic; a gripping sense of the magnitude of the moment, without ever dropping his audience into resignation or pessimism. It was the least showy and, by some distance I think, the most moving and powerful of all his remarkable speeches, for its eschewal of rhetorical flamboyance was done in the service of a higher goal: the rebirth of what he called in his stirring peroration 'common purpose', meaning the reassertion of mutuality without the compromise of individuality.

It is this insistence of being one's brother's and sister's keeper as a pure American ideal, the questioning of what an 'ownership society' means, that was so heartening. What Obama seems to be after is not just the reawakening of national community, but altering what an election campaign actually is. 'You can make a big election small,' he said, witheringly, of the decades of Lee Atwater, Roger Ailes and Karl Rove. The time is too serious, the stakes too high, to tolerate that kind of politics. After cataloguing the Bush administration's manifold failures, something happened to his voice that, in the months that I have followed him since the Iowa caucuses, I have never heard: a ferocious roar of fury bellowed into the microphone. And the word that formed in the fire of his indignation was, simply: 'ENOUGH!' It was a Shakespearean moment that shook the 80,000 rigid, and ought to have disabused any Republicans of the idle assumption that they are taking on a remote, effete intellectual who doesn't have the wherewithal for bloody political combat.

So Obama is betting on the word's enduring power as a reformer of American life. Historically he has good reason for, from the beginning, words and texts have constructed American realities, not the other way round. The spell cast on Americans by the mantle of words goes all the way back to the first Great Awakening in the 1740s when flocks thrilled to Methodist preachers such as George Whitefield. Evangelical passion remains a brilliant strand in the weave of American discourse, but when it made way for the reasoning of the Enlightenment deists and unitarians who made the revolution, another element of American speech-power sounded loud and clear: the reverence for classical oratory.

The Republican bet is that all this is a thing of the past; that, self-evidently, we live in the age of images, and words are just the add-ons to the beguilement of the eye; that all we have are soundbites. Obama's is the more stunning gamble; that so far from the digital age killing off the reign of the word, it has actually given logos a whole new lease of life.

As I write this, the diapason of Martin Luther King's rhetoric on 28 August 1963 rolls over the stadium again, while beside me a row of bloggers writing for *blackamericaweb.com* tap their keyboards. In downtown Denver the places where energy spilled over were certainly not the citadels of CNN or the networks, but the spaces occupied by the Daily Kos, Wonkette and the rest. The blog and the great speech are the low and the high of the enduring dominion of American words; and Obama is betting that words still have the force to remake politics, and even government. Obama is Dick Cheney's worst nightmare, for he represents the antidote to the unanswerably laconic. Has there ever been a politician who revelled in deadly quietness quite so much as Cheney?

Ravelled up inside that gamble is another daring hunch: that, of all Americans, Obama is uniquely qualified to braid together the two great strands of national rhetoric. On the one hand, that of black redemption: saturated with scriptural passion; the eloquence of Martin Luther King (whom in a wonderful conceit Obama simply called 'the Preacher'); the language that altered what Lyndon Johnson believed and did. And on the other, the rhetoric of American classicism: Lincoln's, Franklin Roosevelt's and Jack Kennedy's. From these distinct threads he is hoping to make a new American fabric of speech.

On this evening, though, Obama knew he had to make his words do two things: go on unsparing attack against his opponent, and somehow become a natural extension of the everyday life of suffering Americans. The attack speech, delivered with sombre coldness, did the job. Taking his high concerns to regular Americans was the tougher assignment. Knowing there could be no point in making Obama sound like a trucker faced with foreclosure, the campaign hit on the clever device of having a parade of indisputably middle-class Americans, some long-time Republicans, deliver their grievances to camera. The populist voice comes right from the *populus*.

What Obama did is to touch the nerve of what he knows most Americans care about: old-fashioned virtues – the 'dignity of hard work'; the promise of fair reward for that work; patriotism; the 'promise' that if they live right and do right, their children will reap the reward of that promise. 'That's why I am here,' he said, 'that's what I think every time I tuck my children up at night.'

Suddenly Obama becomes not a politician but a dad, who needs no prompting to understand the heroism of everyday life. In another agile counterpunch at the Republican accusation that he is no more than a 'celebrity', Obama, speaking of the sacrifices of his mother and grand-parents, said: 'I don't know what kind of lives John McCain thinks that celebrities lead, but this has been mine. These are my heroes.' And equally suddenly McCain turns into the patrician who isn't sure how many homes he owns.

In contrast to Al Gore's sententiousness and John Kerry's high-minded elegance, Obama is light on his feet and deadly with his jabs, a pre-emptive warrior. A parade of generals and admirals attest to his fitness to be commander-in-chief, but more spunkily he says: 'If John McCain wants to have a debate about who has the temperament . . . to serve as the next commander-in-chief, that's a debate I'm ready to have.' From this unlikely investment of authority, he says to McCain: 'Let us agree that patriotism has no party . . . so I've got news for you . . . We all put our country first.'

Obama is staking the whole house on a belief that the times are so serious, the damage wrought in the past eight years so grave, that for once the American voters are hungry for a reborn sense of national community, and a president who embodies it. It's common-place that the problem for McCain is that he is too old, and for Obama that he's too young. But one of the transformations that happened in this speech was to make Obama seem a whole lot older, or at least more grown-up, than McCain. As he himself says, his call for a rekindled sense of common purpose can be written off as so much 'happy talk'. The campaign can go straight downhill to its customary depths. But the Republicans had better practise an unac-customed economy of derision, for after Obama's severe magnificence, an attack on his style carries the risk of churlishness: the grim snicker of the crabbed.

Bye-Bye, Dubya

Guardian, 3 November 2008

'Forgotten but not gone' was the way in which the supremo of Boston politics, Billy Bulger, liked to dismiss the human irritants he had crushed beneath his trim boot. The same could now be said for the hapless forty-third President of the United States as the daylight draws mercifully in on his reign of misfortune and calamity. How is he bearing up, one wonders, as the candidate from his own party treats him as the carrier of some sort of infectious political disease? How telling was it that the most impassioned moment in John McCain's performance in the final debate was when he declared: 'I am not George Bush.'

Where, O where, are you, Dubya, as the action passes you by like a jet skirting dirty weather? Are you roaming the lonely corridors of the White House in search of a friendly shoulder around which to clap your affable arm? Are you sweating it out on the treadmill, hurt and confused as to why the man everyone wanted to have a beer (or Coke) with, who swept to re-election four years ago, has been downgraded to all-time loser in presidential history, stuck there in the bush leagues along with the likes of James Buchanan and Warren Harding? Or are you whacking brush in Crawford, where the locals now make a point of telling visitors that George W. never really was from hereabouts anyroad.

Whatever else his legacy, the man who called himself 'the decider' has left some gripping history. The last eight years have been so rich in epic imperial hubris that it would take a reborn Gibbon to do justice to the fall. It should be said right away that amid the landscape of smoking craters there are one or two sprigs of decency that have been planted: record amounts of financial help given to Aids-blighted countries of Africa; immigration reform that would have offered an amnesty to illegals and given them a secure path to citizenship, had not those efforts hit the reef of intransigence in Bush's own party. And no one can argue with the fact that since 9/11 the United States has not been attacked on its home territory by jihadi terrorists; though whether or not that security is more illusory than real is, to put it mildly, open to debate.

But against that there is the matter of hundreds of thousands of Iraqi civilian casualties, more than 4,000 American troops dead, many times that gravely injured, not to mention the puncture wounds and mutilations inflicted on internationally agreed standards of humane conduct for prisoners – and on the protection of domestic liberties enshrined in the American constitution. If the Statue of Liberty were alive, she would be weeping tears of blood.

If Bush himself has been largely kept out of sight, his baleful legacy has been visible in the McCain campaign. McCain has made much of his credentials for independence of mind, a claim which once was credible given his support for immigration reform and opposition to Bush's tax cuts. But somewhere along the road to the Republican nomination, all of this became less important than the lessons of the Reagan-Bush-Rove political playbook which, with the exception of the Clinton election of 1992, seemed to have a track record of unbroken success.

McCain knew this from bitter personal experience, having been on the receiving end of Bush lowball politics in the South Carolina primary in 2000. Coming out of a convincing win against George Bush in New Hampshire, he was stopped in his tracks by a smear campaign conducted through push-poll phone calls in which people were asked whether they knew that the daughter McCain had adopted from Sri Lanka was in fact the illegitimate child of an affair with a woman of colour. Now you would think McCain could never reconcile himself to a politician capable of those kinds of tactics. But there he was in the campaign of 2004, stumping the country for the incumbent, ingratiating himself with the conservative base he knew he would need, even as his old Vietnam buddy, John Kerry, was being coated in slime by the Swift Boaters.

Whatever misgivings McCain might have had about adopting the hardball tactics of his 2000 adversary have long since disappeared before the blandishments of classic Bush-style operatives like Rick Davis and Stephen Schmidt. 'Do you want to be pure, or do you want to win?' they must have asked right after the nomination. Ditching Joe Lieberman as a running mate and unleashing pitbull Palin was his answer.

So even while George Bush is kept at arm's length from the campaign, his campaign style lives on as Obama is stigmatised as a terrorist-friendly stealth-socialist, too deeply un-American to be let anywhere near the Oval Office. 'He just doesn't see America as we do,' says Sarah Palin, trying to wink her way into Dick Cheney's seat. McCain is betting the house that this way of doing politics has at least one more hurrah left in it, and we will find out in the early hours of Wednesday morning whether he is right.

The Bush presidency is the spectre haunting the feast in more than tactics. Although every conservative administration since Ronald Reagan has promised to deliver, through supply-side stimulation, economic growth without bloated deficits, they have never been vindicated in their blind faith in what Bush senior once rashly called 'voodoo economics'. Consistently, they have brought the US Wall Street crashes and recessions along with massive deficits; and yet somehow, the stake that history attempts to drive through the heart of their economic theology never puts the ghoul away.

No weight of evidence to the contrary has ever shaken the totemic belief that tax cuts can grow the economy robustly enough to compensate for drastic shortfalls in revenue. George W. Bush clung to this belief even as the Clinton budget surplus was converted into a mountainous deficit, and John McCain continues to parrot the same belief with the shining face of a true believer.

Not even Gibbon could supply a story as fatefully bizarre as the ultimate consummation of Reagan-Bush conservatism, its last act: the most massive shift of financial power from the private to the public sector since the New Deal. Rather like the Pope deciding that all along he really wanted a bar mitzvah.

If you look at this saga as the history of a dynasty, it's come full circle. For, believe it or not, there once was a time when Bush politics was about centrist moderation. Dubya's revered granddad, Prescott Sheldon Bush, son of an Ohio railroad executive and Senator for Connecticut from 1952 to 1963, was punished in the Catholic towns of industrial Connecticut for his connection with Planned Parenthood. Not only that, but he was a trustee of the United Negro College Fund, the kind of institution that made the eventual career of Barack Obama conceivable.

But the Bushes have always been selective about idealism. And even at the height of the Kennedy-Johnson apogee, Prescott and George Herbert Walker Bush were turning the pages of Barry Goldwater's *Conscience of a Conservative*. They could smell the wind-direction changing. The future of Republican money and Republican power lay elsewhere; with Texas oil. Hence the migration to Midland Texas of George Herbert Walker Bush and his makeover into a Texan who knew the ways of the corporate world; and how to bring about the Great Cosiness between government and business that seemed like the perfect feedback loop: money to power, power to money; tax breaks for the corporations; donations to those who might command the heights.

This is the politics George W. Bush inherited, and he has been its faithful disciple; to the point of purging it of any remaining traces of pragmatism. It is astounding to hear right-wing talk-show bloviators rant about the predicament of the Bush administration being caused by its failure to carry out the true conservative agenda. For there never has been and never will be a more doctrinally faithful instrument of the creed. Never mind the hanging chads of 2000, the Cheney-Bush administration seized the moment to bring on the Goldwater-Reagan Rapture in which government was once and for all got out of the way of business.

So it hasn't really been all George Bush's fault, the stupendous American fiasco. He came to power armed with an ideology that was about to crash and burn; that was, years before the present tumult, already fatally disconnected from historical reality. It was on his watch that American government needed reinventing. It was responsible government that was needed in Iraq and Afghanistan; government that was desperately needed in New Orleans after Katrina, while all George Bush could manage was a fly-by. It is government that this most anti-governmental of all American administrations is learning that is needed now to save the United States from a second Depression.

In his heart of hearts I actually think the shell-shocked Dubya, somewhere in the bowels of his presidency, knows this. But he is nowhere to be found, and so on goes the mad rant that healthcare

reform and progressive taxes are the Trojan horse for socialist revolution. To which those who have another view altogether might want
to say, fear not, for yours, as a Republican president once said, is a
government of the people, by the people. And really it will not perish
from the earth.

The British Election, 2005

Guardian, 5 May 2005

It was when Michael Howard shifted into the conditional mood that I knew which side of the Atlantic I was really on. 'On Friday,' he said, 'Britain could wake up to a brighter future.' COULD? You mean . . . it might not happen? If this had been Detroit or San Diego or Dubuque, incredulous staffers would have rushed the candidate off the podium for emergency reprogramming. 'Will, Michael,' they would chant patiently at him until he Got It. 'Never, ever so much as breathe a possibility of defeat.' But this wasn't Dubuque, it was the Ashford Holiday Inn, and the Somewhat Beloved Leader was addressing the party faithful on how, probably, all things considered, he might, with any luck, and showery periods on Thursday, even the score by full time.

Howard's vision of a briskly spring-cleaned Albion was meant as a rousing clarion call, but it had all the resonance of a tinkling bicycle bell in a country lane. I was just a few hours off the jumbo from Newark, New Jersey, but it felt like dropping down the rabbit hole and emerging into parish-pump politics. Compared with the engorged rapture, the fully orchestrated Hollywood production numbers; the serried ranks of Raybanned Secret Service Men; the ululating good 'ole boys, the big-hair hoopla, the bra-popping, pompom-waggling cheerleaders, the Spandex highkicks; the tossing ocean of flags; the relentlessly inspirational gospel songs; the banners as big as a wall; the parade of uniforms (any uniform will do – firemen, police, marines, traffic wardens, apartment-house doormen); the descending chopper blades; the eventual appearance of the Awaited One to swoons of joy and exultant whoops of messianic acclaim; compared to the whole delirious cornball razzmatazz that passes for democratic politics in the great American empire, Ashford on a bank-holiday weekend was utter Ambridge. Thank God. Except he too was mercifully missing from the general election.

After the stifling incense-choked sanctimoniousness of American politics, getting back to Britain was like coming up for air. Or was I just nostalgic; childishly elated to be on the electoral roll for the first time, after twenty years of residential disenfranchisement? Maybe I was succumbing to antiquated memories of campaigns past: traipsing house to house for Harold Wilson in the brickier zones of Cambridge in 1984; exhilarated that we were at last on the threshold of seeing off the Tories who'd been Her Majesty's government ever since I'd become aware of politics. (Many years on, I'd seen The Enemy close up. Tripping over a rug in the Christ's College senior common room, I rose to find myself face to face with Harold Macmillan's whiskers. 'There there,' Supermac drawled, not missing a beat, 'gratitude understandable; prostration quite unnecessary.') Little did he know. In 1964 we were the New Model Army in Morris Minors, interrupting *Housewives' Choice* to drive aproned grannies to the polls, transforming, as we thought, a forelock-tugging squirearchical Britain into the bracing social democracy of George Brown, Barbara Castle and Roy Jenkins.

There had always been a streak of political feistiness in our family. Living in Margaret Thatcher's Finchley, my father had been so furious at the presumption of whomever it was that had put up a Conservative sign in front of his block of flats, suggesting collective allegiance, that he'd hung from the window balcony of number 26 the biggest Labour-party banner he could find. No one spoke to him in synagogue for months after that. So, yes, coming home politically probably meant returning to unrealistic expectations of face-to-face, high-street, argy-bargy oxygenated polemics. But even if it fell short, it would still feel like red meat compared to the white-bread pap I'd had to consume in the last election I'd covered for this paper: Bush v. Kerry, 2004; primetime-ready brand marketing, punctuated only by sleazebag character assassination.

I'd heard reports that British politics had been invaded by focus-group, market-tested campaigning. That, between Lynton Crosby and Maurice Saatchi, the Tories were playing the American game, eavesdropping on Basil Fawlty in the snug and turning his pet peeves into electoral policy. Are you drinking what I'm drinking, squire?

But if slick persuasiveness was the idea, Howard's performance at Ashford suggested there was more work to be done. After a sly warm-up speech by Damian Green, the local MP, the Somewhat Beloved Leader entered to the stirring chords of 'Victory at Sea', composed for television in the early 1960s by the true-blue American Richard Rodgers. Was this a good idea? Tory party as HMS *Victory*, fine. Pity about the 'At Sea' bit, though.

There then followed what in America would be called the Stump Speech, except that 'stump' with its evocation of cigar-pulling down-home wisdom, cookie-bake homilies and a feverish orgy of baby-kissing, isn't really mid-Kent. To rapt silence, broken only by aldermanic murmurs of assent, the SBL painted an apocalyptic picture of a New Labour Britain – *Blade Runner* with tea – in which pensioners no longer feel free to go to the shops in safety, where MRSA pullulates in hospitals unchecked by Matron, where a critical swab shortage holds up urgent surgery, a Britain where the police are doomed to standing around on street corners sucking on pencils as they complete interminable questionnaires while platoons of drunken yobs, Shauns of the Undead, run amok in the high street, pillaging Starbucks and sacking Boots.

Under his government, Howard pledged, the police would be liberated from pencil duty and set free to 'invade the personal physical space' of the yobs (protected, presumably, by rubber gloves obtained from Matron). SWABS not YOBS: who could possibly disagree?

Several times we were promised a government which would roll up its sleeves (though those of Howard's blue shirt remained elegantly buttoned). Then came the really worrying bit. SBL's voice dropped, the eyes moistened, the smile widened. Acute observers could instantly recognise the onset of a Sincerity Attack. 'I love my country.' Then he told us how he truly feels. About himself. About Britain. Proud. Immigrant roots. State school. Really proud. Work hard. Do well. What Britain's all about. Not layabout.

This sort of thing is of course obligatory for American campaigns where the 'story' of the candidate – a combination of autobiographical confession and patriotic profession – is the *sine qua non* of 'making a connection with the voters'. But in Ashford, among the flowery frocks and jackets flecked with dog-hair, the narrative seemed wetly embarrassing. Then exit to reprise of 'Victory at Sea' and sustained (if not exactly deafening) applause. The faithful were giddy with excitement. Well, almost all of them. One loyalist with a bottle-green flying-ducks tie was still barking over the State of the Country. 'Are you optimistic about Thursday?' I asked tentatively. 'I TRY to be,' he conceded, 'though I was going to desert the sinking ship.' 'Where to?' 'Montenegro.' 'Montenegro?' 'Yes, Montenegro. Not many people know this, but the wine is wonderful and —' (he whispered confidentially) '— they have the most beautiful women in the world. Though, of course, they do tend to be a bit hairy.'

As indeed do the campaigns in these endgame days. Not that you'd guess it watching Howard taking a walkabout on his own patch. For once the sun shone benevolently on his progress. ('We arrive; it rains. It always rains,' said one campaign Eeyore on the battle bus.) Howard was bouncily affable as he trotted down Folkestone high street, a place inexplicably bereft of the roaming hordes of ruffians and mendicant asylum-seekers he says infest New Labour's derelict Britain. Surely he can't mean the ubiquitous Ecuadorian pan-pipers (are there any left in the Andes?) who warbled away while the SBL closed in on constituents, for an economical hand-pump (pensioners got a concerned left hand on their arm too) adroitly avoiding, in short order, the Green party table overstocked with belligerently pacifist eco-literature; giggly girls stuffed into jeans shouting their resolution to vote for the Official Monster Raving Loony party; and burps and hoots from acne-stricken yoofs dressed, bafflingly, in Boston Celtics kit.

As the Leader ducked into Celeste, 'A Taste of Heaven on Earth', for lunch, I was left marvelling at the village-green cosiness of it all; unthinkable in the United States where the candidate would be flanked by a wall of myrmidons with imperfectly concealed shoulder holsters, and would never ever be unplugged from the earpiece through which staff would prompt his every reply. ('Remember, Michael, WHEN we win, not IF!') As for the Monster Raving Loony party, they would be in a Secure Holding Facility, not munching on ham sandwiches ten feet away from the Leader. But in Folkestone, the sun glinted off the sea, vagrant scavenging gulls wheeled around the battle bus (send 'em home) and the violent grunge-hole of Howard's Albion seemed a long way away.

What is it that draws British politicians down to the sea? Conferences in Blackpool and Brighton; a rally for the Labour party in Hove? In America they go to the major markets: conventions, then, in Chicago, Los Angeles, New York, not Cape Cod or Virginia Beach. I was at the only exception, forty years ago, Lyndon Johnson's coronation in Atlantic City, where, amidst the toffee vendors on the boardwalk, porky-pink straw-boatered men from Mississippi with wilting bow ties pretended not to notice the civil-rights demonstrators. At the moment of apotheosis, LBJ, the Hidden One, rose majestically on to the stage on a hydraulic platform as thousands of minute plastic cowboys descended on parachutes from the convention-hall roof. 'All the Way with LBJ,' the Democrats roared. And they did; all the way to Hué and Saigon and the helicopters on the roof.

But whatever's wrong with this election, it isn't hubris. No one was shouting 'If you care, vote for Blair' in Hove last Sunday. In fact they weren't shouting at all. Everything and everyone, except David Blunkett, who gave new meaning to the word unrepentant, was a tad defensive, beginning with the lighting of the stage – not exactly shameless red, more softly fuchsia, the kind of ambient glow that lap dancers use to juice the tips.

The audience in Hove town hall resembled an almost ideological parade of domesticity: babies had tantrums; toddlers toddled, primary-schoolers kicked balls around the back with New Labour dads.

Blunkett eschewed altogether the much-vaunted masochism strategy in favour of unapologetic balls-of-brass: 'You know why they're attacking Tony Blair?' No, go on, tell us. 'Because Tony Blair is the greatest asset the Labour party has.' He even told a story against himself involving blindness and flirting, which somehow managed to make him endearing.

The comedian, Jo Brand, warming up for Blair, was rather more equivocal. She gave him just one stick-on star for achievement, but two for effort. She would vote Labour, she conceded, but there were some, well, a lot of really, things she wasn't too keen on – the small matter of a dodgy war, for instance. But, you know, you wouldn't want Michael Howard, would you?

Stateside, this less-than-ringing endorsement would be a cue for loud music and dimming of stage lights, while Brand was swiftly escorted from the podium and conveyed to a long and richly deserved vacation. Instead we got, by way of reminding us that someone in this outfit (Darth Campbell?) could play electoral hardball: a video evoking the Dark Side of the Tory leader; a brilliantly mixed little cocktail of malice (take one part Poll Tax and one part record unemployment, top with ice and shake) that could have had the campaign heavies in New York and Washington beaming with satisfaction that at last the Limeys have learned something about negative campaigning.

But what would they have made of the Prime Minister, next up, irradiated with the fuchsia glow, in full The Passion of the Tony, go-on-give-it-to-me mode. Look, he understands the three Disses: as in -enchantment, -agreement and -illusion. But really, come on, that's real life, not just politics. And there's so much to be proud of. The faithful agreed. Two rather small 'If you value it, vote for it' banners waved back in puppyish salutation.

But whatever elixir had been downed that night did the trick. By the Monday-morning press conference at, yes, a primary school, Blair was back in punchy, shoot-from-the-hip form, as he did what he likes doing best, pouring ridicule on the Tories' inability to do the sums; Howard's and Oliver Letwin's fitness to be CEOs of Britannia, Inc. The Prime Minister and the Chancellor then went into their alto and tenor sax riffs, the bright and the baggy, Blair at his most engaging, the Chancellor at his most solidly Gladstonian. As Brown upbraided the Tories for being insufficiently faithful to Margaret Thatcher's fiscal prudence, the map of Cuba on the classroom wall with its slogan of '*Socialismo o Muerte*' drawn in the Caribbean seemed to turn redder by the minute. Or perhaps I just imagined it.

Then followed questions from the press, the only feature of which that might have been recognisable to American reporters would have been the well-practised habit of leaders to disarm questioners by remembering their first names. In the White House press room (a calculatedly dismal prefab in the grounds) it might have the effect of defanging the journalists with mock camaraderie; but not in Wimbledon at nine in the morning. Even in the dress code of the press conference – jackets and ties for both party leaders (who'd suited up from the calculated, open-necked informality of the walkabouts) – there was the unspoken recognition of the ritualised, gladiatorial nature of the exchange. 'Right, James (or Brendan or Andrew).' 'Yes, well, going on about the danger of letting the Tories in if you vote Lib-Dem, isn't that the wife-beater sneering, "You'll stay, you've got nowhere else to go"?' To this kind of question, it's safe to say, the famous Dubya lightness would not have responded well. Instead: the telltale dilation of nostrils, the giveaway smirk behind which plans for No Future Admission would already be being finalised. Instead, both Brown and Blair laughed and it was not at all the laugh of someone about to be sick.

The ability to take this kind of take-no-prisoners irreverence on the chin; indeed, to expect it, is breathtaking to visiting reporters from the US, where oppositional politics (such as it is) is mired in a tar-pool of tepid glutinous reverence, where Democratic fury has been frightened into Milquetoast bleating by pre-emptive Republican accusations of 'divisiveness'. If John Humphrys is thinking of a late career move across the pond, he should forget it.

But then again, what must American observers make of the fact that it's Blair and Brown who are given to evoking the New Deal (albeit vintage 1997, not 1932) rather than Democrats who, with Bush prosecuting a deeply unpopular 'reform' (gutting) of social security, ought to be rallying to defend what little is left of it with their last breath? The spectacle of all three parties (for Howard, pledged to abolish student fees, would be identified as well to the American left-of-centre) campaigning on their own particular approaches to fine-tuning the welfare state is enough to fill the neutered American opposition with envious despair. They look at a government standing on a record of economic success, committed to defend public services – the mere mention of which, in the US, would likely trigger the opening of a File in the Department of Homeland Security – and, even with the long trail of muck leading from dubious intelligence reports and suspiciously altered legal advice about Iraq, they listen to the ferocity of Blairophobia and scratch their heads. (At which point perhaps they should remember LBJ for whom no amount of virtue prosecuting the great society exonerated the sins of Vietnam.) But if Blair wakes one morning and feels one prick of the pincushion too many, he might well consider a career move across the pond where he'd be a shoo-in for the next governor of New York. We're already assuming Mayor Clinton. The dynamic duo, then, reborn on the Hudson! Can't wait.

Most wondrous of all, perhaps, is the conspicuous absence in British hustings rhetoric of the one campaign helper without whose assistance no American candidate can possibly hope to prevail, namely God. But then the election is being held in a country where, unlike the US, it is assumed that Darwinian evolution is actually incontestable scientific fact, rather than just a wild hunch that has to compete with Creationism for space in textbooks and lessons. The G word finally got uttered in the Lib-Dems' last press conference before the election. 'So, Charles, do you think you'll be making another run as leader in 2009?' 'God – and my colleagues and constituents – willing,' Kennedy cheerfully replied, invoking the deity with no more theological conviction than if someone had sneezed and he'd said, 'God bless you.' And he would, wouldn't he? On parade at the press conference were all the virtues of his party and leadership: disarming honesty, cornflake-crisp optimism; milk-of-human-kindness concern for, inter alia, pensioners, students, the landscape of Britain and doubtless the Scotties and red deer that roam it.

Was I – after only a few days impersonating a political reporter – becoming, perish the thought, a tad cynical? Or was Kennedy's niceness somehow worrying? Lust for power? Not a sniff. Killer instinct? I don't think so. Even an attempt to congratulate him on the decapitation strategy provoked a denial that he'd ever thought of any term so brutal. If he doesn't want to be confused with Robespierre, perhaps Kennedy ought to spend a little time with Machiavelli. At the press conference, I asked whether he was happy to go into the election positioned as the true centre-left party. He smiled and said well, yes, the Lib-Dems were indeed progressive. Progressive as in heirs to the great reforming post-war Labour government and the bitterly unrealised dreams of the Wilson years? Well, yes, he acknowledged, apparently quite happy to slip into history tutorial mode, but I should remember that those achievements were built on the foundation of the Liberal-party reforms of the people's budget, old-age pensions, Lloyd-George/Churchill years before the First World War. Back to the future then with the Lib-Dems!

It was fabulous, this sit-down chinwag as if we were both sipping pints. And perhaps that's what Kennedy likes doing in his crofter fastness. Jean-Jacques Rousseau would have endorsed this pastoral version of politics, for he warned that while popular democracy was the only right and just political system, it could only prosper in republics of 25,000 or fewer – the size of eighteenth-century Geneva. However low the turnout today, it will be rather more than that. But coming from America where the manipulation of the millions presupposes the priority of commodity marketing, massive up-front investment, saturation advertising, the reduction of politics to the soundbite and the photo-op, a British election looks rather closer to Rousseau's ideal. In these few days I've heard colleagues say they've never seen an election more remote from the people, to which I can only reply: try coming to Baltimore or Minneapolis.

There was, though, at least one big American-pie mob scene to sample: Howard's monster rally out in Docklands. There, I met America's most prolific and famous blogger, Markos Moulitsas, who has never seen British politics at first hand before. He marvelled at the absence from the proceedings, not just of the big campaigner in the sky, but also of flags, bands, the whole pumped-up operation of patriotic euphoria and snake-oil pitches, without which the business of American politics is just so much grey newsprint and paid-for televenom.

Not that this event was low-key. Since Ashford, the SBL had had a slight but telling makeover. The shirt-cuffs now were definitely open; the shirt itself was pink; the tie had been banished. He was ACTION MAN with the ACTION PLAN! He was ready to be ACCOUNTABLE, and to prove it he announced a calendar of achievements, designed with wonderfully meaningless specificity. On 6 June 2006, mark my words and your diaries, the British Border Patrol WILL start patrolling! (What's wrong with 5 June?)

But this heady vision of a new Britain got the crowd on its feet, and, yes, they were cheering. For the new Britain turned out, in fact, to be the old Britain: cricket and courtesy, picnics and politeness, yob-free, swabs aplenty, and to prove it, as the SBL unburdened himself once more of a profession of love of country, there began the low rumble of unmistakably British Music. He ended unequivocally. The backroom boys had done their job. There will, after all, be a brighter tomorrow, starting Friday. The cheers got as riotous as English cheers can get. Elgar's 'Nimrod' powered up and Howard drank in the glory, rode the crescendo all the way to the exit, for one sovereign moment, elated, omnipotent and wholly unconditional.

Virtual Annihilation: Anti-Semitism on the Web

From Ron Rosenbaum, *Those Who Forget the Past: The Question of Anti-Semitism,* 2004

How was your Mother's Day this year? Mine didn't go so well. Call mother. What's up? 386 headstones is what's up, she says: Plashet Cemetery, East Ham, yesterday. Perpetrators arrested. A shock, I say. I'm not shocked any more, she says. And she's right.

Why should we be surprised that the ancient paranoia – or, rather, the proper Jewish anxiety about anti-Semitism – should have survived both the reasonings of modernity and the testimony of history? This is, after all, a time (and a country) where, or so opinion polls tell us, more people than not reject the scientific validity of the theory of evolution. (In some quarters, Darwinism is regarded, along with secular humanism, as another conspiracy of the Elders of Zion.) But then America is not the only country in which children are made precociously knowing, while adults are made credulous. It was a French book, after all, that recently became a best-seller by asserting that the al-Qaeda attack on the Pentagon never happened and that photographs which suggested it happened had been digitally doctored by the CIA. Where once it was naively supposed that 'images never lie', the sovereign assumption of the digital age is that they never tell the truth. Truth morphs; Elvis is alive; there were no gas chambers at Auschwitz.

The digital communications technology that was once imagined as a universe of transparent and perpetual illumination, in which cancerous falsehoods would perish beneath a saturation bombardment of irradiating data, has instead generated a much murkier and verification-free habitat where a google-generated search will deliver an electronic page in which links to lies and lunacy appear in identical format as those to truths and sanity. But why should we ever have assumed that technology and reason would be mutually self-reinforcing? The quickest visit to, say, a site called *Stormfront* will persuade you that the demonic is in fact the best customer of the electronic.

It is only in America that we imagine history as a series of cultural supercessions, each one comprehensively victorious in the totality of its effacements. Thus, in this processional view of the past, Native American society is supposed to have been obliterated by a colonialism which in turn yields to individualist and capitalist democracy. Except, of course, that it doesn't, not entirely; and much time is spent, and blood oft times spilled, tidying up the inconvenient anachronisms. In Europe, on the other hand, especially at the end of the last century, so rigidly serial an approach to cultural alteration has been suspected to be not much more than textbook convenience.

In Europe, ghosts have an impolite way of muscling their way into times and places where they are unexpected – which is why, for example, the cultural emblem of the first great industrial society in the world, Victorian Britain, imprinted on railway-station design and museums of arts, crafts and science, was the medieval pointed arch. It was, to be sure, an emblem of resistance as much as appreciation. So the pointiest of the champions of Christian Perpendicular England – Thomas Carlyle – unsurprisingly also turns out to be the fiercest in his hatred of (his words) Niggers and Jews. The great and the good of Victorian Britain could take both the friends and the enemies of the machine age in its stride. So the age that fetishised rootedness, while at the same time making fortunes by displacing mass populations, made the wilfully deracinated, the *juif errant*, the special target of its disingenuousness. Bonjour, M. Melmotte. Hello, Henry Ford.

To grow up British and Jewish is, by definition, not to be especially confounded at the obstinacy of atavisms refusing to lie down in the tomb of their redundancy. The protean persistence of anti-Semitism came home to me early. I was just seven, I think, when I first saw the writing on the wall. The wall in question was one of those crumbling red-brick affairs blocking off a view of the tracks on the Fenchurch Street line connecting London with the Essex villages lining the north bank of the Thames estuary. They were not quite suburban, though Jewish businessmen like my father had moved there out of the burnt-out wreckage of the city and the East End where they still kept warehouses and offices. They were part fishing villages, part seaside

towns, part dormitory cottages and mansions; yellow broom in the
spring, blowsy cabbage roses in the summer; the smell of the unload-
ing shrimp boats and the laden winkle carts dangerously, excitingly
treif drifting over the tide. But every morning those Jewish businessmen would take the Fenchurch Street train, and one morning my
father took me as far as the station. And there on that wall, in white
letters, faint and fugitive, but, since the day was cloudy (as they often
are in the Estuary), glaring in the grey morning light, two cryptic
letters: 'PJ'.

Nothing more; no 'PJ loves ST'; just the letters alone. So of course I
asked my father about their meaning, and I remember him reddening
briefly and telling me it was just some old *khazarei* – to forget about
it, it didn't matter any more. This, of course, made me determined to
decode the crypt, and it was, I think, my cheder teacher Mrs Marks,
the same teacher who got me to dress up in miniature tuxedo as Mr
Shabba (the eight-year-old bride was Mrs Balabooster), who looked me
in the eye and told me that it stood for 'Perish Judah'; and that it was
a relic of some bad old days in the 1930s when the fascists and Arnold
Leese's Britons had marched not just in Stepney and Whitechapel and
Mile End, but right down to the end of the line, to where the Jews had
dared penetrate the sanctum sanctorum of Englishness: pebble-dashed,
herbaceous bordered, tea-pouring Westcliff and Leigh on Sea.

'PJ' scared the hell out of me not because it smelled faintly of
Zyklon B (I'm not sure I knew much about that in 1952, despite the
missing relatives on my mother's side), but because my generation,
born in the last years of the war, would only get their crash course on
the Holocaust a little later in the London *shul* library, where Lord
Russell of Liverpool's *Scourge of the Swastika*, with its obscenely
unsparing photography of bulldozed naked bodies, opened and shut
our eyes. But I had read *Ivanhoe*, indeed I had seen Elizabeth Taylor
as Rebecca, and so the archaic, declamatory quality of the graffito
spoke to me of the massacres at York, the canonisation of little St Hugh
of Lincoln, Richard I's coronation slaughter in London in 1199. The
persistence of the uglier strain of medieval paranoia in my island
culture seemed, while not exactly fish and chips, not something wholly
alien from British tradition, notwithstanding Disraeli, *Daniel
Deronda*, and the Victorian high hats and morning coats that for some
reason marked the official Shabba morning dress of the notables of

our synagogue. Some of the same writers I most enthusiastically read as a child – Hilaire Belloc, G. K. Chesterton, John Buchan, all of them armoured warriors for holy tradition – turned out a bit later, on closer inspection, to be also the most relentless perpetuators of anti-Semitic demonologies.

Still, there was a moment of innocence. It came in 1951, in the cheerfully technocratic Festival of Britain, which seemed to announce an exorcism of barbarian phantoms. Never mind that it coincided with the first panicky revival of racist fascism in Britain, mobilised against Caribbean immigration. We were told that technology – and especially new kinds of communications technology – would diffuse knowledge, and knowledge would chase away superstition, destitution and disease. It would fall to our generation, the most confidently booming of the Baby Boomers, to make good on the promises of the Enlightenment – of Voltaire, Franklin and above all Condorcet. Modernism's start in the first half of the twentieth century had somehow fallen foul of red-fanged tribalism, but we were the children of techne, of the dream machines of the *philosophes*. I remember one of my history teachers, who, in fact, bore a startling resemblance to Voltaire, saying to our class of thirteen-year-olds, 'Well, lads, we don't know what the rest of the twentieth century has in store, but I guarantee that two of the old legacies are finally done for – revealed religion and ethnic nationalism.' So much for history's predictive power.

And looking so much like Voltaire as he did, he should perhaps have known better, since Voltaire, as we know from Arthur Hertzberg, Peter Gay and others, was the prime case of a *philosophe* who thought one way and felt another; who positively nursed the worm in the bud; who believed in the transformative power of reason up to a point, and that point was where it concerned Jews. It was not just that Voltaire believed that the condition of being able to treat Jews humanely was the mass abandonment of their Judaism by the Jews, and that he was understandably pessimistic that this would ever happen; it was also that *au fond* he believed that, even if the Jews could be persuaded to discard what made them religiously and culturally Jews, there would always be some sort of insuperable racial or even biological obstacle to true assimilation.

The notion that the benevolent illuminations of the Enlightenment

would in due course be bound to eradicate superstition and prejudice
– both those said to be held by the Jews and those undoubtedly held
against them – was compromised not just by the disingenuousness of
its apostles, but by the feebly mechanical nature of their prescience.
What failed them was their dependence on wordiness; their belief in
the inevitable and permanent supremacy of textual logic; their faith
in the unconditional surrender of fables to the irrefutably documented
proof. He who could command critical reading – and critical writing
– would, in such a world of logically driven discourse, command the
future, and that future would be one in which rational demonstration would always prevail over emotive spectacle; just as the same
epistemologists thought that the Protestant logos had vanquished
Catholic charisma. But of course it hadn't. Nor did the Enlightenment
banish the fairy-tale so much as become, in the hands of the brothers
Grimm, its most psychologically aggressive reinventor. What would
unfold, in the age of the industrial machine that ensued, was precisely
the astonishing capacity of technology to promote and to project
fantastic mythologies, rather than to dispel them.

From the outset, of course, the machinery of sensationalist stupefaction – the dioramas, and panoramas, the Eidophusikon – was the
natural handmaid of the sublime and the terrible. As Victorian Britain
became more colonised by industry, so its public became greedier for
spectacles of disaster, brought to them as visceral entertainment: the
simulacra of Vesuvian eruptions; the collapse of the Tay Bridge; an
avalanche in the Simplon. More ominously, the paradox of a modernist
technology co-opted to attack modernism became, in the hands of its
most adroit practitioners, no longer so paradoxical. D. W. Griffith, who
specialised in the manipulation of immense crowds and the apocalyptic collapse of imperial hubris, was all of a piece with the chivalric
romancer of the Ku Klux Klan. Mussolini simultaneously embraced
the piston-pumped ecstasies of Marinettian Futurism and the most
preposterous, Cinecittà-fabricated colossalism of Roman nostalgia.
Ultimately, of course, Albert Speer would deliver for Hitler a Cathedral of Light, where annihilationist rant would be bathed in arc-lit
effulgence; and Leni Riefenstahl would begin her epiphany with a
kind of aerial-cinematic Annunciation, the Angel of the Totenkopf
moving through the skies and casting an immaculately shadowed
simulacrum down on the ancestral sod.

From which it is surely just a hop, a skip and a click to the consummation of cyberhatred – to the welcoming page, for example, of the Czech-based *Jew-Rats*, where its designers, appreciative of their predecessors' knack for cutting-edge media, proudly declare, rather as if they were offering a year's warranty, that 'National Socialism was always known for its all-round, quality propaganda.' At *Jew-Rats* you can download not only the old favourites, *Der Ewige Jude* and *Triumph of the Will*, and elegiac interviews with George Lincoln Rockwell, but also try your hand at games such as *S. A. Mann, Rattenjagd* and *Ghetto Blaster*. Or try the home page of Resistance Records, which features a video game called 'Ethnic Cleansing' whose champions are Terminator-style armoured gladiators and whose targets, helpfully visualised at the top of the page (lest casual visitors confuse them with, say, Muslims or Bosnians) are Julius Streicher caricatures of Jews, complete with standard-issue *Der Stürmer*-ish extruded lips and hooked proboscis.

Just as Romantic-Gothic sensationalism fed on the victories that the optical scored over the textual, so the creative forte of digital media has been the projection of electronic violence and encrypted runes, the most archaic motifs of human culture – Manichaean battle, objects of occult veneration and ecstatic, occasionally hallucinatory vision – all delivered in liquid-crystal read-outs. One kind of elemental plasma is translated into quite another kind. The online game *Nazi Doom* is, in fact, just an adapted (and slightly pirated) version of the emphatically non-scientific Gothic Space Fantasy Games, *Doom, Final Doom* and the rather oxymoronic *Final Doom II*. The optimistic dream of the Enlightenment that technology and addictive fantasy would be in some sort of zero-sum game relationship turns out, as Walter Benjamin predicted, to be precisely the opposite case.

I do not mean to suggest, of course, that the digital world is typified by the engineered delivery of the irrational; only that it is not exactly inhospitable to its propagation. Cyberspace is itself the work of much cerebration, but its most elaborate fabulists are certainly devoted to the primacy of the visceral over the logical. They know their market. Against instantly summoned, electronically pulsing apparitions – the Celtic crosses of the White Power organisations such as Aryan Resistance, or *Stormfront*, the mid-1990s creation of the ex-Klansman Don Black – reasoned argument is handicapped, especially in any competition for the attention of alienated adolescents, for whom the appeal of barbarian action is precisely its violent rejection of book-ishness. The ultimate Gothic fantasists, the mass murderers of Columbine High School, are known to have been visitors to these websites.

It is a commonplace now to observe, with Jay Bolter, that the triumph of the Web represents the overthrow – for good or for ill – not just of linear narratives, but also of the entire system of Bacon-ian and Cartesian systems of classification, with their explicit commitment to hierarchies of knowledge. The universe of deep cyber-space is akin to whatever lies way beyond the orderly alignment of the planets in our own relatively parochial solar system. Instead it launches the traveller along pathways of links to indeterminate desti-nations, to the wormholes of epistemology; and along the route the digital argonaut is exposed to a furiously oncoming welter of inco-herently arrayed bodies of information. The engineers of hate-sites know this, and they depend on catching the aimless surfer who might stumble, for example, on an ostensibly orientalist health site called *Bamboo Delight*, including (really) the *Skinny Buddha Weight Loss Method*, and be directed through a single link to the neo-Nazi *Police Patriot* site designed by Jew Watch and Stormfront.

The Web is, by its very nature, uncritically omnivorous. All it asks is to be fed with information. It has the capacity to monitor its input only through the clumsy and ethically controversial means of censor-ship, so that (I am told) in Germany, when asked for sites responding to the search 'Mengele', the Web will refuse to deliver them to the user. But the notion that any sites can somehow be adequately scruti-nised, much less policed for misinformation, fraud and lies, is already both electronically and institutionally impossible. If you search Google or *www.alltheweb.com* for the Protocols of the Elders of Zion, you will be greeted on the first page by many hundreds of entries (many of which are now devoted to reporting and debating the Egyptian tele-vision series called *Horse Without a Rider*, which notoriously treated them as an historical event), not by the Anti-Defamation League, but by Radio Islam's invitation to download the entire foul and forged text, along with *The Jewish Conspiracy against the Muslim World* and Henry Ford's *The International Jew*. The Church of True Israel, and the anti-New World Order ravings of Henry Makow, Ph.D. (inventor of the word game Scruples), website *www.Savethemales.com*, regard Judaism as a mask to disguise the international hegemony of the Khazars. All these will line up for the attention of the unwary long before any sort of critical commentary is reached.

Nor could anything possibly be further away from the epistemological conventions, according to which arguments are tested against critical challenges, than the Net's characteristic form of chat, which overwhelmingly takes the form of mere call and response to which there is never any resolution, or conclusion, merely a string of unadjudicated utterances and ejaculations. Digital allegiances can be formed, then, not through any sort of sifting of truth and falsehood, but in response to, or in defence against, a kind of cognitive battering. And the virtual reality of the Internet, as Sherry Turkle, Les Back and others have pointed out, has been a gift to both the purveyors and the consumers of paranoia. It offers an electronic habitat that is simultaneously furtive and exhibitionist; structurally molecular but capable, as the user is emboldened, of forming itself into an electronic community of the like-minded. It is then perfectly engineered, in other words, for Leaderless Resistance and the Lone Wolf, the recommended model for zealous racists, Neo-Nazis and White Power warriors who are hunting, like Timothy McVeigh, in solitude or in very small and temporarily linked packs. Instead of slogging up to the camp in Idaho and Montana, digital Stormtroopers can assemble in their very own virtual Idaho, download the Horst Wessel *Lied* and electronically bond.

The Web is also, of course, a mine of useful information for the aspiring neo-Nazi, not just in the selection of human and institutional targets, but also in the resources needed to strike them: everything from artisanal ammonium nitrate to the much more wired offensives against the race enemy, involving intensive electronic jamming known as 'digital bombing' to targeted systems of contamination and sabotage. Taken together, the 500 or so websites in the United States built to proselytise for anti-Semitic and racist causes constitute a virtual universe of hatred, protean enough to hunker down or to reach out as the moment requires, encrypting, when necessary, its most bilious messages so that they become accessible only to those with the decrypting keys (a tactic adored by the secrecy fetishists), or aggressively and openly campaigning when that seems to be the priority. Once inside the net, you can log on to Resistance Records and download White

Power music or order CDs from the online catalogue; you can link to the ostensibly more mainstream racist organisations like the British National Party (who have just trebled their representation in local government elections); you can reassure yourself that the HoloCost or the Holohoax never happened and is just another disinformation conspiracy designed to channel reparations to the ever-open maw of the international conspiracy of Jew Bankers. You can order up your Nazi memorabilia or Aryan Nation warm-up jacket with all the ease of someone going shopping for Yankee souvenirs. And most ominously of all, out there in cyberspace you can act out games of virtual anni-hilations, with none of the risks or consequences you would incur in the actual world of body space.

In the circumstances, it is perhaps reassuring that, according to the best and most recent estimates, active regular visitors and inhabitants of anti-Semitic and racist websites may amount to no more than 50,000 or 100,000 at most. It is possible to argue, I suppose, that it is better that the paranoids lock themselves away in the black holes of poisoned cyberspace than act out their aggressions and delusions in the world of actual flesh-and-blood humanity; but that is to assume that Stormfront troopers and crusaders of the Church of True Israel will never make the leap from clicking to shooting. If there is anything that we have learned from this peculiarly delusional moment in our history, surely it is that today's media fantasy may turn into tomor-row's cultural virus. And in the world of wired terror, head-counts are no guide to the possibility of trouble, which comes, as we have already learned to our dreadful cost, very much in single terrorists rather than in battalions.

However abhorrent, the real threat posed by electronic hatred may not in fact, I suspect, be the hard-core of rabidly delusional anti-Semites and racists, who may, alas, always be with us. It is rather from the elec-tronic extension of the paranoid style to much bigger constituencies of the aggrieved, who see in its basic world view – a global conspiracy of money, secular and sexual corruption – a perennial explanation for their own misfortune, for their own sense of beleaguered alienation. The transpositions then become easy. For the Rothschilds, read Goldman Sachs and the IMF; for the Illuminati, read the Council on Foreign Relations. As Henry Ford said of the *Protocols of the Elders of Zion*, 'All I know is that it fits events.' Nor is this habitual imprinting of the old template on contemporary events a monopoly of the left or right. In fact, *les extrêmes se touchent*: anti-globalisers meet the anti-immigrants; anti-Americanism meets America First; America First meets America Only.

What they share is a freshening and quickening of the rhetoric of violence, the poisoning of the airwaves as well as cyberspace. Ultra-chauvinist blow-hards habitually demonise on air those whom they take as insufficiently patriotic as 'scum' or 'vermin', who need in whatever manner to be locked up, deported or generally done away with. 'Who are these contaminating aliens lodged in the bloodstream of the body politic?' Lovers of multilateralism or the United Nations, and any sort of faggoty liberal intellectual who professes a self-evidently diseased scepticism and exercises a disguised but claw-like grip over the media. Jews? Goodness no. Just people who happen to talk too much and think too highly of reason.

Talking and Listening

TBM and John

First published in Peter Mandler and Susan Pedersen's,
Private Conscience and Public Duty in Modern Britain, 1994

You always remember where it was that you first read the books that changed your life.

I first read *Macaulay: The Shaping of the Historian* in September 1976 in rocky, Medusa-infested coves on the Aegean islands of Hydra and Spetsai. While Macaulay was storming the Whig citadel of Holland House, Mavrocordatos and his fellow pan-Hellenes were launching armed fishing boats from those thyme-scented bays against the Turkish fleet. But such was the spell cast by John Clive's book that my imagination did not drift towards Missolonghi or Navarino. It was elsewhere, in virtuous Clapham, industrious Leeds and pullulating Calcutta. Later, John would give me a respectable cloth-bound signed edition of his book. But it is the dog-eared, suntan-oil-stained paperback hauled around the islands that I truly cherish. For it was in its pages that I first began to comprehend the deep wells that produced the glorious gush of Macaulay's famous *vehemence*. And it was in its pages that I first encountered John Clive.

It is the mark of a truly powerful biography to leave the reader vexed with the author for ending it, robbing him of a companion with whom he has become easily familiar. And by the time I reached 'In more ways than one, Zachary had cast a long shadow' I was all the more sorry to have Macaulay abruptly removed after a mere 500 pages of close acquaintance, especially since I longed to dog his footsteps through Italy; eavesdrop on his Cabinet gossip in 1840; commiserate with his electoral defeat in Edinburgh; sample his rich satisfaction at the record sales of the *History*; listen as he recited his rhymes to his niece Baba Trevelyan and marched the children past the giraffes of Regent's Park, the waxworks of Madame Tussaud's or (to little George Otto Trevelyan's bored dismay) the masterpieces of Eastlake's National Gallery.

I consoled myself with the knowledge that before too long I would meet the famous National Book Award-winning author whom I supposed I already knew pretty well. The jacket carried no photograph, but from the elegant, penetrating prose, the controlled sympathy shown towards Macaulay, the rigorous analysis of his intellectual formation, the shrewd delineation of his life as a political and social animal, I assumed that John Clive would turn out to be an understated, impeccably turned-out Harvard professor. His sense of humour, I thought, would be gentle and loftily Jamesian; someone who carried his colonial name with an air of Brahminical Bostonian *savoir faire*. The biographer's relationship with his subject, whose public mask he had removed to expose the conflicted, passionate and often troubled private man beneath, had to be, I supposed, that of a sympathetic doctor who would calmly listen and offer spoonfuls of cool understanding to his distracted patient.

So much for my powers of literary deduction. Two months later, John knocked (or rather pounded) on the doors of my rooms in Brasenose, tripped over the door-sill and fell spread-eagled on my couch. After we had exchanged flustered apologies, it took about five minutes and a cup of tea (which John drank as if it were a famous vintage, enquiring after brand, store of origin, length of brew) for me to see how spectacularly wrong I had been. The name 'Clive' remained mysterious (as it did for many years), but it didn't take a genius to see that my rumpled guest, who was enjoying his tea and cake so visibly, was hardly a representative of the Boston class, famous for its cool detachment and sensuous self-denial. By the end of an hour I was in a state of delighted amazement that the historian whose extraordinary work I had so admired had also become an immediate friend. After John departed (without further hazard) I ran through the character description which now replaced my hopelessly misjudged extrapolation from his prose style. The historian I had met was warm-hearted, affectionate, voluble; mischievously hilarious, gossipy; clumsy, and self-indulgent. His speech moved from embarrassed stammering to flights of eloquence, the sentences broken with puns and rhymes and even snatches of song performed with exaggerated operatic trills. In the mouldy dimness of the Oxford room his large eyes sparkled with pleasure at a well-taken idea or a well-turned phrase and, at the delicious prospect of routing a common enemy, he would smack a fist into his palm with boyish exultation.

But I had run through this anatomy of a personality before, hadn't I? It was John's account of Macaulay.

The best thing I know on the problems of biography is Richard Holmes's *Footsteps*. Its premise is the inescapable *glissade* between biography and autobiography. Are there any biographers who never ask themselves why they have chosen their subjects; whether, indeed, their subjects have not in some disconcerting sense chosen *them*? Why indeed, you might ask yourselves, have the contributors to this very volume adopted their own particular historical doppelgängers?

Among the many virtues of Holmes's book is that it makes these conundrums explicit. Its confessional voice, tracking Robert Louis Stevenson through the Cévennes (albeit without donkey), Shelley in Lerici, Mary Wollstonecraft and Gerard de Nerval in Paris, is made tolerable by Holmes's own acute self-consciousness of the naivety of these pursuits. In one of the most powerful passages of the book, the denial of total identification is suggested to him by the belated discovery of the very bridge over which Stevenson had crossed the Allier River to reach the little country town of Langogne. It was visible but unattainable, 'crumbling and covered with ivy'. The biographer's efforts to overtake the footsteps of his subject would always be thwarted by such obstacles. The best that could be expected was 'to produce the living effect while remaining true to the dead fact . . . You stood at the end of the broken bridge and looked across carefully, objectively into the unattainable past on the other side. You brought it alive, brought it back, by other sorts of skills and crafts and sensible magic.'

Yet part of that 'sensible magic', Holmes concludes at the end of his Stevenson essay, is the willingness to experience a 'haunting' of the kind he himself went through in 1964 in the Cévennes. This means not only approaching the life of the subject as closely as possible, but actually inventing a continuous dialogue between biographer and subject; a sustained conversation with the writer 'talking back' to his alter ego. Such a process necessarily involves identification and projection for, Holmes says with disconcerting candour, 'If you are not in love with them you will not follow them – not very far, anyway.' And, to be sure, those biographies designed from beginning to end as combat most often end as a vehicle for the author, rather than an exposure of the life, or else simply co-opt their subject as endorsements for the author's favourite cause. No one could ever accuse Richard Holmes of that kind of literary hijacking. But his claim that the biographer should become a virtual literary twin of the subject, distinct yet extremely closely related, is of a piece with the attempt to recover the contingencies that shape a life, not to see it from its birth as somehow predestined to follow a particular path. Only if the subject can be disentombed from his obituary can the unpredictable turns, which John often reminded his readers could somehow be the crucial determinants of a life, be given their real due.

Holmes knows, of course, that this close engagement can never be the whole story. For if the biographer must pursue identification for his story to have inner truth and conviction, he must also disengage if it is to have coherence and understanding. This is especially true of historical biography where authors are inescapably caught in a notoriously tight hermeneutic circle. For while their subject's career is necessarily, and to some degree, the product of his culture and society, it may well, during his own lifetime, have decisively shaped the character of that culture.

So whom had I met on that Oxford autumn day in 1976: the biographer or the biographee? Was my own imagination still so imprinted with his image of Macaulay that I was now fancying it perpetuated in the person of the historian's historian? Had John Clive's own life been so leased out to Macaulay to create his book that it had been returned to him decisively altered by the encounter? Or was it just that this was a literary marriage made on Parnassus, the perfect fit, a miraculous transfer of intelligence and sympathy from one Cambridge to the other?

How close were those natural affinities? In the Clapham Sect little Tom had been celebrated as an extraordinary prodigy, composing Latin poems and assuming a precociously grave manner. To Lady Waldegrave's solicitous enquiry after he had had hot coffee spilled over him by her maid, he replied, 'Thank you, Madam, the agony has somewhat abated.' The instantaneous completeness of his memory was found startling; his quickfire speech almost an excited gabble; his appetite for learning apparently insatiable. Yet his natural exuberance gave his father, Zachary, cause for concern that it might lead him into acts of abomination like reading novels. Hence the energies of the boy were contained within a high stockade of grim Evangelical righteousness.

The little boy with the fair hair and chubby cheeks who hung on the least sign of affection from his mother Selina, and gloried in the performance of parlour recitations, was first entrusted to the zealous Hannah More for the right mixture of godliness and good learning. Then, at twelve, he was packed off to an austerely correct Evangelical boarding school at Little Shelford, near Cambridge, where he suffered agonies of homesickness and discovered that not all Wilberforces, especially not the small thug-like representative at Reverend Preston's School, were paragons of Christian piety. To letters that John Clive describes as 'blotted with tears' Zachary responded with cold consolation. 'He did not find any comfort in Zachary's reminder that Christ had left His father for thirty years and had encountered many troubles yet faced them cheerfully.'

In the Berlin of the 1920s and '30s, Hans Kleyff grew up in almost the opposite atmosphere of patriotic assimilation: Biedermeyer furniture; *Küchen, Kinder und Kultur.* Where Macaulay's cultural performances were in essence always dramatic and rhetorical, in the kind of house typified by the Kleyffs the highest expression of *Bildung* would necessarily have been musical. (The first prize that John won was for music and both he and his brother Geoffrey were accomplished performers.) While Zachary Macaulay's exacting and fervent faith coloured his entire public life, and was a creed drummed relentlessly into the head of his son, Bruno Kleyff's relaxed Judaism barely intruded at all into the social rituals of his metropolitan, professional world. Synagogue, John often recalled, was principally the occasion for his father to sport the Iron Cross he had received for his service in the First World War. And that belief in the civilised compatibility of German culture and Jewish origins remained obstinately in place (as it did for so many of that community), even as the monstrous savagery of National Socialism began to proclaim it a biological impossibility. So where Zachary and Selina Macaulay *chose* to embrace the moral identity of Outsiders, saints walking upright among the sinners of the slave-holding empire, the Kleyffs were turned into fugitives only by the most violent horrors the century had to offer.

For John it was the Fatherland, not the father, that stripped him of the familiar assurances of a bourgeois childhood. Though he would experience the harrowing ordeal of his father's arrest, it was a boyish humiliation that brought home to him the true nature of the punishing barbarism of the Third Reich. For inevitably, the Nuremberg laws caught up with the traditions of the *Gymnasium* and John, along with other Jewish boys, was forbidden to go on the annual boat outing on the Spree. Wounded by the ostracism, burning with tears, John always remembered that day as the beginning of exile.

Did his family's experience at the hands of the Nazis make John warm to the Whig whose maiden speech in the House of Commons was an appeal to remove the bar against Jewish Members of Parliament? In fact, Macaulay took the subject further by writing an eloquent and influential essay in the *Edinburgh Review* against 'the Civil Disabilities of the Jews'. Yet John's treatment of the whole topic is tantalisingly and uncharacteristically sketchy. And given his extraordinary critical penetration of almost every *other* aspect of the young Macaulay's life, it is also strangely incurious. The speech and the essay may well, as he claims, show 'at their best [the author's] commonsense', but whether they also 'get to the root of the matter' is more debatable. For although Macaulay characteristically punctures the most fatuous prejudices against the Jews, and especially those that implied their unassimilability in English society, he is not without decided prejudices of his own. He does not, for example, follow the lead of the French revolutionary legislators who argued for emancipation on the grounds that its consequence would be to dissolve the separateness of the Jews within the political nation. (Indeed it may be to Macaulay's credit that he baulked at this patronising liberalism.) But he argued instead that *since* the Jews had so much property and economic power it was inexpedient to deny them the political influence that went with them. Of course this 'interest group' reform Whiggism was of a piece with his view on extending representation to incorporate industrial constituencies, and he may well have felt about the burghers of Leeds whom he would represent as he did about the Goldsmids and the Rothschilds. But then again, possibly not.

In any case there is one revealing piece of evidence about Macaulay's real attitudes towards the Jews, in the form of a letter written to his sister Hannah at virtually the same time (the summer of 1831) that he was writing his essay for the *Edinburgh Review*. It describes a costume party given by a wealthy Jew to which Macaulay went in ordinary dinner dress, and it shows the young lion of Whig society at his worst, sniggering in corners with the likes of Strutt and Romilly at the ridiculous parvenus got up as Turks and Persians. Occasionally the patricians would take time off from condescension to ogle the 'Israelitish women' like the 'angel of a Jewess in a Highland plaid'. And even when he got to bed that night, Macaulay writes to Hannah, it 'was some time before I could get to sleep. The sound of fiddles was in mine ears and gaudy dresses and black hair and Jewish noses were fluctuating up and down before mine eyes.'

For some reason John Clive's account omits this incident entirely, even though George Otto Trevelyan's *Life and Letters* includes the letter and though it had exactly the kind of brilliant historical colour that he splashed over the pages of his biography. Indeed when he was reminded of the letter by a friend and colleague, John's first instinct was to express scepticism about whether any such letter or any such event existed. Could it have been that his own feeling for London and Oxford as tolerant worlds, where the 'Whig grandees' of his own time mixed on easy terms with the inner circle of German Jewish intellectuals who made up the core of John's favourite *Stammtisch*, softened the edges of Anglo-Jewish history?

Certainly John looked back on his asylum in England as a crucial moment in the trajectory of his whole life, even though he seldom talked about its details. His family lived in Buxton, the old spa town of the Derbyshire Peaks near Matlock (that Macaulay knew very well), and where other German Jews had settled, sometimes under a kind of official surveillance, designated, however absurdly given their circumstances, as 'enemy aliens'. John went to school at Buxton and at some point in these years Hans Leo Kleyff turned into John Leonard Clive, his grandly imperial name some protection at least from the predictable misfortunes of being a Jewish refugee with a German accent in an English public school. Was it at this time that he fell in love with English (rather than British) culture, with its patterns of speech and the sounds of its voices, with the stuttering horsiness and the plummy gentility that he loved to mimic later on?

In any event Buxton was not, for John Clive, what Cambridge was for Macaulay: the place where a fresh social and intellectual identity was established *against* the grain of his family background. Periods of real hardship followed in New York, where at one point the Clives made ends meet by stapling teabag tags, possibly the only manual craft that John ever mastered. The gutsy vitality of New York, even in wartime, encouraged another side of his personality: earthy, pleasure-seeking and flamboyant. To the pianist who played (and sang in a husky baritone) Schubert lieder, and who could pound out choruses of the Victorian hymns, was now added the ivory-tickler of Cole Porter and Gershwin standards. In our house ''S Wonderful' or 'You're the Top' got the full cabaret treatment while a large pastrami on rye waited on top of the upright.

By an amazing quirk of fate, the institution that really had the same formative impact on John as Cambridge had for Macaulay, was the US Army, or rather the not especially typical research unit of the OSS assigned to analyse German politics and strategy for military intelligence. That unit, as Barry Katz's fine book has shown, was staffed with historians, many of whom were to remain John's closest friends and, in other crucial respects, his intellectual mentors and peers: Felix Gilbert, Carl Schorske, Stuart Hughes and Franklin Ford. At the University of North Carolina, as a student on a special scholarship, he had mostly read English literature. But in the OSS he was brought directly into the company of a whole group of distinguished and brilliant historians in the making. It was, moreover, a group that deployed their analytical and critical faculties for an incontrovertible political good. The fact that a crucial inner core were all, like John, refugees from the great German-Jewish culture obliterated by the Nazis only added to their solidarity. It also reinforced an urgent Thucydidean sense that history could speak directly and decisively to the most powerful crises of the human condition.

Thucydides also remained Macaulay's ideal historian: analytically concentrated, critically sharp; unapologetic about history as the origins of the contemporary; unsurpassed as a narrative craftsman and rhetorician. At the age of twenty-eight (roughly the age graduate students now complete their doctorates) Macaulay was cocksure enough to announce just what history was, what was wrong with its modern practice; and to prescribe how it might be improved. That improvement would, in his view, be essentially literary since history was 'a debatable land. It lies on the confines of two distinct territories. It is under the jurisdiction of two hostile powers . . . Instead of being equally shared between its two rulers Reason and the Imagination it falls alternately under the sole and absolute dominion of each.' (Later the same year in his essay on Hallam, Macaulay would characterise the division of history as one part poetry, one part philosophy, or in yet another formulation of the same idea, as part map-making, part landscape-painting.)

John shared exactly Macaulay's notion that 'History in its state of ideal perfection' should be both poetical and philosophical. But he did not always have Macaulay's ebullient confidence that the reconciliation of those two sensibilities could be accomplished, osmotically, by a Scottian immersion in the texture of sources. Though it is hard to think of any historical biography which more brilliantly accomplished this synthesis of literary craft and historical analysis than his *Macaulay*, the union of skills did not come effortlessly. When he enrolled in David Owen's seminar in British history as a first-year graduate student at Harvard in 1946, he thought he might work on Disraeli's novels (a subject which would, I think, have been a perfect choice). But the professor, whose work had principally been in the field of local government and Victorian philanthropy and whose temper was, by turns, mordantly sardonic and austerely remote, rapidly disabused him. The young Clive was instead set to work on the Poor Law Amendment Act of 1834 since that, as he himself explained in a Foreword to a posthumously published book of Owen's, was a way to 'get you into parliamentary papers'. Seeing his student immediately crestfallen, Owen urged him to 'Cheer up, you'll be reading the London *Times* as well.'

In the same essay John expresses gratitude to Owen for emphasising the historian's necessary engagement with institutional and political sources. But though he plunged into research for both his major books with the most painstaking thoroughness, he sometimes felt it more duty than pleasure, especially when compared with the speculative and playful qualities of free historical writing that came to him with such grace and brilliance. Even in his first book, *Scotch Reviewers* (1957), that deals with the early history of the *Edinburgh Review*, it is the passages that sketch the personality of its great editor, the pint-sized and pugnacious Francis Jeffreys, that dart from the printed page.

So however conscientious he wanted to be in respect of mastering the most intricate historical circumstances – and in Macaulay's political heyday in the 1830s and '40s, they were to a layman phenomenally complicated – it was always likely that the power of John's biography would be that of a gripping human history. He was also fortunate, as he was the first to admit, that in G. O. Trevelyan's famous *Life and Letters* he had a wonderful springboard from which to launch his own enquiry. As a nephew of Macaulay and a Victorian Eminence in his own right, Trevelyan discreetly circumnavigated some of the most delicate aspects of his uncle's life. But in many places he is surprisingly forthright about his uncle's mercurial personality. Indeed Trevelyan's declared purpose in writing his book was to show that the Statesman and Historian conventionally accused of righteous self-satisfaction, both with himself and with his Times, was in fact a man of the most exacting and often self-mortifying passions.

There were, however, certain moments in Macaulay's life from which Trevelyan not only averted his own gaze, but directly informed the reader he would pass on to more seemly and edifying matters. Together with the superlative and exhaustive job of editing Macaulay's papers done by Thomas Pinney, this left John in a perfect position from which to revisit the storms and stresses of the career. Where Trevelyan had presented Macaulay's turbulent emotional life as a darkened background to his public life, John made it the *clavis interpretandi*. Above all it was to be a family history, as those closing words about Zachary suggest, and one written with all the engagement, compassion and insight of one of the great Mitteleuropa sagas of bourgeois dynasties: Mann, Fontane, Schnitzler and Zweig, as it were, come to visit the Clapham Sect.

And Sigmund Freud too, of course. Not that John's reading of Macaulay's relationships with his mother, father and sisters is in any sense mechanically Freudian. But given his gathering revolt against Zachary's moral authoritarianism, his adoring devotion to his mother Selina and above all his disturbingly inflamed love for his sisters, the central drama of the book could not help but be acutely psychological.

Neither Tom nor John ever married. After his father died, the centre of John's personal life was his older brother Geoffrey, a philosophy professor and, by all accounts, an accomplished cellist. But Geoffrey Clive was also a diabetic who suffered a brutally withering form of the disorder, going blind before dying in 1975. I don't mean to make crass analogies here between John's devotion to Geoffrey, which in any case I only knew of as part of his memory, and Macaulay's almost operatic possessiveness towards Hannah and Margaret. But it seems to me inconceivable that the closeness of the brothers did not, to some degree, enrich the compassion and depth of understanding that John had for Macaulay's own intense sibling relationships.

At the heart of that relationship, John makes clear, was the overgrown boy Tom's craving to find a domestic nest that would give him the emotional and even physical succour that the bleak righteousness of Zachary and Selina's Clapham virtue had denied. With Hannah (whom he even rebaptised as 'Nancy') and Margaret, he was able to do all the prohibited things: joke, caper, confess weakness; show off; preen himself on his brilliance, chastise himself on his inadequacies, and, both on paper and in person, talk on and on and on, mostly on the subject of Tom, without fear of interruption or contradiction. The bonds which attached his sisters to his own life were, then, intensely selfish. Macaulay felt that his entertainment value, the reflected light that shone from his own political and literary brilliance, and his repeated utterances (all perfectly sincere) of passionate and undiluted love, were enough recompense for all they were supposed to do for him. But those kindnesses and services comprised a long list: from tending his political wounds, humouring his caprices, invariably endorsing his prejudices and, not least, keeping house.

Self-conscious to the point of obsession with what he thought was his ugliness and corpulence (neither of which appears especially off-putting in any of the known likenesses), Macaulay decided, fairly early on, that he would eschew a sexual or conjugal relationship. Those energies that might be dangerously compromised by such tangles would instead be harnessed to the drive of his political and literary career. And as for love, of which he truly possessed a natural abundance, that would find expression in what he imagined to be the purest possible form: that of a brother for his sisters.

It is quite impossible for a modern reader to take in the elemental passion of many of those letters and not find them, at many points, implicitly incestuous. Macaulay's tone to both of them is, in the idiom of the time, that of a lover who goes well beyond the norms of brotherly affection. When Margaret became engaged, his response (expressed to the other sister) was one of jealous outrage and hurt.

For the most part John's biography surveys these storms and stresses with humane precision, often allowing the extraordinary correspondence to speak for itself. In fact at times authorial intervention seems almost excessively suppressed, given the drama unfolding in the letters. In 1834, for instance, Macaulay decided that he would have to accept the post of one of the Secretaries-in-Council to the Governor-General of the East India Company in Calcutta, for purely financial reasons. Announcing this fact to the remaining single sister Hannah (his 'Nancy'), he also asks her to go with him to India, a request that was in fact an act of outrageous selfishness and which was initially greeted with horrified disbelief. Of course, Macaulay couches his request in such a way that it would be *possible* for her to deny him, but only at the prohibitive price of reneging on her own loyalty and love. All in all, the letter is a classic of moral blackmail.

The biographer refrains from saying anything like this. Perhaps he knows full well that Macaulay would be punished many times over for his selfishness when Hannah finds *her* own husband in Charles Trevelyan, one of Tom's colleagues in the civil administration in Calcutta. Moreover, the letter he sends on this occasion back to Margaret in England, full of despairing (if belated) self-knowledge about the futility of the idyll he had created for himself, unmarried sisters ministering for ever to the needs of their genius brother, is so tragically dark as to make any editorialising gratuitous. But is it possible, also, that John, who lived his life in a series of surrogate families, who was virtually adopted by them as an honorary brother and uncle, ate at their table, sang to their children, watched ball games and movies with them, was fed and cared for by them, understood this heavy loneliness at an emotional and psychological depth that could not be registered in the conventions of an historical biography?

Though Margaret's death in 1835 threatened for a while to throw Macaulay into an abyss of depression, this is not a story of unrelenting sorrow – the sad face beneath the public mask of Victorian good cheer. Macaulay never recovered the gregariousness of his Holland House days in the 1820s when he had been the toast of Whig Westminster. But much of his life, until his death in 1852, was spent in the domestic circle of Hannah and Charles Trevelyan and their children to whom he was the irrepressibly high-spirited uncle, regaling them with poems and stories and outings and treats. At one point Macaulay even attributed his ability to make history popular to the fact that he spent so much time talking to small children. That he could do this with a magically assured touch, utterly without condescension, was because there was always a large, overgrown child in the adult Macaulay himself: greedy for affection and praise; easily stung and wounded; just as easily delighted and excited; lavish with his emotions and wicked with his literary nose-thumbing.

John never got to write of this Macaulay: the 'Uncle Tom' whom his first biographer George, when still little 'Georgie' Trevelyan, had no idea was in any way famous or distinguished beyond the fact that he now and then wrote books. But my own children got to know and love their 'Uncle John'; to hear *his* poems, and stories, and songs; laugh at his jokes; humour his rituals; tease him with the threat of his most detested foods (a long list that included honey, olives and any vegetables unknown to his mother's kitchen in the Berlin of the 1930s). Once when I attempted to cook him his favourite dessert, Salzburgernockerln, an impossibly oxymoronic confection of ice and hot custardy interior, I saw my daughter Chloë catching John in an expression of shut-eyed rapture and later asking me, 'Daddy, what did you *put* in that?' For them he was utterly memorable; a child-man; a walking explosion of affectionate and wonderfully uncoordinated humanity.

One of his very closest friends and colleagues has noted that John had a great genius for friendship. And though we who still bitterly miss him understand this first of all as something he added to our personal and domestic lives, it might be argued that that gift actually had powerful and positive consequences for his historical writing. In one of the most dazzling essays in his last book, 'The Great Historians in the Age of Cliometrics', he has Gibbon, Macaulay and Carlyle, each in their own manner, discuss the cutting-edge issue of correlations between sibling numbers and the incidence of baldness among Ohio clockmakers. The pastiches are realised with deadly precision. But as hilarious as they are, they could only have been produced by someone who had become an affectionate familiar of the great men; had listened carefully to the mannerisms of their diction; whose impersonations would then be marked by loving attentiveness.

In another essay in *Not By Fact Alone* (1989) John does his best to give cogent intellectual reasons why we should go on reading the great historians: as exemplars of narrative, tacticians of argument and so on. But in the end he always reverted to the sheer pleasure of their company. Burckhardt, Michelet, Parkman, Henry Adams, Tocqueville and even Marx made up this precious *Stammtisch* of great historians, along with the British writers. The delight with which he samples them, follows their moves, relishes their ingenuity, wallows in their eccentricity, basks in the warmth of their vitality, was much the same as the unalloyed happiness he exuded at a table of eloquent, gabbling, laughing friends. By the same token he would roll his eyes in despair when banal monotony engulfed any sort of institutional meeting, which meant that there was a good deal of eye-rolling from his corner along with a peculiar gesture of taking off his wristwatch and dangling it by the strap, as if he could see his life ticking away in inconsequential tedium.

Yet there was much more to this than a kind of intellectual epicureanism. For at heart John believed that historical wisdom only deserved to endure if it had a proper quotient of wit, force and literary power. That was why he was so depressed by the vast cargo of drab, congested and hectoring prose that he thought weighed down the learned journals. By contrast there was obviously something irresistibly joyous even in the most outrageous adolescent crowing of the young Macaulay who announced a new publication (*The Etonian*) thus:

> Some of us have no occupation, some of us have no money, some of us are desperately in love, some of us are desperately in debt; many of us are very clever and wish to convince the public of that fact . . . we will go forth to the world once a quarter in high spirits and handsome type and a modest dress of drab with verse and prose criticism and witticism, fond love and loud laughter . . . Our food shall be of the spicy curry and the glistening champagne − our inspiration shall be the thanks of pleasant voices and the smiles of sparkling eyes.

When I arrived at Harvard in 1980 I myself thought John's reverence for these past masters exaggerated and his determination to pass on their legacy to his students, a gently old-fashioned kind of work, canonical and aesthetic, not at all in keeping with the vogue for cultural history done by those roaming the jungles of symbolic anthropology. How callow and obtuse I was! For even before he died, and certainly ever since, I can think of nothing more important than to convey the enduring power and wisdom, form and substance of the great masters. Far from cramping the style of students, direct contact with the immense range of creative imagination inscribed in their texts liberates them for any and all possibilities of historical expression. To my belated delight I have found that most undergraduates would gladly trade all the dense theoretical discussions of 'narrative strategy' and 'cultural methodology' for a few pages of the seductive gossip of Herodotus or the dazzling mischief of Edward Gibbon. For as long as this matters, historians and many others will read John Clive with huge pleasure and instruction.

Isaiah Berlin

Review of Isaiah Berlin: *Flourishing: Letters 1928–1946*,
edited by Henry Hardy, *New Republic*, 31 January 2005

In February 1942, Isaiah Berlin, thirty-two years old, sat in a Jewish
religious court in New York City, listening intently to the case of a
one-legged octogenarian *schnorrer* whose amputated limb had gone
missing after surgery. This, as Berlin recognised, was no joke. Unless
the leg was buried in hallowed ground, preferably close to the rest of
the old boy, come the return of the Messiah, it could not be reunited
with the rest of him. A while without his leg, he said, he didn't mind;
fifty years, say, okay, even 100, 200 maybe, but to go around on a
wooden leg for all eternity? Understandably bemused, the judges (one
of whom Berlin noted was called, sublimely, Justice Null) wondered
out loud what the court could do about it. 'That's what I want to know,'
the *schnorrer* replied. After deliberation the rabbi and the justice came
up with a solution. A token piece of the old man – a fingernail, say –
would be buried with due solemnity declaring that, in the unavoidable circumstances, it would stand in for the leg. On the day of
resurrection, the Almighty, surely impressed by the judgement of the
court, would accept the substitution, and the reassembled man would,
with any luck, stride off into the everlasting.

In the letter to his parents, back in solid Hampstead, Berlin, famous
for his relish of the human comedy, described the scene without a trace
of condescension, much less farce. 'The thing was really most pathetic,'
he wrote, using that last word literally. 'A man condemned to wander
about on one leg for eternity, unenviable even in Paradise.' But what
touched Berlin was not just the plight of the old man, but the inspired
improvisation of the two judges, faced with an apparently impossible
request. Short of the ideal solution – the recovery of the missing leg –
their task was to find some way in which the pain and fear of the sufferer
could be eased, and this they satisfactorily accomplished. By Berlin's

lights, this was humane intelligence operating exactly as it should; authority applied to its supreme duty: that of minimising suffering.

If reading this glorious collection of Berlin's letters is, predictably, a heady experience, it is also hearty. Not in the British sense of cheery muscularity (definitely not Berlin's thing), but in the sense that the letters reveal an intellectual sensibility in which uncompromising analytical clarity was uniquely married to an unshakable faith in the moral instincts of humanity. Abstract ideas, free-floating in their own rarefied sphere of discourse, unmoored from historical place and moment (the philosophical fashion when he arrived in Oxford in the early 1930s), became, for him, a kind of high intellectual aesthetics. In the hands of its nimblest practitioners, like J. L. Austin, the performance was a marvellous thing to behold, but in the end, as Berlin realised while crossing the Atlantic in the belly of a bomber in 1944, it was play, not work; at any rate not his kind of work. So while *Flourishing*, packed with letters which, on top form, put Isaiah Berlin in the same rank of epistolary artists as Evelyn Waugh or Kenneth Tynan, can be enjoyed as the most delicious kind of literary and intellectual confectionery (a form of nourishment Isaiah was the last to discount), the book is best read as a *Bildungsroman* of the twentieth century; the strenuous journey of an exceptional mind towards its own self-realisation.

Isaiah Berlin is most famously remembered (especially in Britain) as an unparalleled intellectual phenomenon: the encyclopaedic memory and prodigious intellect delivering high-velocity aperçus, at a rate that left audiences gasping: a bassoon on speed. The first time I saw him lecture in the late 1960s, on the tortured relationship between Tolstoy and Turgenev, he prefaced his remarks by declaring: 'Ladies and Gentlemen, I must warn you that I speak very low and very fast, so if you fail to understand me, would you please indicate this by some eccentricity of behaviour.' Since the caveat was itself delivered the same way, no one took him up. All of Berlin's most dazzling qualities were on pyrotechnic display that evening: the sharp-focused illumination of literature as social thought; the representation (almost a re-enactment) of the cultural world from which that literature had sprung; the poignant incommensurability of ultimately irreconcilable tempers (a Berlin speciality, whether of writers or nations). As he warmed to the subject — as usual without a note, much less a text, the eloquence unfaltering – his expansiveness lit the wintry Cambridge evening. (It had been a prophetic choice when he had named the high-school magazine he founded at St Paul's: *The Radiator*.) Narrating some of Tolstoy's high moral absurdities, Berlin mugged, his broad face turning impishly deadpan, shamelessly milking the laughs. As for his two protagonists, especially Turgenev, who functioned as a ghostly (and sometimes disturbingly close) alter ego for his own anxieties and insecurities, Berlin not so much explored their personae as inhabited them; the basso profundo turning less, or more, emphatic depending on which of the two was getting his moment: the head shaking in mock disbelief; a hand tucked into the vest of his three-piece suit, then emerging in mildly Ciceronian gestures of advocacy. As a performance of the drama of ideas, the lecture was for the connoisseur of the genre, delectably operatic.

Which, some recent critics claim, is all that there really ever was. Reviewed coolly, without benefit of the sentimental reverence generated by a rich body of Berlin anecdotal lore, his whole body of work is said to amount to less than the sum of its parts. This demurral, offered as an astringent reaction against the excesses of Isaiolatry, was entirely predictable, especially in Britain where dimming haloes, especially posthumously, is something of a national pastime, but it could hardly be more obtuse. Far from Berlin's central intellectual preoccupations havering weakly between the hard poles of analytical philosophy and political practice, they can be seen, now more than ever, as unerringly located, precisely at the point where ideas catch dangerous fire: in the realm of social religion. Far from the issues with which he struggled – the tragic irreconcilability of liberty and equality; the social and psychological roots of tribal and national allegiance, to name but two – being extended footnotes to the long nineteenth century (where, certainly, Berlin felt at home), they could hardly be more germane to the tortured perplexities of our own immediate and future situation. When Tony Blair asked Berlin whether he truly believed 'negative liberty' (the removal of coercive constraint) sufficed without the complement of 'positive liberty' (a universally agreed good, reachable through collective rational self-determination), he was paying homage, rather than lip service, to the perennial importance of the distinction first essayed in Berlin's *Two Concepts of Liberty*. Doubtless Berlin would have answered, 'You may well be right', but even supposing you are, not to recognise the pursuit of whatever greater good the Prime Minister might have in mind would entail the sacrifice of some element of liberty, would be to bury his head in the deepest dune.

Nor is there anything about 2005 which would have made Isaiah Berlin repent of the insistence, reiterated in so much of his work, on the historicity of ideas; their particularity in time and place; their obstinate resistance to universalisation. The naive fancy that one-size-fits-all democracy could be transported from the Potomac to the Tigris; or that any sort of system of ideas could be held to be objectively 'timeless' and thus deliverable independently of specific cultural circumstances, would have filled him with grim disbelief. The notion that a *war* might be fought on such deeply mistaken premises would have left him shaking his head (and he did this as rapidly as his speech patterns) in dire dismay.

Though I'm not sure he would have welcomed the classification, Berlin was, in his way, an anthropologist of cultural allegiance; prepared to engage seriously with precisely the kind of ideas which ought to have repelled him: those which were the least cosmopolitan, the least rational, the least amenable to easy resolution through agreed ends. It would have been easy enough for him to write about Voltaire or Benjamin Constant. Instead he gave Counter-Enlightenment anti-rationalist writers like Joseph de Maistre and J. G. Hamann their full due. It was the airy thinness of mechanistic Enlightenment rationality, its failure to speak to the deeper impulses of memory, language and mythology, which, however alien to his own cast of mind, Berlin recognised as potent epistemological facts and which sent him to Vico and Herder. Those exasperated by the reluctance of Sunni Iraqis to be reasonable and take their coming electorally rendered punishment on the chin could do worse than to read Berlin on the tenacity of social magic in the allure of tribal nationalism.

Not that the message would be cheering. Early on in his stay in the United States, where he arrived first in 1940, hoping to move on to Moscow (via Japan), Berlin realised that his sceptical, tragic view of history made him a cultural misfit. In both New York, where Berlin was employed at the British Press Service in Manhattan, and in Washington, where he became Head of the Political Survey section at the embassy, he blinked at the sunlit intensity of American optimism.

Though he genuinely admired American energy and forthrightness, the mistaken conviction that exhaustive iteration was the same thing as understanding depressed him. Ultimately he thought that the national passion for the unequivocal could only be sustained through an exercise of eye-shutting make-believe akin to a children's party game; the conversion of the world from what it was to what America wished (fingers crossed and scarlet slippers clicked) it would be. If not actually inhuman, this optimisation of the world, he thought, was nonetheless a willed self-deception about the reality of human behaviour, namely that there were no conflicts which, with the application of enough goodwill, money and robust determination, could not be resolved.

But for Berlin, even then, it was the beginning of public wisdom to accept that there were indeed a multitude of evils which, in fact, were not open to resolution since arguments of persuasively equal validity could be made for each side. Hello Belfast, hello Jerusalem. Accordingly, the job of statecraft was not to liquidate those differences (for that would seldom happen), but to contain them; to find a space in which *acceptance* of irreconcilability would not require mutual annihilation. However unarguable as historical fact and however timely for our own instruction, this, it need hardly be said, is not the kind of message likely to feature in American inaugural addresses. Better the vacuous uplift of the inspirational nostrum than the sobering descent of the incontrovertible truth.

Not surprisingly, then, there is some mischievous Berlinian ambiguity to the title that his exemplary editor, Henry Hardy, has given to this book of letters. 'Flourishing' was Berlin's habitual communiqué to his parents, Mendel and Marie, to calm their perpetual anxieties about his health and fortunes. In these repeated reassurances he was the touchingly dutiful Jewish son; so much so that, on occasion, Isaiah actually reproached *them* for not writing, cabling, calling. But sometimes, especially from New York, he signalled 'flourishing' when he was anything but. Stuck in his British Press Office on the thirtieth floor of the Rockefeller Center, appointed to liaise with American Jews and Labour Organisations, Berlin missed the banter and gossip of his Oxford friends so desperately and became so despondently guilty about the triviality, as he then saw it, of his contribution to the war effort that at one point his feelings turned suicidal. On another occasion, discovered by his parents to have been hospitalised with pneumonia while sending off yet another 'flourishing' letter, Berlin protested that in fact he *had* flourished before he hadn't, and that, in any case, a New York hospital bed was an enviable idyll: terrific food, nothing to do but read, no one bothering him.

Yet of course Isaiah Berlin did *flourish*, not just in the sense of thriving as Mendel and Marie Berlin hoped, but in the sense of delivering a bravura passage of brass in the reedy plainsong that was philosophical Oxford in the 1930s. Though he happily plunged into a post-Wittgensteinian ethos, drunk on the over-excited discovery that language and the unstable apparatus of cognition might constitute the only available reality, Berlin — who hardly lacked for speech-acts — registered his presence substantively, not just rhetorically. When Isaiah was in a room, no one needed to ask, in the E. M. Forster parody of J. L. Austin, yes, but how do we know he was *really* there? Not that the pleasure he had in being 'Shaya' made Berlin in any sense a *flâneur*. He detested narcissism almost as much as philistinism. And in some aspects of his life, not least his early relationships with women, he could be brutally self-protective: happier as their non-stop cuddly talking bear than as their lover.

As the letters make plain, the epicurean jauntiness came early. The headlong rush of talk on which the equally fast flow of ideas would be borne; the exhilarated delight in gossip as art form; the long steeping in music, especially Mozart, the composer who, for Berlin, ideally married hard-edged classical brilliance with passionate sublimity; the voracious pleasure taken in food, all the indulgent wallowing in the small quotidian happinesses of life like a hippo in warmly gurgling mud, aligned him with his hero Alexander Herzen who believed (along with at least half of Tolstoy's brain) that the point of life was the daily living of it.

He was, in fact, that unlikely thing: a seriously happy Jew. It may well be, as some biographers have suggested, that the eight-year-old Isaiah was afforded his pessimistic view of history, and his aversion to immediate misery inflicted in the name of a proclaimed future good, by witnessing the 1917 revolution in Petrograd. But there's little sign that the triangulation of his personality between its Russian, Jewish and English components ever made him uneasy about the wholeness of his identity. Identities, he would have scoffed, are seldom whole, not the interesting ones, anyway. It may be, as it seemed to Guy de Rothschild, that he 'floated inside his clothes', but there's no doubt that Isaiah Berlin was perfectly comfortable in the solid suiting of a middle-class, north-west London English Jew. The synagogues he attended with his parents, in Bayswater, Hampstead and Golders Green, were, architecturally and socially, testaments to the determination with which bourgeois Anglo-Jews staked their claim to a stable place within the institutions of late-imperial Britain. The interiors were (and are) oak-panelled; the windows neo-Victorian stained glass; the '*yad*' pointer for the Torah readings made from Hatton Garden sterling silver; and the synagogue's official notables, the 'wardens', dressed in black silk top hats and seated in their very own closed pew, the 'box' – solemnly opened and shut each time one of them emerged to mount the steps to the ark.

There was no reason, then, for Isaiah, or his parents, to suppose that doors would be barred against him, provided, that is, he was sensible about which to knock on. So no Eton or Winchester for Isaiah, but the day-school of St Paul's, in London, itself an intense forcing house of intellectual distinction; then Oxford, but not the aristocratic preserves of Christ Church or Magdalen, but Corpus Christi, neither the most dazzling of the colleges nor the drabbest. After graduating (first in Classics 'Greats'; then in Politics, Philosophy and Economics, both with Firsts), Berlin moved smoothly to a lectureship in philosophy at New College. Although in later life he would often say (usually when he was out of Oxford) that he was never happier than in academic life, like many of the most gifted, he paused at the crossroads, not least because he thought New College a depressingly dull place and also because he was tantalised by what seemed, for a while, to be a job offer on the *Manchester Guardian*. When, to his acute disappointment, the job failed to materialise, Berlin took the bull by the horns and entered the notoriously stiff fellowship examination for All Souls, the only Oxford college with no students. No Jew had ever been elected to All Souls, and Berlin's own father attempted to cool his son's expectations by telling him it would be a miracle if it happened. It did. *The Jewish Chronicle* heralded the achievement as another hurdle vaulted; the Chief Rabbi of Britain, Dr Herz, a famous pillar of the conservative establishment, sent congratulations (albeit addressed to 'Irving' Berlin).

Isaiah was already The Phenomenon: unstoppably voluble, eloquent; notoriously ardent; playfully poetic rather than drily cerebral in his intellectual enthusiasms. No wonder so many of his earliest, best friends were Irish: the Lynd sisters, Sigle and Maire, daughters of a writer whom Berlin had met when they had been living in the Warden's Lodge at New College. They were clever, fine-boned, fair-haired, wistful, sardonic, playful; with a good deal of steel beneath the rain-soft complexions. (Both Lynd sisters ended up in the Communist party.) How could the owlish, portly, intense young Jew not fall? He did. Sigle was the first of his real passions, though apparently not so much as a touch passed between them. Her younger sister, Maire, became a lifelong intimate: someone more than a friend and less than a lover; someone to whom Berlin could pour out the contents of his heart as well as his head from time to time. That Maire liked to be known as 'B. J' – for 'Baby Junior' – gives an accurate sense of the circle in which Isaiah felt happiest in the mid-thirties: teasing, faux-worldly, companionable; a fizzing cocktail of chummy brilliance laced with a dash of backbiting bitters at the expense of those judged Not Really Us: among them the relentlessly self-promoting historian A. L. Rowse; the blustering, bullying Richard Crossman, not yet a Labour party politician, whom Isaiah hated and later diagnosed as a 'left-wing fascist'.

His letters at this time occasionally give the uncomfortable impression of playing to the gallery: I Say, I Say-er doing his turn as Entertaining Pet Hebrew ('my dear, you know how *frightfully* clever they all are'):

Dear John,

Not a breath passes here where all is very still. I am about to write a tractate on God chasing his own predictions for you but am so idiotically busy that I haven't been able to find a cool hour yet . . . The only piece of really stimulating gossip there is the unmentionable fact [do be careful] that the President being weak and dying demands blood. The Fellows gallantly offered theirs . . . Hardie was found to have none to offer. Pidduck and Phelps though something was running furiously in their veins were discovered in its not being blood but some sharper, inferior liquid.

But this was June 1933 and through the rest of the decade, ugly political reality kept breaking into the glaring brightness. When Adam von Trott (later executed as one of the July 1944 Rastenburg bomb plotters) defended the Third Reich against charges of persecuting the Jews, Isaiah was at first incredulous and then indignant. On one of his summer pilgrimages to Salzburg he ran into his first authentic Nazi: 'a great corpulent creature in the official brown uniform, with a red & black Swastika on his sleeve, & wearing a small black demi-astrakhan hat with silver symbols embroidered thereon: he was very drunk, rolled into my café, and was led out by 3 waiters'. Yet there is still a disconcerting lightness to his tone when he writes of such things. (Von Trott is given a mild reproof; the brownshirt treated as an amusing curiosity.)

But the acutely observant Berlin is nonetheless beginning to sharpen his focus, both about those at whom he looked as well as himself. In Palestine he described the kibbutzniks to Felix and Marion Frankfurter as 'the old 1848 idealist type of person who somehow do work the land by day & read poetry by night without making it seem impossibly arty and affected. I like them better than I've ever liked any body of men, tho I couldn't live among them, they are too noble, simple and oppressively good.' Much of the surliness of British officials (neither malevolent nor benevolent) towards the Jews, Berlin diagnosed as stemming from a resentment of their usual imperial role of *Kulturträger* to the natives having been usurped by dentists from Cracow, demoting the pukka pashas to the status of glorified traffic cops. Hence the romantic eagerness of the British to adopt the role of protector of the noble Arabs *against* the pushily disruptive Jews and their Mitteleuropa culture of coffee, cake and *Kinder*.

The Frankfurters, whom Berlin met in Oxford, were among the correspondents who provoked him to take the letters to an altogether different plane than that of mercurially entertaining tongue-wagger. For the young Stephen Spender, Berlin became an acute and ruthlessly honest literary critic (not least of Spender's own work), nailing Aldous Huxley's disingenuousness at contriving sinister moments:

> we are used to war horrors, consequently he produces a scene in which the mangled remains of a terrier plop down from an aeroplane on two lovers naked on a roof & spatter them with blood. Quiet horror is a speciality of the French in the last century but whereas Baudelaire and Huysmans do so for purely artistic reasons & standing aloof from it present it without comment, Huxley, a puritan moralist makes a sort

of propaganda of it & merely lowers & sordidifies [*sic*] the scene. One is touched or nauseated or pierced in some way but not moved or at all profoundly affected or made capable of seeing something or understanding anything save abstract general propositions.

No one brought out the best in Berlin's letter-writing as consistently as the Anglo-Irish novelist, Elizabeth Bowen, whom Isaiah first met when, on one of his trips to Ireland with his Anglo-Irish Oxford girl-friends, he was taken to her house in County Cork. Much later, Isaiah would himself contribute to the deflation of Bowen's reputation by claiming that he had always found her novels unreadable: a doubly unbelievable disclaimer, since at the time he waxed feverishly enthusiastic about *The House in Paris* and *Death of the Heart* ('your novel robs me of sleep at nights; it is colossally absorbing') and with good reason for they are two of the strongest books Bowen ever wrote, glittering with precisely the kind of gritty physical characterisation and unflinching psychological insight that Berlin admired.

So when he wrote to Elizabeth Bowen, he raised his own writing to Bowenite heights, often producing literary scene-painting that resembled some of the more confessionally autobiographical moments from Tolstoy or Svevo. Extracting himself at the Paris zoo 'opposite the Python' from the pathetically attached Rachel 'Tips' Walker, a former pupil, whom Isaiah had very definitely Led On, he wrote to Bowen with self-dramatising candour:

We went on aiming at each other, missing mostly, with desperate gravity. Dear me. I can't possibly marry her. She thinks I can. We should be miserable at once. The last scene in which I forced myself to be sensible & pedestrian & analyse the situation calmly & declare that I must stop was awful beyond words. I always found I had to begin afresh & talked almost of the weather, to begin with. Then a silence. Then I would get up & make as if to go. We both felt that something had to be said. We gulped and floundered & I felt unscrupulous & a cad. The climax was reached when she inquired how far my recent declarations resembled my final end with Sigle Lynd? It was past all bearing.

The women Berlin most admired were the opposite of poor 'Tips' (who ended in a mental hospital): strong-minded; unabashed;

verbally quick on the draw, like 'B. J' Lynd; Bowen (whom, Isaiah believed, could hold her own with doubtful types in London and Dublin pubs), Virginia Woolf, who intimidated him with what he thought was the most beautiful face he had ever seen in his life; and Gertrude Stein, who took the smirk right off the face of Oxford undergraduates by telling 'them what was wrong with their lives, asked them what schools they were at, embarrassed them, trampled on them and winked a great deal at Alice B. Toklas'. Bowen's Court improbably became a kind of home from home for the Russian-Jewish Oxford philosophy don, who got into his wellies and even onto a horse to trot along the 'violent green' lanes. It was there in the summer of 1938, while Neville Chamberlain was shuttling back and forth to Berchtesgaden, that Berlin finally completed his short book on Marx, commissioned five years earlier by H. A. L. Fisher for the Home University Library. In the intervening years the work had become an ordeal since Berlin was simultaneously mesmerised and repelled by Marx himself: aghast at recognising traits of single-minded ferocity combined with thin-skinned sensitivity that he acknowledged in himself; deeply alienated by Marx's determinism at the same time as he was in awe of the adamantine coherence of the philosophical edifice he had constructed. For summers on end he procrastinated his way around Europe: the south of France; Dublin; Venice ('so delightful and silly to go in a gondola through a fairly squalid canal & realise this is like a v. second rate novel & then suddenly hear Chopin played from the window of a not very beautiful palazzo & realize that one is part of a sentimental and ridiculous film set'), conspicuously not polishing off the manuscript. But while evading the hairy, chilling presence of Marx somewhere over his shoulder, Berlin fired off volleys, usually to Elizabeth Bowen, of dead-on observations about almost everything else – the problem of defining a highbrow when only highbrows did; Stuart Hampshire's affair with Freddie Ayer's wife Renée; his thrilling discovery of Herzen (who functioned as a kind of anti-Marx for Berlin through the Russian's ironic 'gentlemanliness' and 'unsqualid disillusionment'); the ultimately alienating quality of Henry James's characters, 'all jittering because their private world may be taken away from them (the ultimate tragedy is when it is)'; James's unwitting reinforcement of the stereotype that 'we – the

intellectuals, the sensitives, the observers, the persons who discuss
– are all cripples; able to peer from all sorts of unusual angles . . .
but thereby we deprive ourselves of the right of life which James
vaguely accords to the rare normal figures who occur at the edge
of his world . . . Everything he [James] says is true, piecemeal, so
to speak but false in the aggregate.'

The odd thing is that Berlin was, finally, buckling down to his
Marx book while so many of his friends were, perforce, choosing
sides; Stephen Spender joining the Lynds in the British Communist
party; others taking the Spanish Civil War as a litmus test of allegiance. But Berlin thought and wrote about Marx as if he was
encountering him in the middle of the nineteenth century. This had
the intellectual virtue of not anachronistically projecting back on to
Marx everything that had been done in his name, but it gave the
book – which appeared after the war had begun – an inevitable air
of over-detachment from the monstrous historical drama that was
being played out in Europe.

Ayer and Hampshire went off to war. Berlin, who had always been
an unequivocal and impassioned anti-appeaser, was rejected as physically unfit for military service and chafed at the unreality of donning
endlessly on (more Kant, more Locke) as one country after another
fell to the Blitzkrieg. He soothed his frustration somewhat by recording, Waugh-like, witty reports from the ivory battlements. 'Maurice
(Bowra), if in a lower-keyed register, is still making the same jokes as
before . . . He is in charge, I believe, of some 160 postal workers. So
our mails are safe at any rate. David Cecil still runs in and out with a
voice like a crate of hens carried across a field.' Striking in the letters
of this time is the total absence of any sort of apprehensiveness, much
less panic, as Britain was finally left alone to face the apparently
invincible Third Reich. To American friends like the Frankfurters
he insisted that England was absolutely not done for, and let those like
Auden (who had scuttled away while pretending some act of cultural
diplomacy) have it:

> Personal survival is no doubt a legitimate end; one fights while one
> can & then one either dies or escapes. I am not a soldier & can't be one
> and am in certain respects highly exposed, if only because I am a Jew
> & have written on Marx: I shd do my best not to be caught: if I could

induce some institution in the US to invite me I would. But cold blooded flight is monstrous. And indifference to a conflict on the outcome of which all art and thought depend, repulsive and stupid ... I perceive that I am being violent and unusually public minded. That is perhaps a genuine change. The private world has cracked in numerous places. I should terribly like to help in the great historical process in some way.

The way, however, proved elusive. Berlin, usually nobody's fool, was comprehensively suckered by one of British history's flashier wicked jesters, the amoral, bibulously charismatic Guy Burgess, already in the stable of Soviet intelligence (along with Anthony Blunt and Donald Maclean, whom Berlin also knew without any suspicion that they were communists, much less agents). Eager to get to Moscow himself, Burgess concocted a scheme by which he and Berlin would go together, the latter as a Russian-fluent press attaché-cum-local-expert who might report back to the Foreign Office in London, perhaps on the prospects of detaching the Soviet Union from the non-aggression pact. For Berlin, this seemed just the ticket, and talks with other acquaintances in the Foreign Office in London were encour-aging enough for him, paradoxically, to book a passage west to Washington from where, it was said, the trip to Russia would be arranged. In the event, someone smelled something not quite right (Burgess's notorious intimacy, not with the NKVD, but with the whisky bottle perhaps) and Berlin's own credentials were compro-mised along with his dodgy friend. Instructions came from London. Do not, repeat, not send B and B.

The ignominious collapse of his Russian mission left Berlin stranded, first in Washington, then in New York, and much chastened in temper – both by the starkness of the world crisis in 1940 and 1941, envisioning the flames of the Blitz at home, and feeling guiltily fret-ful about his distance from it. His sparkly correspondents dim and disappear into the night of the war; no more letters to Stephen Spender or Elizabeth Bowen. Overwhelmingly, the letters that survive through-out Berlin's war years in the United States are to his parents and, after the habitual reassurances of his continuing to flourish, assume a graver, more straightforward tone. They also, quite often, tell pardonable whoppers (as children will do) about his true state of mind, which was deeply homesick for England and often sharply alienated from the America in which he found himself. It was not only his parents whom he benignly misled. To Marion Frankfurter, in August 1940, Berlin drew a contrast between Anglo-French over-sophistication and American directness wholly flattering to the latter. 'I am myself a little disturbed by this terrific [American] clarity and emphasis,' he conceded, 'where nothing is taken for granted, everything is stated in so many unambiguous terms, no secret seasoning is tasteable . . . But it is superior to the nuances and evasions of England and France. Aesthetically inferior but morally superior. It destroys art but conduces to life, liberty and the pursuit of happiness.' To one of his old Oxford pals, Shiela Grant Duff, however, he wrote more candidly that 'I cling to the English desperately. I passionately long to come home. England is *infinitely* preferable to the best discoverable here.' More poetically telling, Berlin often compared himself to a melancholy holdover from the *eighteenth* century, confronted with the raw factual world of the nineteenth, unable to withhold his admiration for its iron grip on the future, yet at the same time deeply repelled by a version of mankind which somehow had edited out precisely the weaknesses and contradictions that were, for him (as for Turgenev and Herzen), the essence of being human.

Which is to say, of course, the essence of being Isaiah. For both the views expressed to Marion Frankfurter as well as those to Shiela Grant Duff were authentic Berlin. The inability to reconcile these two halves of his cultural personality, or to have one prevail over the other, and, finally, his hostility to any *reason* why one or the other should triumph, marks not only Berlin's liberation from his long captivity, toiling in the dense and gloomy woods of the Marxist dialectic, but also an early inkling of what would become the hallmark of his own prudentially pessimistic pluralism. The fact that Berlin would go on to articulate a prescriptive philosophical ethic born of his own autobiography does not, of course, necessarily weaken its claim to truth; just the contrary, as the obstinately Romantic half of him would doubtless insist.

This did not mean, though, that the 'daily living' of these contradictions was, for Berlin, especially easy. A brief period of leave in England in 1940 ('the happiest months of my life') only made the distance between British and American values seem more oceanic than ever. Returned to New York, to the job with the British Information

Service, Berlin acknowledged that since 'I wish to help with the war' he had no choice but to apply himself to the job at hand – of enlisting American Jews to use their influence in assisting FDR's undeclared war – he nonetheless declared himself to Maire Gaster as 'nearer to dissolution in my life than ever before'.

More than anyone else it was Chaim Weizmann, the President of the World Zionist Organisation (and Manchester University chemist), who arguably saved Isaiah from a more serious crack-up and who exemplified, to a degree that Berlin came to find heroic, the historical necessity of suppressing the pangs of *Weltschmerz* and Just Getting On With It. On first meeting Weizmann in England, Berlin was curiously unimpressed. Perhaps the Zionist was too much the unreconstructed Russian Jew, relatively (compared to Isaiah himself) unvarnished with the patina of Oxford Common Room cleverness, for Berlin to warm to him right away. However, witnessing Weizmann's inexhaustible determination to make the aims of the Allied war effort congruent with the establishment of a Jewish national homeland; his relentless campaigning and the infallible passion and eloquence he brought to it; the shrewdness of his pragmatism sustained without compromising the nobility of his ideals, Berlin inevitably became lost in admiration. Here was, he thought, an indisputably great man, someone out of the nineteenth century, with the looks of a 'very distinguished, rather tragic camel', but the charisma of a Mazzini or a Garibaldi. Most of all Berlin saw in Weizmann – whose cautionary gradualism was born of an intense devotion to Britain, which in no way diluted his commitment to Jewish self-determination – the perfect exemplar of the man of felicitously mixed feelings. Well before the war was over – and those mixed feelings became precisely the reason why Weizmann would become marginalised by more militant nationalists like David Ben-Gurion – Berlin was defending him against their impatience. Anti-British policies that seemed to have the virtue of urgency, Berlin thought, would, in the end, turn out to be more damaging than beneficial to the long-term interests of Jewish Palestine.

Pearl Harbor made the work of championing the cause of British survival to American-Jewish opinion redundant. Berlin was moved to the embassy in Washington with the reverse commission of explaining American policy and politics in weekly reports sent to the Foreign

Office (and sometimes, as it transpired, to Churchill). His style – and reputation for brilliant candour – was set in July 1942 in a justifiably famous early report, listing in twenty-three paragraphs just what it was about the British which, notwithstanding the hero-worship of Churchill and the near-universal admiration for their behaviour during the Blitz, made his countrymen so unappealing in some quarters of American opinion. Berlin's talent for cultural summary, deployed for the good of the alliance, was on brilliant display here, especially pene-trating when it cut to the quick of English cultural snobbery. Contradictions being, of course, at the heart of every stereotype, Amer-icans managed to dislike Britain for being *both* trapped in a rigid class structure and for 'going red'; for being both too 'adroit for simple, honest Americans' at the same time that they were rigid in their defence of obsolete empire. The British were both nervously reserved about 'tread-ing on American corns' and yet too free with 'over-civilised English accents', aggravating the American suspicion of being patronised by a country that supposed itself culturally superior.

And so on. Just what policy-makers were supposed to do with these insights, of course, was another matter. Nonetheless, the incisiveness of Berlin's weekly reports became legendary in London and the reason for the famous conversation at lunch at Downing Street, in which Churchill quizzed the understandably startled Irving Berlin on his views about American politics and the state of the world in general. Disabused of the mistake, Churchill dined out on the story and Isaiah himself thought it wonderful, the wonderfulness decreasing every time the British Ambassador, Halifax, repeated it, sometimes forcing Berlin to tell the tale himself.

In Washington Berlin settled into a routine, much of which was using dinner parties as a listening post, the gleanings from which would be converted into his reports. Provided he actually got to the dinners (a hilarious letter of apology to a Brazilian diplomat chroni-cles an evening of unparalleled haplessness at failing to find her address), Berlin revelled in his lionising as the wittiest, smartest fellow in town. No wonder, for only Isaiah Berlin could dispel exaggerated fears that Harold Laski was the *éminence rouge* at the heart of a sinis-ter socialist Jesuitry by telling Americans that Laski was merely 'a harmless megalomaniac'.

As the war wound to its end, Berlin's reputation for analytical acuity made him in demand for a post-war job in government. Arnold Toynbee, whose historical outlook (not to mention his anti-Zionism) was the polar opposite of Berlin's, offered him a place in the Foreign Office Research Department: a prospect which he rejected right away as an existence toiling in 'the sunless cave of inhibited professors'. Towards the end of 1945 he finally got his wish to go to Russia, where, in Leningrad, he had the encounter with Anna Akhmatova, sexless (for she was no longer the startling, bird-like beauty of earlier years) but nonetheless love-struck, a meeting which changed both their lives and to mark which Akhmatova inscribed a poem for Isaiah.

The letters from Russia, though, are the only major disappointment in the book: entertaining on the antics of Randolph Churchill, but strangely silent on almost everything that mattered. On the social and material ruin of Leningrad after the siege, there is little; of the enormity of Soviet tyranny, then playing out the spasms of its most insane cruelties, nothing at all. Akhmatova herself appears more an item of cultural tourism than the heart-stopping epiphany their meeting actually was.

But then Isaiah Berlin's future had been set, and it was not going to be in America or Russia (though he was now uniquely placed to write something of global significance about the fate of British culture between the two colossi). It was in that bomber, going back to England in 1944, forbidden to sleep 'because there was some danger of falling on the oxygen pipe and so suffocating', that he found his true vocation. 'There was no light and therefore one couldn't read,' he later told Henry Hardy, in one of the interposed spoken commentaries which wind beautifully through the book like a twist of silk, 'one was therefore reduced to a most terrible thing – to having to think, and I had to think for seven or eight hours . . . from Canada to England.'

What Berlin thought, above all, was that 'I really wanted to know more at the end of my life than at the beginning' and that pure philosophy 'which taxed the intelligence of man to the highest degree' was not somehow for him. 'I didn't want the answers to these philosophical questions with that degree of urgency with which a true philosopher must want them.' Instead he had discovered that he wanted to reconstruct how social and political ideas became generated in a particular place and time and then how they operated in the flesh-and-blood world of history.

And he also knew, with the decisiveness that his immersion in history had brought, that the last places such illumination would be yielded were in official research departments, where humane intelligence toiled for the powerful. He would, then, go back to Oxford.

And there Isaiah Berlin stayed for the rest of his life, unrepentant of the decision, dismissive of the view that in so doing (to the chagrin of Weizmann among others) he had somehow turned his back on real political engagement. For Berlin, the academy would never be a site of mere cultural gaming. It was, rather, the place where liberty — defined as freedom from any sort of coercion — could be lived; and where the challenge of choosing between life's contradictory impulses could be faced with clear-eyed courage.

J. H. Plumb

Foreword to *The Death of the Past*, 2003

The past may or may not have been dead when J. H. Plumb pronounced its obsequies, but to those of us who were taught by him in Cambridge in the 1960s, the author was unforgettably, alarmingly, alive. Whatever stereotypes those of us arriving at Christ's College in 1963 might have had about history dons, a first encounter with Jack Plumb in his rooms – a small man with a perfectly round, bald head, seated in a big armchair, nattily dressed in a three-piece, crisply tailored suit, a high-coloured Jermyn Street striped shirt and bow tie – swiftly saw off the cliché of tweeds and amontillado. Display cases poured brilliant light on to Sèvres porcelain in kingfisher blue and rose pink. The walls were filled with Dutch still-life and genre paintings: a young man with a weak chin and get-me whiskers; a mournful bar-girl with too much sallow cleavage; an arrangement for hock and lemons. Not a bottle of sherry to be seen, but decanters of Château Figeac, often. When Plumb spoke, and especially when he chuckled, as he often did, the effect of Voltaire in the Fens was complete. But there was, however, a serious price to be paid for all this epicurean dazzlement bestowed on clever but slightly stunned youth: intellectual survival under intense and unsparing fire.

Plumb was famously, tigerishly, combative; though also affable and witty, his conversation punctuated by bursts of laughter at the follies of humanity past and present, of which academia itself, he made clear, offered the richest trove. His temper was naturally quizzical, sardonic, gleeful. But it was impossible, amidst the gales of irony that swept through the room on the subject of some hapless figure, not to be nervous that one might be next for the Treatment. The slightly exophthalmic eyes, glittering from behind his spectacles, would fix steadily and expectantly on whomever a Plumb question, joke or challenge alighted. Abashed thoughtfulness was not a possible response, nor was any sort of laboured earnestness. Anyone suspected of Being Serious About Religion was subjected to a philosophical barrage of teasing which could sometimes turn punishingly picador. Most of the wounding, though, happened in the intense hour or so of history supervisions in those rooms, when we read our essays, our hearts sinking to our boots should Jack begin to fidget ominously in the yellow-upholstered armchair. When it went well, the praise was fulsome and went straight to our giddy heads like champagne. But for some, it seldom did go well. Come six in the evening, the remains of large undergraduates (for this was then a rugby college) could be seen collapsed in trembling exhaustion in the College Buttery after an unhappy hour with Plumb, dosing themselves with healing pints of Watneys, repenting solecisms uttered on the Merovingians (for Plumb loved teaching outside his speciality) and swearing never to go through it again.

But of course we invariably did. There was, for a start, always the prospect of the occasional magical supervision, when he would spend half an hour analysing the form, as well as the content, of a paragraph or two; juggling, like the nimblest editor, with the rhetorical structure of the essay, suggesting how it could gain more punch and conviction were paragraph four to have been the opening, and so on. Towards the end, sometimes over those hard-earned glasses of claret, an encyclopaedic range of bibliographic suggestions would tumble out, many of them eccentrically original. A tentative essay on the cultural backwash of the discovery of the New World drew from him amazement that I had read neither Redcliffe Salaman's *History of the Potato*, nor Geoffroy Atkinson's *Nouveaux Horizons de la Renaissance française*, the latter a book which lived up to the winning peculiarity of its author's name by tackling Montaigne and the *Pléiade* via a lengthy discussion of the implications of Indian nudity for the theology of the Catholic reform movement.

Our own trials by fire culminated in the ritual of the Plumb after-dinner seminar. The seriousness of the event was marked by its being convened, not in the sitting room, but on the other side of the stairs of 'O' staircase, in Jack's dining room. A Sheraton table, the polish high enough for us to see our fretful faces embarrassingly reflected, was laid with a tall Paul de Lamerie silver candelabrum. Silver bowls brimmed with fruit, including a strangely incongruous banana. Two decanters of claret rested on the sideboard which, once the speaker had finished his paper, would be brought to the table to do the rounds. For forty minutes or so either Roy Porter, Geoffrey Parker, Andrew Wheat-croft, John Barber or I would hammer and stammer through our stuff, each of us using whatever kind of rhetorical persuasiveness we could muster amidst the intimidating antiques. Roy's speciality was jokes at which he'd be the first to chortle (and they were usually very funny). Geoffrey Parker fortified himself with armour of unassailable and esoteric scholarship. Schama, as usual, depended overmuch on adjec-tival overload and overwrought atmospherics to conceal the shakiness of his hypotheses. (*Plus ça change.*) In the candle-lit glow one always knew if things were going well. JHP's not twanging an elastic band, for instance, was definitely a good sign, as was his not turning his chair sideways to commune with the smirking likeness of Sir Robert Walpole on the wall.

After the reading came the listeners' turn to respond, or else. The claret and fruit circulated (Porter and I usually doing unspeakable things with the grape scissors, an instrument for which London lower-middle-class life had inadequately prepared us). The diplomatic psychology of the discussion was tricky: too fierce in our criticism and we would sacrifice a friendship; too cosy or indulgent, then we risked disbelief and raillery from Plumb. So we generally told the truth. At the end of the circle of comments, Jack would supply his own, and belie his reputation for fierceness by generous helpings of praise for the student's research and his grip on the subject, even while raising questions about both evidence and analysis which not infre-quently turned the whole exercise inside out and upside down. Whatever else happened in those seminars, we all learned the art of vigilantly sympathetic attentiveness, which has stood me, at any rate, in good stead in over thirty years of teaching.

But aside from pedagogic style, was there a 'Plumb' philosophy of history, evident in these bracing hours of instruction, and faithfully represented in *The Death of the Past?* In the mid-1960s, it seemed to be an obligation for every historian worth his salt to make some sort of utterance on what history was and wasn't, many of them a response to, and exasperated refutation of, E. H. Carr's *What is History?*, a book which its countless critics (all of them in the right) see as the mailed fist of determinism lurking in the velvet glove of a faux-scepticism. Herbert Butterfield, G. R. Elton (Plumb's particular nemesis) and

many others had all put their methodological oars in, but what is striking about so many of these *professions de foi* is their un-self-examined
address to the converted. Their working assumption (fair enough in
the 1960s, when the escalator from A-level history to undergraduate
history to graduate history to that first Research Fellowship was
serenely uninterrupted by anything resembling a power outage from
the employment *Zeitgeist*) was that academic history would continue
to be the dominant discipline of both the humanities and the social
sciences; its scholarly gravitas weightier than the study of literature,
yet somehow more imaginatively creative than sociology or economics. For Elton, the question 'who cares?' would have been not so much
impertinent as unthinkable. The issue was not to legitimise the discipline so much as to issue a stringent manual for its professional
practice.

For the worldly Plumb, though, with his relish for, and brilliance
at, popular history writing and journalism, especially in America
where he was the leading literary light of *Horizon* magazine, there
was no question of history resting smugly on its laurels. Dragged inside
the professional stockade, he believed, history would atrophy into an
arid scholasticism. 'What do they of history know,' I remember him
borrowing from E. M. Forster (who had in turn creatively pilfered
Kipling), 'who know only other historians?' For Plumb, history was
either a public craft or it was nothing; and in this spirit he was
constantly urging on us books he cherished which had been written
by historians either rejected by the academy or who had chosen to
work outside it. Iris Origo's *Merchant of Prato*, Barbara Tuchman's
The Guns of August and Frances Yates's work on neo-Platonist
hermetics (very much an eccentricity in the 1960s) all come to mind.
While others cringed at the belletrism they imputed to C. V. Wedgwood, Plumb welcomed her to High Table and introduced us
personally to that elegant, surprisingly astringent mind.

The battle lines were decisively drawn for us at Christ's: the encyclopaedic and the omnivorous (us) versus the arid and the parochial
(them); history seen as an enquiry into the human condition (us) versus
history assumed to be the unfolding epic of English (not even British)
governing institutions (them); history which embraced the literary and
the imaginative without ever forsaking the hard tests of documentary
evidence (us) versus history which treated strong writing as a fig-leaf

for analytical mushiness (them). And while Plumb was adamant about
the indispensability of the archive, neither did he fetishise it. The
archive was, he insisted, startlingly anticipating Arlette Farge and
Pierre Bourdieu, a social institution, with its own invented practices,
hierarchies of significance, both human and documentary, and which
was as much the product of a particular culture as its shaper. *Caveat
lector!* The notion that the historian's task consisted entirely of archae-
ological self-effacement before the bedrock of archival truth − a
mole-like digger of nuggets and gobbets − he found not so much professionally deluded as betraying an almost pathetic want of critical
self-consciousness.

Yet it was precisely Plumb's abiding and unapologetic sense that
history lived for others, not just for itself − that it was, at root, a civic
vocation, not a monastic profession − which snared him in all kinds
of contradictions, some of which are exposed, others glossed over in
The Death of the Past. The central message of the book − that history,
practised as a truly critical discipline, was the enemy of a 'past' in
which liberty of thought and action was forever in thrall to the
claimed authority of ancestral prescription − actually pointed its readers in two directions at once. On the one hand, history, construed as
the study of human society, needed the input of professionals, saturated in, and invigorated by, the methodologies of the Annales school,
especially Bloch and Braudel, if it were to break free, simultaneously
from a culture of sentimental deference to heritage and from the
airless claustrophobia of Gobbet Land. On the other hand, none of
that would make any difference to the survival of history as a public
craft, unless that new professionalism could be translated into
genuinely popular writing. In principle, there was no reason why this
little miracle should not happen, and Plumb's ambitious multi-volume
History of Human Society attempted to do just that. But as an advertisement for a new, yet genuinely popular, history, the series never
really took off, not least because the quality of its writing, while seldom
exactly pedestrian, never really made for page-turning, either. The
project, stalled before its ambitions could be realised, remained obstinately encyclopaedic rather than genuinely innovative. Several
volumes only brought home the truism that Braudels, Blochs and
Febvres, capable of achieving a synthesis of narrative and social analysis, of ethnography and textual exegesis, were painfully scarce.

Narrative drive and the force of events – precisely the history repudiated by Braudel as the artifice of dull practitioners in favour of the slow heave and shift of tectonic-plate forces – were in fact the *sine qua non* of bringing readers back to history and thus liberating them from 'the past'.

And Plumb, a supremely accomplished narrator, knew this. However much he may have asserted the equivalence of the history of the potato with the history of the British (or American) Civil Wars, in his heart of hearts he didn't believe it. In fact, at the height of the mode for social history in the Annales style, Plumb could be found insisting on the power of speech-acts to shake and shape the destiny of communities and nations. If, in some of his great lecture performances (as in his work on Walpole), he might suggest that parliamentary rhetoric was a veil behind which the grind of monied interest did its business, on other days he would impersonate the histrionics of a Fox or a Chatham with precisely the opposite conclusion in mind. His considering intellect, then, may have pointed him away from the power of argument and ideology, but the vitality of his temperament and his deep engagement with the mystery of language pointed, always, towards it. That, indeed, was the gravamen of his ferocious argument against Lewis Namier, whose obsession with interest over ideology Plumb thought a simple mistake about how humans behave.

None of which prevented Plumb from accomplishing an important and even lasting little polemic in *The Death of the Past*. But as so often with him (as with many of the finest historians) what he says is less significant than the way that he says it. Though Plumb clung to the notion that history had to be more than just the exercise of the pleasure principle; more than merely the inspection of the generations of humanity; that it ought, really, to bring about some sort of epistemological and cultural alteration; he was actually hard-pressed to define what such an alteration might be. While all his pupils would agree that a world without critical history would be dangerously worse off, in the end, Plumb, like many of us, remained stymied by an aesthetic in search of a didactic.

Rescuing Churchill

Review of *Churchill* by Roy Jenkins, *New York Review of Books*, 28 February 2002

The last thing George Orwell published was a May 1949 review of Volume Two of Winston Churchill's memoirs of the Second World War, *Their Finest Hour.* You might expect him to have been allergic to its chest-thumping patriotism, its flights of empurpled rhetoric; but not a bit of it. Churchill's writings, Orwell observed, bestowing the most meaningful accolade he could manage, were 'more like those of a human being than of a public figure'. Though in 1939 Orwell had been suspicious of Churchill's belligerent rhetoric and ominous potential for a personality cult of his own, by the time he came to write *1984*, it was not Big Brother who would be baptised Winston, but the doomed renegade, 'the last man'.

Churchill may have been born in Blenheim Palace, but Orwell was right to grant him the gift of the common touch. When the Prime Minister toured the scorched and shattered remains of Bristol after a particularly hellish air raid in April 1941, a woman who had lost everything and was awash with raging tears, on seeing the jowly face and cigar, stopped crying and waved her hanky, shouting herself hoarse, 'Hooray, hooray!' Along with the millions of his compatriots, Orwell believed that, more than any political, or military, gifts, it had been Winston's exuberant humanity – egotistical, erratic, histrionic – as well as his long career as a word-warrior, that had taken a people, shaking with trepidation, and made of them comrades in arms.

Of a piece with that humanity was Churchill's large capacity for self-mockery. Orwell also recycled the story that Churchill followed up 'we will fight on the beaches' with 'we'll throw bottles at the b——s, it's about all we've got left', but that the candid addition was buzzed out by the quick hand of the BBC censor just in time. The story was apocryphal, but the point was that such Churchilliana existed at all. No leader who made jokes against himself was in much danger of turning dictator. In the same vein, Clement Attlee, the Labour party leader who served in his War Cabinet and who could, at times, be a fierce critic, commented not long after Churchill's death that he was 'a supremely fortunate mortal', but that 'the most warming thing about him was that he never ceased to say so'.

But the comedian and the tragedian lived within the same surprisingly delicate skin. The challenge facing any biography added to the groaning shelves of Churchill histories is somehow to do full justice to the Promethean character of its subject, the richly lived (not to say gluttonously engorged) career, without ever being a slave to its mystique. Mere character delineation – easy enough in Churchill's case – won't suffice. The hard work is to demonstrate exactly *how* the outsize Churchillian personality, so truculent, so impulsive, so often profoundly wrongheaded, became, in the dark spring of 1940, just what was needed for national survival. There's no doubt that Roy Jenkins has risen splendidly to this challenge, succeeding, much better than many biographers before him, in bringing to life Churchill the political animal, whose impatient appetite for power, and strenuous exertions to secure it, are often hidden beneath the grand opera of his speechifying. He was smoke, certainly, but he was also mirrors. And Jenkins catches Churchill's studied self-inspection with the sure-shot sharpness of an expert portraitist, a Karsh who has the cheek to stare back.

His big book appears at a doubly interesting moment. The popularity of biographies of heroic but unimpeachably democratic leaders on both sides of the Atlantic owes something, obviously, to the present craving for both public reassurance and political education. The temptation is to return Karl Rove's call and deliver an anatomy of charisma, stripped down to interchangeable parts, available for selective cannibalisation, and rebuilt to cope with the Crisis of the Week, the very stuff (as Churchill might have said) of that most egregious waste of time and money: leadership seminars. Perennially shrewd politician (even, or rather especially, in his eighties) though Lord Jenkins is, he also knows that the cloth from which Churchill was cut is deeply unsuited for modern imitations. (Who, these days, writes his own speeches, much less has the guts to begin one: 'The news . . . is *very* bad'?) So he preserves and celebrates Churchill in all his titanic, unreproducible peculiarity; the storms of petulant fury rage along with the cherubic smiles. Jenkins's angle of vision is that of undeluded, critically intelligent appreciation, wisely informed by his own lifetime of governing experience, neither adulatory nor hyper-sceptical.

His biography also coincides, though, with a moment when Churchill revisionism shows signs, perhaps welcome, of running out of steam. The genre began with the most cumulatively powerful and perceptive book ever written on the daunting subject, *Churchill: Four Faces and the Man*, published in 1968, only three years after his death, when the marble at Bladon churchyard was still shining white. Such collections usually suffer from curate's-egg syndrome, with some good pieces and some bad; not, however, when its authors are A. J. P. Taylor (on the statesman), Robert Rhodes James (on the politician), J. H. Plumb (on the historian), Basil Liddell Hart (on the war leader) and Anthony Storr (on the 'Black Dog' bipolar depressive). While the memorable book was in no way a hatchet job, the authors were nonetheless determined to look at their subject without stars, or tears, in their eyes. While they all acknowledged his indispensability, they were equally forthright (as was Churchill himself) about his many failings. For Plumb (notwithstanding the fact that he had worked on the proofs of the last volume of *The History of the English-Speaking Peoples*), the histories that won Churchill the Nobel Prize for Literature were just so many anachronistic swashbuckling failures, Gibbon's orotundity married to Macaulay's complacent insularity. Liddell Hart thought he had been excessively criticised for disasters in the First World War, but not nearly enough for the Second World War, not least because he had rewritten its history so selectively. And A. J. P. Taylor pointed out with typically unsparing sharpness that the man who, during the 1930s, had so obstinately and so noisily resisted the demise of empire, especially in Asia, actually guaranteed its collapse in 1941 by starving its defences of fighter planes, warships and manpower, in favour of the North African theatre and, less forgivably, the catastrophic attempt to take on the Germans in Crete.

As the tomes of Martin Gilbert's multi-volume Churchilliad arose in the 1970s and '80s like some massive biographical Stonehenge, revisionists, as if in resistance, became correspondingly more audacious. Robert Rhodes James's book *Churchill: A Study in Failure, 1900–1939* made the fair point that had, in fact, the taxi that struck Churchill on Fifth Avenue in 1930 hit with lethal force, his career would indeed have been judged on its impulsive blunders (the Dardanelles in 1915) and its quixotic devotion to deservedly doomed causes – the gold standard, the British Raj in India, the constitutional viability of King Edward VIII. Likewise, Paul Addison's fine scholarly history of Churchill's career in domestic politics and government pulled no punches about his tendency to favour trigger-happy solutions for difficult problems – calling out the troops in 1911 and 1926 to deal with industrial strikes, for example.

A step very definitely too far, however, was taken by John Charmley, whose *Churchill: The End of Glory* (1993) was the most ambitious attempt yet to reach up and pull the giant from his pedestal, but which succeeded only in having his full weight collapse back on the author. Starting with Taylor's insight that the most intransigent defender of the Raj had ironically ended up being the inadvertent instrument of its downfall, Charmley added to it fresh research about the tentative suggestions mooted in the War Cabinet by Lord Halifax in the gloomy days of late May 1940, when France was on the point of collapse, for an approach through Mussolini, to discover what Hitler's terms might be.

The premise of any such negotiations was the proposition, raised as early as 1937 by von Ribbentrop in a private conversation with Churchill when the latter was still just an MP, that Hitler would be prepared to leave Britain's insular sovereignty and its empire intact, in return for a free hand in Eastern Europe. By 1940 this hegemony was to be extended through the whole continent, and Churchill's response – superlatively chronicled in John Lukacs's moving *Five Days in London, May 1940* was the same as it had been three years earlier: indignant categorical rejection.

Charmley, appealing (as self-appointed revisionists invariably do) to the calculus of national interest rather than to 'emotive' morality, argued that if imperial self-preservation, not to mention freedom from postwar economic and military dependence on the United States, was British policy, it might have been better to take the deal. But as Geoffrey Best's excellent, concise new biography (which has had the bad luck to appear at the same time as Jenkins's) points out, even supposing that British national independence, courtesy of the Third Reich, would have fared any better than the French, especially when it came to the little matter of saving Jews from the gas chambers, there is an air of quaintly naive parochialism about Charmley's assumption that the Raj (already exposed by Gandhi as intrinsically ungovernable) would somehow have been granted a stay of execution thanks to the Swastika and the Rising

Sun. It is, in fact, to Churchill's imperishable credit that, faced with the alternatives of hanging on to the scraps of empire, courtesy of Adolf Hitler, or fighting to the end, whatever long-term damage might accrue to British power, he unhesitatingly opted for the latter. Even for its most conspicuous eulogist, better by far an 'end of glory' than the end of freedom.

What, then, moved Lord Jenkins, at a time in his life when less compulsively prolific souls would be booking their poolside loungers in the Bahamas, to enter this crowded fray? According to his own disconcerting admission, he was moved less by any gladiatorial impulse or by the discovery of new information than by the avoidance of anticlimax in his literary résumé following his richly merited success with *Gladstone*. Then, too, there seems to have been the desire to decide whether or not Churchill was indeed Top Prime Minister, a determination made at the very end of the book with Jenkins duly awarding him prime space in the pantheon. Whatever the motives, Jenkins's qualifications are unarguable. Like Churchill, he has been very much a cat who has walked on his own. Both were long kept at arm's length from their party's leadership by suspicion about their loyalty to its core principles. (Arguably Churchill would never have been Prime Minister but for the war.)

Both also put ideas above party allegiance, and they were, in fact, the not dissimilar ideals of anti-Marxist liberalism and state-sponsored social reform, a combination once thought to be an anomaly in the polarised struggle between capitalism and labour, but which, a century after its birth in the early twentieth century, actually looks very much like becoming, at least in Europe, king of the zeitgeist. Churchill was a penal reformer; Jenkins an early campaigner against capital punishment. Both men suffered at the hands of the more puritanical elders of their respective parties for their unapologetic celebration of the pleasures of the table and the cellar. It's hard not to believe that Churchill wouldn't have been pleased by this most epicurean biography, in whose pages no memorable bottle ever goes uncorked. It's certainly the only Churchill biography in which the phrase 'a very remarkable Liebfraumilch', quoted from the recitation by Churchill's aide Jock Colville of the menu on the *Queen Mary* in 1944, seems as inevitable as 'blood, toil, tears and sweat'.

But one affinity beyond all others seems to tie the knot between author and subject: their intertwined careers as both historian and politician, which make the distinction between history as lived event and history as report of that event moot. Nor, in either case, has this been a matter of alternative vocations; the writing used as compensation, both psychological and pecuniary, for the loss of office and power (as it was with Clarendon). Jenkins's career as a thoughtful, elegantly readable political historian goes back almost fifty years. As a schoolboy in the late 1950s, I read and admired his biography of Charles Dilke, the nineteenth-century radical imperialist who self-destructed in a sexual scandal, and his brilliant account of the Liberal government's onslaught on the House of Lords, *Mr Balfour's Poodle*, before I knew much about Jenkins as a rising Labour party politician. Virtually all his books (until this one) have been, one way or another, commentaries on one of the two issues which have most engaged him in public life: the complicated, sometimes tortured, relationship between liberal democracy and social justice, and Britain's relationship with Europe. The writing has informed the career and vice versa.

So too with Churchill. Before 1945, it had emphatically not been a case of the politician exploiting his reputation to launch a literary career; rather the other way around. From the time he went to Cuba in 1896 to his exploits on the north-west Indian frontier, Sudan and South Africa, shamelessly exploiting his and his mother's social connections to put himself on the front line over the objections of local commanders, Churchill reinvented the war correspondent as both fighter and writer. And the more he scripted his destiny, the more outlandishly heroic it conveniently became, culminating in his escape from a Boer prisoner-of-war camp in Pretoria, followed by a trek through the veldt to liberty, before, it goes without saying, re-enlisting.

Copy flowed from his pen to popular British newspapers like *The Daily Graphic* and was then expanded into three substantial books in which Churchill, perfectly judging his readership, managed to combine ripping yarns with romantic laments for the nobly fallen foe. (He was moved to indignant protest when, after the battle of Omdurman, during which he'd taken part in the famous, nearly suicidal charge of the 21st Lancers, he learned that the commander, Lord Kitchener, had desecrated the tomb of the defeated Islamic jihad leader, the Mahdi, mutilated his body and used his skull as an inkwell.)

Recognising a fellow compulsive scribbler, Jenkins can't help be impressed by the single-mindedness with which Churchill went after contracts and royalties, and the adroitness with which he translated his maverick persona into bankable political capital. But when he returns to Churchill's later work, it's more to register his entrepreneurial savvy, running battalions of researchers and landing fat advances to pay for the country house at Chartwell, than to ponder with much sustained curiosity how history profoundly shaped his sense of political purpose. No British statesman since William Pitt the Elder was more deeply marked by so providential a view of his nation's past, and by extension a conviction that his own political life was to be spent in its perpetuation. His account, to be sure, is the conventional sea-girt epic of Protestant parliamentary liberty, unfolding as if through divine dispensation from Magna Carta to Mr Gladstone and related by Macaulay and Henry Hallam, whose books Churchill first greedily consumed between sets of polo in India.

The history was national rather than monarchic and, despite Churchill's birth, not especially aristocratic. (As a Liberal colleague of Lloyd George's attack on the veto power of the House of Lords, Churchill was hot to press for its abolition as an absurd anachronism.) This history was Churchill's religion. Its saints and martyrs spoke to him on a daily basis. When he met with Franklin Roosevelt on board HMS *Prince of Wales* in Placentia Bay in Newfoundland, in 1941, Churchill chose, for the concluding hymn, sung by the mingled ranks of American and British sailors, 'O God, Our Help in Ages Past'. The reason was that it had been sung by Cromwell's Ironsides as they buried the parliamentary tax resister John Hampden, killed in action against the royalists. *That* was his reply to the 'Horst Wessel Lied'.

It's fashionable, not to say mandatory, for serious, critical historiography to write off English parliamentary history as so much 'elitist', self-congratulatory, Whig teleology. But when Churchill returned again and again to the Manichaean confrontation between liberty and tyranny, and to the canonical moments in the British past when despotism had been resisted (the Armada in 1588; the Camp de Boulogne in 1803), those convictions were infectious, not just because they were so heroically articulated, but because they were not, in fact, false. If people wish to know why exactly we are fighting, he told his listeners in 1941, let them abandon the war and they will very soon find out!

In the service of these – to Churchill – self-evident historical truths, he could resort to outrageous acts of casuistry, characterising, for example, Britain's terrifying isolation after the fall of France as the 'honour' which had fallen to Britain of being Germany's 'foremost foe'. His strategy was to compliment his listeners – whether on the BBC or in the House of Commons – by always assuming that they all shared this lofty ideal, when for many millions the main aim of the war was to get through it in one piece, preferably without one's house in rubble. The flattery worked (as it did on FDR, who was co-opted by correspondence as a fellow defender of democracy). In no time at all, the British public *did* come to believe that on its resolve turned the fate not just of national survival, but the fate of democracy. It's this fundamental Churchillian generosity, half-cunning, half-instinctive, which also accounts for the otherwise inexplicable failure to tell the truth in his war memoirs about the deep divisions in the War Cabinet over whether to go it alone or to sound out 'Signor Mussolini'. In 1948, with Neville Chamberlain dead, Churchill could so easily have taken the personal credit due for stifling the last gasp of the appeasers, but he preferred instead to pretend that they were, in their heart of hearts, always on his side.

Roy Jenkins's jaunty narrative seldom pauses for reflections of this kind, much less to give Churchill's eloquence the kind of close analytical scrutiny offered in, for example David Cannadine's illuminating preface to the Penguin edition of the speeches, or the extraordinary essay by Isaiah Berlin entitled 'Mr Churchill in 1940', which doesn't even rate an appearance in Jenkins's bibliography. 'If somebody asked me what exactly Winston did to win the war,' Clement Attlee wrote, 'I would say, "Talk about it."' And although it was important that Churchill attended to the supply of ships and planes and men that would defeat the Axis, he was also the only leader who could take on the Führer's manic logorrhoea and wipe the floor with it. Jenkins has a tendency to take at face value the weaponry of Churchill's oratory, a unique, at times almost Shakespearean marriage between the grandiloquent and the puckishly conversational, even though these spoken masterpieces were the product of countless hours of labour. (His friend F. E. Smith joked that Winston spent the best part of his life preparing impromptu speeches.) As a writer he could be either flat-footed or twinkle-toed, but when he was on song he was unbeatable. Who else would have described the collapse of the old monarchies in 1918 as a 'drizzle of empires falling through the air'? At Harrow, wrote Churchill in his dazzling and often

funny *My Early Life*, 'I got into my bones the essential structure of
the ordinary British sentence – which is a noble thing.' But Jenkins
sometimes betrays a tin ear for the succinct earthiness which, even at
its most theatrically lime-lit moments, made it, as Orwell recognised,
a true language of the people. Compare the two on his stint in the
Cuban war in 1895. Churchill writes, 'We are on our horses, in uniform;
our revolvers are loaded. In the dusk and half-light, long files of armed
and laden men are shuffling off towards the enemy.' Jenkins writes of
Churchill's being 'under mild fire' on his twenty-first birthday: 'This
he regarded as a very satisfactory concatenation.'

Nor would Lord Jenkins be seen dead in the company of psycho-
biographers, so don't go looking here for speculation about
Churchill's reliance on silk underwear, his invention of the velveteen
siren suit, essentially, as startled witnesses reported, overgrown baby
rompers, the oral fixation of the cigar, lit or unlit, or the strenuous
over-compensation (as with Theodore Roosevelt) for the thirty-one-
inch, hairless chest, or the pursuit of oratory as a campaign of
conquest over the stammer and the lisp.

There's a clubby smoothness about Jenkins's prose, which isn't much
interested, either, in walking the growling Black Dog of Churchill's
fits of self-annihilating depression, or pondering his moments of truly
apocalyptic pessimism, both before and after the Second World War,
when he imagined bombs raining from the sky in an immense, even
universal immolation. While Jenkins duly notes the baleful influence
of Churchill's father, the glowering, embittered Lord Randolph, on
the insecure, physically delicate boy, he omits the one story that most
dramatically conveys the pathetic intensity of Churchill's efforts to
prove himself worthy in the eyes of his unspeakable parent.

Writing from Sandhurst Royal Military Academy (where he'd been
sent, having been judged too stupid and idle to amount to anything
in the law), Winston confessed, in a state of abject terror, that he had
wrecked the gold watch his father had given him, not once (when
another cadet ran into him), but twice (when it had fallen from his
fob pocket into a pond). Correctly anticipating the cannonade of cold
fury, the denunciations for incompetence, irresponsibility and all-
around worthlessness that would come his way, Winston mounted a
desperate salvage operation with the same manic energy with which
he would later conduct world wars – mobilising a company of infantry,

then a fire engine, to dredge the pond, finally diverting the headwaters before retrieving the mud-caked timepiece, irreparably ruined. All he could do was to prostrate himself before his father's wrath in one of the saddest letters he ever wrote. To his father's implacable denunciation, 'I would not believe you could be such a young stupid. It is clear you are not to be trusted', Winston bleated: 'Please don't judge me entirely on the strength of the watch. I am very very sorry about it.' More than sixty years later, after his Nobel Prize and his elaborately hagiographic biography of Lord Randolph, he was still trying to justify his life to the bug-eyed bully. One of the last pieces he ever published – mentioned by Jenkins – was 'The Dream', in which a phantom Lord Randolph materialises in front of Winston as he dabs at a canvas, the father baffled by the inexplicable affluence of the wastrel's house until the son proudly recounts the history of his prodigious career.

This still leaves a lot of Churchill's hectic life for Roy Jenkins to write wonderfully about, and he unquestionably does. Few writers know more about the heady days of the great reforming Liberal governments of 1906–16 than the author of an earlier, fine biography of H. H. Asquith, and Jenkins lucidly charts Churchill's desertion of the Tories followed by his meteoric rise through ministerial ranks from a colonial Under-Secretary to the Board of Trade, to Home Secretary and, finally, the Admiralty. Jenkins gives the tyro proper credit, along with his friend and mentor Lloyd George, for pushing through a raft of progressive reforms – labour exchanges, unemployment insurance, mine inspection improvements.

But like Robert Rhodes James and Geoffrey Best, he rightly points out that more than once in his career in government Churchill was the author of policies he later attacked as short-sighted. Thrice he was the impassioned advocate of reduced arms expenditure, as Tory, Liberal and Tory again, and thrice again (in the naval arms race immediately before the First World War, in the 1930s and in the Cold War) he was gung-ho for rearmament. Though he took the lion's share of blame (not altogether without justification) for the catastrophically botched attempt to force the Dardanelles in 1915, he somehow escaped whipping entirely for the almost equally appalling fiasco of the Norwegian campaign of 1940.

Field Marshal Alanbrooke, his bird-watching, pious Chief of Imperial General Staff, in his withering private diaries, often portrays

Churchill as strategically incompetent, deaf to informed counsel, violently abusive to subordinates, and pig-headed in standing by opinions all too often arrived at without even a modicum of familiarity with their logistical implications. Sometimes — as when he claims Churchill's famous 'Action This Day' memoranda suggested greater familiarity with detail than was actually the case — Alanbrooke is unduly harsh. But it is true that, from 1943, the relentless comings and goings over the Atlantic, along with equally gruelling trips to Russia and North Africa, took a toll on Churchill's clarity and grip. In Cabinet meetings his attention wandered and he was capable of rambling on to no particular point, bluffing his way through matters he had failed to prepare for by reading the proper papers. Pushed beyond endurance by this lackadaisical inattentiveness, the normally equable Attlee was goaded into sending Churchill a memorandum of disgusted protest and reproach. Increasingly fatalistic about Britain's inevitable subordination to American and Russian global power, Churchill enjoyed victory much less than he had anticipated.

But unlike his opposite number in the Bunker, much less the man in the Kremlin, Churchill took the criticism on the chin and would snap out of his brandy-lubricated bouts of gloom, summoning ministers to his bedside for morning conferences where he would hold forth, deep in breakfast crumbs and war maps, attired in his red-and-gold dragon robe like some omnipotent mandarin. And as even his most severe critics conceded, all his shortcomings were as nothing compared with the supreme accomplishment of giving Britain the collective will to fight at the time no one else would or could, and when opinionated observers like Ambassador Joseph Kennedy assumed it was not a case of whether the country would capitulate, but when. Alanbrooke would be on the verge of speaking his mind and then Churchill would have him to dine and he would marvel at the Prime Minister's buoyant courage and iron resolve.

What he may have lacked in micro-managerial attentiveness he more than compensated for by moral clarity. During the 1930s, when it was the political norm among the appeasers to hold their noses and turn a blind eye to what the Nazis were doing to the Jews, commenting, in effect, that doubtless it was all very deplorable, but what did one expect in a world which also boasted Mussolini and Stalin, Churchill understood the incommensurability of Nazi bestiality and unhesitatingly said so, over and over again. After Kristallnacht he was unembarrassed to shed tears while describing the torments in a culture which looked on such demonstrations of emotion as dreadfully bad form.

But then, one of the many reasons to be grateful to Roy Jenkins's fine book is to be reminded of Churchill's fundamental decency, the quality that made Orwell forgive him his anti-socialism and his sentimental imperialism. Though limited in education and social experience, Churchill nonetheless had no difficulty in translating his own romantic feeling for nationality to the aspirations of other cultures. It was natural, then, for him to end up the friend of Michael Collins as well as F. E. Smith, Chaim Weizmann as well as Emir (later King) Abdullah, and to see that a two-state solution in both Ireland and Palestine was the only way to satisfy equally legitimate longings for homeland.

In this, as in so many other aspects of the twentieth century, Churchill was a good deal more prescient than the clichés about his octogenarian dotage usually allow. Arguably the very best chapters of Jenkins's book are the last ones dealing with the late 1940s and '50s, after the victorious war leader had been rewarded with the stinging electoral defeat of 1945. Jenkins argues persuasively that even if, when re-elected in 1951, at the age of seventy-seven, Churchill did have a tendency to treat his 'Auld Lang Syne' government as a reunion, he had adjusted his historicist insularity to envision a Britain both enthusiastically pan-European and committed to the Atlantic alliance. The latest chapter of the providentialist story, then, was Britain's indispensable bridge-making between Europe and America.

His last cause, motivated by the certainty that any kind of nuclear exchange would presage the end of human history, was the diplomatic campaign fought doggedly but fruitlessly between 1953 and 1955 to defuse the Cold War. His last speech to the House of Commons before retiring as Prime Minister, ostensibly devoted to a White Paper on Defence, was prepared with excruciating care and was full of dark visions fitfully lit by flashes of optimism, the 'zigzag lightning' which Asquith had identified as the sign of his genius. Its rhythmically intoned peroration sounded, as Churchillian rhetoric had so many times before, the mighty chimes of his call to perseverance: 'Never flinch; never weary; never despair.' It's the achievement of Roy Jenkins's book to let us hear this voice again; to liberate the man from the mausoleum.

Churchill as Orator

Guardian, 20 April 2007

It was well after midnight on 7 February 1787 when Richard Brinsley Sheridan, MP, got up in the House of Commons to flay the hide off Warren Hastings, the impeached governor of Bengal.

The chamber was packed to the rafters, notwithstanding the fifty-guinea price for tickets. By the time Sheridan was done, it was six in the morning and no one had moved.

But virtuoso marathons of oratory weren't at all unusual in that distant golden age of eloquence (and they were a lot more fun than the Castro all-nighter).

Arguing for law reform in 1828, another celebrated silver-tongue, Henry Brougham, clocked six hours and three minutes and again no one budged. But then they both knew their spellbinding craft backwards.

Brougham had written essays on oratory (his favourite being Demosthenes) and at Edinburgh University had heard the great master of rhetoric, Hugh Blair, whose published lectures supplemented Cicero's *De Oratore* as the two great primers of studied eloquence, ancient and modern.

Sheridan took his stagecraft into the chamber, fulfilling Cicero's ideal that the orator should resemble Rome's star tragedian Roscius: 'When people hear he is to speak all the benches are taken . . . when he needs to speak silence is signalled by the crowd followed by repeated applause and much admiration. They laugh when he wishes, when he wishes they cry.'

When did you last hear a speech that good? Tony Blair's epideictic performance at the Labour-party conference last year won admiration even from his foes, but by and large the digital age is cool to rhetoric and, as the enthronement of the blogger suggests, prizes incoherent impulse over the Ciceronian arts of the exordium and the peroration.

State of the Nation addresses to the US Congress – that theatre of sob-sisters and ra-ra patriotism – most usually confuse passion with sentimentality, and since they are worked up by industrial teams of speechwriters, lack one of the elements thought indispensable to great oratory: integrity of personal conviction, the sound of what Cicero, following the Greeks, called ethos.

The robotically choreographed antics in which Democrats and Republicans alternate standing ovations every five minutes is the opposite of the free-spirited audiences Cicero had in mind submitting themselves to the persuader's art.

True public eloquence presupposes a citizen-audience gathered into a republic of listening. But our oral age is iPodded for our customised egos, an audience of one. Headphone listening seals us off, cuts connections.

Then there is that peculiarly British thing about grandiloquence, happier, for the most part, absorbing it in the theatre than in the public realm, where, as Winston Churchill found for most of his career, it was thought a symptom of his showy shallowness, his inconstancy, his addiction to hyperbole; in short, everything a man of sound policy was not.

But of course, speeches were what he did supremely well. Self-conscious that he'd never been through the upper-class nursery of eloquence, the Oxbridge Unions, Churchill fed off the great tradition of British politicians who had prevailed over the laws of understatement and pragmatic sobriety.

He communed with Cromwell, Chatham, Burke and Fox, Brougham, Macaulay and Gladstone, studying their master speeches for instruction on the oral economy of vehemence; when to let pathos, the appeal to passion, rip, and when, as Hugh Blair insisted, to make it retreat. And in one moment, the catastrophic late spring of 1940, this lifetime of rhetorical education and mercurial performance finally paid off.

Churchill's words went to war when Britain's armed forces seemed to be going under and had less wordy politicians like Halifax scurrying for a compromise with the triumphant Axis.

But, though he felt 'physically sick' at the Cabinet meeting of 26 May, when the horrifying magnitude of the German sweep to the Channel, coupled with King Leopold's Belgian capitulation, was sinking in, Churchill was adamant.

'No such discussions are to be permitted' was his response to suggestions to evacuate the royal family to some distant dominion of the empire.

When Kenneth Clark proposed taking the cream of the National Gallery's collection to Canada, Churchill shot back: 'No. Bury them in caves and cellars. None must go. We are going to beat them.'

The rehearsal for his great performance in the House of Commons on 4 June was to the full Cabinet (helpfully minus Halifax) in which Churchill passionately declaimed, 'We shall go on and we shall fight it out here or elsewhere and if at the last the long story is at an end it were better it should end, not through surrender but only when we are rolling senseless on the ground.' (Hugh Dalton added that Churchill had actually said 'when each of us lies choking in his own blood'.)

Ministers thumped fists on the table; some rose and patted him on the back. Defeatism – for the moment – had been held at bay. The long speech to the House of Commons a week later was meant to pre-empt any further thoughts of compromise with the 'Nahzies' (a wonderfully, calculatedly dismissive pronunciation) and to turn the mood of the country from despair to resolution.

Josiah Wedgwood thought it was worth 'a thousand guns and a thousand years' and he was right. It embodied both ethos (noble candour) and pathos (vehement passion) in equal degree and its inspirational persuasion depended fundamentally on one rhetorical tactic: honesty.

Unusually, Churchill dispensed with an introductory exordium and went straight to his narrative of the German blitzkrieg on the north, as if he were writing one of his military histories.

No one minded the mixed metaphor 'the German eruption swept like a scythe stroke'. Interspersed amid the lengthy storytelling was heroic relief, albeit in tragic mood: the futile four days of resistance in Calais (ordered by him). 'Cheers' reported the *Guardian*.

Then followed, in Churchill's instinctively archaic manner, what he thought would have been – and what still sounded like – 'hard and heavy tidings' of the encirclement. He trowelled on the despair, 'the whole root and core and brain of the British army . . . seemed about to perish on the air'. But the 'about', of course, allowed his transition to the 'miracle of deliverance' account of Dunkirk for which Churchill switched tenses, consciously emulating the Chorus from

Henry V: 'Now suddenly the scene is clear and the crash and thunder has if only for a moment died away.'

'Wars are not won by evacuations,' he cautioned, but then followed another of his romances of the 'island home'; the valiant airmen compared to whom 'the Knights of the Round Table, the Crusaders – they all fall back into the prosaic past'.

Each time Churchill appeared to be describing calamity, he made sure to punctuate it with gestures of improbable defiance. There had been 'a colossal military disaster', but 'we shall not be content with a defensive war' (cheers).

He could not guarantee there would be no invasion, but he summoned up the Clio again to remind the House that Napoleon too had been a victim of that delusion.

Even that might have gone differently had the winds in the Channel veered differently. But as the great speech moved to its unforgettable peroration, Churchill was giving all who heard it and beyond the sense of historical vocation, a calling against tyranny, that he felt so deeply himself. 'We cannot flag or fail', and from his Cabinet speech: 'We shall go on to the end', followed by the incantatory lines: 'We shall fight on the seas and oceans', and the rest. To hear the recording of the speech is to be amazed all over again at the fine-tuning of the performance since Churchill deliberately lowers his pitch for much of the 'we shall fight' repetitions, in softly heroic lament, a reproach, perhaps, to the unhinged vocal histrionics of his arch-enemy.

Only with 'we shall never surrender' did the voice suddenly produce a mighty Churchillian growly roar; the full-throated resonance of the roused beast.

It is still magically easy to conjure him up: the glasses down the nose; the bottom lip protruding in pouty determination, shoulders stooped, his very un-Ciceronian body language of patting both hands, all five fingers extended, against his chest, then, as Harold Nicolson reported, down his stomach all the way to his groin.

Standing like that, he looked, Nicolson wrote, like 'a solid, obstinate ploughman' as if the earth of Britain itself defied the worst that Hitler could throw at it.

Nicolson's wife, Vita Sackville-West, wrote to him that even when recited by a news announcer, the speech sent 'shivers' (of the right kind) 'down my spine'.

The reason, she wrote, 'why one is stirred by his Elizabethan phrases, that one feels the whole massive backing of powerful resolve behind them, like a fortress, [is that] they are never words for words' sake'.

She was right. They were words for everyone's sake. They were the lifeboat and the blood transfusion. They turned the tide.

The Fate of Eloquence in the
Age of The Osbournes

Phi Beta Kappa Oration, Harvard University, 3 June 2002

The extraordinary honour of being asked to deliver the oration to the
Phi Beta Kappa chapter, and so become part of a tradition that runs
from Ralph Waldo Emerson to Anthony Appiah, was only *slightly*
qualified by being misinformed by the Dean of Undergraduate Education that her own Phi Beta Kappa orator had been Kermit the Frog. Now
since I manifestly lack both the philosophical depth of Kermit and the
wisecracking irreverence of Appiah, I wondered what could have
possessed whichever guardians of the chapter to imagine that I could
do the job? To another Harvard graduate I wondered out loud, in fact,
and he gave me the answer, which I'm still not sure is a compliment.
'You do,' he said, 'have a certain way with the spoken word.'

Quite what that way might be remains to be seen, or heard, but
I'm prepared to concede that this might be so, since I was told this at
a very early age by my father who thought that, however I'd come by
it, I'd got what in Britain was called the 'gift of the gab'. He had it
himself in abundant measure, having done his time as a soapbox orator
in Hyde Park and the East End of London in the 1930s, where he
carried on talking and talking as Oswald Mosley's fascist blackshirts
pelted him with rotten eggs and the occasional rock. 'A Jew's ultimate
weapon is his mouth,' he insisted, even though my mother added that
the ultimate weapon was, just occasionally and of course temporarily,
disarmed by its collision with a large hairy fascist fist.

I was about ten when I began to be drilled in the bootcamp of public
rhetoric, beginning with a trip to the theatre to see Richard Burton
play Henry V. Though there were no Harfleurs in our neck of London
to attack, a few weeks later there I was, in grey flannel short trousers,
perched perilously on a chair in our living room waving a broom

handle around, and lustily urging the troops to hurl themselves against the breach 'or fill the walls up with our English dead'. When this was recited at our elementary-school concert, between items understandably thought more suitable, or at least less bloodthirsty, for ten-year-olds, the reaction, when I finished, was one of stunned silence broken by furious applause from my actor-manager father. Some years earlier I had responded to all this voice-work by hitting him where I knew it would hurt most. I went on speech strike, going Trappist – for about five months, I seem to recall, remaining defiantly taciturn through a procession of speech therapists and psychotherapists, verbalising only to the gardener and swearing him to silence.

There are those who will tell you I've not shut up since. But this precocious sense of being afflicted with a pretty much incurable case of logorrhoea has actually left me with mixed feelings about the condition. On the one hand, it's hard not to relish the exhilaration of doing one's thing as a language animal. 'Nothing is so akin to our natural feelings as the rhythms and sounds of voices,' says Cicero in *De Oratore*, 'they rouse and inflame us, calm us and soothe us and often lead us to joy and sadness.' 'SPEECH! Speech!' wrote one of the greatest of all its American practitioners, Frederick Douglass, reflecting how he himself had been virtually reborn and certainly emancipated through his own dawning self-consciousness of being a natural orator, and how he had gone on to revolutionise public diction: 'the live, calm, grave, clear, pointed, warm, sweet, melodious human voice . . . humanity, justice, liberty demand the service of the living voice.' But it's precisely those for whom eloquence at the service of truth is an indispensable condition of a free society who are also most likely to fret at its apparent atrophy. The eloquent, of course, have been complaining about this at least since Quintilian (in the second century AD). Rhetoric that was both beautiful and virtuous, they lamented, was degenerating into either self-serving demagoguery, florid ornamentalism or the stumblings and mumblings of the inarticulate – Osbournes in togas – all of which heralded, in the most pessimistic view, the onset of a kind of slavery; the captivity of the powers of speech and the freedom of audience by the forces of diction-management. Listen to a culture flooded by platitude or vastly amused by grunts of dopey incoherence, they would say, and you will hear the bleating of the doomed.

Are we ourselves in that peril? Are we a culture washed in cacophonic fury, but signifying not a whole lot? Can Eminem or a gangsta rapper get away with what they get away with because the barked and shouted violence mocks and deafens any kind of response? Are *we* (as distinct from the licensed manufacturers of presidential rhetoric) even *capable* – especially in a moment of danger – of articulating to ourselves, to the nation, to the world, just what it is that's worth arguing over, fighting for or defending? Is the designed discontinuity of contemporary life – the indispensability of programmed obsolescence; fashion-turnover; the machinery of the market; the obsession with speed (faster, computer, *faster*); with instant drive-through gratification (I want that cheeseburger and I want it NOW); with the disposable over the durable; the strobe-lit subliminally registered broken-faceted reception of sensation – hopelessly incompatible with the voiced thoughtfulness we need if we are to figure out what it is exactly that holds us together against terror? If we can only articulate the meaning of calamity through the waving of flags and choruses of 'America the Beautiful', does this mean that tragedy has a short shelf-life? Would it have been better for all of *you* – made even better citizens of you – if you had been required to take not Expository Writing, but Expository Speaking?

It's a fair bet your forebears of Phi Beta Kappa thought so. For the chapter/fraternity was established as a community of spoken thought and debate; for the express purpose of sustaining classical scholarly values inside and, more urgently, outside the academy. An *American* scholar, it optimistically presupposed, was someone for whom the pursuit of knowledge was conditional not on escape from the contamination of the public world, but active engagement with it. Browse the forbidding pages of the published Phi Beta Kappa orations – not just at Harvard, but at Chicago, Columbia, Cornell – and you'll step into an ongoing Platonic symposium on civic virtue. Now this kind of wisdom does not, of course, come in soundbites. A roughly calculated average running time for those orations was, I would say, an hour and a half (so those of you nodding off at the back, count yourself lucky that my masters today shackled me to twenty-five minutes). On the other hand, those nineteenth-century brethren of yours were treated, quite often, to really scintillating, opening exordia. Try this zinger from Harvard's best – President Charles Eliot in 1888: 'I purpose to examine some parts of the experience of the American Democracy with the intention of suggesting the answers to certain theoretical objections which have been urged against democracy in general and of showing, in part, what makes the strength of the democratic form of government . . .'

Eliot's turgid earnestness was actually out of character with Harvard's traditions – especially Phi Beta Kappa traditions – which perhaps more than anywhere else in the young Republic personified the truism that, as the first Boylston Professor of Rhetoric and Oratory from 1806 to 1809, John Quincy Adams, put it, 'eloquence is power'. Adams believed that the young Republic was in an historical state of political grace – something he could dream about in post-revolutionary eastern Massachusetts – akin to fifth-century Athens or the halcyon years of the Roman Republic; where voices which allied rhetoric to virtue could prevail over faction and brute force. 'Where prejudice [has] not acquired an uncontrolled ascendancy,' he wrote, 'the voice of eloquence will not be heard in vain.' Though, like most of his generation of Harvard graduates, Adams had been trained in rhetoric through the works of Hugh Blair and the eighteenth-century Scot Lord Kames, his own manual for modern orators turned away from the belletristic manner back to what he thought of as a neo-Ciceronian flinty vernacular; designed to plead before the courts or sway a crowd. The tragedy of his life was that although he was nicknamed 'Old Man Eloquent' and although he *looked* as though you could set his bust alongside Demosthenes and Cato the Elder, and although his speaking style was with 'kindled eyes and tremulous frame', the organ itself was apparently shrill and piercing. In an age of the honey-smooth oratory of the young Daniel Webster and John Calhoun, Adams's presidential speeches, which sounded fine when he rehearsed them before the Cabinet – his Farewell to Lafayette or the panegyric to the Erie Canal – seemed barked at, rather than voiced to, the public. And as a President who stood accused of getting the office by a back-door Electoral College manoeuvre, John Quincy was a perfect target for the oncoming Andrew Jackson, who made an issue precisely of Adams's high-pitched classical diction, targeting it with his own populist anti-highfalutin Hickory-Military vernacular. A century and more before the equally glistening dome of Adlai Stevenson (the spiritual descendant of Adams) was attacked as eggheadedly un-American by another no-nonsense ex-general, Dwight Eisenhower, Adams too suffered from seeing what he'd always imagined to be the virtues of the detached, incorruptible proconsul stood on their head as symptoms of effete loftiness.

Now Adams got his faith in the persuasive power of eloquence directly from his father John, the second President, who would drill him in Cicero and Pericles whether walking the farm tracks at Quincy or the canal footpaths in revolutionary Amsterdam. And John Adams, as lawyer, schoolmaster and politician, felt himself to be the guardian of a long tradition of inspirational rhetoric which went all the way back to the Calvinist sermons of Thomas Hooker and the Great Awakening performances of Jonathan Edwards. The power of that charismatic preaching came from the faith that eloquence was saved from egotism, in so far as the mouth that was its instrument was merely a sounding board for the word of God. Moses, of course, had been a stammerer before that word had touched him. Likewise the Great Awakeners were no more than the organ of some higher natural truth. For John Adams's generation coming of age in the Boston of the 1760s, prophecy and politics became fused. It was not so much injustice that they saw in British policy as iniquity. In the unlikely figure of James Otis and the even unlikelier cause of writs of assistance – the legal warrants used by the British to search for contraband – Adams thought he heard and saw a vision of reborn civic virtue. Otis was then thirty-six, his style of speech as he argued against the writs before the heavily wigged and robed justices 'quick and elastic', 'his apprehension as quick as his temper'. For Adams, his was the voice of the natural American; the lost voice of Ciceronian virtue. The fact that Otis's 'passions were painted in his face' seemed to correspond precisely to Quintilian's doctrine that the speaker must feel, emotively, the truth of what he utters if he is to persuade his listeners. Had Otis worn a virtuously dishevelled toga, he could not have won Adams more completely.

All the great orators of the revolutionary age – Sam Adams, Patrick Henry in Virginia, and the first great rhetorician of the post-revolutionary House of Representatives, the now-forgotten Harvard graduate Fisher Ames, said to be the most silver-tongued of all – were famous for their controlled flamboyance; the calculation of a manner that was said to be 'natural' or 'easy', but which managed to achieve often outrageous theatricality without being accused of affectation. They were hams – think of that invisible dagger Patrick Henry plunged over and again into his breast – but they were hams for liberty.

Winning 'hearts and minds', as Adams claimed had been the case, was not *just* the victory of liberty over imperial coercion; it was the vindication, as he and Jefferson believed, of classical republican rhetoric over brute military muscle. The critical role played by French military power – inconveniently the product of a self-interested Catholic despotism – was underplayed in favour of the legend of the mass mobilisation of the people through the sonorities of virtue. And the vocal Founding Fathers believed they were redeeming, among other things, the tradition of Greco-Roman eloquence itself, which in Britain had degenerated into ornamental disingenuousness. Latter-day Ciceros like Edmund Burke – significantly Irish, not English – had attempted to stop the rot. But public diction had decayed into luxury. For the austerely civic Americans it was, on the contrary, a necessity, their first line of defence. An entire generation thought of themselves as 'Massacre' orators, after the Boston Massacre (in which an accident was transformed by indignant oratory into an emblematic confrontation between innocence and occupation).

To that generation, American eloquence worked because it so obviously exemplified Quintilian's definition of an orator as a *good* man who speaks well. They also subscribed to the Aristotelian assumption that the power of rhetoric was in inverse relationship to the self-sufficiency of brute force. Where that force was coercive, mouths and ears were shut. Sparta was taciturn; Athens eloquent. The ideal Athenian leader was the hero who spoke beautiful and impassioned truths – Pericles. But their American descendants also cherished the tradition because the power of eloquence presupposed the freedom to be persuaded; to be reasoned with; to be moved. Cicero's natural theatre was the Senate in which those of like mind would literally stand together, and the job of the orator was, equally literally, to *move* them to a different position. A vote was, of course, a voice. For Cicero, for the Adamses, for Jefferson – and of course for the Lincoln of the Lincoln-Douglas debates – a republic which took the arts of persuasion seriously was not just a free state, but one which could contain difference of belief without resort to mutual extermination. The opposite to that humanely pluralist eloquence is commandment authorised by fiat or revelation and executed through coercion. Terror is, in every sense, dumb.

If the preservation of a public life tolerant of difference is one reason why we should cherish eloquence, the second reason, scarcely less important, and the logical outcome of the first, is that it reconstitutes community without sacrificing liberty. If the founding fathers of public American speech were concerned, in the first instance, to use it to differentiate a free from a tyrannised society, their heirs in the nineteenth century worried about the republic falling apart, either in fratricidal division or into a mere aggregate of mutually conflicting interests.

The great moments of nineteenth-century public eloquence were when orators believed – and made their listeners believe – that for the duration of their discourse, using all the tools that Isocrates, Demosthenes, Cicero and Quintilian had given them – they could reconstitute a mere crowd, a gathering of individuals, into a community; and that that supra-individualist cohesion would survive their dispersal. This is what converted individual abolitionists into a shoulder-to-shoulder brethren; and what Frederick Douglass, who had learned some of his rhetorical magic from them and from his own reading and practising, took on his travels, not least to Britain in 1845–7 where, in Cork, Belfast, Dundee and London, he tried to persuade his listeners that they were part of an indivisible movement to extirpate an abomination from the face of the earth. The most sublimely enduring speech which took, as its mission, the attempt to remake national community over the partially buried bodies of those who had died for it, was of course Lincoln's Gettysburg address – its two minutes preceded by Edward Everett's two-hour performance. (It had been Everett, not Lincoln, who had been the star attraction and for whom the event had been postponed from 23 October 1863 to 19 November in order to give the Harvard President and ex-Secretary of State adequate time to prepare.)

Doomed to be remembered as Lincoln's interminable warm-up act, Everett's speech is, in fact, in its own way – a recitation of the narrative of the battle followed by an appeal for eventual reconciliation – not half bad. But arguably, one of the great and now completely forgotten moments when eloquence was summoned to mobilise national community took place here, at the Phi Beta Kappa Alpha chapter of Harvard, almost exactly 140 years ago, when George William Curtis – *Harper's* journalist and war veteran – delivered the oration on 17 July 1862, a speech which we know was repeated at least forty times around New England that grave autumn. Curtis's aim was to insist on

the indivisibility of liberty and equality; to take away from the seced-
ing states their claim to the rhetoric of freedom, which he
characterised as fraudulent since it was inseparable from the preservation of slavery, and restore that rhetoric to true American
nationality: an inclusive nationality based on the assumption of
common humanity. To *be* American was to celebrate this. If this had
never before been achieved, the enterprise only grew in significance:

> The achievement of all other nations should be only wings to Amer-
> ican feet that they may hasten to heights that Greeks and Romans,
> that Englishmen and Frenchmen and Germans never trod. Were they
> wise? Let us be wiser. Were they noble? Let us be nobler. Were they
> just? Let us be juster. Were they free? Let our very air be freedom . . .
> Let those who will, despair of that perfect liberty with which God
> made us all free. But let us now, here, in the solemn moments which
> are deciding if there is to BE a distinctive America, resolve that even
> were the American system to fade from history, the American princi-
> ple should survive immortal in our hearts . . .

Freedom, Curtis insisted, was the natural right of all, not some, men
– and he came out swinging against discrimination on grounds of sex
as well as race. 'We will never again forget, God help us,' he ended, 'that
the cause of the United States is the cause of human nature, and the
permanent life of the nation is the liberty of *all* its children.'

Now if this speech and its orator have been relegated to the realms
of the unremarkable, perhaps it's just because for the generations when
eloquence *was* power, rhetoric of this degree of truth and power *was*
actually unremarkable; or at least those who could practise it were, if
not exactly two a penny, then thick on the ground. Can we say this of
our own time? Is the question absurd when the 'arts of communication' (and God knows there are abundant seminars going by that
name) presupposes the shortest of attention spans? Go to Widener
Library and look under 'elocution' or 'oratory' and you will be led to
the Miss Havisham of the public arts: tome after tome gathering dust;
relics of a time when mastery of rhetoric was not just a sign of the
educated citizen, but also the ladder, as Frederick Douglass found, of
true social mobility. If you want to learn the arts of persuasion now,
you go not to Cicero and Quintilian, but the Business School Library

where you can pick up the latest technique of negative advertising. Some of the greatest of the twentieth-century rhetoricians saw this coming. In 1912, Teddy Roosevelt waxed eloquent on the need, above all, to outlaw corporate money donated to political campaigns (as well as the critical need to regulate the accounting practices of big business and use state power to conserve the environment).

It was the management of persuasion in the interests of corporations which struck Roosevelt as most ominous for the fate of democracy. Implicit in his anxieties was the prophecy of synthetic eloquence; not the mobilisation of active, participatory citizenship, but its opposite: its convenient abdication to professional opinion-formers. Of course there is nothing wicked about professional speechwriters. The Greeks had rhetores who for payment produced speeches for public orators. Andrew Jackson's best stuff was written by Chief Justice Roger Taney. And Samuel Rosenmann turned them out for Franklin Roosevelt. But there is, I think, a difference between the collaboration of say, Seward and Lincoln, on drafts of his speeches, and the industrial fabrication of purpose-designed speeches, produced by White House Nibelungen toiling in the mines of rhetorical gold – eight full-time writers for Ronald Reagan and a complete staff of fourteen. If we were to take a contemporary check on Cicero's famous five constituents of oratory, what would we find? An *inventio* – the main idea dreamed up and carefully monitored by the staff; *dispositio* – the arrangement, tailor-made for television and punctuated by gestures to 'real-life' heroes inserted into the gallery; *memoria* – supplied by the invisible teleprompter; *actio* – style, the oxymoronic down-home gravitas, studded with reassuring simplicities; and finally *elocutio* – delivery, finely judged to reassure that the incumbent can complete sentences, but equally finely judged to make them short. 'I want four-letter words,' demanded Lyndon Johnson of Richard Goodwin, 'and paragraphs four sentences long.'

And who is to say that they are wrong? If I'm right that the survival of eloquence is the condition of both a free political society and a coherent community, we do need to cherish it. But we also need to hotwire it to contemporary diction, without, I hasten to say, turning into the kind of political rap parodied by Warren Beatty's last film: a public discourse that lies somewhere between Demosthenes and Ozzy Osbourne. And one of the most powerful qualities of such a discourse will be, as Lincoln knew at Gettysburg, knowing just when to stop.

Barack Obama

Independent, 23 January 2009

'They said this day would never come,' he began as he faced the ecstatic throng in the downtown Convention Centre in Des Moines on 3 January 2008. This was the night Barack Obama became a force to be reckoned with. It was a party without food or drink, but no one needed either. They were juiced with jubilation, the din of it bouncing off the precast concrete. The packed crowd, hooting and hollering, was mostly (this was Iowa) white: all shapes, ages and classes. But amid them were plenty of African-Americans, schoolkids in buttercup-yellow T-shirts, silver-haired matrons, tall college boys, who, before the appearance of the candidate, had been rocking and rapping and singing and swaying. They were the gospel choir of The One and the crowd rode the elation as if this was a revival meeting, which in its way it was, the body revived being that of the United States of America.

Obama can play heart and he can play head. He's the classical orator as well as the preacher of call-and-response. That evening he was pitch-perfect; letting the emotional electricity surge before cooling the voltage. He spoke in calculated measures, light on his feet, the basketballing candidate with the nifty jump shot, head turned slightly aside as if tuning in to history's promptings: 'I hear you, Abe, I hear you, Martin; message coming in loud and clear.' Then square on again to the crowd, the gaunt gravity broken by a flashing collusive grin; everybody a brother and sister. Right now he owns American rhetoric. And until he came along the standard response of the hacks was to say he's welcome to it, who cares?

In the age of the television spot and the Web, formal speeches seemed a redundant luxury; so much embellishment; nothing to do with the engineering of power. But lo and behold, it turned out that words were the fuel that turned the pistons after all. George W. Bush's inadequacies with language had stopped being a sign of sterling inner strength, or even an endearing comedy. In the age of Hurricane Katrina and the war in Iraq, words failed him and so he failed America. The country, it turned out, hungered for *logos*, but not the pabulum of standard operating procedure for election campaigns, much less talk radio rant. What it wanted were words to bind up America's wounds; words such as Lincoln and Franklin D. Roosevelt managed; words which, in the midst of calamity, could remind the nation of the resilience of its history; the possibilities of a decent future.

So Obama is both blog and blarney; the melder of old and new in American democracy. His footsoldiers leave no email address undisturbed, but they also knock on doors to get voters registered; veterans to the polls. They can spin a sharp slogan with the best, but their man knows how to be Cicero when the occasion begs for it. That evening in Des Moines, the rhythm of the sentences was scrupulously scored. The last word of that opening sentence, counter-intuitively falling in a downbeat, the irony allowed to register, throwing the crowd its hit of underdog glee.

'They' who thought the 'day would never come' were the thunderstruck operatives of what, until this very evening, had been assumed to be the unstoppable Hillary machine. But it was also the media hacks who had long awarded her the nomination and had written off Obama as too professorial, too liberal, too black and yet not black enough. (The Clintons still had the allegiance of most of the black Democratic leadership.) Obama's campaign, the conventional wisdom had it, would be the candidacy of doomed wholesomeness: losers' granola; the Bill Bradley of 2008. Obama was Campus Man, catnip for the sophomores, all finesse and no killer instinct, who would fold as soon as he realised politics was a contact sport. 'They' were even some of the Obama campaign people themselves, who, not quite predicting the magnitude of the result in Iowa, had failed to organise any security for the celebration. No metal detectors, no watchful men in metallically bulked suits. He was, after all, still a 'Hopeful'. Best not to get deluded. Give it a shot, end up with the second spot on the ticket? Not so bad.

'They' were the Republican opinion-makers who had been salivating at the opportunity of a Clinton nomination. Dirt-diggers primed and raring to go, who resented this inexplicable, irritating disruption to their plans. But this was the greatest wrong-footing in post-war electoral history. Beneath all the prime-time bloviation that night, the dismissals of the Iowa result as nothing more than a web-geek wonder, you could pick up a faint but unmistakable tremor of unease. Could it be that something stupendously unsettling in the political order was actually taking place? What was that sudden subsidence beneath the feet? Just an untoward event or a political sinkhole about to swallow the entire Roveian Republican ascendancy, along with the doomed Bush presidency? Were things really that *weird?* Was it all up with the Age of Reagan? As the campaign rolled on through Hillary's fighting comeback, Obama's capacity to brush off everything thrown at him and his unmistakable growth into presidential suit-size drew reluctant admiration from his foes. This was serious. This was real.

There is no point asking whether Obama would have made it were the times not so out of whack. History made him and he made history. It's the test of a formidable politician that he or she can smell opportunity in unfolding disaster and has the resolution to brush aside those who live by more conventional timetables. It has already been said that it's Obama's misfortune to be the first African-American president at a time of acute national crisis. But you can bet he doesn't see it that way; rather as the gift of challenge. Sometimes – as in 1860 with Abraham Lincoln and 1932 with Franklin D. Roosevelt – the man and the moment do meet. This is one of those occasions, all the more miraculous for occurring at a juncture when the United States must urgently accomplish two goals usually supposed to be in mutual contradiction. On the one hand, America has to rediscover common national purpose; on the other, it must re-engage with the world. Matters have moved so far and so fast from the sovereign assumption of George W. Bush's presidency – that America needed to shrug off the diplomatic niceties of the rest of the world if it was to assert its national interest and protect its security – that the active reintegration of the United States into the global community is now held to be a *condition* of American recovery.

The woeful side of interdependence has been exposed by financial debacle; but it's now Obama's task to turn it into a strength. Obama's mantra has been that, historically, mutual regard has been as much the American way as rugged individualism. Acknowledgement that we are our brothers' and sisters' keepers, he often says, is what we owe to those who want to stand on their own two feet, but who have been disabled by circumstances not of their doing, whether that is a missing father, a neglected school or a catastrophic spike in unemployment. That same truism could be applied from the developed to the developing world; and to the need for concerted international action to arrest climate change. After a long period when attending to others' concerns has been stigmatised as a soft aversion to the exercise of power, Obama wants to reassert mutuality not just as a bona-fide American ideal in the tradition of Wilson, Franklin D. Roosevelt and George Marshall, but one that serves American interests more reliably and more morally than military heft.

It is burden enough that he has to carry the desperate expectations of a damaged United States on his shoulders, but Obama can scarcely avoid a sense around the world that he is the answer to its prayers as well. That somehow he can manage to be a miracle-worker in the Middle East, in Afghanistan and in Latin America. The impossible assignment comes along with what he has wryly called his 'funny name'. For better or worse he is supposed to be President of the planet. Through Barack Hussein Obama run culture lines that connect Kenya with Kansas; ethnically complicated Polynesian-Asian Hawaii with black south Chicago; Scots-Irish bloodlines with a touch of Cherokee on his maternal grandmother's side. His and Michelle's daughters, Malia and Sasha, bring together west and east Africa; the atrocity of the slave ships with his Luo father's voluntary immigration. It's safe to say that he was not elected President because of this cosmopolitan richness. But it's equally true – and remarkable evidence of the American capacity for national redefinition – that it did Obama no harm, either. Once they had recovered from their shock at not getting Hillary Clinton as their long-desired Democratic nominee, the movers and shakers of the Republican party must have gleefully assumed that Obama's name – along with the rich possibilities for its branding him as un-American, not to mention his skin colour, his association with radical preachers and an unrepentant anti-Vietnam-War underground militant – precluded any possibilties of his actually winning the presidential election. Americans, ran the received wisdom, might flirt with his exoticism (the usual code word for race) and his intellectual elitism, but they would never actually put him in the White House. Whatever they now said about George W. Bush, they *had* wanted to have a beer with him, had valued and voted the affability factor, the reassuring sense that somehow he was 'one of them'. Would regular white folks in the heartlands of Indiana, Colorado and North Carolina really think Obama was one of them?

Perhaps the most astonishing fact about the election of 2008 was that by an emphatic majority, if not a landslide, American voters judged someone called Barack Hussein Obama, whose complexion in no way resembled the preceding forty-three presidents of the United States, to be the patriot to whom they wished to entrust the fate of the country at a time of grave peril. Instead of the decorated Vietnam prisoner of war with the hero's story, the public voted into power a lanky African-American intellectual. On the eve of his inauguration, close to three-quarters of the population – a number far greater than those who voted for him – expressed confidence in the prospects of his leadership and administration. Obama's goal of transcending bitter partisanship, of leaving behind the triviality of mutual abuse for a politics of substance – the stance that in every campaign has been discounted as naive – turned out to voice a national craving that, with the avalanche of disasters falling on America, became simply irresistible. The idealistic visionary turned out to be the smart politician.

Whether this delicate flower of national solidarity will survive the deepening recession or a war gone bad in Afghanistan remains to be seen. But even before a word of what must be the most anticipated inaugural speech since John F. Kennedy in 1961 has been uttered, Obama has accomplished something indispensable for the immediate condition of the country: he has restored public trust in the integrity and competence of American government. Against the self-accelerating disintegration of confidence in institutions assumed, as a matter of course, to be more or less dependable – banks, insurance, the stock market, the property market – the mere fact of the Obama administration offers a fixed point around which belief in American reinvention can make a credible stand. Given the ignominy into which the Bush-Cheney administration has fallen, its almost complete loss of legitimacy and credibility, would this have been the case with *any* incoming administration? Almost certainly not, for the manifold crises that have befallen the United States have had at their core a resistance to the notion that there could be any virtue in acts of the federal government other than those undertaken to secure American power. George W. Bush's fatal alternation between contempt for government

and panic-stricken plunges into its arms are the logical consummation of the philosophy of Jeffersonian individualism paramount since
Reagan. The undisguised masterplan was to use deficits to starve
reprehensible (and, as the conservatives saw them, self-perpetuating)
public institutions – such as Public Broadcasting, the Department of
Education, the Environmental Protection Agency – of funds and so
doom them to such impotence that they could be liquidated to nary a
bleat of protest. Thus the bureaucratic behemoth would be shrunk to
its irreducible minimum – and lo, in the burial ground of the New
Deal, a thousand flowers of enterprise would bloom unimpeded by
the thorns and tares of regulation.

So ran the true religion of the right. So it was hardly a surprise
that the Iraq invasion followed the same game plan. As this view insists
that the default mode for every culture worldwide is democracy and
capitalism, once the Baath party and Saddam Hussein were removed,
the allegedly Western-leaning, enterprise-oriented Iraqi culture would
vault to dynamic liberation and its stability and prosperity would
become self-sustaining. The feedback loop was unarguable. Freedom
would ensure integrity; infrastructure – and temporary security needs
– would be funded by oil revenues; and a nucleus of Western entrepreneurial culture would take hold in the benighted autocratic,
theocratic Middle East. The stagnant pond in which the insects of al-
Qaeda bred would be drained and life would be grand in Mesopotamia.

It's hard to think of a moment in American history when ideological blinkers got more fatally in the way of an administration's capacity
to see the true direction of national history. Iraq desperately needed
more and better government, not less. What it got, for many years
following the invasion, was an exploded infrastructure in which masters
of outsourcing roamed at will. As the United States has learned to its
bitter cost, financial institutions needed more careful regulation, not
less. A cyclone of economic imperatives has swept away the bad odour
hanging over government since Ronald Reagan declared it to be the
problem, not the solution. Ask Detroit's automobile-makers and you
will find that Bill Clinton's declaration that 'the era of big government
is over' turns out to be premature. Government has been recalled,
presided over by a chief executive who is unapologetic about its obligations to the socially vulnerable while being under no illusion that its
long-term job is to manufacture automobiles or run the banks.

Republican attempts to demonise Obama as a stealth socialist about to impose a radically alien welfare state on the land of the free failed to strike a chord with a majority of American voters. The reason was that, unlike John Kerry, Obama avoided being boxed into the stereotype of the remote patrician intellectual aloof from the mundane hurts of the average Joe and Jane. Paradoxically, Obama escaped this snare (also eluded by the authentically down-home, chicken-fried Bill Clinton) by not pretending he was something he wasn't. No one was going to buy a version of Obama that was NASCAR and Bud six-pack. But the tried and true conservative tactic of unleashing the mistrust of cleverness, of tarring it as suspiciously metropolitan, failed them. Not only because the results of its most glaring counter-example in the forty-third President were all too fresh, but also because Obama embodied a politics that reflected 'the way people actually live their lives', as he put it in *The Audacity of Hope*. Palin kept yelling that Obama hadn't actually *done* anything, other than strutting his Harvard Law School stuff into the Senate, and in the debate with Joe Biden she turned his record of 'community service' into a joke, as if it were no more than a liberal cookie-bake sale. Obama (though not the street-tough Biden from Scranton, Pennsylvania) was oddly passive in response, but nonetheless the message got across that in south Chicago he had organised tenants to demand basic decencies of life from the Housing Authority.

Those were not trivial matters: removal of asbestos; provision of dependable sewerage; minimal security against the predation of drug gangs; public schools that were invested in learning rather than being teenage holding pens. This was why in Iowa a television-crew driver, raised as a farm boy on a small spread in the south of the state, described Obama's appeal to me as 'down-to-earth'. A way with words, the sharp mind, didn't undercut that impression. They are of a piece with his conviction that intelligence is not necessarily unpatriotic, that education is an American liberation, and that no government need apologise for securing for its least-fortunate citizens the education and healthcare that make the realisation of the American dream something more than an empty piety.

Two places provided Barack Obama with his unfashionable belief in the possibility of a doctrine of public justice and social benevolence that would accord with, rather than betray (as the right had it), American idealism. Those places are Hawaii and the urban black church. They were the making of Barack Obama, though neither of them has been of much interest to commentators on this side of the ocean who, when they pay any attention, dismiss them as two symptoms of American fantasy: the loud shirt and the credulous hallelujah. But fail to understand them and you will never get the forty-fourth President.

Hawaii was as formative for Obama as rural Illinois was for Lincoln. It's the state that regularly appears in the top deck of administrations spending most per capita on education, healthcare, public transport; a state unembarrassed about government activism. None of which makes Hawaii any sort of social paradise. It's precisely because the ethnic wound opened when the kingdom was annexed in 1898 (largely at the behest of the pineapple mogul Sanford Dole) refuses to heal — because the relationship between natives and *haole* whites remains that of colonised victims and imperialists — that the challenge for government to close the gap between extremes of wealth and poverty has remained perenially urgent. The brutality of modern Hawaiian history makes for a state with a restless conscience. All the historical ingredients that made mainland Americans allergic to civic government — above all, the frontier that allowed pioneers to indulge their fantasies of Jeffersonian self-sufficiency — were glaringly absent from modern Hawaiian history. If the islands weren't quite Sweden in mid-Pacific, nor were they the wilder West.

They were, in fact, as much Eastern as Western. Native codes of *kapu* — what was forbidden and the power of traditional law to enforce punishment and maintain asylum — followed by the Asian devotion to family paternalism and governing omniscience, generated a different kind of attitude to public ethics than in the rest of the United States. And although the colonising presence of industrial farming and ranching companies followed the classic pattern of unregulated capitalism, even Sanford Dole and his heirs affected the Hawaiian manner of paternalist obligation. Two other institutions — the strong presence of both Protestant and Catholic church missions and their schools; and the American Armed Forces — only reinforced this unembarrassed sense of an ethical order containing the excesses of an entrepreneurial culture. If anything, Hawaii's reputation as a pleasure dome only made the public determination to contain its hedonism within the bounds of social regulation stronger. Hawaii's story runs counter to American mythologies in so many ways. Instead of unlimited space and a fiction of permanent abundance, it has always been aware of the pressure of population on limited space and finite natural resources. Though there has been ecological havoc wrought by both dense settlement and the destruction of native species by animal colonisation, the Hawaiian way has been to be aware of the costs of the damage and to take steps to arrest it. Tourists get confined to their beach pens on Waikiki, so the last Nene geese can make it on the rainforest hills of western Kauai. Anyone familiar with the wasted terrain of Lana'l and western Moloka'l with its black plastic sheets, torn and blowing in the wind, relics of pineapple plantations long since abandoned, will understand Obama's passion about the stewardship of the global environment. You could scarcely imagine anyone with a background less like the oil drillers of Midland, Texas.

Then, too, Hawaii scrambles the ethnic game in ways that would always make Barry Obama, as he was then, ultimately impervious to the obligations of race-identity politics. Oahu, the island of Obama's upbringing, means 'The Gathering Place', but those who were gathered were exceptionally complicated in their cultural identity. Portuguese and Basque whalers fetched up in Hawaii, as did the Russians and British. The islands are imprinted with Asian strains, but none of them match, much less meld; even though Filipinos and the first wave of Japanese migrants came in virtual bondage as sugarcane workers. Some of those who toiled under indentures were Chinese, but they gravitated quickly (as they did on the Pacific coast of the mainland) to dry-goods stores, launderers, road-builders and cooks. Different generations of Japanese wear the distinctions of their history carefully and precisely; the earliest immigrants now a cut above (rather like convict chic in Australia) later cohorts, including those patriotic Americans who suffered the humiliation and privation of internment after Pearl Harbor, often condescending to the hordes of tourists from Tokyo and Osaka who flood the islands at vacation time. One thing, however, the many Asian-Pacific cultures did share and that was the twinned belief in unremitting bootstrap hard work and the pricelessness of learning.

Growing up black in Hawaii was a whole lot more auspicious than in, say, Alabama or south-central Los Angeles, but it was certainly no picnic. Nearly all of those Asian cultures rubbing up against each other shared a disdain for Africans, distinct from white American racism, but an affliction all the more rankling in what, day by day, must have seemed the easy-going pace of Oahu society. What came as a particular blessing to Obama then was the simple fact of cherishing parentage, meaning his mother and grandparents. Barack Obama Sr and Ann (real name Stanley) Dunham could fall in love at university in Honolulu and their union be relatively uncontroversial compared with states where black–white marriages were still a criminal offence, because Hawaii's attitude was relaxed in such matters. In his gripping autobiography, *Dreams from My Father* (a book so beautifully written that it seems inconceivable it came from the hand of a politician, which, at the time he wrote it, he was not), Obama is unsentimentally clear-eyed about all this. His father and mother, in their respective ways, embodied authentic, if ultimately contradictory, beliefs about American redemption. Barack Sr, the son of a goat-herding Luo chief, came to the United States as the epitome of upward mobility through the American opportunity. But it was the pursuit of that same goal that took him away from the conjugal nest when he was offered another scholarship, this time to Harvard. What he left was not so much an African-American as American-African son, just four years old. Ann, on the other hand, represented something like the opposite instinct: that of America as a liberal commonwealth of social conscience. (Her mother, Obama's 'Toot', characterised Ann as an Adlai Stevenson liberal Democrat, secular and utopian.) In her own passion for America as school project, Ann reached back to the ideals of Emerson, Bronson Alcott and New England instruction, even though she and her parents were from the world of the Great Plains. During her second marriage in Indonesia, she would rouse the small Barack – seven or eight years old – at four in the morning for crash lessons that would supplement the shortcomings of local schooling.

Obama's education was formative in more than a purely pedagogical sense. It made him wonder: was he to be Barry or Barack? What *was* the relationship of a child of Kansas and Kenya to the history of African-Americans; their slavery, persecution, segregation and liberation? Should he escape that history or embrace it? Could *America* escape or embrace it? Oahu's elite schools owed something to the British model as much as the American: uniforms; loyalty codes; heavy-duty homework; and when his mother sent him back to the island to live with Gramps, the moody, unfulfilled furniture salesman and the indomitable, dynamic Toot, Obama went to one of Hawaii's most serious hothouses of talent, Punahou School. Amid the white shirts and dark ties, teenage self-romance was bound to go black and so he did, complete with Afro, basketball, hard music and a smattering of dope. *Dreams from My Father* is pre-emptively candid about all this. Scoring off the forty-second President's procrastinations on the same subject, Obama writes: 'I did inhale. That was the point.' The abrupt and very brief reappearance in Hawaii of Barack Sr, who threw his weight around in Gramps and Toot's Honolulu apartment like some visiting district collector from the British Empire, must have only made the boy's role confusion worse. Was he supposed to admire the missing patriarch or drive a stake through his heart?

At Occidental College in California (chosen because a girlfriend had gone there), Barack got the uppermost of Barry. Black politics and Malcolm the charismatic martyr were irresistible. But what Obama took from Malcolm X (he must have *read* the autobiography rather than just invoking it) was the slain leader's resistance to role-assignments for Black Men: by black Islam, by militant radicalism or by Martin Luther King's Christian exhortation. Obama began to see the addiction to victim-rage as a liability. It was unclear, though, what might replace it. Columbia University, where he transferred for his junior and senior year, doesn't seem to have given him the answer he was looking for. There were more great books; a headlong dive into political theory. But although Harlem was on his doorstep and part of him wanted to lose his doubts east of Morningside Park, his black and white angels continued to wrestle in his head. For some months after graduation, Obama worked as an apprentice consultant to a business corporation in Manhattan. He suited up and bought the briefcase. Hair neatly cropped, he was the African-American In the Office. When he shared his yearning to do something that brought him closer to the tough realities of black life in the cities, the African-Americans who worked at the low-paid cleaning jobs told him they didn't need any more social workers – what they needed were brothers who 'made it', who brought the bacon home to the hood.

Barack came of age with the news of his father's death. Obama was twenty-one, living a mournful, solitary life on a block of East Harlem 'treeless and barren, lined with soot-coloured walk-ups'. Later, he would learn from his half-sister that there had been a sorry decline.

Barack Sr, the gifted goatherd's son who had made it to Harvard, had been an oil-company executive, then a government economic advisor in independent Kenya. But he had paid a heavy price for standing up to Jomo Kenyatta over the Kikuyu monopolisation of offices at the expense of the Luo. His own job had gone; penury and depression followed and in their train, inevitably, multiple women and heavy drinking. By the time he managed a sad, slow climb back, he had been consumed by humiliation and resentment. The tragic picture liberated Obama from that indeterminate vision of the missing but charismatic father on whom he could project some sort of heroic wishful thinking. Now he knew he needed solid connection; the 'hunger for community' that later he would accurately believe America itself craved.

He would find it in south Chicago, though the road to solidarity and success was hardly paved with yellow bricks. Working for the Developing Communities Project, run by a Jewish convert to Catholicism, Jerry Kellman, in the tough projects of Roseland and Altgeld Gardens was an apprenticeship in heartbreak. Trying to mobilise tenants to claim rights to basic services, Obama endured empty meeting halls; hardened cynicism from the city; disbelief among the black churchmen who wrote him off as another naive, over-educated kid who would high-tail it back to a fancy job when he realised he couldn't build Jerusalem overnight on the south side of Chicago. But just the fact that the first black mayor, Harold Washington, was in office, along with deep reserves of tenacity and the famous Obama unflappability, along with the refusal to back off from the improbable, got him through many of these trials. He earned respect the hard way. And through working with the churches – the vital link to the neighbourhoods – Obama found religion the social way, with Jesus the ethical teacher. Once inside, he made the instinctive, historical connection with the entire history of black self-determination, from the secret slave churches in the south through to the great temple establishments that ran schools and cared for the sick and pretty much everything during the century of Jim Crow segregation. He began to tune in to its melodies and cadences; the music itself, but also the mighty instrument of its preaching, without which the civil-rights leaders would have been muffled or distant apostles. From being a listener, he became a speaker, so that when the accusations against

Jeremiah Wright's unhinged anger threatened to derail his campaign in March 2008, it was the most natural thing in the world for Obama to deliver the finest of all his speeches, in Philadelphia, in which he undertook to help white America face and understand the long history through which race, religion and the politics of salvation were all braided up together.

So Barack Obama became an interlocutor, discovering that without compromising his own history he could disarm paranoia and make people of opposite minds and backgrounds listen to each other. At Harvard Law School, where he had gone to acquire the sharp knowledge he would need, whether he stayed in community work or, as his inner voices (and friends) were telling him, tested the waters of politics, he became the first elected black president of the *Harvard Law Review* because he was already seen as someone who transcended partisan alignments. In a bitterly divided institution, Obama was elected with the help of conservatives who saw him as a maker of consensus rather than someone who endorsed radical positions as a duty to his race.

This is how it has gone on ever since. Stereotyped over and again as a presumptuous outsider whose unapologetic reverence for knowledge somehow was supposed to make him tone-deaf to the needs of regular people, Obama has mobilised those who were tired of hearing that the way things had to be was the way they had always been. That went as much for black city and state politics as for the kind of presidential campaign his own was organised to confound. When he went back to Chicago, taking a job in a law firm specialising in civil-rights cases, rather than the high-paying corporate position that would have been offered on a plate, there was no question about either his understanding of, or his credibility with, the districts of south Chicago. Marriage to Michelle Robinson, who had gone from a working-class background to Princeton, did no harm to perceptions of Obama as someone whose understanding of, and credibility with, neighbourhood politics was unimpeachable.

It's true that astonishing breaks have come his way. During the campaign for the United States Senate in 2004, first his Democratic opponent, the billionaire Blair Hull, became terminally mired in a bad divorce; then his Republican opponent, Jack Ryan, was exposed as forcing his wife to have sex in public in heavily equipped swinger clubs. This did not go down well with the party faithful. More often, though, Obama has made his own luck. Taking on a veteran black politician, Alice Palmer, for a seat in the Illinois Senate seemed a wild gamble designed to separate him for good from exactly the constituency he would have to count on for any kind of political career beyond the city. But time and again, he has caught the change in wind-direction, projected himself as new life for an enervated body politic, whether city, state or country, and time and again he has managed to put together a coalition of support across race, class and the cultures that are presumed to divide the United States into two permanently alienated warring camps. Last year, Indiana was in his column.

He is not all mouth and mind. Though his opponents liked to caricature him as someone who talked the talk while ducking votes, his time in the Illinois Assembly and his shorter tenure in the Senate were certainly not short of evidence that he knows how to deliver legislation that makes a concrete difference to people's lives. In Illinois, hundreds of bills bore his sponsorship and many of them, though unglamorous, were of the utmost importance: securing state funding for free mammograms and prostate screening, for example. In the Senate, he teamed up with the pillar of orthodox Republican foreign policy, Richard Lugar, to sponsor legislation dealing with the security of nuclear waste and to tighten oversight of nuclear materials that might have gone astray inside or outside the United States. What could be more important than that? Well, saving the nation, I suppose. (Let's leave the world out of it for the moment, shall we?) No election campaign or no curriculum vitae could guarantee he is up to the task. But last October, when everything fell apart and the dread phrase 'uncharted waters' kept on issuing from the lips of stricken veterans of US political and financial life, Americans recognised a stark difference in the capacity of the two men they were being offered as potential presidents. John McCain imploded in meaningless histrionics, suspended his campaign and marched to Washington to do, as it turned out, nothing in particular. Obama kept his cool. When he opened his mouth it was to say things that, on the whole, made sense to the confused and the panicky. It was a good enough omen to win him the White House.

Calm intelligence will be the necessary but insufficient condition of bringing the United States out of its economic trough. At a time when public faith in those who were entrusted with money, power, credit and weapons has utterly collapsed, it falls to Barack Obama to restore belief in the history and destiny of the American experiment. Who could conceivably be in a stronger position to do that?

So as he took the oath of office on the Bible that Abraham Lincoln used in 1861, Obama at last began wiping clean American history of its ancient taint: the promise of equality and liberty, made by the Founding Fathers at the same time that it was denied to its slaves and their shamefully oppressed descendants. A day later, on 21 January, his government was installed on the fiftieth anniversary of Martin Luther King's great Washington speech, and Obama can now say to whoever will listen that it is truly a dream no longer postponed. All of America can be embraced in that recognition, just as all of America, those who voted for him and those who did not, was uplifted by his election.

None of which guarantees he will be the President his country and the world is hoping for. But I'm prepared to take a bet he will.

Performing

Richard II

Almeida programme, 2002

The word 'theatre', in our modern sense of a playhouse, makes its debut in English literature in Act V, Scene II of *Richard II*. Reporting on the drastically different reception given by Londoners to the ascendant Bolingbroke and the fallen Richard, the Duke of York thinks of them as competing performers:

> As in a theatre, the eyes of men
> After a well-grac'd actor leaves the stage
> Are idly bent on him that enters next
> Thinking his prattle to be tedious
> Even so, or with much more contempt, men's eyes
> Did scowl on Richard.

And this is apt because *Richard II* is intensely concerned with the performance of sovereignty: the relationship between stage presence and authority. The play asks its lead to act the part of someone who is, himself, acutely conscious of the need to act, and who, in his Big Moments, is overcome, not so much by stage fright as by a paralysing insight into his own mortal humanity. On the battlements of Flint castle in Act III, York is momentarily struck by the fact that, despite his dire predicament, Richard still looks the part of a king: 'his eye, / as bright as is the eagle's, lightens forth, /Controlling majesty; alack, alack, for woe, / That any harm should stain so fair a show.' But after thundering at the presumptuous Northumberland and delivering one of the play's many accurate prophecies that his deposition would inaugurate generations of slaughter, the grass bedewed 'with faithful English blood', Richard collapses, almost incomprehensibly, into a vision of his own annihilation, buried beneath the king's highway 'where subjects' feet / May hourly trample on their sovereign's head'.

Flooded with a sickening understanding of the false consciousness of majesty, Richard, whose entire life up to that point had been conditioned by it, surrenders the crown to Bolingbroke who (until the very last lines of the play) is plainly not much bothered by self-knowledge. In York's chilling account of the London procession, it is evident that Bolingbroke has become an overnight impresario of political bullshit, marketing his fake humility before the adoring throng.

> Whilst he, from one side to the other turning,
> Bare-headed, lower than his proud steed's neck,
> Bespake them thus 'I thank you countrymen.'

From very early on in its performance history, *King Richard II* spoke to an issue on contemporaries' minds: the difficult contrivance of 'majesty' – a title which the historical Richard was the first English king to require of his subjects. Too little of it, and the country as well as the person was demeaned; too much, and the country would be governed by megalomania rather than justice. 'I am Richard the Second Know ye not that?' Elizabeth told the antiquary and geographer William Lambarde when he presented her with his *Pandecta*, a compilation of rolls and muniments stored in the Tower of London. The utterance sounds oracular, but it was actually delivered in a rare moment of touching vulnerability. A few months before, the aged queen had survived a botched rebellion, led by her sometime favourite the Earl of Essex. He had gone to the block, but the crisis must still have been very much on her mind for when her gaze caught Richard II's name on Lambarde's list of kings, she reminded him that one of Essex's supporters, Gellie Meyrick, had paid to have the play performed 'forty times in streets and open houses' as a way of softening up the public for a deposition. It's possible that this was not Shakespeare's version, since the astrologer Simon Forman reported in 1611 having seen a *Richard II* which, unlike Shakespeare's play, featured scenes from the Peasants' Revolt. But Elizabeth was defensive enough about the whole subject of the ill-starred king to send Sir John Haywarde, whose history of Henry IV contained an account of the deposition, to prison for his pains in 1599.

Not surprisingly, then, as long as the Queen was alive, Shakespeare took care to publish the play without the great deposition scene in Act

IV. But he would certainly have been aware when he was writing the play in the mid-1590s that many contemporaries thought the catalogue of miseries in that dreadful decade to be a replay of the 1390s. Once again, England seemed militarily weak with a new Armada in the offing. Once again, punitive taxes were being imposed while a succession of catastrophic harvests had sent food prices sky-high. There were food riots in London and other towns in 1596. And once again England seemed ruled by a sovereign who had lost touch with reality, preferring to listen to the drooling encomia of court flatterers while Faerie-Land was sewn with gibbets. In the same year that Shakespeare probably completed the play – 1596 – a man in Kent was arrested for declaring it would 'never be a merry world until her Majesty was dead'. No one could hear John of Gaunt's bitter death-bed complaint about an England 'leas'd out' and its king become 'landlord of England' without thinking of the furious protests against monopolies and patents sold off by the crown in the last years of Elizabeth's reign.

But if the Queen had ignored her low-boiling point long enough to read, or actually see, Shakespeare's play, she could hardly have taken it as a blank cheque for deposition.

Following Raphael Holinshed's *Chronicles* (in their second augmented edition) Shakespeare dutifully goes through the case for his removal – the arbitrary dispossession of the Lancastrian inheritance, and the indulgence of flatterers who are said to have come between Richard and his conjugal duty to sire an heir. (There's not a shred of evidence, other than his childlessness, that the historical Richard was gay, although I suppose any monarch who commissions a cookbook and insists that his courtiers eat with their spoons was bound to be thought suspiciously un-English.) But except perhaps for his jocular callousness towards the dying John of Gaunt (in reality a far more detested figure than the King), Shakespeare is at his least convincing when labouring to turn Richard into a ruthless land-grabber who deserves his come-uppance. Disaster falls on England and on the King for nothing much more serious than bad refereeing, bad timing (the Irish expedition) and for having the cheek to use the Lancastrian inheritance to finance it. As soon as matters go swiftly downhill, the play picks up pace and persuasiveness. Much more compelling than the extended 'sceptred isle' travel-bureau panegyric orated by Gaunt is its rhetorical bookend: the Bishop of Carlisle's apocalyptic vision of the fatal consequences of usurpation: a country drowning in blood:

> Disorder, horror, fear and mutiny,
> Shall here inhabit, and this land be call'd
> The field of Golgotha and dead men's skulls.

Death is everywhere in the play – 'graves, worms and epitaphs' already on Richard's mind when he is barely back on dry land. In fact, the drama is perhaps best thought (especially by the sixty-something Queen Elizabeth) as an *Ars Moriendi*: a preparatory treatise on how to die, wholly right for a history set in the world of the Black Death. Richard learns the hard way. But he does learn, and near the end asks his weeping queen also to 'learn, good soul,/To think our former state a happy dream'. Richard's eagerness to embrace his Christ-like sacrificial martyrdom was a logical end for the historical ruler, who did indeed suffer more than somewhat from a Messiah complex, understandable (if not forgivable) in an age desperate for saviours. It's a pity, really, that Shakespeare opted for the predictable thug-attack to polish him off, since the more historically plausible end of the King – death by starvation – would have given Richard a chance to meditate more fully on the provisional nature of majesty, indeed of earthly life itself, and to become absorbed most completely into his transfiguration as a Plantagenet Buddha.

Henry IV, Part II

Note for the Royal Shakespeare Company production, 2008

Among the Histories this is The tragedy. It is, not least in the cool tightness of its writing, right up there with Dane, Moor and Scot. At its pitiless end, no bodies litter the stage. Something much worse has happened: the annihilation of hope; the banishment not just of plump Jack Falstaff, but of delusion. What remains? The naked machinery of power in all its grinding metallic cruelty; the tinny blare of trumpets tuning up for the new king's murderous cross-Channel excursion, courtesy of his father's deathbed counsel. And Shakespeare appearing as himself at the very end offering a mordant shrug, 'My tongue is weary; when my legs are too, I will bid you good night.'

Only those half-asleep in the stalls imagine that *Henry IV*, Part II is somehow an 'add-on' to Part I. It certainly is woodwind to I's brass, but the plaintive minor key that plays throughout is the tip-off to II's darker profundity. II needs I to set up the vanities – history, amity, loyalty, appetite, mirth, battle – because II's job is to rip them all to shreds. The muscular heft of history gets collapsed into rumour, false comfort, ill tidings. Unlike I, not only is there no point to the plots and rebellions, but those who enact them know there is no point, except some sort of remorseless execution of a fatal cycle. So the protagonists on both sides – the dying king, the melancholy Archbishop of York – spend time wrestling with the unquiet ghost of Richard II, whose deposition and murder have condemned them all to stumble around forever sleepless like the grimly insomniac king.

Not a hoot, then, even with Falstaff at its heart? No, but something important remains amid the cold political ashes: memory. Part II is better called a memory play than a history; it is the most lyrical Shakespeare ever wrote. And it needs the most delicate touch in its direction and acting to draw out the autumnal pathos. The most heartbreakingly vivid scenes come from the mouths of the old as they spirit themselves back beyond the ache of their brittle bones to the lusty lads and lasses they still feel themselves to be. Whatever else ails them, their memories are as bright as gems: 'Thou didst swear to me upon a parcel-gilt goblet sitting in my Dolphin-chamber at the round table, by a sea-coal fire, upon Wednesday in Wheeson week when the prince broke thy head for liking his father to a singing man of Windsor . . .' prattles Mistress Quickly, never forgetting Falstaff's promise of betrothal – and we see the moment in all its hopeless glory. 'Then was Jack Falstaff, now Sir John, a boy and page to Thomas Mowbray, Duke of Norfolk,' reminisces Shallow to Silence, and we suddenly see the juvenile, perhaps slender Jack. Time rustles in the lines like fallen leaves.

What makes all this bearable is a scene of intense sweetness, a love scene all the more tender for being ostensibly dressed in farce, and the purer for being set in Mistress Quickly's brothel. After the raillery – and brutal it is, with much talk of diseases – between Falstaff and Doll Tearsheet, they become creakily amorous for old time's sake: 'Come I'll be friends with thee Jack; thou art going to the wars and whether I shall ever see thee again or no there is nobody cares.'

Falstaff defends Doll against the rampaging Pistol, then verbally sets about the Prince and his friend Ned Poins, 'a weak mind and an able body', not knowing they are listening in disguise. The affronted then get their satisfaction by cackling at the ancient venery:

> Poins: Let's beat him before his whore.
> Prince: Look, whether the withered elder hath not his poll clawed like a parrot.
> Poins: Is it not strange that desire should so many years outlive performance?

To which Falstaff, oblivious, gives the retort that redeems the entire play from the cynicism that sometimes seems to chill it, a single moment of instinctive, unembarrassed humanity: 'Kiss me, Doll.' And she does, for unlike princes and kings, the whore is true: 'By my troth, I kiss thee with a most constant heart.'

Martin Scorsese: Good-Fella

Financial Times, 30 October 2009

It's just as well that the couch I'm sitting on is plump and hospitable or I might have fallen off it when Martin Scorsese tells me that the real inspiration for the tone and voice of *Goodfellas* was not *Scarface* or *Public Enemy*, but *Kind Hearts and Coronets*. Oh, right, Alec Guinness in drag, Joe Pesci in murderous hysterics, I see. But then, when you think about it for a minute, the revelation makes perfect sense. The note of black glee in Ray Liotta's interior monologues ('As far back as I can remember I always wanted to be a gangster') is not that far away from Dennis Price's cool plan to murder his way into the landed class that presumes to despise him. They share the smirk of superior knowledge, the contempt for the chumps who do things the regular way. Mayhem and chuckling are never far apart in either the British post-war comedies or Scorsese's opera of mischief. Stick a fedora on Dennis Price or Alastair Sim, unclip the accent and they could breeze downtown. The wiseguys in *Goodfellas* spend even more time laughing than killing. Sometimes the uproar is so unhinged that it looks like de Niro, Liotta and Pesci will dislocate their jaws, like pythons guffawing as they digest a goat.

In his sixties, Scorsese is at the height of his powers, which is saying something. After a long day in the cutting room working on a pilot for a television drama series about Prohibition-era Atlantic City, his conversation is still high-octane, the enthusiasms sparks, that catch the weighty pack of his idea-loaded imagination. Lately, he's got a lot to be happy about. His new movie, *Shutter Island,* based on a thriller by Dennis Lehane, scheduled for release early in 2010, is set in an institution for the criminally insane off the Massachusetts coast, a pile that makes the hotel in *The Shining* or Motel Bates look like day-trips to Disneyland. Scorsese built the set around the shell of the old hospital. The gurneys were still there, the stainless steel of the cafeteria giving off a bad glint. 'You walked in and you could feel it, the disturbance,' he says. Ben

Kingsley and Leonardo di Caprio (doing most of his own stunts) stalk and scuttle through it like cat and rat, and the storm-blasted island turns in a performance of thunderously Calvinist gloom. If there were an Oscar for best acting role by a landscape, Shutter Island would be a shoo-in. For the first time Scorsese had to work with those pesky extras, trees. 'Never worked in a forest before. Hard to get the shots, no room for dollies and tracks.' In many ways the movie, a crazy quilt of dreams and terrors, was a tall order. A week into filming the director realised what he was up against, the fiendishly complicated layering of Lehane's story asking him to 'make three films at the same time'. Maybe Scorsese works best when most stretched, for the result of all the perfectionist head-scratching and pitch-in ensemble acting is a triumph of what you might call heavy entertainment, but only in the sense that bits of *King Lear* are too.

And like everything Martin Scorsese does, *Shutter Island* is enriched by its director's encylopaedic memory of the cinema. Nothing so laborious as 'homage' gets inserted; there are no billboarded visual quotations, but it's as though Scorsese has internalised the entire history of the medium, turning himself into a one-man archive on which he can draw for inspiration in whichever genre he happens to be working. Sometimes even the admirers forget his astounding range. The same director who made the agonised *Raging Bull* and the manic, temple-pounding *Bringing Out the Dead* also made the exquisitely patient *Kundun*, the camera letting a small boy come at his own pace to the realisation of what it meant to be the Dalai Lama. The guiding light of Satyajit Ray seemed to be at Scorsese's shoulder when he dissolved the camera into the chosen boy's point of view. So which movies guided him this time? 'Oh, for the atmospherics, the way of setting mood: *Cat People, I Walked with a Zombie* and *Out of the Past*,' he says, as if I was bound to know all about the work of Jacques Tourneur. Caught out like an undergraduate claiming to have 'looked' at the assignment rather than actually to have done it, I make a quick hit on YouTube after our meeting and there are the Tourneur films, moodily off-kilter, tautly scripted, nagging little shards in the psyche.

This total immersion works curatorially. Scorsese doesn't just make individual movies, chasing box-office and the annual-award madness, though he'd be inhuman not to want both. But he has always felt lucky to be able to work in the art to which he's been addicted since, as a bronchial altar boy, he sat bewitched in the Saturday-morning movie theatre darkness, or watching on black-and-white television (as I did an ocean away in London) Alexander Korda costume movies like *The Private Life of Henry VIII* or David Lean's *Great Expectations*, in which John Mills was scared pipless by Magwitch and Jean Simmons as Estella stomped on our balls even before we had any.

Never taking this good fortune for granted (it was an outrageously long time before The Movies finally returned the favour with Oscars), Scorsese has done everything he could to look after the memory bank. He has been a major force in the conservation and restoration of decaying and damaged film; devoting special care to films which meant a lot to his own education as student and practitioner. Olivier's *Richard III* he first saw in a black-and-white television broadcast, but it was shot in a process called VistaVision, and he is currently restoring a surviving print to its original splendour. The winter of discontent will never look so sunny. Meanwhile, the 'crawl' that opens the film, 'England, 1485 . . .' etc., sits in his personal treasure trove in New York along with the Red Shoes from Michael Powell's masterpiece. In between feature films he and his long-time friend and editor-collaborator Thelma Schoonmaker, who was married to Powell and whose perfect touch is all over *Shutter Island*, are putting together a documentary chronicle of the British cinema from the late 1940s to the gritty neo-realist films of the early '60s: Karel Reisz's *Saturday Night and Sunday Morning*, Tony Richardson's *Loneliness of the Long Distance Runner* and Lindsay Anderson's *This Sporting Life*. Like his Italian documentary, the work will be unapologetically personal and when I hear him summon up the shade of Ian Carmichael (*I'm Alright Jack* is a favourite), the improbability of the young Scorsese, spending time in the world of the Lawrentian slagheaps and the two-ups, two-downs, strikes me all over again. But for Scorsese, the fried eggs and rolled-down nylons, footy in the smoke and puke in the pubs, brought a scuffed-up truth of documentary realism to Ealing, Pinewood and Elstree, much as Rossellini, de Sica and Visconti did for the fantasy world of Italian films. He may be the only director who can invoke *Rocco and His Brothers* and *This Sporting Life* in the same sentence, as if it were obvious they were rivers flowing into the same deep sea of social drama. Talking about them, I have a presumptuous hunch and wonder out loud if the bone-crunching sound track of the rugby-league movie, with Richard Harris's skull smashing against other mangled faces, had any influence on the way Scorsese recorded and shot the boxing devastation of de Niro's Jake la Motta in *Raging Bull?* A pause. Ever the tactful gent, he replies, 'Maybe, yes, maybe!'

Sure. But generosity comes naturally to Scorsese. So it shouldn't be surprising that he agreed to participate in the Rolex Mentor and Protégé Arts Initiative – one of a group (other distinguished mentors work in theatre, literature, dance, music and the visual arts) – that gives younger artists the opportunity to learn something about their vocation by directly experiencing a work-in-progress. (Stephen Frears was a Rolex Mentor in 2008.) The lucky young director who got to spend precious time, months of it, with Scorsese at work on *Shutter Island* is Celina Murgan, an Argentinian with two films already on her résumé. Scorsese chose her from a shortlist of three, impressed by a film she had made about teenagers doing their thing in a gated community after the parents had gone. 'I sat there, and around twenty-five minutes into it, I realised this was something; that, almost casually, she had created a world that already seemed to have been there, no starting, no stopping.' A benevolent chuckle and 'Of course that's a different sensibility, not the way *I* work, but . . .' And it was exactly because he does things differently, generates the worlds he creates out of the plot, that Scorsese, so open to other ways, picked his lucky protégé. Murgan got to go to the shoot of *Shutter Island* as often as she wanted and must have seen the toughest of movie-making challenges bloom into something extraordinary; the actors reaching hard; the director revising and revising again as things went along. Could she talk about particular shots? 'Sure, sometimes, to the assistant director.' She was welcomed to the cutting room, to the sound mix and, exceptionally, even to rushes – 'not always . . . I like to speak freely to Thelma'.

There's a back story to this great gift. Murgan – and many others, it turns out – are getting the chance that the young Scorsese was himself denied. In the 1960s, a young film student in NYU School of the Arts, Scorsese badly wanted to get experience first-hand from a master. Elia Kazan – whose *On the Waterfront* and *East of Eden* were just the kind of epics of social pain he revered – was visiting the school. Scorsese, script in hand, made an appointment. He arrived ten minutes late at the great man's office. Kazan had his coat on, listened to the young enthusiast, riffled cursorily through the script and wished him luck. Indies hardly existed in New York, other than John Cassavetes's company that produced

Shadows. There was nowhere to go and no one to help a novice through an apprenticeship. Scorsese, without any ill will, thought at that moment, 'If ever I was in Kazan's position, I'd do something to help.' So starting with *Taxi Driver*, he brought novices onto the set, sometimes youngsters with absolutely no experience of film-making beforehand, and into the crew as apprentices, 'So long as they didn't get in the way of the actors and knew when not to speak up.' Some of them decided film wasn't for them, but others began their career this way and went on to make good features and stay in touch. I'd never heard of such a thing, directors normally being ruthless about keeping 'outsiders' away from the set. But Scorsese was, and is, different. He makes outsiders insiders and all he asks for is rapt attentiveness. So, I ask him, which films after *Taxi Driver* did he open to this kind of apprenticeship. 'All of them,' he says. 'Anyone else do this kind of thing that you know of?' Scorsese smiles, shrugs.

Which only reminds me that to spend any time with him is to be in the presence of someone for whom his hard craft is an exacting labour of love. He burns with the anxiety and pleasure of that knowledge like a perpetually glowing coal. And some lucky people get to draw close to the warmth. His ten-year-old daughter Francesca, for example, to whom he's showing the British comedies of the 1950s that still fill him with delight. 'Does she get it, the wickedness?' I ask. 'Oh, *The Ladykillers*, she and her friends they all love it. There's this moment when there's a fight going on and the little old lady comes in and they *stop fighting*! They *stop*!' Scorsese laughs like the connoisseur of mischief that he is – and like the ten-year-old he once was, watching that malarkey unfold for the first time. One thing is for certain; he's the *perpetuum mobile*; he doesn't do stop.

Charlotte Rampling

Harper's Bazaar, January 2010

There's a crunchy moment in *The Night Porter* when Charlotte Rampling lays a trap for her ex-concentration-camp guard, played by Dirk Bogarde, which involves him walking over broken glass. He does so and smiles. Ten minutes into the interview with her and I know how he felt. The lacerations are minor, the attractions powerful. But there are moments when it feels bloody. It's not that Rampling is openly hostile; just giving off waves of someone enduring a minor indignity, like a dental check-up. To be fair, she had been perfectly frank about her distaste for interviews, telling me that one reason she doesn't do many films is that she finds 'the exposure' tawdry. 'There are so many things I hate,' she says, offering a steely smile. I grin back weakly, hoping I'm not the most recent addition to what's obviously a long list.

Call me a cynic, but is there not a smidgen of disingenuousness here? Is she not – for all her smouldering disdain through photoshoots – just the teeniest bit complicit in this perennial curiosity about whether she still has 'the Look'? (She does.) Doesn't she actually enjoy the gasps of disbelief that the body which in the 1970s turned men into warm puddles on the floor is still, at sixty-three, a thing of beauty? Probably. But you believe her when, tightening her lip a little and making a face as though she's swallowed something dodgy, she talks wanly of the rounds of film promotion – talks, that is, while avoiding eye contact and mostly directing her words diagonally across me to the restaurant wall. Still, at the start of a year that promises a number of high-profile Rampling performances – in films including an adaptation this September of Kazuo Ishiguro's *Never Let Me Go,* co-starring Keira Knightley and Carey Mulligan; Danny Moynihan's satire on the London art scene, *Boogie Woogie,* in spring; and, coming this autumn, the latest from American auteur Todd Solondz, *Life During Wartime* – she will surely have to gird herself for the inevitable run of 'exposure'.

For a time, installed in a corner booth at the upscale London restaurant where we have agreed to meet, we just contend in awkwardness; she doing her cat impersonation, me the floppy old terrier who just wants to woof and play. But then, when I ask her in earnest (for this is what actually interests me) about how she came to be the mind-blowingly great actress she is, she emerges from under the hedge of her frowning, and turns directly towards me as if surprised that anyone – for a *magazine* article – would want to talk about how she came by her craft.

Then it suddenly becomes a very different story; a story, in fact, of how her life and art have flowed into each other, for she's not shy about talking about some chapters – at least of her own family history, rather than her married life and loves – weighted though it is with trouble and sorrow.

Her father Godfrey Rampling died last year (aged 100), and no degree in advanced psychoanalysis is needed to understand that he was the true north on Rampling's compass. It was from him she got her backbone and physical bravery. 'Made you climb walls, did he?' 'Oh, everything,' she says, 'We [she and her sister] couldn't be wimps.' He saw in Charlotte the tomboy; the fighter, the one who in some way might be an athlete. Godfrey ran the second leg in the 400-metres relay at the notorious Berlin Olympics of 1936, and is captured in Leni Riefenstahl's *Olympia* winning the gold for Britain. The runner immediately behind him had fallen ill and was way behind when Godfrey took the baton and carved his way through the pack. 'He *was* beautiful,' Rampling emphasises, looking wistfully into the distance. 'They said he ran like a god, and they were right.' He paid a price for his heroics. A leg went out, and was never quite the same again.

Rampling was born ten years later, in Sturmer, Essex (I greet her as a fellow Essexian and she smiles in mildly snobbish surprise, 'Really?'). Her father had already become remote or, in her own word, 'frightening', disappearing into silent distances that seem to have translated into emotional intimidation. In fact, he was as much frightened as the frightener. 'Of what?' 'A haunting,' says Rampling, sighing a little. 'He began to carry the weight of the world on his shoulders.' The load of it crushed him into periodic depressions, which his daughter felt the burden of, growing up first in Fontainebleau, where her father was stationed for NATO as a lieutenant colonel with the Royal Artillery (and where she was part-educated, becoming fluent in French); and perhaps even later, at a distance, at the girls' boarding school St Hilda's in Bushey, Hertfordshire.

The playpen of the late Sixties was, of course, the antidote to all this patriarchal gloom, and like so many other cool stunners, Rampling played hard. 'I did everything very young,' she says. She worked as a model before being spotted in a Cadbury commercial and cast in Silvio Narizzano's 1966 classic *Georgy Girl* as the impossibly fine-boned, hard, hot number, against Lynn Redgrave's adorable dumpy duckling who eventually gets the man.

Then came the shattering moment when the Swinging stopped. Her twenty-three-year-old older sister Sarah fell ill while pregnant, gave birth prematurely, fell into a steep depression and shot herself. Shortly after, their mother, who had always been very close to Sarah, suffered a stroke, and was left severely disabled. In a matter of weeks, Rampling, now in her early twenties and with the world about to be at her feet, was robbed of the two people she loved most in the world. (Her grief was disrupted by her father's insistence, so as not to upset her mother during her long, painful rehabilitation, that the truth of Sarah's suicide remain a secret. The official version would be that she suffered a cerebral haemorrhage.)

It's not surprising that acting became a way of changing the subject, moving into someone else's skin. If the part called for it, Rampling would do pain, not be its victim. It was while she was shooting an Italian film with Gianfranco Mingozzi in 1968 that Luchino Visconti spotted her and cast her in *The Damned*, his epic tale of dynastic corruption at the beginning of the Third Reich. As the Jewish daughter-in-law of the only liberal scion of the family, Rampling was pitch-perfect: tender, poignant and desperate (a rebuttal to those who think of her as mostly sexy-tough). I tell her that I've always thought one of the remarkable things about her career has been its range; and though it's the truth, this is not something she's used to hearing.

It's a paradox. On the one hand, she insists that somehow there has to be something in the part that is also of her. On the other hand, she was crucially guided by Visconti to understand the psychological morphing needed to make a performance credible. (We enjoy a brief Visconti love-in when I reveal that some of my earliest movie passions as a teenager were *La Terra Trema* and, especially, *Rocco and His*

Brothers, which took me weeks – if ever – to get over.) When she murmurs of his charisma and handsome, Marxist-aristo charm, it's obvious that he became for her the warm-blooded fatherly mentor. When, in *The Damned*, she had to play a scene pleading for the life of her children, she went to Visconti in despair, saying she had no idea how to do it, that she couldn't do it. 'Listen, Charlotte,' he said, 'you don't have to have *done* anything like this. You must just *believe* you have done it.' Later, standing right beside the camera as she acted, he urged her: 'See behind the eyes. See behind the eyes . . .'

Without Visconti's guiding hand, then, there would have been no *Night Porter* and no international fame. It was Dirk Bogarde, the tortured male lead in *The Damned*, who saw she could play something quite different, and working with the director Liliana Cavani devised the script and plot for the strange, terrifying, sadomasochistic fantasy that became *The Night Porter*. Rampling recalls putting Visconti's advice to the test early by having to do, right at the start of the shoot, 'the fucking concentration-camp scene. I had to *sing*.'

For all the thunderstruck acclaim she received for the film, life was not altogether plain sailing. Many parts came along, many of them mediocre. Her first marriage (to actor Bryan Southcombe) broke up when she fell headlong for rock composer Jean Michel Jarre. It was mega-force love, and articles regularly appeared about the Beautiful Couple's romantic life in Paris. But every so often, in the 1980s, she would hit a reef, falling into what sounds like the same depression experienced by her father. Being cared for by her husband, she'd recover, only to sink into the terror of its return.

There must have been a moment when Jarre had had enough, as he took up with a younger civil servant, and in 1997 Rampling's second marriage ended. Then, in 2001, her mother died, and it freed something up in her. She became much closer to her father, moved by his kindness and love for her mother. ('It was his redemption,' she says.) And, when the truth about her sister's suicide was let out, she was at last allowed to grieve.

The join between Rampling's emotional life and working life became sewn together by the great French indie director François Ozon. She says, looking back on her career, that her best films have been 'a documentary of me'. (Indeed, without the deep stain of her personal drama, her acting would just be an affectation, the calculated projection of 'the Look'.) But in her two films for Ozon, *Under the Sand* (2000) and *Swimming Pool* (2003), she reached for, and achieved, something much more profound: the sensuality of melancholy; the embodiment of the angry wound.

In *Under the Sand* especially, in which she plays a childless, affectionate wife whose husband disappears on a beach in south-west France while she has her eyes closed sunbathing, Rampling's capacity to play the light moments – bursts of wilt-inducing laughter in the midst of sex, breezy certainty in the gathering distress – give the drama its full tragic force.

She also loved playing Miss Havisham in a BBC adaptation of *Great Expectations*, reading Dickens and looking up David Lean's classic to prep; and had the part of graceful, sexually potent middle age nailed. 'They suited me,' she says of roles in films like Laurent Cantet's 2005 *Heading South*, about a professor who travels to Haiti for sex with the local young men.

But you somehow don't want Rampling just to corner the market in sexually compulsive crosspatches, though she is said to perform brilliantly in a hotel-bedroom scene as a rich, unhappy sexual predator in the upcoming *Life During Wartime*. Still, the work she has done lately – including a feature about street dancers in England called *StreetDance; Never Let Me Go*, in which she plays the enigmatic and haunted headmistress Miss Emily; and a comic turn in *Boogie Woogie* – seems to draw on that capacity for range that Visconti first saw in her. 'But I just don't get that many parts,' she says, 'not the scripts I can be bothered with.' After her sister died, she swore she would not make films 'just to entertain'. And if there have been projects in the past that have fallen short of that lofty principle, there's no doubt that, in her early sixties, she no longer has truck with the mediocre.

It's dark now, out there on the rain-slick London street; and gradually the lights are being dimmed in the Italian restaurant. The tape recorder goes off. I order glasses of white wine. She demurs for a second and then is happy when I overrule her. She is off later to see her friend Kevin Spacey's play of *Inherit the Wind* at the Old Vic. With her velvety voice, it's not surprising she has done theatre both in London and Paris – a Marivaux and the unedited, terrifying version of Strindberg's *Dance of Death*. But now she wants to talk a bit about my childhood, not hers, and we do, friendliness replacing professional curiosity. She has stopped looking at the wall. 'What am I going to do to pass the time?' she teases, giving me the full-on charm. I am speechless. Then the angel passes, and back comes a self-satirising version of Grumpy Puss. 'Will it be good?' she worries of the play. It's the audience, not the actors, she's already taking exception to. The massed sitting, the clapping . . . 'You know I *hate* places where people all do the same thing.' The fact that she laughs at her own vehemence is a sure sign she really means it.

Clio at the Multiplex

New Yorker, 19 January 1998

'We have come to understand that who we are is who we were,' says Anthony Hopkins, impersonating John Quincy Adams at the climactic moment of Steven Spielberg's *Amistad*. He says this in front of a bust of his father, John Adams, seen in soft focus. A muted trumpet sounds over the rhetoric, vaguely invoking patriotic sacrifice. Hearts around the theatre swell like popcorn. In reality, Adams's address to the bench on behalf of the abducted Africans of the *Amistad* took eight hours, spread over two days. Spielberg works on a broad canvas, but not that broad. His movie boils the speech down to a five-minute appeal to the Founding Fathers, and, in particular, a cheerful assertion of the compatibility of liberty and equality enshrined in the Declaration of Independence. When Jefferson duly appears (in bust form), we are evidently *not* meant to think of the unrepentant Virginia slave-holder. In fact, since the closing speech does little else but make that ringing appeal to ancestor worship, we're asked to believe that it was enough to sway the justices (the majority of them slave-holders) into upholding the decision of the Connecticut court, thereby freeing the captives.

As a clinching argument about the legality of treating the Africans as born slaves or born free, this makes no sense, not least because the case turned neither on the morality nor on the legality of slavery in America, but on the slave *trade* on the high seas. The *Amistad* Africans had been abducted from a British protectorate and shipped to a Spanish colony in clear violation of a treaty between the two kingdoms which prohibited the traffic. John Quincy Adams did end his great address with an appeal to the past, but it was an appeal to the independence of the Supreme Court, and invoked John Marshall and his colleagues, men apparently with too little name-recognition for Hollywood. As for his peroration, 'I can only ejaculate a fervent petition to

Heaven that every member [of the Court] may go to his final account with as little of earthly frailty to answer for as those illustrious dead', it, too, may not have the ring of the box office, but it was a masterpiece of psychological cunning. One of the most odiously adamant of the Southern Justices, Philip Barbour, died in his sleep between the beginning and the end of Adams's speech, thus presenting Adams with a perfect opportunity to remind the rest of the bench of an even Supremer Court waiting for them.

It's an opportunity that Spielberg passes up. Instead, he concocts the feel-good fantasy that JQA's appeal to ancestry was borrowed from Cinque, the leader of the shipboard slave rising – that between the Mende wise man and the Massachusetts rationalist (the two never met) there existed the unspoken bond of warriors for freedom. Possibly the most important moment in the movie is also the most fabulously fictitious. Cinque, sitting in Adams's library (in those far-off days presidential libraries were places where ex-presidents actually read books), reassures his champion that they will not go into court alone. 'No, no, we have right at our side,' Adams says hurriedly. '*No*,' Cinque gently admonishes the ex-President. 'I meant my ancestors . . . I will call into the past . . . and beg them to come . . . And they must come, for at this moment, I am the whole reason they have existed at all.' Adams stares back at Cinque, mutely grateful for the insight. His eyes water with deferential illumination. Spielberg holds the shot and holds the shot, flagging its Significance.

You can't altogether blame Steven Spielberg for the piety. As a relatively recent convert to ancestor worship himself, he seems to have realised that in late-second-millennium America he has his work cut out for him, and he has applied his brilliance as a storyteller to getting it done. But lining up a row of busts of the Founding Fathers as a way of cueing up patriotic nostalgia only brings the difficulty of history-in-America into sharper focus. After all, those same patriarchs were in the business of repudiating, not venerating, the past – of creating a nation that was conspicuously liberated from the weight of the past's authority. And at the same time that the film invokes the need to keep the memory of ñational history alive, it has a lot of fun with America's invention of political modernity. Martin Van Buren, looking like an affable chipmunk in Nigel Hawthorne's enactment (the real Adams, dedicated to vigorous swims in the Potomac, called Van Buren 'inordinately fat'), is gleefully depicted as the archetypal creature of the hustings, complete with baby-kissing and Nixonian full-arm salutes, a deliberate contrast with the flinty, philosophical JQA. Yet Adams, after his own blighted presidential tenure, showed himself to be a belated but adept convert to political populism, jumping into the muckiest popular campaign of his day − anti-Masonry.

So when Hollywood history claims that in ancestor veneration lies our redemption from the culture of the short shelf life, it only sort of means it. *Amistad* is just the most recent, and most impressive, example of filmed history as costume civics, chronicles of latter-day saints and martyrs, right in line with *Glory*, *Malcolm X* and *Michael Collins*. If movie history is to get produced as box office with a conscience, it must serve one of two purposes: explain the Origins of Us or act as Augury of What Is to Come. But this kind of history, whether designed as the genealogy of identity politics or as prudential political-investment service, seldom escapes the contemporary world that it claims to transcend. Even in a production as painstakingly researched as *Amistad*, entrapment within the contemporary is suggested by a multiplicity of careless details, not enough in themselves for any except the most pedantically correct historian to get steamed over, but cumulatively betraying a tin ear for the obstinate otherness of the past. While both the nocturnal shipboard musical party that sails past the newly liberated *Amistad* and the velocipede that rides past the astonished Africans who thought themselves home carry a certificate of impeccable research, the film's writers hardly notice (any more, I guess, than the audience does) utterances inconceivable in 1839. 'Sure you do,' Pete Postlethwaite says when Cinque denies knowing anything much about African domestic slavery. *'Yesss!'* the defence team cheers when it wins its verdict in court. 'Is there anything as pathetic as an ex-President?' jeers a member of Van Buren's entourage, meaning John Quincy Adams. In 1839, that would have been an expression of sympathy, not of derision.

But perhaps the writers did notice all these details and intend them to narrow the distance between the past and the present, making history more user-friendly. This would explain the relentless tide of tepidly inspirational chorales that washes over the action, much like the musical accompaniment to a Party Convention bio-documentary eulogising the nominee: Sigh here. Weep here. Chuckle here. A*men!*

here. Hence, too, some of the casting, which recycles familiar faces in the roles to which previous Hollywood productions have assigned them. Meet Morgan Freeman once again as the noble but uneasy intermediary between white and black culture. Say hello to Matthew McConaughey as the cutely presumptuous lawyer, whose courtroom savvy is belied by his rumpled but winsome demeanour. (The real Roger Baldwin was a distinguished advocate, a Yale man, and the grandson of a signer of the Declaration of Independence.) Most peculiar of all, the urge for familiarity seems to involve the assumption that history, especially American history, calls for Brits in costume, Masterpiece thespians, thereby giving the unintended impression that the Revolution never actually happened.

Historians ought not to gripe too much about these anomalies. A recent and excellent anthology of their commentaries on historical movies, *Past Imperfect*, edited by Mark Carnes, is a litany of complaint about distortion (*A Man for All Seasons*), naive lack of interpretation (*Gandhi*), and the passing-off of conspiracy theory as documented evidence (*JFK*). But if 'historical consultant' has generally come to mean a low-rent databank for producers in a hurry, rather than any real conceptual or creative role in the shaping of a credible historical narrative, the academy must take at least some of the blame, for having largely abandoned, until recently, the importance of story-telling as the elementary condition of historical explanation. Story-telling (aside from its exacting formal demands) lies at the heart of historical teaching and ought to be as much a part of the training of young historians as the acquisition of analytical skills. When the historian Natalie Zemon Davis, for example, who is herself gifted at and sensitive to the subtleties of narrative, got involved in the making of Daniel Vigne's *The Return of Martin Guerre*, that involvement was apparent in every frame, in the way the actors wore their village clothes – not clothes fresh from the wardrobe department or soiled for the day, but evidently lived-in, frayed and patched hand-me-downs. Vigne and Davis reconstructed the texture of rural provincial life in sixteenth-century France, its rites of passage and its rough justice as remote from modern experience as if the story had been African, rather than European. As a result, the crucial trial scene, at the end of the movie, was a long way from being Perry Mason in doublet and hose, yet lost nothing of its dramatic power for being historically credible.

A true feeling for period, then, should never be confused with pedantically correct costume-and-decor detail. It's possible to get all the minutiae right and still get the dramatic core of a history wrong. And here's a trade secret. The right stuff, whether the historian is trawling through the archives or prowling the set, is to have a hunch for the illuminating power of the incidental detail. At the climax of the true *Amistad* history, Spielberg missed, somehow, an astounding story that ought to have been a director's dream. Just as John Quincy Adams, a few days before he was to argue the case before the Supreme Court, alighted from his carriage in front of the Capitol (still, incidentally, *without* its dome), a violent burst of gunfire made his horses bolt. The first demonstration of the Colt repeating rifle was being performed in the Capitol yard. Adams's coachman was thrown to the ground, and the following day he died of his injuries. For the devoutly religious statesman, there could have been no more shocking witness that Providence was watching over the unfolding drama. Colts, carriage horses and Calvinism – the kind of historical collision undreamed of in scriptwriters' fiction.

All history is a negotiation between familiarity and strangeness. No one put it better than Thomas Babington Macaulay when, in 1828, at the ripe old age of twenty-seven, in a famous book review (which the omnivorous John Quincy Adams is likely to have read in *The Edinburgh Review*), he presumed to define history as divided between reason and imagination: 'a compound of poetry and philosophy'. What Macaulay yearned for was a perfect marriage between those two contrasting modes of apprehending the past. But he was not optimistic about seeing that ambition realised, even in his own dazzling and exuberant prose. Instead, he viewed history as a relentlessly contested battleground between regiments of analysts and story-tellers, with him stuck in a no-man's-land as the polemical bullets whistled over his head. In the meantime, he lamented, the best stories were being told to the biggest audiences by historical novelists, the auteurs of their day, and none of them more accomplished than Sir Walter Scott, the Spielberg of the Tweed Valley, whom most academic historians disdained, but whom Macaulay deeply envied and admired. In a beautiful aside, Macaulay compared Scott to the apprentice of a medieval master of stained-glass windows working in Lincoln Cathedral. The spurned apprentice went about collecting the shards and fragments discarded as worthless by his master, and assembled them in a window of such blazing splendour that the master not only acknowledged the superior genius of his pupil, but killed himself out of humbled morti-fication. Scott, Macaulay says, is the inspired opportunist who understands how to use the materials despised as trivially anecdotal by the philosophical historians. And, while Macaulay yielded to no Cambridge don in his insistence on the indispensability of reasoned interpretation, he saw the fate of history in popular culture as condi-tional on its self-appointed masters being prepared to reacquaint themselves with the imaginative skills of the story-teller.

Macaulay knew that both treatments of history – 'map' and 'painted landscape', as he characterised them – were hallowed by venerable pedigrees. He acknowledged Thucydides, for all his powerful narra-tive art, to be the founding father of history as the political science of the past, unapologetically engaged in explaining the great crisis of his age: the Peloponnesian War. Like Spielberg's writers, Thucydides had no hesitation in putting in the mouths of protagonists such as Peri-cles the sentiments he *thought* they would have uttered even if there was no record of their speeches, or any recollection on his part of what had been said. Neither for Macaulay nor for Thucydides was there the slightest anxiety that the record of the past might be fatally distorted by the enthusiasms and preoccupations of the present, or that the primary mission of history was indeed to explain and recount the Origins of Us.

But Macaulay knew that there was another kind of history, a history that emphasised, poetically, the otherness of the past, its obstinate unfamiliarity, the integrity of its remoteness. Indeed, he knew that the great exemplar of this kind of history; with its naive sense of wonder and its promiscuous muddling of myth and ritual, report and document, was Herodotus, the figure whom Thucydides acidly criti-cised as forfeiting credibility through an indiscriminate use of sources, and whom Macaulay, neatly standing the title of patriarch on its head, adroitly characterised as a 'delightful child'. Most historical writers, both inside and outside the academy, will, I think, own up to both styles – the rational and the poetic – and perhaps even acknowledge that the original attraction was as much romantic as analytical. For some of us, it's the byways, rather than the highways, that unexpect-edly turn out to be the more profound routes of illumination. And those of us who are prepared to surrender to the informing detour cherish history, as the late Dame Veronica Wedgwood confessed, for its 'delightful undermining of certainty'.

If American culture is suspicious of candid confessions of uncertainty, Hollywood's history-makers, by and large, have wanted nothing to do with it. Who needs story lines that don't know where they're going, a cast of characters in which the nice and the nasty seem disconcertingly indistinguishable, and where the business at hand seems to have nothing to say to the issues of the day? Outside Hollywood, though, there have been powerful history movies, created in the poetic, not the instructional, mode. These are the films that have respected the strangeness of the past, and have accepted that the historical illumination of the human condition is not necessarily going to be an edifying exercise and that memory is not always identical with consolation. These are also films that embrace history for its power to complicate, rather than clarify, and warn the time traveller that he is entering a place where he may well lose the thread rather than get the gist. Worse yet, the decor of the poetic history movies, while rich in authenticity, is often bleak and raw in aspect, resistant to the glossy patina of its antique furniture.

The best movies in this mode – Luchino Visconti's *The Leopard* (1963), Miklós Jancsó's *The Round-Up* (1965), Roberto Rossellini's *The Rise to Power of Louis XIV* (1966), Andrei Tarkovsky's *Andrei Rublev* (1966), Werner Herzog's *Aguirre: The Wrath of God* (1972) and Yves Angelo's *Le Colonel Chabert* (1994) – not only are dedicated to reconstructing vanished worlds, in all their unruly completeness, but challenge the truisms of linear history, where the order of events is progressive in both a temporal and a moral sense. In curmudgeonly fashion, they hint that later is not necessarily better. Equally, though, such films accept the unavoidability of the past, the thinness of the soil in which our forebears lie buried. They don't so much reach out and grab the past in the name of the present as perform miracles in the opposite direction: have the present waylaid by the past. Rossellini's film used amateur actors in its faithfully ritualised tableaux of court life at Versailles, so that the 'performance' of Jean-Marie Patte as Louis XIV eating alone on his dais with the public watching was utterly remote from a star turn, something that seems unlikely when, any day now, Leonardo DiCaprio does the Sun King at your multiplex. It was the genius of Visconti to cast Burt Lancaster against type, as the fatalistic Sicilian aristocrat in *The Leopard*, so that his previous screen personae simply disappeared without a trace into the world of nineteenth-century Risorgimento Italy. Those are the kinds of movie history that enjoy confounding expectations, roughing up the neatness of our contemporary self-satisfaction. And, as often as not, they have something to say about what is at the back of every historian's mind: the relationship between the living and the dead.

The most eloquent of recent films to have done all this is Yves Angelo's tour de force *Le Colonel Chabert*, based on a novella by Balzac. Angelo was the cinematographer for another remarkably faithful historical reconstruction, *Tous les Matins du Monde*, the story of the seventeenth-century bass violist and composer Marin Marais, and is blessed with perfect historical pitch. Like *The Return of Martin Guerre*, *Le Colonel Chabert* concerns a figure who, having been presumed dead on the battlefield of Eylau, in 1807, returns a decade later and attempts to have his survival acknowledged in law and in society. Unlike the sixteenth-century peasant, though, Chabert (played, again, by Gérard Depardieu, who must have worn the clothes of every generation after the Black Death) is repudiated by his wife. She has survived the debacle of the Napoleonic Empire and has made her peace with the Restoration by marrying an ambitious aristocrat with a squandered fortune but an ancient pedigree. She wants nothing to do with the tattered phantom of her past, a social embarrassment and a political peril.

No one knows an *historical* establishing shot like Yves Angelo. The first frames of *Le Colonel Chabert* transport the viewer directly and shockingly into a vanished world (while also announcing the story's theme: the battle between entombment and endurance), and they do so by annihilating a cliché of cinema history, the gorgeousness of Napoleonic military spectacle. Grimy fingers, seen in close-up, scrabble through uniforms encrusted with mud and blood, ripping the frogging, hunting the valuables. It is Eylau, the day after. A piano plays an adagio from a chamber piece. Mutilated horses are thrown on bonfires. Boots, sabres, helmets and cuirasses pile up in tarnished hecatombs. The camera knowingly quotes from the period's own representations of disaster the Napoleonic hagiography of Baron Gros, Géricault's severed limbs and heads, Goya's puddles of blood and sightless eyes – but without any preciousness or pedantry. Eventually, the camera tracks back to a panorama of death, almost casually observed, peasants busily scavenging the corpses amid the dirty snow, surviving officers dragging bodies to communal burial pits.

In the greatest ten minutes of Depardieu's career, Chabert tells his story to the lawyer he wants to recruit to his cause. Left for dead, he was buried in a mass grave. His mind flickers back and forth between the Napoleonic glory days and the squalid nightmare of their eclipse, and he speaks of the horror of being taken for mad, of incarceration in German asylums. Angelo has no need to picture these on camera, but he must provide convincing reconstructions of two historical milieus: the world Chabert has left, and the world in which he now finds himself marooned – that of Restoration France, in which the first condition of legitimacy is selective forgetfulness. That world, pitilessly cynical, and governed by an ex-émigré culture that is grossly venal and preposterously snobbish, is sketched with a fidelity both to Balzac and to historical truth. Mme Chabert, now a countess, adjusts an earring of grey jasper decorated with a Greek-revival figure, revealing a taste more of the Empire than of the Restoration. The destitute children of army officers killed on the battlefield are taught sabre slashes with wooden sticks by an unrepentant and impoverished Bonapartist who befriends Chabert. An entire world is conjured up on the narrow fault line between victory and calamity, between recall and oblivion. There are no heroes, no tear-pricking diapasons of grandiose music. When Napoleonic military brass sounds, its metallic bravura has the jangling noise of history's black jokes.

Is it possible for an American movie-maker to produce anything remotely like *Le Colonel Chabert*? Is anyone at DreamWorks up for, say, *The War of 1812*, where British and American governments compete in a meaningless carnival of folly and hubris while the White House burns and men's lives are sacrificed for no reason at all?

The question of what befalls a history movie that nonetheless hews more to the poetic than to the instructional mode of historical narration is raised by the case of *Kundun*, Martin Scorsese's undersung masterpiece. *Kundun* may have begun its life being as much of a good-cause movie as *Amistad*. Its central figure, after all, is the unquestionably heroic, Nobelised figure of the Dalai Lama. And even though we're unlikely to see Michael Eisner in saffron any time soon, the atmosphere of Buddhist worthiness circulating in Hollywood can hardly have hurt its chances of being taken on by Disney.

But what Scorsese has accomplished is a work that has absolutely nothing to do with its ostensible billing as 'epic'. Like all great movies made in the poetic mode, it approaches its subject indirectly, backing into history rather than declaiming the theme. Its real story is about the abrupt *arrival* of history, both in the life of a small child and in the life of the culture he is supposed to personify. These linked narratives turn on the loss of innocence and the loss of freedom, not themes calculated to ingratiate themselves with the American movie-goer.

Like Angelo, Scorsese has invented a disconcerting visual language that flows naturally from his subject and does the necessary work of shaking the audience loose from habitual expectations of what a history movie is. The film is painted in the brilliant colours of the sand mandala, an ideogram of Buddhist contemplation, with Nirvana at its centre. The reconstitution and dissolution of the mandala, part of the Buddhist belief in the chain of existence, at the movie's poignant end becomes a metaphor for the fate of traditional Tibet itself. There is a dreamlike, ritualised quality to Roger Deakin's cinematography, and the non-actors who speak Melissa Mathison's deceptively simple lines do so with an integrity that takes the film out of the realm of produced enactment and into that of orally transmitted chronicle – the beginning of history itself. 'Tell me,' the two-year-old future Kundun says, insisting on hearing yet again the story of his birth, and Scorsese, as much as the child's family, obliges.

Like Angelo, Scorsese can't resist quoting history, but in his case it's the history he lives in: the archive of the cinema. There are elements of Satyajit Ray in the infant's-eye-view of the world at the beginning; clattering footage from a Méliès fantasy to punctuate the growing up; the brutal Agincourt scene from Olivier's *Henry V* playing as the walls of history press in on the young man; a tragic variation on the Atlanta crane shot from *Gone with the Wind* as the Dalai Lama dreams of slaughtered monks. While Tibet is pulled inexorably, as a captive, into the modern world of war and propaganda, the camera angle adjusts to modern necessities, but still halts on the far side of movie conventions. The sympathetically embarrassed Chinese general attempts to converse with the Dalai Lama, but is met with impassive silence. The debris of the modern world now gets mixed with the wreckage of tradition. Newspapers are read, but a living oracle, shrieking and hissing in prophetic convulsions, indicates the route of escape.

Throughout the movie, there are shots of startlingly compressed eloquence: a child Dalai Lama is literally framed against a high window of the Potala palace, simultaneously eminence and prisoner; a rat lapping at the water during a ceremony is allowed under Buddhist principles to continue his business undisturbed while the priests go about theirs; the Dalai Lama in his robes, summoned from a Peking bathroom to an audience with Chairman Mao, wipes his spectacles (inherited from the previous incarnation) before patiently attending to the wisdoms of the Great Helmsman, delivered from a well-upholstered couch. These are the pictures from which history is constructed, with the kind of intuitive delicacy that only a natural narrator understands.

The most enduring historians have always valued the necessary alliance between picture-making and argument. Sometimes they have relied on actual illustrations, like the unknown maker of the Bayeux Tapestry, and the propaganda genius who in 1803, 800 years later, decided to exhibit the tapestry as part of Napoleon's attempt to represent himself as the latter coming of William the Conqueror in the planned invasion of perfidious Albion. As often as not, though, historians have been content to shoot their scenes and paint their pictures in their writing. These were the histories that imprinted themselves on my mind when I began to get the history bug. Sometimes such auteurs worked in improbable places. The Venerable Bede, in his monastery at Jarrow, tells the seventh-century story of the West Saxon assassin sent to kill the virtuous King Edwin of Northumbria. To make sure the contract is done right, the hit man paints his double-edged dagger with poison. But at the last instant, faster than you can say 'Secret Service', a loyal thane throws himself in the way of the killer. The dagger passes right through the body of the retainer and pierces the King, who nonetheless survives to become a Christian convert.

To option this story, please contact <u>Bedeworks@Clio.edu</u>. Yes, that's right, edu.

True Confessions of a History Boy

National Theatre programme essay for Alan Bennett's *The History Boys*, May 2004

Yes I was, and still am. I blame it on my teachers whom we always called masters. One of them still writes to me, spotting egregious errors on a page or a TV script and gently correcting them at which point I revert to the 12-year-old dunce in grey flannels and snake belt, and go stand in the corner, flushed with shame.

The first master, at primary school, was a man of gaunt, wolfish features who reserved his occasional smile for History Boys of Promise and who thought it all right if I really wanted to do a history of the Royal Navy, the main point of which were the cigarette card illustrations: Golden Hind, Victory, Ark Royal, WD & HO Wills, Gallagher, Dunhill. He was followed at secondary school – one of the Oxbridge hatcheries Alan Bennett's Headmaster yearns to rival – by a history master committed to having us all experience, at first hand, the terror of the Dark Ages. Dressed in RAF uniform, he would bring a heavy metal ruler down on the desks of inattentive 'toads': Hengist and Horsa, boy, WHACK, Ethelred the Unready, boy, SLAM! One day, when his aim was off, a toad got it right on the knuckles while looking out of the window during the Battle of Hastings. We couldn't wait for the Renaissance to arrive but apparently it wouldn't until the Third Form.

The history masters of the Upper School divided into the Wisecrackers and the Uncles and both were magic. The Uncles really cared; perhaps about their part in the hatchery production quota, but what they cared most about was our distant kinship with the shades. In their charge we got to know Mazzini and William Jennings Bryan and Masaryk as if they were in the room. Hullo, Tamas, pull up a chair and tell us what really happened. With the wisecrackers (including the deutero-Voltaire) we chuckled at the antics of the mighty – that Charles I, what a ninny – and specialised in the foibles that brought them down to earth. It was bliss to know that Pitt the Younger couldn't hold his drink (especially in the House of Commons) and dawn to be alive when we learned that Bismarck's voice was falsetto. 'Blut und Eisen' we would shriek as we headed for the Fives Courts for a quick fag (of the nicotine not the pubescent kind).

But the Love That Dared Not Speak Its Name was certainly around in Cricklewood where the school stood (though its official address for the Headmasters' Conference was, needless to say, 'Hampstead'). A brilliant and gentle geography master was suddenly removed from teaching the climate and produce of Indonesia and then from the staff altogether. He was, the Head announced at assembly, 'not well' and so not well that no-one should attempt to communicate with him, even though he undoubtedly deserved our sympathy.

And we were lucky enough to have our own unforgettable, incomparable, Hector; erotically ambiguous, effortlessly charismatic, dazzlingly erudite. And like Hector, all the history he thought we would ever need, and much more besides, was in the literature he set before us. He didn't enter the lives of the History Boys until the school had made a move from the grit and grunge of Cricklewood to a suburban pastoral farther north, where it instantly invented a pukka public school 'house' for boarders. This was the last straw for us urban cowboys, already in grief and shock at being exiled from the Beeferie (Willesden Green) and from the House on the Corner which we were sure was an Irish brothel. (Why we lurked there, I'm not sure; possibly on the off-chance that someone would emerge one day and announce a Schoolboys' Discount?)

Public schoolboys we emphatically did not want to be. They were the enemy. There was a real one up the road, and when its inmates, on parole, came to our History Club our hearts went out to them for they were an anaemic, pimply-gangly bunch, all snot and blazers, evidently cast down by their incarceration in bosky Hertfordshire. Though our Hector had come to us from a Real Public School, and though he was, in fact, a deep-dyed aristocrat with actual land and an eccentric pa who did himself in with an ancient hunting gun while we were reading A-Level *Hamlet*, Hector was, for us The Glamour of the World. He had toiled in Greek bauxite mines, had been a Scots Guard, had sat at the feet of the immortal Leavis, all of which made us pay attention when he spoke of Empson and Eliot and Donne and

Dryden. His voice, a baritone as smooth and dark as buffed porphyry, could explode, when amused (and he was, a lot) into a girlish giggle. It was not Golders Green. It was not even Hampstead. Nor were his clothes. Leather-patched tweed and flannels and our Hector were strangers to each other. When we opened the door to our first class we beheld (rather than saw) a figure, dressed entirely in black (this was well before black was Black), perched, cross-legged on a table. The face was startlingly handsome; the nose Roman, the eyes blazing. Rows of desks had been replaced by a circle. He was, naturally, in the centre.

Yes it was an act, but we all signed up for parts: the shy but book-ish closet philosopher (not me); the worldly tough-guy (not me); the versifying sixth form pseudo-Thom Gunn (not me); in fact, the Dakin, the Posner, the Scripps (or rather the Rebbe Shkripovich) (not me). And, my God, we worked for our prince of letters: if the essay was Donne, we damned well gave him Herbert too; if the essay was Shel-ley, we showed off our intimacy with Keats's prose. Without warning, entire lessons would be replaced by sessions listening to the Sanctus from different Masses: Bach, Brahms, Fauré. We went to hear the Czech Philharmonic with him and there was a party at his flat in Kens-ington (or was it Belgravia?). He was romantic, dangerous and perhaps a bit much, but we couldn't get enough of him.

But I was a History Boy, and come A-Level and Oxbridge time, I made my choice, albeit with some torment. Hector took it badly as if betrayed, and barely spoke to me for months; the flashing smile replaced by a thin-lipped expression of indifference which cut to the quick. Many years later at a garden party I told him that much of the rest of my life had been spent trying to make the choice between liter-ature and history moot, and reminding him of Carlyle's dictum that 'history is the only poetry were we but to get it right'. He smiled the old smile, benevolently unconvinced.

Picturing

The Matter of the Unripe Nectarine: High Ground/Low Ground and Ruskin's Prejudices

Christ Church Symposium, on the centenary of Ruskin's death, Oxford, 7 April 2000

I suppose we don't expect our prophets to be reasonable, which is just as well, since this is the way that Ruskin offered his considered judgement, in the first volume of *Modern Painters*, on Dutch landscape painting:

> The great body of them is merely to display manual dexterities of one kind or another and their effect on the public mind is so totally for evil that though I do not deny the advantage an artist of real judgement may derive from the study of some of them, I conceive the best patronage that any monarch could possibly bestow upon the arts would be to collect the whole body of them into a grand gallery and burn it to the ground.

Why *did* Ruskin hate Dutch painting so much, and with a vehemence and intensity he sustained over many years, returning to the subject in volume five of *Modern Painters* as a way of constructing a portrait of everything he believed art should not be? It's no mystery, of course, that his attacks on Dutch art were of a piece with his deeply felt anti-commercialism. But it's worth noting at the outset that Ruskin's equation of Dutch painting with ignobility, with the amoral reproduction of mechanically derived effects, those '*manual dexterities*', was emphatically *not* the view of critics elsewhere in Europe, especially in France, who otherwise did share much of Ruskin's hostility to capitalist philistinism. And in this respect at least, the prophet turned out to be false, for the one thing that *Modern Painters* did not generate was modern

painting, and what Ruskin has to say about Dutch painting almost inadvertently tells us why. Authentically modern art – that is to say, and here
I'm following Clement Greenberg's famous definition, painting that
embraced its two-dimensional flatness, painting that self-consciously
rejected a transparent relationship between objects and their representation – was not the child of Ruskinian criticism, but of the French
critical tradition in which all the things that Ruskin most hated – the
indifferent rendering of contemporary material life – turned out to drive
the modernist revolution. In that respect at least, 1900 has to be seen as
the last year of an old, rather than the first year of the new modernist
century.

For Ruskin, of course, painting was normative or it was nothing. Its
reach to beauty was only possible to the degree to which it also reached
for truth. With this in mind he launched his attack on Dutch painting,
as the epitome of stale meretriciousness. He was withering about seventeenth-century Dutch art in general, the 'various van somethings and
Back somethings', seeing it as devoted to the mechanical reproduction
of cheap lighting effects, the random accumulation of mindless anecdote. He complained of its vacancy of ideas and, most damning of all,
its reduction of a calling to the status of a *trade*. Potter, Berchem, Backhuizen, Willem van de Velde the Younger and, most surprisingly, Jacob
van Ruisdael (so passionately admired in Germany and France) all came
in for a beating at the hands of Ruskin's big stick. Rubens was taken to
task in a very particular and telling way, and Rembrandt seldom alluded
to at all, although Ruskin evidently liked the master's landscape etchings and drawings, as well he might. Of Rembrandt's paintings he had
virtually nothing to say except that he thought the greatest of all was
the self-portrait of the artist and his wife in Dresden, which we now
know to represent Rembrandt and Saskia as the Prodigal Son and his
Whore in a Tavern, but which Ruskin, in keeping with his pathetic innocence about the nature of connubial bliss, believed to be the artist and
his wife 'in a state of ideal happiness. He sits at supper with his wife on
his knee flourishing a glass of champagne with a roast peacock on the
table.'

Ruskin's most savage denunciations, though, were reserved for his
particular bête noire, Aelbert Cuyp. Perhaps this was because Cuyps
were represented in the Dulwich Picture Gallery, which, close to
Ruskin's paternal home, must have been an exceptionally important

place of initiation for him, assembling as it did so many more paintings than Eastlake's fledgling National Gallery. It was there that Ruskin saw one particular Cuyp and read William Hazlitt's description of it, which raised his hackles. In the chapter on 'The Truth of Skies' in volume I of *Modern Painters*, Ruskin let Cuyp and Hazlitt both have it. Skies were, after all, a crucial subject for Ruskin, for whom the perception and description of sky was a contact point between painterly practice and intimations of the celestial, which inspired some of his most beautiful drawings. Just before getting on Cuyp's case he cites the lovely remark made by Dickens in his *American Notes*, when lying on a barge deck and looking, as Dickens felt, not at but *through* a pure blue sky. Ruskin too was exacting in his account, not just of blue skies, but of what happened to those skies when they were flooded by different kinds of radiance, at dawn, at sunset, at high noon. He certainly knew that when commonplace admiration was voiced about Cuyp's grand production numbers, sooner or later it was his skies – their tonal warmth; their golden saturation – which was supposed to clinch the matter. So it was precisely this quality in which all of Cuyp's habitual meretriciousness was he thought exposed, on which Ruskin concentrated his critical gaze:

> Look at the large Cuyp in the Dulwich Gallery, which Mr Hazlitt considers 'the finest in the world' and of which he very complimentarily says 'The tender green of the valleys, the gleaming lake, the purple light of the hills have an effect like the *down* [Ruskin italicises this for full withering effect] on an unripe nectarine!' I ought to have apologized before now, for not having studied sufficiently in Covent Garden to be provided with terms of correct and classical criticism. One of my friends begged me to observe the other day that Claude was 'pulpy', another added the yet more gratifying information that he was 'juicy' and it is now happily discovered that Cuyp is 'downy'. Now I dare say that the sky of this first-rate Cuyp [Ruskin had no more damningly backhanded compliment than a 'first-rate Cuyp'] *is very like an unripe nectarine: all that I have to say about it is, that it is exceedingly unlike a sky.'*

Perhaps Ruskin *should* in fact have spent some time in Covent Garden, in which case he might have noticed – and it would still have served his purpose in attacking Hazlitt – that nectarines (unless Victorian fruit was different from our own) are conspicuously smooth and un-downy on their skins, and that it was the red-golden colour, not the texture of their surface, that Hazlitt was after, in coining his doomed simile. But the producer of fake sunsets, compounded by the egregiously inattentive critic, epitomised for Ruskin everything that was wrong about conventional bourgeois taste – the craving for gaudy theatrical effects not found in nature, the willingness of the technically proficient painter to supply them, and the complicity of the critic in praising them. 'It is difficult to conceive how any man calling himself a painter could impose such a thing on the public and still more how the public can receive it.'

It is odd, though – or then again perhaps it is calculated – that in all his diatribes against Cuyp, Ruskin should have failed to notice or say anything about the fact of his hero Turner's immense and glaringly obvious debt to the very same detestable Cuyp. If the *point* of harping on about Cuyp was precisely to achieve a *dissociation* between Turner and the Dutch master – that Ruskin felt was inappropriately lodged in the public mind – then he completely, and quite uncharacteristically, fails to address the issue specifically. It's much more likely, I think, that Ruskin failed to register the awkward fact that so far from Turner understanding the Dutch tradition as something to be aggressively discarded in pursuit of the higher truths of his own landscape painting, he repeatedly turned back to it as a source of deep interpretative inspiration. Unlike Ruskin, who did his best to avoid the Low Countries, except in so far as he was obliged to disembark en route to the High Countries where his heart lay, Turner returned to Holland again and again: the first time in 1817, then in 1825; and in 1840–42, just prior to the publication of the first volume of *Modern Painters*, in 1843. Turner had been there for three successive years, not just as a traveller of course, but as a working artist, his sketchbook filling up with drawings. Paintings which drew deeply on Dutch art for their inspiration, and composition, punctuated crucial moments in Turner's career. The very first painting that he had ever shown in public, in 1796, a marine painting of fishermen, was famously closely modelled on a Willem van de Velde the Younger. The painting with which he gained a public following when it was exhibited at the British Institution in 1801, *Dutch Boats in a Gale, Fishermen Endeavouring to Put Their Fish on Board*, was likewise indebted to van de Velde, and was in fact commissioned by the Third Earl of Bridgewater (a huge fan and collector of Dutch marine paintings) to hang alongside his own van de Velde.

Of course Ruskin might well have retorted that it was precisely the taste of a canal-builder like Bridgewater which had deformed, happily not fatally, the young Turner's early prospects and healthy sense of independence. But he would have had a harder time with the painting exhibited in 1818 as a direct result of Turner's first journey to Holland the year before, and which justifiably won him an even greater fame: *Dort, or Dordrecht. The Dort Packet-Boat from Rotterdam Becalmed.* For it was blindingly obvious that the great picture, immediately and expensively bought by Turner's most devoted patron Walter Fawkes and hung in the music room of his Yorkshire house, was a fulsome act of homage to Aelbert Cuyp. Turner had seen Cuyp's *Maas at Dordrecht* when it was shown at the British Institution in 1815 and it may well have been that he was so struck by it as to make a pilgrimage (for there was no other reason to go to Dordrecht, which was quite out of the way for a British traveller), to the very site at the junction of the Scheldt and Maas from which Cuyp (and van Goyen) habitually painted their estuarine scenes.

Turner's painting ought to have been absolutely abhorrent to Ruskin, for, quite apart from its reproducing a classically Cuypian late-afternoon blue-gold sky, it was, after all, a picture of people, a very *low* kind of people by Ruskin's standards, reduced to doing absolutely nothing in the absence of wind. That is of course the magic of the piece: the sense of utter stillness in a world that was habitually busy. The twin emblems of the painting's play on movement and immobility are the bird skimming across the surface and an item straight from Ruskin's worst nightmares of Covent Garden – a single cabbage floating imperturbably on the oily surface of the river.

And there were plenty more 'Dutch' Turners to come: a whole sequence of them in the 1830s and '40s, in which the paragon was not Cuyp, but Jacob van Ruisdael. It doesn't say a lot for Ruskin's own attentiveness to, or familiarity with, the whole range of Dutch painting that he regrets that Ruisdael never turned his hand to painting rough water, when in fact English collections had countless examples of Ruisdaels in precisely this vein and which were so clearly the departure point for many of Turner's most powerful choppy-seas pictures, including the stunning *Port Ruysdael* of 1827, now in the Mellon Center for British Art at Yale. (How much of a gesture of homage did Turner have to make before Ruskin would acknowledge it?)

There was another aspect of these sea paintings which was obviously inconvenient for Ruskin's determination to make Turner the embodiment of everything Dutch art was not: namely their Whiggism. *The Prince of Orange, William III Embarked from Holland and Landed at Torbay, November 4th 1688 after a Stormy Passage* was exhibited at the Royal Academy in 1832 and was thought then – and now – to be an allegory of the Parliamentary Reform Act of the same year, a campaign into which Turner's patron, Walter Fawkes, MP, threw everything he had. Whether or not William III's 'stormy passage', dramatically sketched in on the left of the picture, did refer to the proceedings in Parliament, there's no doubt at all that Turner meant to make a connection between the canonical scripture of the Glorious Revolution and the consummation of that tradition of Whig liberty in the act of 1832. The picture, then, is a supreme instance of Turner doing something which Ruskin's view of him precluded: drawing inspiration from the tradition of Dutch painting, especially its dramas of light and darkness, in order to make visible an historical theme which, at least in the terms of its sympathetic protagonists, was morally and constitutionally heroic.

When Ruskin returned to the attack in volume V of *Modern Painters*, published of course in 1860, he had not seen any reason to moderate his hostility. Quite the opposite in fact. The last part of the book, 'Of Inventions Spiritual', which contains some of Ruskin's most wonderful literary pyrotechnics, is a critical review of the landscape tradition in European painting, beginning with the lofty heroes – Titian and Veronese – and ending with the low villains, or rather the clowns, as Ruskin calls them more than once, not just Cuyp but new targets of his excoriation: Teniers and Wouwermans. Rubens, who gets to share a chapter with Cuyp, is not treated to quite the same roasting, but he is patronised by Ruskin in, if possible, an even more deadly manner, as 'a healthy, worthy, kind-hearted courtly-phrased Animal – without any clearly perceptible traces of a soul except when he paints his children'. And it is not just in Rubens, but in Dutch painting generally, this obstinate earthiness, which for Ruskin makes Netherlandish art finally so irredeemable. The whole *point* of art being, for Ruskin, the transcendence of the material conditions of its production, Netherlandish painting was something which remained locked up in so much pigment, canvas and linseed oil. It was only to be expected, then, that when Dutch painters turned to animals, they should treat them as so much material stock-in-trade, the seventeenth-century equivalent of air-brushed lustrous advertising copy: 'Paul Potter their best herd and cattle painter does not care even for sheep but for wool; regards not cows but cowhide', incapable of perceiving 'any condition of an animal's mind except when it is grazing'. Veronese, on the other hand, seems to have a direct line to what Ruskin calls 'the spiritual view of the dog's nature', while 'the dog is used by Teniers and many other Hollanders merely to obtain unclean jest; while by the more powerful men, Rubens, Snyders, Rembrandt it is painted only in savage chase or butchered agony'.

The two chapters which follow are best summed up by Ruskin's opening of chapter VIII in which he contrasts Wouwermans and Fra Angelico – 'Having determined the general nature of vulgarity we are now able to close our view of the character of the Dutch school.' And Ruskin's preceding chapter on distinguishing between vulgarity and gentility is one of the least rewarding and tendentious in the entirety of *Modern Painters*, soaked in a kind of moral snobbery which on the page at least reads even more odiously than the regular social kind. But by this point there is absolutely no stopping him in his Manichaean opposition between the forces of good and wickedness. The 'Hollanders', as he calls them, turn out to be defective painters because they lived in a defective world: a world of cabbages and wool. It is a stupid world, bound to create stupid art in the literal sense of inducing stupor in those who behold it: Cuyp, of course, a 'brewer by trade' whose work 'will make you feel marvellously drowsy'; a world, too, from which God has been completely banished. In their 'pastoral landscape we lose not only all faith in religion but all remembrance of it. Absolutely now at last we find ourselves without sight of God in all the world.' As a view of Jacob van Ruisdael's mature landscapes, this reading would be forgivable in its obtuseness, I suppose, if the overwhelmingly self-evident spirituality of so many of those great paintings, most obviously of course with the two versions of the *Jewish Cemetery*, remained generally obscure to nineteenth-century critics. But of course they didn't. At least since Goethe and Hegel, if not before, Ruisdael's obvious transcendentalism had been the subject of innumerable essays and critical investigations: none of them, I suppose, read or at least taken on board by Ruskin. But as he warms to his task Ruskin reveals himself, I think, to be part of that strain, not entirely pleasant in nineteenth-century moral criticism, which is intent on pinning down and pinning the blame on specific historical moments when the Christian inheritance was sold off for pieces of silver. It's worth quoting this extraordinary passage in full: 'being without God in all the world,' then:

> So far as I can hear or read, this is an entirely new and wonderful state of things achieved by the Hollanders. The human being never got wholly quit of the terror of spiritual being before. Persian, Egyptian, Assyrian, Hindoo, Chinese, all kept some dim, appalling record of what they called 'gods.' Farthest savages had – and still have – their Great Spirit or, in extremity, their feather idols, large-eyed, but here in Holland we have at last got utterly done with it all. Our only idol glitters dimly in tangible shape of a pint pot and all the incense thereto comes out of a small censer or bowl at the end of a pipe. Of deities or virtues, angels, principalities or powers in the name of our ditches, no more. Let us have cattle and market vegetables.

Perhaps none of this would matter for Ruskin, had not this art of cattle and vegetables managed to infect landscape painting ever since, nowhere more completely than in England. Perhaps he was thinking of Crome and the Norwich school; perhaps Gainsborough. In any event Ruskin declares, 'the whole school . . . inherently mortal to all its admirers having by its influence in England destroyed our perception of the purposes of painting' (in particular a proper sense of colour; Ruskin was adamant that in a land without sunshine it was only to be expected that the only colour interest would be to extract 'greyness' and 'shininess').

Something had happened between writing volume I and volume V of *Modern Painters* to make Ruskin apopleptic about the Dutch disease in landscape. It happened, I believe, in 1857: the year of the Manchester lectures which became *Unto This Last*, Ruskin's headlong assault on the barbarities of liberal capitalism, and also the year when he began to work on the completion of *Modern Painters*. And the event was the mother of all blockbusters, held on the old cricket ground at Old Trafford and known as *The Art Treasures of the United Kingdom* (although an enormous number of works were in fact lent from abroad, as well as the cream of private collections within Britain itself). Evidently designed to be a riposte to the Paris Exposition Universelle of 1855, in what had become an alarming competition of exhibitionist one-upmanship, the Manchester exhibition was, for the art world, what the Great Exhibition of 1851 was for everyone else. The scale itself was gargantuan: 2,000 paintings, 1,200 of them Old Masters, from Byzantine icons all the way to Turner, as well as sculpture, decorative art — ceramics, enamels, terracottas, bronzes, glass, armour, ivories; watercolours, drawings, etchings and photographs. A railway line and station had been constructed expressly to transport visitors to the show (without, however, a four-hour wait on opening day) and disembarked them right in front of the exhibition. A great processional boulevard led to the immense iron-and-glass cathedral of art (just the sort of architecture, of course, abominated by Ruskin), the 'nave', as it were, 700 feet long by 200 wide, each branch of the crossing 400 feet long, with galleries running around them and a huge ceremonial space for a full orchestra at the crossing itself. A hundred thousand meals were served daily, 300 roast chickens an hour, a feat duly applauded in the national press. Once Queen Victoria and Prince Albert had lent their names to the organising committee, the £75,000 needed to underwrite the show appeared magically from the Bank of England. Ten thousand two-guinea season tickets had sold before opening day on 5 May. The Queen herself arrived on the twentieth anniversary exactly of her accession, on 30 June, together with the Prince Consort and a number of her children, including Vicky and her betrothed, the Crown Prince of Prussia. It was, of course, raining. This was Old Trafford in June after all.

The ceremonial centrepiece of the show was, naturally, a procession of historical portraits celebrating the grand continuities of British history: kings and queens to be sure (including Holbein's sublime miniature of Anne of Cleves, which Horace Walpole thought his greatest masterpiece), but also of course the great pantheon of cultural worthies: Shakespeare, Newton, Locke, Dr Johnson and, rather surprisingly, Oliver Cromwell and John Hampden. But the curator in charge of the Old Masters' collection, culled from the great and the good among the British aristocracy and plutocracy — the dukes of Devonshire, Buccleuch, Richmond, Northumberland; from Scotland: Breadalbane, Lothian; and on and on (and occasionally plain citizen collectors like John Walter, the journalist writing for *The Times*) — was none other than Gustaf Waagen, the director of the Berlin Museum, who in 1854 had been publishing

his exhaustive inventories of the Old Master paintings in private collections – still an extraordinary source for our understanding of the history
of taste. And although Waagen ensured an astonishing representation
of Italian painting – Giotto, Pollaiuolo, Mantegna, Masaccio, Leonardo,
Michelangelo, Dürer, Titian, Tintoretto, the Caracci and so on – it was
northern painting which really excited him, and which he mustered at
Manchester in profusion and quality. Twenty-eight of what were then
thought to be Rembrandts: three from the Queen, four from the Marquis
of Hertford (core of the Wallace Collection), the double portrait of Jean
Pellicorne and Susanna van Collen, the great grisaille of *John the Baptist
Preaching* (now in Berlin), *Floris Soop* and so on. But also a huge haul
of precisely the pictures for which Ruskin had such deep repugnance –
a crowd of Cuyps including the great view of Nijmegen from Woburn
Abbey, Queen's Hunters; also a mass of Hobbema, Potter animal pieces
and the execrated Wouwermans. And twenty Jacob van Ruisdaels,
including the *View of Bentheim* in John Walter's collection; the
pollarded oak, and marsh and waterfalls as well as a whole number of
stormy marine paintings which would have confirmed for Ruskin the
connection between the Dutch master and Turner.

The list, of course, is not the point. It goes on and on. What the
Manchester show affirmed, to a degree that must have set Ruskin's teeth
on edge (despite the inclusion of a *hundred* Turners) and sent him back
to further rounds of denunciation, was the pride of place given to
precisely the kind of paintings that he believed were destroying the
vitality of *true* painting in England. The Manchester exhibition must
have seemed to Ruskin, despite all those Turners and a sprinkling of
the Pre-Raphaelites, a repeat performance of the tawdry vulgarity of
the Great Exhibition six years before, but perhaps even worse because
it suggested so eloquently the essential imperviousness of English taste
to the sacred reawakening launched by the Pre-Raphaelites: the tyranny
of polish. The immense presence of Dutch art could only have
confirmed him in his judgement that it was, essentially, manufactured
interior decoration for the plutocracy. It's hard not to read *Unto This
Last* and not see it as Ruskin's specific counterblast to the orgy of vulgarity, the loss of gentility represented by the iron-and-glass cathedral at
Old Trafford.

Nor does it come as a surprise to learn that incomparably the best –
not necessarily the most exhaustive, but certainly the most perceptive

– report on the Manchester exhibition comes from the pen of a French critic, then living in exile in Holland under the adopted name of 'Willem Bürger' – Bill Citizen – and that critic was of course the great Théophile Thoré. (It's odd that no one has thought to write a parallel life of Ruskin and Thoré, since their passions were so similar and their influence almost equally profound.) Though they're slight in length, Thoré's two introductory chapters to his *Trésors d'Art en Angleterre* (published at amazing speed in London – in French – in 1858) are little gems of insight, since he sees right away to the social argument made by the *fact* of the Manchester show. Faux-naïf, he begins by asking why – at least for the convenience of foreigners – such an important exhibition wasn't located in London, a mere two hours' train journey from Dover, and then of course answers his own question. The idea is a parade of the *educational* pretensions of industrial capitalism in its own back yard, specifically a kind of pedagogical gift donated from capital to labour, from the entrepreneur to the worker. And it must be an expressly *British* enterprise at that – hence the deliberate distance, so Thoré thinks, from the Channel and the North Sea, and the enormous prominent space given to historical portraiture, historical miniatures and artefacts illustrating the continuity of British history. In continental Europe, the implication is, according to Thoré, you have revolutions. In Britain we have exhibitions. This ostensible union of classes is made all the more solid by the fact that the community of collectors increasingly cut across the formal stratifications of class in England – as far as owning great Dutch paintings is concerned, the journalist John Walter and Sir Robert Peel (or, rather, by 1857, his widow) were every bit the peer of the aristocratic Cavendishes, Grosvenors and Russells.

Thoré evidently has mixed feelings about all this, because while he's genuinely lost in admiration at the smoothness with which this propaganda stunt is handled by the businessmen of Manchester, in alliance with the broad acres of the rest of England, the old revolutionary in him rankles at '*his*' favourite art – Dutch art – being shamelessly exploited as an emollient for discontent. For it was not fortuitous that Thoré had chosen the Kingdom of the Netherlands for his place of exile (rather than Victor Hugo's Guernsey) from the police state of the Second Empire. It was not just Dutch art that was the attraction – although that was of immense importance to him – but the kind of society Thoré, in common with many other old revolutionaries, believed to have survived in the Netherlands, a society at the opposite pole of the metropolitan corruptions of Paris and London, or the industrial brutalities of Lille and Manchester. The best account of this French vision of the Netherlands is in an extraordinary book written by a now undeservedly forgotten writer, Alphonse Esquiros, who spent 1855 in Holland and who published *La Néerlande et la Vie Hollandaise* four years later. Esquiros was an old revolutionary comrade of Thoré, a cell-mate at Sainte-Pélagie where they had both done time for offending the censors under the July monarchy. Though his family was well-to-do haute bourgeoisie, the paternal house remained right in the centre of the Faubourg Saint-Antoine and thus in the middle of the bloodiest action of the June days in 1848. While Thoré was editing *La Vraie République* together with George Sand and the Saint-Simonien Pierre Leroux and contributing liberation manifestos to the *République des Arts*, Esquiros was opening his house to the wounded and dying hauled directly from the barricades.

After it was all over, and the warriors of the new France were all either in prison, exile or discreet silence, they cast around for some sort of light in the general darkness and, perhaps improbably, perhaps not, saw in Holland a culture in which bitter social division, plutocratic hegemony, cultural intolerance and the bureaucratic state were all miraculously absent. The northern Netherlands seem to have missed out altogether on the Industrial Revolution (in contrast to Belgium). Its little towns – Haarlem, Delft, Rotterdam and Gouda – all little miracles, so they thought, of self-government. In the writing not only of Esquiros but another utterly infatuated admirer of the Dutch, Jules Michelet, the *trekschuit*, the tow-barge, became the symbolic opposite of the railway locomotive. In the slow, horse-drawn barge, time and space, they thought, remained astonishingly in balance, its languid schedules utterly incompatible with the urgent clock of industrial production; and within the *trekschuit* were accommodated all types and conditions, with none of the glaringly inegalitarian class separations that marked the compartments of the railway train. The first thing that all the Francophone pilgrims did on disembarking from the train (in which, perforce, they were compelled to arrive in Holland) was to get on the *trekschuit*. Likewise the individual cargo-barge symbolised something else of supreme significance for the French Hollandophiles: the sanctity and autonomy of the nuclear family on which they believed true social happiness depended. (It's striking how little Ruskin has to say about this issue.) Jules Michelet, another of the most passionate devotees of the Dutch, and a personal friend of the great archivist historian Groen van Prinsterer, described the tow-barge (in a purple passage which in places almost anticipates the *bateau ivre*) as a 'Noah's ark': '*C'est l'arché de Noë, qui doit contenir toute une famille, homme, femme, enfants, animaux.*'

To these writers and critics, then, Holland was an unforced, organically cohesive community; precisely in fact the kind of society which Ruskin, and before him Pugin, imagined had existed in Christian medieval England and which he wanted to reintroduce through the Guild of St George. But in reinstating, as they imagined, the integrity of the medieval craft guilds along with neo-medieval design and painting, Ruskin, the Pre-Raphaelites and the Guild Socialists were reaching back across a great span of time in which the actual lived experience of work and worship had been irrevocably lost. But the French enthusiasts of small-town Dutch culture were, they supposed, witnessing a continuity they thought had never actually been broken. And granting a large degree of wishful thinking – especially in respect of the larger cities like Amsterdam – they were not entirely wrong. The northern Netherlands was one of the very last cultures in western Europe to experience the Industrial Revolution. Compared with Holland, Ruskin's Switzerland was Coketown.

The eulogists of Holland had not arrived at their improbable social epiphany overnight. What makes their position so diametrically opposite from Ruskin's is that while our Prophet read what he supposed to be the essentially prosaic and (his favourite word) 'carnal' nature of Dutch painting to be evidence of a hopelessly debased and vulgar culture, immune to any possibility of the spiritual life, French writers in whom art criticism, social evangelism and political activism were married to at least the same degree as Ruskin, came to precisely the opposite conclusion from the same evidence! Years before they were eyewitnesses and reporters on Dutch society, these critics, banded together as *Jeune France*, were impassioned devotees of its art, including its landscape painting.

Many of those who would become the champions of Dutch painting in France in the 1830s were first exposed to it when they were very young in the great aristocratic collections which passed, sometimes by force, to the new Louvre – the collection of the Marquis de Vaudreuil, for example – as well as in the loot brought to Paris by the wagons of Napoleonic triumph. It was through that more doubtful route that the great treasures from the Stadholder William V's collection, including the great Potter in The Hague and a number of Ruisdaels, were first seen by Michelet who never forgot them. After 1815 these canonical works disappeared in two directions: the expropriated works properly repatriated back to the royal collection in The Hague (the nucleus of the Mauritshuis) and in much greater numbers (from, for example, the Prince de Conti and the Choiseuls) into the collections of the aristocratic magnates of Britain, via the auctions and sales inventoried by John Smith.

So when the writers, poets and artists of *Jeune France* were looking for counter-paradigms around which they could rally against the academy, the lost treasures of Dutch art were one of their first thoughts. Though they might come to despise it in the end (and not all did), the railway train got them from Paris to Antwerp and eventually to Utrecht by the late 1830s and early '40s. And another crucial technological breakthrough – lithography – helped them publish the works of the Dutch masters in their periodicals, none more important than Arsène Houssaye's *L'Artiste*, which published art criticism by Théophile Gautier, Gérard de Nerval, Félix Pyat, Petrus Borel, Eugène Delacroix and of course the young Thoré.

The qualities which these writers saw in Dutch art, and which they held to be socially and morally redemptive, were precisely those which Ruskin read as evidence of the degenerate vulgarity of the culture: namely its earthiness, its rejection of grand or sacred narrative; its rejection of received assumptions about the beautiful and the ugly; the willingness of artists to consider themselves as proximate to their subjects, however drunk or debauched or dirty or violent those subjects might be. They also, of course, indulged in a great deal of wishful thinking – nourished by the anecdotal early eighteenth-century biographies of Dutch artists by Arnold Houbraken – as to their autodidact background. Rembrandt – their favorite farouche – was firmly lodged in their imagination as the miller's son with flour in his hair, marrying the peasant girl Saskia. And in keeping with Romantic assumptions about the indivisibility of personal temper and painterly style, they also read imaginary connections between those biographies and aspects of handling – van Goyen's notorious propensity for gambling thus became an explanation for the loose sketchiness of his style and his rejection (as was then thought) of under-drawing; Dou's apparent manic fastidiousness was of a piece with the gem-like licked finish of his genre paintings and still lifes, and so on.

Most important of all, though, the writers of *Jeune France* were attracted to the greatest work of Dutch art for what they called its '*poésie*': and here again both Potter and Jacob van Ruisdael played a crucial role. Poesy (for which these writers were at least in part indebted to their readings of German idealism) meant the intimation of unworldly things from the close inspection of the worldly; the implication of interiors from the avid description of surfaces. So that while Ruskin took Potter's cows to be evidence that all the Dutch cared for was a kind of merchant's inventory of leather on the hoof, Arsène Houssaye could write of the same painting that Potter 'fixes nature itself on the canvas as if it were a mirror . . . he [Potter] proves triumphantly that cattle have a soul, a spirit, even a mind (*pensée*), that these animals speak to you with their eyes, their movement, their postures (*attitudes*)'. Lammenais, the arch Christian mystic socialist in this company, felt precisely the same way. Jacob van Ruisdael was, just as Goethe had thought (Houssaye again), '*le poète des coeurs blessés* . . . the poet of wounded hearts; he is not just copying nature; he is giving it its soul'. Ruisdael is 'sad, dreamer, poet above all'. Thoré went even further. In 1844 he compared Ruisdael's *Little Tree* with Michelangelo's sculpture for Lorenzo de Medici known as *The Thinker* – so that the '*petit buisson*' attempting to find some peace amidst the agitations of nature became anthropomorphised as a tragic hero – an association which, it's safe to say, definitely would not have occurred to Ruskin.

But then Thoré had already decided – as he wrote in an essay on Adriaen van Ostade in 1847 – that Dutch painters of the golden age exhibited a kind of peculiar mysticism, suspended between the material and the immaterial worlds: 'The Dutch of Ostade are . . . more Christian than one would ever imagine, practising the spirit of the Gospel, the detachment from earthly vanities, equality and fraternity.' So while, for Ruskin, Dutch painters betrayed their shallow attachment to the surface appearances of this world through their vulgar concern with finish, for his French contemporary art critics, they were the pioneers not of the finite but the infinite world.

These two stances, about as opposite as one might imagine, were I suppose partly conditioned by the nature of the enemy to be attacked. In France, in the 1840s and '50s, it was still, by and large, classical academicism, or the stale posturings of the *style troubadour*. The earthiness of Dutch painting, by contrast, became obviously important for the painters who set themselves most resolutely *against* the grandiose histories and florid portraiture of the official Salons — painters as diverse as Daumier and Millet, and the *plein air* Barbizons (Corot and Rousseau). Dutch pictures were as yet very thinly displayed in the Louvre and even scarcer in the grand collections of the plutocracy. The late 1850s were the time when both of those situations changed. In England, on the other hand, the enemy was to be found in the bourgeois and aristocratic houses, which were positively stuffed full of Dutch art since the auctions of the post-Waterloo years. And it was in that over-upholstered milieu that Ruskin believed the taste for Cuyp and Ruisdael had deadened both private and public sensibility.

Whatever the reason for these strikingly opposed responses, their effects on the critical discourse about the nature of Dutch art were, I think, serious and long-lasting. Ruskin's brutal dismissal of Dutch art as, at best, so many painted lies about nature and, at worst, the painterly equivalent of the forces of Antichrist, deserving nothing better than being consigned to a great incineration, in effect left the field to writers like Mrs Anna Jameson, whose massively popular books on painting measured Dutch art for the degree to which it was 'charming' or not. Unshakably established as part of moneyed taste, writing about Dutch painting in England became (as it certainly had not been in the eighteenth century) almost exclusively a matter of disputes about authentication, and the development of simple chronologies of style from 'early' to 'late'. It was quite unthinkable, for example, that a serious study of Dutch art should play any part at all in the meditations of those critical communities which seemed in the year of Ruskin's death, a century ago, to be pointing towards the future — the aesthetic movement and Arts and Crafts. As far as Dutch painting was concerned, Ruskin had done something much more fatal than burned the lot of it — he had made its study the exclusive province of connoisseurs. It had become an intellectual dead end, the subject of parlour talk.

Across the Channel, something like the opposite was true. The early and acute insights of Thoré, Houssaye and Esquiros had blossomed in two extremely powerful ways. First, Thoré's own impassioned promotion of the work of Frans Hals generated a completely new understanding of his portraiture (close in many ways to Riegl), and his rediscovery of Vermeer had led him to see hard archival-based documentation as the next step towards proper historical reconstruction of the lives and working conditions of the artists which he himself realised he had over-idealised. The first major archival publications about Dutch painting that I know of were thus the production of a French specialist and friend of Thoré's, Henri Havard. Second, and perhaps in the end more fundamental to the future of thinking and practising art, the critical insight that Dutch art did *not* thrive on a transparent or literal relationship between the objective material world and the manner of its representation, but rather posed an enormous question mark over that representation, was astonishingly fertile for thinking about the function of painting in general. It was, in ways incomprehensible to Ruskin, who insisted over and over again that the painter's job was to do no more but no less than represent the truth of nature, the bud of modernism. It was in precisely the artificiality – the 'lies' told about nature in so much Dutch painting – that the way forward actually, for better or worse, lay. And in this respect, forgive me for saying, it was Jacob van Ruisdael, Rembrandt van Rijn and Théophile Thoré, and not John Ruskin, who turned out to be the real prophets of Modern Painting.

Dutch Courage

Guardian, 23 June 2007

Feeling conjugally challenged? Look at Frans Hals's double portrait of Isaac Massa and Beatrix van der Laen in the National Gallery's forthcoming *Dutch Portraits* show and, instantly, all will be right with your corner of the world. The graceful painting, silvery with intimate affection, documents one of the great changes in the history of European marriage: the possibility of the shared smile – the *glimlach* revolution. Not that lipwork had hitherto been out of the question for portraiture. But *La Joconde* she isn't. Leonardo's thinly knowing smirk implies private knowledge, to be decoded only through the proprietorial collusion of patron and painter. But Hals's newly married couple, Beatrix sporting both betrothal and wedding rings on her right hand, advertise their mutual pleasure openly for our shared celebration. They incline to each other and, through their self-identification as a harmonious pair, radiate that sympathy outwards through the picture plane towards us. Behold, the painting says, as Isaac holds his hand to his heart, the very picture of proper Christian marriage in which duty also happens to be pleasure.

To gauge the magnitude of that alteration you can look at Jan Claesz's twin portraits in the exhibition of a married couple from the first decade of the seventeenth century. The figures are still rigid with conventions of social duty, above all that of engendering, the human bond entirely subsumed by the obligations of decorum.

Precisely because, during the seventeenth century, the Dutch travelled that journey from iconic formalism, through a period of easygoing naturalism, back to refined family ensembles dressed to display patrician rank and classical taste, the National Gallery show is an opportunity to reflect on the evolution of the genre itself. As patrons reminded painters (including Rembrandt) whom they thought had been altogether too free with artistic licence, likeness was their first duty. But as Richard Brilliant argued in his elegant book, *Portraiture*, the artist has often interpreted that job as the likeness of an idea, a sense of a person, rather than the laborious imitation of physiognomic detail. Roger Fry complained of a Sargent portrait of a British general that he couldn't see the man for the likeness. He was commenting at a time when a portrait was thought to be the capture of a bundle of psychological characteristics stamping the unique quality of a person, which could be read through facial expression and body language, and then transcribed on to the canvas as a sign of essential self. This was no more than a subjective hunch about a person, masquerading as some deeper objective reality. But it meant that modern portraiture has generally been imitation complicated by interpretation.

Centuries earlier, before the Romantics inaugurated the cult of the unrepeatable self, the work of the portraitist was to represent the imagined mask of, say, the scholar (Holbein's Erasmus), the Doge (Titian's Andrea Gritti) or the virtuoso courtier (Raphael's Castiglione); all of them personifications rather than revelations. But between the normative icon of the Renaissance and the naked ego-show of the nineteenth century, bolder portraitists such as Hals nudged the decorous expectations of their patrons towards informality while never quite disobeying the obligation to represent something (wealth garnered in virtue, for instance) as well as someone. Then, enter the Haarlem smile, hallmarked not just by Hals, but by followers such as Jan de Bray, whose happy couple, the printer Abraham Casteleyn and his wife Margriet de Bancken, perpetuate the Halsian manner well into the 1660s, with the adoring *huisvrouw* (housewife) leaning towards her husband, while he gestures with creamy complacency towards us.

Just why Haarlem should have broken the solemnity barrier is a mystery, though perhaps the conjunction of breweries and textiles, both giving a glossy shine to things, the humanist slant of its academies removed from Calvinist-canting Leiden, had something to do with it. But the Haarlem painters also knew that the line between the sympathetic smile and the coarse grin, with teeth exposed, was the severe boundary that separated portraiture from genre painting. The most famous of all Hals's paintings, *The Laughing Cavalier*, is, in fact, neither. And no wonder, for the raucous guffaw, with its noisome reek of herring and onions, was the sign of low-lifes, both the people and the pictures.

The van der Laen marriage portrait is something else again, on one level an omnium gatherum of all the stock marital pieties that could have been pulled straight from a domestic-morality manual such as Jacob Cats's *Houwelyck*. Beatrix leans against her solid spouse in a gesture of trusting subordination to his considerable substance. At her feet, inevitably, trails ivy, the symbol of fidelity, while behind the couple a vine, the emblem of fruitful devotion, twines itself around a sturdy trunk. The partners were famously loaded: a prosperous Russian trade merchant married to a local heiress. But what would otherwise be an egregious display of conspicuous fortune is carefully offset by sartorial signals of their old-fashioned homeliness. The sharp clothes may flash with Hals's silky light, but they are sober Christian black and Beatrix sports the kind of aggressively unfashionable millstone ruff which, by the 1630s, was more likely to be found encircling the neck of a matron. And if raw money is modified by old piety, it's also polished by culture, hence the display of their poetic pretensions, embodied by the garden, the kind of place extolled in the gently Arcadian love poetry of P. C. Hooft, complete with Italianate pavilions, classical statuary and fountains.

But Hals has moved the picture well beyond an anthology of allusions. The scene is bright with human as well as botanical nature; the smiles seem spontaneous rather than assumed. In an exquisite touch of intimacy, Hals has the fine silk of her hair escaping her under-cap, the *ondermuts* that was seldom thought proper for portraits, but whose delicate pink seems to rhyme with her rosy complexion. His ability to convey this move to warm informality was technical as well as conceptual. Inspired perhaps by Rubens (for the Flemish presence was strong in Haarlem), Hals's handling of paint was itself looser than anything that had yet appeared in Dutch art, the darting hand suggesting the energetic innocence of impulse.

Of course, the balance between bravura and decorum was always delicate. Hals's portrait of the twenty-something plutobrat Willem Coymans obliges the patrician by incorporating his coat of arms – the black cattle that made him an urban *kooi-man* (cow-boy). But by describing the translucent fallen collar and the gold-embroidered coat through a web of dashing, hectic strokes, Hals manages to give Coymans the look of unbothered insouciance, making his improbable expression of thoughtful self-regard a tad more credible.

We're constantly being cautioned by the anachronism cops not to read

backwards and trawl through Dutch art for the ancestry of modern
bourgeois informality. And if it's countervailing images of Calvinist
sobriety you want, you'll find enough dutiful sobersides in the show.
(Casteleyn and de Bancken turn up again in startling profile as Calvinist clones.) But the curators have been right, for the most part, to go for
the graceful flash, in the work, for instance, of the satiny Cornelisz
Verspronck, which briefly lit up the Low Countries and lingered to haunt
the archivists of European memory – Proust, Claudel, Zbigniew Herbert
– as the sorry old continent staggered from butchery to banality. Their
observation that the seventeenth-century Dutch painters, stereotyped
by Hollandophobes like Ruskin as incapable of rising above the
prosaically material, illuminated the poetry of daily life turns out to be
right. For a generation or two, the Dutch did move art on, and through
it ennobled quotidian humanity, investing two genres in particular –
landscape and portraiture – with the force of natural truth. That
happened because the kind of patrons – the Church and the court –
that were least interested in nature fell away as serious players in the
Dutch art market. Instead, there were just punters, you and me, tens
of thousands of us, who, if we were, say, in whalebone or the rye trade,
could afford a few guilders on a Van Goyen riverscape, or a bit more
on an image of ourselves, a *contrefeitsel* – us edited into grandeur, or
piety or marital devotion or cultured finesse, but us all the same.

Which is not to say that the painters on show at the National Gallery
– even Rembrandt – were free to do their thing any way they saw fit.
Some had been to Italy, and even those who hadn't (like Rembrandt)
were acutely conscious of the idealising strictures of classicism. At each
end of the spectrum there were those unbothered by the conflict – pure
Italianisers or pure parochialists – but the strongest were somewhere
in between and struggled not just with the conflicting demands of imaginative idealism and natural truth, but with a similarly exacting conflict
between the obligations of social form and the lure of vitality. In some
of the most powerful portraits, dynamism – the implication of movement – has the upper hand, even when the subject is actually standing
quite still. So Andries de Graaf, the potentate of Amsterdam money and
politics, in Rembrandt's slick version of him in 1639, gets the full
gentiluomo treatment, leaned against a truncated classical column, legs
elegantly contrapposto, his trim frame exuding silkily understated
nonchalance. But the billowing swathe of his right sleeve seems to take

on a rhetorical life of its own, as if blown by the Dutch breezes, imply-
ing the dynamic citizen-hero that Rembrandt presumed de Graaf
wished to personify. He may have presumed wrongly, as de Graaf was
one of those who expressed his unhappiness with the master's efforts.

The trade-off between grandeur and energy, monumentalism and
the life-force, became even more problematic when artists were commissioned (at a lucrative rate per head) to paint group portraits. Adding to
the challenge was the requirement, understood as built into the contract
(and famously ignored by Rembrandt in *The Night Watch*), to produce
acceptable individual likenesses at the same time as communicating the
collective ethos of the company. This is still a tough call for corporate
photographers (whether of company retreats or the school cricket team),
who do exactly what the most mechanical of the Dutch portraitists did
in the late sixteenth and early seventeenth centuries: line them up along
the picture plane till they run out of heads, or else stack them up in
terraced rows. To make the job still more complicated, group portraitists
had to register niceties of rank within the companies, so that at a militia banquet no one would confuse the captain with his lieutenants.
Unsurprisingly, the results were inhumanly wooden, an additive
arrangement that managed, in the memorable phrase of Rembrandt's
student van Hoogstraten, to make the sitters look as if they could all be
decapitated with one sweep of the sword.

There was one further non-negotiable requirement made of group
portraits. In addition to documenting the internal coherence of the
company, they also had to engage with those who stood before the paintings, blessing their good fortune that the fate of Amsterdam or Haarlem
was in such capable, confidently civic, inexhaustibly virtuous hands. The
great Austrian art historian Alois Riegl, in the work he wrote on Dutch
group portraiture in 1902, believed this two-way stretch to represent a
breakthrough in the genre, reconciling as it did the internal, but locked-
off, coherence of Italian art with the outwardly directed exuberant show
of the Netherlands. For the first time, so Riegl believed, the connection
between subject and beholder had been brought together in compositions that invited cross-frame attentiveness. That might be true, but it
was also a genre of inspired social fraud, for this bond between Them
and Us came into its own precisely at the moment when the regents of
the Dutch towns were becoming a caste of unaccountable oligarchs. Ah,
the whoppers that faux-naturalism commits.

The pictorial strain of doing all these things simultaneously, having multiple figures participate in a credible scene – chatting, drinking, charitably condescending to orphans or the aged, anatomising – at the same time that they bond with us, was a severe formal test of the available talent. The unavoidability of tables in banqueting pieces meant that figures who would otherwise be showing us their backs have to turn round or lean at forty-five degrees, a move not all group portraitists could convincingly bring off. In merely workmanlike hands the paintings either coagulate in a congested scrum or else fall apart. Hals and Rembrandt were not the only virtuosi who could pictorially multitask. Nicolas Pickenoy and Thomas de Keyser, both represented in the National Gallery show, were dependable workhorses in the genre, but their efforts to make the ensembles come credibly alive are tentative and always play second fiddle to their obligations to deliver likeness and rank. Even Hals, the supreme virtuoso of space and figure-juggling, could buckle under the strain. *The Meagre Company*, the Amsterdam militia piece in the show, is by two hands: Pieter Codde's as well as Hals's, because of a two-year row with the militia officers over whether Hals would finish it in Amsterdam or have it sent back to Haarlem where he was nursing, so he said, a bad leg. (They believed he was stalling for more money.) Exasperated, the company of crossbowmen turned to the local talent, Codde, who may have been in the militia himself. But Codde proved not much more dependable, spending a night in jail in irons along with the maid with whom he was conducting an affair. The double-painting breaks in two, precisely at its gallant centre figure. To the left is Hals's assured flash and dash; to the right, Codde's painfully laboured attempts at spontaneity. No wonder Codde never went near full-length figures again.

The two Rembrandt group portraits – *The Anatomy Lesson of Dr Nicolaes Tulp* of 1632 and *The Staalmeesters: Syndics of the Clothmakers' Guild* from three decades later (1662) – bookend his Amsterdam career and are both stupendous masterpieces that would alone be worth the price of admission. Throwing caution to the winds, Rembrandt bet on making collective dramas that embodied the ethos of the group, while not compromising either on likeness or the connection made from the painting to beholder. But the balance between attention within and attention beyond the frame could not be more different. In the Tulp, all eyes within the arrowhead arrangement of intense concentration are locked on to the professor-anatomist, who dissects the flexor muscles while demonstrating their action with his own free left hand. A single figure at the top of the pyramid, a pentimento revealing that originally he was hatted, looks at us while pointing to the criminal corpse in a concessionary gesture to memento mori. We anatomists are good, but let's not get above ourselves; we all end up like that. But Rembrandt, at least conceptually, has smuggled himself into the scene with the implication that the painterly dexterity needed to bring off the painted anatomy lesson was analogous to the demonstration itself.

The same covert self-insertion happens even more ingeniously in *The Staalmeesters*. It was long assumed that the drama of the scene, with one of the quality-control men rising to his feet, must have been in response to someone entering the chamber of their deliberations and, so Riegl thought, saying something that provoked a response. A cooler generation of critics thought this was so much fantastic projection and insisted this was 'just five gentlemen in black sitting for their portraits'. But four years ago, in a stunning insight, Benjamin Binstock argued that since Rembrandt's initial study drawings for a composition (which he later abandoned for the present arrangement) were made on account-book paper, it was very likely that those drawings were made in the very book we see depicted on their table, thus making artist and sitters true partners in the composition. The two figures, one of whom gestures at a page the other holds, are thus debating the making of art – this work of art.

This subtle visual essay in the collaboration between painter and patrons would have been just the thing to tempt Rembrandt as an exercise in vindication, since he was doubtless still smarting from his greatest fiasco four years before, when his painting of Claudius Civilis and the oath of the Batavians had been rejected by the regents of the town hall, leading him to mutilate the masterpiece. The connection between the two, Binstock further argued, is not just their similarity as groups around a table, but the fact that *The Staalmeesters* was painted on the rough herringbone canvas intended for a replacement for the repudiated Batavians. It gets even better. If the syndics are paying attention to the drawings in the book and then to someone in the room, that someone must surely be Rembrandt himself, so that the syndics are actively glancing from book to painter, taking in the changes he has made to the very scene that we now see. This is a gesture of co-option beyond anything Riegl could have imagined. The master has put himself in our shoes, and vice versa, in a quality-control drama of composition. The syndics are still checking the cloth, but it is in fact the weave of a canvas.

The secret of *The Staalmeesters* can stand for the peculiar genius of Dutch art at this moment in its history; one that wore its prodigious ingenuity lightly. What seems to be the most straightforward visual culture turns out to be a Chinese puzzle; an endless enquiry into the observation and representation of seen things and people. The Dutch were obsessed with nature all right, but very often, and with a confounding depth, that turns out to be the nature of picturing itself.

Rubens

Guardian, 22 October 2005

The thing about entitling your show *Master in the Making* is that it assumes a public already sold on just what it was that got made. But that couldn't be less true in the case of Rubens. In any given museum on any given Sunday, the empty gallery is invariably 'Flemish, 17th Century', where gatherings of massively upholstered nudes shift their dimpled weight opposite a collision of horses and carnivores, while by the door an obscure and pallid saint embraces his martyrdom with rolled-up eyes. Punters enter, take a quick gander, assume the proper expression of the glazed, the cowed, the awed and the baffled, and then accelerate towards the door marked 'Rembrandt'.

Which is a shame, since there are peculiar exhilarations to be found in Rubens that are reproduced nowhere else in baroque art: the strenuous manipulation of sensation, even profound emotion, through purely pictorial muscle; incomparable draughtsmanship; eye-popping colour. Not for Rubens the darkling palette and the stripped-down casting of Caravaggio (though he took much else from the master whose scandalously naturalistic *Death of the Virgin* he tried to buy for the Duke of Mantua), nor the introspective psycho-probes of Rembrandt. Rubens is all about meaty animal energy and high-voltage design, the play of what one seventeenth-century biographer called his *furia del pennello* – the fury of the brush.

But Rubens's surging line was never simply a virtuoso flourish. It was always put at the service of the controlled orchestration of bodies in motion. And as a colourist, no one since Titian and Giorgione came close. Whether he was confecting the most delicate flesh tones or throwing screaming vermilion at the canvas, it was with an eye to modelling forms rather than just filling them, thus making the ancient and tedious battle between *disegno* and *colore* moot.

Put all these gifts together and you get what contemporaries came to recognise as an incomparable marvel – the 'god of painting', as one of those recommending him for an Antwerp altarpiece in 1609 wrote. When he is operating at the height of his powers – as in the Courtauld oil sketch for the *Descent from the Cross*, or the adorably nipple-guzzling *Roman Charity* from the Hermitage – Rubens knocks the stuffing out of you, altering your breathing pattern.

So will this show at the National Gallery be that kind of conversion experience? If it turns out that way – and anyone who loves Rubens and wants to make the enthusiasm infectious must dearly hope so – it will be a triumph of art over concept. For the exhibition is very high-minded: it is so relentlessly bent on tracking each and every influence that went into the evolving artist's manner (though it omits some of those that meant most to him in his earliest days, such as the woodcuts of Holbein and Tobias Stimmer) that at times it seems in danger of disappearing up its own erudition. There are great and good things to be learned here about Rubens's compositional technique, but the over-whelming emphasis on process has tilted the choice of works towards those that can be unpacked as a cluster of compositional drawings, sketches and alternative versions. So we get two versions of *Susanna and the Elders*, neither sensational, rather than Rubens's self-portrait with his first wife, Isabella Brant – a hymn to conjugal fertility – which certainly is.

There's something airless about a show conceived and executed from a place so deeply internal to the academy of connoisseurs that you can practically smell the Chardonnay. In short supply (for the most part) is what, far more than this bit of Raphael or that bit of Michelangelo, actually made Rubens Rubens: what the painter would have called *wellust* and we – because English doesn't have a name for it (goodness, I wonder why?) – would call *joie de vivre*, a hungry instinct for the flesh.

I suppose you have to admire the unfashionable courage of an exhibition so single-mindedly cool to history or biography. I'm among the ranks of those who think the pendulum has swung a little too far away from formal analysis and towards historical context in recent years, so that the pure visual charge of art has sometimes been suffo-cated beneath data-bloated compendia of prices and patrons. No danger here, though, of stooping to vulgar context. No danger of letting the visitor know, for instance, that Rubens grew up in the most bloody theatre of religious war in Europe; that his father – a Protestant convert! – was imprisoned and nearly executed for an affair with the Princess of Orange; that his most important Antwerp teacher, Otto van Veen, criss-crossed confessional lines between Calvinist Leiden and militantly Counter-Reformation Antwerp, or that the painter's early life was a succession of personal, as well as painterly, dramas. Granted that the early *Battles of the Amazons* aren't despatches from the front; granted that they owe much to Leonardo's *Battle of Anghiari*. But isn't it interesting, nonetheless, to wonder whether the bristling cavalry that appears incongruously behind the classical figures don't owe something to Rubens's response to contemporary history?

This isn't just a quibble about wall captions. It's hard to think of a painterly career more tightly entwined with the great events of his time, as well as with the classical pedigree of his craft. And many of those events go straight to the heart of his 'making'. Rubens, after all, first became an artist in Antwerp – a city in which the legitimacy or illegitimacy of sacred image-making had driven men to violence. Nine years before Rubens was born, Calvinist iconoclasts had smashed statues, ripped paintings from the walls of the cathedral. There was a Catholic restoration, but before Rubens was apprenticed there had been another return of Protestant whitewash before it was finally and permanently restored to the Catholic Counter-Reformation. So the intense fervour of Rubens's religious painting is not just art, but spiritual weaponry. And his early career is as much a journey through a war zone as a prolonged exercise in the absorption of classicism.

In fact, the formative period in Italy from 1600 to 1608 is problematic in ways more fascinating than a genealogy of influences can possibly suggest. Like all aspiring artists in Rome, Rubens devoted himself to studying the sculptured riches of antiquity and duly drew the usual suspects: the *Farnese Hercules*, the *Laocoön*, the *Apollo Belvedere*. But the curators are right to insist on his brilliantly expressive amendments, all designed with a view to animating the sculpture. According to his eighteenth-century admirer Roger de Piles, Rubens warned against 'the effect of stone'. He undoubtedly agreed with his brother Philip who wrote to him: 'Away with that apathy which turns men not into human beings but rather into iron, into stone, a stone harder than the Niobic stone of mythology which overflowed with tears.' Rubens's work, then, became an articulate dialogue between classicism and naturalism.

It was also a decisive intervention in the stale dispute between what northern and southern painting were supposed to be. Most famously, Michelangelo, in a conversation with Francesco da Olanda, had let it be known that Flemish artists were tremendously good at painting trees and grass and peasants, the implication being that they were mere skilled illusionists rather than true artists possessed by the divinity of an idea. More than any other Flemish artist before him, Rubens would decisively overthrow the stereotype, establishing himself as a supreme history painter. Without ever apologising for his own gift for earthy naturalism (the sublime landscapist is already evident in detail from early works), he cast himself as a palette-toting humanist philosopher: the *pictor doctus*, the learned painter.

It's a pity, then, that the person most influential in this vocational reinvention – his brother Philip – is largely missing from the exhibition, notwithstanding the fact there are two group portraits that bring the brothers together, one of which happens to be a knockout masterpiece. For Rubens – unlike the archetypal caricature of the isolated melancholic genius (Michelangelo, Caravaggio, Salvator Rosa) – was the most sociable and fraternal of artists. In Rome he mixed with the likes of Dr Johannes Faber, who treated him for a bout of pleurisy and who was, among other things, a friend of Galileo, and a naturalist who had written works on dragons, serpents and parrots.

Fraternity and friendship for the Rubens brothers was not just a sentiment but a philosophy: a golden chain of connections binding like-minded men to each other, and to their teachers in the recent and remote past. The dazzlingly beautiful and moving *Four Philosophers*, painted in the year of Philip's premature death in 1611 and now in the Pitti Palace, anthologises all the deepest thoughts and emotions that made the young Rubens tick. In a classical niche is a vase of four tulips – two open, two shut – not just the northern bloom par excellence imported to the world of the classical south, but emblems of two living and two dead men. The dead are Philip and his teacher, the neostoic philosopher and philologist Justus Lipsius. But the chain stretches further, for behind Lipsius and beside the tulips is a bust then thought to be of Seneca, the stoic who counselled men to bend but not break under the worst that fate and history could bring your way: war, tyranny, plague and untimely death. In the end there would be redemption, so images of Roman antiquity and Roman Christianity (a marbled pillar and a view to the church of St Theodore on the Palatine) are paired, while behind the foreground figures stands the no longer quite so young Pieter Paul Rubens, swathed in black.

If the *Four Philosophers* couldn't make the journey from Florence to London, the irony is all the more acute because Rubens, as the exhibition makes clear, did a great deal of travelling before returning to fame and fortune in Antwerp in 1608. Hired by Gonzaga, the Duke of Mantua, to paint a gallery of 'beautiful women', he managed to get leave to go to Rome where he lived, eventually, with Philip in the northern artists' neighbourhood near the Piazza del Popolo. Every so often he would report back to Mantua, sometimes travelling with the Duke to Genoa. There he painted stunning full-length portraits of Genoese aristocratic women, one of which shines in this exhibition: it is a piece of unapologetic costume glamour, the sumptuously loaded brush creamily caressing its subject. Rubens made studies of the Genoese palazzi and obviously loved the flash opulence of a banking republic in which brassy glitz was made elegant by the trappings of classical grandeur. It was like home, but with pomegranates and parrots rather than cheese and ale.

However, official travel brought trials that would test Rubens's neo-stoical powers of resilience. Sent by the Duke of Mantua with a gift package for the King of Spain and his favourite, the Duke of Lerma (the usual thing – crystal vases full of rare perfume, horses so glossy and well bred they travelled inside their own carriages, original paintings and copies), Rubens endured the nightmare of unpacking the art to find it half-destroyed by damp. The Mantuan minister, who didn't much care for this wet-behind-the-ears envoy displacing him, suggested that he rush off a landscape or two the way Flemings did. Instead Rubens painted the *Heraclitus and Democritus* included in this show, not just to display his philosophical credentials, but – since one scowls and the other laughs at the twists of fate and follies of men – perhaps also as a wry piece of autobiography. The artist who one day would enjoy his reputation as the prince of painters and the painter of princes already knew how to handle power.

None of this would matter were he not also on his way to becoming a great history painter, which is to say the artist of spellbinding

altarpieces. Back in Rome, he was lucky with his timing. The Orato-
rian order was looking for someone to decorate their church. Annibale
Carracci had given up painting, Caravaggio was on the run and Guido
Reni was too untested. Rubens had his chance: he took several cracks
at it and, when it failed because of the intense reflectiveness of the
light, took out his neo-stoic manual of adaptability and did them something on slate instead.

Then he returned to Antwerp, breathing a little freer after the
conclusion of a truce with the Dutch. In two years he knocked off two
transcendent masterpieces – the *Raising of the Cross* and the *Descent
from the Cross* – which, if all other Rubens paintings were to go up
in flames, would still ensure his claim on the adulation of posterity.
Of course, those altarpieces, which are triptychs in the old Flemish
style, can't travel. But the National Gallery exhibition provides a rich
insight into the ways in which Rubens worked towards what became
the grand spiritual machines of the big altarpieces, by means of
preliminary studies, drawings, sketches and the 'pocketbook' in which
he encyclopaedically gathered images, organised by subject.

What is so striking about those multiple try-outs is the way in which
the improvisatory freedom – the rushing force of the pen and brush
– manage to be translated so completely to the large-scale works.
Rubens's hand flies, but the works are in the best sense weighty,
whether conveying the agonising upward heave of the cross – all sweat
and raw sinew – or the burden of the crucified Christ dropping onto
the blood-red caped figure of John the Evangelist.

The best passages are classicism fleshed out by naturalism: a barking hound, a winding cloth gripped in the teeth of someone at the
head of the cross; brutality and pathos, momentum and stillness held
in perfect equipoise. For these moments alone it's worth trekking
through the mediocre apprentice pieces, and hacking aside the under-
brush of scholarly interventions, to get to those stupendous instants
when, in front of his *Massacre of the Innocents* or *The Death of
Hippolytus*, your eyes widen, your pulse races and you agree that the
master has indeed been made.

Turner and the Drama of History

New Yorker, 24 September 2007

Poor old Turner: one minute the critics were singing his praises, the
next they were berating him for being senile or infantile, or both. No
great painter suffered as much from excesses of adulation and execration, sometimes for the same painting. *Slavers Throwing Overboard
the Dead and Dying – Typhoon Coming On* had, on its appearance at
the Royal Academy, in 1840, been mocked by the reviewers as 'the
contents of a spittoon', a 'gross outrage to nature', and so on. The critic
of *The Times* thought the seven pictures – including *Slavers* – that
Turner sent to the Royal Academy that year were such 'detestable
absurdities' that 'it is surprising the [selection] committee have
suffered their walls to be disgraced with the dotage of his experi-
ments'. John Ruskin, who had been given *Slavers* by his father and
had appointed himself Turner's paladin, not only went overboard in
praise of his hero, but drowned in the ocean of his own hyperbole. In
the first edition of *Modern Painters* (1843), Ruskin, then all of twenty-
four, sternly informed the hacks that 'their duty is not to pronounce
opinions upon the work of a man who has walked with nature three-
score years; but to impress upon the public the respect with which they
[the works] are to be received'.

The reasons for both the sanctification and the denunciation were
more or less the same: Turner's preference for poetic atmospherics over
narrative clarity, his infatuation with the operation of light rather than
with the objects it illuminated. His love affair with gauzy obscurity, his
resistance to customary definitions of contour and line, his shameless
rejoicing in the mucky density of oils or in the wayward leaks and
bleeds of watercolours – these were condemned as reprehensible self-
indulgence. Sir George Beaumont, collector, patron and, as he
supposed, arbiter of British taste, complained noisily of Turner's
'vicious practice' and dismissed his handling of the paint surface as

'comparatively, blots'. The caustic essayist William Hazlitt was especially troubled by Turner's relish of visual ambiguity: the sharp line
melting into the swimming ether. Contrary to Ruskin, Hazlitt thought
it was unseemly for Turner to fancy himself playing God, reprising
the primordial flux of Creation. Someone, Hazlitt commented, had
said that his landscapes 'were pictures of nothing and very like'.

But that is precisely what we *do* like, do we not? Turner's art of conjuring something from nothing, and then (unlike God) having the temerity
to deposit the working trace of that mysterious process on the canvas,
has made him a paragon for modernists. He seems to have understood
picturing as a collaborative process between the artist's hand and the
beholder's eye, in which the former laid down suggestive elements and
the imaginative observer assembled them in his mind to make a coherent subject. Sometimes he would help the process along, sometimes not.
But he was much taken by the indeterminacy of the exercise, by forms
that escaped resolution. The sobriety of the hard edge became, one has
to think, a sign of conceptual banality, a weakness in the mind's eye. For
him the purest form, and one that he repeatedly returned to, was also
the most naturally unstable: the rainbow.

Taken to task by an American buyer for the indistinctness of the
very beautiful 1832 painting *Staffa, Fingal's Cave* – Hebridean cliffs
veiled by streaming rain and sea spray – Turner, through an intermediary, begged the American's pardon, for 'indistinctness is my fault'.
But, as that vice turned – for his modernist apostles – into a virtue,
the script changed, and Turner was apocryphally made over into the
defiant independent who had wanted the American to know that
'indistinctness is my *forte*'.

It's often said that Turner had only two true subjects: the anatomy
of light and what Ruskin nicely called the 'palpitating' vitality of paint
itself. His learned preoccupation with optics, the struggles to analyse
and represent the diffusion of light, fathered a poetry of radiance, and
grandfathers him into the ancestry of Impressionism; his emotively
weighty manipulation of pigment did the same for Expressionism. So
it is the Turners that most affronted the stuffy Victorians, mired as
they were in anecdotal sentimentality and ponderous literalism, with
which we most easily identify: pictures big with prophetic courage,
the inkling of an alternative life for paint. With Turner, so this story
goes, the story doesn't matter; it's the opera of the drenching colours,

the unloosed play of the brush, the gouge of his untrimmed thumb-nail scoring a groove through the sticky pigment – that's his claim to immortality. Why should he give a fig about all those gods and heroes and Scriptures and battles?

Except that he did, obstinately and passionately, as the National Gallery's show in Washington blazingly demonstrates. The procession of phenomenal narrative pictures that constitute its core makes it clear that we do Turner no favours by pinning the tinny little medal of First Modernist on him. Subject matter meant a great deal to him, and if claiming him for the poetry or the physics of light blinds us to the seriousness with which he yearned to be Britain's first great history painter, he would not have thanked us. What, I believe, he wanted us to see was that, as far as the monumental oils were concerned, all his radical formal experimentation – the trowellings and the 'mortary' quality of the paint surface that his critics complained of, the scrap-ings and rubbings and stainings – was at the service of those grand narratives. It's correct to think of light as his subject, but when he was most ambitious, light was a protagonist in an epic narrative of creation and destruction – an Anglo-Zoroastrian burn-out.

Regulus, for example, tells a gruesome tale probably drawn from Oliver Goldsmith's *Roman History*, which Turner had in his library. The tragic hero Marcus Atilius Regulus was a Roman consul-general who, captured by the Carthaginians in the First Punic War, was released on parole and sent home to persuade his countrymen to sue for peace. Instead, Regulus urged the Senate to fight on, but, being an honourable gent, returned to Carthage to face the music. To punish him for violating their trust, his captors cut off his eyelids and stood him in the noon sun to go blind. Then they locked him in a barrel with the nails pointing inwards to finish the job.

Turner originally painted the picture in 1828 in Rome, where he took a lot of abuse for histories in which you couldn't make head nor tail of the action. Stung by the criticism, Turner shelved the paint-ing until, nine years later, he sent it to the winter show of the British Institution, in Pall Mall. There, according to contemporary witnesses, he confounded his peers by coating the picture with lumps of flake-white: 'He had two or three biggish hog [bristle] tools to work with and with these he was driving the white into all the hollows, and every part of the surface. This was the only work he did, and it was the finishing stroke.' At the end of the attack, the sun, a fellow Academician reported, was a protruding disc of pigment like a 'boss on a shield'. Even though the white has yellowed somewhat, we can still see this intervention as an enactment of what happened to Regulus: the scalding of the retina, the light that switches off vision – white-out. Viewers complained that Regulus was nowhere to be found, but although there is a characteristically perverse miniature figure that might conceivably answer to the tragic hero, it's more likely that Turner simply virtualised him into the murderous glare. That heavy-handed business with the white pigment wasn't just a proto-Expressionist performance, but a calcu-lated fit between manner and matter.

For Turner, light was not just the enabler of vision. Especially in his histories, he conceived of it as a dramatic actor: the vehicle of emotive as well as optical illumination; the agency of romantic disori-entation or, in its absence, the demon of eclipse. And all these states of vision were personal and local, the spectacles of his own story. For Turner, the ultimate subject was always the history of Britain, and he felt that subject in his marrow. Yes, he travelled, relentlessly. Yes, there was Venice and Mount Cenis, and the Loire and the Alps, the Rhine and the Rhône and the Seine. But he always came home; at heart he was a self-conscious British patriot and, more than that, a Londoner, born and bred a five-minute walk from the Thames.

He was born on St George's Day, 23 April, celebrated as the birth-day of both Shakespeare and the Prince of Wales. It was the spring of 1775, the week of the 'shot heard round the world' at Lexington Green. So he came to maturity when Britain, shaken by the American debacle, turned to territorial memory for a romantically reinvented bond of nationhood. Geography was history and history was destiny. The young Turner, tramping the countryside in the 1790s, often sketched or painted in watercolours Gothic ruins or vaults where balladeers imagined ancient canticles being moaned in the moon-beams, mossy limestone crypts housing the sleep of ancestors: Ewenny Priory, Tintern Abbey, Stonehenge. The Napoleonic Wars triggered a burst of antiquarianism; greaves and helmets long rusted shut were extracted from dung-floored barns, given a lick of grease and polish, and reassembled to stand guard in the manorial hall.

Commercially astute, Turner knew that there was a ready market for this fabulous junk, but, in any case, he loved it himself. When, in 1802, it was time for a submission that would mark his acceptance as a full member of the Royal Academy, he offered a bardic romance: Dolbadern Castle, in Wales, the prison of the Welsh prince Owain ap Gruffydd, who had been locked up by his brother Llywelyn. The ruin was just a plain circular tower squatting on a modest hillock, but Turner gave it the full Romantic treatment, upping the altitude, lowering the point of view, backlighting the tower and setting it on a plinth of rock, crowned with scudding clouds. As in *Regulus*, the tragic hero of Dolbadern became virtualised, personified this time in craggy stone, not blinding light. Turner was interested not in the deeds of the heroes, but, rather, in the ways in which their memory might be visually transmitted to posterity. It was as though mere flesh and blood, however handsomely booted and spurred, weren't quite sufficient, and neither was the art that purported to celebrate them – better to embody them in rocks and ruins.

His approach to war, too, was radically unheroic. The norm for battle pieces was to memorialise the genius of command and the gallantry of the ranks. Turner had tried this, in 1800, with an innocuous version of the battle of Seringapatam, in southern India, where serried lines of scarlet coats advance on the distant citadel of the Sultan of Mysore. But what he really liked, in common with much of the British public, was a good disaster. Around 1805, a series of calamities – the Plagues of Egypt, the destruction of Sodom, shipwrecks, the panic-stricken and the prostrate – begin to populate his large dark, thunderstruck canvases. In all these gloomy efforts, the human figures are limp, almost invertebrate, their faces summarised in a few caricatural strokes and their bodies weirdly attenuated, as if in a new Mannerism. Turner was not, as sometimes charged, an incompetent figure painter. He had spent years in academic drawing and in his early career had produced conventionally modelled studies. But when it came to the big oils he chose to stylise them, as if in self-conscious repudiation of the classical tradition. (And here it does seem legitimate to see that rejection inaugurating something that would end up with Matisse's *La Danse* or *Les Demoiselles d'Avignon*.) For Turner, the distortions were the agents of narrative: the representation of the figure as victim, the disarticulated plaything of history's mischief.

In the case of the spectacular action painting *The Battle of Trafal-*

gar, Turner did his homework, going to Sheerness to see the hulk of Nelson's flagship, HMS *Victory*, and carefully sketching its splintered beams. But he threw the research away to compose, in 1806, an astounding enactment of the chaos of war at sea, using a viewpoint high up in the mizzenmast shrouds, where, although ostensibly on the British man-of-war, the beholder can as easily imagine himself in the roost of the French sharpshooter who kills Nelson. The entanglement of the ships of the line, like so many lumbering dinosaurs locked in belligerent slaughter, is described through an inchoate massing of sails, each impossible to connect to any vessel in particular. It's a maritime traffic jam, a smoke-choked pile-up with nowhere to go, no visible stretch of *sea*! And, in case people weren't already confused, Turner made matters worse by collapsing two discrete consecutive episodes into one: the French surrender, indicated by the tricolour laid on the deck of Nelson's flagship, and the canonical climax of Trafalgar, Nelson dying, stretched out amid the huddle of his grieving officers. *Victory*'s victory becomes pyrrhic, the tragedy embittering the triumph.

The Duke of Wellington fared no better than Nelson. In 1817, Turner, after visiting the site of the bloody victory over Napoleon, at Waterloo, chose instead to paint the harrowing aftermath: a nocturnal carpet of corpses lit by the sulphurous glare of a rocket, with grieving wives and sweethearts, some of them carrying infants, searching desperately through the human debris. It is a return to the distraught Niobes of the Greeks, the wailing woman as personification of calamity.

Tragic poundings – fires that cleansed, extinctions that were the prelude to rebirths – became the great theme of Turner's mature epics. It was as though the life cycle of the man born on Shakespeare's birthday were an emblem of England's own fate: history written on the body. Turner was tormented by asthmatic wheezes and joint pains, for which he took the narcotic herb thorn apple (consumed daily through the goop that accumulated in the bowl of his pipe). As middle age advanced, he felt a steady drumbeat of decease, the winnowing of those closest to him. In 1825, his patron and first great collector, the Yorkshireman Walter Fawkes, radical in politics and hospitable in character, died in debt; then, in 1829, Old Dad, whom the son had shamelessly exploited as factotum and workhorse, but who had also

been his bosom friend; then the heavily landed connoisseur and collector (of women as well as of pictures) George Wyndham, the Third
Earl of Egremont, who, after Fawkes's death, had made Turner his
house artist, giving him lodging and studio space. In return, he
painted, rather ambiguously, a series of glimmering rectangular views
of house and park and some of the Earl's business enterprises – such
as the Chichester Canal and the Brighton Chain Pier – designed to be
set in the panelled walls of the dining room. Two of those paintings
Turner elongated, the fish-eye vision emptying the frame and lend-
ing the space a sombre fatefulness. The canal is aligned ninety degrees
to the picture plane, and, on it, a little man hunched in a coat, a
battered hat on his head, sits in a rowboat fishing – one of Turner's
favourite pursuits – as a black-sailed brig moves ominously towards
us, an allegorical self-portrait smuggled into the commission. A note
of elegy seems to hang over Turner's work for Egremont. After going
to the Earl's funeral, in 1837, he painted one of the house's great rooms
in wild disarray, as if the aristocratic world that the Earl embodied
had been attacked by an invasion of light.

Such alterations exercised the most strenuous minds of early Victorian Britain. Many of them, like the architect A. W. N. Pugin and
Thomas Carlyle, eulogised what they imagined to be a lost, devotional,
architecturally Perpendicular, Christian Albion and waxed wrathful
about the materialist hell of the Age of Machinery, with its philistine
utilitarianism and worship of what Ruskin, the sherry merchant's son,
called, contemptuously, 'the goddess of Getting-On'. In an implausible overreading of *The Goddess of Discord Choosing the Apple of
Contention in the Garden of the Hesperides,* Ruskin recruited Turner
as an anti-capitalist, but the truth is that his mills were usually neither
dark nor satanic. His sketch of the town of Dudley, made around 1830,
when the possibility of an English revolution hung in the air along
with bituminous fumes, gives obvious prominence to the emblems of
an older world – church and castle barely holding their own amid the
chimneys. Consuming fires, Turner seems to have thought, were just
the medium through which the country had to pass to come to a new
national life.

When the Houses of Parliament caught fire, on the night of 16 October 1834, Turner, along with a throng of fellow Londoners, rushed to
see the spectacular inferno. Hiring a boat, he bobbed back and forth,

riding the tide, at Westminster Bridge. There had been no foul play, but, since a Parliamentary Reform Act had been passed just two years before, amid loudly voiced fears that, unless it was legislated, the kingdom might, like France in 1830, go down in bloody revolution, the relationship between rulers and ruled was in perilous play. A dominating feature of the two *Burning of the Houses of Lords and Commons* paintings that resulted – one now in Cleveland and one in Philadelphia – is the crowds jamming the embankment and Westminster Bridge, watching, fixedly, the cremation of 'Old Corruption'.

This is another authentic first – the painting of the People. Turner was putting on canvas Burke's definition of representative government as a contract between the past and the present. The past is embodied, as if in a Gothic allegory, in the spectacle of the purifying inferno. In the Philadelphia painting, Turner has augmented this feeling of a political altarpiece by turning Westminster Bridge into a structure that seems cut from alabaster rather than limestone, and appears to liquefy into the flame-tinted water at its far end. But the two pictures also look forward to the great issue of the nineteenth century: the test of popular legitimacy. In the Cleveland painting (the two are united in the National Gallery show), Turner broadens the river so that he can give prominence to the rapt masses in the foreground, dramatising their distance from the burning palace of Westminster. One figure, enigmatically, holds up a sign that reads, simply, 'NO'. This does not make Turner some sort of socialist. It is still Britain, and auspicious unrevolutionary stars are twinkling above the Thames. But the poetics of power did absorb him. And although we often think of Turner as the lyricist of the empty landscape, the truth is that the other Turner, the denizen of the London alleys and pubs, was truly Hogarth's heir, with an unerring instinct for the crowd as social animal.

Every so often, that public-minded, historically fretful Turner thought that Britain should confront ugly truths. The doomed *Slavers* was conceived in just such a proselytising spirit and timed for 1840, the year an abolitionist congress was to be convened in London. But Turner's ambition for a history painting that would achieve, through the medium of marine catastrophe, a moral reckoning had been rehearsed around 1835.

He was, once again, playing with fire, and although that 1835 picture is in a radically incomplete state, it's the skeleton of a masterpiece. Flecked with gobs of phosphorescent cinders raining down from the sky into a storm-churned sea, the huge composition was traditionally given the title *Fire at Sea*. For years, it was underrated and underread as a rough sketch. It is in the National Gallery show, where visitors will find it described as *Disaster at Sea*, which is right, but not right enough. Fifteen years ago the scholar Cecilia Powell recognised that the work depicted an actual calamity, or, rather, a crime: the sinking of the *Amphitrite*, in September 1833. Powell made one simple, vital connection that hadn't been noticed before: the frantic figures wrapped about the broken mast and fallen spars of the rapidly sinking wreck are all women and small children. The *Amphitrite* was a convict ship transporting female prisoners and their infants to the penal settlement in New South Wales. Driven off course by a storm in the Channel, it ran aground near Boulogne and began to break up. It was close enough for appalled French witnesses to offer assistance, but the captain, evidently a stickler for the rulebook, declined, on the ground that he had no authority to land his charges anywhere but their Antipodean prison. He battened down the hatches to prevent just such an escape. In desperation, the women broke through, but to no avail. Though one Frenchman actually swam out to the ship with a line, all of the more than 100 women and children drowned. Three crew survived.

The atrocity was widely reported in the press. Ballads were written and sung about it. Turner could not possibly have missed it, and he responded with a painting of timeless tragic power: the *Guernica* of nineteenth-century British art. The bodies are a curling ribbon of writhing, pathetic, naked *women*, arms flung out to the babes who slip from them into the sea for which − in the transparent film of water washing over a spar − the painter deployed all the prodigious gifts of the illusionism he was thought to have abandoned for poetically pretentious freedom. Turner's bodies are already bobbing flotsam. They are helpless, ugly, manic, and they tear us apart. Our mere witness seems to implicate us in the enormity of the cruelty, the proper effect of all great histories from Caravaggio to Picasso. The pity of the thing is relentless, because of the phenomenal coherence of Turner's draughtsmanship, the violence of the storm and the desperation of the victims − who should be flying away, centrifugally, but instead are sucked into the whorl of the merciless elements.

We'll never know why Turner never finished or exhibited the painting. Perhaps he did finish it and this is it. At any rate, the *Amphitrite*
was among the 300 or so oils left in his studio when he died, in 1851,
and so it was included in his bequest to the nation. Turner was the first
painter in the history of art to give his work to the public, rather than
to a church or a patron – and this, too, speaks to the intensity of his
devotion to the cultural life of the British people. Ruskin was at least
right about that.

In the century and a half since Turner was buried, in St Paul's
Cathedral, the British have loved him with a grateful ardour that has
nothing to do with his place in the genealogy of modernism and everything to do with the poetic visualisation of their history. The year
before last, BBC Radio 4 asked listeners to vote for the greatest painting – from anywhere in the world, any time. The hot candidate was,
unsurprisingly, Constable's *Hay Wain*, that carthorse idyll by a plashy
stream that seems to preserve the English countryside, in all its cow-
parsley, humming-bee, *Wind in the Willows* summery splendour for
ever and ever, amen. But the winner was Turner's *The Fighting
Temeraire Tugged to Her Last Berth to Be Broken Up* (1838), a painting not about the embalming of the British past, but about its
unsentimental coupling with the future.

Although the sky over the Thames is saturated with a nectarine
sunset that seems to mourn the passing of the timber veteran of
Trafalgar, reduced to a pallid phantom (Turner, as always, taking liberties), its masts and furled sails are restored as it is tugged to Beatson's
breakers' yard, at Rotherhithe. Thackeray, who adored the painting,
assumed that Turner had cast the tugboat as the gnomic villain of
the piece, dragging the valetudinarian to its last indignity. But Turner
– especially in his own last years – was not at all hostile to the incoming empire of technology. Quite the opposite: he believed that the
speeding train or the chugging paddle steamer could be turned into
a visual lyric that married time with motion. For that matter, since
the two vessels are sailing upstream, and thus westwards, the vermilion sky behind them, in the east, may actually be a sun*rise*, a fanfare
for the future, not a dirge for the past. That's the wonderful thing about
being British: you can never really tell which is which.

James Ensor at MoMA

Financial Times, 3 July 2009

Oh BELGIUM, man! was Zaphod Beeblebrox's oath of choice when his two heads were pushed right to the edge. But if *The Hitchhiker's Guide to the Galaxy* meant the curse to suggest rain-soaked tedium relieved by stabs of edgy peculiarity, it got Belgium wrong, the tedium bit anyway. This is the country that gave us Bosch and Magritte and, right in between, the feverish thing that was James Ensor. By turns lurid, lyrical, mysterious, sophomorically satirical, intimate, raucous, cerebral, macabre, tender, narcissistic, suicidal, iconoclastic, reverent, supersaturated and washed out – and that's just in the first fifteen years of a half-century career – Ensor is the figure no conscientious chronicler of the birth pangs of modernism can afford to overlook, but also the one whom no one has any idea what to do with.

So good for New York's Museum of Modern Art (MoMA) for giving him the first major show in a very long time, even though the curatorial effort to plug him into the genealogy of modern art turns out to be a futile enterprise. He's catnip for the ism-hunter, since he could do the lot. So the wall-captions and the catalogue assiduously nail this and that picture to the ism *du jour* – Impressionism, Expressionism, realism, surrealism, slathery tachism and pretentious symbolism. But his sensibility was as twitchy as a bat, swooping out of the air and vacuuming up whatever took his fancy on any particular Tuesday.

His whole career, at least the interesting two decades of it, was one long carnival guffaw at the higher seriousness of modernism. You can almost hear the kitschily raffish self-portrait – Rubens on absinthe, crowned by a Quentin Crisp snapbrim trilby, primroses bursting from the hatband – squeal with giggles from the wall at the solemnity of the installation. *Oh Belgium, man!*

And not just Belgium, but Ostend: the place you went to for marine calm when Brussels was just too much fun. Which is what Ensor did after a short stint at the École des Beaux-Arts, where he rehearsed a lifetime's habit of getting on everyone's nerves.

King Leopold's Brussels, grown fat on a deadly combination of voracious African imperialism, Liegeois coal and local waffles, was a pincushion for the avant-garde. Its luminaries – the group who called themselves 'Les Vingt' and their critic-patriarch Emile Verhaeren – were alert to anything, within and without their borders, that would shred the overstuffed upholstery of bourgeois academicism. It was Verhaeren who wrote the first gushing review of Van Gogh and who wanted Ensor to exhibit with Les Vingt. He became one of their number, but was never a team player. So in 1880, when antsy modernists were hungering for a spell in the South Seas or the boulevards of Paris, Ensor returned to his native town of Ostend, from which he would seldom budge for the seven decades of the rest of his life.

Which is not to say that Ostend was a dull backwater of a middling province of a Lilliputian kingdom. It boasted a small-time bohemia, oompah and pickled herring on the promenades, chalky Pierrots and madcap Punchinellos; it had beer and bathing huts and curio shops, one of which was owned by Madame Ensor, James's doughty Flemish mother. His father, not so doughty, was an Englishman of means who no longer had them, and had wanted to plant a theatrical sense of himself between the salt marshes and the slate-coloured sea. In their artist son, the two parental tempers – morose and exuberant – bounced off each other, with mood-swinging results.

The twenty-year-old James moved into the loft above the novelty shop and plundered its inventory, especially its grinning or wailing masks, to brilliantly histrionic effect. It wasn't an especially profound or original insight, the Ensorian perception that the grimacing carnival mask might express the Real Persona while the flesh-and-blood face was merely the mask of social convenience, but only Goya and Daumier had made the masquerade such a penetrating genre of psychological portraiture.

Did the obsession with masks actually produce compelling art? The answers in the MoMA show will surprise anyone who thinks they know the mischievous Monsieur Ensor well. *The Scandalised Masks* (1883) is a throwback to the seventeenth-century genre painting of Adriaen Brouwer (for all his antic iconoclasm, Ensor was a great archivist of the Netherlandish tradition), with the startling difference that instead of two *boers* in a tavern, a half-doped snout-nose looks up to see a clogged and bonneted woman, sinister in dark glasses, coming through a door, clasping a wind instrument. Her gesture, also drawn from low-life painting, is unsubtle, the invitation more ominously castrating than seductive.

Much dalliance with intimiste Impressionism follows, with Ensor freckling his light through the tufty woollen gloom of Ostend parlours. But one stunningly weird picture, called, as if to provoke the burghers, *Lady in Distress* (1882), promises something unsavoury: a Sickert of the dank seaside. She's not so much In Distress as completely out of it: eyes half-closed, body sunk into the feather-bedding as if awaiting a shroud. One window is draped with a sallow fabric; at another, the curtain is pulled back, its swag hooked to the wall. But the light coming through the exposed pane is painted with a clotted flake-white impasto, while the backlight behind the closed drape is suggested by the thinnest of paint stains, scraped back with palette knife and brush handle. Light is dark and dark is light. Welcome to Ensor's *univers pervers*.

Occasionally Ensor takes it easy, and the results are breathtaking. The enormous *Rooftops of Ostend* (1884) is Turner meets Jacob van Ruisdael, yet somehow translated into an idiom that was all Ensor's own. The sky, cerulean and pink, creamy and dove-grey, covers seven-eighths of the canvas, and is passionately worked with the palette knife and broad brush, while the crowded roofs below, in their contrapuntal dance of planes, anticipate Cubist townscapes.

But Ensor didn't give a hoot for where he was supposed to stand in the face-off between tradition and modernity. Another revelation of the show is the enormous, monumental charcoal drawings, with their multiple quotations from Ensor's art-god, Rembrandt. Ostensibly scenes from the New Testament, they are set by the artist in a Belgian carnival, complete with high-hatted bandsmen. And if the loss of the Son of God amid the seething throng seems a modern caprice, Ensor knew very well that it looked back to swarming pictures by Bosch and Bruegel, in which the indifferent brutality of the crowd engulfs the redemptive presence of the Saviour.

Ensor himself never really felt redeemed, and after a while the jokes in which genre figures, and his own self-portraits, are replaced by skeletons wear even thinner than the rattle of bones. His mind was too frantic, its demonic energy never crystallising around a painterly language in which form and content marry without acts of self-conscious main-force. He means to jangle, but in the end the cacophony enervates rather than illuminates.

Every so often, though, there are treats when he seems to reach back to the boy who must have watched the waves roll in to the beach: a little version of the Battle of Waterloo, with numberless toy-soldier riders hurled against each other, and, at the other extreme, a cartoon-ish beach scene, complete with smiley-faced Mr Sun, an array of bathing huts, the dip and bounce of beach bums, two men snogging in the foreground – the whole 'ooh missus' malarkey of the thing a little cartwheel of pictorial joy. And you think, this may not be vanguard art, but it has the quick of life in it.

Rembrandt's Ghost

New Yorker, 26 March 2007

In April 1973, the month that Picasso died, he was asked to choose an image to be used as a poster for a show of recent work at the Palace of the Popes, in Avignon. He picked *The Young Painter*, an oil sketch he'd done a year earlier, at the age of ninety – a vision of his dewy beginnings, not his bitter end. The look is naive and apparently artless, but the hand that draws it is heavy with memories, not just of a Barcelona boyhood, but of the archive of painting. The apple-cheeked youth recalls another young painter at the outset of his career, the twenty-three-year-old Rembrandt, picturing himself and his calling around 1629, in a panel not much bigger than this page. The faces are unmistakably similar: gingerbread-clownish beneath a wide-brimmed hat; snub nose; eyes stylised as ogling black holes, as if drawn by a child. The captured moment, in both images, is solemn; the young men pause before their work, brushes in hand, as if locked in a creative trance. A raking light, the illumination of an idea, strikes their faces. 'I don't paint what I see,' Picasso was given to saying. 'I paint what I know.' Rembrandt, his picture tells us, felt the same way: the mind instructing the hand.

It was an unlikely pairing – the cerebral modernist who had made a point of expelling sentiment from painting going wistful over the master whose every brush mark was loaded with emotion. But the fixation was real. The shelves in Picasso's studio at Mougins, in the South of France, were packed with Rembrandtiana, including all six volumes of Otto Benesch's edition of the drawings. And though Picasso could not have seen Rembrandt's little panel at first hand (it was in Boston), he must have plucked that archetypal image of setting forth from one of his books. Radical remaker of art though he was, Picasso always balanced his iconoclastic instincts with a compulsive historicism. In 1936, he had agreed to become absentee director of the Prado, while Madrid was under fascist siege. Constantly measuring himself for admission to the pantheon, Picasso evidently felt that taking down the masters also meant taking them on, and in his time he had mixed it up with, among others, Grünewald, Poussin, Cranach, Velázquez, Goya and El Greco. At the end, though, it was Rembrandt of whom, according to his friend and biographer Pierre Cabanne, he spoke 'ceaselessly'. The haunted self-portraits of those final years, all stubble and cavernous eye sockets, were surely prompted by the series of pitilessly truthful mirror images that Rembrandt executed in his last decade: a dispassionate scrutiny of time's ruin recorded in heavy jowls and pouches. Occasionally, as in the self-portrait as St Paul (in the Rijksmuseum), Rembrandt arched his eyebrows in an expression of quizzical self-recognition, the chastened sinner who might yet imagine redemption. Picasso's face-making, on the other hand, is showy with self-contempt: so many glaring skulls.

Rembrandt first appeared in Picasso's visual imagination in the 1930s, as Janie Cohen points out in her essay 'Picasso's Dialogue with Rembrandt's Art', in the volume *Etched on the Memory*, at a time when the Spanish artist was making an ambitious 'suite' of 100 prints for the dealer Ambroise Vollard. Two qualities in Rembrandt's print-making had sparked a sense of comradeship across the centuries. First, there was the experimental freedom that Rembrandt allowed himself – sketching ideas on the etching plate and then reworking them, adding other designs, sometimes related and sometimes not – so that the overall image developed organically. A 'trial' etching might have a face, a tree and a single eye (his eye) on the same plate, and Picasso imagined this multiplicity of visions as an antecedent for his collage play with discontinuous fragments of objects. But Picasso also identified with Rembrandt's complicated relationship with his models, making them objects, indistinguishably, of aesthetic curiosity and erotic possession.

Picasso's riffs on Rembrandt are all about lusty looking; in his version of Rembrandt's *Jupiter and Antiope*, he casts himself as the horned *Faun Unveiling a Sleeping Woman*, one hand lifting a bedsheet, the other reaching for a voluptuous breast. Rembrandt's original is in fact a bolder and weirder exercise in erotic inspection, the god in faun form leaning over the woman's gently exposed nakedness with an expression of disconcerting benevolence. His gaze, emphasised by a touch of deep-scored drypoint at the eyes, is concentrated entirely on the darkly cross-hatched groin, whose details Rembrandt (after Titian, the greatest soft-porn tease in art) has made tantalisingly invisible. But it's Rembrandt who takes most pains to wipe any hint of the ornamental from his nude. Antiope's chubby chin is lifted, her mouth slightly opened as if in a snore, snouty nostrils upturned, an arm wrapped about her head exposing tufts of armpit hair. Picasso, too much the fastidious classicist to linger on armpits, merely summarises the sleeper's face, in the manner of his countless nude paintings of his mistress Marie-Thérèse Walther.

These two obsessions – experimental print-making and the gaze of disingenuous desire – came together at one serendipitous moment. In 1934, while Picasso was preparing a plate with multiple profiles of Marie-Thérèse, the etching ground cracked. According to his friend and dealer Daniel-Henri Kahnweiler, Picasso improvised around the accident precisely the way Rembrandt was thought to have done in his free-form 'sketchpad' plates, some of which anthologised different images of his wife, Saskia. 'I said to myself: it's ruined,' Picasso noted. 'I'm going to do any old thing on it. I began to scribble. It became Rembrandt.' The doodle did turn into Rembrandt's face, though in all likelihood it wasn't quite the pure accident that Picasso made it out to be. Because his plate of the Marie-Thérèses recalls the Saskias, he was probably, at some level, thinking of Rembrandt before he'd even begun. But, once Rembrandt was summoned, he and Picasso became one and the same. Rembrandt's face on that etching grafts him in the prime of his smiling self-congratulation – complete with curly whiskers and feathered beret – onto the puffier, double-chinned visage of Picasso's own middle age.

Looking at these 'Rembrandt' prints a few years later, Picasso drily commented to his mistress Françoise Gilot that 'every painter takes himself for Rembrandt'. He was right. No artist in the Western canon, not Raphael, not Michelangelo, not even Goya, has been so compulsively co-opted as heroic alter ego as Rembrandt. Painters like Turner, Delacroix and Van Gogh, who self-consciously saw themselves as Rembrandt's apostles, believed that he, more than any other artist, had modelled forms with light and colour rather than with line. The luminous shimmer of paint, not the hard-edged purity of classical sculpture, was their lodestar, and no one, they thought, had liberated its radiance quite like Rembrandt.

There was, to be sure, a good deal of romantic projection involved in seeing Rembrandt as the patriarch of painterly integrity. The poignant trajectory of his biography, from precocious swagger to humiliation, satisfied a sentimental craving for punished temerity. And, while many of the early stories were fanciful (for example, his self-taught simplicity, when in fact he attended both Latin School and, briefly, Leiden University), the documented facts played directly into a narrative of heroic, if not reckless, innovation: the miller's son, mugging in the mirror to get the passions right for his history paintings, and plucked from obscurity by the Prince of Orange's talent scout; the dizzy ascent to fame and riches in money-drunk 1630s Amsterdam, the supermarket of the world; the free-spending owner of prime real estate, dressing himself and his wife in morally dubious poses; a painter who pushed conventions, especially in portraiture and group portraiture; the crash into insolvency and the death of Saskia, of children, of Hendrickje, the companion of his later years; the man, in his sixties, staring again into the mirror, the mugging gone and only humble self-recognition left.

But for every romantic who saw in this career an original free spirit, the inventor of *l'art pour l'homme,* there were severe classicists who condemned his naturalism as self-indulgence. They despised his juvenile relish for the seamier side of the human condition: urinating beggars and babies, cellulite-heavy nudes; copulating lovers in a bed, a fornicating monk in a cornfield. They detested the way he rubbed their noses in a gleeful mixture of the sacred and the profane. Was it really necessary to have a dog defecate in front of the Good Samaritan? It was precisely this contempt for academic propriety – and for the sacred hierarchy of the genres, with its disdain for importing the rawness of daily life into the refined matter of history paintings – which made Rembrandt a hero to the romantics.

The default mode of modern writing about art is to despise any notion of singularity as so much overheated genius-fetishism. So the idea that Rembrandt was the original democrat of subject matter – a maverick who flouted convention to follow the bidding of his muse, and who did push the boundaries of what painting (or, for that matter, print-making) could do well beyond any contemporary conventions –

is dismissed as sentimental anachronism. Perhaps that accounts for the fact that, during the quatercentenary commemorations of his birth, last year, so little attention was paid to what might be called 'the Rembrandt afterglow'. In this coolly empirical view, wary of perpetuating platitudes – such as his supposed indifference to the 'rules' of art, his rough way with some patrons, the self-consciously dramatic manipulation of his paint – the historical Rembrandt was attentive to his patrons and gregarious rather than misanthropic, and abided by the rules of art far more than he sought to violate them. But Gary Schwartz's superb new *The Rembrandt Book* makes plain the disputes between Rembrandt and his patrons over the displeasing difference between what they thought they had commissioned and the delivered work. So it may well be the case that Rembrandt the sociable conformist is more mythical than Rembrandt the 'heretic' (as one of his classicist critics puts it). It has never been in doubt that he wilfully offended classical principles of decorum. Fifty years ago, Seymour Slive's *Rembrandt and His Critics* analysed the strong responses to Rembrandt in the name of upholding the norms of classical decorum. Classicism's first principle decreed that only the representation of ideal forms could give art universal authority, while Rembrandt, these critics asserted, believed the opposite: that only a shockingly unedited version of natural truth could serve art's highest purpose.

This makes Picasso's attraction to Rembrandt even odder, for the Spanish artist was far more of a classicist than a Romantic. Picasso's work of the 1920s and '30s is populated by drawn and painted meditations on the endurance of classicism, and no one performed exercises in the economy of classical line with more elegant finesse. But Picasso was a classicist with a difference: an artist capable of recalling the elements of ideal form precisely in order to puncture its pretensions. Plaster busts sit in his studio across from nudes with mischievously scrambled body parts. A classical head with both eyes seen frontally but situated on a profile isn't really a classical head. The world in which he wandered was Dionysian, prowled by satyrs and Minotaurs – the ominous bestiary that modernist idealism never managed to expel. Picasso recognised in Rembrandt an ancestor of his own dangerous visual intelligence, which could move freely between the aesthetic convenience of the nude and the messier, sexier reality of the naked model: etched images of half-dressed women warming themselves by the stove. Nothing like that stripping truth would happen again until Manet and Degas.

Picasso and Matisse thought there was what they called a 'chain' that connected their understanding of modernism with certain older masters – Velázquez and Goya as well as Rembrandt – who had begun the work of having art ask awkward questions about its own conventions: in this case, the comfortable piety of the nude. That makes Rembrandt's half-naked women (except in the modesty of their undress) the true conceptual ancestors of Picasso's *Demoiselles d'Avignon*, 250 years later. So the inspirational Rembrandt might be at least as important as the historical Rembrandt.

If art's highest purpose was to make visible what Sir Joshua Reynolds called 'invariable' ideas of beauty, Rembrandt was compromised by his earthiness. If art's fulfilment came from the harmonious deployment of light and shade, Rembrandt would be found wanting for the jarring extravagance of his chiaroscuro and his contempt for subtle modulations of tone. If self-effacing absorption within the purity of art's realm was what you were after, Rembrandt's shameless appeal to the beholder, his addiction to the human theatre (often starring himself), the aggressive marks of his own heavy hand were repellently self-indulgent. Reynolds, who was both an admirer and a collector (and who painted a portrait of himself as a young man in an obviously Rembrandtian manner), nonetheless found *The Night Watch* – that explosive, centrifugal discharge of civic energy, at once brilliantly controlled and feverishly liberated – a dismaying, incoherent chaos. He also thought it 'extraordinary that Rembrandt should have taken so much pains' on the *Susanna* in the Mauritshuis in The Hague, 'and have made at last so very ugly and ill-favoured a figure'.

But Reynolds was prepared to forgive Rembrandt his excesses and his wanton disregard for proper finish, because, like many eighteenth-century writers, he considered him a master colourist. When the Romantics acclaimed Rembrandt as an unsurpassed dramatist of light and colour, they turned on its head the assertion that his naturalism belonged to a lesser order of vision than classical idealism. Their message was: Do not confuse common subjects with prosaic painting; Rembrandt proves the opposite – that the divine lives within the husk of mortal things. The critic William Hazlitt, for whom Rembrandt was indisputably 'a man of genius', described him in 1817 as 'the least commonplace in his grossness of all men' and 'the least fastidious of the imitators of nature', for 'he took any object, he cared not what, how mean soever in form, colour and expression, and from the light and shade which he threw upon it, it came out gorgeous from his hands'. Truth to nature, which for Hazlitt was 'the soul of art', was, therefore, the gateway to poetic vision, not the plodding transcription of matter.

Turner was even more emphatic. Rembrandt, he said in an 1811 lecture to the students at the Royal Academy, threw over common subjects a 'veil of matchless colour' so that 'the Eye dwells so completely enthrall'd [that it] thinks it a sacrilege to pierce the mystic shell of colour in search of form'. In other words, forget about traditional drawing and composition. It was as a painter who modelled with light that Rembrandt had done what the critics had declared impossible – revealing, without the clutter of symbolism, the inner mysteries of outward things, including the human form and face. He was the perfect painter precisely because he conveyed both surface and interior, flesh and spirit, body and mind. While Rembrandt's earliest biographers had supposed him to be the illiterate friend of beggars and boors (and Saskia, the burgomaster's daughter, a simple peasant girl), the nineteenth-century writers thought him a profound thinker, *Denker und Dichter*.

They had a point. Rembrandt was, in essence, a conceptual artist, who manifested his ideas not through classical emulation and high finish, but through a sketchy roughness that preserved the lightning strike of what Delacroix called the *première pensée*. It was that direct hit of the imagining mind that distinguished true art, registering the flux of life, its contingent, temporal quality, the buddings and sheddings that gave human existence its majestic poignancy. Paradoxically, slick finish lied about nature and humanity. A broken surface, made with slashes and stabs and unconcerned to cover every corner of the canvas, better caught the emotive reality of lived life, an unpredictable affair, sometimes reticently withdrawn, sometimes so exuberantly full that it could never be contained within the hard-edged line. That was why not just Van Gogh – a besotted idolater of Rembrandt – but a whole succession of practitioners of the expressively loaded brush, from Chaim Soutine to Frank Auerbach, have looked back to Rembrandt as having struck the first great blow to rid art of the callow equation between optical appearance and lived experience.

It was those high-minded connoisseurs the brothers Goncourt who, in 1861, spelled out the relationship between Rembrandt's athletic treatment of the paint surface and the expression of human vitality: 'Never has the human form, living and breathing and beating in the light, been conveyed by the brush as by his.' In Rembrandt's work, 'flesh is painted, heads are drawn and modelled as if they emerged physically from the canvas, through a kind of tattoo of colours, a melted mosaic, a moving swarm of dabs which seems like . . . the palpitation of skin in sunlight'.

The transference of that vitality effect from the geometric reproduction of illusory space according to the rules of Renaissance perspective to the vibrating paint surface itself was the beginning of modernism. And though the broken plumes of Titian's late brushwork and the dashes and blotches of Velázquez's painting were also unprecedented departures from high finish, Rembrandt's modernist devotees were right to hail him as their patriarch, however innocent he may have been of willed novelty. If Picasso recruited Velázquez and Manet to the modernist ancestry, how could he not see Rembrandt as the great inaugurator? All art, to some extent, attempts to stand against the transient nature of human experience by supplying an alternative vitality. But often the laborious attempt at 'lifelikeness' risks ending up duplicating deadness. Rembrandt went the opposite way, achieving unprecedented liveliness by marking his portraits with the spoiling work of time, vitality achieved through the candid acceptance of mortality. That way, the moderns correctly saw, he commanded a peerless ability to register fleshly human presence.

For instance, Rembrandt knew the ostensible truth of local colour to be less important than getting its changing tones as it passed through variations of light and shade; that way, colour itself became organic. Compositions like *The Night Watch*, he gambled, would come alive not through an accumulation of posed portraits, but through their atmospheric integration into an irregularly lit drama. The nineteenth-century painter Eugène Fromentin could not have been more mistaken when he wrote, 'The country, the place, the moment, the subject, the men, the objects have disappeared in the stormy phantasmagoria of his palette.' It was precisely because, in defiance of any precedent, Rembrandt whipped up that storm that the Amsterdam harquebusiers march from *The Night Watch* towards us, from their time to ours, with undiminished élan.

In the 1960s, after a thirty-year absence, Rembrandt came calling again, as Cohen points out, entering Picasso's increasingly morbid meditations on his own place in the pantheon. Picasso had undergone surgery for (depending on your sources) either his prostate or his bowel, but, in any case, a procedure that he thought had made him impotent. It's a commonplace that the artist who liked to masquerade as bull or Minotaur equated sexual and creative potency. (Indeed, one of the Vollard prints depicts a blind Minotaur in exactly the same attitude as the blind Tobit groping across a room in Rembrandt's etching.) If Picasso had made a variation of Rembrandt's *Bathsheba* (in the Louvre) back in the 1930s, he might have incorporated himself into the painter's-eye view, which is also King David's as he spies on the perfect nude's ablutions, watching her read his summons to the royal presence and bed. But in his post-op satirical mood Picasso gave Bathsheba the features of his wife, Jacqueline, while making himself, grotesquely, the grinning maidservant washing her mistress's feet in preparation for the royal rape.

Depicting himself as a dwarfish voyeur unmanned by the proximity of imperious nudes, Picasso had even greater need of his fantasy Rembrandt, the artist enacting his virility with his brush. Rembrandt's startling portrait of himself as the Prodigal Son, unsubtly hoisting aloft a long, cylindrical goblet of wine, while Saskia, in the guise of a plump tavern whore, perches on his lap, became in Picasso's etched version a piece of ornamental pornography. His Saskia wears high heels, tart's lipstick and a lurid grin, and, thanks to the Cubist convention of simultaneous front and rear depiction, can flash all her graphically detailed pudenda.

Picasso had become the emasculated onlooker in a perversely imagined Rembrandtian theatre of the senses; others would have to do his strutting and rutting for him. First, improbably, was the central figure in *The Night Watch*, the well-named, for Picasso's purposes, Captain Frans Banning Cocq. Sometimes Picasso would project a slide of the painting on his studio wall, and from the uproar of that scene Captain Banning Cocq would stride into his drawings, paintings and prints as the Musketeer, gripping his officer's cane, especially when confronted by a mighty nude. In one strangely beautiful aquatint, the Musketeer marches, hand on cane, not across an Amsterdam bridge, but towards another stockinged woman offering herself, thighs splayed, from within a curtained bed.

Picasso's recruitment of Rembrandt as the sponsor for his own immortalisation culminated, three years before his death, in a sacrilegious borrowing from Rembrandt's most theatrical etching, *Ecce Homo*, Pilate's display of Christ before the people. In the Rembrandt etching, the Saviour is brought out as if for a curtain call, hands bound, on a high stage; spectators look out from lead-paned windows, an ill-assorted crowd (in the first five states of the etching) jostling below. Picasso borrowed the proscenium stage show, but replaced the mocked Jesus with himself, turbaned, but pathetically reduced in stature: the impotent potentate. Gathered around him, onstage, in the stalls, peering down from the gods, is the teeming cast of characters who have populated his life and work: nudes on and off horses; incarnations of himself as diapered baby-Pablo; Pierrot-Pablo; and, in imitation of the Musketeer, spear-bearing Pablo. In place of the jeering crowd calling for the crucifixion of Jesus there is, predictably, his seraglio, etched in as many styles as he had had lovers and wives.

Self-mockery (just about) saves this 'Theatre of Picasso', as he called it, from egomania. Picasso probably knew of Rembrandt's disturbing final self-portrait, in which he posed as the Greek artist Zeuxis dying of a fit of bilious cackles as he laughed at the old woman whose portrait he was painting. Among the spectators smiling down at Picasso's final act are the bulb-nosed faces of the Rembrandt-Picasso the painter fantasised he had become.

Rembrandt had the life force in his hands, right to the end. That's why Picasso adamantly refused to think of him – or his other mentor-masters – as belonging to 'the past'. 'To me there is no past or future in art,' he said in the early 1920s. 'The art of the great painters who lived in other times is not an art of the past; perhaps it is more alive today than it ever was.' Timelessness is not always an empty cliché; sometimes, as the ninety-year-old Picasso knew when he reached towards Rembrandt as a tonic against extinction, it is full of sustaining truth.

Anselm Kiefer (1)

Guardian, 20 January 2007

How do you like your contemporary art? A quick hit of juicy mischief, a larky take on mortality, binful of bluebottles, pocketful of glitter, everything you never wanted to know and more about the artist's entrails? Right then, give Anselm Kiefer a very wide berth – because, as the show at White Cube, London, will confirm, he doesn't do droll, he does the big embarrassing stuff, the stuff that matters: the epic slaughters of the world, the incineration of the planet, apocalypse then, apocalypse often; the fragile endurance of the sacred amid the cauterised ruins of the earth.

But lately, the undertaker of history has turned gardener. From deep beneath the loam of memory heaped over the canvas, Kiefer's vast, rutted wastelands have germinated brilliant resurrections: pastel blooms, spikes of verdure sprouting irrepressibly through the skin of a hard-baked earth-rind; or peachy-pink poppies trembling atop spindly black stalks that climb gawkily from bituminous slag. So, notwithstanding the *massacre du jour* served up with the cornflakes in our daily newsprint, for Kiefer in his current redemptive temper, hope really does spring eternal.

He must be the most un-hip artist ever shown by White Cube, the very Sanhedrin of cool; barely a contemporary painter-sculptor at all, if the range framing the contemporary goes from coyly self-effacing minimalism to gaudy showboating. What's more, Kiefer does earth-space, not cyberspace. No Luddite, he nonetheless has let it be known that what he dislikes most about computers is the indiscriminate quality of their memory, a universe of data held simultaneously, accessible at the click of a mouse, permanently available and impervious to either natural attrition or poetic distortion. Since nothing may be digitally forgotten, nothing may be truly recalled.

Much of Kiefer's art represents a resistance to this inhuman virtu-

alisation of memory; its lazy democracy of significance, its translation into weightless impressions. The opposing pole from that
disposability is to make history obstinately material, laid down in
dense, sedimentary deposits that demand patient, rugged excavation.
Kiefer's work burrows away at time, and what it exposes also makes
visible the painful toil of the dig, skinned knuckles, barked shins and
all.

For a German born amid the slaughterhouses of 1945, booting up
could never be glibly electronic. Kiefer became famous in the 1970s
and '80s for his frontal engagements with the totems of German
history: blood-spattered trails befouling the deep Teutonic woods (his
name means fir tree) from which the national culture had been prover-
bially rough-hewn; torch-lit timbered pantheons within which heroes
and anti-heroes lay provisionally interred.

By the lights of the transatlantic avant-garde, Kiefer did absolutely
everything wrong. The choices were clear. Art either had to be hard-
edged in its irreducibly angular minimalism, like Donald Judd's
stacked boxes, which drew their ominous power from being nothing
other than what they were; or else it had to be ecstatically collapsed
into the raw and rowdy universe of signs: op'n'pop, flags and soup tins,
one long cackle at art's valetudinarian pretence to hold the moral high
ground. To grab our attention amid the modern clamour, art needed
to drop the churchiness (especially abstract churchiness), and get out
from under all those centuries of pompous sententiousness and obscure
storytelling. All painting could be was flat-out play (with the emphasis on flat).

Wrestling with his Teutonic demons – and keeping close company
with the likes of Grünewald, Altdorfer and Caspar David Friedrich –
Kiefer could scarcely comprehend, much less identify with, the case
for painterly amnesia, nor with the posturing for lightness and shallowness (he has never been much of a tease). Stubbornly, his art was
always hewed to spatial depth and moral weight, so his landscapes take
anti-flatness about as far as it can possibly go, opening immense vistas
behind the picture, carved furrows on the surface stretching away to
remote distance.

He does not do this innocently, of course. The practice of perspective, invented to imagine a bucolic world where pastoral fancies were
enacted in a neverland of happy radiance, is recycled in Kiefer's land-

scapes to exterminate the fantasy. Kiefer's skies are often black, streaked with the phosphoric licks of a descending firestorm, and what vanishes at the vanishing point are the balmy consolations of rusticity. Bye-bye *Hay Wain*, hello the Somme.

Kiefer also needs immensity in order to frame the ancestral epics of life and death which for him remain art's proper quarry, and which sometimes extend beyond that far horizon into the infinite metaphysical space of the beckoning cosmos, where they interrupt the emptiness with mapped constellations. Events – scriptural, mythic, poetic, historic – are transfigured into written words on the painting, because, for Kiefer, words sanctify the events and figures to which they refer, rather than demystify them.

His seriousness about words, as weighty as the lead from which he forges his books, also puts him at odds with the ironic mode of quotation that has long defined modern art. Instead of mimicking the industrially reproduced comic signage of the mass market, Kiefer marks his pictures with the spidery inscriptions of his own hand, the moving finger quoting, inter alia: Isaiah, Paul Celan, Aeschylus. Wordiness for Kiefer is painterliness. The library and the gallery, the book and the frame inseparable, even interchangeable, in his monumental archive of human memory. Not since Picasso's *Guernica* have pictures demanded so urgently that we studiously reflect and recollect in their presence.

Which may make Kiefer's new work sound like homework (to be severely marked by the forbidding Herr Professor über-Bombast). Nah, thanks all the same, you're thinking, would rather do a day with Damien and Trace. But advance preparation in the *Iliad*, the Kabbalah, not to mention higher scriptural exegesis, is really not the price of admission. For visual drama that (I guarantee) will haunt your dreams, there's no one alive to beat Anselm Kiefer. This is because, along with being a philosopher-poet, he also happens to be a craftsman of phenomenal power and versatility.

For some time, he has been experimenting with work that crosses the boundaries separating not just art and literature, but painting and sculpture. Sometimes (as in the breathtaking *Merkaba*), a *Gesamtkunstwerk* (total artwork) brings together free-standing sculptural elements in stone or lead in continuum with a vertical painted surface, the one acting as a terrestrial transport to the celestial apparition of the other. Some of the paintings on display at White Cube sustain this working method by setting a clump of thorn bushes before an ashy-grey winterscape that speaks (much less ponderously than this makes it sound) of chill death and resurrection. But other paintings – especially in the triptych of confounding masterpieces that, alas, will be travelling to the Gallery of New South Wales in Sydney – have incorporated into the grittily loaded texture of the canvas itself a seething bed of organic (and occasionally inorganic) matter, so that the surface becomes akin to a yeasty humus; alive with golden flecks of straw and hay, twigs, whole branches which poke through the impasto. Another denial of the modernist dogma that authentic paint should never dare to present as anything other than itself.

Kiefer's paint is forthrightly the crusty medium of generation – the baked clay that develops the cracks and fissures from which vegetable life burgeons forth. Even when the paint is, in fact, just that, it is made to clot and coagulate, puddle and pond, or rise in frozen crests as if it were the volcanic material of primordial genesis.

Kiefer's painting, then, is not a representation of some feature of creation so much as a re-enactment of it. And if this sounds a mite up itself, well indeed it is, and none the worse for it. Even if you care not a toss for the esoterica, the richness of classical allusion (such as the catastrophic landscape of the fall of Troy, scarred with explosions of carbon and cobalt, and transmitted via a telephonic connection from Greek peak to peak in mimicry of Agamemnon's beacon signals to faithless Clytemnestra), you can still happily envelop yourself in the blanket of colour and line that fills every centimetre of Kiefer's pictures.

Dazzling, nostalgically psychedelic shots of colour. Beneath the verse from Isaiah that speaks of heavenly mercy, '*Rorate coeli desuper et nubes pluant*' (Drop down ye dew and let the clouds rain upon the just), Kiefer has planted a field of blazing, flamingo-tinted poppies. But the mercy is not unqualified; the flowers are marshalled along perspectival lines all the way to a horizon that is built from raised skeins of greenish-black paint, the corrupted hues of chemical pollution. (Evidently we're not in Monet's picnic country of *Les coquelicots*.) Kiefer's poppies with their black faces can be read interchangeably as columns of warriors or the floral memorials of their fiery entombment. And the petals of the middle distance suggest the flares of combat as much as a field of flowers.

The most startlingly florid of the pictures travels from a paradise garden at its base, with the caked terracotta blossoming in arabesques of brilliant violet, pink and vermilion splashes that coil through the more furrowed landscape. Above it are more verses from Isaiah that open the Palm Sunday liturgy: '*Aperiat terra et germinat Salvatorem*' (Let the earth open and bring forth a Saviour). But Kiefer being Kiefer, there needs be trouble in paradise, so that along the serpentine line of beauty lurks the form of a skeletal snake, its vertebrae constructed from a string of terracotta beads suspended on spinal wire poking from the picture surface. Good and evil, vitality and mortality, thus literally hang sinuously in the balance, it being deliberately unclear whether the serpent is safely fossilised within the sprouting clay, or has shed its casing the better to writhe into freshly devilish incarnation.

This dialogue between martyrdom and resurrection continues into the deeply stirring Palm Sunday installation: eighteen glazed cabinets that house vertically mounted branches of vegetation (mangroves, sunflower pods and dracaenae as well as palms themselves). Stacked atop each other, the cabinets seem not so much vitrines from some botanical museum as the opened pages of a herbiary, Kiefer the tree-man knowingly playing with the conceit of a super-folio, interleaved with sacred revelations. The branches are coated with a thin skin of plaster or white paint so that, at first sight, they seem bleached of life, sapless and forlornly skeletal. But the newly (if tentatively) optimistic Kiefer wants us to register Palm Sunday as a true triumph; the entry to Jerusalem inaugurating the events that lead not just to the Passion but to the Resurrection. Kiefer also knows that, in both pagan and early Christian iconography, the palm with its sword-like branches was known as an immortal tree, which never actually perished but constantly regenerated, a new sheath of fronds budding from the site of a fallen limb. The very earliest representations of the cross in the Coptic Church thus took the form of the living palm. Kiefer has also contrived to display another palm as if it were the feathers of some avian or even angelic wing; a doubly miraculous apparition which, as outsize quill, writes its own revelatory gospel behind the veiling glass.

Like the dirty fields of death sewn with floral brilliance, Kiefer's phantom tree limbs enact a parable of the intertwined fate of nature and humanity. For the erect branches lie or stand against flesh-coloured beds of sand, which in their gracefully voluptuous swirls are unmistakably feminine and invitingly sexual. In one of the most beautiful of the cases, *Hosanna*, the vegetable matter is arranged as a luxuriant pubic tangle; the *prima mater* from which life itself issues. Kiefer has managed somehow (perhaps by treating the case as a kind of bath) to run streams of graphite across the sand and then wash them out to form delicate rills that suggest the ferns and lichens of the first green life to appear on the living planet. Gustave Courbet's lavishly devotional hymn to the pudenda, *The Origin of the World*, is by contrast all frisky slickness. Instead of the erotic quiver, Kiefer gives us a heart-stopping moment, as we suddenly read those marks as simultaneously biological and cosmological, micro and macro; a vision of deltaic capillaries, the pulsing veins and branches of an estuary as seen from an orbiting camera, or up close, the fronds waving gently through a transparent wash of nourishing water.

This is as good, I think, as art ever gets: mystery and matter delivered in a rush of poetic illumination. That Kiefer's work happens to engage with almost everything that weighs upon us in our tortured age – the fate of the earth, the closeness of calamity, the desperate possibility of regeneration amid the charred and blasted ruins – and that it does so without the hobnailed tread of pedestrian polemics, is just one of the many marvels for which we have to thank, yet again, this most indefatigable of modern magi.

In Mesopotamia: Anselm Kiefer (2)

Catalogue essay for the Anselm Kiefer exhibition
Karfunkelfee and the Fertile Crescent, White Cube,
October–November 2009

Anselm Kiefer is talking about bricks. They were, he says, the first toys he remembers playing with: putting something together, one thing above the other, fashioning walls, a place of shelter. He had pulled the bricks from the debris and rubble to which his home town had been reduced by wartime bombing. As it happens, I remember something of the sort myself: my father walking me through the blackened ruins of the East End and the City of London, policemen yelling at me as I kicked balls around bomb sites. Around Stepney, houses still had whole walls torn away, the ruins looking down on patches of weedy grass and bent railings twined with convolvulus. There were piles of bricks everywhere, shattered and sooty as if refired in the kiln of the Blitz. German planes had done this to my city; our planes had done that to Kiefer's. I remember, in the short-trouser years of the early 1950s, compulsively playing with children's brick sets. The best of them boasted actual miniaturised bricks and real cement mortar that I mixed in the kitchen sink with a tiny trowel. Later came the famous Bayko brick sets, grooved Bakelite rectangles that you slid down metal rods to make small houses, or, if time and ambition allowed, mansions, factories, cathedrals. That's what kids did in the years after the war. We ran around the dim streets shouting, kicking stuff in and out of the gutters, and then we went home to build things.

One of Kiefer's perennial obsessions is how history, the Nietzschean demon of havoc, chews up habitat. The maker of art is also the tumbler of edifices. The motif stalks through Kiefer's early masterpieces of the 1970s, like the scarred and begrimed emptiness of the *Märkischer Sand* (1980), stretching to the vanishing point, so that perspective itself becomes the enabler of terror and lament. But other homelands romanticised by picturing are equally grist to the massacre mill: the woodland depth of the *Teutoburger Wald* (1978–80), for instance, where the Roman legions of Varus were annihilated by the Germanic tribes. In all these meditations on hubris, on the scarifying incisions and abrasions that power scores into the earth, houses of shelter and domination – towers, lodges, ziggurats – suffer some sort of stress fracture, from within or without. Constructed from the raw materials over which they loom – sand, clay, stone – they totter, shatter and crumble, returning to the elements from which they were constituted. Bricks that arose from mud fall back to the slather whence they came. Form loosens into unform; unform implies form.

For Kiefer, built structures – including the densely textured deposits of his own works – are always contingent and provisional, and subject to the erosion of time and the caprice of the elements, including human elements. Famous for his challenges to curatorial preciousness – in fact, to the presumption that art must be about permanence – he installs sculptures and sometimes *paintings* outdoors (in the courtyard of his Paris studio, for example) to see what the weather might do to them. (A set of his San Loretto paintings are there right now.) Air, light, wind and rain are co-opted as collaborators in this resistance to finish. Sometimes you see Kiefer's mixed-media pieces locked down in gallery space, like so many tethered King Kongs or blinded Samsons, hulking, shaking their chains, with the pent-up feel of something that wants to break out from polite enclosure. Much of Kiefer's work – like the *Shevirat Ha-Kelim* (the Breaking of the Pots) – has this uncontainable spill; a self-destabilisation, a falling off from the two-dimensional mooring of the wall into our own space.

History's dislodgements, and the subsequent reoccupations of nature, are ancient subjects for Western art – as for scripture and literature – always burdened with tragic foreknowledge. The half-built helical shell of Pieter Bruegel the Elder's *Tower of Babel* (1563) would, for any Renaissance beholder, have implied its own destruction. In Giambattista Piranesi's Roman *veduti*, the overgrown ruin, choked with creepers and bristling with moss and weed, is the subject, not the original architecture. J. M. W. Turner's *Dido Building Carthage* (1815) unsubtly foregrounds the vegetation into which the vanquished empire will decay. It was after visiting Roman ruins in Campania, at Baia and Pozzuoli, that in 1832 Thomas Cole was able to paint his moralising cycle on *The Course of Empire* for the kind of patron acutely conscious of the contingent nature of architectural pomp: the Manhattan merchant Luman Reed.

But Kiefer is acutely aware that nothing beats the twentieth and twenty-first centuries for spectacles of construction and demolition: Albert Speer and *Slaughterhouse Five*, the Kuala Lumpur Tower and 9/11; colossalism matched by incineration. But into his funeral pyres and sulphurous fields of annihilation lately has crept a note of redemptive brightness; germinations poking through the ash; blooms of sharp colour – flamingo, coral, carnation – blossoming through the sedimented strata. Destruction rains down on those big canvases, but from the cake-cracks, pits and chasms nature burgeons. And, as always in Kiefer's work, the modern loops round the aeons to be met by the primordial and mythic. Half-buried, half-exposed within the scarified fields of slaughter, trilobitic forms of early creation lurk. Lately, or so it seems to me, Kiefer's cosmology has taken an ecological turn, inflected with planetary pathos. Inside the vitrines of *Palmsonntag* (2006), Kiefer set branches of palms and other ancient trees, opened like leaves in a book and covered in a ghostly skin of plaster: the botanical lifecycle of seed and bud trapped in a pallid carapace. The beds on which these botanical phantoms arc were drifts of sand, laved in muddy water, allowed to pond and cake, resembling satellite images of deforested silted estuaries – places where human culture began and where its end might be heralded by ecological self-strangulation.

This drawing together of beginnings and endings – these sites that exist simultaneously as cradle and graveyard – continues to haunt Kiefer, caught at a moment in his own time-span when vitality and mortality are nudging up against each other more than our generation likes to admit. While he has been brooding on Mesopotamian origins and endgames, Kiefer has also been producing a series of exceptionally beautiful compositions, triptychs and diptychs enclosed in glass vitrines that revisit one of his earliest and most compulsive themes: the depths of the German woodland. This, too, has been, immemorially, a site of origination and termination. Through the 1970s, Kiefer, whose blankly scorched book was titled *The Cauterisation of the District of Buchen* (1975), returned again and again to an historical memory from which mythic tribal difference sprang: the annihilation of the Roman legions of Varus in the Teutoburger Wald by Germanic warriors. Names and portraits, rendered as if in wood-cut (and sometimes actually so), of the genealogy of this myth of beginnings – from the hero Arminius to romantic poets like Stefan George – snaked through the forest depth, and over a path spattered with blood or dirtied snow. The treatment of pictorial depth itself was a beckoning to memory, and without any consolatory implication that by taking that path some sort of healing transcendence might be achieved. Whatever Kiefer's histories are about, they certainly aren't about cheaply bought closure.

Kiefer's new work retraces some of those apparently inescapable obsessions without merely reiterating them. The form in which the woodland space is housed has changed from the implication – through the line of perspective – of interminable depth, to the box-vitrine: visible but untouchable. The tall glazed cabinets suggest the display cabinets of nineteenth-century natural historians, but, set side by side with no intervening space, also the opened pages or, as we might say, folios of a book. Memory has become, literally, boxed in; the relatively shallow space further obstructed by masses of leafless thornbush climbing the frame, interposed between the beholder and the wood-land depth. Snagged or impaled on this memory briar are doll-scale dresses and costumes, while giant cuspids – the teeth that tear, punc-ture and rend – lurk in the undergrowth. At the base of the snarled growth, memory unspools, the serpent in the garden taking the form of a length of film on which photographic images are printed on lead, Kiefer's favourite medium for embodying things that, heavy as they are, imply slippage and shape-shifting: the ultimately unfixable imprint of time.

The allusion is, of course, to another kind of literary folk memory: the fairy-tales collected and published in 1812 by the Brothers Grimm as *Kinder- und Haus-Märchen* – especially Hansel and Gretel, aban-doned by their mother to feral beasts and the infantiphage witch. (In one particularly haunting composition, Kiefer suspends a floating costume with an empty hood – half monastic habit, half rustic dress – over the wood-space; a presence equally readable as guardian spirit or demonic ghost.) The *ur*-habitat becomes a place of imperilled inno-cence; grisly outcomes postponed or executed. But it is also the primal dwelling place turned into an unsafe shelter. Kiefer figures the tree trunks with broad, slashing, pitchy-black strokes, sometimes leaning towards each other to form an arboreal pointed arch. Knowingly encyclopaedic, these 'organic' proto-architectural leanings recover an entire literature on the origins of Gothic architecture, which its eighteenth-century archivists insisted followed the spontaneous intertwinings and sylvan tunnels of the deep woods and were somehow thus normatively closer to the natural world than to the classical masonry imposed upon it. But there was as Joseph Rykwert and others have reminded us – also an extensive literature on 'primitive classicism' going all the way back to Vitruvius, claiming that its elementary forms – columns, entablature and pediment – themselves originated in rustically modified tree forms: the open-air sacred grove turned into the built temple. Republican Rome apparently preserved such a crude timber temple to remind itself amidst the pomp of its masonry of the rude origins of its virtue and power.

The fate of early dwelling places, the construction and deconstruction of the abodes of culture, seems to preoccupy Kiefer, especially when he shifts his own places of residence and work. The first time I saw his desert-pyramid forms was at the Gagosian show in downtown Manhattan in 1998; the monumental fruit of work done at Barjac in the South of France where, after a period of desolate self-mortification (as in the 1991 painting *Zwanzig Jahre Einsamkeit*), his creative drive had begun to show a phenomenal power surge. The Gagosian exhibition *Dein und mein Alter und das Alter der Welt* (Your and My Age and the Age of the World) was named after a line from Ingeborg Bachmann's poem 'Das Spiel ist aus' (1954). It enacted a monumental link between the Austrian poetess who had also been responsible for introducing German readers to the work of her lover and doomed hero, Paul Celan, whose own *Todesfuge*, written in 1945, had had an incalculable effect on Kiefer's interpretation of German fate and the Holocaust. But in the form of an immense stepped pyramid, half-lost in the swirl of sand that adhered to its abraded surface, Kiefer was also knowingly engaging with the first love poem that Celan had sent to the twenty-two-year-old Bachmann in 1948, *In Aegypten* (In Egypt), in which the old erotic-thanatic intricacies of the ashen-haired Shulamith and the golden-tressed Margareta reappeared: *Du sollst die Fremd neben am schönsten schmücken / Du sollst sie schmücken mit dem Schmerz um Ruth, um Mirjiam und Noëmie.* (Bejewel the stranger who sits beside you most beautifully / Bejewel her with pain for Ruth, for Miriam and for Naomi.) The drifts of scouring sand covering the half-built, half-unbuilt pyramid put in play the tension between solidity and instability, dwelling and rootlessness. In another poem from *Ober Gerauchschlos* (Above Soundlessness), Celan had conjured up the *Sandvolk* ('Sand people', and sometimes also 'Urn people') dwelling in an ultimately barren place beneath an unsparing sky, their lives watered by the tears of their eyes, the ground beneath their feet shifting grains.

Kiefer tells me that not one of the overwhelming paintings shown at Gagosian sold, and that, as he remembers it, the reception, even from critics who had admired his work, like Peter Schjeldahl, was largely hostile. In retrospect this seems astounding, though not surprising. The immense, half-eroded structures, which appeared simultaneously to arise from and collapse back into barren waste, constituted a one-room epic with which the usual opening-night rituals – Manhattan black kit, glasses of white wine – seemed an uncomfortable fit. The troubled-travels of Celan and Bachmann in and out of Egypt – one lover dying by water, the other by fire – could not have seemed further away, for all their inscriptions on Kiefer's great paintings.

It was a test, I suppose, of whether heavy-load maximalism could register at a time when impish minimalism was king of the contemporary art world. The union of art and history had been decreed uncool. Conceptualism sprouted even – or especially – when the concepts were themselves jejune. Desert Storm was a memory; 9/11 and another Iraq campaign were not even bellicose prophecy. One of the paintings from the 1998 exhibition, *Für Ingeborg Bachmann. Der Sand aus den Urnen* (For Ingeborg Bachmann: The Sand from the Urns), is being shown again at White Cube, where it is, however, surrounded with the brickwork paintings that make up *The Fertile Crescent* series. Seeing the stacks of Kiefer's bricks again, laid down in the sand, reminded me that on that earlier opening night in Manhattan I had thought, for some reason, of another hod-load of bricks: Carl Andre's *Equivalent VIII* (1966), bought for the Tate Gallery in 1972. The bewildered or furiously obtuse response to Andre's neatly continuous bed of 120 bricks laid on the floor forced its defenders into an explanation of serial minimalism, but it's fair to say that the high concept of art from which all trace of art-ness, as well as the shaping hand of the artist, had been expunged proved a hard sell to the narrative-hungry British public.

Kiefer, on the other hand, has consistently been the most un-modular of contemporary artists; the least likely to be satisfied with an extruded grid as a sufficient expression of immanent form; the least likely to withdraw the shaping hand of the artist from his work as if it were a contaminant. On the contrary, Kiefer's gestural brushwork is aggressively artisanal, Rembrandtesque, bereft of hard-edged rectangularities, loaded not just with the dense matter of painterly construction, but an unapologetically personal relationship with the histories therein embedded. So Kiefer's bricks are *made* in their clayey, puddly muddiness as he works. Differential drying rates echo the process by which loose clay or mud hardens and cakes, the density of the pigment forming tessellated deposits and stacks. Anything less modular could hardly be conceived of. The work both in its elements and as a whole is organic and shifting like memory itself. Bizarrely, some of it makes me think of John Ruskin's beautiful, if operatic, approach to geology in which solid rock exposes the volcanic tumult responsible for its prehistoric creation. Only Ruskin could describe slaty crystalline as 'quivering', but he would, I think, have understood and enjoyed the charge of mineral energy that Kiefer brings to his brickwork. In this sense, the fertility of Mesopotamia, the slow-motion kinesis of its estuaries, carries through to the edifices that were raised on its river banks. And as if in acknowledgement of this organic relationship with the landscape that produced the hanging gardens of Babylon or the ziggurats of Ur, Kiefer's tesserae are alive with mineral animation. Even when whole fields of them are laid down on an extensive landscape (as in fact they do dry in simple Indian brickworks), the bed, in *Ninife* (2009) for example, heaves, buckles, writhes as if the bricks and topography on which they rest undulate in erotic connection. That would indeed be the Mesopotamian way.

Kiefer's fascination with the ambiguities of construction and deconstruction lead him to treat his brickworks synecdochically; they are fragments that imply the whole. Rising stacks appear as the initial elements of an eventual pyramid; while the walls of the building behind them represent a structure that is both maker and made. Its arched openings and high walls suggest a simple brick factory akin to those which Kiefer himself saw and photographed in south India. But they also imply the grandiose imperial towers and citadels of Chaldea, Assyria and Babylon, which rose from the mudflats only to fall, each in their turn, at the hands of successor empires. The flaring, rusted, hard-fired passages in the ground of some of these paintings, or the half-ruined, ragged-edged turrets, complete the cycle of historical births and deaths in which Kiefer discovers the history of our own times as well as the archaeology of antiquity. Where writing and cultivation and law and architecture began is also where war and annihilation achieved epic consummations. In *Die Siebte Posaupe* (2009) and in the largest painting from *The Fertile Crescent* series, unmistakably fortress-like buildings shed their brick skins as if sloughing off their Babylonian power, to be reduced once more to rubble.

If this seems unsurprising in a German artist, it's not just because of a life that began its memories amidst smouldering rubble and destruction, with *Trümmerfrauen* (rubble women), sweeping amidst the debris for the bricks that might yet make an *Anfang* (beginning) out of a Ground Zero. It's also because it was German archaeology that transformed the study of the ancient Near East. 'Fertile crescent' was a phrase coined at the turn of the twentieth century by the first – and prodigious – American Egyptologist, James Henry Breasted. But the Midwestern Breasted had studied archaeology in Berlin, and his scholarly, impassioned location of the origins of 'Western' culture in the great river societies stretching from the Nile to the Euphrates was an overwhelmingly German enterprise. It was German Assyriologists like Robert Koldewey who first mapped out a credible chronology for the succession of Mesopotamian civilisations, and who also understood that the primary building element from which their mighty and fallen monuments had been made was, indeed, unfired mud brick. When he excavated cuneiform-inscribed brick vestigial walls, Koldewey believed he had discovered the Hanging Gardens of Babylon. His site was all wrong, for the Greek historian Diodorus Siculus clearly locates the gardens beside the Euphrates itself, but in most other respects Koldewey and his German colleagues got it right. The great brick walls – probably of a storehouse – were erected sometime in the reign of Nebuchadnezzar II, towards the end of the sixth century BC: the same period in which the First Temple in Jerusalem was destroyed.

More modern Assyriology has confirmed, though, that unfired

brick structures go right back to the identifiable origins of building itself; perhaps as early as the *fourteenth* century BC, according to the historian of Mesopotamian building materials, Peter Moorey. This kind of information, linking the earliest conceivable structures of shelter, power and ceremony with an unchanged technology that can still be seen today in parts of India, needless to say delights and inspires Kiefer, confirming, as it seems, the ribbon of time within which epics of construction and deconstruction – work arising from floodplain mud and returning to it – unfold along a continuous arc.

That the most recent adventure of military havoc took place in 2003 amidst utter indifference to the conservation of memory will only have reinforced Kiefer's instinct about the conjunction of disaster across the aeons.

From time to time – especially in New York – complaints are voiced about contemporary art's failure to produce some sort of adequate response to the world-shattering moment of 9/11. But it seems naive to expect an equivalent to Goya's *Third of May 1808* (1814), or Picasso's *Guernica* (1937). The risk of banal illustration and moral incommensurability with the magnitude of the massacre is great enough to persuade artists to stay their hand. But anyone in search of a resonant meditation on the instability of built grandeur, on the chronicles of heady calamitous risings and tumblings that constitute the narrative of humanity from Ur to Manhattan, would do well to look hard at Kiefer's *The Fertile Crescent*. As usual, he is incapable of making trivia.

John Virtue: The Epic of Paint

Catalogue essay for *John Virtue: London Paintings*, National Gallery, March–April 2005

There's something missing from John Virtue's skylines: the London Eye. And that's not just because he dislikes the featherlight airiness of the wheel, so at odds with his bituminous, Dante-like vision of a beaten-up, endlessly remade city of men scarred by the damage of history. Virtue's London is more battlefield than playground; his angle of vision the angel's hover rather than the child's expectation of ascent. But his aversion also stems from what the Eye represents: bubble-glazed, sound-sealed enclosure, an encapsulated rotation to postcard epiphany; sites turned into sights and those sights visually itemised rather than bodily encountered. Up it inexorably goes, carrying the happy hamsters, far, far above the grunts and grinds of the town, far, far above London. What Virtue most hates about it – I'm guessing – is its name: the presumption of vision. What his paintings do is take on the hamster wheel; insist that Virtue's vision is the real London eye. Instead of detachment there is smashmouth contact; instead of mechanically engineered, user-friendly serenity, there is the whip-saw excitement of the city; its rain-sodden, dirt-caked, foul-tempered, beery-eyed, jack-hammered, traffic-jammed nervy exhilaration. Instead of a tourist fantasy, there is a place.

These paintings are punk epics: gritty; brazen with tough truth. You don't so much look at them as collide with them; pictures which smack you into vision. This is what all strong painting is supposed to do: deliver a visceral jolt, half-pleasure-hit; half-inexplicable illumina-tion. It's what Rubens, Rembrandt, Turner, Francis Bacon, on top form, all manage. We gasp 'knock-out' and we mean it pugilistically; that we've taken a body blow. But instead of reeling groggily under the impact, we seem to have been given, Saul-Paul-like, a brand-new set of senses. We look at the world differently, we register experience differently, and we wonder how the hell this has been done, with something so economical as canvas streaked with paint; in Virtue's case *black and white* paint? And the answer is not to credit Virtue's paint with resolving itself into something we recognise as previously seen (even if that something is Nelson's Column), but rather to realise that those painted forms are themselves the material of new vision.

Virtue's work is a stunning reminder of what truly powerful painting can yet achieve. The obituary of painting has been written so many times that declaring it premature has itself become a tedious piety. But the dirge drones on: the woebegone longing for the titans of yesteryear, for the Pollocks and de Koonings and Rothkos, under whose auspices paint, liberated from representation, did its own thing, was declared the Life Force. When the usual British suspects (Freud, Hockney, Hodgkin, Auerbach) are wheeled on for refutation of the Death of Paint, and the words 'vigorous' or 'constantly inventive' get uttered, it's with a note of gratuitous appreciation that the club of patriarchs can still turn it on, notwithstanding (it's implied) their veteran years and settled ways. There are, for sure, paint-handlers of prodigious power and originality around among the upstart young'uns – Jenny Saville; Cecily Brown; Elizabeth Peyton; and in a very different key, Rebecca Salter (notice the gender?), but it's also true that painting still seems to feel a need to make a case for itself against exhaustion. That it so often makes that case by ironising its relationship with photography – by fabricating images of such hyper-reality that their synthetic quality simultaneously owns up to the artifice of picturing while implicating photography in the duplicity – is just another symptom of painting's fragile confidence. Gerhard Richter, for instance, works in two minds and two moods: the one a defiant, slathering ooze of viscous abstraction; the other a more nervous and self-conscious dialectic with past masters (Vermeer and Van Eyck) and with today's bad news. Anselm Kiefer, on the other hand, in his most recent metaphysical venturing, has increasingly needed free-standing sculpture and sculptural effect on his canvases, if only in the cause of liquidating the formal boundaries between vision and touch.

'Pure' two-dimensional painting, at its most defensive, seems to have been boxed into a shrinking space between, on the one hand, video art and photography (against which a century ago it could unapologetically define itself) and, on the other hand, sculpture. If the nineteenth- and twentieth-century avant-garde was dominated by painting, with sculpture in an auxiliary relationship, specialising in monumental rhetorical statements whether Rodin or Henry Moore, Giacometti or Zadkine, the hierarchy in our own time seems to have been completely reversed. Whereas painting was once the medium through which the separation between the signs of the world and the work of art could be overthrown, it's usually sculpture these days which makes the most aggressively subversive moves. The fact that the definition of sculpture (Richard Serra's torques, but also Sarah Lucas's car wrecks constructed from unsmoked cigarettes) refuses nailing down only adds more kick to its anarchic exuberance. Once the solid citizen in the studio, sculpture is now the wicked imp of invention. In Britain, its compulsive leitmotif is eros and thanatos, sex and death, but with death the runaway favourite, possibly because the practitioners of the morbid joke are far enough away from its reality to be able to imagine it as a real hoot. The favoured tempers in which these endlessly reiterated obsessions are rehearsed are elegy (Rachel Whiteread) and irony (Damien Hirst).

Irony-connoisseurs are going to have slim pickings amidst the heroically rugged work of John Virtue. For his paintings have been made as if much of contemporary art, or rather the *fashion* of contemporary installation art, had never happened, or at best are a facile distraction from more solidly enduring things. Good for him. Irony is poison to his passion, for his work draws not on death, but life; in the case of the epic paintings he has made while looking at London, the life of a bruised city, caught in the warp of time. But the *élan vital* of Virtue's work also owes its strength to another celebration: of the life of paint itself. Which is why, when you look at a John Virtue, be it one of his 'landscapes' or his London pictures, you see more than the Exe Estuary or St Paul's Cathedral. You see John Virtue himself, in the act of painting, the work a permanent present participle of storming creativity. The modish word to describe such action is 'marks', but that implies discrete traces of remote activity. In Virtue's case, the more you look, the more you see the paint in a state of turbulent self-animation: dripping and drizzling, stabbing and dabbing, like a feverish sorcerer's apprentice. To say that Virtue and his work are unstoppable is to say many things, all of them apposite. But the most important tribute that can be paid to him is to acknowledge that in an art culture comatose from ironic overkill he has asked the straight question – what can paint actually do? And then he has set about supplying an unrepentant, triumphal answer.

Though Virtue's work is fashioned without any thought of the critics in his head, its implications are, in fact, momentous for the debate about the direction of painting in the digital age. The rap against Abstract Expressionism was always about its solipsism; the heady conviction that painting was no more than the manipulation of the materials which constituted it. It was at the point when freedom from figuration – the adrenaline rush of egotistical all-over energy – turned into pseudo-spiritual loftiness, especially with colour-field stainers like Morris Louis and Barnett Newman, that those who yearned for modern painting to embody visual experience of something other than itself began to complain of aesthetic asphyxiation. The take-it-or-leave-it upyoursishness of high abstraction, its priestly *noli me tangere* distance from social experience and from the indiscriminately raucous universe of signs, its warning notices posted against what it imagined to be the mindless crud of pop culture (movies, advertising, the whole gamut of capitalist gimcrackery) began to seem monastically barren. Against that visual scholasticism on rushed the storming postmodernist carnival: Johns's flags and beer cans; Rauschenberg's shrieking collages; Rosenquist's wall-length Cadillacs and mustard-loaded hot dogs; Lichtenstein's comic strip *WHAAM!* 'The world,' as Leo Steinberg nicely, but demurely, put it, 'was let back in again.' How sad, then (and in retrospect, Warhol and his factory of stoned cuteness was a culprit in this), that work made as a breakout from narcissism should somehow reinforce it, posing archly, relentlessly, mercilessly, the dullest question in the world: 'Is it art?' Surely, and I say this imploringly, we no longer give a toss?

Certainly, John Virtue has more important things to care about, perhaps the most important of all being his move to make the dichotomy between modern painting and modern picturing moot. The party line for Abstract Expressionists (or at least their scribes and seers) could be summed up in a nutshell: the more painting, the less picturing there has to be; the *integrity* of painting depending, unconditionally, on the repudiation of picturing. By picturing I mean not just the attachment to description (for evidently that is not John Virtue's thing), but the evocation through the brush of something *about* a seen place, person *or* object. The seen something might not be the apparent surface characteristics of the place, person or object, so that the 'seeing' might be within the mind's eye, rather than a retinal report. So that we might well say that what John Virtue depicts is not London at all, but an idea of London, a sense of London (though not, I think, an *impression* of London). To acknowledge that much is not, for a moment, to compromise the 'reality' of how his eye, his hand and his paint coordinate, but on the contrary to insist that the reality they together make, the reality of a *painting* of London, is, in fact, the only reality worth having, at any rate in the National Gallery.

What John Virtue has made possible is a reunion of painting and picturing, no longer in a relationship of mutual depletion, but something like the opposite – mutual sustenance. No one standing in front of one of his big canvases could think that the force with which they deliver his vision could possibly be communicated in any other way: not digitally, not photographically, certainly not sculpturally. Nor, once seen, can that vision be subtracted from the sense of what London is or, for that matter, what painting is. In our visually over-surfeited but still mysteriously undernourished age, this is not bad to be going on with.

So what is it exactly that Virtue pictures? Well, nature, culture, history – that is, the history of his own craft as well as of the world – and the interlacing of them all in our visual imagination. Even on the evidence of the Exe Estuary paintings, he has never been a pastoralist. Cud-chewing serenity is not exactly the stuff of those roaring black and whites even when, ostensibly, they begin with solitary reflection. In 1958 Frank O'Hara did an interview with one of Virtue's heroes, Franz Kline, in which Kline also confessed himself to be incorrigibly in the stir of things, the artist telling O'Hara, 'Hell, half the world wants to be like Thoreau worrying about the noise of traffic on the way to Boston, the other half use up their lives being part of that noise. I like the second half, right?' Even when he has drawn by the side of a flowing stream or on a gantry swaying above the Thames, I think Virtue, too, is most moved by the buzz of the world; whether gnats humming in the tall grass, the gaseous tremble on the filmy pond or the pullulation of the urban hive. Instinctively, he draws no distinction between history and natural history. So too, like Kline again (and, for those who rejoice at having spotted Virtue's 'source' in Kline's instinctual black-and-white visual operas, one need only quote Brahms congratulating those who detected a touch of Beethoven in the finale of his fourth symphony – 'any fool can see that'), 'I don't feel mine is the most modern, contemporary, beyond the pale kind of painting. But then I don't have that fuck the past attitude. I have very strong feelings about individual paintings and painters past and present.' Which, in Kline's case included, on the positive side, Rembrandt, Bonnard and Toulouse-Lautrec, and in Virtue's, Rembrandt, Turner, Claude Lorrain and Goya.

A catty little debate about Kline turns on the degree to which he is to be thought of as a purely abstract painter or rather as one among many in whose work traces of figuration deliberately lurk; especially since titles like *Crow Dancer* might be read as a tease to identify primitive forms within the heavy onslaught of brushstrokes. But to participate in the quarrel is to miss the point about Kline since the force of his work is precisely to problematise the notion of 'pure' abstraction, and to translate seen (or felt) experience into an independent realm of painted gestures. *Meryon* (1960–1) may have started with the clock tower in Paris, mediated through a nineteenth-century engraver, but Kline's armature completes its Gothic ruin and resolves it into something elementally different.

Equally fruitless would be an argument about whether Kline, or for that matter, John Virtue, are painters of instinct or calculation, since the answer to both is yes. Much of the energy of Virtue's work does come directly from its improvisatory technique; so that the brushstroke seems always to have been freshly and urgently laid. Virtue is a draftsman through and through, yet the sweeping grandeur of his designs is less a matter of carefully calibrated delineation (the passages in his work I like the least are those where he makes linear architectural summaries, however freely rendered), but rather of his involuntary obedience to the accumulated patterning of a lifetime's working practice. His technique is painterly liberty guided by self-education. This makes him that rarest of birds in the studio, the wholly free disciplinarian.

In this complicated negotiation between chance and calculation, it so happens that Virtue has a revolutionary predecessor, the extraordinary eighteenth-century painter, Eton drawing master and print-maker, Alexander Cozens. In his moments of deepest perplexity (and there were many moments in his protean career when he was unperplexed and produced work of great banality), Cozens was exercised by the dissipation of the energy of the *idea* of a work, in the long process of its meticulous execution. This he thought a particular problem with landscapes, where a free sketch from nature would inevitably lose vitality as it was worked up in the studio, often at far remove in time and place from the drawn image, and, according to classical desiderata, guaranteed to drain away its spontaneity. (The phenomenally rich record of Virtue's sketchbooks documents not only the force of fleeting circumstances on his subject matter – light, wind, position – but also his determination to sustain that immediacy in the vastly amplified forms of the paintings.) Through serendipity (for him, the only blessed path), Alexander Cozens happened on a technique he thought might arrest this fatal stagnation of energy and which he called, in a publication, *A New Method of Assisting the Invention in Drawing Original Compositions of Landscape.* Observing the accidental patterning made by a soiled piece of paper, and recalling Leonardo da Vinci's musings on the associative suggestiveness of streaked stones, Cozens took this arbitrary staining as a cognitive tease from which to work up a fully imagined design. In the *New Method*, the stains became Cozens's 'Blots', which provoked from his critics derision and the accusation that he was simply a charlatan.

Cozens was surely responding to Lockean theory about the initially unmediated force of sensory impression, as well as to the lure of the unfettered imagination, so dear to his friend the Gothick plutocrat William Beckford. But this did not make Cozens an entirely impulsive dabbler. His own description of the blots navigates carefully between intuition and calculation: 'All the shapes are rude and unmeaning as they are formed with the swiftest hand. But at the same time there appears a general disposition of these masses producing one comprehensive form, which may be conceived and purposely intended before the blot is begun. This general form will exhibit some kind of subject and this is all that should be done designedly.'

Cozens goes on to justify his *New Method* by claiming it helps stamp the *idea* of a subject (he means this, I think, Platonically, as the original abstract concept of a subject) and is even bolder (or more romantic) by writing that the preservation of that living Idea is itself 'conformable to nature'. By this he does not mean there is a direct match between the concept of a representation and the objective facts of physical form, but rather something like the very opposite: that we are all prisoners (Plato and Locke again) of our machinery of cognition, and *that* is the proper form which the artist should seek to imprint on paper or canvas.

This may sound like an overly philosophical view of the modus operandi of so meaty a painter as John Virtue; yet it's surely not far from the mark. What Virtue gives us is not a visual document of London (in the manner, say, of Wenceslaus Hollar) built from the accumulation of reported details, each in fastidiously gauged and scaled relationship to each other, so much as an overwhelming *embodiment* of London; closer to an East End pub knees-up – the trundle of an old bus grinding its way through the night streets; the peculiar whiff of fresh rain on rubbish-filled streets; the jeering roar of a stand at White Hart Lane (or Highbury); the brimstone glare of a line of Doner KebabChicken-FishnChippy takeaways – than to a Prospect by Canaletto. Virtue's St Paul's is not Wren's architectural 'gem', it's the pre-bleached, grimily defiant mascot of cockneydom: black, hulking, a bit thuggish. And just as he turns the bleached dome black, he equally stunningly turns the dirty old river white. But (as with Kline again) Virtue's blacks and whites aren't polarised absolutes: they drip and smear each other with gleeful impurity; much of the white flecked with a kind of metropolitan ashiness that gives the paint guts and substance; much of the black, streaky and loose, like road tar that refuses to set. His is, in fact, a smoky London, even if painted long after the epoch of the great pea-soup fogs. His vade-mecum is Dickens, not Mayor Livingstone (though an earlier unreconstructed Ken would love these pictures).

Virtue has often sung his ode to pollution; the artist's friend. Whether to embrace or reject the begrimed air, the half-choked light has historically sorted out the men from the boys in London painters. Whistler loved it, of course, though he gussied it up as a dove-grey penumbra hanging moodily over Chelsea Reach. Claude Monet was in two minds about it, cursing it from his room in the Savoy in 1899 for blotting out the fugitive sun. Yet by far the strongest of his paintings – completed in a studio a long, long way from the Thames – were the greeny-grey early-morning images of crowds tramping and omnibussing their way to work over hostile bridges, unblessed by even a hint of watery sunshine. The beatific tangerine sunsets which Monet inflicted on other paintings in the series, on the other hand, glimmer over the Houses of Parliament with a risible absurdity that could only be forgivable as the product of some mildly narcotic stupor.

Likewise, it's a symptom of their meretriciousness – their tyranni-
cal prettiness, their utter failure to connect with anything that ever
made London London – that almost all of the paintings produced
between 1747 and 1750 by Giovanni Antonio Canaletto feature radi-
antly cerulean skies. It may just have been that Canaletto was lucky
enough to work during days – we have them, to be sure – of empyrean
blue hanging over the Thames, but his obligation to sunny optimism
extended beyond mere pictorial ingratiation. Canaletto was working
for aristocratic patrons like the Duke of Richmond, heavily invested
in the building of Hanoverian London, and whose education on the
Grand Tour led them to reconceive the port city as the heir to Venice,
Amsterdam or even Rome. Hence the earlier import of Italians to do
London views – Antonio Joli and Marco and Sebastiano Ricci, for
example – since their brief was to confect a fantasy metropolis in
which classical memory united with commercial energy. Church
façades bask in toasty Latin sunlight, the terraces of grand houses
backing on to the Thames are populated only by ladies and gents of
The Quality, and the river itself is barely disturbed by the occasional
barge. Westminster Bridge, then under construction as a pet enterprise of the Duke of Richmond, was presented by Canaletto as a
framing device, the Thames seen through one of its spectacular arches,
both brand-new and somehow mysteriously venerable in the manner
of a Piranesi *veduta*. The truth, however, was that the bridge was hated
by a good section of London artisans and tradesmen, particularly the
watermen who saw in it their impending redundancy. As visual para-
digms of the New London, then, Canaletto's display pieces were
(unlike Hogarth's prints or John Virtue's paintings) emphatically not
for the 'middling sort' of people, much less the plebs. This aristocratic
preference for poetic fancy over social truth reached a *reductio ad
absurdum* with Canaletto's follower, William Marlow, painting in 1795
a *capriccio* in which St Paul's has been transplanted to a faithfully
rendered depiction of the Grand Canal in Venice.

We tend to think of Turner (another of Virtue's heroes), or at least
Turner the Brentford boy and happy waterman, as the antidote to all
this Italianate picturesque contrivance. But of course Turner was as
drunk on visions of Italy, and Venice in particular, as any of the *piccoli
canaletti*, and was quite capable of turning out editions of the Thames

which washed the scummy old stream in a bath of sublimity. And he was never above pleasing patrons, either. The direct ancestor of his 1826 *Mortlake Terrace*, now in the Frick Collection, painted for the nouveau-riche William Moffatt, with its peachy light and strolling gentlefolk is, indeed, Canaletto, and beyond him, the Dutch city painters of the seventeenth century. Related concoctions like Turner's 1819 *Richmond Hill on the Prince of Wales's Birthday*, or the 1825 watercolour of him sketching the serpentine curve of the river and the city about it from the summit of Greenwich Park, are best understood (and forgiven) as patriotic-civic allegories; omnia gathera of the memories, sentiments and loyalties called forth by the London prospect; but this time more in the nature of an implied historical pageant, insular and cocky rather than hybridised and Italianate. And, here, too, the debt is more to the Dutch celebrations of the *genius loci* – Esaias van de Velde's wonderful *View of Zierikzee*, and of course Vermeer's Delft – than to a mechanical reiteration of Roman glories, both departed and resurrected.

At least Turner was struggling to marry up authentic Cockney Pride, an experience of place, with a reimagined painterly aesthetic, rather than simply make the city a creature of swoon-inducing beautification; something which the punky smut of London will always, thank God, resist. It was not the American-ness of Whistler which led him to treat the river as aesthetic trance, but perhaps his permanent and increasingly desperate yearning to be in Paris, yet condemned to languish amidst the likes of William Frith and Augustus Egg as The American in London. The only way to survive was to flaunt it, and this Whistler did by becoming a painterly revolutionary in spite of himself, effectively annihilating his subject for a mood-effect. The rockets fall in gorgeous nocturnal obscurity somewhere, who cares, in the vicinity of Cremorne Gardens. The Gardens were a London pleasure haunt and a particular bête noire of John Ruskin as, of course, was Whistler himself and this painting in particular, for which the word effrontery seemed to the self-appointed guardian of visual truth to have been coined. But to make a Cremornian painting, to present art as epicurean delectability, a luscious dish for the senses, was precisely Whistler's point, one which, again, Paris might have taken as a compliment, but which London found somehow (it couldn't say *exactly* how) indecent.

A great gap opened up in modernism, then, between London as

the site of aesthetic cosmetic and London as the site of raw document; in the nineteenth century between the butterfly effects of Whistler and the reports from the underworld of Gustave Doré; in the twentieth between the visual histrionics of Oscar Kokoschka and in the 1950s the startling photographic streetscapes of the mind-blowingly gifted Nigel Henderson. Leon Kossoff and Frank Auerbach did wonders in regrounding vernacular visions of the city in the worked density of paint, but even they were not quite ready to take on the totemic sights and memories of the war-ravaged city in the way Virtue, born two years after the doodlebugs had done their worst, could. (In fact, the spirit of painterly liberty in the 1950s had its own strong reasons to go nowhere near anything that could be thought of as paying lip service to a Festival of Britain-like cavalcade.)

But that fastidiousness sealed off modernist painting of the city from the broader public whose need was, and may always be, celebratory, not darkly suspicious, or furtively pathological in the Sickert way. And it's the muscular innocence of John Virtue's picturing (along with the bravura of his paint-handling); his instinctive relish of the ant-heap swirl of London; his shockingly brave determination to make work which the untrained eye can immediately engage with, which has helped him achieve something no other painter of or in London has ever managed, a truly populist expressionism. That an entire ensemble of his huge, as well as his merely impressively large, paintings should be hung together in the National Gallery as if in the Hall of Honour in the palace of some prince of Baroque, so that they are experienced as a cumulatively intoxicating rush of spectacle, only makes their deeply democratic quality the more miraculous.

But then Virtue has not been holed up like Monet in the Savoy Hotel, nor taking the morning air like Canaletto with the Duke of Richmond these past few years. Instead, he has been swinging from a gantry, or perched precariously on the roof of Somerset House, London's mean drizzle on his head; its cinders flying in his face; taking the measure of the city very like his cynosure Turner, in his non-Mortlake moments, right between the eyes. The fine frenzy that pushes Virtue along is wonderfully documented in his sketchbooks, but the challenge for him has always been somehow to transform those immediate responses in the studio into something that both registers and transcends its subject matter. In this most difficult of painterly goals he has, I believe, triumphantly succeeded, allowing us to read the great white daub at the heart of so many of his paintings as intrinsically related to its figural source in the Thames. At such moments of recognition, the pulse of the Londoners among us, especially, will race a little faster. But the reason to be most grateful for these epic masterworks is precisely for their resistance to visual cliché, even to cockney sentimentality; for their faithfulness to a London eye that actually sees beyond London. So we must also read the white daub as a white daub; the most thrillingly satisfying white daub conceivable, ditto the great racing black strokes; the gale-force whirl of the brush. Back and forth we go, then, through the picturing and the painting; the two in perfect step, doing the Lambeth Walk, oi! It comes as no surprise, then, to learn that that just happens to be where John Virtue lives.

Frans Hals,
*The Marriage
Portrait of Isaac
Massa and
Beatrix van der
Laen, c.* 1622.
Rijksmuseum,
Amsterdam.

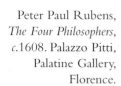

Peter Paul Rubens,
The Four Philosophers,
*c.*1608. Palazzo Pitti,
Palatine Gallery,
Florence.

J.M.W. Turner, *A Disaster at Sea,*
'The Wreck of the Amphitrite', *c.* 1835.
Tate Gallery, London.

J.M.W. Turner, *The Burning of the
Houses of Lords and Commons*, 1835.
John Howard McFadden Collection,
Philadelphia Museum of Art, Philadelphia.

James Ensor, *Scandalized Masks*, 1883.
Royal Museums of Fine Arts of Belgium, Brussels.

Pablo Picasso,
'Ecce Homo', After Rembrandt
from Suite 156, 1970.
Tate Gallery, London.

Picasso At Work, c. 1970.

Anselm Kiefer, *Karfunkelfee*, 2009. White Cube Gallery, London.

Anselm Kiefer, *Shevirath Ha Kelim*, 2009. White Cube Gallery, London.

John Virtue, *Landscape No. 711*, 2003–4. Marlborough Fine Art, London.

Donald Rumsfeld, Secretary of Defense, Washington, D.C., May 7, 1976.
From *The Family*, a portfolio of 69 portraits. Photograph by Richard Avedon.

Avedon: Power

Guardian, 27 September 2008

Was there ever such a pretty wart? There it sits beside the noble nose, the solitary imperfection in Richard Avedon's impossibly beautiful portrait head of Barack Obama, taken in 2004 when Obama was the wunderkind of the struggling Democrats. You look at the clever, artless, eager child preserved in the star orator, civic gravity and American ardour overlaid on the same face, the open collar an advertisement of moral transparency, and two equally wistful thoughts come to mind. How long ago *that* seems; and how sad it is that the greatest of America's portraitists in any medium isn't around right now to fulfil his project of shooting 'Democracy' in action. But Avedon died, aged eighty-one, in mid-shoot, not long after photographing Obama. He was excited about the work (there was not much about life that didn't excite him); and he talked about 'Democracy' capturing politics as it played out in the lives of regular Americans, rather than a gallery of Players. But on the evidence of some of the pictures, he became drawn to an emblematic freak show; a polemic of the peculiar, easy pickings for an artist with Avedon's sardonic eye. So, predictably, we have the Republican Conventioneer costumed as Lincoln, but emitting the icy glare of an executioner; or the bovine high-school blonde who seems constituted entirely from dairy matter, the satin spikes of her diadem crumpling on her brow, a lazy eye turning her impersonation of the Statue of Liberty into farce. Only in the portrait of 'Specialist John H. Copeland', photographed at Fort Hood, does monstrosity get complicated by pathos. The image of the young soldier separates at the neck. Below is the American empire; the line-backer frame in camouflage fatigues, impossibly bulked up and weighed down by flak jacket; massive gun; a mesh kitbag; above the collar-line, a fresh-faced kid in a buzz cut, doing his best to perfect a roadblock glower, but triggering only an urge to make him a quick cup of cocoa.

Avedon never made any pretence to objectivity; the notion of the dispassionate lens he wrote off as delusion. His work, he frankly confessed, was at least as much about him as his subjects: a vast collective self-portrait of the compulsions he projected on to America's faces and figures. In person Avedon was a merrily humane optimist, warm-blooded and gregarious; to know him was to love him. But he was no sentimentalist and there was a Daumier streak in him: coolly contemptuous of the political masquerade even while he was enthralled by its performances. Like Daumier, he thought that lies and cruelty settled like a crust on the physiognomy: passive cosmetic surgery gone wrong. All he had to do was to supply a lit exposure of the particular features in which moral intelligence or its absence had been inscribed.

As hip as he mostly was, Avedon was, at root, an old-style Jewish moralist whose texts were written in freckles and furrows, pits and pocks. Sometimes those marks and blemishes, which stood out so sharply against the indeterminate white sheet against which his faces posed, were lit as poetic expressions of the persona. So the much mottled but kindly moon-face of John Glenn, astronaut turned Ohio Senator, becomes itself a benign planetary surface. Avedon took delight in tweaking – or annihilating – the expected icon. Ronald Reagan, whose beaming smile warmed millions with its avuncular easiness, he trapped in lower-facial corrugation, as if the firming of power had been withdrawn in retirement along with the presidential motorcade. 'Looking good,' Nancy is said to have murmured as Reagan stood on the chalk lines he had asked Avedon to supply, looking anything but. The gaze off yonder Avedon may have wanted to suggest rueful reflection, but our retrospective knowledge of Reagan's mental fade into Alzheimer's gives the image an altogether different charge. Confronted by his famously affable beam turned into a mask of porky smugness as if fattened at the trough of self-satisfaction, Karl Rove got all steamed up, accusing Avedon of setting him up to look 'stupid'; the arch-amBusher ambushed.

To which, I think, Avedon would have replied with his most roguishly winning grin that all his portraits were collaborations; and that nothing about the meeting of photographer and subject was calculated in advance: not the clothes, not the hair, not the body language. People came as they were. But the truth is a little more complicated than that profession of guilelessness. Avedon did in fact have certain *idées fixes* about the essential whomever; and then, through some astonishing act of photographic magic against that white paper, could make clothes, expression, collude in imprinting the essential them. Accompanied merely by the innocent act of sticking his left hand in his pocket, the trademark glasses a smidgin off kilter, Henry Kissinger's expression assumes the defensiveness of no-penetration concrete berms erected around an American embassy. For all we know, there may have been moments when Kissinger (who can be voluble) let his guard down and surrendered to the Avedon charm offensive. But the caught image is of someone guarding state secrets deep in his trousers. Equally, it's hard not to let what we now know of Donald Rumsfeld's years of catastrophic military bungling cloud our take on Avedon's young myrmidon of the Ford administration. But the insignia of the Organisation Man, whose openings are strictly limited – the slightly superior amusement registered in the narrowing eyes, the dangerous haircut and the barely unzipped attaché case – are already there. Could it be my imagination, or are Rumsfeld's swept-wing lapels converging at the one-buttoned jacket, a cunningly coded sartorial blueprint of the Stealth bomber to come? . . . Nah . . .

Avedon's was a literary and dramatic sensibility more than an aesthetic. Every face, every body came with a potential narrative to tease out. Sometimes, in his own mind, sitters were twinned in some deep and weighty history even when they faced the camera alone. The Carter-Ford election was fought all over again in his studio; Carter, at ease in his loosely fitting Christian simplicity, Ford (slightly unfairly) made to scowl as if a different and nicer man were struggling to break through the stony carapace. Deeper still is the duet of Adlai Stevenson and Dwight Eisenhower, a chapter to itself, in Avedon's visualisation, of post-war American history. The curriculum vitae tells us that Stevenson, the last heavyweight intellectual in Democratic politics before the Arkansas Kid, was twice loser; Ike the winner; which immediately sets up expectations of Avedonian role reversal. And so it seems. Stevenson, photographed when he was Kennedy's ambassador to the United Nations, at the acme of his rhetorical force (especially deployed against the Castro-Khrushchev missiles), looks to his right, but his face is alive with confident wit; the unembarrassed pleasure of a life vindicated. The old boy is blessed with the benison of Camelot. By contrast the post-presidential Ike seems flaky pastry: the eyes unfocused. Stevenson's glance is sideways and down, a man on top of his form; Ike's is distant and upwards, lost in meditation. But it was, in fact, Eisenhower who in his old age had the more important things to say: his farewell presidential address the famous warning against the coming of the self-perpetuating 'military-industrial complex', the beast that would consume American liberty. So Avedon bestows on him the dreamy saintliness of some ancient buddha already mourning his vindication.

The studio was Avedon's theatre, with sitters encouraged to perform and the maestro as the genial director. The only time I went there myself for a group photo of *New Yorker* writers paying homage to their departing editor, the atmosphere was festive, beckoning drinks on a side-table. Avedon orchestrated the afternoon unwinding, encouraging us into showtime exuberance (in our case not a challenge). When the right moment came, he stood beside, not behind, the large-format camera, never taking his eyes off us, a party to the party, and caught the family jubilation just so. It was, I think, his Shakespearean sense of life as play that made him Olympian and intimate at the same time. His strongest pictures tease out the inner, optimised image we all carry around within ourselves, hoping that it might have some relationship to the way others see us: strong, wise, finely featured. But then Avedon puts that naively glamorised version in a dialogue with what he sees himself; the result being, in the subjects with which he had most sympathy, a marvellous dialogue between inner and outward countenance: the anima and its vital casing.

The effect, when successful, is to evoke presence more distinctively than any other photographer who has ever turned their hand to portraiture; more powerfully than Matthew Brady, Julia Margaret Cameron, August Sander or Alfred Stieglitz. For like Rembrandt, Avedon caught the shorthand signature of an entire life and the pose became a print of individual spirit. There *is* Senator Daniel Patrick Moynihan, his face lit with Erasmian amusement at the incorrigible human comedy, the dunderheaded obtuseness of political clods incapable of seeing the finesse of politics as he did, or of taking on the obligation to thought that came with the acquisition of power. Well, well, he would say, nursing his shot glass, marvelling at the mess of it all, bow tie askew, arms akimbo, the Irish-American lilt on the edge of a chuckle, would you believe it? And you look at Avedon's picture, the Senator to the life, and yes, you do.

Cooking and Eating

Cool as Ice

Vogue, August 2007

Summer 1956. Anthony Eden is dreaming dangerous Egyptian dreams which, in the following autumn, will send what little remains of the British Empire right up the creek (aka the Suez Canal). But we don't know about that and, if we did, we wouldn't care. It's the last day of school. We've seen off the eleven-plus, and out there in pebbledash London, beyond the gritty little playground of our primary school, beyond the black spiked railings hung with tendrils of bindweed, there's a siren chiming. Bing-bong, bingety bongety bong. Mr Whippy is calling and we, short-trousered, snake-belted, grimy-kneed, snot-nosed, want what he's got. We want a Ninety-Nine; God, how we want it: that shaggy-bark chocolate stick plunged into a mound of air-pumped chalky glop, which would be called vanilla were it not to defame the dark bean. But then we weren't too organic, not in 1956. So we charge out through the rusting green gates and break into our version of 'La donna è mobile':

> My name's Anton-i-o
> I sell ice cream-i-o
> Down your back-alley-o
> Tuppence a lick-i-o.

The delirium of ice cream is inseparable from juvenile glee; the uninhibited indulgence of the mouth. To get your tongue round a dollop is to become instantaneously childlike again, whatever your age; to cop a mouthful of lusciousness that magically marries opposites: fruit and dairy, the tart and the voluptuous; a shot of excitement meets a scoop of all's well. Yes, yes, doctor, we know the taking of the cone-heaped mound in our greedy gobs makes us blissed-out babies again, tripping down mammary lane: slurp, lick, suck, even, on occasions, drool and slobber. But it's more complicated than milky regression.

Mouthfeel — that's the trade term for the *sine qua non* of a satisfying product. Boardrooms of serious persons in suits will sit around — with tiny plastic spoons? — sliding the stuff in, rolling their tongues around it. Their brows will furrow and their lips purse as they assess texture, smoothness, density, whether the paste is too granular or too unctuous. They will pronounce judgement on the brightness or dullness of flavour; on whether the product has legs. But that's not what James Joyce would have wanted from mouthfeel, is it?

Imagine Molly Bloom doing strawberry flavour: 'A plop in the mouth, and down it goes and more I want more and the stink of the earthy summer and oh there yes there is the silkymilkysmooth mouthfeel and I feel the ice and my heat melts it and then yes I smell the torn berries and my tongue searches for the seeds which arent there . . .' Or, you know, something along those lines.

Not quite your mouthfeel? Come on, you know there's nothing like ice cream to give you that shot of guilty pleasure. Though I am partial to a tart sorbet — rhubarb, mango and the perfect lemon — you need the fatty voluptuousness of ice cream to make you really happy on a drizzly Monday in June. It shoves sense (and thoughts of diet) aside. You don't eat ice cream, you gorge on it. Open wide and dream — perhaps of the perfect, but as-yet-unrealised flavour? Mine would be made from the two most mysteriously succulent Edenic fruits I've ever eaten, both in the Dominican Republic: the milky-fleshed *caimito* — a flood of scented flavour, ethereally light; and its opposite, *nispero* — the unappealingly leathery brown skin concealing a bronze-coloured, honey-tasting flesh.

Where you are and with whom you're eating has much to do with the pleasure quotient. After a sudden storm off the coast of southern Brazil, our day-trip sailboat put in to a bay where the water was churned turquoise. The rain hammered down on the pink sand, but there was a small hut with an overhanging palm roof and under the shelter someone offered us coconut ice cream from the boat. It seemed like Dido's dessert.

When I was growing up in Golders Green there was no question which brand of ice cream was for nice Jewish boys and girls. Joe Lyons's Dairy Maid had been founded by Isidore and Montague Gluckstein of Whitechapel in partnership with Barnett Salmon and old Joe himself. Joe's ices were then British and Jewish, just like us! So we loyally but unenthusiastically sucked on our Orange Maid: the drink on a stick which parents kept on telling you was good for you, and the livid pink-and-white Mivvi, with its secretions of crimson goop – the Shirley Temple of the ice-cream world. The opposition – Wall's – could not have been more deeply *goyische*, since they also made pork sausages and pallid pies packed with gristly-grey mystery mince. The assumption at home was that, somehow, something of the piggy-wiggy must have crept into their Neapolitan Bricks. Which of course made the temptation to dally with the forbidden food irresistible. Heston Blumenthal may think he's the pioneer of bacon ice cream, but for us it was already there in the fabulously sinister form of a Wall's Tutti-Frutti.

The strenuous modern urge to come up with flavours that will make ice cream sexy seems redundant when all that is really needed for the stuff to tickle our fancy is intensity. Getting that intensity suspended in a smooth paste of frozen cream is enough of a feat without wasting time on sensationalism. The past masters of ice-cream making knew all about the lure of the savoury. Frederick Nutt's *Complete Confectioner of 1789* offered thirty-two flavours, including barberry, brown bread, damson and Parmesan cheese, which turns out to be nothing more than a frozen soufflé and lacks the conviction of his 'grape' flavour (actually made with elder, the *grappe de sureau*). If it's serious shock-ice you're hunting, you need to hop on a plane to Otaru Unga in Hokkaido, Japan, where apparently you can sample their chicken-wing, horse-flesh, sea-urchin, squid-ink, crab and (less dauntingly) pickled-plum and cherry-blossom flavours. Beside those exercises in kamikaze infusions, our home-grown Purbeck's Chilli Red seems hopelessly sedate, its speckling of hot flakes neutralised by the ocean of fatty Dorset cream. A few of the modern curiosities do actually work, especially in New York: Il Laboratorio del Gelato's Toasted Sesame Seed is wonderful because the custard seems to have been infused, not just scattered with seedy mix-ins. Larry's in Washington DC has a halvah ice cream which isn't at all bad. And another idea whose time you might think ought never to have come is Mario Batali's Olive Oil, but it's actually rather seductive, the little beads of oil hanging glossily on the salty cream like green sweat.

What is it about frozen desserts that tempts makers into these adventures in the gratuitous, instead of concentrating their ingenuity on nailing, say, the perfect pistachio?

A classic instance of something that should have been killed on the drawing board is the work of a team of marketing geniuses who must have thought it would be really cool to stick their perfectly good fruit sorbets in plastic tubes, thereby realising what may be the single worst packaging idea in food history. The result is called Ice Pulp. You can either shove the thing directly in your mouth, as if you suddenly remembered you'd forgotten to brush your teeth, or else you can squeeze a fat worm of blood-orange or mango sorbet on to – what exactly – a spoon, a fruit, a friend?

Would the Emperor Nero have gone for Ice Pulp? In the more fanciful ice-cream histories he is credited with being the original Mr Whippy, despatching teams of moaning slaves to the Apennine peaks to fetch back straw-wrapped wagonloads of ice, which would then be flavoured at his table with honey, pulped fruit, or possibly the remains of critics rash enough to under-praise his poetry. It was the sheer labour-intensive, conspicuously wasteful grandeur of the whole enterprise, the improbability of conserving ice in hot climates, that made it a royal project in the first place. An early recipe survives from the reign of the Mughal Emperor Akhbar, and though the predictable tales of Marco Polo bringing the taste for frozen sherbets back from Mongol China are apocryphal, it seems likely that Renaissance Europe got the iced-fruit habit from the Arab-Moorish presences in Sicily and Spain.

But there was – and is – nothing very complicated about the technology for making this most paradoxical of delights. Believe me, if I can do it – with just a little cylinder that sits in the freezer overnight while the infused custard or fruit syrup is chilling, and which then takes a mere twenty to thirty minutes of electric paddling to turn itself into ice cream or sorbet – all of you can, too. A relative newcomer to the genre, I've whipped up some not-half-bad ice creams – ginger and honey, green tea, fig and brandy, and the 'scalded apricots' of Elizabeth Raffald's 1769 recipe. My only advice: don't skimp on the egg yolks – Thomas Jefferson prescribed six for his vanilla – and never use low-fat milk. Sorbets are even more of a pushover. And if you can't serve them in the cups and glasses made of ice that feature in the Victorian cookbooks, put a few assorted scoops of rhubarb, lemon and blood-orange in a tall wine glass and you'll put a smile on the faces of kids of all ages sitting at your table.

In America, once the great ice king of Boston, Frederick Tudor, had discovered that pine sawdust was the perfect preservative for mass-packed ice and began to sell it commercially, and once sugar had gone from a luxury to an everyday commodity, a whole culture grew up around the rituals of home-made ice cream. The weekly batch involved the whole family, romping kids to stooped grans, taking turns with the churning paddle as the harvest of peaches, picked from the tree, formed itself into a fragrant mouthful of perpetual summer. The fact that the churning required attention even when others were off at church only made the treat more wickedly irresistible; homely and sinful at the same time: a Tom Sawyer picket-fence moment, bathed in shoo-fly innocence.

The American hunger for ice cream has always been an ache for a prelapsarian way of life that never was. Successive brandings have spoken to whichever paradise seems to have been most poignantly left behind. Great Depression? Right, invent the Good Humor (choc) Bar. In the Sixties, Reuben Mattus created the fake Scandiwegian brand of Häagen-Dazs, with its meaninglessly hovering umlaut, to comfort a country still crying over its murdered president. Home-style ice-cream makers have always looked for hills to nestle in, rather than be Nestléd, so Ben and Jerry resettled amidst the Green Mountains of Vermont in the late Seventies. The high-minded folksy earnestness in which the Ben & Jerry's brand wrapped itself was an obituary for the acid age: the iconography of the tubs with their self-righteous screeds and vaguely R. Crumb graphics servicing the fantasy that the thrusting yuppie was, at least as he gobbled Cherry Garcia, in Woodstock for ever.

On Main Street, the soda fountain had been a ra-ra American insti-tution, a defining fixture of the town since before the Civil War; a souser-free anti-bar where milky wholesomeness took the peril out of bobby-soxers' scarlet lipsticks. The places themselves shimmered with splendour, boasting ornate gilt-frame mirrors and towering chrome fountains. The post-war, post-welfare-state version in Britain was the milk bar. Its antiseptically tiled walls – intended, I guess, to be redolent of the dairy – were closer to a scrubbed-down NHS ward. The juke'n'jive espresso bar soon meant that its days were numbered. But before we got to drainpipe trousers, we sat there in the mournful brightness with our boatloads of banana splits, on which reposed snail-like deposits of ersatz cream. Choc ices, in the back row of the cinema between snogfests, were our best friends, since one could carry on biting, affecting cool indif-ference, as a free hand set off on its voyage of exploration.

The days of toxically lurid lollies like the unsubtly rocket-shaped,

horizontally banded (lime, lemon, strawberry) Zoom, the Jelly Terror,
Mr Merlin's Magic Purple Potion, Lord Toffingham (with its tongue-
beckoning toffee drip) and the unforgettable Lolly Gobble Choc Bomb
are long gone. In place of the thrillingly irradiated industrial-waste
aesthetic we have the return of the bucolic: flavours that take you back
to Ambridge and the village fete. In place of Mrs Thatcher (who worked
as a chemist for Lyons), we have thatched-cottage memories; our own
version of sempiternal Albion where the bumblebees hum and Ratty
sculls the stream. So September Organics (based near Hereford, and thus
at one with the cows) offers a Blackberry and Apple Crumble flavour,
and its Brown Bread (another standard recipe of the eighteenth-century
books) is about the first I've tasted that actually brings off that elusive
combo of yeasty-crumby-creamy. But it's possible to be led too far up
the hedgerow. Cinnamon, as my co-tasting friend Cassata pointed out,
is a volatile spice and needs to be almost dangerously fresh to infuse into
the waiting custard. Often, as with pistachio nuts, the temptation is to
compensate for fugitive flavour by aggressive roasting which releases a
coarsely augmented version of the flavour. Over-sweetening is another
trap into which otherwise perfectly good ice creams fall, but then I'm
someone who would much rather sample Dentist's Mouthwash Sorbet
than be forced to consume a tub of Butterscotch-Anything.

My very first experience of what real ice cream might actually taste
like was in the late Fifties in Glasgow, where an Italian community ruled
the vans. Marine Ices on Haverstock Hill in north London is one of the
last outposts of that unapologetically fruit-creamy world. But first-hand
experience of the *gelaterie* of Florence, Lucca, Orvieto, Rome and Naples
has developed in me the craving for something as close as possible to the
vivid, unclouded flavours that sit in the stainless-steel basins of
Pasqualetti, Perché No and Badiano. Oddono's of Bute Street in Kens-
ington does a pretty decent approximation, even if we are expected to
congratulate them on their vanilla hailing from Madagascar, their pista-
chios from Sicily. The most successful crossovers are marriages between
English memories and Italian tradition. But there's still nothing in the
shops to compare with the brilliant Ciao Bella brand available in and
around New York, nor with the even more spectacular stuff coming out
of Jon Snyder's Il Laboratorio del Gelato on the Lower East Side. Were
their Prune-Armagnac, their Fresh Mint, their Vanilla Saffron and their
Strawberry, which tastes more of strawberries than most strawberries do,

not so palate-blowingly fabulous, you couldn't forgive the pretentiousness of their brand name. But they are. Nothing I've ever tasted in Britain
comes close, with one sensational exception: an Elderflower Crush Sorbet
made by the terrific Jude's somewhere around Winchester. Most of their
product – chocolate, mango – is good, but the elderflower number, which
dances its way down your greedy gullet and which still has you begging
for more, is about as close to perfection as modern *gelato* will ever get.

Is it possible to get a bit too worked up about ice cream? In the dawn
of the Häagen-Dazs epoch (which did promise flavours that were
'orgasmic'), Gael Greene, the food critic of *New York Magazine*,
claimed that it was 'not excessive to rank the ice-cream revolution
with the sexual revolution, the women's movement and peace for our
time'. 'Great ice cream,' she wrote, as if declaiming the Gettysburg
Address, 'is sacred, brave, an eternal verity.' Jeez, Gael, it ain't *that*
good, but okay, it's pretty damned close.

Ice-cream recipes

Blood-orange and rosewater sorbet
Makes 6–10 portions

150g caster sugar
750ml freshly squeezed blood-orange juice
100ml orange juice
100ml lemon juice
2 tbsp orange zest
1 tbsp rosewater (or to taste)

Put the sugar and 100ml of water in a small saucepan on a high heat.
Bring to the boil and stir until the sugar dissolves.

Turn the heat down and stir for about three minutes until the syrup
thickens. Transfer the syrup into a bowl, add the juices, zest and then
rosewater and stir well. Allow the mixture to cool and set in the fridge
for at least four hours, or overnight.

Pour the fruit syrup into an ice-cream maker and follow the manufacturer's instructions.

Note: the rosewater will make this a fairly soft-spooning sorbet.

Carrot, apricot, cardamom and saffron kulfi
Makes 6–10 portions

500g carrots, peeled and cut into small chunks
200g sugar
250g good-quality (Turkish) dried or fresh, stoned apricots
150ml whole milk
150ml evaporated milk
½ tsp saffron threads, crushed
20 cardamom pods
50g pistachio nuts

Put the carrots in a small saucepan and add just enough water to cover them. Add 100g of sugar, bring to the boil and then turn the heat to low and cook slowly for twenty minutes, uncovered, stirring occasionally. Add the apricots and cook on a very low heat for another twenty-five minutes, adding a little water if necessary. Purée the carrot-apricot mixture in a blender, check for sweetness and put to one side.

Boil or microwave the whole milk on a high heat for fifteen minutes. Use a spatula to stir and scrape down the sides to mix any 'skin' into the milk. Repeat this for three more fifteen-minute batches. Add the evaporated milk and remaining sugar to the mixture and cook for a further ten minutes. If a rubbery skin has formed, this time remove it.

Crush the saffron using a pestle and mortar and add to the milk mixture. Leave to cool for twenty minutes.

Pound the cardamom pods in the mortar to release the black seeds, discard the skins, then crush the seeds well. Put the pistachio nuts into the mortar and crush coarsely. Add the nuts and seeds to the milk. Stir the carrot-apricot purée into the saffron-cardamom thickened milk, then transfer the lot into a bowl and leave to chill in the fridge for at least four hours, or overnight.

Pour into an ice-cream maker and follow the manufacturer's instructions.

Serve this in chilled glasses, with sliced fresh mangoes and papayas, sprinkled with a little freshly squeezed lime juice.

Cinnamon and honey ice cream
Makes 6–10 portions

1½ cinnamon sticks, broken in half
250ml full-fat milk
650ml cream
2 tbsp powdered cinnamon
3 tbsp clear honey
6 egg yolks
50g caster sugar

Put the cinnamon sticks in a small frying pan on a medium-low heat and dry-roast until they release their fragrance. Be careful not to burn the sticks. Then put the milk, half the cream and the sticks into a medium, heavy-based saucepan and whisk in the powdered cinnamon. Bring almost (but not completely) to the boil, stirring constantly. Reduce the heat, add the honey and stir for a further five minutes so that the cinnamon can infuse. Take off the heat. Leave to stand for five minutes, then remove the cinnamon sticks.

In a bowl, whisk the egg yolks with the sugar until the mixture is pale yellow.

Whisk 50ml of the hot milk mixture into the egg and sugar; then add the rest. Return to the pan and stir over a low heat for seven to ten minutes until the custard coats the back of a spoon. Take off the heat and leave to cool thoroughly.

Taste for fragrance. If it's a little underwhelming, this is the moment you can, if you like, add some super-high-quality powdered cinnamon. It will fleck the ice cream, but what's wrong with that?

Whip the remainder of the cream in soft peaks and fold into the mixture. Chill for at least five hours in the refrigerator or, better still, overnight.

Turn the mixture into an ice-cream maker and follow the manufacturer's instructions.

Serve with brandy snaps.

Note: cinnamon loses its strength very easily, and for this recipe to work the spice needs to infuse the custard. So if, when you open the jar or bruise the end of a stick you don't get a fierce shot of fragrance, buy some fresh.

Sauce of Controversy

Guardian, 26 November 2008

What is the single, best word to describe the pleasure of a great bolognese sauce? Rich. And right now, in lean economic times and at the start of a long, cold winter, we will be wanting some of that richness, won't we? Which must be why sales of 'mince' are up 16 per cent. It's an easy, irresistible, almost childish pleasure: the ground meat dissolved into a dark blood-red sauce until they are one and the same; no hacking, slicing or cutting needed; a slurpy goodness; the oily bolognese hanging on to the slippery pasta; guaranteed joy in a world that's just ruled it out.

In 1973, the National Theatre put on a production of the Neapolitan playwright Eduardo de Filippo's *Saturday, Sunday, Monday*, in which a family falls apart along with the meat sauce. A character played by Laurence Olivier was at the centre of it all, but the real star was the *ragù*: actually cooked onstage, filling the theatre with the narcotic aroma of sizzling onion, garlic, tomatoes and meat. The acting was terrific, but who cared? Audiences applauded and rushed out to the nearest trattoria – only to be disappointed by a garish, thin, red concoction.

You don't want that, but what do you want; or rather whose *ragù* or meat sauce? It's a subject that can start fights among partisans. I've borrowed this and that from hostile parties and over many years of experiment developed a version that brings you a bowlful of Italian splendour in icy times.

First, and most essentially, you need time. Bolognese sauce isn't fast food. If you're assuming you can get home late, fry up some minced beef, bung a can of tomato purée on it, let it sit for ten minutes and cook the spag, you might as well go to the sub-standard local Italian after all. Think of the real bolognese as a party of shy ingredients who need careful introducing to each other if they're going to get happily intimate. You will need forty minutes to an hour to get every-thing going. and at least another hour for the sauce to develop its gorgeousness. If you have a whole afternoon, better still, or if you can cook a big batch and leave it to combine and develop (preferably not in the fridge) overnight, so much the better.

Other than time, here's what you must have: three different kinds of meat: veal, beef and, in some form or other (minced loin, or sausage or pancetta), a bit of a pig. Some classic recipes insist on hamminess as in pancetta, but it depends on whether you want that cured quality or not. It's certainly not as essential as the mashed chicken livers which, in a true bolognese sauce (such as Elizabeth David's on page 323), are really oblig-atory: they give the dark substance and pungency you're after. If you have liver-haters in the house, don't tell them; they won't notice.

The procedure – which also calls for the cook to drink something happy-making, say a Morellino de Scansano – is always the same. Sauté your *odori*: onion, garlic, parsley, finely chopped carrot (quite a lot of that), celery (ditto). Then remove them to a bowl while you're browning the meats; drain some (not all) of the fat; return the meat; add chopped peeled tomatoes and a tablespoon of purée; salt, pepper, oregano, a smidgin of thyme, ditto basil. Sauté the chicken livers separately until just the brown side of pink, mash them up and add to the pot. Then add beef or chicken stock. Bring to a simmer.

Now the second Big Decision faces you – the wine: red or white? Both are actually fine, but they make for a different style of sauce. The red can be aggressive, which works if you are on a two-day bolog-nese, as it will have time to be fully absorbed by the other ingredients; but, if you're going to be eating it the same evening, use white and let it just help the meat melt.

About half an hour before serving, grate a little Parmesan cheese into the sauce and let it blend – irrespective of whether you're going to sprinkle more on the final dish.

Last trick – don't drown the spag in the sauce. The oily grains should hang on the pasta rather than smother it.

And cook enough to freeze a load. You will be grateful on those long, dark winter nights. Or mornings. I've had it for breakfast and, believe me, it will change your whole day. Sometimes I've even spooned it down cold. So sue me.

Or try one of these classics:

Marcella Hazan's version
Serves 4–6

1 tbsp vegetable oil
4 tbsp butter
½ cup chopped onion
⅔ cup chopped celery
⅔ cup chopped carrot
¾ lb ground beef chuck
salt
fresh ground black pepper
1 cup whole milk
whole nutmeg
cup dry white wine
1½ cups canned Italian plum tomatoes, torn into pieces, with juice
1¼–1½ lb pasta (preferably spaghetti), cooked and drained
freshly grated Parmigiano-Reggiano cheese at the table

Put the oil, three tablespoons of butter and the chopped onion in a heavy 3.3-litre (6-pint) pot and turn the heat to medium. Cook and stir the onion until it has become translucent, then add the chopped celery and carrot. Cook for about two minutes, stirring the vegetables to coat well.

Add the ground beef, a large pinch of salt and a few grindings of pepper. Crumble the meat with a fork, stir well and cook until the beef has lost its raw, red colour.

Add the milk and let simmer gently, stirring frequently, until it has bubbled away completely. Add a tiny grating, about an eighth of a teaspoon, of fresh nutmeg and stir.

Add the wine and let it simmer until it has evaporated. Add the tomatoes and stir thoroughly to coat all the ingredients well. When the tomatoes begin to bubble, turn the heat down so that the sauce cooks at the laziest of simmers, with just an intermittent bubble breaking through the surface. Cook, uncovered, for three hours or more, stirring from time to time. While the sauce is cooking, you are likely to find that it will begin to dry out and the fat will separate from the meat. To keep it from sticking, add half a cup of water as necessary.

At the end of cooking, however, the water should be completely evaporated and the fat should separate from the sauce. Taste and correct
for salt.

Add the remaining tablespoon of butter to the hot pasta and toss
with the sauce. Serve with freshly grated Parmesan on the side.

Elizabeth David's version
Serves 6

85g uncooked bacon or ham (both fat and lean)
butter
1 onion
1 carrot
1 small piece of celery
225g lean minced beef
115g chicken livers
3 tsp concentrated tomato purée
1 glass white wine
salt and pepper
nutmeg
2 wine glasses meat stock or water
½ a tsp nutmeg, freshly grated if possible

Cut the bacon or ham into very small pieces and brown them gently
in a small saucepan in about 15g of butter. Add the onion, the carrot
and the celery, all finely chopped. When they have browned, put in
the raw minced beef, and then turn it over and over so that it all browns
evenly. Add the chopped chicken livers, and after two or three minutes
the tomato purée, and then the white wine. Season with salt (taking
into account the relative saltiness of the ham or bacon), pepper and a
scraping of nutmeg, and add the meat stock or water.

Cover the pan and simmer the sauce very gently for thirty to forty
minutes. Some cooks in Bologna add a cupful of cream or milk to
the sauce, which makes it smoother. I add a light sprinkle of nutmeg.
Another traditional variation is the addition of the ovarine or unlaid
eggs which are found inside the hen, especially in the spring when
the hens are laying. They are added at the same time as the chicken
livers and form small golden globules when the sauce is finished.

When the *ragù* is to be served with spaghetti or tagliatelle, mix it with the hot pasta in a heated dish so that the pasta is thoroughly impregnated with the sauce, and add a generous piece of butter before serving. Hand the grated cheese round separately.

Cheese Soufflé

Guardian, 2 March 2009

In 1958, when I was thirteen years old, the days of the midweek seemed to melt aimlessly into each other. Saturday night couldn't come fast enough: winkle-pickers, drainpipe trousers, hanging around Golders Green bus station eyeing the birds and doing a bit of back-combing. But I didn't need a diary to tell me how far away the weekend was. The evening aromas coming from the kitchen as I struggled with my Latin verbs would check off the days.

Wednesday brought a pungent sheepy smell emanating from the greyish lamb and barley soup my mother optimistically called Taste of the Garden of Eden. Expel me, please. Haddock in the air? That would be Thursday. Eaten cold, two days later, for breakfast, it wasn't all that bad. When the fried flakes started to glow with a slight morning iridescence, the thing turned edible. The faintest whiff of roasting garlic? That would be what my sister and I uncharitably dubbed Friday Night Memorial Chicken; a venerable object smeared on the breasts with a dab of Marmite meant to cheer the bird up as it emerged defeated from the oven. Rattling inside the little cavity was that one solitary clove of garlic: the exotic knobble that my mother conceded as a romantic touch amid the iron regimen of her unvarying weekly routine.

So when I learned to cook in the 1960s, the discovery of food was always about experiment: an aversion to routine of any kind. There were certain trusty books at hand; my guides and mentors – Elizabeth David's *French Provincial Cooking* and *Italian Food*, and Simonne Beck, Louise Bertholle and Julia Child's *Mastering the Art of French Cooking*. And I quickly learned that there were some things I did better than others – bouillabaisse, *soupe au pistou*, *stufato di manzo* (Italian beef stew) – but I shunned anything resembling a familiar repertoire: a bistro edition of my mother's kitchen. So I would recklessly take chances with dinner parties on dishes I had never tried before. Sometimes they worked; some-times they didn't.

Zwiebel, an Alsatian onion tart from Elizabeth David, had exactly the buttery-golden texture and voluptuous ooze running to the walls of the pastry shell, but a beef Wellington served up to impress his-torians was a glutinous ruin. Undaunted, the riskier the combo of pastry and whatever it was, the more I was up for it. It took a few disas-ters with a classic Russian salmon *koulibiak*, but on the third try at a summer dinner party in my neo-brutalist Cambridge don's rooms, I pulled it off, passed the vodka and watched as conversation stopped and guests forked their way to quiet joy.

Years later, with small children running round my American kitchen, cooking was still ordained as adventure. Living in New England, the family was going to eat seafood – and I didn't mean fish fingers. In late February, the very first tiny, intensely sweet shrimp of the season would be driven down from Camden, Maine, by a ruddy-faced fisherman who would park his van on a suburban hill, pack a huge plastic tub of them for a few dollars, and we would gorge through the weekend, sucking the meat from the delicate shells. Then there was lobster, the scariest imaginable food for children, which we educa-tionally set before them. We cracked a claw open for my four-year-old daughter, who was leaning towards the glistening oily white flesh when a cry of horror came from my smaller son sitting in his high chair. 'No, Chloë! Don't put it in your mouth,' he wailed, staring in horror at the lurid marine cockroach. She did.

But, even as I turned into an unstoppably crazed gazeteer of world cuisine – Maghrebi *maqluba* (upside-down aubergine and rice casse-role), Burmese *beya kwaw* (split-pea fritters) that fell apart in the pan – I knew it was unfair to recruit my kids as fellow gastro-explorers in the name of principled eclecticism. Small children are nature's little conservatives. They are warmed by fulfilled expectations. They have favourites in the kitchen – and why deny them? So I developed some dishes that could satisfy my longing for complicated exercises in flavour fusions, but still be food that the children loved: a lemony-chickpea chicken stew first encountered in Claudia Roden's Middle Eastern books, and the much-requested *raan*, a Kashmiri roast lamb dish in which the joint is marinaded in three separate coats: a garlic-and-roast-spice rub; a paste of saffron, crushed pistachio and almonds blended with yoghurt; and finally, a sumptuous drizzle of honey. After two (or preferably three) days tight-wrapped in film in the fridge, out it comes and slow-roasts (or rather disintegrates beneath its nutty-spicy-sweet golden mantle of flavours) and you have something that's both main course and pudding all at once.

Raan was all very well for the weekend (marinade Friday night; eat on Sunday), but the more hectic family life became, the more I needed a range of dishes that would make them happy as they smelled the cooking when they came in from lacrosse or science lab on a bleak muddy evening in February, or while they got stuck into homework. They had to be dishes that wouldn't take an age to prepare (though dinner was usually around eight, two hours after most American kids had eaten, allowing their friends to stop round for a second supper). And it had to be a meal I wanted to shop for, after a day's teaching or writing.

Getting to know the shopkeepers makes a difference, turns a transaction into a gossip with friends. At the Korean greengrocer I want to know when the New Jersey asparagus might show up in May, but also how Monica is doing off in Montana with her one-year-old. At the butcher's in Chappaqua, they'll find me a rabbit for a pasta sauce, but I worry how Tony manages after losing his wife in a battle with cancer. At Harold's place they'll be smoking sturgeon and whitefish and complaining it's been too long since they saw me, while across the street at Mount Kisco Seafood I'll talk cricket with Pauly from India, but baseball with Brian and Joe even though they're Yankees fans and I'm a diehard Red Sox loyalist. We switch to Pink Floyd or politics and they tell me the Copper River salmon from Alaska is in – and only for a precious two weeks. So I'll take a long beautiful fillet and power-roast it in the oven with a light crust of fine-chopped fresh herbs.

The trick is to set the roasting pan, liberally greased with butter (olive oil, if you must) and a layer of herbs, in a fierce oven, say 225°C, until the green stuff is on the turn of crisping. Then you set the fish on top, skin-side up, for just four minutes for a piece about 1.5cm thick, until the skin peels off with just the touch of a knife. Turn, season and cover the now exposed side of the fillet with more herbs (parsley, coriander, thyme, even tarragon – just not rosemary) and roast for another four. The fish cooks perfectly, buttery and golden-crispy on the outside, perfectly juicy inside. Kids of all ages, even fish-haters, love it.

So the herby salmon became an item in the repertoire I swore I would never have. But actually family cooks need these staples; together they make a kitchen portrait of their table life together. And with any luck, as they grow up and leave home and start their own kitchens, the children will take those food memories with them. There is an Italian meatloaf — *polpettone* — that I made a lot, which, before he became a vegetarian, my son liked so much that he wrote his college application essay about father—son bonding in the hunt for the perfect meatloaf recipe, ending with the triumph of the *polpettone rustica*. It's a homely, lovely thing; a coarse blend of veal and beef, into which you knead some chopped-up stale white bread, soaked in milk, a few grams of finely grated Parmesan, a beaten egg and that's about it. But then instead of packing it into a loaf tin, you make a freeform Swiss roll or big sausage of it, roll it in flour and carefully set it in a casserole of foaming butter or oil together with a couple of sprigs of thyme, a bay leaf and a sage leaf. You let the roll bubble and brown a little, add a glass of white wine or (better for some reason) dry vermouth and then put it in a 180°C oven with the lid off. After thirty minutes take the pot out, and carefully turn it over with spatulas (wooden are best, as non-flexible) and let it cook another thirty to forty minutes. Serve with some sauté potatoes and a *salsa verde* and you can guarantee supper bliss.

There are other indispensable items in the Schama repertoire: a wonderful simple dish of flattened chicken fillets dredged in paprika and cayenne cornmeal, fried and set on a bed of rocket that has been doused in chopped summer tomatoes, their juice marrying with some good olive oil and a little sherry vinegar, the whole thing crispy and sloppy, hot and fresh, all at the same time. Then there are swordfish steaks marinated in an Asian blend of soy, mirin, grated ginger, garlic and chopped spring onions, and barbecued for seven minutes a side.

But what the kids moaned for, craved, especially in dark winter months, was the simplest of all: a cheese soufflé. Simple? Yes, it could hardly be simpler, and also virtually infallible as long as you have a dependable oven. The prep takes perhaps twenty minutes; the cooking, filling the kitchen with luscious, toasty-cheesy aroma, another twenty-five to thirty minutes, during which time you can make a salad or a pan of spinach to cut against the voluptuous ooziness of the soufflé. So the whole thing takes maybe forty-five minutes – a doddle for hard-pressed cooks in midweek. And though soufflé cooking scares people off – what if it fails to rise? (it never does) – the only art you have to learn is the difference between mixing and folding the cheese-yolk mixture into the beaten whites.

Once you've tried it, you'll know there's nothing to it and, unless you're a cholesterol timebomb, it will be at the heart of your very own family repertoire too.

Cheese soufflé
Serves 4

6 eggs, separated into 4 yolks and 6 whites
2 tbsp butter plus tsp for greasing soufflé dish
1½ tbsp plain flour, plus dusting for the soufflé dish
200ml milk
170g grated Gruyère
2 tbsp Dijon mustard
1 tsp salt
50g finely grated Parmesan

For accompaniment
Either watercress salad with walnuts and a drizzle of balsamic
dressing, or shredded cavolo nero crisped in the oven for 10
minutes with 3 tbsp olive oil

Pre-heat the oven to 190°C. Butter a large (1.8l) ovenproof soufflé dish and dust with flour.

Separate the eggs: whites into a large bowl, yolks into small one.

On a medium-high heat, melt the butter in a large saucepan; add the flour and blend with either a wooden fork or a small whisk, stirring all the time for two minutes, so that the mix doesn't form lumps. It should make an elastic goop.

Add the milk and continue to stir or whisk for about four minutes until the mixture forms a dense creamy mass – the béchamel.

Add the grated Gruyère and stir until smooth. Remove from the heat. When tepid, whisk in the egg yolks, mustard and salt.

Beat the whites preferably by hand with a balloon whisk, but an electric beater works just fine, until they form soft and floppy peaks.

Using a flexible plastic or rubber spatula, fold the cheese-mustard mix into the whites (or vice versa, it really doesn't matter). What does matter is that you fold, not beat or aggresively stir. Folding just means diving the spatula to the bottom of the bowl, lovingly bringing it up and over again to blend the mix. It's always much better to undermix than lose air by thrashing it into submission.

When the mixture is nicely married, pour into the buttered, flour-dusted soufflé dish. It should fill all but 1cm below the lip. With a knife, cut a circle in the top of the mix – to create a crown – and sprinkle over the finely grated Parmesan.

Set the soufflé dish in the oven and turn the heat down immediately to 175°C.

While the soufflé is cooking, assemble a simple salad – watercress or rocket with a light dressing, a little acid to cut against the creaminess of the soufflé.

Bake for twenty-five minutes before peeping. Test doneness with a skewer. It won't collapse. If the skewer comes away cleanly and, depending on whether you want an oozy, flowing centre or a drier soufflé, stop right there or cook for another four minutes. Serve with the watercress salad or a dish of crsipy cavolo nero or spinach.

Simmer of Love

Vogue, February 2008

Whoever would have thought that a writer as bony as Virginia Woolf would be the one to extol the majesty of beef stew in all its gloppy glory? In *To the Lighthouse*, Woolf transforms a dinner party, wretched with unspoken strong feeling, into a moment of tender communion. What accomplishes this miracle? A Swiss maid sets down on the table a big brown pot of *boeuf en daube*. Suddenly, everything and everyone is enveloped in the welcoming fug of meaty steam. Aromas of bay and wine hang benevolently over these tediously self-absorbed types. Flinty minds liquefy. The ladle ladles, they all tuck in, human sympathy descends on the refined company. They begin to resemble actual human beings. The beleaguered hostess, Mrs Ramsay, is so swoony at her 'triumph', through which egotism has melted into the 'confusion of savoury yellow and brown meats' lying in the casserole, that she commits a white lie, claiming the dish is 'a French recipe of my grandmother's' when in fact it is (needless to say) the creation of her cook, Mildred.

And, for a moment, you, too, reader, are held in a contented drool. Unless, that is, you are a cook – which, you then suddenly realise, Mrs Woolf could not possibly have been herself. *Boeuf en daube? Yellow* meats? *What* 'yellow' meats? A chicken foot lurking in there along with the beef and onions, is there? And then the credibility of the scene falls apart just like a lengthily braised joint, except less appetisingly. For now you also recall that, a few pages previously, Mrs Ramsay had been agitated that her diners would not assemble on time because, she worries, where a *boeuf en daube* is concerned, 'everything depended upon being served up to the precise moment they were ready. The beef, the bay leaf and the wine – all must be done to a turn. To keep it waiting was out of the question.' But this description, from the most fastidiously observant English novelist of the twentieth century, is exactly what a *daube* is *not*.

Stews are the most forgiving dishes. Under their tight-shut lid they can be allowed to simmer away for hours on end, provided they don't dry out – which they won't if you buy cuts with enough fat to lubricate the slowly dissolving tissue, and so long as you poke your nose in the pot from time to time to check for dwindling juice. Stews seem to possess an organic vitality independent of the cook. Left alone overnight, even in the fridge, benevolent unions and fusions happen, so that the longer they go on, the better they get. Eating a stew on the day it's cooked is okay. Eating it the day after is an improvement, and spooning down a bowlful for breakfast two days later is a wholly different experience from cornflakes. It's this steady gathering of richness, the accumulating intensification of flavour that, over the centuries, made stews a rare sustenance amidst the emaciated life of the rural poor, for they could be simmered in an iron cauldron over a slow fire, or set in a bed of cinders waiting to be devoured after a long day of herding or harvesting. They are the dish *par excellence* of cultures without timepieces.

Early French cookbook writers like Menon, who equated social stability with the culinary traditions of the *terroir*, praised the *marmite perpetuelle* – the perpetual poultry-pot, never allowed to be emptied or taken from the heat, so that the broth left from the long poaching of one bird would then welcome the arrival of the next, which in turn would contribute its own golden oozings, on and on for ever in a great unbroken chain of nourishment. When the *marmite perpetuelle* seemed to have vanished from rural cuisine at the close of the nineteenth century, its elegists thought the end of true cooking was nigh.

How odd is it that being 'in a stew' is a description of sweaty anxiety when, in fact, the food is a balm for the fretful: a slow, voluptuous yielding, long bundles of fibre softening in a gently bubbling bath of oily wine or, in the Flemish *carbonnade*, yeasty beer. We think of stews as wintry comforts but they are sure-fire proof against dirty weather, hot or cold. The most satisfying *daube* I remember making was in the summer of 1972 when an ugly Mediterranean storm-system stalled over the Côte d'Azur, where I was holidaying with a girlfriend in a walk-up rental in Cagnes-not-really-sur-Mer. The place wasn't much to talk about, but the tiny kitchen boasted a mighty *marmite*. After an overnight marinade of the beef in local olive oil (no cold-pressed extra-virgins known in 1972, not to us anyway), barnyard-smelling red Minervois wine, a tablespoon of vinegar and a fist of herbs and garlic, we rendered some cubed bacon in the morning, softened some carrots in the fat so they took on a vivid glaze, and let the usual mess of sliced onions and garlic go gently translucent. I had brought along with me the bible of all novice cooks, Elizabeth David's *French Provincial Cooking*, and it was her *daube provençale* that we made, throwing in a greasy slab of salt pork, some sprigs of thyme and parsley and oregano, bay leaves from the tree outside the old limestone house, a handful or two of black olives, a few bashed peppercorns and some curls of orange zest. The storm growled overhead in an inky sky, wooden doors in the hilltop village banged, and stray cats screeched in the lightning. Wishing the stew a happy simmer, we went to bed, the scent of Provençal thyme welling through the rooms. Every so often we'd get up to slurp the mysteriously harmonising concoction from a big old spoon or throw some rough cognac on the surface, setting light to it for cheerfulness's sake, hoping not to incinerate the rental. It was meat and drink, breakfast, lunch and supper, that sumptuous *daube*. We wiped bowls with hunks of stale baguette or ate it on beds of slippery noodles, beads of oil glimmering on the pale ribbons as the feast saw off the bullyboy thunder. The festive, recklessly amorous Elizabeth, we thought, would have approved.

So if there's joy promised in the consumption of a richly cooked stew, why don't we see more of them on the menus of ambitious contemporary restaurants? Partly, I suppose it's because their messiness doesn't sit well in a plating culture that wants you to ooh and aah at the exquisiteness of presentation; a thin tile of (please God, no) sea bass, skin side up, its silvery surface demurely crisped at the edges, perched just so on a plinth of spinach while teeny-weeny broad beans do a dainty little dance around the perimeter of the dish. Cute. Stewing meat of whatever kind is never cute; it's the slob on the plate, leaking incontinently towards the beckoning mash. But gastro-aesthetes are wrong to write off stews as simple stuff. Done right, they are complex compositions, but they are, certainly, earthy: redolent of the farmyard and not for the dainty. In Oklahoma some years ago, I was treated to a bowl of burgoo. Even if the squirrel was, as I suspected, yard-kill, who cared when it luxuriated in a brick-colour smoky sauce of chipotle chillies, plum tomatoes, garlic and beer? A true *civet* — whether classically of hare or any other four-legged critter — is defined by two additions to the pot: the onions or chives from which the dish gets its name, and the blood of the animal stirred in before final reheating. Among American cowboys, as my friend Blanquette reminded me, sonofabitch stew, made from brains, tripe, hooves, innards, tongue and 'mountain oysters' (balls, to you) – in fact, anything that doesn't get to be hamburger – is still prime rodeo fare.

There's also the sense among contemporary chefs that *boeuf bour-guignon* and its kindred stews are old hat; along with the paprika-lurid goulashes and *coqs au plonk* that featured heavily in the Paris *bistros* of the Fifties, like Chez Allard and Louis XIV on the place des Victoires, and which gave Anglo bohemians groaning from limp veg and leathery beef the impression they had arrived in a real-food world. In the Sixties those dishes, served with halfway decent bread, became the staple of the first London 'bistros' I could afford, like the Chanterelle in Chelsea, places where (unlike today) you went to be *un*seen, except by your roman-tic prospect. Never mind the flouncy waiters in their blood-red shirts, a plateful of *coq au vin* seemed a declaration of class war on the aristo fare at toffish places like the Mirabelle, with their anaemic sole sitting in a puddle of béchamel. We smoked Gitanes hung on our nether lip, Belmondo-style, across from turquoise-eyeshadowed dates dragging arti-choke leaves through their incisors.

Or, courtesy of Elizabeth David, Jane Grigson and, later and more dauntingly, Mesdames Bertholle, Becks and Child's *Mastering the Art of French Cooking*, we would whip up our own versions of *boeuf bour-guignon* on a solitary, erratically sputtering gas ring in a college staircase kitchen, much to the horror of the Cambridge cleaning ladies, who smelled nasty habits along with the nasty garlic.

And it was a bonus that those of us who were historians were, we thought, cooking (in the most legitimate way) our research, as well as vice versa. High politics turned us off as much as *haute cuisine*. Instead, we marinated ourselves in Fernand Braudel's history of the food migra-tions of the centuries; the Europeanisation of exotic foods like sugar or spices like pepper and cloves. The revolutions we really rated as world-changing were the appearance of the American potato and tomato, not the storming of the Bastille. Redcliffe Salaman's epic history of the tuber was a must-read (it still is). Before long our cook-books were also our texts of history and ethnography: Alan Davidson's stupendous works of encyclopaedic scholarship; Elizabeth Ayrton's *The Cookery of England*, which introduced us to cooks like Gervase Markham in the seventeenth century, Elizabeth Raffald and the punchy Hannah Glasse in the eighteenth. In the British Museum Reading

Room I'd play truant from teaching undergraduates Abelard or Eisenhower and dally instead with Robert May's *The Accomplisht Cook*
(1660) or Varenne's *Cuisinier Français* (1651). And gradually I became
aware of the epic battle between Spit and Pot. Spit People were aristocratic roasters; birds and beast, trussed and turned; Pot People were
the plebs: lengthy braisers.

There was never any doubt I was a Pot Person. The closest my
mother – who grew up in the Jewish East End, and whose idea of lamb
stew was something worryingly thin and grey – ever got to rhapso-
dising about food was when she described taking the iron pot of *cholent*
(the stew of meat and vegetables – which, if done right, had raw eggs
in their shells buried within) to a communal baker's oven before the
onset of the Sabbath on Friday night. Nothing, she said, was quite like
taking the lid off the *cholent* pot by the time the family got back from
synagogue the next day. '*Taam gan eden*,' she would murmur dream-
ily – 'The taste of the Garden of Eden.'

Stews are the inclusive food, uniting multitudes – your family, your
friends, your tribe – around the same capacious, endlessly nourishing pot.
When the Grand Constable of the Dauphiné, during a time of religious
war at the end of the sixteenth century, wanted to win friends and allies,
he'd bring his *grande marmite* to town and put on a spread for 500. A
surviving recipe written in his hand calls for, among other ingredients,
160 pigs' trotters (a good source of gelatine thickening), 100kg of beef,
40 bottles of red wine, 24 of white, 32 chickens and 25kg of mushrooms.
But this was small potatoes compared to the great *sancocho* of Caracas,
in which, earlier this year, in a mass demonstration of Chavezian state
philanthropy (or megalomania), a single pot containing 5,000kg of meat
and 7,000kg of vegetables, including yucca, okra and plantains, bought
the loyalty of at least 17,000 satisfied Venezuelans.

Stews are bringers of contentment to a discontented world. I don't
know of any other kind of food, except perhaps freshly baked bread
and cakes, guaranteed to fill a kitchen with such a sense of abundance.
They violate all the cool modern conventions, for they demand fat and
time and copious carbs – mashed potatoes or parsnips, pasta or bread
– to soak up the juicy mess. You'll have skimmed much of the killer
grease half an hour or so before serving, so there's no obligation to
cleanse the palate with anything sharply green. Don't even think about
spinach, though the collapse of a summer salad on an oily plate is one

of the table's great acts of surrender. Forget about anything leaner or meaner (like green beans): that's like inviting Lent to the carnival. And as the winter nights close in and the craving for those unctuous, oozing, life-sustaining stews becomes irresistible, do yourselves a favour: make a large pot at the weekend and it will last all week, nourishing your very own Perpetual Pot of Pleasure.

Stew recipes

Boeuf en daube provençale
(Remembered and adapted from Elizabeth David)
Time: 3 hours 30 minutes (plus marinating time)
Serves 6

1½kg stewing beef, cut into 2½cm cubes

For the marinade:
2 tbsp olive oil
2 medium carrots, coarsely sliced
1 stick celery, finely chopped
2 cloves garlic, finely chopped
3 medium shallots, finely chopped
1 tbsp rosemary, chopped
1 tbsp thyme, leaves stripped from sprigs
1 tbsp flat parsley, finely chopped
12 peppercorns, cracked
a pinch of salt
1 bottle robust red wine – Gigondas or Cahors

For the stew:
plain flour for dusting
1 tbsp olive oil
200g streaky bacon or pancetta, diced
2 garlic cloves, smashed but not chopped
2 bay leaves
1 tbsp fresh thyme
4 good-quality anchovies, minced (optional)
zest of ½ medium orange
50g good-quality black olives

125g mushrooms
75ml cognac
fresh parsley, finely chopped, for garnish

Prepare the marinade one or two days in advance of serving the *daube*: heat the olive oil in a frying pan and sauté the carrots, celery, garlic, shallots and herbs on a medium-low heat for about three minutes, until the herbs release their aroma.

Put the beef in a bowl, combine with the marinade, season with the pepper and salt and add the wine. Cover and leave overnight. If steeping longer, turn the meat in the marinade every few hours.

When you are ready to cook the *daube*, use a slotted spoon to remove the beef from the marinade, pat dry on paper towels and dust with flour.

Pre-heat the oven to 125°C, gas mark ½.

On a medium heat, heat the oil and fry the bacon or pancetta in a casserole until it begins to crisp. Remove the bacon from the pot and set aside. Turn up the heat and brown the beef in batches.

Return the bacon to the dish, add the beef and marinade, and then the garlic, bay leaves, thyme, anchovies (if used) and zest. Put on the lid, place in the oven and cook for at least three hours, until the meat falls apart.

About thirty minutes before serving, add the olives and mushrooms, and continue to cook. Warm the cognac in a ladle, pour over the stew and set it alight.

Garnish with parsley and serve from the pot with bread or flat noodles – the traditional Provençal way.

Chickpea-lemon chicken stew with couscous
Time: 1 hour 30 minutes (plus soaking time)
Serves 4

425g chickpeas (prepare as below, but if you are short of time, use tinned and drain and rinse well)
1 small onion, peeled
2 garlic cloves, peeled

For the stew:
4 tbsp light olive or safflower oil

2 large onions, thinly sliced
4 cardamom pods, cracked
2 tsp turmeric
1 tsp cumin seeds
3 garlic cloves, crushed
1 tsp ground cumin
½ tsp cayenne
½ tsp ground ginger
1 tsp coriander seeds, coarsely crushed
1 organic chicken, cut into 8 pieces
the juice of 3 lemons (if possible unwaxed)
250ml chicken stock
1 lemon (preserved if possible), cut into pieces
15 green olives, pitted
salt and freshly ground pepper, to taste
fresh parsley or coriander for garnish

Prepare the chickpeas before cooking the stew: place them in a colander and rinse well. Then put them in a bowl of cold water at room temperature and soak overnight. Transfer to a saucepan over a medium heat, add the whole onion and garlic cloves, bring to the boil, then remove from the heat and leave to soak for two to three hours, until almost tender.

Heat two tablespoons of the olive oil in a tagine or casserole dish on a low heat and sauté the onions, cardamom pods, turmeric and cumin seeds for ten minutes, until the onions are soft but not brown.

Add the garlic, ground cumin, cayenne, ground ginger and coriander seeds, turn the heat up to medium and fry for a further three minutes.

Remove the spiced-onion mix and set aside in a bowl. Add the remaining two tablespoons of oil to the casserole and brown the chicken pieces on a medium heat for about ten minutes, until golden. Season with a little salt and pepper, then add the lemon juice and chicken stock to the pot so that the chicken pieces are fully covered.

Put a lid on the pot and simmer on a medium heat for thirty minutes.

Drain the chickpeas. Add to the stew with the lemon chunks and olives. Simmer for a further thirty minutes, until the meat is beginning to fall off the bone and the liquid has become a thick sauce.

Serve the stew in bowls, spooned onto a pile of couscous, and garnish with finely chopped fresh parsley or coriander.

My Mother's Kitchen

Observer Food Magazine, 11 October 2009

It was when my mother minced the tip of her forefinger into the *klops* that I realised her cooking owed more to enthusiasm than finesse. No, I'm wrong. It was when she decided not to bother to *search* for the little piece of alien flesh amidst the beef, but carried on kneading the meat with the onions, that I got a sense of her priorities, at the top of which was Just Getting It Over With. I was nine. The kitchen intrigued me for it seemed some sort of battlefield in which my mother laid about various ingredients until they surrendered and accepted their fate in a long, hot oven. She would never have used the term *batterie de cuisine*, but she took pride in the more fearsome of its implements, in partic-ular the heavy-duty steel hand mincer, which, after it had been polished to military brilliance, was attached to the kitchen table. All kinds of food went down its helical screw-mouth: translucent cod and haddock fillets on Thursdays for the *gefilte* fish; unusual extra chicken breasts for fried balls served up sometimes on Sundays, and the mid-week jumbo meatballs, the legendary *klops* of her strenuous attack. Into the screw were also fed lashings of onion and, if she was in a mood to lighten the fish or chicken, a beaten egg or two. I don't remember her crying out in pain when she pulled her slightly chewed-up finger out of the mincer, though there was a hearty Yiddish curse or two sent in its direction. Like Basil Fawlty scolding his Mini, she had Warned It Before and now it would just have to take the consequences. Into the sink went her finger; on to the slightly drippy wound went an Elasto-plast and on she went with the *klops*. At nine I could (on select occasions) be a sanctimonious little perisher and knew that I could put a stop to the inexorable grinding by asking her whether the ground fingertip was, in fact, kosher, and if not, would it write off the whole dish – one of my father's favourites? I also knew that she would brush the objection aside with one of her more devilish laughs and that would be the end of it, other than swearing me to silence as Father and my older sister tucked into the *klops*.

Later, when she worked as the Field-Marshal of Kosher Meals on Wheels in the Jewish East End, getting up before dawn to travel across London to see all the housebound got their lunches, and relished every minute of it, I realised that it was not the food that was my mother's foe so much as the domestic kitchen itself. A bundle of animal energy in a pretty little package, she just was not cut out for the middle-class housewife role in which she had got somehow stuck, and all the displaced, ferocious energy, and slightly manic, often comical, action drama just needed a bigger stage to operate on. As far as I could tell, Trudie had always been this way. As a little girl, Chaya Gittel – the name she went by in Whitechapel and Stepney – had the startling looks that made people want to chin-chuck her or (for her), worse, pinch her cushiony cheeks: black curls and cobalt-blue eyes; a killer combo. But when she was made to dress up, and the curls were trained into ringlets, people found out in a hurry she was more spitfire than angel. Her father, my grandfather Mark, the only one of a gang of Lithuanian-Jewish brothers who stopped in Stepney rather than moving north to Liverpool to catch the New York ship, was a butcher. So when Chaya, over furious protest, was forced to dress up in silks and satins imported at great expense from my grandmother's Vienna relatives for Special Occasions, my mother's way to make a tomboy statement was to take the butcher's shears and slash it to ribbons. The thrashing she got made her repent not one bit. She set her jaw firmly and swore she would do it again.

Perhaps it was the butcher-shop childhood that did it, but my mother grew up seldom relishing food; and certainly holding herself apart from the fatty wallowing in the joys of the Jewish table, which she looked on, often, with undisguised contempt – even, or especially, when she was forced to cook it. Food and its relentless preparation was somehow a chore, an enemy of life. During the war she worked for de Havilland aircraft, Girl Friday to test pilots, one of whom used to take her for spins in his roadster, a bottle of Scotch handy in the glove box. She got to like un-Jewish things: Thames Valley pubs and good hard Cheddar with the odd dark vein running to the rind. My mother thought the test pilot an ace and always laughed at the memory of his fine madness. He ended in a ball of flame, but that only made the story perfect as far as she was concerned.

In her girlhood Chaya befriended a turkey whose lame strut — a ritual impurity — had saved it from the slaughterer's knife. She called it 'Loomie' — the Lame One — and taught it to limp up and down the stairs. Girl and bird bonded with terrible intensity and spent much time in each other's company. Then, inevitably one day, Loomie disappeared, sold by my grandfather to a gentile colleague for a destiny with Christmas. My mother threw one of her majestic tantrums, barricaded herself in her birdless room, emerging only to grab her younger brother and attempt to run away south, dragging her teary-eyed little sibling all the way past London Bridge on the road she hoped ended in Brighton, before being picked up by an amazed but kindly copper. All her life she stayed wary of butchers, and had the Insider's Knowledge to make their lives miserable should she suspect they were overcharging for poor cuts and stringy quality. Burly men in stained aprons from Stamford Hill to Temple Fortune would hide behind the *Wieners* or hurry to the cold room when they saw Trudie barrel through the glass door. I sometimes thought the curse of the Lame Turkey hung over her entire treatment of poultry, especially the terminally overcooked Friday-night chicken, whose ghastly pallor was enlivened by a coating of Marmite so that it emerged from the oven looking like a society matron who had been mistreated at a tanning salon. Within its cavity rattled a lonely duet of garlic cloves, an exotic concession to my father's savoury cravings.

My father belonged to a different Jewish food tradition — Rumanian with a dash of Sefardi ancestry — so that rice, dried fruit, and stuffed vine leaves (with the more Ashkenazi sweet-and-sour cabbage substituting in my mother's version) were dishes that made him happy and, above all other things, I think, aubergines; still not easy to find in the 1950s. My mother eked out the joy of the aubergine, sometimes making a purée laced with more garlic than she usually found acceptable, and stuffing them with minced beef (without, so far as I know, the addition of human parts) in which the spices of my father's mother's kitchen — cinnamon and allspice — played a dangerous, appetising part.

When she felt she was not Under Obligation, Trudie could turn out some good simple things. Her pride and joy, a thick, glutinous lamb-and-barley soup she called 'Ta'am Gan Eden' — the Taste of the Garden of Eden — never quite lived up to its billing as far as I was

concerned; the muttony pungency of kosher lamb somehow obliter-
ating the stewed vegetables. But she made wonderful egg noodles to
go with the chicken soup that preceded the *Poulet à la Marmite*; and
I would help her slice the egg-rolls into quarter-inch strings and lay
them out on greaseproof paper. Every so often I would steal one of
the yellow ribbons, popping it in my mouth before the high-speed
hand of my mother slapped it away. Then there were the fried fish
balls: Sefardi Jews' gift to Britain (for everywhere else in the Jewish
world, *gefilte* fish is poached). Whatever the precise mix of egg, matzo
meal, onion and spices that went into the devouring mincer, my
mother got it right, and the smell and sound of the discs, going tawny
brown in their bath of hot oil, was when I wanted to be in the kitchen.
As far as I was concerned, she never made enough, for though they
were fried on a Thursday, I would gobble one down for breakfast the
next morning and by Saturday, somehow (though my mother
complained about their lengthy residence in the fridge), they had
taken on some mysteriously enriched flavour that was, for me, heaven
to the palate. In synagogue that morning, my hair slicked up into a
pompadour hardened with a secret recipe of Brylcreem and Uhu glue,
deep in discussion about the fortunes of Spurs and the fabulous Valen-
tine twins up in the gallery whom we ogled from below, I knew that
I smelled faintly of haddock beneath the Old Spice. But you know
what, dear foodies, I didn't give a damn.

Mouthing Off

Oxford Food Symposium, September 2009

There's not much I won't or can't eat. I've eaten crocodile in Holland; barbied kangaroo at Uluru and mountain oysters in Cody, Wyoming. But tongue, even though Fergus Henderson in his recipe for 'Ox Tongue and Bread' lyricises about its slices as 'like little angel's wings', has always tested my gag reflex. (Come to think of it, I'm not sure I'd want little angel's wings in my mouth either.) Lambs' tongues are a particular problem – like pigs' tongues, so I'm told – because, being pretty much the same size as our own, a confusing subject and object of mastication, one stands a fair chance of biting the former rather than the latter. Given that tongues are dense with cell receptors (fifty to a hundred for each so-called bud), the experience – as you all know – can be acutely painful and bloody. But there's another telling aspect to my lingophobia, which is all to do with the separate, but (I want to argue) connected functions of the tongue, that, in my case, precludes the possibility of consumption. Biting one's tongue is an act expressing pre-emptive remorse in the mouth, where the tongue is in fact the processing agency of pleasure. And more significantly for those of us in the word business, the fear of tongue-biting seems to me an anxiety about muting the organ of articulation without which our experience of food seems (whether this is right or wrong is the subject of these remarks) incomplete. So it's the threat of damaging or mutilating the multi-tasking organ which is both the instrument of utterance and consumption that is at the root (not to pun) of my tongue-anxiety, I suppose. Do any of us here really want to eat our own words?

La langue, is of course a gastro-structuralist's dream, especially when allied to the palate; though in its connection between language and eating, one that seems not to have occurred to Saussure himself. He may or may not have read Brillat-Savarin's *Physiologie du Goût*, but he never seems to have reflected on the fact that, assuming *la langue* (as he coined it) is the prior wiring that makes *la parole* – individual utterance events – possible, it is actually the elemental experience of taste, registered on the tongue's cell receptors, which gives rise in the infant to sound-communication; and that, further evolved, is the defining characteristic of what distinguishes humans from dumb beasts. We are, as has often been noted, the language animal. But it's probably only in this symposium that two of the tongue's three purposes – taste and speech – can be thought of as functionally connected; one kind of experience informing and structuring the other.

Almost all of the nerve endings in a newborn are centralised in tongue and mouth, so that the former acts as an astonishingly precocious processor of information coming from the maternal breast and its milk. The hunger instinct and what to do about it is activated there, but babies also use their tongues expressively to register difference of mood and wants. In this sense, from our very earliest days, 'utterance', however basic, and consumption are tongued. The infant sucks, generates a sound, but in turn that sound, learned by the baby as a signal to prompt parental attention, will cue up a feed. It is, you might say, a perfect feedback loop and the most elementary bonding between using the tongue to consume and the tongue to communicate. Scientific studies have shown – and the experience of many parents will have borne it out – that during that first year of life a baby is surprisingly omnivorous, using the tongue and palate to explore, in addition to breast milk, an extraordinary range of sensations across the four taste categories of sour, sweet, salty and bitter (and perhaps, who knows, even including umami). Our own daughter at this very early stage liked nothing better, we discovered – in contravention to all the received wisdoms about the baby-food purées – than blue cheese (Stilton in particular), lemons, olives and (on, I hasten to say, the rare occasions when she got a chance to sample it) caviar. Likewise, much early language originates in response to flavour. Our daughter's first identifiable word, both descriptive and commanding, was 'apple' (or rather 'a-boo'). It seems to be only beyond the first year or fifteen months that the dislike for some strong food flavours sets in and a much more conservative separation between likes and dislikes, much of it almost certainly socially learned from siblings and beyond, modifies the initial lingual adventurousness.

So does all this biological and behavioural information make the case from which we can begin our proceedings here, that if our defining characteristic is indeed as language animal, the lingo compulsion does actually get under way with mother's milk; that as soon as we eat, we feel the need to make some noise about it, a sound that will end up as verbalisation and, eventually, writing. It's certainly the case – as I'll want to argue in a little while – that we do seem culturally and socially wired for this connection, and that while beasts roar with hunger or grunt with satisfaction, our own feeding process demands something more complex. It's been a standard form of commentary by relatively sophisticated travellers, observing those whom they think of as relatively unsophisticated natives, to make a point of commenting on the savagery of eating in speed and silence, akin, they usually say, to animals. That at least was the view of the many travellers to the United States in the nineteenth century, especially the French and the English who, like Colonel Basil Hall, Fanny Trollope and Dickens, never passed up an opportunity to comment on the velocity and utter silence with which Americans, especially on the frontier, in river boats – but also in large taverns and hostelries – ate. In 1827 in Memphis, Tennessee, Mrs Trollope observed her fellow diners at a hotel eating 'in perfect silence and with such astonishing rapidity that their dinner was over literally before ours began . . .'; (when) 'they ceased to eat they darted from the room in the same moody silence which they had preserved since they entered the room . . .' As for their successors, 'the only sounds were those produced by knives and forks with much chorus of coughing'. In subsequent commentaries of this kind words like 'animal' or 'scarcely human' were applied to this habitual scene. From the beginning, as seen by foreigners, America was the habitat of social regression: the land of silent as well as fast food.

In contrast, the instinct to register relish through description and discussion – to make a commentary on what was being eaten part of the digestive process – has been established as a protocol of civility. As soon as there are texts, there are food compulsions, not least of course in the Bible, which can fairly be characterised as food-obsessed, whether in the morphology of taboos, complicated distinctions in Leviticus and Deuteronomy between clean and unclean, but also of course in prophetic poetics. At almost every critical turning point of scriptural teleology, outcomes presumably fated by that mercurial crosspatch Jehovah turn on food choices: the fruit that evicted men and women from the paradise garden; the fratricide of the horticulturalist against the pastoralist (an argument over which form of oblation was satisfactory to the deity); the mess of pottage that disrupted the family hierarchy and delivered priority to Jacob; Samson's honey, the Baptist's *wild* honey and locusts; the Singer of the Song's pomegranate fixation, as we might reasonably call it – and on and on. The point is not just that, in the infancy of culture, food allusions and narratives merely occur, but that they are heavy signifiers of outcomes. Much, as Margaret Visser would say, 'depends on dinner'.

So if we accept that in culture, rather than nature, there can be no eating, and perhaps no cooking, without talking and writing, the manner of utterance in speech and on the page bears a heavy load of signficance, whether in rhetorical spectacle (like television); the language manners of menus (the subject of another contribution to the symposium and a subject that obviously repays close semiotic reading); or the growth of the vocalising habit in waiting staff which in the United States, perhaps to reverse that earlier reputation for taciturnity, has become a kind of social preaching often done by not-very-good performers. A chosen diction, an affect of language – and this is usually very self-conscious – carries with it a code of values about the nature of the food and its preparation. The A-line decorum with which the heavily frocked Fanny Cradock presented her cooking lessons on television in the 1950s made it plain that they were meant for the women who aspired to be epitomes of bourgeois propriety. (Though for some of us, this programmed role-playing was strangely, perhaps wonderfully, subverted by Fanny's androgynously deep voice, especially when she put the whiskered Johnny in an apron.) At something like the opposite pole, a half-century later, Gordon Ramsay's 'F Word' compressing – let's say it, shall we, and strip it of its coyness – sex and alimentation, fucking and feeding, not to mention the insertion of fuck into almost every moment of embattled cooking, is a possibly over-strenuous way of proclaiming (whether we agree or not) that earthiness is a signifier of social authenticity, a combative liberation from the culinary preciousness of haute cuisine. Since Ramsay's game is, the implication goes, unquestionably well hung, his is cooking for, by and with the People.

Other choices of diction and tone summon up other messages.

Fergus Henderson, in *Nose to Tail Eating*, tells us 'How to Eat Radishes at Their Peak'. 'Pile your intact radishes onto a plate and have beside them a bowl of coarse sea salt and the good butter.' Now no one is in any danger of confusing a recipe written like this – in fact the choice of recipe itself – with anything written by the Eff-Chef or Jamie Oliver. But there's something about that insistent definite article – '*the*' good butter. What 'the good butter' does sound like, *very* like, is John Evelyn's treatise on salad, the *Acetaria*, published in 1699, or in fact any cookbook from post-Baconian (no pun intended again) England of the seventeenth and pre-Romantic eighteenth century – Gervase Markham or Hannah Glasse. 'Take a faire carp and scour him well,' etc. Together with Henderson's aphorisms passed off as dispassionate culinary science and zoology: 'Woodcock defecate before they fly, so they can be roasted with the guts in, which heightens the flavour.' (I bet it does.) The message not so deeply coded is that Henderson's cooking is benevolently archival and is all about a return to the imagined English pastoral of Parson Woodforde or Squire Western, in which nature, slaughter and cooking, blood and guts, snout and tripe, were assumed elements in the native kitchen and table. There are moments in Henderson's asides as well as instructions that don't quite add up – as in the requirement for Jellied Rabbit: 'Use tame or particularly beautiful wild rabbits for this' – as if we would ever be in a position to reject wild rabbits that weren't *particularly* beautiful; but it doesn't matter because the nativist visceralism of his food regime is so romantically distinctive and strong. The backward historicist journey, away from fusion, faddism and fashion, is meant, I think, as consolatory therapy for contaminated urbanism. 'Even just writing this recipe down,' he says of his Fish Pie, as if presenting himself as someone who, notwithstanding blood and guts, is prone to attacks of urban neuralgia, 'its soothing qualities have quite' (notice that Wildean '*quite*') 'restored me from the fragile state in which I was.' We don't really need the confessional tone to make the pie; but we register it as a delineator of authorial personality: the poetic romantic butcher-cook seeking to reattach English cooking to its pre-industrial roots.

It won't take much prompting, for any number of these gastro-dialectics to come to mind, so many of which were expressed in self-conscious choices of linguistics. It wasn't just what Marinetti had to say when he spat in the eye of *la cucina di nonna*, but the way that he said it. But you can't beat the pioneers of 'fooding' – Alexandre Cammas and Emmanuel Rubin – for exploiting the implications of language to communicate their version of an eating and cooking revolution.

Le style est l'homme même . . . the very neologism of 'fooding' is of course not accidental. Using *franglais* not just casually, but as the masthead of a manifesto, is a gesture comparable to Marinetti's choice of diction but perhaps even more aggressive, since it confronts not just the classicism of haute cuisine and its *langue*, but even more particularly of course the romance of *terroir*, over the past decades something of an obsession on both sides of the English Channel. In this sense 'fooding', the *mot*, attacks the presumptions of two sorts of assumed superiority: the hierarchy of the old school and the fables of provincial authenticity; the mysteries of the earth that are said to be the antidote to die-stamp globalisation (though *dico* does actually praise *terroir* and the slow-food movement). Cultural nationalism in France has such a high stake in its food regimes that of course, as Cammas and Rubin well know, to overturn it in favour of a kind of promiscuous cosmopolitanism is to reach for the most transgressive strategy imaginable, in thinking of not just gastronomy's but France's place amidst the cultures of the world and in particular those of the Anglo-Saxon world; the sense that France is somehow holding out the promise of regional richness against the debased thinness of globalisation.

Fooding practices – the shameless embrace of the snack, the brief, intensely concentrated hit of food before moving on to somewhere and something else, preferably from an absolutely different food culture – intentionally violate much of the holy writ of *gastronomie*: concentration, slowness, uniformity, coherence, meditative pleasure and even, or rather especially, the hierarchy of courses beginning with savoury appetiser or hors d'oeuvre and ending with sweet dessert. (That deconstruction also operates, of course, in the programme of Ferran Adrià and his followers in the United States, like Grant Achatz.) But what strikes me about *fooding* now is how much the lingo effect is crucial to their subversion. In 2004, Cammas and Rubin published *Fooding, le Dico*. Classically French in wanting to create a lexicography of a moment and a manner, it violated for a start the definition of what a dictionary *was*, at least by relatively modern standards, following the spectacularly brilliant '*Dictionnaire égoïste de la littéra-ture française*' of Charles Dantzig in being '*dictionnaire totalement subjectif*'; though it's the kind of subjectivity that in a way recalls pre-*Encyclopédie* Voltaire.

In the *dico* you'll find potted biographies of the new heroes, Adrià, Moreno Cedroni and Victor Arganzonis – '*Che Guevara du barbecue*' – along with shout-outs to those who, like Anthony Bourdain, have at some point violated the protocols. But there are also entries on 'crumble'; Duralex glass; 'jerk chicken' (*à consommer sans modération sur fond de steel bands déchaîné, au célèbre carnaval londonien de Notting Hill);* and '*sardines à l'huile*' *(les sardines en boîte ont perdu leur image trash cabanon pour devenir une nourriture éminemment bobo, symbole du retour aux plaisirs simples).*

The overthrow of '*gastronomie*' for 'fooding' is the most dramatic instance, I suppose, of normative proclamation in the remaking of food culture, but all these examples are instances where language-acts are not just incidental to, but inseparable from, the constitution of food universes. It may be that right now we are suffering from lexical gourmandism; have become too logorrhoeic for our own good, whether it's the almost unimaginable proliferation of food journalism and cookbooks; the multiplication of television food programmes (I plead guilty as an accomplice to some of this); the appalling habit (marked in the United States) of training waiting staff to deliver lengthy disquisitions and sermons on their specials – often, and inaccurately, with the personal pronoun attached (as in 'my seabass today comes with wild rice and a stuffing of celery root and rutabaga'); or even a verbalised *explication de texte* on how to construe the menu and its philosophy (this happens in Tom Colicchio's Craft and, I'm sorry to say, in one of my favourite places in the world, Dan Barber's Blue Hill at Stone Barns, where the tableside lecture reaches almost the point of theology). Then there is the menu itself – a work, all too often, of faux-literature minus any obligation to obey the basic rules of syntax. In exasperation I've made it my own rule of thumb – and I recommend it to you – never to order any item described with more than one verb. And the redundancies I've never been able to get, but which get lodged in the repertoire – 'pan-fried' for instance. Where else are they going to fry it – in a bucket?

Could it even be – and I hesitate to mention this at the food symposia

– that, as Michael Pollan has recently suggested and I've long thought, we have got to the point of diminishing returns, of an inverse relationship between the second-hand consumption of words about eating to the first-hand experience of cooking it, or even reflectively eating it? A kind of ersatz gastronomy has arisen (the so-called 'gourmet' kitchen) in which cooking and eating experienced in restaurants and in journalism are . . . about celebrity chefs – but never taking the culture home. This may be because too many restaurant critics aren't themselves cooks.

The sheer ubiquity and quantity of food-wording has also lowered the bar of quality ('Best Food Writing' anthology, most of the writing was feebly anecdotal) to the point of almost complete depleted exhaustion. So that there are, in effect, two food-word cultures operating side by side; one empty and ephemeral, the language itself casually or reflexively set down, and then a surviving remnant of a different genre – that presumably we are all here to honour – which sees the experience of food as a way of illuminating the nature of human behaviour, habit, mindset; to set out what exactly it is that humans do, not only when they feed, but when they register their feeding on the speaking tongue and the writing mind. What in the end *is* that language reaching for that I argued earlier was somehow behaviourally, if not actually biologically, wired to cooking and eating – and, for that matter, farming and butchering, or hunting and gathering? The answer surely is fixing through a kind of verbal re-enactment; which means it's an act of translation from one sort of experience to the other, in the sure knowledge that much – perhaps the essence – will indeed be lost in translation, as it is indeed lost in comparable verbal exercises when we try to speak or write about music or sex, but without any diminution of the compulsion to try. At its most egregious is the negotiation made in wine description in which complex perfumes are rendered as what they are not and could never have been, but the approximation of which makes a kind of olfactory shorthand – thus 'cedar', 'blackberries', 'leather', and many more nonsensically summoned aromas.

That's a mere matter of convenience, the more improbable the sensory allusion – Roquefort, gunpowder – the more prodigious the reputation of the nose in question. But real seekers after translation are trying, however futilely, something different, for at some level we are all enticed by the possibility that encoded within the fix established by even inadequate re-enactment is the promise of perfect repetition (which also seldom happens in music or sex). And sometimes, what gets lost in *actual* translation has its own unmistakable richness.

Take this wonderful item, for instance, supplied from Z. Guinaudeau's *Fez*, in the recipe for Mchoui kindly given to me by my friend, the brilliant cook and cookbook writer, Alice Sherwood:

Choose a young sheep, fat but not too big. *Bsmillah*. Plunge the knife into the carotid and let the blood spout out to the last drop. Wash the gash in the throat seven times. Make a hole with the point of the knife just above the knee joint of one of the back legs between flesh and skin. Put a stick through this hole and turning it round, start to loosen the skin. Through this opening blow till the air gets to the forelegs and makes them stick up. The sheep will then swell and stiffen as though it had been a long time in water . . . Quickly while an assistant stops up the hole cut the skin between the legs and skin the sheep like a rabbit. Be careful not to cut the trotters or the head and respect the horns . . . Hang up the hide to clean; put aside the liver and heart and hang them up. Give the tripe to the women who will scrape, rinse and put it to dry.

Or the wonderful and related Choua:

Divide the head in two having first cut with scissors and singed the wool which still remains stuck on the skin. With a chopping knife dig out the horns. Tap and shake this pitiful mask to oust any worms that may still remain in the mouth and nose of the animal. Take out the brains, clean them with ashes then plenty of water . . . The part much appreciated is the eye. You insert a finger delicately in the socket; a quick turn of the nail and the orb will fall out, extricate it and eat, well seasoned with salt and cumin.

Now what these passages do, it seems to me, is to succeed through the sheer clumsiness, you might say the sheer *failure*, of translation. Put another way, the translation of the experience survives or is owed to the mistranslation of the idiom. The original language – which is richly rhetorical, Muslim, tribally poetic – preserves the social totality of the experience; the union of butchery and cookery – without the inevitable flattening, the cultural dilution that happens when a cross-idiom translation goes more smoothly; the rough original. What we have here is the whole picture untouched; the crawling worms in the nose.

This rich description of what it is we do when we plant, harvest, slaughter, butcher, knead, bake, roast and consume ought not, of course, to be left to the inadvertent payload of inadequate translation. The strongest food writers aim exactly for that wraparound translation effect. It's seldom that they are restaurant critics or recipe collectors and publishers. The philosopher Michael Oakshott was much given to saying that while you could reduce cooking to a recipe, you couldn't do the same with politics. Many of us, as my friend Adam Gopnik pointed out, would reverse that truism: it's cooking which defies reduction to recipe; politics, alas, is reduced all too easily.

So how to convey that socially inflected rich description without always sounding like an anthropology seminar? The very best writers – those in a class of their own – have embedded their cookery – and their recipes – in remembered experience; part memoir, part re-enactment. And when I say embedded, in Elizabeth David's case, at least in the most prodigious of all her books, *French Provincial Cooking*, this is literally true – in the layout of her best books, ingredients and cooking procedures are – deliberately, I'm quite sure – made to disappear inside the text of the essay in social recollection or the gastronomical archive. David had a famously liberating, free-and-easy attitude towards recipes as strict instructions, asking the British to try stripping down a dish to its essentials, a 'primitive' version, or to experiment with flavour augmentations if the simplified version lacked savour. To *get* at a recipe, say, for an *anchoïade,* you have to go by way of M. Caramelo at La Réserve in Beaulieu . . . 'expensive, solid, elegant in an old-fashioned way . . . the anchoïade here was outstandingly good and I remember, in spite of the immense portions served, ordering, much to the amusement of the head waiter, a second helping. When I returned to the restaurant a few days later he was ready with my double portion of anchoïade even before I had even asked for it.' Or to get to the wonderful passages on daubes you have to go via Pierre Huguenin, *Les meilleurs recettes de ma pauvre Mère* . . . 'During the holidays at Gemeaux . . . when we arrived at my grandmother's dark kitchen on Sunday after Vespers it was lit by a ray of sunshine in which the dust and the flies were dancing and there was a sound like a little bubbling spring. It was a daube which since midday had been murmuring gently on the stove, giving out sweet smells which brought tears to your eyes . . .' The effect of David's heaped remembrances is to turn any individual dish into a kind of archive of social experience and its record – so that companion figures show up through her pages – Pomiane and the ubiquitous Curnonsky; Abdre Croze, an obscure mayor of Saint-Rémy for the bouillabaisse; a gathered company through time. And it was this Proustian act of poetic fusion, along with the invitations – which (unlike Julia Child) often lived up to the cult of simplicity (invoking Escoffier) that Elizabeth David constantly advertised – which first really got me and some of my generation cooking in the 1960s. What we felt truly translated in her paragraphs was remembered sensuality.

Which cues up and leaves the best for last, I suppose, the greatest food writer who has ever lived, or at least written in English: Mary Frances Kennedy Fisher, whom even the supercool authors of '*le dico*' revere for the sublimity of her prose. In MFK, Elizabeth David's tendency to embed the recipe within memory, archive and ethnography became even more completely dissolved. You don't, I think, really go to her for the recipes – I'm not sure I have ever actually cooked one. What you do go to her for is the exactly rendered experience of human hunger, passion, devouring; and for an as yet absolutely matchless, poetic talent (and I use this term carefully, because it seems to me that Mary K did actually have that enviable talent for conjuring sharp and sensuously registered precision out of thin air that is the poet's forte). Here, for instance, from a justly famous (or it had better be), tiny essay, called cleverly 'Borderland', which finds her in Strasbourg with Al Fisher in February, in a freezing, 'cramped dirty apartment across from the sad zoo, half full of animals and birds frozen too stiff even to make smells'. Now there is a recipe – of a sort – buried in this essay, but MFK sets up the bleakness of the place she's in (at a polar extreme, you'll note, from Elizabeth David who never wrote about cold, grim places), in order to introduce her 'dish', if we should call it that: 'tangerine sections warmed on the radiator'. 'My pleasure in them is subtle and voluptuous and quite inexplicable. I can only describe how they are prepared.'

Now listen to the way this 'recipe' is communicated: a kind of literary seduction, a thing done with mind and eye and tongue, absolutely self-conscious – again in the poetic vein – the seductive effect of allit-eration, with all kinds of details that have not a lot to do with the tangerine treatment, but everything to do with the material presence of the woman herself who is fingering them:

> In the morning, in the soft sultry chamber, sit in the window peeling tangerines, three or four. Peel them gently, do not bruise them as you watch soldiers pass, and past the corner and over the canal towards the watched Rhine. Separate each plump little pregnant crescent. If you find the Kiss, the secret section, save it for Al.
>
> Listen to the chambermaid thumping up the pillows and murmur encouragement to her thick Alsatian tales of 'l'intérieur'. While she mutters of seduction and bicyclists who ride more than wheels, tear delicately from the soft pile of sections each velvet string. You know those white pulpy strings that hold tangerines into their skins? Tear them off. Be careful.

You are then supposed to lay out a newspaper on the hot radiator and lay the sections on them so that they plump up in the heat. They perfume the room. Night comes on and 'the soldiers stump back from the Rhine'.

> The sections of tangerines are gone and I cannot tell you why they are so magical. Perhaps it is that little shell, thin as one layer of enamel on a Chinese bowl that crackles so tinnily, so ultimately under your teeth. Or the rush of cold pulp just after it. Or the perfume. I cannot tell.
>
> There must be someone, though, who knows what I mean. Proba-bly everyone does because of his own secret eatings.

Here, next to nothing is lost in translation and, because of the perfect word-play, the shell crackling under one's teeth like Chinese enamel followed by its opposite, the rush of cold pulp, we are, for a moment, in MFK's body, indeed in her mouth. Which is as good a place as anywhere to end.

Remembering

Omaha Beach

Financial Times, 13 June 2009

For the integrity of democracy, this was the worst of weeks and the best of weeks. Fresh-cut flowers laid on the graves of D-Day heroes were barely beginning to wither when the misbegotten whelp of Mosleyism got its first seats in the European parliament. In London, Gordon Brown was shedding ministers like leaves from a tree attacked by death-watch beetle. I was in Dublin beside the oily Liffey for the Writers' Festival. There, I quickly discovered, the Irish were confronting their own demons, every bit as corrosive to public faith in their governing institutions as the expenses scandals in Britain.

To mangle Tolstoy, while every economic boom is the same, every economic bust implodes in its own peculiar way, throwing up gobs of squalor in its wake. In Britain we have long told ourselves that, while we may be a bit frayed at the edges, by God we know how to run a parliamentary democracy. But now the culture that gave us Gladstone versus Disraeli has sunk into the taxpayer-funded dredged moat where bottom-feeders lurk in terror of the exposing hook and line.

In Ireland the capacity of the moral bog to swallow public trust may be even more profound. The official report, published last month, on the maltreatment of children in Ireland's 'Industrial Schools' was all anyone wanted to talk about in Dublin. From 1940 through the 1980s, tens of thousands of children were victims of physical and sexual abuse at the hands of lay staff and teachers in institutions run by Christian congregations. In its dry understatement, the report is one of the most horrifying documents of systematic social cruelty to be published since the war. Children despatched there by the Irish courts as 'unruly' were treated as feral beasts, beaten with instruments designed to inflict maximum pain.

The betrayal of public trust amounted to a shocking collusion between Church and state to look the other way. Lay perpetrators would be reported to the Gardai, but seldom prosecuted, and members of religious orders known to have committed atrocities on their wards were dealt with within the Church. But now all the sweaty procrastination has been swept away in a great tempest of public fury, not least because Irish taxpayers are going to have to foot the €1.3 bn (£1.12 bn) bill for reparations to traumatised victims. This is the collateral damage of great social and economic implosions. When one kind of public credit – the assumption that investment trusts are not frauds; that commercial banks can actually cover their obligations to depositors; or that the people's representatives aren't slurping at the public trough – comes apart, the entire social contract can unravel at dizzying speed.

Which was a good reason to go to Normandy for the sixty-fifth anniversary of D-Day and register the unequivocal good of which democracies are equally capable along with habitual acts of infamy. Historical commemorations are always tricky things, never more so than in the case of great battles. Those who fought them often tell us who didn't how hard it is to convey the reality in narratives, be those reports a day or a half-century later. And so we euphemise. Military history maps with their arcing arrows trap the unbearable reality of dismembered boys within a code of antiseptic graphic conventions. Those little shaded boxes shadow-box with the truth.

Added to this is the muffling effect of ceremonious decorum. But in this particular case, expectations that our new American Pericles would soar above funerary platitude ran the opposite risk of turning the occasion into yet another exercise in Obamania. Posters in the window of the local tourist office featuring Potus in cool threads and proclaiming – apparently the idea of the mayor of the city – 'YES WE C(AEN)' only added to the foreboding.

The biggest invasion was by re-enactors. On the evening of 5 June, the front at Grandcamp-Maisy, between Pointe du Hoc and Omaha Beach, had D-Day-vintage Jeeps in tan paint parked opposite the sea wall. Inside the Brasserie du Guesclin, Frenchmen and young women impeccably uniformed for 1944 tucked into their *foie de lotte marine* and *turbot grillé*. From GI uniforms there came, disconcertingly, voices that hailed from Bremen or München-Gladbach. It's a well-meant gesture against oblivion, but somehow deaf to the music of time. Most of the re-enactors – in their late twenties and thirties – are too old, their trousers too sharply creased, too fabulously *buff* to impersonate the skinny kids of D-Day, in the grip of animal instincts of self-preservation. When it comes to the bidding of memory, less is more.

Later that evening, I stretched out on a wooden *chaise* in a Norman manor-house garden, fleshy roses blooming on the limestone walls, and let the emptiness carry me back to the tens of thousands packed in the transport ships sixty-five years ago — trapped, panicky and seasick — on the bobbing tide while Eisenhower decided it was go; to silk parachute gear dropped over the heads of tow-haired quarterbacks from Milwaukee. As the first stars came out, a wind soughed through the Normandy oaks and then, suddenly, the fading horizon eerily flared and the stillness was struck by the dull boom of fireworks from distant Utah Beach. But the dogs of the Calvados didn't know the noise was innocent thunder, and yipped and yowled as their forebears did all those Junes ago.

Weather was a famous obsession of the D-Day planners, forcing Ike to postpone the landings by a day. But the meteorological gods were kind to the veterans, many in wheelchairs, some magnificently spry and upright, crowding into the American Cemetery at Colleville-sur-Mer. So the sun shone on the affable curls of Tom Hanks; the band struck up 'Moonlight Serenade'. The 'Battle Hymn of the Republic' followed, rendered with such mournful beauty that our hearts were already in our mouths. Anticipation hung in the air along with Potus's chopper which, heralded by rotor wind, spinning eddies of new-mown grass over the heads of the crowd, finally descended.

Speech Idol then got under way with Nicolas Sarkozy delivering a blinder, full of unembarrassed poetic passion; summoning up images of twenty-year-olds on their ships caught in silence; silence hanging as well over the German machine-gun nests that awaited them. Was this *Sarko*, invoking the tears of parents bidding their sons farewell? Was this the gigolo of the Elysée forcing us to see bodies rolling in the soaking sand? *Evidemment.* The peroration was even more astonishing coming from a successor of Charles de Gaulle, as Sarkozy laid a rhetorical bouquet of heartfelt gratitude on the graves of the dead and the heads of the living.

So truth, in the tragic genre, had against the odds already been spoken, and was only briefly forced to take a back seat to gung-ho platitude when the Canadian Prime Minister Stephen Harper quoted a soldier whom, he claimed, couldn't wait to get to Omaha Beach. Gordon Brown rallied with a moving vision of the liberating armada, but then scuttled it with large invitations to honour their memory by Making the World a Better Place. Exit Thucydides, enter Hallmark Cards.

As usual it fell to the Historian-in-Chief to get to the heart of the matter: asking why D-Day still meant so much to us. It was, he said, the sheer improbability of success. However appalling the cock-ups of that day, this could not be true when the immensity of the American and British industrial smash-machine was brought to bear against the overstretched Reich. But Obama's second answer nailed it: that, for all the imperfections and flaws of the Allies, the absolute moral clarity that bound together the men of 6 June, the obligation to resist and uproot a regime that had been fed on the appetite for 'subjugation and extermination', radiated a redemptive glory over the human condition. *Mirabile dictu*, decency is possible. And such historical outcomes, said the Historian, summoning his own inner Tolstoy, do not happen according to any grand historical design. They are merely the aggregated acts of countless individual human agents who for one moment were lit by the simplicity of moral purpose.

So, when you are all losing your cornflakes on the unedifying news of the day, just hold that imperishable event close, honour the wrinkles that were once just twenty-year-olds trying to make it to the end of the beach and, while they were at it, made the world a better place.

Gothic Language: Carlyle, Ruskin and the Morality of Exuberance

London Library Lecture, 12 July 2008

When Ralph Waldo Emerson was giving a course of lectures in London in 1831, Carlyle did his new friend the honour of going to hear him and, of course, chaffed him for being so cowardly as to read from a prepared text instead of facing the terror and exhilaration of impromptu – Carlyle's own preferred style. No terror, no life force. So, I thought, in honour of one of the Presidents of the Library I should do the same and then I thought, well, no, the occasion is quite terrifying enough already, and besides *that* kind of life force may not be what the patrons of the London Library need on an evening in July, or at any rate such a lecture, even though it might take unanticipated and thrilling twists and perhaps even on occasion rise to a Carlyean level of romantic vehemence but go on and on rather like this Carlyleo-Ruskinian sentence and feel in the end quite as long as *The French Revolution*. So apologies in advance for this quasi-reading.

This is probably the only audience in London to whom the question 'why does no one read Ruskin and Carlyle any more?' would be a gross impertinence. But then we know that London Library readers aren't exactly the common clay, so just to confirm my suspicions about everyone else I went round the corner to Waterstone's and asked if they happened to have anything, anything at all by Carlyle? 'FIRST NAME' was the response of the kindly person at Information as she tapped the computer. And there was every single title with a big fat Zero by their side indicating not on shelves, not in inventory, no orders placed; no demand. Ruskin fared only slightly better with a travellers' edition of *Stones of Venice* and that was it.

Though Kenneth Clark, sixty years ago, made a valiant effort to prescribe 'Ruskin for the Modern Day', no one paid it much heed and the green volumes of *Modern Painters*, never mind *Fors Clavigera* and *Munera Pulveris* go on gathering title dust. There are I suppose plenty of reasons NOT to read Carlyle. In particular, it probably doesn't help that his biggest fan in the 20th century was Hitler. And Carlyle was an equal opportunities hater, detested Jews as much as Negroes . . . (he called them something different) – so it was rather delicious when I discovered that Hotel Carlyle in New York (itself a wondrous oxymoron when you think about it) was named in honour of the great man by its builder Moses Ginsberg. Ruskin is a byword for sniggering about sex; and preciousness. But when I nonetheless assign both of them to students at Columbia what they gag on right away is the language. In a course on what I loosely call Earth Writing, I assigned them the page on Slaty Crystalline in volume 4 and they probably hadn't expected to read this:

> And behold as we look farther into it, it is all touched and troubled like waves by a summer breeze, rippled far more delicately than seas or lakes are rippled; THEY only undulate along their surfaces, – this rock trembles through its every fibre like the chords of an Eolian harp – like the stillest air of spring with the echoes of a child's voice. Into the heart of all those great mountains, through every tossing of their boundless crests, and deep beneath all their unfathomable defiles, flows that strange quivering of their substance.

Or how about Carlyle in the introduction to *Cromwell*, attacking Drysasdust antiquarianism:

> Dreariest continent of shot rubbish the eye ever saw, confusion piled on confusion to your utmost horizon's edge, obscure, in lurid twilight as of the shadow of death, trackless, without index, without fingerpost or mark of any human foregoer – where your human footstep, if you are still human, echoes bodeful through the gaunt solitude peopled only by somnambulant Pedants, Dilettants and doleful creatures, by Phantasms, errors, inconceivabilities, by Nightmares, Norroys, griffins, wyverns and chimeras dire . . .

' "What the hell is *that?*" is pretty much the usual response: 'Prose run mad' as Thackeray put it – and he was a friend; embarrassing poetry? Yes in both cases perhaps. For it was precisely this determination to make the distinction between the poetry and prose moot, to create what some of you might still think of as a Frankenstein of a genre – poetic non-fiction; but at any rate a style of prose writing that concerns itself with some of the defining characteristics of verse: an attention to cadence, to the sonorities of words, sentences leaping from the matrix of syntax to do their own thing in aid of what Carlyle praised in Ruskin as 'melody of utterance' and in another moment as 'poetic indignation'. What bound them together as a 'minority of two' (Carlyle's characterisation in 1865) was their impatience with empty grammatical decorum. Such writing – very often the writing of their critics – amounted they thought to a kind of literary embalming, a film laid over the raw vitality of history, or painting. Both Ruskin (the young Ruskin at any rate) and Carlyle struggled for years with what we might call a problem of translation: how to catch and fix that subject matter without rendering it inert. Doing justice to the original meant, they romantically thought, more than simply total immersion in its lived reality but as much as a muscular re-enactment – of the French or Puritan Revolutions; or the construction of a painting by Tintoretto or Turner, or even, when Ruskin fancied himself privy to the design of God (which was much of the time), entering into the mystery of his terrestrial creation and producing something as oxymoronic as lyric geology. The issue for both of them was not so much that writing about history and art was second-hand; almost all non-fiction would share that quality; but that revelling in the second-handedness was prized by the guardians of the trade as a model of the report well-written, the work well done. To be distant was, in that view, elegant, trustworthy, sound; when to be close, they believed, was to be true. Their passion was engaged in the redefinition of clarity: to replace the reliability of distance with the unreliable but more faithful experience of proximity. The clarity of distance proceeded from the superiority of hindsight. But Carlyle in particular yearned to make the reader humble in the face of ultimately inscrutable providence and thus recover through rude force, the uncertain outcomes of history and art, to set the reader down again on the edge of undetermined possibility. And this, for Carlyle and Ruskin, was always more than an aesthetic challenge. To make readers exult, tremble, panic once more, whether in the workshop of Tintoretto or the National Convention, was to rescue them from the besetting sin of intellectual complacency; history as the unfolding of inevitability. It was also to remake the historian's vocation as resistance to disappearance; 'the etiolation of human features into mouldy blank', as Carlyle put it of the seventeenth century.

To put it another way; the writing rules of the Johnsonian eighteenth century had been above all committed to transparency and harmony. The brute chaos of the world mastered as knowledge. That knowledge was cool in its dispassion. What Ruskin and Carlyle wanted to generate was a different kind of knowledge; one that proceeded from warm-bloodedness; one that proceeded from total absorption in its subject to the point of letting go of the usual mechanics of perception. What was commonly taken to be vision, comprehension, they believed was – a word they both liked – 'owlish'; a form of blindness, for it did no more than measure surfaces. It was not so much sight as surveying. Though they revered the masters who had ventured afresh with language – Wordsworth and Coleridge above all, and with some reservations Hazlitt – they still felt that none of the conventions was capable of pulling the reader into uncomfortable, attentive, proximity; the abolition of body space between past and present, subject and object. On the other hand, if some sort of diction could be fashioned that attacked the automatic quality of reading, the reader might be provoked into a kind of creative partnership with the writer, become sparring partners in a battle for the recovery in language of lived experience. Only that way, Carlyle believed, could what the Dryasdusts had doomed to be the 'grand unintelligibility of the Seventeenth Century' become audible once more. And the writing that did this work might itself be read as confrontationally heroic; its scars and scrapes, nicks and cuts, all unapologetically registering the force of the travail needed to make it. In some sense, the rugged endeavour of that work itself was meant to become a moral exemplum for readers. For both of the seers, noble handwork was the only salvation to a culture otherwise in thrall to the die-stamp of the machine, the aim of which was uniformity.

Carlyle is always wanting, as a preliminary tactic, to obliterate the mediocre; scorch through its defensive primness. So it's not surprising, then, that fire is the natural element of what he imagines to be a resurrection of the lost Gothic-native vigour of old English prose. When you read *The French Revolution* you smell smoke. Images of fire – bituminous, carboniferous – lick through its pages. Sometimes its very words seem printed in hot soot; the world consumed by the revolution, as Carlyle writes, is 'black ashes'. Mirabeau is a *'fiery fuliginous mass which could not be choked or smothered but would fill all France with smoke. And now it has got air, it will burn its whole smoke substance, its whole smoke-atmosphere too, and fill all France with flames'*. Paris doesnt just fall to the revolution in July

1789, it burns: '*Let conflagration rage; of whatsoever is combustible! Guard rooms are burnt, Invalids mess rooms . . . straw is burnt three cartloads of it hauled thither, go up in white smoke; almost to the choking of Patriotism itself; so that Elie with singed eyebrows had to drag back one cart . . . '* An entire chapter is – for no reason the subsequent narrative clarifies – called 'Flame-Pictures' . Revolutionary events do not just happen, they ignite, and in a great climactic passage just before the onset of the Terror (though admittedly the book has more climaxes than it does pages) France itself becomes a '*kindled Fireship*'. The Girondins and the Jacobins ? '*Here lay the bitumen stratum, there the brimstone one; so ran the vein of gunpowder of nitre, terebinth and foul grease.*'

You might say it was a Romantic commonplace, this playing with fire, when speaking and writing of epic events, though you won't find it in Wordsworth's version of the French Revolution nor in Romantic history before Carlyle because he single-handedly invents the genre. Critics habitually (and sometimes without quite sensing what they're doing) characterise Carlyle's style as pyrotechnic; the simultaneous blazing forth of vehement heat and blinding light springs from what we might call his Presbyterian Zoroastrianism; the sense that fire is the element of destruction and rebirth. Remember that he learned German in the first instance to read geology and it seems likely to me that in the great debate over the origins of the world, and in particular its mountains, Carlyle is certain to have been a vulcanist rather than a neptunist. He loved it when metaphors turned material, so naturally he was among the massive crowd (which included Ruskin's hero Turner) watching the Houses of Parliament burn down the evening and night of 16 October 1834. It was about a month after Carlyle had begun work on *The French Revolution* and on that particular day he'd been working (reluctantly) with the Dr Dryasdusts in the British Museum, returning home to Cheyne Row with his usual 'museum headache'. Looking from his back windows he noticed the angry red glow, opened them, inhaled the acrid smoke and hurried off as fast as he could to join the crowds on the Embankments. Though he heard some of the spectators complain that 'it didnt make a good *fire*', it was certainly hot enough for Carlyle's – as for Turner's – imagination to see the incineration as a cleansing of the fetid sty of corruption, from which phoenix-like some purer form of British constitution would surely arise. That the destruction of the house of Old Corruption had been caused by the burning of tally sticks, the record as Carlyle saw it of accumulated iniquity, only made it all the better. It seems likely, then, that he transferred the 'flame-picture' he had directly witnessed to the conflagration of the French monarchy.

But even had Parliament not burned, *The French Revolution*, would have been a work of spontaneous literary combustion, because of course, *it did.* Behind all of Carlyle's obsession with flames lay the trauma of his own manuscript being literally consumed by them. On the evening of 6 March 1835, John Stuart Mill, friend and kindly, if often baffled, review editor, paid an unannounced late visit to Cheyne Row, along with his beloved Harriet Taylor, and stood distraught on the doorstep barely able to get any words out (even more unusual for Mill than Carlyle). This was entirely understandable, since what he had to say was that the only manuscript of Volume One of *The French Revolution* (up to the Flight from Varennes) had been accidentally destroyed by a maidservant at his – or it wasn't clear – Mrs Taylor's house. The servant had apparently thought it was fire-kindling. Now it says a lot for Carlyle's genuine affection for Mill that he didn't immediately think there was something fishy about this account – unfinished though the manuscript was, it was still mighty big, and how much paper do you need, after all, to start a fire in a middle-class London parlour? Jane Welsh Carlyle had her suspicions that Harriet Taylor might have had a hand in this and that Mill was gallantly taking responsibility for her disaster, but they were rejected out of hand as unworthy and unlikely by her husband. Carlyle even unconvincingly claimed that it had actually been a relief to hear Mill's news, as he had initially thought he had come to announce that he had run off with Mrs Taylor.

But a night of great anguish followed in which Carlyle felt 'something cutting or hard grasp me around the heart'. In the morning he resolved to persevere and – shortly after – to accept Mill's anguished offer of money to sustain him through the unexpected additional time that he would need to complete the work. Again one has the impression that Carlyle, more feeling than he sometimes let on, did this at least as much out of a wish to be tender to Mill's burden of guilt as of a need to pay his bills (though that need was certainly always exigent). He proceeded to write the first section of Volume Two and then, the hard part, go back to the beginning and start over with Volume One. Like any of us faced with such a Sisyphean task, he suffered terrible ordeals of doubt; idealising what had been lost for ever to the flames as the irrecoverable original, hundreds of pages of *mots justes*, beside which the remembered version he was now actually writing was a pallid simulacrum, the impostor of necessity. He would write feverishly but then become blocked by panic; during one period lasting many weeks, capable only of reading low romances on the couch, 'the trashiest heap of novels available'. In late spring he consigned the rewrite to a drawer, calling it 'a mass of unformed rubbish'. With the summer of 1835 came a renewed burst of energy to replace what he always described to his brother Jack (who, possibly unfeelingly, gave Carlyle a vivid description of the eruption of Pompeii) as his 'poor burnt manuscript'. By the end of August he'd finished, went to see his family in Scotland, watched the flame-tail of Halley's comet and sent the manuscript to Mill (who'd kept his distance from Cheyne Row for some time) to read.

Mill would indeed read it and praise the 'prose-poem' to the skies both to Carlyle and in print when he reviewed its publication in 1837. How much this was an act of reparation or the truthful candid judgement of friend and editor, neither of them would ever be able to judge. But for both of them the saga of destruction in the flame, and rebirth as Word-Phoenix, had a very particular significance. While we will never know what the first manuscript of Volume One was like, it seems unlikely that the book as written was some sort of pale ghost of its original, for it spoke with unrepentant literary aggression against the conventions, even Romantic conventions, of the day: the weird sublimity, the drug-rush hyperbole, the manifold transgressions against grammar, syntax, word order, the confrontational lapel-grabbing relationship with the reader ('O beloved brother blockhead'); the ecstatic ejaculations and fulminations; the wild and wandering digressions, all of which had already made Carlyle unsellably notorious or at the very least an acquired taste. How about this for the procession of the Estates General:

> Yes in that silent marching mass there lies Futurity enough. No symbolic Ark like the old Hebrews do these men bear: yet with them too is a Covenant; they too preside over a new Era in the History of Men. The whole Future is over there, and Destiny dim-brooding over it, in the hearts and unshaped thoughts of these men, it lies illegible, inevitable. Singular to think they have it in them, yet not they, not mortal, only the Eye above can read it — as it shall unfold itself in fire and thunder, in siege and field artillery, in the rustling of battle banners, the tramp of hosts, in the glow of burning cities, in the shriek of strangled nations!

Steady ON, you might yourselves be saying, and it was Mill who, after reading *Sartor Resartus,* which it's safe to say was almost certainly not his cup of tea, and after trying to edit Carlyle's long essays on Cagliostro and the Diamond Necklace, tried to do so himself in ways more likely to appeal to the author than the literary Lord Jeffrey's advice that he should simply 'try and write like a gentleman'. Here is a typical passage from 'Cagliostro':

Meanwhile gleams of muddy light will occasionally visit all mortals, every living creature (according to Milton, the very Devil) has some more or less faint resemblance of a Conscience; must make inwardly certain auricular confessions, absolutions, professions of faith – were it only that he does not yet quite loathe and so proceed to hang himself. What such a Porcus as Cagliostro might specially feel and think and be were difficult in any case to say, much more when contradiction and mystification designed and unavoidable so involve the matter . . .

Mill in response: 'About that Cagliostro and that Teufelsdreck, by the way, it has frequently occurred to me of late to ask of myself, and also of you, whether that mode of writing between sacrcasm or irony and earnest be really deserving of so much honour as you give it by making use of it so frequently. The same doubt has occasionally occurred to me respecting much of your phraseology, which fails to bring home your meaning to the comprehension of most readers so well as would perhaps be done by commoner and more familiar phrases . . . the style would often tell better on the reader if what is said in abrupt exclamatory interjectional manner were said in the ordinary grammatical mode of nominative and verb'. 'No surgeon can touch the sore places in a softer hand than you do', Carlyle wrote back to Mill, and continued poignantly that 'I daily reflect on this with great sorrow, but it is not a quarrel of my seeking. I mean that the common English mode of writing has to do with what I call the hearsay of things and the great business for me in which I alone feel any comfort is recording the *presence,* bodily concrete coloured presence, of things for which the Nominative and verb as I find it here and Now refuses to stand me in stead.'

What Carlyle was aiming at, he made clear to Mill, was to write prose poetry; because the matter of *history* was too profound, too cosmically disorderly to be confined to the utilitarian neatness habitual to those whom Carlyle derisively called the 'cause and effect' people. The 'right history of the French Revolution', Carlyle wrote to Mill in 1833, would be 'the grand poem of our times', and the 'man who could write the Truth of that were worth all other writers and singers'. Mill warned Carlyle that if he persisted he would face a rough ride, for 'the prejudices of our utilitarians are at least as strong against some of your writings as those of any other person whatever'. But Carlyle protested that this was the only way he knew and the only way he wished to impart, and enact, history. He knew he would offend every convention of literary decency but in the spirit of the Gothic Romantics he revered, like Schiller, Jean Paul Richter and Schlegel, unruly violent energy registered the upheavals that shaped historical outcomes. He told himself that 'if the things come out from the right place, I say to myself it will go to the right place. It is a simple plan this but a desperate one.'

In the end Mill accepted Carlyle's reinvention of historical voice to the extent of using, in his enthusiastic review of *The French Revolution*, precisely the term — 'epic prose poem' — that had made him scratch his head in the first place. But other guardians of the way history — and prose writing more generally — ought to be written, like John Sterling (usually a friend), remained decidedly unentranced, objecting to the 'headlong capriciousness . . . the lawless oddity and strange heterogeneous combination of allusion'. Carlyle's style was 'positively barbarous' and among his neologisms, Stirling, editor of *The Atheneum*, in particular, hated 'environment', 'complected' and 'visualise' as the affectations of a wilful obscurantist. Carlyle wrote back that 'if one has thoughts not hitherto uttered in English books, I see nothing for it but that you must use words not found there, you must *make* words.' Stirling, like many other critics, thought it was Carlyle's immersion in German literature that produced the interminable sentences, the prodigious superabundance of expression which gives harshness and strangeness; the '. . . jerking and spasmodic violence; the painful subjective excitement'.

Those thoughts, demanding heightened forms of utterance, began as Carlyle in his twenties began to dip into history himself: the usual suspects, Hume, Voltaire, Gibbon and Smollett's *Complete History of England*. Gibbon's style he found intermittently entertaining, but in the end the self-conscious orotundity, the ironic polish, seemed to him more to do with a kind of self-admiring verbal strut than a true effort to embody the matter at hand. And it mattered a great deal, I think, that the young Carlyle was reading the canon of 'philosophical history' — in Edinburgh and then beginning to write in Craigenputtoch, for those were two quite different Scotlands. It was exactly Enlightenment Scotland, with its eirenic cultural climate; its commitment to universal truths unproblematically discoverable through rational inquiry, which were somehow a thin medium with which to represent the drive of much history. Unless, that is, the whole point of history was, as the rationalists and empiricists claimed, 'philosophy teaching by experience'. But that was to make history no more than a demonstration of propositions arrived at a priori in the logic chamber. The choice of prose for such exercises would certainly be classically Johnsonian: grave or witty, balanced, restrained, never exclamatory.

But Carlyle belonged to an entirely different Scotland – that of the Presbyterian Calvinism of the south-west border country, and, to him, the most natural diction was Scripture and the first true history the Bible of the Authorised Version. Scripture, with all its thunderings, exordia, calls to judgement, and prophetic passion, which he felt had a more archaic and therefore more instinctively direct connection to that which it narrated than the decorously Augustan forms in which most contemporary historical writing seemed lengthily marinaded. Then Carlyle read Homer, and his convictions about the polite artificiality of most eighteenth-century history only strengthened. In part this was because he believed that the recounting of history was an instinctive, ubiquitous and even involuntary human act. 'A talent for history may be said to be born with us, as our chief inheritance. In a certain sense all men are historians. Is not every memory written quite full with Annals where joy and mourning, conquest and loss, manifoldly alternate . . . ?' There is no recounting of an hour, a day, a year, Carlyle thought, which does not take the form of historical narration, be the subject paltry or grand. 'Our very speech is curiously historical. Most men, you may observe, speak only to narrate, not in imparting what they have thought, which is indeed often a very small matter, but in exhibiting what they have undergone and seen, which is a quite unlimited one. Cut us off from narrative, how would the stream of conversation, even among the wisest, languish into detached handfuls . . . Thus, as we do nothing but enact History, we say little but recite it.' Since our lives are constructed in such narrations of a verbal, improvised, and undecorous kind, so should the history of public deeds and great matters preserve that spark of naturally untutored report.

Conventionally decorous prose was, Carlyle believed, the opposite from the broken-faceted literary vitalism he was groping his way towards; being just the serviceable prose of cerebral self-confirmation. It would be writers who abandoned themselves more freely to the flux of history, and to the dense plenitude of the human past – its ungovernable commotions – and who somehow battled their way to a style that registered that inchoate turbulence, who would more easily bring together the magic moment and the rolling of the aeons. In 1830, two years after Thomas de Quincey had pronounced the art of rhetoric in English prose writing dead, Carlyle published the first of two essays on history, setting out what might be expected of it. Above all, he attacked the self-referentiality of most historical language; its mistaken supposition that submitting the partiular to some pre-determined notion of the general was tantamount to the assignment of significance:

> Alas, do our chains and chainlets of causes and effects which we so assiduously track through certain hand-breadths, years, square miles, when the whole is a broad deep immensity, each atom 'chained' and complected with all. Truly, if it is Philosophy teaching by experience, the writer fitted to compose it is hitherto an unknown man . . . better it were that mere earthly histories should lower such pretensions more suitable for Omniscience than human science . . . and aiming only at some picture of things acted, which picture itself will at best be a poor approximation . . .

In the disingenuous guise of a turn towards methodological modesty, the satisfaction of merely painting 'a picture of things acted', Carlyle was in fact, of course, proposing a titanic ambition: to reinvent history entirely. For if the first job was dense picturing, the Enlightenment loftiness would have to go. When you read Gibbon you heard him and only him. To be sure you certainly heard Thomas Carlyle in his work, but when he got to work using every tool in the repertoire of sensuous memory – music, smell, colour, texture – you heard everyone else too, and the din was transporting.

> See Camille Desmoulins, from the Café de Foy, rushing out, sibylline in face; his hair streaming, in each hand a pistol! He springs to a table; the Police satellites are eyeing him; alive they shall not take him, not they alive him alive. This time he speaks without stammering: Friends, shall we die like hunted hares? Like sheep hounded into their pinfold; bleating for mercy, where there is no mercy, but only a whetted knife? The hour is come; the supreme hour of Frenchman and Man; when Oppressors are to try conclusions with Oppressed; and the word is, swift Death, or Deliverance forever. Let such hour be well-come! Us, meseems, one cry only befits: To Arms!

Let universal Paris, universal France, as with the throat of the whirlwind, sound only: To Arms! To Arms! yell responsive the innumerable voices: like one great voice, as of a Demon yelling from the air: for all faces wax fire-eyed, all hearts burn into madness. In such, or fitter words does Camille evoke the Elemental Powers in this great moment . . . – Friends, continues Camille, some rallying sign! Cockades, green ones – the colour of Hope! As with the flight of locusts, these green tree-leaves; green ribands from the neighbouring shops, all green things are snatched and made cockades of. Camille descends from his table, stifled with embraces, wetted with tears: has a bit of green riband handed him, sticks it in his hat.

Now, aside from Carlyle's cosmic interpellations, which come fast and furious, this long passage does everything he promises in his new history: it propels the reader abruptly into the immediate physical presence of the event. It heightens the effect by conscious use of poetic devices – the aspirate alliteration of the 'hunted hare' (spondees were a speciality, though not here); the inversions and repetitions that convey precisely the breathless, deathless self-dramatisation of the revolutionary protagonists' 'Alive they shall not take him, not they alive, him alive' – we by the way have to supply the commas that make voiced sense of that; but which also re-enact Desmoulins's imperfect conversion from stammerer into orator; the melodramatic sententiousness: 'swift death or deliverance forever' (absolutely authentic to the moment, then, and the place – remember, the Palais Royal where all this is unfolding is a site of theatres and burlesques as well as speech making); Carlyle's unmatched feel for expressive etymology, his cunning in its deconstruction so that he italicises the *well* in 'well-come', preserving and reinforcing the precise semantic load of 'bien-venu'. And, then, not least there is the organic vitalism, by metaphorical indirection; a spectacular vision, at once close up and panoramic, of the city swarm, a huge sudden pullulation, the snatch of leaves to use as cockades, an unstoppable mass of voracious creatures taking to the air, 'the flight of locusts'. (And one could go on ad infinitum within this single passage, and on almost every page, with close readings that would reveal a richness of utterance and complexity of poetic strategy that make comparisons with his idols, Milton and Dante, not entirely ridiculous.)

What Carlyle has done here – and in all his historical writing – is to replace what he takes to be the falsely contrived persona of the dispassionately Olympian narrator with the impassioned oracular poet-bard, a modern

Herodotus or Livy- a persona unembarrassed to become part of the action himself; a protean companion in written speech who, by turn, may dissolve himself into the protagonist (in this case Desmoulins), only to re-emerge as either choric stage-director – 'So hangs it, dubious, fateful in the sultry days of July', or 'On, then, all Frenchmen that have hearts in your bodies! Roar with all your throats of cartilage and metal, ye Sons of Liberty' – or (this about the September massacres and the uneasy relationship between atrocity and the words that must inadequately convey their report) as judicial interlocutor: 'That a shriek of inarticulate horror rose over this thing, not only from French Aristocrats and Moderates, but from all Europe, and has prolonged itself to the present day, was most natural and right. The thing lay done, irrevocable; a thing to be counted besides some other things, which lie very black in our Earth's Annals, yet which will not erase therefrom . . . Well may mankind shriek, inarticulately anathematising as they can. There are actions of such emphasis that no shrieking can be too emphatic for them. Shriek ye; acted have they.'

Carlyle described *The French Revolution* as a revolution of a *book* in itself, which, having heard a lot of it now, you might for better or worse agree, depending on how you feel about revolutions; a book, he said, thinking of the incendiary ordeal he had to go through to write it, 'born out of blackness and sorrow'. Its stuttering diction, its whirling, convulsive shakes and spasms, were meant to trample on the literary complacencies, but also of course to present the writer in some sort of mysterious deep kinship with his subject. The historian posturing as hero did not preclude moments of selective self-effacement. Much of this alternation between egotism and self-annihilation Carlyle took from his German Romantics. His early biography of Schiller, published in 1825, was, at the same time, a genuine effort to sketch a portrait of Promethean loneliness, but also mapping the journey that writing ought to take, from examining the surface of the world into its more invisible wellsprings. *Sartor Resartus* was his retort to what he called 'the gospel according to Richard Arkwright' – or, in 'Signs of the Times', the mechanical age. Vocation was to isolate the cladding of the external world, 'the flowery earth-rind', but then to peel it away to expose the elements that truly mattered; the infinite rolling ocean of existence, within which the external world was a mere islet. In this manner, it was what the French Revolution revealed when it tore away the politeness of the world, what Carlyle called 'the age of Imposture', that was both horrifying and exalting, but which, above all, was real.

That journey from exterior surfaces and commonplace responses, towards something more impalpable, bonded Carlyle not just to the German romantics but to American transcendentalists like Emerson, with whom Carlyle became an improbably close friend and correspondent. More than once in response to Emerson's adoring blandishments Carlyle seriously considered making a journey, like so many of his literary contemporaries, to the United States, only to pull back when he suspected himself of doing it for precisely the base mercenary reasons he deplored in everyone else. And, besides, despite the good Transcendentalist of Concord, Mass., Carlyle in the end suspected America to be supremely the land of low appetites and money-grubbing, only a bit more successful at those enterprises than the British. What he failed to see – and this is partly bcause in his formative years American writing meant, mostly, Washington Irving, and for him (for all of us), worse, Fenimore Cooper, whom he wrote off as a Leatherstocking Walter Scott – was the histrionic strangeness of that country's literature; the entitlement that Hawthorne, Melville (*Moby Dick* and *The French revolution* could have been written by the same hand I sometimes think) and the ejaculatory Walt Whitman gave themselves to cut absolutely free from British presumptions about what strong writing was. Whether or not Carlyle ever read them (and there's no evidence that he did), their own oracular, broken, encyclopedically heterogeneous manner; their gift for re-making or ignoring syntax; their embedding poetic meter in the heart of prose, certainly owed something to the way they read him.

The most eloquent tribute of this unlikely kinship, the sense that Carlyle had freed them from deference to English politeness, came from Henry David Thoreau, who actually read the *Complete Works* to that date while living in his sylvan hermitage on Walden Pond between 1845 and 1847.

Emerson had given him the books and had told Thoreau how badly received many of them had been, *Sartor Resartus* above all. Thoreau wrote that he knew very well the kind of 'aged and critical eye' that could not make head or tail of Carlyle's style, which to them 'seems to abound only in obstinate mannerisms, germanisms and whimsical ravings of all kinds ... we hardly know an old man to whom these volumes are not hopelessly sealed.' But Thoreau took Carlyle's language as natural as the rough New England countryside to which he compared it. (It was, he implied, the only thing worthwhile to have come out of England since Wordsworth and Coleridge). 'The language they say is foolishness and a stumbling block to them, but to many a clear-headed boy they are plainest English and dispatched with such hasty relish as bread and milk' . . . 'Not one obscure line or half line did he ever write. His meaning lies plain as the daylight, and he who runs may read; indeed, only he who runs and *can* read can keep up with the meaning'. What Thoreau found deeply moving, so *American*, in Carlyle was his populist enlargement of the literary voice; to cover a whole world of sound – 'He can reduce to writing most things – gestures, winks, nods, significant looks, patois, brogue, accent, pantomime, and how much that had passed for silence before does he represent by written words. The countryman who puzzled the city lawyer, requiring him to write among other things his call to horses, would hardly have puzzled him; he would have found a word for it, all right and classical, that would have started the team for him.'

What Thoreau appreciated about Carlyle was his ability to liberate language from its gentility; and make its ideas seem 'but freshly living, even the body of it not having passed through the ordeal of death . . . the smallest particles and pronouns all alive within it'. But also, of course, Carlyle's heroic Gothic rudeness; the humour 'vigorous and titanic', the challenging, not to say confrontational, relationship with the reader, 'O beloved blockhead brother of mine'. And possibly, more than anything else, the sense that Carlyle's writing was never ever mechanical, stamped and pressed from any sort of die; that it reached back into the humus-damp earth and had the sappy vigour of a young tree.

Thoreau's perception of what Carlyle wanted to do with the language, but also to literary culture in the Anglophone world, was accurate. In 1838, the year after *The French Revolution* appeared, Carlyle published a long essay on Scott, ostensibly a review of John Gibson Lockhart's seven-volume biography and vindication of his father-in-law. It was a mostly merciless put down of Lockhart (whose book on Burns he had praised), whose pointless copiousness provoked Carlyle to comment, 'There is a great discovery still to be made in Literature, that of paying literary men by the quantity they do not write' (in which case, of course, Carlyle would have been worse off than he was). Then the damning verdict, defining faint praise: 'he has accomplished the work he schemed for himself in a creditable workmanlike manner. It is true his notion of what the work was, does not seem to have been very elevated. To picture-forth the life of Scott, according to any rules of art or composition so that a reader . . . might say to himself "There is Scott, there is the physiognomy and meaning of Scott's appearance and transit on this earth, such was he by nature, so did the world act on him, so he on the world" . . . this was by no manner of means Mr Lockhart's plan.' But then Carlyle went on to skewer poor dead Scott as an exemplum of what a serious writer and serious writing should not be. Scott, in effect, was irredeemably prosaic, led by ambitions that were entirely worldly, content to live on the surface. 'His power of representing things . . . his poetic power, like his moral power, was a genius in extenso, and we may say not intenso. In action, speculation, broad as he was, he rose nowhere high, productive without measure as to quantity, in quality he for the most part transcended but a little way the region of commonplace. It has been said "no man has written as many volumes with so few sentences that can be quoted." Winged words were not his vocation'. What could be said on Scott's behalf was that he knew what he was, was free of cant, and had a 'sunny current of true humour and humanity, a joyful sympathy . . . the truth is, our best definition of Scott were perhaps that if he was no great man then something much pleasanter to be, a robust, thoroughly healthy and withal very prosperous and victorious man'.

He was, Carlyle implies, a perfect fit for the age, but the age of veneer which called out for attack-writing to strip it away. Better by far to separate oneself from its anodyne pseudo-accomplishments, aim for something else entirely, something rugged, shambling, unco-ordinated, and do so in a tongue that would shake the reader awake into new vision; to have writing, just so much paper and printer's ink, nonetheless force the reader into the urgent immediacy of his or her own fate.

The way, then, that Carlyle *talked* to Britain was to summon the past to upbraid the present for its vain, shallow, sense of time; to attack the vainglorious quality of its self-admiration which he diagnosed as moral indolence; a failure of the shared imagination.

If Carlyle's verbosity has, I fear, proved infectious, to the point of making the no less verbose Ruskin disappear, I want, at any rate, to finish with him. It's the right way round, I think, to take Carlyle first because, without him, there is no question that Ruskin would not have come to his own unembarrassed poetic diction; would not have waged war on the desiccated conventions of art writing, thank you Sir Joshua Reynolds (Hazlitt always honorably excepted, although Ruskin didn't), just as Carlyle waged war on the empty nostrums of history. They shared much of the bigger enterprise, the preaching of the salvation of handwork over machine manufacture; the mistrust of classicism; the sanctification of profuse ornament as embodying the connection of man and nature, a connection threatened by the tyranny of mensuration; a sense that the ultimate enterprise was to make the sheer plenitude of human existence (as well as the transcendence of landscape) the expression of God's benevolence (or, in Carlyle's case, his stern sovereignty).

But instead of making himself the embodiment of arduous creativity, constantly playing to the gallery, Ruskin in *Modern Painters* of course displaced all that Promethean recklessness, obstinacy and suffering onto the slightly surprised shoulders of his god Turner. There is, you'll doubtless be happy to hear, no time to talk about this in any detail – many have before me – Robert Hewison, Wolfgang Kemp, and others. But what sometimes seems to me to get taken for granted is the performative quality of Ruskin's writing in *Modern Painters*. He's after the same thing as Carlyle's *French Revolution*; namely, unparalleled immediacy; the sense of Being There, but the 'There' is not just, or sometimes not at all, a reproduction of Turner's making of the work so much as Ruskin's personal unmediated encounter with it. But that's an encounter at a level of almost madness-inducing intensity and total immersion, to the point at which Ruskin – how consciously we'll never know, since, unlike Carlyle, he seldom if ever feels he must answer for his style – writes exactly as he supposes Turner must paint; with a kind of gorgeously incontinent abandon. When he wrote about Turner's *Land's End* in the last book of Volume One of *Modern Painters*, he deluded himself into thinking that what he was doing was analytical description, dense ekphrasis, if you like. But what he was actually doing was word painting, word singing in Carlyle's sense, in which the rhythmic music of the paragraph is everything. If it's a poem, it's a tone poem – Ruskin the impassioned conductor controlling the orchestra of alliteration, assonance, allusion, sudden metaphor, the words and the water they describe rolling over each other. It's hard to remember when you hear this that he is just describing a picture – and in some senses of course he isn't; or rather, the picture is of the storm-tossed author's nerve endings:

> . . . the Land's End, the entire order of the surges where every one of them,
> divided and entangled among promontories as it rolls in and beaten back
> part by part from walls of rock on this side and that side, recoils like the
> defeated division of a great army, throwing all behind it into disorder,

breaking up the succeeding waves into vertical ridges which, in their turn, yet more totally shattered upon the shore, retire in more hopeless confusion, until the whole surface of the sea becomes one dizzy whirl of rushing, writhing, tortured, undirected rage, bounding and crashing and coiling in an anarchy of enormous power, subdivided into myriads of waves of which every one is not, be it remembered, a separate surge but part and portion of a vast one, actuated by internal power, and giving in every direction the mighty undulation of impetuous line which glides over the rocks and writhes in the wind, overwhelming the one and piercing the other with the form, fury and swiftness of a sheet of lambent fire . . .

STOP! STOP! you cry, and, dear, patient, fellow London Library Readers, I actually have.

A History of Britain: A Response

American Historical Review, June 2009

If I confess to some astonishment at writing this response, it is only because I am even more astonished – and moved – that the *American Historical Review* judged a fifteen-part television series worthy of sustained critical consideration in the pages of an *AHR* Forum. I would be churlish not to preface my comments by first thanking all three commentators for the intellectual generosity with which they approached their subject, and for the marked absence of condescension towards a project which, had they tackled it themselves, they would, I believe, have discovered to be every bit as exacting as any more conventionally scholarly project.

It is eleven years since I started work on *A History of Britain*, nine years since the first film shoot in Orkney, and six years since the last episodes were broadcast on terrestrial channels in Britain and the United States. (Although, gratifyingly, the series has had a continuing life on cable broadcasts and on DVDs, both as an educational tool and as popular entertainment.) So looking back on the enterprise from this distance is, for me at any rate, something of an exercise in cultural history itself. But it is also an opportunity to reflect on the part that the television documentary plays in diffusing historical knowledge; provoking debate and enriching the common culture with a sensibility informed by the past could not be more timely. For the scholarly community is surely at a crossroads in considering the forms by which history is communicated within and beyond the academy. The digital moment is no less pregnant with consequences for the survival of the interpreted past than was the transition from oral to written word in antiquity, and from written to print culture in the Renaissance. Whether we like it or not (and I have my own load of mixed feelings), we are unquestionably at the beginning of the end of the long life of the paper-and-print history book. The exigencies of economic austerity are likely to only hasten a process that is already under way. Print books will of course survive their eventual demise in the market-place of knowledge, and monographs custom-printed from digital sources will doubtless endure as physical objects, perhaps even on library shelves. But in shorter order than the profession has yet taken in, most history will be consumed, especially beyond the academy, in digital forms: on interactive websites; as uploadable films; from elec-tronic museum sites, archives and libraries – a prospect towards which most university scholars seem (at best) cool, and to which we are taking precious few steps to acclimatise future generations of historians.

While I was working on *A History of Britain*, moved by the possi-bility of passing on some insight to students about the ways in which scholarly history might be popularised for much broader audiences without compromising its integrity, I was rash enough to propose an optional graduate seminar called 'History beyond the Academy'. I thought I might actually offer instruction on script-writing, on devel-oping treatments and budgets for a variety of hypothetical projects: radio documentaries, digital textbooks, interactive public exhibitions, children's books, films. Further, I imagined that along with disciplined practical instruction about these skills, such a class would debate the long and complicated history of the relationship between scholarly and popular writing. I have always tried to preach what I have prac-tised: that the two lives of a historian, within and without the academy, are mutually sustaining, each necessary for the other to flourish, and that without their interdependence we are doomed to an intellectual half-life, cut off from the nourishment of, and responsibility to tend the curiosity of, the non-academic world. The proposal was greeted in some quarters with polite dismay as an act of pedagogical subver-sion. 'Do you want to create second-class citizens among the students?' was one rhetorical question put to me by way of dissuasion. (For the record, I persisted and, some years later, though only *once*, taught the course as planned.)

It was from this conviction that our calling not only invites us but requires us to reach beyond the academy that I undertook, with great trepidation – and exhilaration – *A History of Britain*. Although it is sometimes referred to as 'The BBC History of Britain', my caution-ary resort to the indefinite article was of course not casual. Whatever the outcome of the series, my role as narrator and interpreter presupposed the provisional, candidly subjective character of the project. I have never pretended otherwise. In fact, it was, I confess, a slight impatience with the assumption (in, for example, Ken Burns's documentaries) that a multiplicity of voices somehow guarantees balance or authentically interpretative pluralism that provoked me, perhaps perversely, to raise the hermeneutic stakes by offering one historian's vision. As all the commentators have pointed out, there were many inherent dangers in the approach, not least narrative arrogance. But I deliberately set out to challenge what seemed to me the unexamined assumptions of pseudo-balance presupposed by the choir of talking heads approach.

It doesn't require much knowledge about film-making to realise that the impression of openness given by replacing a single voice with a quartet or more is, in fact, just that. Unless one of those voices supplies the script (at which point pluralism ceases), the director selects those whom he or she chooses to be heard. What is said, how much of a voiced comment is heard, and where it gets cut into the body of the film is invariably an auxiliary of the directorially written script, and its effect is conditioned by its relation to the visual archive. In these documentaries the single director is the historian, whatever the captions may say. And the edit is the final draft. The scripts for *A History of Britain*, on the other hand, were entirely mine. There was no 'vast team of researchers', just a single junior colleague per film, usually the assistant producer, who also had to deal with locations, fixers and the usual production multi-tasking that makes documentaries possible. So, for better or worse, almost all of the research work that went into those scripts was my own. The determination of locations was likewise a collegial process, with discussions about how this or that site might work with evidence and storyline. If not on a shoot, I was part of the editing process by which the 'pieces to camera' were integrated with archival evidence, attending screenings of the cut through its many stages or making edit suggestions long-distance. I worked with the composer John Harle and directors on the score, and in some cases on the dub itself. For critics who think I had already arrogated too much authority to my narration, I suppose this hands-on integration into the production compounds the sin. But faced with the choice between, on the one hand, a role that restricted me to on-camera opinions, with the creative history really being made by directors and editors, and, on the other hand, the possibility of more total immersion, I had no doubt which approach would be more satisfying and, for the audience, more honest.

A History of Britain was never purely monovocal. But instead of cutting to colleagues, the films were thickly seeded with contemporary voices, from Orderic Vitalis to George Orwell, sometimes deliberately offering competing versions of the same event. And when dispute was material to the historical matter – for example, in Oliver Cromwell's treatment of Irish prisoners of war and civilians – I did my best to present both sides of the argument, without, however, disingenuously abdicating my role as arbitrator of evidence, the same persona that we all habitually adopt in our writing. What I did not want was for the films to turn into seminars, for those are two incommensurately distinct forms of communication. (For that matter, just how genuinely open the professorially led seminar ever is to a democratic plurality of opinion is quite a question, as Pierre Bourdieu has reminded us.) But given that my task was to try and create a broad popular audience for the narrative of British history, and to hold it week after week, my choice was to eschew an echo chamber of authorities in favour of a companionship in which the narrator took viewers along with him on a journey of shared illumination. When the opinionated voice provoked, the provocation was, I hope, always candid, stirring debate, counter-argument and dissent, often robustly expressed on the website, which was itself richly supplied with both general and scholarly essays, many of which took healthy exception to my own version.

In this kind of project, story must come first, the handmaid and condition of analytical debate, not the other way about. This is no more than to follow the obvious rule set out by the historians of antiquity, and it corresponds to the most rudimentary phenomenological understanding of the way non-scholars order the experience of time. Re-presenting (with all the knotty issues of evidence retained) is one of the most complex and demanding tasks that historians can set themselves, even though professional scholars, wary of narrative theory, sometimes imagine it to be the amateur version of the discipline. Story is the thread that connects our scholarly work with the listening, reading public, and we break it at our peril. To weave those threads into a rich fabric, the executive producers (Janice Hadlow and Martin

Davidson, both thoughtful historians in their own right) and I believed that a single unapologetically opinionated writing and speaking voice could create and retain a mass audience, the breadth of which was commonly said at that time to be unavailable to television history. Many commentators cite the great example of Kenneth Clark's *Civilisation* as a model, to which I would also add the more inspirational example of Jacob Bronowski's *The Ascent of Man*, and Alistair Cooke's stunning tour de force *America: A Personal History of the United States*. But at the time of the planning of a television history of Britain, that tradition of personal essay had all but died out. This was not entirely the case, since writer-presenters such as Michael Wood remained a model of what could be done in this medium, but it was still largely true that the interpretative single-voice form had been written off as a vestigial remnant of oak-panelled patrician broadcasting. Democratic television, on the other hand, was assumed to be fly-on-the-wall actuality: a day in the police station, the trauma room or the schoolroom in the deadpan style of Fred Wiseman, and often very brilliantly realised for television by directors such as Roger Graeff.

But at the very heart of the kingdom of fly-on-the-wall, there were subversives – Michael Jackson, then controller of BBC2, and Janice Hadlow, then in charge of one of the two history divisions of the BBC – who nourished a suspicion that if you stood the received wisdoms on their head, you might be closer to the truth. Their belief, widely dismissed at the time as quixotic, was that there was a pent-up public demand for a single-voiced, chronologically ordered history on the grand scale, richly informed by social and cultural history but unapologetically *évènementielle*, when the events in question happened to be of the order of magnitude of the Norman Conquest, the dissolution of the monasteries, the Civil War, the Industrial Revolution, the Irish famine, and so on. And not just on television, but in schools around Britain, where history was being rationed to perhaps two hours a week at best, and where the curriculum was set out as a series of disconnected modules known as 'Hitler and the Henries', the non-academic public was being starved of just such a grand narrative.

I never intended the series to be empty of social history, still less of the experience of 'the people', as Miri Rubin and to some extent Linda Levy Peck charge. Nor was it. But television is a work of the eye, and the life of the people necessarily had to be embodied in what could be looked at: dwellings and artefacts – the tiny, profoundly poignant Saxon church at Bradwell; the surviving remnant of a lost Catholic world in the rood-screen paintings at Binham Priory; the shocking photographs of the Indian famines of the late nineteenth century taken by missionaries; and, as Peck kindly mentions, the unspeakably moving tokens left by mothers depositing their infants at the Foundling Hospital. The very first images seen (other than the tidal shore) were of the village of Skara Brae and the hearth and ornaments made in that world remote both spatially and temporally from the Anglocentric world. And if, at the end of the film, the camera moved in on the exquisite 'Alfred Jewel' in the Ashmolean, it was both as a materialisation of royal sovereignty and to convey a sense of the precarious allegiance to that earliest of English courts on the part of those who beheld it. We took viewers into a fifteenth-century manor house, the deserted cottages of Irish famine victims, the fields of Bengali cultivators, the homeless shelters of London in the Slump. Equally, where the voices of people remote from the centre of power were available and integral to the bigger plot, we did our best to make them heard: from the world of the Roman legionaries on the Hadrianic frontier preserved in the Vindolanda tablets, to the anonymous Irish monk who believed he might be the last survivor of the Black Death, to Leveller women and the victims of Peterloo.

So what, exactly, needs defending here? The decision to fill the second episode with the story of the Norman Conquest, or the third with the struggle between Church and state in the reigns of the Angevins? If so, I readily plead guilty as charged. Professor Rubin wanted a much more intensive dose of social history and a good deal less narrative of the powerful, but of course at the heart of many of the formative dramas were insurrections against the mighty – from the Peasants' Revolt to the Puritan revolution to Chartism – that we could hardly have been more conscientious in examining. But it is true that our remit was to put social flesh on the history of power, for contests over power were what ultimately created Britain.

In the end, though, ostensible dichotomies between narrative and analysis, between political and social history, exist more in the methodological imagination than in historical practice. Film-making is the best instructor in the meaninglessness of that divide. Meeting the technical demands of a medium where it is imperative that one assumes no prior knowledge of a subject or period, while refraining from patronising the viewing audience, is itself a serious education in the economy of explanation. In any given programme, there would be self-evidently major issues – Cromwell's treatment of the Irish, Jacobitism, the Sepoy rebellion – all of which, if the historian is doing his work properly, presuppose familiarising the audience with the responsible protagonists, their ideologies and actions – before it is possible to introduce debate. All this takes time, narrative care and a respect for the intrinsic dramaturgy of the medium. Films are not consumed like books and cannot be written like them. (Which is why I wrote three companion volumes, precisely to expand the scope of what I was able to compass in a bare fifty-eight minutes.) Within the covers of a book, readers may move back and forth as attention and interest prompt. In the television documentary, propulsive visual and spoken energy is critical. In these respects, the medium is actually something of a throwback to pre-professional forms of historical narration, all the way from Herodotus, the crafting of narrative that *performs out* its analysis rather than headlines it. It must use scholarship responsibly without ever subjecting the audience to a sense of their being examined or overburdened with scholarly dispute, yet it must speak to that audience's trust that the narrator has earned his credibility with knowledge.

So there is, in fact, a poetics of television history, which needs to be respected if the form is to accomplish its own particular kind of communication – for millions rather than thousands. Such a poetics presupposes a strictly non-fiction dramaturgy, bound together by a clear and compelling narrative arc, and its making is quite as formidable a challenge as, say, the formal composition of post-Ciceronian oratory. Documentaries never work as a succession of loosely stitched-together sequences about this and that matter, social or political, each given their ration of minutes according to some preconceived hierarchy of significance. The distinction is the difference between even the most skilled lecture and a film able to retain its audience from beginning to end (a tougher assignment on television than in the cinema, given the freedom to wander between choices). Profusion risks confusion, and confusion is the harbinger of boredom, which in turn is the cue for a switch to Monday-night football. Peter Stansky remembers the scintillating lectures delivered by A. J. P. Taylor as television performances, but those happened more than forty years ago, in a different cultural universe. Since then, the challenge to deliver knowledge, argument and non-fiction stories through the digital media has become much more formidable, and if historians want to reach an audience beyond the academy (of course it's possible that the vast majority do not), then some attention has to be paid to the particular demands – and rich opportunities – offered by long-form documentary film and video.

One historian's inclusiveness is another's unforgivable omission, of course, but in any event, the pursuit of inclusiveness is the death of plot. To take a specific instance of what Professor Rubin surprisingly dismisses as the 'antics of kings', the foregrounding of the great conflict over law, and the relative authority of Church and Crown which was at the heart of the matter in the Henry II–Becket dispute, needed setting up (as did the history that would culminate in Hastings and Domesday) so that viewers, the vast majority of whom would not have known much about the Angevins, could become familiar with the parties and persons involved. And of course there are occasions when the fate of not just the state but the people hangs on the person of the prince. I own up to believing – as forthrightly stated – that however prepared by religious dissent since the Lollards, in the end the English break from Rome was an act of the redefinition of sovereignty executed by a monarch desperate for a male heir. It seems peculiar to have to defend this view as antiquated. All that matters is whether it is true. That Anne Boleyn also happened to be a learned Protestant is material to this issue, and I tried to say as much. But the notion that that programme paid no attention to the experience of the world beyond the court is an inattentive reading of the film, and I appreciate Professor Peck's alternative view. Equally, of course, the issue of issue for Elizabeth I was one that would affect the entire fate of English religion. What we were doing with 'The Body of the Queen' was, as is often the case in the whole series, 'debate by stealth', in this case applying the questions set out in Ernst Kantorowicz's *The King's Two Bodies* about the distinction between the body natural and the body political (made moot in the Queen's case), as well as much more recent literature on gender and sovereignty, to the fatefully intertwined story of Elizabeth and Mary Stuart. Those who wanted to experience the film as an engagement with the politics of gender, the reproductive biology of sovereignty as it played out across the Anglo-Scottish border, could do so; those who wanted to sit back and drink in an astounding dynastic drama could do that, too. I don't see any need to apologise for our attention to the second kind of demand. Both kinds of audience were entitled to their respective needs, and we tried our level best to satisfy them without compromising scholarship or debate.

All this took hard work. I confess to being a little surprised that in her account of the meetings with BBC producers during an earlier version of the project, Professor Rubin rather airily divided up the labour into what she imagined historians would, or rather would not, do, and what 'the production team' would tackle, the more strenuous labour, she implies, being undertaken by the latter. But for this historian, at any rate, both the magnitude of the challenge and the satisfaction of creation rested in that division of labour being made moot, in the historian doing his best to master the exacting craft of television film. This means, at the bare minimum, relearning script-writing as an entirely different exercise from book-writing, one that not only has to be constantly responsive to what the viewer is looking at, but has to be conceived, from the outset, as a series of visual sequences, each one itself a succession of shots, understanding, in fact, the syntax of the cut. (I am personally allergic to the meaningless dissolve except in instances where it dramatises the memory link between past and present. In one of the episodes in my most recent series, *The American Future: A History*, for example, we mixed through from a shot of a stony creek on the Gettysburg battlefield to a Civil War photograph of the same site with a dead soldier lying in the gulley.)

I don't altogether disagree with Peter Stansky's objections to the clumsiness of poorly enacted reconstructions. Done badly, they can induce cringe-making alienation from the historical moment rather than realise the ambition of bringing the viewer close to it. But sometimes a kind of film synecdoche or emblematics can work powerfully on the viewing imagination, especially when both approaches have a connection with the documentary and cultural report. So, for example, a shot of a single bonnet bowling along a field in the aftermath of Peterloo worked, I believe, quite well in summoning the ghosts of the massacre, since contemporary reports commented on the clothes of the victims left behind in the panic. Instead of a wide shot of the Cabinet War Rooms (very much a museum of a moment), we used shots of apparently incidental details – a row of coat hooks, an ashtray – to convey the whole.

And when rooted in a strong sense of the iconology of the period, emblematics can visualise a historical scene far more expressively than either a shot of a document or a low-budget piece of acting. To convey the fury of Henry II at the defiance of Becket, for example, we used close-up shots of a hawk's beak opening and shutting (to the rhythm of unseen proffered mice), an image entirely in keeping with the spirit of royal bestiaries and the falconry of which the King was fond. We used the same kind of technique with a white peacock's display to suggest the significance of charisma for the Elizabethan court, making the kind of connections between plumage, virginal whiteness, the elaborate ruffs of court dress and the grandiose paintings that captured them, all in a single shot. And sometimes less is simply more. To convey the plight of the fugitive Mary Stuart from Scotland, we took up position at exactly the right place, near Workington on the Cumbrian side of the Solway Firth, where the Derwent flows into the sea. But there was no boat and no fake Queen of Scots. All the camera did was to track slowly along the shore, shooting the slow lap of the waves while the commentary evoked the documented record of her sorry condition. The eyes of the viewer saw tidal water, but their mind's eye saw the Queen.

I can't emphasise enough that these aren't 'tricks' designed to bewitch the viewer into historical romance. The royal hunt, the reality of exile and the relationship between power and display are all serious historical matters on which matters of sovereignty turned. The same sort of attentiveness inspired the idea of illustrating, albeit briefly, the effects of the Black Death with emptiness and absence, unattended farm implements, or the Popish Plot with the playing cards that were circulating at the time. In many instances, the careful building of the visual and narrative structure of a film turned on the realisation of a unifying conceit. The last programme in the series had somehow to give a sense of the fate of the British Empire from the turn of the twentieth century to the Second World War, a feat of economy that would have been impossible had we tracked conscientiously through from the Liberal governments of Edwardian Britain to the Labour victory of 1945 and everything in between. Instead I decided to concentrate on what two utterly different figures made of the destiny of Britain in the age of economic disaster and totalitarian aggression: Churchill and Orwell, to begin with Churchill's death and to end with Orwell's. But as the fifteenth programme in a long, sustained narrative also had to serve as coda, the director, Clare Beavan, and I decided that the style would give the feeling of Mass Observation documentary, black and white even when it was actually not. And the mood would be an engagement with elegy, a deep strain in British writing, prose and verse, and the binding conceit would be the lament for, or resistance to, ruin.

Sometimes serendipity is the best ally. I had been filming a sequence (in the end dropped from the edit) for the late-eighteenth-century episode at the Royal Naval Dockyards at Chatham. Between shots of masts and spars, during the inevitable waits for the location to be lit, I wandered into a warehouse-cum-dry-dock that was, in fact, half-breakers' yard, half-repository of rubbish, inhabited mostly by pigeons and piled high with the debris of centuries: cannonballs; a motor launch broken in two; a 1940s vintage limousine covered with feathers and bird droppings; bits of submarine. Seen from a high platform above, it was a wonderland of imperial redundancy. And it gave us both a sequence near the beginning of 'The Two Winstons' and our poetic motif. Off we went, the director and I, hunting for abandoned and boarded-up country houses and, most challengingly, an airfield of the right Second World War vintage that had not been converted for more modern use. After a very long search, we found one in Norfolk, complete with original control tower and broken windows, Tannoy speakers, and long grass growing in the cracks opened in the runways. Eureka! For the defiant Churchill speeches of 1940 at the time of the Battle of Britain, we needed neither the much-viewed archive footage of the Prime Minister nor photo stills of the 'Few' by the side of their Spitfires, much less a Winston impersonator in a dubious homburg. All we needed were yawning-wide shots of that airfield, open and desolate to the flat country, and the superlative *vox humana* of Churchill sounding over the East Anglian wind. What we were fighting against, of course, was familiarity. Running the film archive would simply have made that problem worse, because it would have subconsciously cued up the imminence of the eventual victorious outcome. What Clare Beavan and I wanted to restore was a sense of the terrifying loneliness of the British at that moment. Ghostly emptiness was the way to do that, with not so much as the faintest sound of cranking aircraft engines to cut the admixture of bravery and fear. Behind the sequence, of course, was the usual serious historical issue: the yen by Halifax and others to find a way to settle with the Axis without compromising the empire. Pulling the viewer into a mood that had nothing of the bulldog breed about it would, we hoped, restore contingency to the history.

Now, I recognise that this account may seem a long way from what most of the readers of the *American Historical Review* recognise as the work of the historian. Our first duties are to nourish our academic community and our research, to ensure that future generations of historical scholars are sustained and encouraged and that new paths of research and debate are opened. Courses have to be taught, dissertations examined, articles and books written, appointments made. In making the fifteen episodes of *A History of Britain* for the BBC, I had to ask for exceptional generosity of leave from my kind colleagues at Columbia University, although between the three spells of shoots, I returned to campus as working professor. But the main obstacle to broadening our conception of what it means to be a historian in the digital age is, I think, force of habit, the axiomatically self-reproducing nature of the profession – the sense that, somehow, popular and scholarly history are mutually depleting. I can only say that everything I did and everything I learned while making these films led me to believe that the very opposite is true: that the two arms of our métier are mutually strengthening, and that without an abiding sense that we can work to make the past live for the public, we will doom ourselves to an intellectual graveyard: that of the connoisseurship of the dead.

The Monte Lupo Story

Review of *Faith, Reason and the Plague in 17th-Century Tuscany* by Professor Carlo M. Cipolla, *London Review of Books*, 18 September 1980

Professor Cipolla's new book, *Faith, Reason and the Plague*, puts one in mind of a Florentine *espresso*: minuscule in size; briefly stimulating in effect; and extortionate in price. At £7.50 for eighty-five pages of text, his readers will be shelling out eight pence a page, a tariff which, I couldn't help but calculate, would have put my own first book in the shops for around £65 a copy. Not for nothing, then, is he renowned as the most economical of economic historians, specialising in small books on big subjects – literacy, population, technology and the like. Many of these have brilliantly succeeded in dealing with complex historical problems within the space of a nutshell. In this case, however, the shell is altogether more imposing than the nut.

The book comes expansively inflated with puffery in two styles: the High (or Reverential) Puff and the Low (or Fastidious) Puff. The High Puff asks us to believe that the book 'is of immense historical importance' as 'it presents a picture of the real life of ordinary people who constituted the overwhelming majority of the population of pre-industrial Europe . . . on whose shoulders the high civilisations of the Renaissance, the Baroque and the Enlightenment were built'. In other words, without taking into account the plague victims of a Tuscan hill village in 1630–1 or, by extension, anything that ever happened to anyone at any time between 1400 and 1800 – our contemplation of Michelangelo, Bernini and Voltaire is callow and impoverished. The Low Puff refers more tactfully to 'spare' prose and 'deft' strokes, evoking the warbling of the piccolo rather than the swell of the *vox humana*.

I should in fairness add that for your £7.50 you get three appendices (one transcribed from an earlier work); a bibliography of fifteen items, thoughtfully printed in very large type and stretching over two pages; lists of contents and figures taking a page apiece; and a good deal of white surface area, all contributing to take the page-count into three figures. Professor Cipolla helps this along by interpolating between his more strictly historical observations strangely delphic utterances of the sort one usually associates with Christmas crackers: 'loneliness is the price a man has to pay when in a position of power'; or, in more cybernetic vein: 'there are people who because of their biomass, physical dignity or psychic energy easily assert their authority on others'. Apart from ruminations on biomass deficiency, there are the obligatory frequency diagrams designed to translate the perfectly obvious into the statistically awesome, and illustrations which are verbally recapitulated in the text. But all the cladding and padding and wadding and stuffing can't conceal that this is a very short book about a very small town over a very brief period in time. To be blunt, it is a footnote cranked up into a Cecil B. de Mille production.

Given the extreme simplicity of the episode recounted, even eighty-five pages seem a bit luxurious. Far from Professor Cipolla telescoping its details, he has elongated them into a historical shaggy-dog story with a correspondingly inconclusive pay-off. Its outlines can be summarised semaphorically in the manner of those invaluable contents lists in nineteenth-century history books. Plague hits Tuscan village of 500 souls in 1630; Florentine health magistracy puts formidable Dominican in charge of quarantine; opposition from truculent inhabitants who resent their already rudimentary subsistence further confined by irksome restrictions on movement; resurgence of petty crime; mortality recedes with winter cold; monk departs; plague revives early 1631; mayor fails to enforce regulations, dies in harness; monk recalled as attempts to ban religious procession meet with angry resistance from local priest and populace; procession goes ahead; quarantine stockade at one of the city gates vandalised at night; outraged roving commissioner summons insomniac busybody who claims to have witnessed the misdeed, but (it being night) fails to identify culprits; witness rather than vandals thrown in jail until story believed; culprits undiscovered, plague recedes again; monk departs again; commission concluded inconclusively; end of story.

Professor Cipolla fleshes out these bare bones with some striking characterisation, but much of it is of the kind sneered at by historians when they encounter it in historical novels. When unsupported by anything except the most circumstantial evidence, there is invariably a resort to the emphatic and the imperative: 'While he rode at an early hour towards the castello, he must have been thinking about those Monte Lupans'; 'he must have been inquisitive by nature'; 'like so many talkative people . . . Pandolfo must have felt pleasantly self-important'. Similarly, when the action threatens to flag, Cipolla stokes it up again by imaginative use of dramatic hyperbole, generally of the Mills and Boon variety: 'He had not slept at all during the night and now in less than twenty-four hours he had experienced the whole gamut of emotions ranging from excited curiosity to the heights of euphoria down to the depths of terror.' Since this refers not to attendance at a witches' sabbath or an auto-da-fé, but to the busybody's nocturnal snooping, followed by his informing and subsequent cross-examination, the reader might be pardoned for thinking Professor Cipolla's threshold of excitement rather lower than average. At the very end of the tale the ghost of the immortal Edgar Lustgarten walks again (scripted by *Monty Python*): 'Who broke down the stockade at Monte Lupo? Was Pandolfo lying when he swore he had not recognised the evil-doers? And what role was played by the carpenter? These are questions that must remain unanswered.'

If the devotee of history-as-thrills is not likely to find much in this book to set his spine tingling, can the scholar learn anything fresh? Given the immense literature on plague and its social impact (to which Professor Cipolla has made distinguished contributions, but on which the massive volumes of Jean Biraben might be thought to have said the last word), it is hard to see that the Monte Lupo story is much more than a minor, if picturesque, addition to our knowledge. It comes as no surprise to discover an individual cleric like the Dominican Father Dragoni transcending the disputes of Church and state over the stringency and propriety of prophylactic regulations, and enforcing the wishes of the latter rather than the former. Humanist or even monastic clergy throughout plague-stricken Europe often gave their Christian pastoral duties a higher priority than they gave to traditional rites, usages and customs. One important aspect of the Counter-Reformation Church was precisely this kind of *attack* on popular ceremony. Nor is it startling to find no positive correlation between religious processions and plague mortality. Ever since Creighton's classic history it has been supposed that by far the most common (albeit not exclusive) agents of transmission were, not other people, but the fleas of *Rattus rattus*.

Carping aside, the most depressing aspect of this offering is what it implies about the pigmification of historical scale. The time has long since passed when historians dealt exclusively with the grand scenarios of power; the life and death of empires and nation states; their wars and revolutions, diplomacy and business. It was a salutary corrective to turn instead to the history of the unsung masses, and from the most recalcitrant and ostensibly ephemeral sources, ingenious and gifted historians such as Richard Cobb, Olwen Hufton and E. P. Thompson have produced masterpieces of historical reconstruction in which the lives of the obscure and the downtrodden are given the front of the stage. There was, and is, a serious purpose in viewing elite culture and its politics from the perspective of the common individual struggling to survive. But this is not the same thing as assuming that *all* historical events have an equivalent call on the historian's attention, or that any scrap of evidence, however inconsequential, which is capable of being written up with a modicum of imagination and literary competence demands rescue from oblivion. On the contrary, much of it could do with being sent straight back there. The indiscriminate celebration of the humdrum threatens to dissolve history into a random aggregate of disconnected episodes, ancedotally related. And the result of such a process is not merely the substitution of a mosaic comprised of myriad, imperfectly fitting chips of the past for a possibly over-coherent picture of Great Events, but an invitation to study the individual fragments as though they each were miniaturised versions of the whole. This 'microcosmic' view – the absolute opposite of Febvre's and Braudel's equally unattainable '*histoire totale*' – is, in effect, a neo-pointilliste heresy of immense positivist vulgarity. Its premise must be that history is comprised of discrete actions and events, each as worthy of study as the next, since each contains within it some element of the universal. At the most banal level – Tolstoy's preference for the cosmic significance of the ear of ripening wheat over the cosmic significance of Napoleon – this is necessarily true. But to conclude, for example, that a study of the distribution of Bolshevik posters in Plotsk is quite as important as a study of the Petrograd Soviet is tantamount to a declaration of war on causal explanation: a relapse into egregious relativism.

It is time, perhaps, to reinstate the significance of significance. Or is it too quaint to insist that the historian's work involves explanation and argument, and that this necessarily entails an evaluation of evidence? And that only when such evaluation, comparison, selection, is undertaken can evidence be brought to bear on a predefined problem or a preconceived hypothesis? Has there been such a loss of nerve among historians that they now swallow uncritically the social anthropologist's dictum that to describe is to explain? For 'thick description' can mean thin understanding, if what is being thickly described has lost its anchorage in the larger measures of time and space.

The signs of a creeping *Montaillou* syndrome are ominous. The local, the anecdotal, the parochial, the gossipy and the intimate threaten to tyrannise historical fashion quite as thoroughly as the public, the national and the political once did. As the demand for 'readable' history becomes a hunt for the scraps and shards, the rags and bones of evidence, from which a good yarn might be knocked together, the historian is in danger of becoming a kind of beachcomber among the casually washed-up detritus of the past. If this goes further we shall revert to what we were before Thucydides had grander ideas: bards, tellers of tales, ministering to a culture terrified by the fragility of the contemporary, and seeking in chronicle an inverted form of augury. Or, less apocalyptically, we may end up as minor entertainers in light prose. Should that happen, the High Puffer's boast that if 'more history books were written like this they would drive novels off the market' will be put to the test. And on the evidence of this kind of tittle-tattle, it will be history, rather than the novel, which will meet with a rude comeuppance.

No Walnuts, No Enlightenment

Review of *The Business of Enlightenment* by Robert
Darnton, *London Review of Books*, 20 December 1979

No walnuts, no Enlightenment, it seems. For, as Robert Darnton tells
us in his epic chronicle of the Life and Times of the quarto edition
of the *Encyclopédie*, it was nuts and resin from the Midi together with
Paris turpentine and linseed oil which made the ink (six monstrous
250-livre barrels) which primed the type which printed the thirty-
six million sheets which comprised the quarto which lowered the price
which Spread the Word which overthrew superstition which disarmed
the Old Regime and inaugurated the rationalist millennium. Or was
it?

Historians have long been given to attributing the French Revolution and all its unholy works to the corrosive influence of the
Philosophes. The counter-revolutionary Abbé Barruel saw the revolution as a conspiracy hatched by malevolent acolytes of Voltaire:
freethinkers and freemasons bent on subverting the authority of
Christian monarchy. Less histrionically, Alexis de Tocqueville shared
the assumption that the diffusion of Enlightenment scepticism had
unfastened the ties of deference and order underpinning the Old
Regime. It was characteristic of the fecklessness of intellectuals, he
argued, to attack established institutions without much bothering
about what might replace them.

For Marxist historians, this approach was unduly generous to
thinkers and scribblers, investing, as it did, the world of ideas with
an autonomy that was unreal. Since, in their view, the revolution was
a product of inexorably shifting social forces, the Enlightenment
could be no more than an expression of that movement: in Ernest
Labrousse's awesome phrase, '*la prise de conscience bourgeoise*'. The
Philosophes were correspondingly relegated to the role of window-
dressers for the ascendant power of the bourgeoisie. One of the many

satisfying results of Robert Darnton's prodigious research has been to dispose of these hoary pieties once and for all. By painstakingly tracking down virtually all of the 8,000-odd subscribers to the quarto, he has been able to show that a preponderant majority belonged to precisely those sections of the French elite that were the first to suffer from the revolution: rentiers; office-holders; landowners with pretensions to cultivation; 'enlightened' clergy; Parlement lawyers. Many of these were noble; very few of them were engaged in anything that could be described as capitalist enterprise. Commercial travellers in pursuit of subscriptions found meagre pickings in the great centres of trade and industry like Nantes and Lille, where they grumbled of philistinism and avarice. In an ancient centre of administration and law like Besançon, though, the mixture of ennobled professionals and *bien-pensant* noble academicians yielded a bonanza for the purveyors of Enlightenment by mail order.

Both the anti-revolutionary and the Marxist views were, in any case, based on bald assertion rather than evidence. Both tended to extrapolate an ethos from an arbitrarily summarised version of the Great Texts, and then assign it significance or insignificance as their preconceptions dictated. But we are all contextualists now. Instead of ruminating in a documentary void on the social resonance of political philosophy, cultural historians look to political milieu and the currency of polemics, to routes and means of transmission and to the vulgarisation, rather than the refinement, of original texts, for clues to an understanding of their impact. While form seems to be of more interest than the interpretative scrutiny of content, and the printer's bench has replaced the philosopher's cell as the focus of attention, this should not be taken as a reaction of vulgar empiricism against the over-rarefied nature of old-style *Kulturgeschichte*. At its best, and when not mesmerised by the nuts and bolts of ideology – the minute enumeration of column inches and censors' pencil stubs – it is an authentically historical way of examining the process by which words become deeds; ideas animate action; and the heresies of one generation transmogrify into the orthodoxies of the next.

In this work of historiographical reorientation, Professor Darnton's magisterial study stands as a major landmark. The measure of his extraordinary achievement is that, for all the countless volumes that have been written on the Enlightenment, his is the first to have understood it, and to have succeeded in describing it, as a social phenomenon. This he has done, not by pondering the exegetical niceties of manuscripts nor by tracing the distribution of the expensive folio edition, but by going directly instead to its 'stepchild', the mass-market quarto: 'ragged, blotchy and unkempt'. Thus he begins where most intellectual historians lose interest: with Diderot's ill-tempered refusal to have anything to do with a proposed revised version, in 1768. This was not because his editorial genius could not bear the prospect of alterations to the sacred text, but for precisely the opposite reasons. He now regarded the whole *Encyclopédie* as '*un gouffre où ces espèces de chiffoniers jetèrent pêlemêle une infinité de choses mal digérées, bonnes, mauvaises, détestables, vraies, fausses, incertaines et toujours incohérentes*'.

The massive work of revision and correction was deflected into the alternative project of the quarto – making the *Encyclopédie* available at a third of the original price to thousands of subscribers. This change of course represented a deliberate entrepreneurial decision to go for quantity rather than quality, and for fast, fat profits rather than lingering scholarly endeavour. And it was in researching the genesis of this momentous enterprise that Darnton hit on a historical goldmine of staggering richness: the papers of the Swiss publishers and printers, the Société typographique de Neuchâtel. Though the STN were to be muscled out of much of the action that followed by the heavy brigade of French publishing, the intricacy and density of their records enabled Darnton to unravel the entire history of the launching, manufacture and marketing of the quarto.

His narrative follows the speeding *diligences* conveying the ill-assorted syndicate of business partners between Paris, Lyons and Neuchâtel, each group wheeling and dealing to outmanoeuvre the other while fending off lightning raids by press pirates profiting from an age innocent of copyright protection. It moves among the peregrinations of rag-pickers scouring Burgundy for the linen shreds needed to produce the mountains of paper consumed by the book, and records the unpredictable behaviour of master printers, downing tools for an impromptu foray into the local cabaret or disappearing down the road towards the beckoning finger of a rival employer offering better wages. The excruciating scissors-and-paste labours of tame abbés, hired to sort, file and rearrange copy, are documented, as are the perspiring journeys of solitary travelling salesmen, working the provinces for orders, attempting to drum up promotion, and greasing the palms of smugglers crucial for the selling of what was still, at least officially, an illegal book. Frustrated booksellers in Montpellier and Le Havre and Dijon fret and fume as promised deliveries fail to materialise or arrive with blotched paper and disintegrating bindings. But finally, at the end of the chain, the subscribing customer, his thirty-six volumes complete (including three of plates), could count himself, for less than 400 livres, as the advance publicity cunningly promised, among the advance guard of modern civilised man: the owner of a work which more than any other had, 'with giant steps', 'accelerated the progress of reason'.

Professor Darnton has marshalled this immense mass of detail with skill and elegance to cause the minimum of pain and maximum of illumination. Quite apart from the challenging nature of its conclusions, it is a work which brilliantly succeeds in clothing the dry bones of history with living flesh. His resourcefulness is such that, on the basis of a single thumb print smearing a page in Volume 15, he was able to piece together the biography of the peripatetic and slovenly artisan who left it there. Over-inking was a dodge used to lighten the formidable task of pulling the press bar, and it was from the irate correspondence of the STN with their contract printer, complaining about the abuse, that this pocket biography was rescued from oblivion.

In the interminable procession of Lives of the Famous – royal and political – which week after week testify to the bankruptcy of the historical imagination, Robert Darnton's magnificent book stands as an inspirational example. Its time-scale is perfectly calculated for the examination of a complex phenomenon in depth: it is not bogged down in triviality, nor does it get lost in the vast deserts of the *longue durée* demanded by the most severe practitioners of 'total history'. Its prose is as sharp as its perception, and for all the texture of its detail, the book avoids the kind of micro-history now favoured by, for example, Emmanuel Le Roy Ladurie, in which the relating of a single episode, garnished with a gloss of elementary social anthropology, is meant to proclaim self-evident significance. This is simply the imaginative re-creation of a momentous enterprise, set in the framework of an important historical argument. As such it will become one of the classics of modern historical literature.

Much of the originality of the book derives from its yoking together – as the title implies – of cultural and economic history. Its account of the launching and management of the huge and unwieldy business of the quarto is essential reading for an understanding of entrepreneurial practice and malpractice in the eighteenth century. The extensive arsenal of extortion, conversion of funds, counterfeiting, blackmail, bribery and press piracy is offered as a record of big-time capitalism in its tooth-and-claw phase. A relatively mild form of everyday dishonesty sanctioned, for example, the use of promotional literature announcing the publication of a new work, together with prices and prospectuses, without the slightest commitment to going ahead, should this preliminary sortie fail to elicit an encouraging response. More serious was the naked blackmail practised by pirates (one with the engaging name of Grabit), who threatened to publish available material at undercutting rates until bought off by the harried publisher at an exorbitant price. Much of what is recorded here suggests the thinness of the line between crime and business, though Darnton's suggestion that this was in stark contrast to a more 'managed' capitalism in industrialising Britain seems open to debate.

Because of the extraordinary assortment of rogues and fools, villains and victims assembled in the book, some of its narrative has the compelling quality of an eighteenth-century morality novel. The backwoods provincial Swiss, turgid with Calvinist probity, innocent of deep guile, but with their nostrils quivering at the scent of profit, plunge headlong into the murky waters of quasi-illegal publishing, only to swim straight into the grateful jaws of the giant (French) predators gliding in the lower depths. That they eventually surfaced again without being swallowed alive, but after being treated to a severe mauling, was less the result of their own astuteness than of the predictable and mutual hostility of the two most accomplished and ravenous sharks: Joseph Duplain and Charles-Joseph Panckoucke.

The two men were not, in fact, interchangeable types. Duplain, the press baron of Lyons, was the more uncomplicated and gangsterish. Specialising in rapid turnover and massive profit margins, he never hesitated to use graft, strong-arm pressure and extortion to secure them. While tyrannising his subcontractors to produce the goods, he was quietly creaming off enormous sums by falsifying his inventory of sales. Even he, however, could go too far and expose himself to lethal counter-attack by his long-suffering and suspicious business partners. Having educated themselves in the kind of tactics that were second nature to Duplain – industrial espionage, sabotage, false greetings of amity – the STN together with Panckoucke sprung the trap for their delinquent partner. In one of the most memorable passages in the book Duplain was confronted with irrefutable evidence of his gigantic swindle, and forced into disgorging 200,000 livres to extricate himself from disgrace and ruin. While this was a colossal sum, and while their cut provided the Swiss with some balm for their wounded innocence and shrunken profits, it was nothing like enough to impede Duplain's progress towards his heart's desire: the purchase of royal office, carrying with it a patent of nobility. And it was a paradox, absolutely typical of late eighteenth-century France, that the semi-criminal buccaneering capitalist should see the goal of all his plots and stratagems as absorption into the class of the landowning aristocracy.

Panckoucke, who had some tart asides to offer on his ex-partner's pretensions to lord it as 'Duplain de St Albine', was an altogether more complex personality. So far from speeding after Duplain down the highway of illicit gain towards noble status, Panckoucke veered off after the quarto away from quantity and back, as he supposed, to quality. In the closing sections of his book, Darnton traces his subsequent career, dominated as it was by the colossal, ruined edifice of the *Encyclopédie Méthodique*, the ultimate work of compilation, arranged according to rules of subject, not the absurd dictation of the alphabet. The 'ultimate *Encyclopédie*' was intended by Panckoucke to replace the solecisms and anachronisms of which Diderot had complained so bitterly. But the effort needed to tackle this work of revision proved so exhausting that it cast a long and dark shadow over Panckoucke's remaining years, growing ever more monstrous like some intellectual Fonthill that threatened to crash down from its precarious foundations and bury its architect amid the debris.

Professor Darnton sees Panckoucke's obsession with the project of the *Encylopédie Méthodique* as an anticipation of the habits of nineteenth-century robber barons for whom 'speculation had become an end in itself'. It is certainly true that the scale of the gamble, costing Panckoucke nearly two million livres and involving 100,000 articles collected in forty-two quarto or eighty-four octavo volumes, dwarfed anything that the Enlightenment had yet produced or even conceived. But rather than this growing out of Panckoucke's admittedly omnivorous appetite for big-time business, it was the product of his fixation that the tomes of the *Encyclopédie Méthodique* would provide the key with which the mysteries of the modern world would be disclosed. In other words, he had come to believe his own promotional literature – an unpardonable lapse for a publisher. He even appears to have cherished the view that the systematic organisation of knowledge, its classification into great monolithic compartments of the intellect, would make men happy and free. '*L'homme devient autant libre plus il a l'esprit cultivé,*' he opined, following Condorcet rather than Rousseau; and he stuck by this faith as his great project hit the reefs and started to founder.

A mighty debacle was in sight long before the Revolution made it a certainty. Deadlines were broken: the brigades of editors assigned responsibility for the mammoth sections into which the work was divided procrastinated, as subsidised intellectuals are prone to do, and failed to deliver copy. Panckoucke's costs sky-rocketed and his subscribers began to defect as he importuned them for more time, more volumes and more subscriptions.

So far from the French Revolution representing the consummation of Encyclopedism, the opposite turned out to be the case. Although Panckoucke initially greeted it with warmth, he very soon felt its adverse effects. The costs of both manpower and materials shot up, and both were diverted to service the more urgent needs of the revolution: broadsides, pamphlets, patriotic ballads and the like. He had been prudent enough to diversify into journalism, but the kind of ephemeral literary flotsam and jetsam washing around the streets of Paris, and soaking up precious print and paper, was anathema to his sense of the weighty and the durable. More galling still, as soon as he had brought out the immense compilation on legal institutions, the revolution wiped the slate clean of antique usages and arcane precedents, thus rendering it useless as a work of reference.

All this was hard to take, and as the revolution turned militant, Panckoucke's huffing and puffing against scurrilous invective and irresponsible fly-by-night printers became more exasperated. Rejected at the polls, he took to advocating the old system of guilds and licences as a way of restoring orderly regulation. This was not simply a case of sour grapes. For all the ostensible 'liberalism' of the *Encyclopédie* enterprise, it turned out in the end to have been crucially dependent on the institutional peculiarities of the Old Regime. A state in which official censorship coexisted alongside actual permissiveness had been ideally suited to Panckoucke's sort of publications. The formal disapproval of the Parlement courts, the occasional book-burning by the public executioner, promoted his reputation as a purveyor of the avant-garde, while the reality of toleration and even encouragement on the part of Louis XVI's court protected him from serious jeopardy. Like much that was dynamic in this period – Atlantic trade, for example – his publishing operated within the interstices of formal institutions where the spirit of modernity was struggling to free itself from the dead weight of antiquity.

Indeed, both Panckoucke and Duplain had needed the power of the French monarchy as an occasional tactical weapon. When confronted by a Swiss-printed octavo which threatened to undercut the quarto just as they had undercut the folio, they used the full muscle of police power to deny the trespassing pocket edition any entry to the French market.

In a more oblique sense, the entrepreneurs, like the authors of the *Encyclopédie*, had worked, not in irreconcilable antipathy to, but in symbiotic relationship with, the Old Regime. They were grateful for its more self-parodying anomalies as points to score off, and like Voltaire in his denunciations of *mortmain*, actually embellished their abuse for propaganda purposes. Many of the King's ministers had long come to acknowledge the truth of much of what the *Philosophes*, and indeed the physiocrats, urged. But with some exceptions, such as the emancipation of Protestants in 1787, their institutional immobilism precluded their being able to do much about it.

No such tacit generosity coloured the militant stage of the revolution which profited from their inadequacy. Instead of embracing Panckoucke's creed of liberating reason, sanctimonious Jacobinism turned violently and with savage repugnance on the luke-warm morality of the *savant* and the *bel esprit*. Academicians were reviled (not infrequently by renegades among their own number) as parasites who in their lust for royal and noble favour had battened on to the verminous cadaver of the old order. Against their celebration of pure rationality were ordained the transcendent values of social piety, simplicity of manners, stoical virtues and righteous anger.

It was only when the fierce flame of this irascibility burned itself out with the Terror that those who had evaded its punishments, or who had at least temporarily colluded in its indignation, surfaced once more in a guise that would have been familiar to Panckoucke. By this time, he had prudently silenced his tirades, but had abandoned the wreck of the *Encyclopédie Méthodique* to his family before dying in 1798. Had he survived just a few years longer, one suspects he would have been gratified by the ethos of Bonaparte's Consulate. For in place of editorial patronage, the state had taken over the management of classified data and had transformed their practitioners – land surveyors, engineers, mathematicians and *polytechniciens* – into the freshly exalted caste of professional experts, showering them with the status and the subsidies which they have never relinquished.

If this extraordinary denouement fails to yield a satisfactory answer to the question I posed at the outset – the connection between Enlightenment and revolution – it may well he because it was, all along, the wrong question to put. If, instead of characterising the revolution as the harbinger of the New Era, one sees it as a convulsion of nostalgic desperation, and its protagonists, not as men with their gaze directed at a scientifically organised or capitalistically managed future, but rather as artisans and landless peasants rebelling *against* the prospect of such a future, then its historical separation from the late eighteenth century and the mid-nineteenth century becomes clearer. And if we formulate a new question – did the Enlightenment and its most ambitious creation, the *Encyclopédie*, help bring to birth a modern world in which aggressive capitalism was to be partnered by scientific determinism, *notwithstanding* the interruptions of revolutionary upheavals? – then, after reading Robert Darnton's thrilling and luminous volume, we can venture a tentative answer. *Oui, hélas.*

Abolishing the Slave Trade in Britain and America: Sound and Fury or Deafening Silence?

Stanford University Presidential Lecture, 2007

When was it exactly during the bicentennial commemorations of the abolition of the slave trade that I became aware of just how much had changed in Britain? Was it when Ghanaian *memnon* horns, alerting villagers to the imminence of a slave raid, sounded from the choir screen in Westminster Abbey? Or was it a little later when a robed young militant writer harangued the Queen in the nave, the monarch rather grandly allowing the shouting to go on for a full four minutes before the agitator was strong-armed out of the abbey. (Hmm, I thought, just try that one in Washington DC and see what happens.) After the service I asked Kate Davson, the direct descendant of William Wilberforce, who read from a speech to the House of Commons, what she thought. 'Oh,' she said rather sweetly, 'I understand so well. The pain never goes away, does it?' That's the Wilberforces for you: Christian to the end.

Or was it when I – the lapsed Jew – found myself standing in the pulpit of All Saints Church, Fulham, on the invitation of its parish vicar Joe Hawes, who had decided, 194 years after the burial of the abolitionist Granville Sharp, to give the patriarch of the campaign the church funeral he'd been denied by the parish priest of the day? There had, apparently, been no love lost between Sharp and the vicar, the latter suspecting the former of Dissenter views about the liturgy even while professing allegiance to the Church of England. So in July 1813 the church funeral was abruptly cancelled, and Sharp was permitted a summary few words by the graveside in the churchyard. To the vicar's intense vexation, all of abolitionist London – black and white – came anyway. The service this year was an act of reparation for the affront;

the eulogist was the aforesaid Jew, and the congregation about as ethnically mixed as you could imagine – among them, however, being
members of the prolific Sharp family, looking (how tenacious these
British genes are) exactly like their evangelical forebears. When the
ceremonies began with one of Granville's own duets played on his own
English horns, preserved – aptly enough – in the Horniman Museum,
the centuries just folded in on themselves in a quantum way and we
were not so much commemorating as virtually re-enacting. (Rather in
the way Collingwood thought all history had, in some sense, to be imaginative re-enactment before it could ever be analytical interpretation.)

But commemoration of the British abolition of the slave trade there
most certainly has been – during March of this year, it seemed almost
24/7: a day of 'Resistance and Recollection' at the British Museum
(readings to schoolkids as well as grand utterances by the likes of Wole
Soyinka); a fine exhibition in Westminster Hall of documents and
artefacts, including the travelling box used by Thomas Clarkson on
his peregrinations around Britain, shackles, yokes, coffee beans grown
by ex-slaves in free Sierra Leone, and the famous *Am I Not a Man and
a Brother* Wedgwood medallion reproduced by the abolitionist entrepreneur in tens of thousands; the print of the Liverpool slaver *Brookes*,
with its sardine-can-packed African bodies, which we know likewise
made its way into thousands of homes around the country; two new
museums of slavery – one in Liverpool, another about to open in the
Docklands in London; my own book about the fate of the escaped
slaves who sided with the British in the revolutionary war turned first
into a ninety-minute television film and then into a stage play, which
has run in London and is currently touring in the North of England.

Now obviously this saturation coverage isn't to be explained merely
as an act of historical piety – and the tone of the proceedings has often
been (this has to be a good thing) clamorously self-interrogatory. Issues
of reparations and apologies have indeed come up (for what it's worth,
if one of my German contemporaries came up to me and said, 'Tremendously sorry about Auschwitz, won't happen again, I promise', and all
that, I'd say, 'Well, if it makes you feel better, right, but it doesn't really
cut it'). More important, though, the commemorations have been an
occasion on which to ask serious questions about national identity and
allegiance in Britain; the legacy of empire; and in particular unsentimental questions about being black and British over the last 200 years.

But in all this vocal theatre of memory, in all the waves of sound and fury, one rather remarkable fact has been completely ignored: Thomas Jefferson signed an Act prohibiting the slave trade to the United States, and by American traders, into law three whole weeks before George III gave the British equivalent the formal royal assent. But you can hardly blame the British for overlooking this, since the commemoration has gone entirely missing on this side of the pond. Google it, and you'll find nothing at all, not even the commemorative stamp that I was told was planned – in the age of universal email about the most exiguous form of tribute imaginable. In fact when Charles Rangel, the New York Congressman and one of the leaders of the Black Caucus, proposed a motion of commemoration and congratulation, it was to the British Parliament, not to his own legislature that preceded it! This recalls perhaps the fact that in 1808 congregations of black churches in Philadelphia sang anthems to the British abolition of 1807, hoping that 'Columbia's chains' would follow – not noticing that they already had. When the General Assembly of the United Nations formally marked the anniversary on 26 March, the American delegate, Richard Terrell-Miller, a white career diplomat whose Senate confirmation preceded the anniversary by nine days, actually failed to mention that the United States had done likewise.

This dramatic contrast between contemporary fanfares and alarums on the one side and deafening silence on the other repeats the pattern set 200 years ago. Researching the debates on the subject in the Ninth Congress in late 1806 and early 1807, Matthew Mason noticed just how much the dog failed to bark in the night. President Jefferson, who – schizophrenic as always on matters of race – was heartily glad to see it pass, referred to it very little in his letters and private papers. What was on his mind – and that of Congressmen and most of the American press – was something they thought much more dramatically important: the capture of Aaron Burr and the unravelling of his conspiracy to detach the western territories from the Republic; and the interference with American commerce posed by the mutual commercial wars of the French and British Empires. Attendance in the House of Representatives and Senate when the abolition of the slave trade was discussed was thin, and the debates themselves were almost never over moral fundamentals, but rather skirted the ethics for intensive examination of the pragmatic details of enforcement. Was slave trading to be a felony or a misdemeanour (with very different penalties prescribed as a result)? What was to be the fate of slaves taken from apprehended ships? Were they to be automatically manumitted? Or treated, in effect, as contraband? Would the measure extend the prohibition to coastal inter-state traffic? On all these questions, exactly as you would expect, representatives from the Lower South were militantly intransigent. Government interference with inter-state trade was taken to be an extension of federal power so gross as to be tantamount to a violation of the constitution, and provoking from John Randolph an explicit threat – in 1806 – of secession. If trading in slaves was to be treated – as northern proponents like Senator Stephen Row Bradley from Vermont, and Representative John Smilie of Pennsylvania wanted – as a felony, the implication was that convicted persons might be subjected to the death penalty. No southerner, said Randolph and others, would ever assent to the execution of one of their number for committing a deed which they would never consider a crime. And since, of course, the vast majority of likely illegal trading ventures would take place at southern ports and in southern waters, the outlook for enforcement was not auspicious. Most ominously of all, for the fate of the Bill, southern representatives set their face against any possibility of liberating slaves taken from captured ships, thus releasing large numbers of black freedmen into their own slave societies. (Remember that from the 1790s onwards states in the Lower South – and some areas of the Upper South – had been doing their utmost to rid themselves by expulsion of troublesome populations of free blacks.) To admit more was, southerners like Peter Early of Georgia insisted, to light the fires of insurrection. It would be, he said, 'an evil greater than slavery itself'. The only recourse beleaguered southerners would have, said Early, was 'self-defence – gentlemen will understand me – [we must] either get rid of them or they of us; there is no alternative . . . Not one of them would be left alive in a year.'

It's important to remember that many of the most forthright and articulate assailants of Jefferson's Act – or rather those who wanted to amend it into harmlessness – were actually either Virginians like John Randolph or Virginians by origin like Peter Early, even though he had moved to and spoke for the Lower South. What the debate – such as it was – at the end of 1806 implied was an early fracture within the leadership of the South itself, and not always just along regional lines. Madison was, as usual on this issue, uncomfortably in the middle –

endorsing the Act, provided it did not cause too much 'inconvenience' to his fellow plantation owners like the President, who sustained his moral schizophrenia to the end. Not least, of course, because Jefferson and Madison – not to mention their faithful correspondent in Massachusetts, former President Adams – well knew that the price, first of Confederation, then of making a Union, then of enacting a constitution, had been deferring to the Lower South on both the trade and the institution of slavery itself. Postponing legislation concerning the slave trade for twenty years had been the condition of making the constitution possible (and there were in 1807 those who refused to accept the law as valid, considering that Jefferson had anticipated by a year the end of that moratorium even though the law was not to come into effect until 1808). This had been the Faustian bargain that had made the United States, and (to mix metaphors) the poisoned chalice that the temporising Virginians – Jefferson and Madison – knew very well would be passed along to their posterity.

Jefferson had a peculiarly corrupted and tortured conscience about all this. His original draft of the Declaration of Independence had included a ferocious paragraph attacking the slave trade – 'cruel war against human nature itself, violating its most sacred rights of life and liberty in the persons of a distant people . . . captivating and carrying them to slavery in another hemisphere, or to incur miserable death in their transportations thither'. That paragraph had been duly stricken from the final draft, 'in complaisance to South Carolina and Georgia', but Jefferson had in any case made this one of the colonists' grievances against Britain by blaming the whole trade on the King – 'the warfare of the Christian King of Great Britain'! Responsibility for the glaring inconsistency between the 'self-evident' truth that 'all men are created equal' and the fact of slavery thus was conveniently displaced onto the person of the offending monarch and his culpable ancestors. Nothing to do with us of course – heavens, no! And now the King and his 'courtiers', as Jefferson liked to call them, were compounding the evil by actually conspiring to foment armed insurrection among the slaves by promising them their liberty if they remained loyal to the Crown. Such diabolical Machiavellianism!

Behind this rich exercise in historical disingenuousness lay the nagging anxiety of the Founding Fathers that to face squarely up to the contradiction between the promises of the Declaration and the reality of the slave economy was to bring the Union down before it ever had a chance of consolidation. This was, of course, merely to postpone what Jefferson and Madison and Adams and many others predicted would be the inevitable conflict, which indeed came to pass a half-century later. It's a matter of deep poignancy, as Pauline Maier saw in her book on the Declaration, that subsequent pragmatists like Stephen Douglas contorted themselves in knots to make the promise of equality something like a utopian principle – a nice idea – never actually to be implemented, or intended for whites only, while for the young Abraham Lincoln, even in his law-practice days in Springfield, it always meant precisely what it said. Not only did Jefferson, as it were, move on to other matters – the Louisiana Purchase – while hoping for the best, but it was during his presidency that an all-time record number of slaves were imported into the United States (many of them on British ships) precisely in anticipation that perhaps the trade would be subject to eventual prohibition.

In some fundamental sense, then, directly broaching the issue in 1806 and 1807 was to toy dangerously with what was perceived as a fragile union. To add sectional bitterness to the divisions that already beset the United States – between Federalists and Republicans over the extent of central power, and to do it at a time when the country was beset with dangers from abroad and at home – was to do damage to an already vulnerable body politic. No wonder Jefferson soft-pedalled it and conceded many of the South's demands. Slaving after January 1808 would not be a felony and would be punished by fines. There was to be no interference with inter-state commerce in humans, and scant provision was made for any sort of naval enforcement of the prohibition. The navy, such as it was, had its hands full keeping American waters free of privateers, or British and French ships taking prizes, without taking further duties on itself. The poisoned chalice was passed quietly on.

Historically, then, the abolition of the slave trade in the United States pointed in every respect to a future of disunion; of national disintegration, a reckoning to be paid in blood. And I suppose that's why there's been so little disposition to celebrate or commemorate it in this anniversary year. But there's something else at work here in some larger sense about the selectivity of public memory in this country, the tendency, especially at a time of – what shall we call it? – military perplexity, to use history for consolation. I was reminded of this by watching episodes

of Ken Burns's egregiously titled PBS documentary series *The War* (as
if only the American experience counted): an immense exercise in
elegiac self-congratulation. Whatever our troubles, there was at least
one war which was fought for indisputably noble motives and which
by and large turned out well. The consolatory and redemptive pay-off
– history as lullaby – is unmistakable. But this was not what the first
authentically critical historian of our tradition – Thucydides – had in
mind for us at all. He was, after all, a general who had taken part in
the conflict he chronicled and that made him not an elegist, but a gadfly
for the complacent. I'm always struck by the passages from the *Peloponnesian Wars* for use in American core curricula – almost always
Pericles's funeral oration, hymning the liberty for which Athenian men
sacrificed themselves – a speech text which may be the only compromised passage in that history since Thucydides, a rebarbative critic of
Herodotus's playing fast and loose with the sources, conceded it was
based on the report of someone who might have heard the Dear Leader.
The real *telos* of the work, as you know, is quite different, a damning
indictment of the Athenian imperial hubris that leads them to Syra-
cuse and catastrophe. The march to self-destruction is the point of the
book and it immediately establishes as a birth-text, Western history as
an exercise in merciless self-criticism; its temper cautionary, its intelligence sceptical, its pay-off – as often as not – tragic. History is the
memory of comeuppance for the next generation; its integrity bound
up with its honesty and its abhorrence of patriotic self-ingratiation.
Thucydides's history – our history – is no one's cheer-leader.

Which brings me, inevitably, to my own countrymen across the ocean
and the place of the moment of abolition in British cultural memory.
Now it's true that the British are hardly exempt from the kind of patriotic self-congratulation – history as moral reassurance – that I've implied
is an issue in its American popularity. It's equally true, though, that disas-
ters like Dunkirk are as likely to be meat and drink for writers and readers
as Trafalgar and D-Day. From Dr Johnson's famous epithet about patriotism being the last refuge of a scoundrel to the ingrained scepticism
against hero-worship in British history, it's also true that the cautionary
temper has on the whole served British commemoration reasonably well.
So although there was certainly an element of back-patting going on in
the commemorations of abolition – especially since it led, after a generation, directly to the parliamentary abolition of slavery itself in 1833

(rather than the opposite in the American case), with figures like Thomas Clarkson agitating for and presiding over both — it's also true that this year has been an occasion for looking into the glass of time darkly, in particular for a re-engagement in the debate over the relationship of slavery to economic power.

What's been impressive, I think, though, is the degree to which the moment hasn't just been a reheating of Eric Williams's *Capitalism and Slavery*, the ur-text which a half-century ago attacked abolitionism as a movement of convenience, made possible only when the Atlantic sugar economy was in decline, made irrelevant by the new laissez-faire manufacturing economy. No scholars (to my knowledge) would seriously try and argue that any longer, nor the indisputability of the timing of abolition occurring at the zenith of the slave and sugar economy, rather than during its decline.

It's precisely because the instrumentalist argument from social expediency (once, but no longer, put by David Brion Davis) can't possibly be empirically sustained that the bicentennial has prompted historians — and the common culture more generally — to engage again with abolition as a moral act; one in which it's just conceivable that the protagonists meant what they said, especially when figures like Granville Sharp, the archdeacon's son, and Thomas Clarkson, intended for the ministry (and who took up abolitionism as a kind of Pauline conversion when he learned about the *Zong* from a sermon preached by Dr Peter Peckard in the Cambridge University Church of St Mary's), invoked Christian religion.

The essential reason why, I believe, the commemoration of abolition became so much an event in the national culture in this year of 2007 is because the debate performed very much the same function 200 years ago. Linda Colley, in *Britons*, has written about the role that the agitation against the slave trade played in creating a kind of national politics, and one which included as political actors for the first time hitherto-excluded constituencies like women. That's absolutely right, but I want to push the argument further and, in contrast to the American sense that anti-slave-trade campaigning was a nation-breaker, suggest that in Britain it was a nation-maker; perhaps, along with the romanticism of the past that took place during the wars against the French, *the* single most powerful force in the making, or rather the remaking — the re-formation — of Britain.

And this was, paradoxically, the fruit of defeat. American victory – won at the price of not pushing the contradiction between the Declaration of Independence and the social reality to the point of threatening the union – made a powerful incentive to let that particular sleeping dog lie, for at least twenty years. In Britain, defeat led to bitter soul-searching, in the first instance on the part of critics of the American war like Granville Sharp, Edmund Burke and Charles James Fox. But the sense in which Britain was the new Nineveh or indeed Sodom, punished for its manifold sins – its corruption, its profanity, but above all its inhumanity to fellow men, reduced to chattels and beasts of burden – was a common refrain in the early rhetoric of the abolitionists. Whereas the fate of the United States depended on *not* grasping this particular nettle, the fate of Britain, the castigators of slavery insisted, was conditional on its doing just that.

And in striking contrast to Congress, skirting around the big moral principles of national self-definition in its debates, those in Parliament were almost nothing but. The orations made in the late summer of 1806 – and perhaps precisely because it was under attack from reformers demonising it as nothing more than the unclean temple of 'Old Corruption' – transformed the Houses of Commons and Lords into a rhetorical theatre for the redefinition of the legislature, and by extension the British constitution – King in Parliament, the Law and the Church working together to extirpate the abomination. Fox – who was junior to Lord Grenville in the government, but its senior spokesman in the House of Commons – began his speech with encomia, not just to Wilberforce, but to his most famous political adversaries, William Pitt and Edmund Burke, both of whom were conveniently dead. (Fox was shortly to follow in September of that year, leaving Grenville to steer the legislation through its final readings the following March.) Waxing magnanimous, Fox quoted Burke: 'to deal and traffick not in the labour of men but in men themselves, was to devour the root, instead of enjoying the fruit, of human diligence'. The 1791 speech of Pitt (his bitterest foe in precisely that year of revolution) was: 'the . . . most powerful and convincing eloquence that ever adorned these walls, a speech not of vague and shewy ornament but of solid and irresistible argument founded on a detail of indisputable facts and unquestionable calculations . . .' Fox summoned the ghosts of the past masters of the House in a demonstration of cross-party unity on this one great matter. A

succession of extraordinary speeches followed, including two of them
– by the one-armed hero of the American war, Banastre Tarleton, and
General Isaac Gascoine, both of Liverpool – against the motion. But it
was left to the brilliant Solicitor General Samuel Romilly to be the most
uncompromising of all about what was at stake, which was nothing
less than the integrity of Parliament and the honour of the nation.
Romilly upbraided the two Houses for delaying as long as they had, since
Wilberforce's original motion was introduced in 1791, exhorting them
to come to a more ethically proper conclusion. Like other orators in the
House, he dismissed the argument that slavery and the traffic had
existed in all cultures and societies since antiquity as being no reason at
all why Britain should not step forth (he implied especially in the light
of American hypocrisies) to embrace the mantle of moral dignity and
end it. (In the Lords, Beilby Porteus, the Bishop of London, one of the
staunchest of the abolitionists, made the point that to argue from custom,
to argue from *is* to *ought*, might as well justify the Chinese practice of
mass exposure of infants to die.) Neither the fate of the Atlantic economy (or of Bristol and Liverpool), Romilly said, nor the possibility that
abolition might simply be a gift to the French or the Spanish empires
at a time when we were at war with them, could possibly justify perpetuating a *malum in se*, this unconscionable evil. The year 1796 had been
set by the House as 'the utmost limit allowed for the existence of that
most abominable and disgraceful traffick and yet it still subsists'. (It was
the fault of the Lords, he said, that the Act had not gone through earlier.)
'I can very well understand that nations as well as individuals may be
guilty of the most immoral acts from their not having the courage to
inquire into their nature and consequences.' But in 1789 Parliament *had*
so inquired and it was:

> established by a great body of evidence that the African slave trade is
> carried on by rapine, robbery and murder and by fomenting wars . . . thus
> are these unhappy beings in order to supply this traffick in human blood
> torn from their families . . . Now sir after all this has been proved, after
> it has been ascertained by indisputable evidence that this trade cannot
> be carried on without the most iniquitous practices, that murder, rapine
> and robbery are the foundations of it . . . that wars are fomented to support
> this traffick; that most disgusting cruelties attend it in the passage of this
> unhappy part of our species from their native home to the place of their

slavery, that they are there subjected to a cruel and perpetual bondage, I do say that this trade ought not to be suffered to continue for an hour; it is a stain upon our national reputation and ought to be wiped away.

When it was claimed that merchants would have to be compensated, Romilly replied, 'ought the debts of the people of England to be paid with the blood of the people of Africa? . . . the people of England are not to consent that there should be carried on in their name a system of blood, rapine, robbery and murder . . . because we must make some compensation to some individuals'.

This was also the nub of Wilberforce's argument – that the issue spoke to 'the inestimable advantages of a free constitution'. When others said the timing was poor because of Britain's continuing involvement in the wars with Napoleon and his allies, Wilberforce (and this was before Trafalgar, and while Napoleon had established an invasion camp on the Channel) retorted to the contrary:

> if ever there was a period in which this country, circumstanced as we are, had an opportunity of setting a glorious example to all the other nations of the earth and of giving a proof of the inestimable advantages of a free constitution, of an enlightened policy and of all the blessings Providence has bestowed upon us, the present is that moment and we ought to hail it with joy as giving us an opportunity of shewing the world that we are not . . . a sordid race looking exclusively to our own interest and pursuing it through the oppression of others . . . but that we are a nation governed by the rules of justice, which are dictated by true wisdom . . . no society any more than any individual can be long upheld in prosperity upon any other principle.

The subtext of this flamboyance, and the targets of its righteousness, were of course the false prophets of liberty – American and French – who paraded their ostensible devotion to freedom before the world while countenancing servitude and despotism. (Napoleon encouraged the slave trade and would formally reintroduce it two years later.)

The motion passed by an overwhelming majority in both Houses, and the final bill by 289 to 16 – in contrast to the exact 60–60 division in Congress over the ban on inter-state commerce, a tie broken against the motion by Speaker Macon from North Carolina. But the alteration of the position in the British Parliament was of a piece with the evangelical reform movement that was attempting to create a new empire, a Christian empire in fact, established, as Romilly said, on virtue rather than interest, or rather through strenuous attempts to redefine the national and imperial interest so that it squared with evangelical notions of virtue and, perhaps even more important – and certainly as popular – newly romantic notions of English (rather than British) history.

This had always been the driving force of the principal campaigners. Granville Sharp had taken up the cause of abducted blacks in the streets of London – in the 1760s – certainly because he believed the plight of slaves was a violation of Christian ethics (there was a great deal of Talmudic hair-splitting in the debates about whether the Israelites had or had not countenanced bondage), but also because he believed passionately in something at least as sacred, that is the unbroken integrity of the English Common Law by which he held (from an Elizabethan case) 'the air of England was too pure for a slave to breathe' – or that once upon these shores all men and women had the same rights to the King's justice. Hence Sharp's unremitting tournament with Lord Chief Justice Mansfield over the status of escaped slaves that had been recaptured by former masters, with the intention of forcible deportation and sale in the West Indies. Sharp's campaigns in the 1770s – fortified at least by his correspondence with American abolitionists like Anthony Benezet and Benjamin Rush – were a reformer's tour of the British constitution. After the law came the Church, whose indifference to the 'accursed thing' (as he called the slave trade) appalled him. Bishops and archbishops were deluged by memoranda and booklets until they capitulated and were converted. After the prelates of the Church, Sharp wanted to recover what he imagined in his Gothic romance to be the pristine forms of democracy: the 'frankpledge' elections of householders to local offices of 'tithingmen' and 'hundreddors', and so on up the chain of governance to a reformed and morally cleansed national representation.

It wasn't just Sharp, of course, but the saints of the Clapham Sect – Zachary Macaulay, Henry Thornton, Hannah More and Wilberforce himself – who saw the campaign against the slave trade as the first act in a great national purification. After the Act went through on 25 March 1807, it was said that Wilberforce turned to Thornton and said, 'Well, Henry, what shall we abolish now?' – and the answer was the lottery! But attacks were launched not just on electoral corruption, but on all manner of social evils, from prostitution to climbing boys and demon gin. Prompted by Malachy Postlethwayte, erstwhile propagandist for the Royal African Company, turned early critic of the trade, then by Adam Smith and finally by the Quaker merchants and bankers – Samuel Hoare and Joseph Woods – an intensive debate was joined as to what was, and what was not, a moral form of commercial activity. In their campaigns to persuade supporters to refrain from using 'slave-made' products, they made much of the addictive and 'enslaving' quality of tobacco and rum that corrupted the freedom of the consumer as much as it was purchased by the blood of those who had laboured to produce it.

And if all this seems somehow marginal now to the main act – the transformation of Britain into an industrial and military empire – that judgement seems, to me at any rate, the anachronistic projection back from a perspective of social science. What the campaign to remake British national identity turned on was as much bound up with moral judgements as the Protestant Reformation and the seventeenth-century Puritan moment. The evangelical movement was the descendant of both of those earlier reformations, and it was of course the nursery of Victorian self-belief that they had indeed managed to reconcile the demands of power, money and Christian morals. That one might think them deluded in this conviction doesn't in any way diminish the force of its original coherence. The fact, too, that after the Irish union of 1801, Great Britain was an indivisible constitution made the reformers believe that what was enacted in Westminster would hold good for the whole country. The centralisation of the British state worked to optimise reform, just as the confederated nature of the American constitution worked against it.

But there was, of course, one respect in which the British reformers of 1807 were no more certain than their American counterparts: whether the abolition of the *trade* was the harbinger of emancipation, or whether it pre-empted serious consideration of it. In the United States, the horror at freeing blacks from captured slavers was in part a matter of precaution against insurrections, but also because politicians from the Lower South argued it would lead to unrealisable expectations of general emancipation throughout. Both Jefferson and Charles James Fox were at pains to deny any such thing was anticipated, much less taken for granted. Fox went out of his way to treat any such imputation as an anti-abolitionist

canard. Even William Wilberforce, notoriously, was at best an extreme
gradualist, who believed that prior property rights could not be interfered
with, and that there had to be a period of education and apprenticeship
before slaves could possibly be trusted with their liberty. Only Granville
Sharp – to his dying day – and the Clarkson brothers were immediate
emancipationists, and it was the re-publication of Thomas's great history
of the abolition of the trade which kick-started, in the 1820s, the
campaign for emancipation itself that culminated in the Act of 1833–4.

That campaign, historians are beginning to emphasise, was a transatlantic one in many respects. It was in London that the great
international Abolitionist Congress was held in 1840, patronised by the
Prince Consort and for which Turner painted his notorious and doomed
Slave Ship. It was in Britain that Harriet Beecher Stowe's *Uncle Tom's
Cabin* found its most rapturous and extensive readership. It was in
Newcastle upon Tyne that Frederick Douglass found his personal eman-
cipators, so that it was logical that the lecture tour, which established
him as the great charismatic orator of abolitionism, took place in 1845
in Ireland and Britain. Speaking to rapt assembly rooms in the places
where the Clarksons had first agitated for the abolition of the trade in
blood – in Manchester and Leeds, Birmingham and London, even in
Liverpool – Douglass imagined a British Empire which lived up to its
promises and which, since 1838, and especially beneath the ensign of
the Royal Navy combing the African coast for slavers, was the true bene-
factor of enslaved Americans. He exaggerated enormously the
colour-blind character of the British, so overwhelmed was he by being
taken into Parliament, to stately homes and cathedrals. (Had he gone
visiting, say, Thomas Carlyle, he might have come away with an entirely
different and less rosy view.) But in one respect he was right: in the stren-
uousness of their determination to make their own moral revolution in
Britain, the saints had refused to sweep under the carpet the most repugnant and morally catastrophic issue of the day. A pity, then, that he
couldn't have been in Westminster Abbey to hear the Queen yelled at
by her Anglo-African subject, for that would have confirmed for
Douglass that, for all their selective sanctimoniousness, the British are,
sometimes, capable of taking the truth on the chin.

A League
of Its Own

Red October

Guardian, 29 October 2004

It was the opening of *Catch-22*: love at first sight. Yossarian? Me. The Chaplain: a grungy hole of a baseball ground called Fenway Park. A chilly Boston night in April 1982, the Red Sox playing the Oakland A's, managed by the somewhat recovering drunk, ex-Yankee Billy Martin. What was I doing there? No idea.

Cricket and football (our football) were my games and would stay that way, never mind that I was living in Boston. Every month my dad had taken me to Lords to see Middlesex – the Comptons, Freddie Titmus, Alan Moss – and I'd happily inhaled the mix of beer tankards and fresh-cut grass while Arthur Schama went blissfully to sleep as the county lost yet again to Sussex (Ted Dexter). In winters it was White Hart Lane – starting early – when Alf Ramsey played for them in his long baggy black shorts, and then into the glory glory years of Nicholson, Blanchflower, Mackay and the dashingly undependable Greaves. So why would I want to waste my time watching glorified rounders in what looked like a terrible dump, its drab paint a bilious grey-green and peeling, just like the girders on the elevated freeway?

Because my friend John Clive had nagged and nagged and I had given in. He was an unlikely Sox fan himself: my colleague in the Harvard history department; biographer of Macaulay; originally Hans Kleyff from Jewish Berlin: big, round, soft and exuberant with dark-brown eyes, and a hoarse chuckle. He loved great historical writing, Apple Brown Betty (a pudding, not a call girl) and the Red Sox. So (grudgingly bemused) I went along for the ride, all innocent of the imminent and irreversible Change in Life, the *coup de foudre*; the date with fate that was about to hit.

My nose got it before the rest of me did. Walking among the mass of the Sox Nation converging on the ballpark, up Yawkey Way, the nose surrendered to the smell of Italian sausage and frying onion peddled from the street stalls. You eat them sandwiched in hot doughy rolls, with screaming yellow mustard dripping out the end, and we did. Holy shit, there was something in those sausages; something that obviously made people happy, for happy this crowd surely was: kids and grandpas; lots of loud Boston women with insecure dye-jobs and square shoulders encased in warm-up jackets that had seen many years of heartache; dads with six-year-olds riding on their shoulders. A crowd pouring through the gates from tough Irish Southie, patrician Marblehead or, like us, from bosky Lexington.

Inside, Fenway was unpromising: a mass scurrying up and down dark and dirty ramps; programmes hawked, the notorious horse-trough toilets already brimming horribly from hours of Yawkey Way beer. But then, the climb up the steps into ballpark heaven: a blaze of golden light; grass as damply brilliant and as soft as a meadow in County Donegal; men in blue-and-red jackets gently warming up; a thuck-thuck as the baseball hit the mitt; an ancient organ that sighed and groaned and wheezed and sang while welcoming us to the inner sanctum of the cathedral; an even more ancient announcer, the late, great Sherm Feller, who from the depths of his avuncular baritone declared, 'Ladies and gentlemen, boys and girls, welcome to Fenway Park', and from the ladies and gentlemen and boys and girls a soft roar of mass pleasure that rippled round the stands, and my cricket-loving, football-doting self was a hopeless, helpless goner; Middlesex and Spurs were yesterday's passions. This, I thought, as I improbably caught the bag of peanuts chucked at me from fifteen feet by the vendor, was where I had to be. This was home.

The Red Sox won that evening: veterans (as I rapidly learned) charging round the bases, such as 'Yaz' Yastrzemski, a high-octane hulk; taciturn Jim Rice, the slugger leaping at the edge of the outfield to hoist in what seemed sure home runs; Dwight 'Dewey' Evans, natty in his trim moustaches, an elegant stance at the plate, cracking line drives through the emerald grass. So we went home happy, but being the Red Sox Nation, morning-after moodiness replaced the brief euphoria. *Catch-22* – we won, but actually we should have lost – began in earnest. There were anxieties about the veterans. How long could this bunch hack it? Was it Yaz's last hurrah? And indeed I had noticed the air of slightly decrepit gentility – like much of Boston – hanging over the team as they chawed their chewing tobacco.

I had no idea, of course, what I'd got myself into. I was still clue-less about recognising pitches, especially from the bleachers or the box seats way out behind third base; couldn't tell a cut fastball from a slider if they hit me in the face. (It takes time, but believe me, it repays study. Great pitchers can turn the ball in mid-air in ways that spin bowlers have scarcely dreamed of.) Much more ominously, I had no idea of the dreaded history: the feckless sale of Babe Ruth to the Yankees by the owner Harry Frazee, reputedly to finance the Broadway musical *No, No, Nanette*; the ensuing 'Curse of the Bambino'; the failure to win a World Series since the Kaiser hung up his helmet.

I vaguely knew of the Yankees–Sox rivalry, but – since the Bronx Bombers were themselves regularly bombing in the 1980s – who cared? I had no idea whatsoever of the saga of torment; the moments of deluded euphoria (Carleton Fisk hitting the walk-off homer in Game 6 of the 1976 series against Cincinnati) before the crushing putdown (the loss of the same series in Game 7); an epic of sustained pain that by compari-son made the pecking of Prometheus look like a day at the beach.

I would learn in the worst possible way: the notorious 1986 World Series against the New York Mets. In the American League Champi-onship series (semi-finals to you lot) the Sox had come from a strike away from being eliminated by the California Angels, when a pitcher called Donnie Moore served a fat one over the plate to Dave 'Hendu' Henderson, who saw it coming with his name on it, grinned one of his gap-toothed grins and sent it away. Stuck with the stigma of being the 'goat', poor Moore went into a depressive slide and committed suicide. We went into the World Series against the Mets high on confi-dence – we had the brilliant pitching duo of Roger Clemens and Bruce Hurst and some of those unbowed veteran hitters from the early '80s. One strike away from Winning It All in Game 6, a ball notoriously trickled through the open gate of Bill Buckner's bandy legs and the Mets came back from the grave. In Game 7 it was our hearts into which the stake was driven.

Years – decades – of roller-coaster elation and despair followed. In the meantime I had done something unforgivable, saddled my own two kids with this infatuated allegiance; taken them to Fenway, shoved peanuts and sausages into their faces, made them do the 'wave'; embar-rassed them with my roaring abuse of visiting Yanks; taught them (yes, I could do that now) the difference between the cut fastball and the slider; in short, pretty much ruined their blameless lives.

This came home to me in the worst possible way, almost exactly a year ago when I took my son, eighteen, and grown prematurely wise in Soxian pessimism, to Yankee stadium to see the seventh and deciding game of the American League Championship. Around the seventh inning, well up on the Yanks, our ace Pedro Martinez pitching, we dared a cautious smile of anticipation. The Yankee fans were leaving in depressed droves; those that weren't were scowling at us or hiding their faces in their hands. Then Martinez, kept in for an inning too long, suddenly folded, surrendering hits. Amidst pandemonium the game tied, and then a homer by the aptly named Aaron Boone won it for the Evil Empire. My son's face was drained of colour, but he was the grown-up attempting to console his unhinged father. So now you know why I was up at 4 a.m. on Thursday morning watching every last pitch of the game with St Louis online; now you can measure the combination of ecstatic disbelief and narcotic jubilation coursing through my veins as our ace closer, Keith Foulke, made the last out.

A bit OTT? Absolutely not, my world-weary cricketing friends. Anything is possible in 2004: the trains will run on time; balmy breezes will drift over Wales in December; the lion will lie down with the lamb; and, oh yes, a Red Sox fan will, come January, be sworn into office as the forty-fourth President of the United States.

Acknowledgements

The author and publishers would like to acknowledge and thank the following publications and institutions. Although the copyright for each piece lies with the author, every effort has been made to trace and contact the relevant primary publishers in each instance. The publishers would be pleased to correct any omissions or errors in any future editions.

Travelling

'Sail Away: Six Days to New York on the Queen Mary 2', *New Yorker*, 31 May 2004

'The Unloved American: Two Centuries of Alienating Europe', *New Yorker*, 10 March 2003

'Amsterdam', an uncut version of the essay in John Julius Norwich, (ed.), *The Great Cities in History*, 2009

'Washington DC', an uncut version of the essay in John Julius Norwich, (ed.), *The Great Cities in History*, 2009

'Brazil', *Financial Times* Diary, 22 November 2008

'Comedy Meets Catastrophe', *Financial Times*, 26 September 2009

Testing Democracy

'9/11', *Guardian*, 14 September 2001

'The Dead and The Guilty: 9/11 A Year On', *Guardian*, 11 September 2002

'The Civil War in the USA', *Guardian*, 5 November 2004

'Katrina and George Bush', *Guardian*, 12 September 2005

'In its severity and fury, this was Obama at his most powerful and moving', *Guardian*, 30 August 2008

'Bye-Bye Dubya', *Guardian* 3 November 2008

'The British Election', *Guardian*, 5 May 2005

'Virtual Annihilation', originally published in Ron Rosenbaum (ed.),
Those Who Forget the Past: A Question of Anti-Semitism, 2004

Talking And Listening

'TBM and John', originally in *After the Victorians: Private Conscience and Public Duty in Modern Britain*, Peter Mandler and Susan Pedersen (eds.), 1994

'Isaiah Berlin', *The New Republic* 31 January 2005

'J. H. Plumb', introduction to the new edition of *The Death of the Past*, Niall Ferguson (ed.), 2003, reproduced with permission of Palgrave Macmillan

'Rescuing Churchill', *The New York Review of Books*, 28 February 2002

'The Lost Art of Great Speechmaking', *Guardian*, 20 April 2007

'The Fate of Eloquence in the Age of the Osbournes', Phi Beta Kappa Oration, Harvard University, 3 June 2002

'Barack Obama', *The Independent*, 23 January 2009

Performing

Richard II, note from the Almeida Theatre Production of *Richard II*, Almedia at Gainsbrough studios, 2002

Henry IV, note for Royal Shakespeare Company production, 2008

'Martin Scorsese: Good Fella', Financial Times, 31 October 2009

'Charlotte Rampling: "A Documentary of Me"', *Harper's Bazaar*, January 2010

'Clio at the Multiplex', the *New Yorker*, 19 January 1998

'True Confessions of a History Boy', National Theatre programme essay for Alan Bennett's *The History Boys*, May 2004

Picturing

'The Matter of the Unripe Nectarine: High ground/low ground and Ruskin's Prejudices', Christ Church Symposium, on the centenar of Ruskin's death, Oxford, 1 April 2000

'Dutch Courage', *Guardian*, 23 June 2007

'Rubens', *Guardian*, 22 October 2005

'The Patriot: Turner And The Drama Of History', the *New Yorker*, 24 September 2007

'Carnival and Cacophony', *Financial Times*, 4 July 2009

'Rembrandt's Ghost: Picasso Looks Back', the *New Yorker*, 26 March 2007

Anselm Kiefer (1), *Guardian*, 20 January 2007

'In Mesopotamia: Anselm Kiefer (2)', Catalogue essay for the Anselm Kiefer exhibition *Karfunkelfee and the Fertile Crescent*, White Cube, Hoxton Square and Mason's Yard, October-November 2009

'John Virtue: The Epic Of Paint', National Gallery catalogue essay, 2007

'Avedon: Power', *Guardian*, 27 September 2008

Cooking And Eating

'Cool as Ice', *Vogue* © The Condé Nast Publications Ltd, August 2007

'Sauce of Controversy', *Guardian*, 26 November 2008

'The Great G2 Recipe Swap: Cheese Soufflé', *Guardian*, 2 March 2009

'Simmer of Love', *Vogue* © The Condé Nast Publications Ltd, winter 2008

'My Mother's Kitchen', *Observer Food Magazine*, 11 October 2009

'Mouthing Off', Oxford Food Symposium, September 2009

Remembering

'Omaha Beach', *Financial Times* Diary, 13 June 2009

'Gothic Language: Carlyle, Ruskin and the Morality of Exuberance', London Library Lecture, 12 July 2008

'*The History Of Britain*: A Response', *American Historical Review*, June 2009

'The Monte Lupo Story', *London Review of Books*, 18 September – 1 October 1980

'No Walnuts, No Enlightenment', *London Review of Books*, 20 December 1979

'Abolishing the Slave Trade in Britain and America – Sound and Fury or Deafening Silence?', Stanford University Presidential Lecture, 2007

In A League of Its Own

'Red October', *Guardian*, 29 October 2004

Contents

Foreword

Nearly without exception, human beings the world over are fascinated by the photograph. A photograph is a timeless, compelling, emotive and honest representation of our world; of the places we've been, the events we've witnessed, the people we've met and loved. The photograph is a reflection of our world and ourselves; our mind's eye projected onto cotton vellum or computer screen. The persistence of vision *ex machina*. Indeed, the photographic image is the true iconography of the modern world.

For the photography enthusiast, these are very exciting times. In the span of less than 10 years, we have witnessed the evolution of photography from a mostly silver halide film-based process to a completely digital process. The individual photographer now has the capability to shoot, 'develop', and create prints using an entirely digital workflow, and completely within the comfortable confines of his or her own study.

This new-found freedom from film and the complicated processing thereof is largely due (of course) to the ready availability of affordable digital cameras and photo-quality printers; but it is due also, in no small part, to the efforts of the people at Adobe Systems. Adobe is committed to empowering the digital photographer by providing the most powerful and excellent tools available for rendering, manipulating and printing digital images. Among the most popular and successful of these tools is Adobe Photoshop Elements.

Although one of the original design intents behind Photoshop Elements was to make many of the most common image enhancement tools more readily available and noticeable to the novice user, there is still much depth behind this initial surface. Fortunately for both Adobe and its customers, talented writers such as Philip Andrews have resolved to explore this depth and, in easy-to-understand language and step-by-step guidance, provide access to you, the reader.

Advanced Photoshop Elements 7 for Digital Photographers is a beautifully rendered and compellingly written exploration of the advanced features and techniques that can be accomplished with Photoshop Elements. Through the use of many sample photographs, screen shots and clearly illustrated examples, Mr Andrews provides us with the tools to turn our images into exciting and compelling works of art.

From careful and thoughtful descriptions of the basics of tonal adjustments and camera and scanner settings to detailed explanations for creating traditional photographic effects such as lith print style reproductions, *Advanced Photoshop Elements 7 for Digital Photographers* will provide you with an entire arsenal of tools for adding emphasis, detail, and clarity to your images and for exposing and enhancing their inherent beauty.

If you love photography as much as I do, you are in luck with this book.

Enjoy.

Mike Leavy
Engineering Manager for Elements products
Adobe Systems, Inc.

Introduction

When Photoshop Elements came out it was assumed by many that, because it was so inexpensive, it would be the sort of program that you could master in a couple of hours – it certainly wouldn't require a huge learning curve and probably, let's face it, a chunky manual to get to grips with it, as its professional sibling, Photoshop, does. But how wrong we were. Budget certainly doesn't mean basic in this case, and Adobe has packed so much into Photoshop's little brother that you really do need an expert guide to get the best out of it, to lead you through all those nooks and crannies and show you all the cool tricks that are not obvious to the casual user.

But who to choose to be that guide? Well for me there's only one person, and luckily for you it's the one whose name is on the cover of this book. Philip Andrews is an enigma. As editor of the UK's leading digital photography magazine I require two main qualities from my contributors: they have to be real experts who possess a truly in-depth knowledge of their subject, and they have to be able to communicate that knowledge in simple layman's terms that anyone can understand. (They also have to be reliable and hand their copy in on time, but that's another story!) Well there are plenty of experts and plenty of communicators, but you'd be amazed at how rare it is to find someone who is both, as Philip is.

Philip Andrews knows Elements better than anyone else I know. He also writes in a friendly, entertaining and non-academic style – despite the fact that he is a senior lecturer in photography. He has a great understanding of the needs of the end user and his knowledge and enthusiasm for digital imaging (and photography in general) shine from every sentence. He's an accomplished photographer too, so he not only talks the talk but walks the walk, and uses many of his own excellent images to illustrate his points.

Having already covered the fundamentals of Elements in his last book Philip now moves on to more complex themes and ideas, things which you might (wrongly) have considered a bit ambitious for Elements. As before he puts the software into the wider context of digital imaging in general and explains the why as well as the how. Once again there's a great linked website that allows you to download some of the images used in the book and try the techniques out for yourself.

With Philip as your guide you'll be using Elements like a pro and making great images in no time.

Good luck.

Nigel Atherton
Editor of *What Digital Camera* magazine, UK

1

The Next Level

There is no doubt that when Adobe decided to release Photoshop Elements photographers the world over rejoiced. Not content with their offerings for entry and intermediate users in the past and ever conscious of the growing digital camera user base, the Adobe boffins created the new package with you, the digital photographer, firmly in their mind. Despite the rumors spread by the 'Photoshop Snobs' that the product was just a cut down version of Adobe's professional package and that any serious editing will need to be completed in Photoshop, users the world over are realizing just how well Photoshop Elements fits their needs.

A true photographer's tool

Adobe had finally heard the cries of the mortals and produced an image manipulation package that has the strength of Photoshop with the price tag more equal to most budgets. Elements gives desktop image-makers top quality image editing and management tools that can be easily used for preparing pictures for printing or sharing via the web or CD. Features like the panoramic stitching option, called Photomerge, and the Photo Browser are firm favorites and were featured in this package before they ever appeared in Photoshop. The color management and vector text and shape tools are the same robust technology that drives Photoshop itself, but Adobe has cleverly simplified the learning process by providing an easier-to-use interface and options like step-by-step interactive recipes for common image manipulation tasks. These, coupled with features like the Smart Brush and Quick Selection tools, Adjust Color Curves and the Convert to Black and White features, make the package a digital photographer's delight.

Beyond the companion introduction title >> *This book is the result of many requests to provide a 'next step' that will take Elements users beyond the basic concepts and skills outlined in the introductory text,* Adobe Photoshop Elements – A visual introduction to digital imaging. *(a) Edition 1. (b) Edition 2. (c) Edition 3. (d) Edition 4. (e) Edition 5. (f) Edition 6.*

As a photographer, teacher and author I was captivated by the simplicity and strength that Adobe has crammed into the package and knew that this was just the sort of image editing program that would satisfy the demands of the digital camera users I met every day. So to accompany Elements, I released a new book which was an introduction to the package and digital imaging in general. Titled *Adobe Photoshop Elements – A visual introduction to digital imaging* it quickly became a best-seller and was followed up with a series of new and revised editions to accompany ongoing versions of the program.

As Elements users became more familiar with the concepts and tools used in the program it wasn't long before I started to receive requests for more advanced techniques than those presented in this introductory text. These were quickly followed by queries about how to position Elements as the key 'image editing component' in a high quality photographic workflow that encompassed capture, management, manipulation and output activities.

Elements is central >>
*Photoshop Elements is the
pivot point for all editing and
enhancement tasks involved in the
production of quality photographic
images. The digital production process
involves four distinct steps –
(a) capture, (b) manipulation,
(c) management and (d) output.*

This book is my answer to these requests. With well over
150 new techniques it provides professional tips aimed
at advancing your Elements skills beyond the basics. It is
presented in a series of highly illustrated step-by-step color
tutorials that show you what can be achieved. The techniques
are discussed in the greater context of professional quality
workflows that cover camera and scanner capture, raw
processing, picture management, panorama production
and quality print and web production. There is even a new
section that looks at how to use Elements as a linked editor
for Lightroom providing an even more comprehensive and
professional workflow for experienced Elements users.

Each technique is cross-referenced with related skills and ideas in
the book and there are on-line resources and video tutorials at the
book's website –

www.photoshopelements.net

Here you can download and practise with many of the example
images, video tutorials and resources used in the production of
the book. Key settings for important dialog boxes are presented
along with the illustrated steps needed for you to complete each
technique. By working side by side with this text, your favorite
image editing program and the associated web resources, you
will quickly build both your Elements skills and your general
understanding of the processes involved in creating quality
photographic images.

3.02 Saving and loading selections
*Suitable for Elements – 1.0, 2.0 | Difficulty level – Intermediate
Resources – web image 3.02 | Related Techniques – 3.01, 3.03, 3.04, 3.05
Tools used – Selection tools | Menus used – Select*

Photoshop Elements thankfully gives you the option to save
all your hard selecting work... can be used again later.
With y...ction...   Save...

Step-by-step >> *The techniques in the
book are presented in a highly illustrated
step-by-step fashion that will progressively
build your Elements skills.
(a) Cross-referenced techniques.
(b) Step-by-step illustrations.*

The comprehensive Photoshop Elements workflow

Over the past few versions of the program Adobe has made massive changes to the way that users work in Elements. These changes have converted Photoshop Elements from simply being a photo editing program into a complete digital photography system.

Now in its seventh revision, Elements provides a total workflow solution from the moment you download your files from camera, phone, scanner or the net, through organization, archiving and manipulation phases and then onto printing or outputting the pictures electronically (online albums, email attachments) or as print. Understanding how the various components in the system fit together will help you make the most of the software and its powerful features.

The Adobe Photo Downloader feature and **Get Photos** command allow you to preview, select and download files from a variety of different sources.

The **Organizer** component (a) of Elements works like a 'super' file browser allowing you to import and organize pictures straight from your camera, scanner, the net or your hard drive.
You can view the photographs via the **Photo Browser** or **Date View** options. Pictures can be grouped into Albums (previously called Collections) and you can find specific images via the unique 'keyword tags' that you attach to the files.
In **Date View** (b) images are grouped and displayed based on the date they were taken.
The **Map View** (c) displays photos according to their location on a map with options to share the referenced map with others.

IMPORT

ORGANIZE

The **Full** Edit workspace contains all the familiar editing and enhancement tools that Elements users have come to expect. It is here that you can take full control over the manipulation and fine-tuning of your pictures. You can also add text, play with layers, create multi-picture composites and combine all manner of special effects with your original photo.

EDIT & ENHANCE

The **Print** options in Elements 6.0 and 7.0 are a little different from earlier versions of the program. You can choose to print individual photos or multiple pictures on a single sheet of paper. You can also preview and print individual pages of the multi-page .PSE document. As an added bonus, when printing from the Organizer workspace, decorative frames can be added to the images right from the Print Multiple Photos dialog box.

PRINT

QUICK EDITS

The **Quick Fix** editor provides a series of one-click or semi-automatic fixes for common problems with lighting, contrast, color and sharpness. All the controls are contained in the one screen for speed and you can configure the display to show before and after versions of the photo.

CREATE & SHARE

In versions 6 and 7, the photo projects options are split into two different categories. You can select the various project options from either the Create or Share panels on the right of the Organizer or Editor workspaces. Entries found here use a step-by-step approach to create such projects as slide shows, VCD presentations, photo album pages and greetings cards and photo galleries.

GUIDED EDITS

The **Guided Edit** mode combines step-by-step instructions with controls and tools embedded into the instructions. This is a good place to learn new techniques or get up to speed on how to use new tools and features.

Elements basics

Most digital image-makers find that there are several enhancing steps that they always perform on a newly acquired picture. These changes are often among the first skills that the new Elements user learns. Despite the fact that this book is designed to build upon such basic techniques I thought that it would be best to revisit them briefly to ensure that we are all working from the same game plan.

For the most part these changes follow a predictable sequence:
Import, Organize, Orientate or Straighten, Crop, Adjust Tones, Alter Color, Apply Sharpness and Save.

These basic alterations take an image captured by a camera or scanner and tweak the pixels so that the resultant picture is cast-free, sharp and displays a good spread of tones.

Importing photos

When opening Elements the user is confronted with the Welcome screen containing a variety of options. From this screen you can choose to organize, edit, get creative or share your pictures. The first step for most Elements users is to import their photos from a digital camera or scanner. This task is generally handled by the Adobe Photo Downloader which will automatically start when a camera or card reader is attached to the computer. The files are downloaded and cataloged in Elements with the utility.

Alternatively you can import files from other sources or activate the downloader manually from inside the Organizer workspace, which is accessed via the View and Organize selection in the Welcome screen. See Step 1. This feature provides a visual index of your pictures and can be customized to display the images in Browser, Date or Folder mode and thumbnails can be sorted by keyword tags, title, media, metadata or collection.

To start your first catalog simply select the Organizer: File > Get Photos and Videos menu option. Choose one of the

Step 1 >> *The Welcome screen provides simple and easy access to different parts of the Photoshop Elements system.*

Step 2 >> *Choose the location of the files to import from the list in the File > Get Photos and Videos menu or shortcut.*

Step 3 >> *Add naming, destination folder and deletion details for the transferred files in the Downloader dialog.*

listed sources of pictures provided and follow the steps and prompts in the dialogs that follow. See Step 2.

Basic organization

When using the Photo Downloader you can add naming, destination folder and deletion details and in the Advanced dialog you can also apply metadata, auto stack, fix red eye and add group tags to photos automatically. See Step 3. After downloading, or importing, the files are previewed as thumbnails in the Organizer workspace. At this time it is a good idea to make use of some of Elements' brilliant organizational features to help manage the files before jumping into editing and enhancement activities. Add keyword tags to your photos by click-dragging existing entries from the Keyword Tags pane onto your photos. See Step 4. Alternatively, add your own Keyword Tag entries using the new option (+ button) at the top of the pane. See Step 5. Adding Keyword Tags to your photos means that you can search for and locate individual files based on this association.

Along with Keyword Tags you can also group your images into Albums (previously called Collections) and Smart Albums that automatically update each time you add pictures to Elements. In version 7.0 you also have the option to synchronize Albums online.

Changing a picture's orientation

Turning your camera to shoot images in Portrait mode will generally produce pictures that need to be rotated to be viewed correctly. Elements provides a series of dedicated rotate options that are available from inside the Photo Browser workspace. Simply right-click the thumbnail and select an option from the pop-up list. See Step 6. While organizational tasks and some simple automatic enhancement changes are handled in the new Fix pane of the Photo Browser workspace, more controllable edits are applied in either the Quick, Guided or Full Edit workspaces. So for the next set of changes the picture is passed to the Editing workspace. Do this by selecting the Go to Full Edit option from the right-click thumbnail menu. See Step 7.

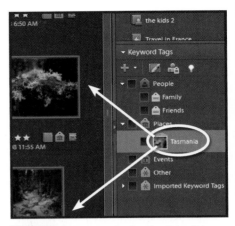

Step 4 >> *Add Tags to the thumbnails by click-dragging the entry from the Tags pane onto the photo.*

Step 5 >> *Add a different Tag entry by clicking the New button and adding details in the Create Keyword Tag dialog.*

Step 6 >> *Orientate the photo using one of the options in the right-click menu of the Photo Browser workspace.*

Cropping and straightening

Most editing programs provide tools that enable the user to crop the size and shape of their images. Elements provides two such methods. The first is to select the Rectangular Marquee tool and draw a selection on the image the size and shape of the required crop. Next choose Image > Crop from the menu bar. The area outside of the marquee is removed and the area inside becomes the new image. The second method uses the dedicated Crop tool that is located just below the Magic Selection Brush in the tool box. Just as with the Marquee tool, a rectangle is drawn around the section of the image that you want to retain. The selection area can be resized at any time by click-dragging any of the handles positioned in the corners of the box. To crop the image click the Tick button at the bottom of the crop marquee or double-click inside the selected area. See Step 8.

An added benefit to using the Crop tool is to not only pre-visualize the crop but also rotate the selection by click-dragging the mouse when it is positioned outside the box. To complete the crop click the Tick button at the bottom of the crop marquee, but this time the image is also straightened based on the amount that the selection area was rotated.

Spreading your image tones

When photographers produce their own monochrome prints they aim to spread the image tones between maximum black and white. So too should the digital image-maker ensure that their pixels are spread across the whole of the possible tonal range. In a 24-bit image (8 bits per color channel – red, green and blue), this means from a value of 0 (black) to 255 (white). Elements provides both manual and automatic techniques for adjusting tones.

The Auto Contrast and Auto Levels options are both positioned under the Enhance menu. Both features will spread the tones of your image automatically, the difference being that the Auto Levels function adjusts the tones of each of the color channels individually whereas the Auto Contrast command ignores differences between

Step 7 >> *Pass the photo to one of the editing spaces by selecting the option from the right-click menu.*

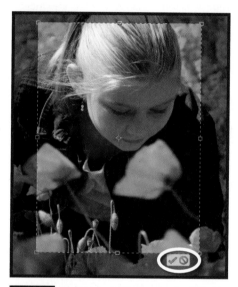

Step 8 >> *The Crop tool gives the user the ability to crop and straighten selected areas of the image.*

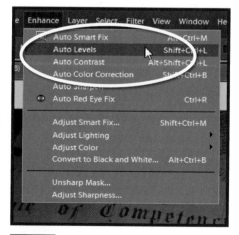

Step 9 >> *The Auto Levels and Auto Contrast functions spread the tones of your image automatically.*

the spread of the red, green and blue components. If your image has a dominant cast then using Auto Levels can sometimes neutralize this problem. The results can be unpredictable though, so if after using the feature the colors in your image are still a little wayward, undo the changes and use the Auto Contrast feature instead. See Step 9.

If you want a little more control over the placement of your pixel tones then Adobe has also included the slider-based Contrast/Brightness and Levels features used in Photoshop in their entry-level software. Both these features, plus the new Adjust Color Curves feature, take back the control for the adjustment from the program and place it squarely in the hands of the user. See Step 10. Jump to the end of the chapter for more details on manual control of tones.

Ridding your pictures of unwanted color casts

Despite the quality of modern digital cameras' White Balance systems, images shot under mixed lighting conditions often contain strange color casts. The regularity of this problem led Adobe to include the specialized Color Cast tool (Enhance > Adjust Color > Remove Color Cast) in Elements. Simply click the eyedropper on a section of your image that is meant to be gray (an area that contains equal amounts of red, green and blue) and the program will adjust all the colors accordingly. See Step 11. This process is very easy and accurate, if you have a gray section in your picture. For those images without the convenience of this reference, the Variations feature (Enhance > Adjust Color > Variations) provides a visual 'ring around' guide to cast removal. See Step 12.

Step 10 >> *The Levels feature provides manual control of the position of white, mid and black tones in your image.*

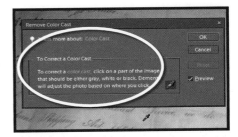

Step 11 >> *The Color Cast tool uses an Eyedropper feature to neutralize color casts in your images.*

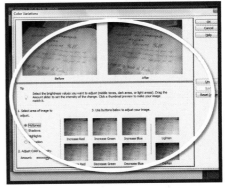

Step 12 >> *The Variations control provides a 'ring around' approach to cast removal.*

Applying some sharpening

The nature of the capture or scan process means that most digital images can profit from a little careful sharpening. I say careful, because the overuse of this tool can cause image errors, or artifacts, that are very difficult to remove. Elements provides several sharpening choices, most automatic, and one with a degree of manual control.

The Auto Sharpen feature found in the Enhance menu provides automatic techniques for improving the clarity of your images. The effect is achieved by altering the contrast of adjacent pixels and pixel groups. Elements also includes the Unsharp Mask filter and the Adjust Sharpness feature, which provides the user with manual control over which pixels will be changed and how strong the effect will be. The key to using these features is to make sure that the changes made by the filter are previewed in both the thumbnail and full image at 100 percent magnification. This will help to ensure that your pictures will not be noticeably over-sharpened. See Step 13.

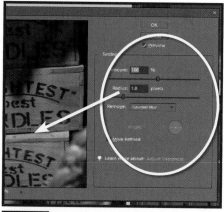

Step 13 >> *Adjust Sharpness improves the overall appearance of sharpness in the image by increasing the contrast of adjacent pixels.*

Saving your images

The final step in the process is to save all your hard work. The format you choose determines a lot of the functionality of the file. If you are unsure of your needs always use the native PSD or Photoshop format. These files maintain layers and features such as editable text and saved selections, and do not lose any picture details due to compression. If space is a premium, and you want to maintain the best quality in your pictures, then you may decide to use a compressed version of TIF or Tagged Image File Format. JPEG and GIF should only be used for web work or when you need to squeeze you files down to the smallest possible size. Both these formats lose image quality in the reduction process, so keep a PSD or TIF version as a quality backup. See Step 14.

Step 14 >> *Elements provides a range of file formats that can be used to save your images.*

Basic Elements workflow

These steps should be the first changes and enhancements you make to new digital photographs. It is upon these basics that the rest of the book will build. So make sure that the sequence and skills included here are second nature before moving on to extending your Elements knowledge.

Basic Elements Adjustments Workflow		
Download image from camera	Import picture from scanner	Open image via Photo Browser
Tag photos (Right-click > Attach Tag)		
Rotate picture (Image > Rotate menu)		
Straighten picture (Crop or Straighten tool or Image > Rotate menu)		
Crop picture (Crop tool or Marquee then Image > Crop)		
Adjust brightness (Enhance > Adjust Brightness/Contrast menu)		
Alter contrast (Enhance > Adjust Lighting menu)		
Remove color casts (Enhance > Adjust Lighting menu)		
Apply sharpening (Enhance menu)		
Save file (File > Save As)		

Book resources and support movies can be found at **www.photoshopelements.net**

Take manual control of your tones >>

One of the most basic, yet critical, tasks for any digital photographer involves adjusting the contrast and brightness of their images. This action is often one of the first undertaken by novices and professionals alike when enhancing newly shot pictures. Well-executed contrast and brightness adjustments can take an 'okay' image and turn it into a dramatic picture.

Though at first glance making these changes seems like a simple task, don't be too eager to play with the Brightness/Contrast sliders. These controls though upgraded in version 6 are often too coarse for quality work. Careful manipulation of the pixels is the key to making quality images and these features don't allow the subtlety of adjustment that is necessary to achieve good results. Instead, employ the aid of either the Levels feature (Enhance > Adjust Lighting > Levels) or the new Adjust Color Curves feature (Enhance > Adjust Color > Adjust Color Curves) when making these changes. Professional digital photographers prefer to use tools like these as they not only provide sliders to alter brightness and contrast but also show a visual representation of the spread of the pixels or preview of the image changes.

Levels adjustments >> *The Levels and Adjust Color Curves features provide fine manual control over the contrast and brightness of your pictures. (a) Before. (b) After. (c) The Levels adjustment used to correct contrast and brightness.*

Advanced tonal control

The first step in taking charge of your pixels is to become aware of where they are situated in your image and how they are distributed between black and white points. The Histogram palette (Window > Histogram) displays the same graph of your picture's pixels as the Levels feature. Viewing the histogram can be one of the quickest ways to diagnose the source of brightness and contrast problems in your pictures.

The left-hand side represents the black values, the right the white end of the spectrum and the center area the midtones (see Levels feature illustrations on page 12). As you may be already aware, in a 24-bit image (8 bits per color channel) there are a total of 256 levels of tone possible from black to white – each of these values are represented on the graph. The number of pixels in the image with a particular brightness or tone value is displayed on the graph by height. Where the graph is high there are many pixels of this tone present in the image. In contrast, low areas of the graph mean that few pixels of this tone can be found in the picture.

Knowing your images

After a little while of viewing the histograms of your images you will begin to see a pattern in the way that certain styles of photographs are represented. Overexposed pictures will display a large grouping of pixels to the right end of the graph, whereas underexposure will be represented by most pixels bunched to the left. Flat images or those taken on an overcast day will show all pixels grouped around the middle tones and contrasty pictures will display many pixels at the pure white and black ends of the spectrum.

These tonal problems can be fixed automatically by applying one of the standard correction features, such as Auto Contrast or Auto Levels, found in Elements. Both these commands re-map the pixels so that they sit more evenly across the whole of the tonal range of the picture. Viewing the histogram of a corrected picture will show you how the pixels have been redistributed. If you want to take more control of the process than is possible with the auto solutions, open the Levels dialog.

Using the Levels control

Looking very similar to the histogram this feature allows you to interact directly with the pixels in your image. As well as a graph, the dialog contains two slider bars. The one directly beneath the graph has three triangle controls for black, midtones and white and represents the input values of the picture. The slider at the bottom of the box shows output settings and contains black and white controls only.

To adjust the tones, drag the input shadow and highlight controls until they meet the first set of pixels at either end of the graph. When you click OK the pixels in the original image are redistributed using the new white and black points. Be careful though as moving the black point slider beyond the first pixels in the graph will convert these tones to straight black, losing any shadow detail that was present. Similarly, dragging the white point too far towards the middle will change delicate highlight details to pure white. Moving the midtone slider will change the brightness of the middle values of the image without changing the black and white points in the image. Altering the output black and white points will flatten, or decrease, the picture's contrast.

Pro's Tip:
Hold down the Alt key whilst moving the black or white input slider and you will see a reversed version of the image showing the pixels that are being converted to black or white by the action.

Basic changes >>
(a) To add contrast drag white and black input sliders inwards.
(b) To reduce contrast drag white and black output sliders inwards.
(c) To darken midtones drag mid input slider to the right.
(d) To lighten midtones drag mid input slider to the left.

Protip for Adjust Curves usage: *Holding Shift while moving the Shadows or Highlights slider lets you move on the horizontal axis instead of the vertical.*

The Adjust Color Curves control

The Adjust Color Curves option provides another way that you can alter brightness and contrast in your photo. Unlike the very basic Brightness/Contrast control, Adjust Color Curves provides separate controls for altering the brightness of highlights, shadows and midtones as well as a single slide for changing midtone contrast.

The feature is divided into two different sections – Style and Adjust Sliders. The Styles section contains several preset adjustments. Selecting one of these entries will apply the adjustment to your photo. The After image shows the enhancement changes.

The Adjust Sliders section contains four controls plus a curves graph that plots the tonal relationships in the picture. Whereas the Styles presets provide a one-click image adjustment, the controls contained here allow multiple, additive, fine-tuning changes. The best approach is to select a Styles preset that matches the change that you are requiring first, e.g. Lighten Shadows, and then fine-tune the results with the Adjust Sliders controls. Pressing the Reset button restores the dialog's control to the default 'Increase Midtones' values.

2

Scanner and Camera Techniques

There is no way to get around the fact that the quality of your final digital pictures is dependent on how well they were captured initially. Poorly photographed or badly scanned images take their problems with them throughout the whole production process and end up as poor quality prints. One of the best ways to increase the level of your work is to ensure that you have the skills and knowledge necessary to create the best digital file possible at the time of capture. This is true for the majority of you who now shoot with a digital camera as well as those who are converting existing photographic images to digital with a scanner.

To help gain this level of control let's go back to the basics and see how factors like resolution and numbers of colors affect the quality of image capture.

The basics – resolution

Most of us, no matter how new to digital photography, are aware that resolution has a direct link with picture quality. It is true that this factor, along with the numbers of colors (bit depth) saved in the file, or captured by the camera, helps determine the overall quality of the image.

The rule of thumb that most new users adhere to goes something like this – the higher the resolution and the greater the bit depth the better the image will be – and to a large extent this is true. High-resolution images with lots of colors are generally better quality than those with a limited color range and fewer pixels, but to understand how integral resolution is to making great digital images we must look a little deeper.

Digital photography basics >> *All digital photographs are constructed of a grid of colored pixels which when seen at a distance combine to form the appearance of a continuous color and tone picture.*

Image capture – input resolution

Computers can only work with digital files. The world as we view it, and as we capture it in silver-based photographs, is not in a digital format. Tones and colors merge gradually from one extreme to another. For the computer to be able to work with such images they must be changed from this 'analog' or continuous tone format to a digital one. Scanners and digital cameras make this change as part of the capturing process.

The scene or print is tested, or sampled, at regular intervals and a specific color and brightness allocated for each sample area. The testing continues in a grid pattern all over the scene, gradually building a pattern of the image which is made up of discrete areas of specific color/brightness. Each of these areas, or samples, becomes a pixel in the resultant digital file.

Resolution at this capturing stage refers to the frequency that samples are made of the image. Generally this measurement is represented as the number of samples taken in a one inch space; for this reason it is sometimes called Samples Per Inch or spi. Unfortunately most scanner software does not use this terminology but prefers to refer to this setting as Dots per inch (dpi). This is a hangover from language used in the printing industry and does more to confuse than clarify the situation.

If you are using a digital camera to capture your image then the resolution will be determined by the sensor, which has a specific number of CCDs set into a grid that is used to digitize the image. Scanner users, on the other hand, are able to control the sampling rate by changing the settings 'in the scanner's dialog box'.

A high sampling rate will result in a higher quality image with a much greater file size. A low SPI will provide a smaller file of less quality. These facts lead a lot of new users to a situation where all images are scanned at the highest resolution possible. Do this and your hard drive will soon be completely used up. High-resolution scans require huge amounts of storage space.

Input resolution >> *High input resolution (a) will produce an image with finer detail than a picture with low resolution (b).*

Input resolutions should be decided on the basis of what the image's final use will be. If the image is to be printed the size of a postage stamp then there is no point scanning at a resolution that will result in a file large enough to print an A2 poster. Remember the end usage determines the scanning resolution, or to put it in a way more easily remembered, 'Know where you are going before you start the journey'.

2.01 How many pixels do I need?

Suitable for Elements – 7.0, 6.0, 5.0, 4.0, 3.0, 2.0, 1.0 | Difficulty level – Intermediate
Related techniques – 2.02, 2.12, 2.13, 13.07

The trick to knowing how many pixels you require is to think carefully about the end product you want to create. As an example, if you want to produce a 10 x 8 inch photographic quality print and you know that the lab you will use to output the image suggests a resolution of 250 dpi, then you have all the information to determine the number of pixels you will need to capture. Essentially the lab is saying that to produce photographic quality they need 250 pixels for every inch of the print. For the photograph to be 10 inches high then your file must contain a minimum of 2500 pixels for this dimension and to ensure the 8 inch width, you will need 2000 pixels. With this knowledge you can adjust the settings on your scanner so that you will end up with a picture file that contains the minimum pixel dimensions of 2500 x 2000.

For digital camera shooters, understanding this concept will not only give you an indication of the maximum print size available from your camera's sensor, but will also allow you to accurately select the correct resolution, or more precisely the correct pixel dimension, setting on your camera for specific tasks. The table below will give you a good starting point.

Chip pixel dimensions:	Chip resolution: (1 million = 1 megapixel)	Print size at 200 dpi. (e.g. photo print)	image size at 72 dpi: (e.g. web use)
640 x 480 pixels	0.30 million	3.2 x 2.4 inches	8.8 x 6.6 inches
1440 x 960 pixels	1.38 million	7.4 x 4.8 inches	20.0 x 13.2 inches
1600 x 1200 pixels	1.90 million	8.0 x 6.0 inches	22.0 x 16.0 inches
2048 x 1536 pixels	3.15 million	10.2 x .7.6 inches	28.4 x 21.3 inches
2304 x 1536 pixels	3.40 million	11.5 x 7.5 inches	32.0 x 21.3 inches
2560 x 1920 pixels	4.92 million	12.8 x 9.6 inches	35.5 x 26.6 inches
2000 x 3000 pixels	6.0 million	10 x 15 inches	27.7 x 41.6 inches
2336 x 3504 pixels	8.2 million	11.6 x 17.5 inches	32.4 x 48.6 inches
2592 x 3888 pixels	10.2 million	12.9 x 19.44 inches	36 x 54 inches

Proposed use	Suggested image resolution
Screen or web use	72 dpi
Draft quality inkjet	150 dpi
Photo-quality inkjet	200-300 dpi
Photo lab output (min)	250 dpi
Photo lab output (max)	400 dpi
Offset printing (good quality)	300 dpi

The suggested output resolution changes for different end uses. For you to accurately capture enough pixels for the end result you desire, you will need to be aware of the resolution requirements for different end products. The table to the left indicates some of the resolution requirements for different uses.

Spreading the pixels >> *In the example, the digital file has dimensions of 800 x 1200 pixels. Though the number of pixels remains the same, each of the prints ranges in size because of the numbers of pixels used to print each inch.*
(a) 16 x 24 inch printed at 50 pixels per inch (ppi).
(b) 8 x 12 inch printed at 100 ppi.
(c) 4 x 6 inch printed at 200 ppi.
(d) 2 x 3 inch printed at 400 ppi.

(a) (b) (c) (d)

Pro's Tips:
• **Know where you are going before you start the journey** – your scanner resolution should be based on the end use of the digital file. A poster will need a higher resolution initial scan, and a bigger file, than a postcard.
• **Balance print quality with practical file sizes** – test your printer to see at what image resolution increases in print quality cease to be perceived. Make this your base image resolution and scan your files according to this setting.

Once you know the image resolution needed for the printer, the final size of the print and the size of your original you can easily calculate the scanning resolution and the total pixel dimensions you need for your digital file. Use the formula in the table below to give yourself an indication of the number of pixels you need for any size print job.

Pro's Scanning Resolution Formulae				
1.	Final image dimensions (pixels)	=	Original image dimensions (inches)	x Scanning resolution (samples per inch)
	3000 x 2400 pixels	=	10 x 8 inch print	x 300 samples per inch
	6000 x 4000 pixels	=	1.5 x 1 inch (135 mm film)	x 4000 samples per inch
2.	Print size (inches)	=	Image dimensions (pixels)	/ Image resolution (pixels per inch)
	15 x 12 inches	=	3000 x 2400 pixels	/ 200 pixels per inch
	20 x 13.33 inches	=	6000 x 4000 pixels	/ 300 pixels per inch

The basics – color depth

This growing understanding of how important resolution is to high quality imaging underpins the continual push by digital consumers for higher pixel output from their cameras. In the last couple of years sensor sizes have pole-vaulted from the diminutive 1.5 megapixels to the more commonplace 8.0 and even 10.0 megapixel models that now fill the shelves of many photographic suppliers. The power to create truly photographic quality output up to A3 size is well within our grasp.

But high resolution is only half the 'image quality' story. The number of colors in an image is also a factor that contributes to the overall quality of the photograph.

Discrete colors (or levels)

Photographs in either print or negative (or slide) form contain a range of subtle tones and colors that blend smoothly into each other. These are referred to as 'continuous tone images'. For instance, in a traditional black and white print it is difficult to see where one shade of gray starts and another one finishes. The effect is a smooth transition from the deepest shadows through to the most delicate highlights.

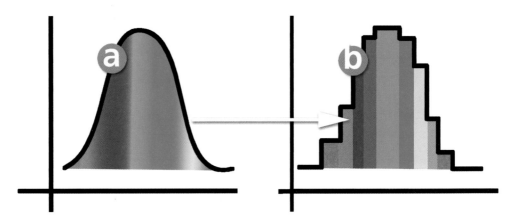

Analog to digital >> *In the capture process, via digital camera or scanner, a continuous tone original or scene is converted into discrete colors that can be represented by a series of numbers. (a) Analog original containing continuous tones. (b) Digital version containing discrete colors.*

In contrast, a digital image is made up of discrete tones and colors. When a scene or a print is captured by a device such as a camera or scanner the continuous original is converted into a digital file. The file describes the image as a series of numbers representing these discrete colors and tones. When we scan a negative or slide, or photograph a scene, we make this conversion by sampling the picture at regular intervals. At each sample point, a specific color is chosen to represent the hue found in the original. In this way, a grid of colors is put together to form a digital version of the continuous tone original.

24-bit color (8 bits per channel)

256 levels of red

256 levels of green

256 levels of blue

= a combined total of 16.7 million colors

48-bit color (16 bits per channel)

65,536 levels of red

65,536 levels of green

65,536 levels of blue

= a combined total of 281,474,976 million colors

8-bit versus 16-bit >> *Digital photographs captured in 16-bit per channel mode contain a greater number of colors than those captured with 8 bits.*

Comparing bits

Each digital file you create (capture or scan) is capable of representing a specific number of colors. This capability, usually referred to as the 'mode' or 'color depth' of the picture, is expressed in terms of the number of 'bits'. Most images these days are created in 24-bit mode. This means that each of the three color channels (red, green and blue) is capable of displaying 256 levels of color (or 8 bits) each. When the three channels are combined, a 24-bit image (8 + 8 + 8) can contain a staggering 16.7 million discrete tones/hues.

This is a vast amount of colors and would be seemingly more than we could ever need, see, or print, but many modern cameras and scanners are now capable of capturing 16 bits per channel or 'high-bit' capture. This means that each of the three colors can have 65,536 different levels and the image itself a whopping 281,474,976 million colors (last time I counted!). But why would we need to capture so many colors?

12-bit capture

Many cameras capture 12 rather than 16 bits per channel. These files contain 4096 tones per channel, as opposed to the 65,536 possible with 16-bit capture. Generally these 12-bit files are captured as raw files and when converted with the Adobe Camera Raw feature, you can choose between producing a 16- or 8-bit converted file.

2.02 More colors equal better quality

Suitable for Elements – 7.0, 6.0, 5.0, 4.0, 3.0, 2.0, 1.0 | Difficulty level – Intermediate
Related techniques – 2.13

Most readers would already have a vague feeling that a high-bit file is 'better' than a low-bit alternative, but understanding why is critical for ensuring the best quality in your own work. The main advantage is that capturing images in high-bit mode provides a larger number of colors for your camera or scanner to construct your image with. This in turn leads to better color and tone in the digital version of the continuous tone original or scene.

'Fantastic!' you say, 'No more 8-bit capture for me, I'm a 16-bit fanatic from here on in'. But there is a catch (you knew there had to be).

Capture commandment >> *If you want the best quality pictures always make sure that your scanner or camera captures in 16-bit per channel or 48-bit mode.*

On most cameras this is referred to as the 'Tiff' or 'Raw' setting. See technique 2.10 for more details on Raw files.

Despite the power and sophistication of Photoshop Elements the program only contains a limited range of editing options when it comes to 16-bits per channel files. Along with Raw file conversion, 16-bit support commenced in version 3.0 of the program. Previously when opening a 16-bit picture the program displayed a dialog warning that it didn't support the high-bit mode and then asked if you wanted to change the picture to an 8-bit form.

In these recent versions of the program the Rectangular and Elliptical Marquee and Lasso, Eyedropper, Move and Zoom tools all function in 16-bit mode. In addition, you can rotate, resize, apply auto levels, auto contrast or auto color correct, or use more manual controls such as Levels, Shadow/Highlights and Brightness/Contrast features. The Sharpen, Noise, Blur and Adjustment filter groups also work here as well.

Does this mean that making enhancement changes in 16-bit mode is unworkable? No, you just need to use a different approach. Read on.

Global versus local enhancement

Because of the limitations when working with a 16-bits per channel file in Elements some digital photographers break their enhancement tasks into two different sections – global and local.

Global, or those changes that are applied at the beginning of the process to the whole picture. These include general brightness and contrast changes, some color correction and the application of a little sharpening.

Local changes are those that are more specific and are sometimes only applied to certain sections of the picture. They may include dodging and burning-in, removal of unwanted dust and scratches, the addition of some text and the application of special effects filters.

This separation of enhancement tasks fits neatly with the way that the 16-bit support works in Photoshop Elements. Global changes can be applied to the photograph whilst it is still in 16-bit mode; the file can then be converted to 8 bits per channel (Image > Mode > 8 Bits/channel) and the local alterations applied. This is the process that the professionals have been using for years and now Elements gives you the power to follow suit.

The advantages of 16-bit or high-bit capture

Here are the main advantages in a nutshell:

1. Capturing images in high-bit mode provides a larger number of colors for your camera or scanner to construct your image with. This in turn leads to better color and tone in the digital version of the continuous tone original or scene.

2. Global editing and enhancement changes made to a high-bit file will always yield a better quality result than when the same changes are applied to a low-bit image.

3. Major enhancement of the shadow and highlight areas in a high-bit image is less likely to produce posterized tones than if the same actions were applied to a low-bit version.

4. More gradual changes and subtle variations are possible when adjusting the tones of a high-bit photograph using tools like Levels than is possible with low-bit images.

Common high-bit misconceptions

1. Elements can't handle high-bit images. Not true. Previous versions of the program couldn't handle high-bit pictures, but since Elements 3.0 the program has contained a reduced feature set that can be used with 16-bits per channel images. And even with this limitation there are enough tools available to ensure quality enhancement of your images.

2. High-bit images are too big for me to handle and store. Yes, high-bit images are twice the file size of 8-bit images and this does slow down machines with limited resources, but if this is

16-bit Workflow

Set camera or scanner to 16 bits per channel or 48-bit mode	Set camera to Raw file format

Photograph scene

Download or import file to the Elements' Organizer workspace with Adobe Photo Downloader

	Open photo in the Adobe Camera Raw feature
Open photo in the Standard Editor workspace	Adjust settings to 16-bit PSD file
	Convert and pass photo from Camera Raw to the Full Edit workspace

16-bit mode – Global Changes

Perform basic cropping and orientation changes with the Crop tool
Alter contrast with the Levels or Shadows/Highlights features
Adjust brightness using the Levels or Shadows/Highlights features
Remove color casts by adjusting Levels settings in individual color channels
Apply basic sharpening using the Unsharp Mask filter
Save a 16-bit archive version of the file

Convert to 8 bits per channel

8-bit mode – Local Changes

Remove dust and scratches with Spot Healing Brush
Dodge and burn specific picture parts
Apply filter changes
Add text
Add image or adjustment layers
Save a finished 8-bit working version of the file

a concern put up with the inconvenience of a slow machine whilst you make tonal and color changes then convert to a speedier 8-bit file for local changes.

3. I can't use my favorite tools and features in high-bit mode so I don't use high-bit images at all. You are losing quality in your images needlessly. Perform your global edits in 16-bit mode and then convert to 8-bit mode for the application of your favorite low-bit techniques.

Ensure quality capture and enhancement with 16-bit and Raw files

1. Unless space is an issue capture all images in the highest color depth possible. This will help to ensure the best possible detail, tone and color in your pictures.

2. If you have a camera that can capture Raw files then ensure that this feature is activated as well, as it provides the best quality files to work with.

Digital shooting technique

With the basics out of the way let's now look at how to manipulate some of your camera's technology in order to create the best digital files possible.

Exposure

Good exposure is one of the cornerstones of great imaging. Whether it be traditional silver-based photography, or the new pixel-centered picture making, getting your exposure right will ensure that you capture the most information possible.

Photographs that result from the sensor receiving too much light are said to be 'overexposed'. They typically have little or no details in the highlight portions of the image and the midtone regions are far too bright. In contrast, pictures that have been captured with too little light are referred to as being 'underexposed'. In these images it is the shadow areas that lose details and in this scenario the midtones are too dark.

The perfect exposure will produce a picture that contains:

- A good spread of tones from light to dark,
- Details in the shadow areas, and
- Details in the highlight areas.

For most shooters, exposure is something that the camera does automatically. You frame the image in the viewfinder, or via the preview screen, push the button down halfway and the camera focuses and adjusts the exposure for the scene. Push the button down fully and the image is captured using the exposure settings selected by the camera.

Generally speaking, letting the camera do the work produces great results, but in some circumstances where the lighting is a little tricky, the 'auto' exposure route can result in images that are either 'under' or 'over' exposed. It's here that the photographer needs to 'step in' and make some adjustments to the exposure settings. Modern cameras have a range of features designed to override the camera's auto exposure settings.

Shadows   Midtones   Highlights

Over- and underexposure >> *The cornerstone of all good photography is accurate exposure. (a) Overexposed images are too light and lose details in the highlights and mid tone areas. (b) Well-exposed pictures have a good distribution of tones over a range from dark to light. (c) Underexposed images have little or no shadow detail as these areas are converted to pure black.*

Exposure control

Two devices – the **shutter** and the **aperture** – control the amount of light that hits your camera's sensor.

The shutter is either an electrical or mechanical device that controls the length of time that the light falls upon the sensor. The longer the shutter is 'open' the more exposure the sensor will receive and, conversely, the shorter the shutter speed the less exposure is received. Shutter speeds have traditionally been measured in fractions of a second and are represented by a number sequence of halves and doubles. With some cameras, one step either way in the sequence is referred to as a change of a 'full stop', other modes step in 1/2 or 1/3 stops, and so multiple steps will be needed to make a full stop change in exposure.

The aperture works in a similar way to the iris in your eyes. The amount of light hitting the sensor, or entering your eye, is controlled by the size of the aperture, or iris, hole. Using a large hole will transmit more light than when a small aperture is in place. Again a series of numbers represent a doubling or halving of the amount of light entering through a given aperture.

This sequence is called F-stops and causes some confusion with new camera users as the scale equates the biggest aperture hole with the smallest F-stop number.

By varying the combination of aperture and shutter speed the camera, or photographer, can adjust the amount of light entering the camera to suit the sensitivity of the sensor. In bright conditions it is normal to use a fast shutter speed coupled with a large aperture number (small hole). Conversely, in low light situations a slow shutter speed and small aperture number (large hole) would be selected.

Mechanics of exposure >> *Aperture and shutter in combination control the amount of light that hits the sensor.*
(a) The aperture opens to allow more light into the camera and closes to reduce exposure.
(b) The length of time the shutter is opened is displayed in fractions of a second.
In addition to these mechanisms controlling exposure they also change the way that the photo looks. The aperture also controls the depth of field or zone of focus in the photo and the shutter manipulates how motion or movement is recorded.

2.03 Exposure compensation

Suitable for Elements – 7.0, 6.0, 5.0, 4.0, 3.0, 2.0, 1.0 | Difficulty level – Intermediate
Related techniques – 2.02

One of the real advantages of photographing digitally is the ability to review your efforts immediately after shooting via the built-in screen on the back of the camera. With this tool it is easy to determine the times when the auto exposure system is producing images that are not quite the perfect exposure. When this occurs you can increase or decrease the amount of light reaching the sensor by using the Exposure Compensation feature.

This control effectively changes the shutter speed or aperture selected in steps of a third of an F-stop (sometimes also called EV – exposure value). Most cameras allow changes of up to plus, or minus, 3 stops. In tricky lighting scenarios I generally shoot a test image, review the results, adjust my exposure compensation settings and shoot again. I continue this process of shooting and reviewing until I am satisfied with the exposure.

A more precise way to determine over- or underexposure is to consult the histogram display of your camera. The histogram can be accessed from your camera's playback menu and it visually graphs the spread of the pixels in the image. This feature takes the guesswork out of determining whether your image has exposure problems.

A bunching of pixels to the left-hand end of the graph usually indicates underexposure and the need for more light, whereas a grouping to the right signals overexposure and requires a reduction in either the aperture or shutter speed setting.

Exposure compensation >> *Many digital cameras contain a special feature that can be used to modify your exposure settings without altering the aperture or shutter speed values directly. This Exposure Compensation control allows you to increase or decrease the overall exposure of the picture.*

Frame-by-frame control

Apart from the absence of film, the typical digital camera has many familiar features. Experienced shooters on the whole have no difficulty understanding technology such as the shutter, aperture, or ISO sensitivity as these options have their traditional counterparts, but most new digital cameras contain several often overlooked functions that are designed to help you produce the 'ultimate images – shot by shot'.

Some of these features include:

• Contrast control,

• Saturation adjustment, and

• In-built Sharpness control.

These controls are now found on all but the most basic entry-level models and provide a level of flexibility that was never possible in the days when 'film was king'.

2.04 Contrast

Suitable for Elements – 7.0, 6.0, 5.0, 4.0, 3.0, 2.0, 1.0 | Difficulty level – Basic

The contrast control is one of the most useful features for the digital camera owner. When you are faced with shooting a beach, or snow scene, on a sunny day the range of brightness between the lightest and darkest areas can be extremely wide. Set to normal your camera's sensor will probably lose detail in both the highlight and shadow areas of the scene. Delicate tones will either be converted to white or black. Changing the setting to 'less contrast' will increase your camera's ability to capture the extremes of the scene and preserve otherwise lost light and dark details.

In the opposite scenario, sometimes your subject will not contain enough difference between shadows and highlights. This situation results in a low contrast or 'flat' image. Typically, pictures made on an overcast winter's day will fall into this category. Altering the camera's setting to 'more contrast' will spread the tonal values of the scene over the whole range of the sensor so that the resultant picture will contain acceptable contrast.

In-camera contrast adjustment >> *Altering the way that your camera records the contrast or the extremes of brightness in a scene can help to ensure that you capture important highlight and shadow details.*
(a) Less contrast setting.
(b) Normal contrast setting.
(c) More contrast setting.

'How do I know if my scene has either too much or too little contrast?' The beauty of shooting digitally is that we can preview our image immediately. In particular check the shadow and highlight areas using the camera's histogram feature. If the display contains pixels bunched at either end of the graph then the picture is too contrasty and will warrant a contrast change and a re-shoot. Pixels concentrated in a group in the center of the graph indicate an image that is too flat and needs to be re-shot using a higher contrast setting.

Pro's Tip: Contrast correction that is applied via your favorite image editing software package is possible and often used, but it is always preferable to capture the image with the best contrast at the time of shooting. This will guarantee you are making images of the best quality.

2.05 Color saturation

Suitable for Elements – 7.0, 6.0, 5.0, 4.0, 3.0, 2.0, 1.0
Difficulty level – Basic

The saturation, or vividness, of color within your images can either make or break them. Sometimes color is the cornerstone of a picture, providing both the focal point and the design for the whole photograph. In these circumstances, desaturated or pastel hues will only serve to weaken the strength of the picture. In contrast, strong color elements can distract from important subject matter, causing the viewer to concentrate on the color rather than the subject of the picture.

Digital shooters can take more control of the color content of their images by selecting just how dominant or vivid the hues will be in their pictures. For shots that rely on their color the vividness can be increased; for those that work more effectively with subdued hues, the color strength can be reduced by way of the camera's saturation control.

Again, the effectiveness or suitability of each setting should be previewed and if necessary, several images with different color settings can be captured and the final choice made later. Though not as critical for retention of details as the contrast settings, it is important to capture as much color information as possible when shooting. This does not mean that you shoot all

Histograms >> *Mid to high range cameras usually contain a Histogram function which displays the spread of the tones in the image. This feature is very useful for determining if a picture is exposed correctly or contains too much or too little contrast. (a) Shadow tones. (b) Middle tones. (c) Highlight tones. (d) High contrast picture. (e) Low contrast picture.*

subjects with maximum saturation; it is just a reminder that if color is important, consider changing the saturation settings to suit your needs and your picture.

 Pro's Tip: Always shoot in Color mode even if the photograph is to be used as a black and white. The picture can easily be converted to black and white in your image editing program at any time and you have the advantage of a color version if ever you need it.

In-camera saturation adjustment >> *Using the saturation control in your camera you can alter the strength of the colors in your pictures. (a) Black and white. (b) Minimum saturation setting. (c) Normal saturation setting. (d) Maximum saturation setting.*

2.06 Image sharpness
Suitable for Elements – 7.0, 6.0, 5.0, 4.0, 3.0, 2.0, 1.0 | Difficulty level – Basic

The digital equivalent of film is a grid of sensors situated behind the lens in your camera. Each of these sensors records the light and color of the image that is focused upon it. In doing so a digital version of the scene is constructed. Despite the high resolution of modern sensors and specially developed lenses, the final image contains a degree of softness that is the direct result of this capturing process.

To help create crisper images the camera manufacturers include in-camera sharpening as one of their auto enhancement tools. Designed to improve the appearance of sharpness across the picture these features enhance the edge of objects by increasing the difference in tones between adjacent pixels. Sound confusing? Just remember that the act of sharpening changes the pixels in your image and just like the other image enhancement tools, too much sharpening can destroy your picture.

How do I know what settings to use? There are two schools of thought for deciding when and where to apply sharpening to your images. Some shooters apply a little sharpening in-camera, using either the minimum or auto setting. Others prefer to leave their images untouched and will use the sharpening tools built into their favorite image editing program to enhance their pictures. I lean towards the second option, as it offers me the greatest control over the sharpening effects and where they occur in my photographs.

In-camera sharpness adjustment >> *Some photographers regularly apply in-camera sharpening to their pictures, but I prefer to leave this task until the images are loaded into Elements where I have more control. (a) No sharpening applied. (b) Normal sharpening setting. (c) Maximum sharpening setting.*

Pro's Tip: When sharpening in your editing program always view the image to be sharpened at 100% so that you can see the effects of the filter at the magnification that the picture will be used at.

2.07 White balance control
Suitable for Elements – 7.0, 6.0, 5.0, 4.0, 3.0, 2.0, 1.0 | Difficulty level – Basic

Our eyes are extremely complex and sophisticated imaging devices. Without us even being aware they adjust automatically to changes in light color and level. For instance, when we view a piece of white paper outside on a cloudy day, indoors under a household bulb or at work with fluorescent lights, the paper appears white. Without realizing it our eyes have adapted to each different light source.

Unfortunately digital sensors, including those in our cameras, are not as clever. If I photographed the piece of paper under the same lighting conditions, the pictures would all display a different color cast. Under fluorescent lights the paper would appear green, lit by the household bulb (incandescent) it would look yellow and when photographed outside it would be a little blue. This situation occurs because camera sensors are designed to record images without casts in daylight only. As the color balance of the light for our three examples is different to daylight, that is, some parts of the spectrum are stronger and more dominant than others, the pictures record with a cast. The color of the light source illuminating the subject in your picture determines the cast that will result.

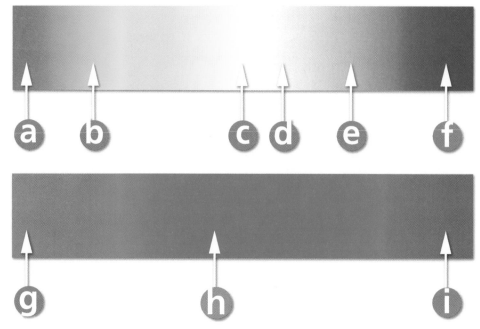

When is white light not white? >> *The color of white light varies from source to source. Our eyes adjust to these changes but the camera will record the differences as a color cast in your pictures. The White Balance feature is designed to rid your images of these casts. (a) Candle. (b) Household bulb. (c) Daylight. (d) Flash. (e) Cloud. (f) Skylight (no sun). (g) White fluorescent. (h) 'Daylight White' fluorescent. (i) 'Daylight' fluorescent.*

Traditional shooters have been aware of this problem for years and because of the limitations of film, most photographers carried a range of color conversion filters to help change the light source to suit the film. Digital camera producers, on the other hand, are addressing the problem by including White Balance functions in their designs. These features adjust the captured image to suit the lighting conditions it was photographed under. The most basic models usually provide automatic white balancing, but it is when you start using some of the more sophisticated models that the choices for white balance correction can become a little confusing.

Most modern digital cameras provide a vast array of options that should have you shooting 'cast-free' in any lighting conditions. The selections include:
- Auto,
- Fine or Daylight,
- Incandescent,
- Fluorescent,
- Cloudy,
- Speed light or Flash, and
- White Balance Preset.

Color casts from different light sources >> *Camera sensors are balanced for daylight. Shooting pictures under non-daylight light sources will result in the color casts we see above. (a) Daylight. (b) Fluorescent. (c) Household bulb or incandescent. (d) Flash. (e) Cloudy day.*

Auto white balance >> *The modern digital camera has a highly developed auto white balance system. It performs well under most lighting scenarios and should be your first choice when shooting under difficult conditions.*

Auto white balance

The Auto function assesses the color of the light in the general environment and attempts to neutralize the mid tones of the image. As with most 'auto' camera features, this setting works well for the majority of 'normal' scenarios. The feature does a great job with scenes that contain a range of colors and tones, but you may strike some difficulty with subjects that are predominantly one color, or are lit from behind. Also keep in mind that some subjects, such as cream lace, are meant to have a slight color shift and the use of the Auto feature in this case would remove the subtle hue of the original.

Apart from these exceptions most cameras' Auto features produce great results that require little or no post-shooting color correction work. So it's my suggestion that if in doubt try the Auto setting first. Check the results on the preview screen of the camera and if there is a color cast still present then move on to some more specific white balance options.

Light source white balance settings

The Daylight (Fine), Incandescent, Fluorescent, Cloudy and Flash (Speed light) options are designed for each of these light types. The manufacturers have examined the color from a variety of each of these sources, averaged the results and produced a white balance setting to suit. If you know the type of lighting that your subject is being lit by, then selecting a specific white balance setting is a good move.

Again, for the majority of circumstances these options provide great results, but for those times when the source you are using differs from the 'norm', companies like Nikon have included a fine-tuning adjustment. With the light source set, the command dial is turned to adjust the color settings.

Fine-tuning white balance >> *With some models white balance settings can be fine-tuned to suit specific lighting scenarios. With this camera plus values add blue to the picture and negative values add red.*

For Daylight, Incandescent, Cloudy and Flash options selecting positive values will increase the amount of blue in the image. Alternatively, negative numbers will increase the red content.

If you have selected Fluorescent as your light source then the Fine-tuning feature will allow you to select one of three different white balance settings. FL1 is suitable for tubes marked 'White', FL2 should be used with 'Daylight White' fluorescents and FL3 is for those labelled 'Daylight'.

2.08 Applying fine-tuning automatically

Suitable for Elements – 7.0, 6.0, 5.0, 4.0, 3.0, 2.0, 1.0 | Difficulty level – Intermediate
Related techniques – 2.07

If you are like me and find manually fine-tuning hampers the flow of your photography – shoot, stop, switch to menu, fine-tune white balance, shoot again, stop, switch to menu ... you get the idea – then check to see if you camera has an Auto White Balance Bracketing option. This feature automatically shoots a series of three images starting with the standard white balance settings and then adding a little blue and finally a little red.

I find white balance bracketing particularly useful when shooting difficult subjects like the hand-blown colored glass in the example. As three separate images are saved I can make decisions about the most appropriate color by previewing them on my workstation's large color calibrated monitor later rather than the small preview screen on the back of my camera in the field.

Auto fine-tuning >> *The White Balance Bracketing option automatically captures several pictures with slightly different color settings. (a) Standard setting. (b) + Red. (c) + Blue.*

Preset white balance options >> *You can obtain a precise white balance setting under mixed lighting conditions by using the Preset or Customize option in your camera. When the feature is activated the camera will analyze a white (or mid gray) card in the scene, neutralize any casts that are present and set the white balance according to the analysis. The images now photographed with this preset white balance setting will be cast-free.*

2.09 Customizing your white balance

*Suitable for Elements – 7.0, 6.0, 5.0, 4.0, 3.0, 2.0, 1.0 | Difficulty level – Intermediate
Related techniques – 2.07, 2.08*

In a perfect world the scene you want to shoot will always be lit by a single source. In reality most scenarios are illuminated by a variety of different colored lights. For instance, what seems like a simple portrait taken in your lounge could have the subject partially lit by the incandescent lampstand in the corner, the fluorescent tube on the dining room ceiling and the daylight coming through the windows. Because of the mixed light sources a specific white balance setting is not appropriate. Instead, you should use the customize, or preset, white balance option on your camera.

Based on video technology, this feature works by measuring the light's combined color as it falls onto a piece of white paper. The camera then compares this reading with a reference white swatch in its memory and designs a white balance setting specifically for your shooting scenario. With the process complete you are now set to shoot your portrait secure in the knowledge that you will produce cast-free images. Always remember though, because this is a customized process, if you decide to turn a light off, or move your subject to another position in the room, then you will need to remeasure and reset your white balance. This way of working is by far the most accurate way to correct the color casts resulting from mixed lighting sources in your pictures.

It takes into account changes in color that result from:

• Light reflecting off brightly painted walls,

• Bulbs getting older,

• Mixed light sources,

• Light streaming through colored glass, and

• Shooting through colored filters.

2.10 Shooting Raw for ultimate control

Suitable for Elements – 7.0, 6.0, 5.0, 4.0, 3.0, 2.0, 1.0 | Difficulty level – Intermediate | Related techniques – 2.02

More and more medium to high end cameras are being released with the added feature of being able to shoot and save your pictures in Raw format. For most users this option on the camera's file menu has no real significance, but there are a growing number of photographers who having tried the new file type vow never to go back to using any other format. They boast of the extra quality and control that is achievable when using Raw for their image making and probably most impressive of all often refer to images in this format as being the closest thing to a digital 'negative' that we have yet seen. But why all this talk about Raw? What does the term actually mean and how can it help me take better pictures?

Raw files >> *Unlike TIFF and JPEG formats, Raw files contain the unprocessed image and shooting data. In many cameras the visual information is laid in the Bayer pattern of the original sensor.*

Back to the beginning

To start to understand the importance of Raw formats we need to go back to the beginning of the capture process. All single shot digital cameras (except those using the Foveon chip) contain a sensor that is made up of a grid of light-sensitive sites. Each site responds to the amount of light that hits its surface. By recording and analyzing each of these responses a tone is attributed to each sensor site in the grid. In this way a digital picture can be created from the range of scene brightnesses that are focused through the lens onto the sensor's surface. Fantastic though this is, this process only results in a monochrome (black, white and gray) picture as the CCD or CMOS sensors by themselves cannot record the color of the light, only the amount.

To produce a digital color photograph a small filter is added to each of the sensors. In most cameras these filters are a mixture of the three primary colors red, green and blue, and are laid out in a special design called a Bayer pattern. It contains 25% red filters, 25% blue and 50% green with the high percentage of green present in order to simulate the human eye's sensitivity to this part of the visible spectrum. In their raw, or unprocessed, format the output from these sensors is made up of a grid of red, green and blue patches (pixels) of varying tones. And yes this does mean that in any individual picture only 25% of the sensor sites are actually capturing information about the red or blue objects in the scene.

Interpolated color

I hear you saying 'But the images that I download from my camera are not split into discrete RGB colors'. This is true. What emerges from the camera is a full color picture which contains 100% red, 100% blue and 100% green pixels. This occurs because as an integral part of the capture process the raw RGB data that comes from the sensor is interpolated to create a full color image. Using special algorithms, the extra detail for a non-red site, for instance, is created using the information from the surrounding red, green and blue sites. This process is called interpolation and though it seems like a lot of 'smoke and mirrors' it works extremely well on most cameras.

When you opt to save your images in JPEG or TIFF formats this capture and interpolation process happens internally in the camera each time you push the shutter button. In addition your camera will also reduce the number of colors and tones from the 16-bit color depth that was captured to the 8 bits that are stored in the file. Selecting a Raw format stops the camera from processing the color-separated (primary) data from the sensor and reducing the image's bit depth, and saves the picture in this unprocessed format. This means that the full description of what the camera 'saw' is saved in the image file and is available to you for use in the production of quality images.

Raw images >> *The image stored in a Raw file is based upon the base data that comes directly from the sensor and needs to be interpolated to create the full color digital file we normally associate with camera output.*

DIY Raw processing

Sounds great, doesn't it? All the quality of an information-rich image file to play with, but what is the catch? Well, Raw files have to be processed before they can be used in a standard image editing application. To access the full power of these digital negatives you will need to employ a special dedicated Raw editor. Photoshop Elements 3.0 was the first version of the program to have such an editor built into the program. Called Adobe Camera Raw this feature is designed specifically to allow you to take the unprocessed Raw data directly from your camera's sensor and convert it into a usable image file format. Chapter 3 is dedicated to the processing of raw files using Photoshop Elements.

Adobe Camera Raw also provides access to several image characteristics that would otherwise be locked into the file format. Variables such as color depth, White Balance mode, image sharpness and tonal compensation (contrast and brightness) can all be accessed, edited and enhanced as a part of the conversion process. Performing this type of editing on the Raw data provides a better and higher quality result than attempting these changes after the file has been processed and saved in a non-Raw format such as TIFF or JPEG.

So what is in a Raw file?

To help consolidate these ideas in your mind try thinking of a Raw file as having three distinct parts:

Camera Data, usually called the EXIF or metadata, includes things such as camera model, shutter speed and aperture details, most of which cannot be changed.

Image Data which, though recorded by the camera, can be changed in the Elements Raw editor and the settings chosen here directly affect how the picture will be processed. Changeable options include color depth, white balance, saturation, distribution of image tones and application of sharpness.

The **Image** itself. This is the data drawn directly from the sensor in your camera in a non-interpolated form. For most Raw-enabled cameras, this data is supplied with a 12-, 14- or 16-bits per channel color depth providing substantially more colors and tones to play with when editing and enhancing than found in a standard 8-bits per channel camera file.

Camera Data
(f-stop, shutter speed, ISO, camera exposure mode, focusing distance etc)

Image Data
(white balance, sharpening, colour mode, tonal compensation)

Image
(full 16 or 12bit colour and tone)

Raw files make-up >> *The Raw file is composed of three separate sections: Camera Data, Image Data and the Image itself. By keeping these components separate it is possible to edit variables like white balance and color mode which are usually a fixed part of the file format.*

Raw File

SCANNER AND CAMERA TECHNIQUES

Raw processing in action

When you open a Raw file in Elements you are presented with the Adobe Camera Raw dialog containing a full color interpolated preview of the sensor data. Using a variety of menu options, dialogs and image tools you will be able to interactively adjust image data factors such as tonal

Select all images

Zoom, Move, White Balance, Crop, Straighten, Red Eye Removal, ACR Preferences, Rotate, and Toggle for Delete tools

Preview

Full screen

Basic, Detail, Camera Calibration tabs

Highlight clipping

Histogram

Capture details

Settings selections

Color temperature controls

Exposure control

Recovery control

Blacks control

Brightness control

Contrast control

Clarity control

Vibrance control

Saturation control

Help

Save image

Zoom level controls

Color depth

Preview of conversion

Apply changes and close

Cancel changes

Apply changes and open in Elements

Queued raw files

Raw files >> When you open a raw file in Elements the Camera Raw editor is activated, providing you with a range of sophisticated controls for the enhancement and conversion of your raw files.
After making your changes, click Open – the plug-in closes and the converted file is placed into the Elements workspace.
(a) Adjust tab options.
(b) Detail tab options.
(c) Camera Calibration options.

Sharpness controls

Grayscale noise control

Color Noise control

The calibration settings used for the color and tonal control of the image.

Camera-based
RAW processing

TIFF
JPEG

RAW file

Computer-based
RAW processing

TIFF
JPEG
PSD

Capture workflow >>
Selecting JPEG or TIFF as your picture's file format means that the image processing is handled by the camera. In contrast choosing the Raw format removes this task from the camera and places it firmly with you and your computer. Working this way means that you have a say in decisions about white balance, contrast, brightness, sharpness and color mode.

distribution and color saturation. Many of these changes can be made with familiar slider controlled editing tools normally found in features like Levels and the Shadows/Highlights control. The results of your editing can be reviewed immediately via the live preview image and associated histogram graph.

After these general image editing steps have taken place you can apply some enhancement changes such as filtering for sharpness, removing color noise and applying some smoothing. The final phase of the process involves selecting the color depth and image orientation. Clicking the Open button sets the program into action applying your changes to the Raw file, whilst at the same time interpolating the Bayer data to create a full color image and then opening the processed file into the Elements Full Edit workspace.

The Raw advantage

The real advantages of editing and enhancing at the Raw stage are that these changes are made to the file at the same time as the primary image data is being converted (interpolated) to the full color picture. Editing after the file is processed (saved by the camera in 8-bits per channel versions of the JPEG and TIFF format) means that you will be applying the changes to a picture with fewer tones and colors. A second bonus for the dedicated Raw shooter is that actions like switching from the white balance option selected when shooting, to another choice when processing are performed without any image loss. This is not the case once the file has been processed with the incorrect white balance setting, as anyone who has inadvertently left the tungsten setting switched on whilst shooting in daylight can tell you.

For a more in-depth look at raw processing steps in Photoshop Elements go to Chapter 3.

2.11 Shooting workflows

Having an understanding of all these camera techniques is one thing but putting them together when you are out shooting is another. To capture the most detail and in the best quality that your camera offers is a multi-step process. The following table summarizes the steps involved in three different approaches to capturing images using the techniques discussed above. The highest quality is obtained by shooting with a Raw file which is then enhanced using a dedicated editor. If your camera doesn't contain Raw capabilities then the next best option is to shoot TIFF and make your adjustments in Elements. If neither option is available then using 'best quality' JPEG will give good results.

Recommended Digital Camera Workflow

Before Shooting	Select highest resolution		
	Pick best color depth (16 bits per channel or 48-bit overall)		
	Select file format – **JPEG**	Select file format – **TIFF**	Select file format – **Raw**
	Choose finest quality (least compression)	No compression	No compression
	Set Color mode (sRGB for web work, AdobeRGB for print work)		
	Set Saturation		
	Set White balance (Either for the dominant light source or using the Customize option)		
During Shooting	Arrange composition		
	Adjust focus (Check Depth of Field)		
	Set exposure (Check Histogram)		
After Shooting	Adjust Highlight and Shadow (Elements)		Adjust Highlight and Shadow (Adobe Camera Raw plug-in)
	Alter contrast (Elements)		Alter contrast (Adobe Camera Raw plug-in)
	Remove color casts (Elements)		Remove color casts (Adobe Camera Raw plug-in)
	Apply some sharpening (Elements)		Apply some sharpening (Adobe Camera Raw plug-in)
	Save processed file (Elements)		Save processed file (Elements)
Image Quality	Good	Better	Best

Scanners >> *The most popular scanners can be divided into two distinct groups. (a) Dedicated film scanners that are designed to record digital files from transparent originals such as negatives and slides. (b) Reflective scanners which are used to convert prints to digital files. Some of the models in this group have transparency attachments which provide the extra ability to scan slides and negatives as well.*

Film and print scanners

It was not too long ago that an activity like scanning was the sole responsibility of the repro house. The photographer's job was finished the moment that the images were placed on the art director's desk. But as we all know, the digital revolution has changed things forever, and scanning is one place where things will never be the same.

Desktop scanners that are capable of high-resolution color output are now so cheap that some companies will throw them in as 'freebies' when you purchase a complete computer system. The proliferation of these devices has led to a large proportion of the photographic community now having the means to change their prints, negatives or slides into digital files. But as all photographers know, having the equipment is only the first step to making good images.

For the most part, scanners can be divided into three distinct varieties – film, print and the more recent hybrid or combination scanner.

Dedicated film – This device is set up specifically for negative or slide capture and is usually restricted to a single format (135 mm x 120 mm/5 x 4 inch). The hardware is not capable of reflective scanning. If your business involves the repeated capture of images of the one film type, a dedicated scanner is a good investment.

Dedicated print – The scanners in this category are the most affordable and easily obtainable of the three types. If you can't afford a digital camera of the quality that you desire and you have loads of prints in boxes lying around the house then spending a couple of hundred dollars here will have you enhancing high quality digital versions of your pictures in no time.

Hybrid – These scanners are capable of both reflective and transmission scanning. This means that the one device can capture both film and print images. Starting life as flatbeds with added transparency adapters, these scanners have developed into multi-function devices that are capable of producing quality files from both types of originals.

2.12 Scanning resolution – 'Know where you are going before you start the journey'

Suitable for Elements – 7.0, 6.0, 5.0, 4.0, 3.0, 2.0, 1.0 | Difficulty level – Intermediate
Related techniques – 2.01

Just as is the case with camera-based capture, the quality of the digital picture that results from our scanning activities is based primarily on resolution and color depth. It is critical that these two factors are carefully considered before any scanning capture takes place.

Scanning resolution, as opposed to image or printing resolution, is determined by the number of times per inch that the scanner will sample your image. The number of pixels generated by a digital camera has an upper limit that is fixed by the number of sensors in the camera. This is not the case for scanner capture. By altering the number of samples taken for each inch of the original print or negative you can change the total number of pixels created in the digital file. This figure will affect both the 'enlargement' potential of the final scan and its file size. The general rule is the higher the resolution the bigger the file and the bigger the printed size possible (before seeing pixel blocks or digital grain).

Scanning resolution (samples per inch)	Image size to be scanned	Output size (pixels)	Output size (inches for print @ 200 dpi)	File size (Mb)
4000	35 mm film frame (24 mm x 36 mm)	4000 x 6000	20 x 30	72.00
2900	35 mm	2900 x 4350	14.5 x 21.75	37.80
1200	35 mm	1200 x 1800	6 x 9	6.40
600	35 mm	600 x 900	3 x 4.5	1.62
400	5 x 4 inch print	2000 x 1600	10 x 8	9.60
1000	5 x 4 inch print	5000 x 4000	25 x 20	60.00
400	10 x 8 inch print	4000 x 3200	20 x 16	38.40

Scanning resolution >> *Adjusting the resolution that you scan at will directly affect the pixel dimensions of your final file. High scanning resolution will create more pixels in the files which translates into bigger prints.*

Does this mean that we always scan at the highest resolution possible? The intelligent answer is NO! The best approach is to balance your scanning settings with your printing needs. If you are working on a design for a postage stamp you will need less pixels to play with than if you want your masterpiece in poster format. For this reason it is important to consciously set your scanning resolution keeping in mind your required output size. See section 2.01 for more details about resolution.

Some scanning software will give you an indication of resolution, file size and print size as part of the dialog panel but for those of you without this facility use the table on page 42 as a rough guide.

2.13 Color depth

Suitable for Elements – 7.0, 6.0, 5.0, 4.0, 3.0, 2.0, 1.0 | Difficulty level – Basic | Related techniques – 2.02

As we have seen already color depth refers to the number of possible colors that make up the digital file upon the completion of scanning. If you have the choice always select 16-bit scanning mode (sometimes called 48-bit – 16 bits for red + 16 bits for green + 16 bits for blue) instead of 8-bit as this provides you with the opportunity to capture as much information from your photographic original as possible. Remember this is true even if you intend to convert these files to 8-bit immediately upon opening. The more accurately the image is scanned in the first place the better quality the down sampled file will be after the conversion has been made.

Scan in 16-bit mode >> *To capture the best detail, colour and tone always scan in 16-bit mode.*

SCANNER AND
CAMERA TECHNIQUES

2.14 Multi-sample

Suitable for Elements – 7.0, 6.0, 5.0, 4.0, 3.0, 2.0, 1.0
Difficulty level – Intermediate

Scanners in the mid to high end range often contain another feature that is designed to increase the quality of digital capture, especially in the darkest parts of the negative or print. Called Multi-Sample Scanning, it is a process where the image is sampled or scanned several times and the results averaged. This approach is particularly helpful when the scanner is trying to penetrate the shadow areas of a print or the highlight parts of a negative. It is in these parts of the picture that a single pass scan will most likely provide a 'noisy' result.

You can reduce this noise by making several scans of the same area and then averaging the result. The theory is that the level of noise reduction is directly proportional to the number of samples to be averaged. Therefore machines that offer a multi-sample rate of '16x' will produce better results than those that only contain a '4x' version. The down side to the technology is that all this extra scanning and averaging does take time. For instance the Minolta

Multi-sample scan >>
Some scanners offer the option of 'multi-scanning' your film original. Select this setting for the best overall capture of difficult negatives or slides, but be warned – using this feature dramatically increases your scanning time.

Dimage Dual III set to 8x Multi-Sample can take up to 14 times longer to make a high-resolution, high-bit scan of a 35 mm negative. For most well-exposed and processed negatives or prints there will be little extra quality to gain from this procedure, but for those troublesome images that seem to have areas of dark impenetrable detail using multi-sample will definitely produce a better overall result.

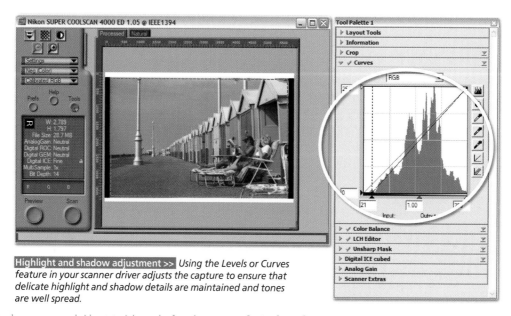

Highlight and shadow adjustment >> *Using the Levels or Curves feature in your scanner driver adjusts the capture to ensure that delicate highlight and shadow details are maintained and tones are well spread.*

AFTER

BEFORE

Contrast changes >> *Flat pictures can be corrected at scanning time by adjusting black and white using the Brightness or Contrast tools in the scanner driver.*

2.15 Highlight and shadow capture

Suitable for Elements – 7.0, 6.0, 5.0, 4.0, 3.0, 2.0, 1.0 | Difficulty level – Basic

With resolution and color depth set we can now scan the image – well almost! Just as exposure is critical to making a good photograph, careful exposure is extremely important for achieving a good scan.

All but the most basic scanners allow some adjustment in this respect. Preview images are supplied to help judge exposure and contrast, but be wary of making all your decisions based on a visual assessment of these often small and pixelated images. If you inadvertently make an image too contrasty then you will lose shadow and highlight detail as a result. Similarly, a scan that proves to be too light or dark will also have failed to capture important information from your print or film original.

It is much better to adjust the contrast, sometimes called gamma, and exposure settings of your scan based on more objective information. For this reason a lot of desktop scanner companies provide a method of assessing what is the darkest, and lightest, part of the image to be scanned. Often looking like the Info palette in Elements these features give you the opportunity to move

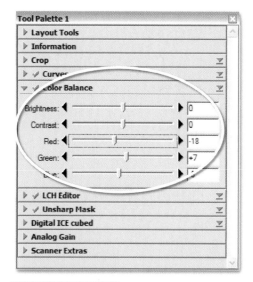

Color cast correction >> *Color casts can be removed from scanned originals using the slider controls found in the scanner driver.*

Removing casts with histograms >> *In the absence of dedicated cast removal sliders careful adjustment of the histogram for each channel can achieve the same results.*

around the preview image pegging the highlight and shadow areas. Other scanner drivers include their own version of the histogram, which you can use to diagnose and correct brightness and contrast problems. With these tools you can set the black and white points of the image to ensure that no details are lost in the scanning process.

For those readers whose scanning software doesn't contain this option, try to keep in mind that it is better to make a slightly flat scan than risk losing detail by adjusting the settings so that the results are too contrasty. The contrast can be altered later when you edit the picture in Elements.

2.16 Color cast correction

Suitable for Elements – 7.0, 6.0, 5.0, 4.0, 3.0, 2.0, 1.0 | Difficulty level – Intermediate

Despite our best abilities some photographs are captured with a dominant color cast that pervades the whole picture. Using the scanner driver's own color adjustment feature you can neutralize this tint at the time of capture. Frequently the scanner software provides a before and after thumbnail of your color adjustments so that you can preview your changes before committing the final settings. Now when the picture is scanned the color balance is adjusted and the color cast removed.

It is true that this process can be handled by Elements using the Color Cast or Color Variations features but, as we have already seen with the camera techniques above, the best quality images are generated when adjustments such as these are made at the capture stage.

2.17 Dust and scratches

Suitable for Elements – 7.0, 6.0, 5.0, 4.0, 3.0, 2.0, 1.0 | Difficulty level – Basic

One of the hidden enemies of quality scans is dust. Though the presence of dust won't reduce the ability of the scanner to record highlight and shadow detail accurately it does decrease the overall quality of the file because the affected area must be retouched later in Elements. No matter how proficent the retouching is, the 'rebuilt' section of the picture that is created to cover the dust mark will never be the same as the detail that existed in the original negative, slide or print. More important, especially for the photographer with hundreds of scans to complete, is the massive amount of time needed to retouch these dusty areas.

Some scanner models will include features designed to remove dust (and scratches) automatically from the picture during the scanning process. This technology when applied carefully can produce truly amazing results. One example is the Digital ICE technology produced by Applied Science Fiction (www.asf.com). Unlike post-capture processing where the dust mark is covered over using samples of other picture detail that surrounds the area, ICE isolates the marks during the scanning process and then proceeds to erase the defects from the picture. As the process is directly linked to the scanning hardware the Digital ICE technology cannot be applied to a dust affected image after it has been captured.

If you are considering buying a scanner then it is worth considering a make and model that incorporates the ASF Digital ICE feature. It's true that the defect detecting and erasing processes do add to the overall scanning time, but the retouching time saved more than makes up for it.

Auto dust removal >> *Features like ASF's Digital ICE can remove dust and scratch marks automatically at the time of scanning. (a) Before Digital ICE. (b) After Digital ICE.*

2.18 Noise Reduction technologies

Suitable for Elements – 7.0, 6.0, 5.0, 4.0, 3.0, 2.0, 1.0 | Difficulty level – Basic

As part of the process of scanning an image, visual errors are introduced into the file that were not part of the original. This is true to varying degrees for both entry level and high end scanners. The most noticeable of these errors is called noise and usually shows up in shadow or highlight areas of the picture as brightly colored random pixels or speckles. Image noise can be caused by a variety of factors including high speed film grain (high ISO), under- or overexposed negatives or slides, lighting conditions with brightness extremes, and image enlargement, as well as the CCD sensor itself. At worst, high levels of noise within a picture cause the image to appear unsharp and less detailed and have the potential to distract a viewer's attention away from the content of the image. To help correct or, more accurately minimize, the impact of noise in our digital photographs, scanner manufacturers like Kodak, Minolta, Nikon and Umax have banded together with software producer Applied Science Fiction (www.asf.com) to include ASF's Digital GEM product in their scanning software. GEM reduces image noise and grain during the scanning process and should be used when standard scanner settings produce noisy results.

Cameras and noise

Scanners are not the only capture devices that can introduce noise into a digital photograph. The sensors in cameras can suffer from the same problems as those found in scanners.

Generally, noise is at its worst in photographs taken with high ISO (equivalent) settings or when the shutter speed is longer than one second.

To help remove the noise in camera-captured pictures ASF also produces a plug-in version of their GEM software that can be activated via the Filter menu in Elements. This version of the software provides a little more control than that provided as part of the scanner driver as it allows separate adjustments for highlight and shadow noise as well as a slider control to alter the sharpness of the picture.

Alternatively, Elements versions 6 contains the Reduce Noise filter (Editor: Filter > Noise > Reduce Noise). As with the GEM plug-in the filter contains several sliders that help balance noise removal and overall sharpness of the processed picture.

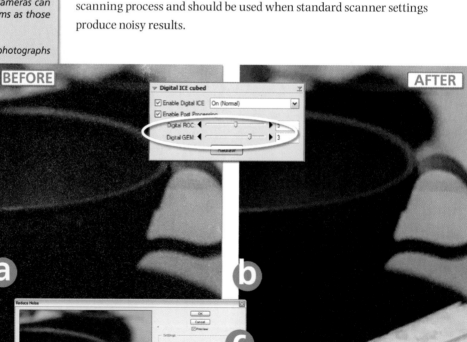

Removing noise >> *Using a technology such as ASF's Digital GEM feature whilst scanning will reduce the appearance of grain in your picture whilst maintaining the sharpness and clarity of the photograph.*
(a) Noise before Digital GEM.
(b) Noise after Digital GEM.
(c) Elements' new Reduce Noise filter.

Re-creation of color >> *ASF's Digital ROC feature re-creates the color lost in original pictures due to fading or incorrect color balance at the time of shooting. (a) Before and (b) after color regeneration.*

2.19 Color regeneration features

Suitable for Elements – 7.0, 6.0, 5.0, 4.0, 3.0, 2.0, 1.0
Difficulty level – Basic

The last feature in the Applied Science Fiction trinity of scanning products is Digital ROC. Starting life as a feature designed specifically for use in the restoration of faded negatives or prints, many scanner operators now regularly leave the ROC option turned on for their non-restoration jobs as well. It provides a fast and effective way to automatically adjust the scanned image to account for over- and underexposure, color casts and, of course, fading. The feature analyses the data from the blue, green and red layers, identifying areas of loss and carefully recreating density and detail. ROC can also be used to restore density to faded black and white prints or negatives if the original is scanned in RGB mode initially.

The product is available as a plug-in for Elements or as part of your scanner software. Most scanners that included ICE and GEM also contain the ROC feature as well. The plug-in offers more control over the color regeneration process by providing slider adjustments for the red–cyan, green–magenta and blue–yellow tints.

Digital ROC for cameras >> *The ROC and GEM components of the Digital ICE suite are also available as plug-ins for Photoshop Elements, providing grain reduction and color balancing options for camera-based images.*

SCANNER AND CAMERA TECHNIQUES

Recommended Scanning Workflow

Before Scanning	Select resolution to suit print needs (samples per inch)	
	Pick best color depth (16-bit per channel or 48-bit overall)	
	Set Color mode (sRGB for web work, AdobeRGB for print work)	
	Set media type (reflection – print or transmission – negative, slide)	
	Set original type (negative, slide, print)	
After Preview Scan	Flip or rotate (if necessary)	
	Crop out unwanted detail (if necessary)	
	Adjust focus (Manual or Auto)	
	Set exposure (Check Histogram)	
	Remove color cast (if necessary)	
	Turn off Dust and Scratch Removal feature	Turn on Dust and Scratch Removal feature (if necessary)
	Turn off Color Restoration feature	Turn on Color Restoration feature (if necessary)
	Set Single Sample mode (Single Pass)	Set Multi-Sample mode
After Scanning in Elements	Adjust Highlight and Shadow	
	Alter contrast	
	Remove color casts	
	Apply some sharpening	
	Save processed file	
Image Quality	Good	Best

2.20 Scanning workflow

Making sure that your negatives/ prints are clean before scanning can save a lot of time spent removing marks from the picture later. Use a soft cloth or a blower brush to remove surface particles before placing the film strip into the holder or the print on the platen. Don't forget to clean the glass of the scanner as well.

Check with your scanner manual to see which way the film should be placed in the holder. Inserting the film the wrong way round will mean that any writing in the picture will be back to front. Place the film in the holder ensuring the strip aligns with holder edges. Insert the film holder into the scanner. For flatbed scanners, place the photograph face down on the glass surface making sure that the edges are parallel with the scanner's edge.

Start the scanner software. You can do this from inside Elements. Simply select the scanner name from the Import (Editor: File > Import) menu. This will open the software that controls the scanner. Some scanners are supplied with a stand-alone version of this software that you can access from your program's menu without having to open an editing package first.

Fixing common shooting problems

Use the guide below to help diagnose and solve shooting problems.

1. Focus not on main subject
Problem: The main subject in the image is not sharply focused.
Cause: This is usually caused by not having the auto focus area on the main subject at the time of shooting.
Solution: If your subject is off to one side of the frame make sure that you lock focus (pressing the shutter button down halfway) on this point before re-composing and releasing the shutter button.

2. Picture too light
Problem: The photograph appears washed out or too light with no detail in the light areas of the print.
Cause: This is caused by too much light entering the camera causing the overexposure.
Solution: You can resolve this problem by adjusting the camera's exposure compensation control so that it automatically reduces the overall exposure by one stop. Shoot again and check exposure. If still overexposed, change the compensation to two stops. Continue this process until the exposure is acceptable.

3. Picture too dark
Problem: The photograph appears muddy or too dark with no detail in the shadow areas of the print.
Cause: Again this is a problem of exposure. This time not enough light has entered the camera.
Solution: Adjust the exposure compensation control to add more light or alternatively use a flash to help light your subject.

4. Subject too blurry
Problem: The main subject, or the whole picture, appears blurry and unsharp.
Cause: When images appear blurry it is usually the result of the subject, or the photographer, moving during a long exposure.
Solution: Use a tripod to reduce the risk of camera shake and try photographing the subject at a point in the activity when there is less movement.

5. Flash off glass
Problem: This problem results from the flash bouncing straight back from the glass into the lens of the camera.
Cause: The flash travels directly from your camera hitting the glass and bouncing directly back into the lens.
Solution: Using available light rather than the flash is one solution. Another is to move a little to one side so that the flash angles off the glass surface away from the camera.

Adjusting for backlighting >> *The camera's exposure system can be easily fooled when there is a source of bright light in the photo and the subject is in shadows. Here the portrait sitter is a silhouette because the camera is basing the exposure on the light coming from the window. To correct this situation:*
1) Move the subject so that they are no longer framed by the window, or
2) Use fill flash to illuminate the subject in the foreground, or
3) Fill the frame with the subject and then take your exposure reading.

6. Portrait too dark

Problem: Instead of a clear picture of your subject framed by the window you end up with a silhouette effect, where the subject is too dark but the window is well exposed. See above.

Cause: When your subject is sitting against an open window the meter is likely to adjust exposure settings for the light around your subject.

Solution 1: Move the subject so that the light from the window falls onto them from the front or side rather than behind.

Solution 2: Use the camera's flash system, set to 'fill flash mode', to add some more light to the subject.

Solution 3: Move closer to the subject until it fills the frame. Take an exposure reading here (by holding the shutter button down halfway) and then reposition yourself to make the exposure using the saved settings.

7. Portrait too light

Problem: The main subject is 'blown out' or too light (overexposed).

Cause: This problem is the reverse of what was happening in the example above. Here the meter is seeing the large dark areas within the frame and overcompensating for it, causing the main subject to be too bright.

Solution 1: Manually compensate for the overexposure by adjusting the camera's exposure compensation mechanism so that the sensor is receiving one, two or three stops less light.

Solution 2: Move close to the subject until it fills the frame. Take an exposure reading here and then reposition yourself to take the picture using the saved settings.

Fixing common scanning problems

Use the guide below to help diagnose and solve scanning problems.

1. Marks on the picture

Problem: The photograph contains marks on the surface after scanning.

Cause: This usually occurs because of dust or scratches on the glass plate on the top of the scanner or on the photograph or negative.

Solution: Clean the glass plate and photograph carefully before placing and scanning your picture. If you still have marks use a retouching tool to remove them (see the Eliminating blemishes technique in Chapter 8 for more details).

2. Color picture appears black and white

Problem: After scanning a color picture it appears black and white on screen.

Cause: The 'original' or 'media' option in the scanner software is set to black and white and not color.

Solution: Re-scan the picture making sure that the software is set to color original or color photograph.

3. Picture is too bright

Problem: The picture looks too bright overall. Light areas of the photograph appear to be completely white with no details.

Cause: The picture has been scanned with the wrong 'exposure' or 'brightness' setting.

Solution: Re-scan the picture, but this time move the brightness or exposure slider towards the dark end of the scale before scanning.

4. Picture is too dark

Problem: The picture looks too dark overall. There is no detail in the shadow parts of the photograph.

Cause: The picture has been scanned with the wrong 'exposure' or 'brightness' setting.

Solution: Re-scan the picture, but this time slide the Brightness or Exposure slider towards the light end of the scale before scanning.

5. Picture looks washed out

Problem: The picture has no vibrant colors and looks washed out.

Cause: The contrast control in the scanner software is set too low.

Solution: Re-scan the photograph altering the scanner's contrast setting to a higher value.

6. Writing is back to front

Problem: The message on a billboard in the picture is back to front.

Cause: The negative or slide was placed into the scanner back to front.

Solution: Turn the film or slide over and scan again.

7. The picture has too much contrast

Problem: The delicate light areas and shadow details of the picture can't be seen and have been converted to completely white and completely black.

Cause: The contrast control in the scanner software is set too high.

Solution: Re-scan the photograph altering the scanner's contrast setting to a lower value.

8. When I print my scanned picture it is fuzzy

Problem: The print of a scanned image is fuzzy, not very clear or is made up of rectangular blocks of color.

Cause: To get the best quality prints from your scanned pictures you must make sure that you match the scan quality (resolution) with the output requirements. A fuzzy or unclear print is usually the result of using a scan quality setting that is too low.

Solution: Re-scan the picture using a higher scan quality setting (resolution).

3

Processing Raw Files

Raw is the new buzz word in photographic circles the world over. Professionals and serious amateurs alike are switching their cameras from the standard JPEG and TIFF capture options to the Raw format. This is despite the fact that doing so will mean that they add another processing step to their digital photography workflow. It seems that the extra level of control possible when processing your own Raw files (rather than letting the camera do the work) is worth the effort. So how do Photoshop Elements users become part of the Raw Revolution? Well this chapter will outline both the workflow and conversion techniques that you can employ to make Raw capture and processing a regular part of your photographic routine.

The Photoshop Elements approach to Raw processing

As we saw in Chapter 2 Raw files contain both the image and metadata along with the actual picture information in a format which cannot be directly opened into Photoshop Elements. Instead the Raw photo is opened first into a conversion utility where global image characteristics such as white balance, brightness, contrast, saturation, noise reduction and sharpness are adjusted before the converted file is opened into the Full Edit workspace. Alternatively the converted file can be saved as an Adobe Digital Negative or DNG file. Once the converted file is opened in the Elements Editor workspace it is no longer a Raw file and can be edited and enhanced just like any other photo.

This approach to Raw processing is often called Convert then Edit as the original Raw file must be converted before any pixel-based or local editing can take place. In contrast other Raw processing solutions such as Adobe Lightroom provide a full Raw workflow which includes editing functions and output to print and web without ever converting the Raw file.

Raw Processing >> The **Convert then Edit** approach is the most popular workflow currently used by Raw shooting photographers. The Raw file is downloaded from the camera and the first task in the process is to convert the file to a type that is more readily supported by photo editing programs such as TIFF or PSD.

3.01 Enabling your Raw camera

Suitable for Elements – 7.0, 6.0, 5.0, 4.0, 3.0, 2.0, 1.0
Difficulty level – Basic

With most Raw-enabled cameras, switching from one capture format to another is a simple matter of entering the camera Set up menu and selecting the Raw entry from the Image Quality or File Format options. With some models you can also make this change via a Quality toggle or switch elsewhere on the camera.

Occasionally there is also a choice between saving compressed and non-compressed versions of the Raw file. Unlike the algorithms used for compressing JPEG files, the method used when compressing Raw files is 'lossless', meaning that all the detail that was captured is retained in the compressed file. Compressing will mean that pictures will take up less space on the memory card, but the process of compression does result in longer saving times. For most shooters this isn't an issue but if you like to photograph sports or action, then the extra time taken to compress the file will reduce the frames per second rate of your camera. In practice most Raw shooters opt for non-compressed files and just buy more memory cards to accommodate the larger file sizes that need to be saved.

CAPTURE FILE SIZE COMPARISONS	JPEG file size (Fine setting)	JPEG file size (Normal setting)	JPEG file size (Basic setting)	TIFF file size	Raw file size	Raw file size (compressed)
Example file 1	2997 Kb	1555 Kb	782 Kb	17708 Kb	9777 Kb	5093 Kb
Example file 2	2466 Kb	1575 Kb	748 Kb	17712 Kb	9776 Kb	4275 Kb

Capture format versus file size >> *The capture format you select directly affects not only the way the file is saved and its visual quality but also the size of the final file. JPEG produces the smallest files but uses a 'lossy' compression system to do so. In the JPEG format you can adjust the level of compression used when saving the photo. In this table the Fine setting uses the least compression and the Basic option the most. Both TIFF and Raw formats preserve all the image detail and any compression used with these formats is 'lossless'.*

There are several cameras on the market that also have the ability to save both Raw and JPEG versions of the same file at the time of capture. This option can be a real time saver if you need to access your pictures quickly, but the feature is less of an advantage if you regularly perform many enhancement steps to your files, as in the end the captured JPEG will not resemble the processed Raw file.

At the big end of town most of the high-resolution camera backs, which are destined for use with medium format camera bodies, only capture in Raw formats. Many make use of dedicated software to control the camera, capture the photo and then process the Raw file. Other manufacturers, such as Hasselblad, Samsung, Ricoh and Leica even use Adobe's DNG format as the capture format, making the transition to Elements a simple one.

In practice – enabling your camera

For the purposes of this workflow example I have included step-by-step instructions for both Nikon and Canon cameras below.

Canon workflow

1. Press the Menu button and turn the Quick Control Dial to select the Quality heading and then press Set; this will display the Recording Quality screen.

2. Next, use the Quick Control Dial again to choose one of the Raw options from those listed. Depending on the camera model your choices may include Raw and Raw + JPEG. Press Set to set the selected capture mode.

Note: Canon cameras divide the controls into two levels: Basic and Creative (advanced). They name these control subsets different 'Zones'. If your camera is currently in the Basic Zone you won't be able to choose any Raw caption options. To do this, you will need to switch to the Creative Zone first, and then alter the Recording Quality. Canon's menu system also varies from consumer to pro models so check with the manual if you are unsure.

Nikon workflow

1. To switch the default capture format to Raw, activate the menu on the back of the camera and then use the Multi-selector control to navigate to the Shooting Menu (second option on the left side of the screen). Use the right arrow on the Multi-selector control to pick menu options.

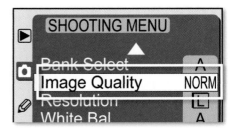

2. From the first page of the menu list, select the Image Quality entry. This will display another screen containing a list of quality options – three JPEG, one TIFF and one NEF (Nikon's version of Raw). At this screen choose the NEF (Raw) heading.

3. Selecting NEF will display a final screen with a choice of two different Raw capture modes – 'Comp. NEF (Raw)' compressed and 'NEF (Raw)' uncompressed. Select one of these options and then exit the menu.

3.02 Modifying your capture workflow for Raw
Suitable for Elements – 7.0, 6.0, 5.0, 4.0, 3.0, 2.0, 1.0 | Difficulty level – Basic

In the previous chapter we looked at the controls that are available to digital camera users that enable them to capture great images. These include such digital-only options as Saturation, Sharpness, White Balance and Contrast Control. Using such features it is possible for the digital photographer to customize their image capture more than was ever possible when film was king. But switching capture formats to Raw impacts directly on the role that these controls play in your digital capture. As we already know factors such as white balance, contrast, saturation and sharpness settings are not fixed in Raw files. These controls are only applied to the file at the time of conversion or after the image exits the Adobe Camera Raw utility and is opened in the Editor workspace. So rather than these factors being applied in-camera, as is the case with JPEG and TIFF capture, they are applied via the ACR utility. In fact any of the adjustments you make to these settings on the camera can be reversed or tweaked in ACR. Remember the white balance illustration? You forget to change from tungsten to daylight and shoot outside. No problem, just make the switch back to the daylight setting in the ACR dialog and the photo is corrected without loss of image quality.

So if these factors are controllable at conversion then should the Raw shooting photographer bother with them at time of capture? This is a good question to which you will receive many answers. Unfortunately many shooters believe that capturing in Raw is a 'fix all' for poor camera technique. Haven't selected the right white balance? No problem, fix it in Raw. Haven't judged the light quite right? Again, not a big deal just fix it in Raw. Nor adjusted your lighting for good contrast? Again, not an issue, there is contrast control in Raw. But to my mind although many factors can be altered in Raw this approach has four main drawbacks:

1. Correctly captured pictures need less correction when converting, saving valuable time.
2. The white balance settings determined at time of capture provide a good starting point for further fine-tuning during the conversion process.
3. If a Raw + JPEG capture mode is being used then the color in the accompanying JPEG photo will better match the processed Raw file as it was more accurate at the time of capture.
4. Correct exposure provides better quality edited images as ideally no shadow or highlight details are clipped when the picture is taken.

Raw capture will fix it!

Raw capture implications on workflow

So what changes to standard capture workflow should the Raw shooter make? Let's examine the impact of Raw capture on some of the standard camera controls.

Resolution – When working with Raw as the capture format, most cameras will not provide the ability to alter the dimensions of your photo. The largest photo possible (one sensor site to one pixel) is generally recorded in the Raw file.

Color Depth – Raw photographers automatically get access to the increased levels of tone afforded by high-bit capture because nominating Raw as the capture format negates the camera's bit depth settings and automatically provides the full depth capable by the sensor. At time of conversion in ACR you can elect the bit depth of the converted file.

Saturation – As the vibrancy or saturation of the converted image can be controlled on a picture-by-picture basis in ACR it is a good idea to leave this camera setting on the default or normal value. This will display your photo with standard saturation in ACR and then give you the option to boost or reduce vibrancy according to the requirements of the photo.

White Balance – Despite the fact that white balance can be losslessly adjusted in ACR it is good practice to match white balance settings with the dominant light source in your scene. This helps to maintain the photographer's own capture skill as well as ensuring speedier color cast removal in ACR, as the camera settings are loaded as default when opening the image. The more accurate these capture settings are the less fiddling the photographer will need to do to ensure a great result.

Contrast – Most cameras have the choice to increase or reduce contrast. The feature is invaluable when shooting in difficult lighting scenarios and saving the results back to TIFF or JPEG files. Raw shooters have the luxury of being able to make these types of contrast adjustments much more accurately and on an image-by-image basis back at the desktop.

Sharpening – Professionals now employ a workflow that applies sharpening at three different times during the enhancement process – at time of capture, during enhancement and then when preparing for output. For Raw shooters adopting this approach means adding a little global sharpening in-camera or at the time of conversion. Both approaches are fine as long as the sharpening is kept to a minimum with the idea that it will be fine-tuned later to account for subject matter and output destination.

Noise Reduction – Reducing noise on the desktop, either during Raw conversion or afterwards inside Photoshop Elements, provides better control over the process and therefore better results than the auto approach adopted by in-camera systems.

ISO – Shooting in Raw doesn't directly affect the selection of ISO setting used for capture. These settings will be based on the available light in the scene or the shutter speed required to freeze or blur motion.

Camera Exposure – Shooting in Raw doesn't change the fact that exposure is key to the creation of high quality images. It is true that the slider controls in ACR provide a great deal of flexibility when it comes to processing the tones in a photo and that this means that slight problems with exposure (under- or overexposure) can be corrected more easily than with other capture formats. What is important to remember though is that this doesn't provide photographers with a license for poor exposure control. The best conversions are made with images that are well exposed.

3.03 Using the Adobe Photo Downloader
Suitable for Elements – 7.0, 6.0, 5.0, 4.0, 3.0, 2.0, 1.0 | Difficulty level – Basic

Over the history of the development of Photoshop Elements one of the most significant additions to the program has been the Organizer workspace. This feature provides a visual index of your pictures and can be customized to display the images in Photo Browser Mode, date mode or sorted by keyword tags or album (collection). Unlike the standard file browsers of previous editions which created the thumbnails of your pictures the first time that the folder is browsed, the Organizer creates the thumbnail during the process of adding your photographs to a collection.

To commence downloading your Raw files and, in the process, create your first collection, simply select the View and Organize option from the Welcome screen and then proceed to the Organizer: File > Get Photos and Videos menu option. Select one of the listed sources of pictures (camera or folders) provided and move through the steps and prompts in the dialogs that follow. If you are sourcing your files from a camera or card reader then the Adobe Photo Downloader (APD) automatically starts when you attach these devices, removing the need for you to go to the Get Photos menu to start the downloading process.

Option 1: Getting your Raw files from camera or card reader

To demonstrate the process let's start by downloading some photographs from a memory card or camera. This will probably be the most frequently used route for your Raw images to enter the Elements program. Connect the camera, being sure that you have first installed the drivers for the unit. Alternatively you may wish to eject the memory card from the camera and insert it into a card reader that is already attached to the computer. The Adobe Photo Downloader utility should automatically start; if it doesn't then

Downloading files >> *Raw files can be imported directly from the camera or by inserting the memory card into an attached reader.*

manually select the From Camera or Card Reader option from the File > Get Photos and Videos menu.

After attaching the camera, or inserting a memory card into the reader, you will see the Adobe Photo Downloader dialog. This is a utility designed specifically for managing the download process and has both a Basic and Advanced dialog mode. The **Basic Dialog** is displayed by default. The first step is to select the location of the pictures (the card reader or memory card in the camera) from the Source drop-down menu in the top right of the dialog. The first photo in the group is shown as a thumbnail on the left of the window. Below this area is the Import

Settings section where you can choose the folder location for the pictures that are downloaded as well as options to create new subfolders, rename photos and delete successfully downloaded files. There is also a checkbox for activating the new Automatic Download feature which imports photos directly from card reader or camera, bypassing the Adobe Photo Downloader dialog and instead using the import options saved in the Camera or Card Reader preferences (Edit > Preferences > Camera or Card Reader).

Clicking the **Advanced Dialog** button at the bottom left switches the window to a more sophisticated version of the feature. Here all the photos on the card/camera are previewed and you have the additional options of fixing red eyes, creating photo stacks and adding group tags

Adobe Photo Downloader >>
The Adobe Photo Downloader or APD utility is used to transfer images from your camera or card reader to your computer. In the process you can rename, add tags, remove red eye, apply metadata, and suggest Photo Stack groupings.

and metadata information automatically as files are downloaded. By default all pictures on the card will be selected ready for downloading and cataloging. If for some reason you do not want to download all the images then you can deselect them by unchecking the tick box at the bottom right-hand of the thumbnail.

After selecting the options in either the Basic or Advanced dialog click the Get Photos button to transfer the pictures. After the process is complete Elements will tell you that the files have been successfully imported.

Option 2: Loading Raw files from an existing archive, disk or drive

Acting much like the File > Open option common to most programs the Get Photos and Videos > From Files and Folders selection provides you with the familiar operating system browse window that allows you to search for and open pictures that you have already saved to your computer. You generally have the option to view your files in a variety of ways including Thumbnails, Tiles, Icons, List and Detail Views using the drop-down menu from the top of the window.

However, for Windows XP users, the Thumbnail option will only display small previews of your Raw files if the Microsoft Raw Image Thumbnailer and Viewer utility is installed. This is available free from http://www.microsoft.com/windowsxp/using/digitalphotography/prophoto/Raw.mspx. Vista users will only be able to preview their raw files in Windows Browsers after installing a Raw file CODEC available from the camera manufacturer's website.

Users can also elect to automatically fix red eyes or suggest photo stacks here as well. After selecting the image, or images, you wish to import into Elements, select the Get Photos button.

How to multi-select the files to import

To select several images or files at once hold down the Ctrl key whilst clicking on the pictures of your choice. To select a complete list of files without having to pick each file in turn click on the first picture and then, whilst holding down the Shift key, click on the last file in the group.

Disable the Adobe Photo Downloader

1. Select Organizer: Edit > Preferences > Camera Or Card Reader.

2. Deselect 'Auto Launch Adobe Photo Downloader on Device Connect'.

Enable the Adobe Photo Downloader

1. For Elements 6.0/7.0 users select Organizer: Edit > Preferences > Camera Or Card Reader.

2. Select 'Auto Launch Adobe Photo Downloader on Device Connect'.

Enabling the Automatic Download option in Adobe Photo Downloader (APD)

1. Choose the Automatic Download option from the APD Basic or Advanced dialogs. The downloader will commence automatically the next time a card/camera is connected.

2. Select Organizer: Edit > Preferences > Camera Or Card Reader and set the preferences for the download in the Files and Download sections of the dialog.

Activating and deactivating APD

3.04 The Adobe Camera Raw interface

Suitable for Elements – 7.0, 6.0, 5.0, 4.0, 3.0, 2.0, 1.0 | Difficulty level – Basic

Before commencing to process our first raw file, let's take a close look at the Adobe Camera Raw feature as it appears in Photoshop Elements 7.0. The ACR dialog, the user interface between you and what goes on inside the Camera Raw plug-in, provides tools to adjust, process, convert and save raw files. After opening a raw photo from inside either the Organizer or Editor workspaces, this dialog will be displayed.

Adobe Camera Raw interface >> *Features of the Adobe Camera Raw dialog box in Photoshop Elements 7.0.*

1. Preview area.
2. White balance settings.
3. Tonal controls.
4. Auto option for tonal control settings.
5. Color controls.
6. Detail tab containing the sharpness and noise options.
7. Zoom tool.

8. Hand tool.
9. White balance tool.
10. Crop tool.
11. Straighten tool.
12. Red eye removal tool.
13. ACR preferences.
14. Rotate buttons.
15. Mark for deletion button.
16. Queued raw files.

17. Save button.
18. Bit depth options.
19. Shadow and highlights clipping warnings.
20. Preview checkbox.
21. Camera Calibration tab containing the Camera Profile menu.

The ACR dialog can be broken into four separate areas: 1. Preview. 2. Image adjustment controls. 3. Raw file queue. 4. Toolbar.

The feature's window is broken into four distinct areas:

1. A preview of the file is displayed in the center of the dialog. Any editing or development changes made to the file will be reflected automatically in this preview.

2. A queuing area for raw files awaiting processing. This area of the dialog is only present when multiple raw files are selected for opening and is new for Photoshop Elements 7.0.

3. Controls or settings area. This part of the dialog contains all the processing and development controls for altering the look of the color, tone, sharpening and noise in the photo. The settings are grouped under two tabs – Basic and Detail. A new third tab called Camera Control lists Camera Profiles that are available for the current image. A histogram graph is also displayed here.

4. The toolbar sits at the top of the dialog and houses options such as the Zoom, Hand, Crop and Straighten tools.

The Help and Save buttons are located at the bottom left of the window. In the center is the bit depth menu and on the right, are the Done, Cancel and Open Images buttons. To ensure that you have the best selection of tools to use on your raw files, make sure that your ACR plug-in is always up to date. See section 3.05 for more details on how to obtain and install the latest version of the plug-in. By way of introduction let's look at each of these work areas in turn.

The preview space

The preview displays the changes you make to your image via the develop or enhancement settings. Any adjustment of controls are reflected immediately in the preview image, providing a visual reference to the effect of the alterations. The preview can be enlarged or reduced in size to suit the screen area available. When making some changes, such as Sharpening or Noise

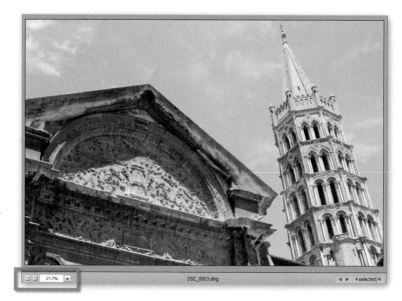

The preview >>
The preview image in ACR's dialog is capable of being magnified to a range of levels. The current magnification value is shown in the bottom left corner of the window.

Reduction, the preview should be magnified to at least 100%. At this zoom setting, you will be able to preview the results of the adjustments of these controls.

There are three ways for you to change the magnification level of the preview to 100%:

1.   Double-click the Zoom tool,

2.   Select the 100% entry from the zoom menu at the bottom left of the dialog, or

3.   Use the Ctrl+ to magnify or Ctrl - to reduce the size of the preview to the zoom value in the window at the bottom left of the dialog.

Zoom to 100% >>
The zoom menu at the bottom left of the dialog provides a variety of zoom levels for quick access.

Image adjustment controls

The right-hand side of the ACR dialog is reserved for the core adjustment features.

Histogram

A full color histogram is located under the RGB values. The feature graphs the distribution of the pixels within your photo. The graph updates after changes are made to the color, contrast and brightness of the picture. By paying close attention to the shape of the graph you can pre-empt many image problems. The aim with most enhancement activities is to obtain a good spread of pixels from shadow through midtones to highlights without clipping (converting delicate details to pure black or white) either end of the tonal range.

Image tones and histogram shapes >>

The histogram in ACR shows the distribution of pixels across the image. Areas with the most pixels are the tallest areas of the graph. The shape of the histogram indicates the look of the picture.

1. *An overexposed image has a histogram with the pixels bunched to the right end of the graph.*

2. *Conversely, underexposed photos have pixels pushed to the left.*

3. *Flat or low-contrast pictures typically have all their pixels grouped in the middle.*

4. *High-contrast photos or those that have 'clipped' highlights and shadow areas usually have many pixels at the extreme ends of the graph.*

5. *For the best results, with most images, you should always aim to spread the pixels between the maximum black and white points without clipping any of the image pixels.*

This is not the case for all photos though. Take, for instance, the case of a black cat in a darkened room, the correct histogram for this photo will show a bunching of the pixels towards the left side of central, whereas a shot of the ski slopes, also correctly exposed, will display most pixels to the right of the histogram graph.

The Basic tab

Below the histogram is a tab area containing two options – Basic and Detail. The Basic tab contains all the tone and color controls. On the other hand, the Sharpening and Noise Reduction features are grouped under the Detail tab. Here we will concentrate on the controls under the Basic tab.

Image Settings menu

The Settings drop-down menu is displayed by clicking the Settings button on the right side of the Tabs. The menu contains the Image Settings, Camera Raw Defaults, Previous Conversion, Custom, Clear Imported Settings, Save New Camera Raw Defaults, and Reset Camera Raw Defaults entries. Here are some more details on each entry:

The Settings menu >>

The Settings menu contains options for saving or recalling image settings associated with specific cameras.

Image Settings: The Image Settings option restores the original settings of the current photo. Use this selection when you want to reverse changes that you have made and wish to restore the photo to its virgin state.

Camera Raw Defaults: This option applies a group of slider settings that are default values associated with a specific camera and photograph. When a photo is opened for the first time, the settings and white balance will be altered to Camera Raw Defaults (based on the camera model) and As Shot (based on the camera settings used for the photograph), respectively.

Previous Conversion: Another option in the Settings drop-down menu is Previous Conversion. This setting stores the 'last used' values for all controls and is an efficient way to apply the enhancements used with the previous image to one currently open in the dialog. Using this option will help speed up the conversions of a series of photos taken at the same time under the same lighting conditions. Simply make the adjustments for the first image and then use the Previous Conversion option to apply the same settings to each of the successive photos from the series in turn.

Custom: Moving any of the slider controls such as Temperature or Tint sliders under the White Balance menu automatically changes the settings entry to Custom. Once the settings have been customized for a particular photograph the values can be saved as a new Camera Raw Default entry using the save option in the pop-up menu accessed via the sideways arrow next to the Settings menu.

> **Pro's tip:** As ACR recognizes the raw file created with different cameras the new Camera Raw Default will be applied to only those photos captured with the specific camera that the settings have been saved for.

White balance correction

White balance is used to correctly balance the color of the scene to the lighting conditions at the time the shot was taken. Leaving white balance set at As Shot means you elect to keep the white balance values that were used when taking the picture.

As you know, one of the advantages shooting raw is that this setting is not a fixed part of the picture file. Altering the specific white balance setting at the time of raw conversion is a 'lossless' action. This is not the case if you have used an incorrect setting and have shot in JPEG or TIFF. Use either of these two formats and the white balance setting will be fixed in the file and can only be changed with destructive adjustments using features like Color Variations or Remove Color Cast. In this regard raw shooters have much more flexibility.

White Balance drop-down menu: For instance, if you selected a Daylight setting in-camera and think that Shade or another white balance preset may be closer to the actual lighting conditions you may select one of the options from the list of presets under the White Balance drop-down menu. Moving either the Temperature or Tint sliders switches the setting to

Custom. These controls are used for matching the image color temperature with that of the scene.

Temperature slider: The Temperature slider is a fine-tuning device that allows you to select a precise color temperature in units of degrees Kelvin. When an image is too yellow, meaning it has a lower color temperature than you prefer, move the Temperature slider to the left to make the colors bluer and compensate for the lower color temperature. When an image is too blue, or higher in temperature than you prefer, move the slider to the right to make the image warmer, adding more yellow compensation. So, left is to make image colors cooler and right is to make image colors warmer.

Tint slider: The Tint slider fine-tunes the white balance to compensate for a green or magenta tint. Moving the Tint slider to the left adds green and to the right adds magenta. This control is often used to neutralize a color cast caused by lighting from fluorescent tube or strip sources.

White Balance tool: The quickest and perhaps easiest way to adjust white balance is to select the White Balance tool and then click in an area that should be neutral gray or even amounts of red, green and blue. For best results, use a dark to midtone as the reference and be careful not to click on an area with pure white or specular highlights. These will produce unreliable results so keep away from the bright highlight areas of highly reflective or chrome surfaces. One suggestion for working with neutral gray is to:

White Balance control >>
When an original file is opened for the first time in the dialog, the settings and white balance values will be set to Camera Raw Defaults (based on camera model and make) and As Shot (determined by the camera settings at the time of capture), respectively.

1. Click on the White Balance tool.
2. Move the White Balance tool cursor over a midtone area which should be neutral gray (e.g. textured white area) but contains a color cast in the preview.
3. Click on the image location to neutralize the cast not just in the selected area but in the whole photo.

WB tool workflow

Making tonal adjustments

Below the white balance controls are the Exposure, Recovery, Fill Light, Blacks, Brightness, Contrast, Clarity, Vibrance and Saturation sliders which are also available for making adjustments to raw files. Adobe has positioned these controls in the dialog so that when working from top to bottom you follow a specific enhancement workflow. For this reason you should follow these steps in order:

Tonal changes workflow

1. Set the white clipping points using the **Exposure** slider.
2. Set the black clipping points using the **Shadows** slider.
3. Use **Recovery/Fill Light** controls (if needed).
4. Adjust the overall brightness using the **Brightness** slider.
5. Adjust contrast using the **Contrast** slider.
6. Use the **Clarity** slider to adjust local contrast.
7. Boost specific desaturated colors with the **Vibrance** slider.
8. Adjust saturation, if needed, using the **Saturation** slider.

Tonal adjustment sequence >>
Adobe has positioned the slider controls that adjust the tones within the image in the order (top to bottom) that they should be applied within the ACR dialog.
The Exposure and Blacks sliders should be used first to set the white and black points in the photo. Use the Alt/Option keys in conjunction with these sliders to preview the pixels being clipped and to accurately peg the white/black points. Or alternatively switch on the Shadows/Highlights Clipping Warnings which perform the same function whilst leaving the full color preview visible.
Next lighten or darken the photo using the Brightness slider. Unlike the Exposure control this slider doesn't affect the white and black points of the image but rather adjusts the appearance of the photo by compressing or extending the altered tones.
Recovery and Fill Light sliders are new for this release of Elements' ACR. Use the Recovery control to rebuild highlight areas where one channel has been clipped. The Fill Light slider brightens mid to dark shadow areas.

Exposure

The Exposure slider adjusts the brightness or darkness of an image using value increments equivalent to f-stops or EV (exposure values) on a camera. An image is underexposed when it is not light enough or too dark and it is overexposed when it is too light. Simply move the slider to the left to darken the image and to the right to lighten (brighten) the image.

What do the f-stop or EV equivalents indicate? An adjustment of -1.50 is just like narrowing the aperture by 1.5 (one and a half) f-stops. Moving the slider 1.33 places to the left will dramatically darken an image and to the right the same amount will result in a bright image. If you have to move more than two full stops in either direction this probably indicates your settings at capture were inaccurate. Making adjustments beyond two stops starts to deteriorate image quality as invariably shadow or highlight detail is lost (clipped) in the process.

For those of you who are interested, the Exposure slider sets the white clipping points in the image. Clipping shows as values creeping up the left (shadow) and right (highlight) walls of your histogram (and red and blue areas in the image if shadow and highlight previews are turned on), and occurs when the pixel values shift to the highest highlight value or the lowest shadow value. Clipped areas are completely black or white and contain no detail. As you want to maintain as much detail in the shadows and highlights as possible your aim should always be to spread the picture tones but not to clip delicate highlight or shadow areas.

Blacks (Shadows)

Moving the Blacks or Shadows slider adjusts the position of the black point within the image. Just as was the case with the Exposure slider you should only make shadows adjustments when the clipping warning is active. This will ensure that you don't unintentionally convert shadow detail to black pixels. Remember movements of the slider to the left decrease shadow clipping. Moving it to the right increases or produces clipping.

Brightness and Contrast

The Brightness slider is different to the Exposure slider although both affect the brightness of an image. Brightness compresses the highlights and expands the shadows when you move the slider to the right. When adjusting your photos your aim is to set the black and white points first and then adjust the brightness of the midtones to suit your image.

R: 208   f/22   1/125 s
G: 250
B: 11   ISO 200   100 mm

Highlight and Shadow clipping warnings >>
To ensure that you don't accidently convert shadow or highlight detail to pure black or white pixels ACR contains two different types of 'Clipping' warnings.
1. When the Shadows and Highlights Clipping Warning features are selected at the top of the Histogram graph, areas of highlight clipping are displayed in the preview as red and shadows as blue.
2. Holding down the Alt key whilst moving either the Exposure or Shadows sliders will convert the preview to black (for Exposure) or white (for Shadows). Any pixels being clipped will then be shown as a contrasting color against these backgrounds.

Contrast adjusts the spread of the midtones in the image. A move of the Contrast slider to the right spreads the pixels across the histogram, actually increasing the midtone contrast. Conversely movements to the left bunch the pixels in the middle of the graph. It is important to adjust the contrast of midtones after working on exposure, shadows and brightness.

Recovery

When a photograph is overexposed one of the consequences can be that the lighter tones in the image lose detail and are converted to pure white. This process is called clipping. Digital images are created with details from three color channels (red, green, blue). In situations of slight overexposure, when only one channel is clipped, it is possible to recreate the lost detail with the highlight information from the other two (non-clipped) channels. The Recovery slider attempts to recreate lost highlight details in such cases. Moving the slider to the right progressively increases the degree of highlight recovery.

Recovering highlights >>
The Recovery slider is used for correcting clipped highlights. With the clipping warning activated it is easy to see problem highlights (1). When moving the slider to the right, ACR will attempt to reconstruct clipped details from the information stored in the non-clipped channels (2).

Fill Light

The Fill Light slider is used to lighten the darker tones in a picture without affecting the middle to highlight values. Use this control to brighten backlit subjects or boost shadow details. The beauty of this control is that the changes it makes do not generally impact on mid to highlight values.

Pro's tip: In some instances you may need to readjust Exposure and Blacks sliders after Brightness, Recovery, Fill Light and Contrast to fine-tune your enhancements.

Boosting shadows >>
The Fill Light slider manipulates the mid to dark tones in the photo. Moving the slider to the right pushes these tones towards the highlight end of the histogram, lightening them.

Clarity

Located along with Vibrance and Saturation controls at the bottom of the Basic panel, this new slider produces localized contrast changes to otherwise flat images.

Rather than adding contrast to the whole image by stretching the tones between black and white points, Clarity works on changing contrast on the detail in your photos. There are many sophisticated, multi-step, sharpening techniques that produce similar effects but thankfully Adobe has managed to squeeze much of their contrast-increasing abilities into a single control. Moving the slider to the right increases the effect.

Adding contrast using the Clarity slider >> *The Clarity slider gradually increases the contrast of details in the photo.*

Vibrance

The Vibrance slider is a new addition to the Basic panel of Adobe Camera Raw. Like the Saturation control, Vibrance controls the strength of the color in the photo. Movements to the right boost the color and movements to the left make the vividness of the hue more subtle. But unlike the Saturation slider, Vibrance manages these changes selectively, targeting the least saturated colors and protecting (to some extent) skin tones.

This makes the new control the first tool to reach for when you want to boost the color in your photos. The results are easier to control and less likely to display posterization or color clipping from over-application than the traditional Saturation control.

Saturation control >>
The Saturation slider controls the strength of the color within your raw photos.
(1) Dragging the slider all the way to left (-100) will remove all color from the photo, creating a monochrome picture.
(2) A value of 0 is the default setting where the saturation is neither boosted nor reduced.
(3) Moving the slider all the way to the right to a setting of +100 produces twice the saturation of the normal or default setting.

Saturation

If desired, the Saturation slider may be used to adjust the strength of the color within the photo. A setting of -100 is a completely desaturated monochrome image and a value of +100 doubles the saturation. Watch changes in the histogram when you move the Saturation slider in either direction.

Auto tonal control

When first opening a picture ACR will adjust the tonal controls to an average setting for the picture type and camera make/model. When the Auto setting is selected, ACR examines the picture and adjusts the controls according to the images' content. When these settings are in place, moving the associated slider will remove the selection but these values can be reinstated by selecting the check box again.

ACR auto options >>
(1) A single Auto button is provided with the version of ACR that ships with Photoshop Elements 7.0.
(2) There are individual Auto options for Exposure, Shadows, Brightness and Contrast controls inside earlier versions of the ACR dialog.

Sharpening, Luminance Smoothing and Color Noise Reduction

Sharpening (Amount, Radius, Detail, Masking), Luminance Smoothing and Color Noise Reduction are all controls that can be accessed under the Detail tab.

Sharpening

Sharpening is an enhancement technique that is easily overdone and this is true even when applying the changes at the time of raw conversion. The best approach is to remember that sharpening should be applied to photos as the very last step in the editing/ enhancement process and that the settings used need to match the type of output the photo is destined for. In practice this means images that are not going to be edited after raw conversion should be sharpened within ACR, but those pictures that are going to be enhanced further should have a small amount of subtle sharpening applied in ACR and specific output sharpening applied later using the specialist filters in Photoshop Elements.

Detail Tab controls >>
The Detail tab contains both Sharpening and Noise Reduction options.

When a picture is first opened into the ACR the program sets the sharpening and noise values based on the camera type and model used to capture the image. For many photographers making further adjustments here is an exception rather than a rule as they prefer to address sharpening in the Editor after cropping, straightening, enhancing, resizing and going to print.

The inclusion of two new controls in the Detail section of the Camera Raw dialog contributes substantially to the user's ability to fine-tune the sharpening in their images. Added to the existing Amount (strength of the effect) and Radius (number of pixels from an edge that will be changed in the sharpening process) sliders is the Detail and Masking controls. Both sliders are designed to control which parts of the image the sharpening effect is applied to. As with all sharpening techniques ensure that the preview is set to 100% before playing with the new controls. In fact, this magnification level is essential if you are to see the masking previews mentioned below.

Moving the Detail slider to the right increases the local contrast surrounding edge areas and therefore enhances the appearance of details. Moving the slider to the left decreases the effect and also reduces the appearance of halos.

The Masking control interactively applies an edge locating mask to the sharpening process. Sharpening through an edge mask is nothing new but encapsulating the process in a single slider control is. A setting of 0 applies no mask and therefore all detail in the photo is sharpened. Moving the slider to the right gradually isolates the edges within the photo until, at a setting of 100, sharpening is only being applied to the most contrasty or dominant edges in the picture. Holding

Sharpening preview options >>
After magnifying the preview to 100% there are four different preview options available when holding down the Alt keys and sliding one of the Sharpening sliders.

down the Alt key (at 100% magnification) as you move the slider previews the masked areas, allowing you to fine-tune exactly where the sharpening is being applied. Remember no sharpening is occurring in the black parts of the mask, in the areas masked by gray tones only partial sharpening is being applied and in white mask sections the full effect is revealed.

As well as including a mask display option, in the latest version of ACR you can also preview the settings for the other sharpening sliders. Holding down the Alt keys while moving the Amount slider displays a 'luminosity only' version of the image so that you can gauge the sharpening effect without the distraction of color. This preview also reminds us that in the latest version of ACR sharpening is applied to detail only and not the color information in the photo. When the Alt/Opt keys are used with the Radius slider the preview highlights the 'edges' in the image that will be sharpened and the width of the sharpening effect.

Noise Reduction

ACR contains two different noise reduction controls. The Luminance Smoothing slider and the Color Noise Reduction control. The Luminance Smoothing slider is designed to reduce the appearance of grayscale noise in a photo. This is particularly useful for improving the look of images that appear grainy. The second type of noise is the random colored pixels that typically appear in photos taken with a high ISO setting or a long shutter speed. This is generally referred to as chroma noise and the effect is reduced using the Color Noise Reduction slider in ACR. The noise reduction effect of both features is increased as the sliders are moved to the right.

ACR noise reduction controls >>
Along with the masking options for Sharpening, the ACR design team also took the opportunity to tweak the noise reduction algorithms in the latest release of the product. Though the effects are not as dramatic as those possible via other methods, the changes are definitely an improvement.

Raw file queue

The third section of the Photoshop Elements version of the ACR dialog only appears when you select multiple raw files inside the Organizer workspace and then choose the Full Edit option from the right-click menu. The selected files are opened into the ACR dialog and listed on the left-hand side of the main workspace. This function, though available in the Photoshop version of ACR, was only introduced to the edition that ships with Photoshop Elements in version 6.0.

Queued Raw files >>
When selecting multiple raw files to open in Photoshop Elements the pictures are listed on the left side of the Adobe Camera Raw dialog.

In general, only one image can be selected from the grouping, and displayed in the preview area, at a time. All changes made to the image settings are applied to the selected photo only. Users can move from image to image making the necessary enhancements before clicking the Done key to apply the changes without transferring the files, or Open to display the converted pictures in the Full Edit workspace. But this is not the only way to work with the files.

Synchronizing enhancements across multiple files

The Select All button at the top of the queued files can be employed for a more efficient workflow. With this feature enhancement changes made to a single photo can be applied across the whole range of images queued in the dialog.

Applying changes across multiple raw files

1. For best results, start by multi-selecting files from the Organizer space that have similar characteristics or were shot under the same lighting conditions.

2. Next, open the pictures in ACR by selecting the Full Edit option from the right-click menu. The ACR dialog opens with the selected files listed as thumbnails on the left.

3. Now select a single photo from the queue that is indicative in tone and color of the whole group. With this photo displayed in the preview area, choose the Select All option from the top of the dialog.

4. Proceed to make enhancement changes to the previewed files as you would normally. Notice that these changes are also applied to the other photos in the queue.

5. The changes made to all the photos can then be fine-tuned to suit the characteristics of individual images (if needed) by selecting each picture in turn and adjusting the controls.

6. If no changes for individual files are necessary, then the selected photos can be saved, using the Save Images button, transferred to the Edit workspace with the Open Images option or the enhancement settings applied by clicking the Done button.

Applying changes across rated raw files

1. In addition to being able to apply image changes across all the queued files by choosing the Select All button, it is also possible to adjust a subset of the files listed. Start by reviewing each of the queued files in turn by clicking onto the thumbnail on the left of the dialog.

2. During the review process rate those files that you want to adjust as a group. Do this by clicking the star rating section located under each thumbnail.

3. Once the review process is completed and all files to be enhanced as a group are rated, hold down the Alt key and choose the Select Rated button at the top of the queued list. Notice that this action selects only those files with a star rating attached.

4. Now you can set about applying the changes to those selected as before.

5. If you want to remove an image from the Rated grouping simply click on the no rating option under the thumbnail.

Step-by-step

The ACR toolbar >>
Photoshop Elements users have access to a range of tools via the toolbar at the top of the ACR dialog.
1. *Zoom tool*
2. *Hand tool*
3. *White Balance tool*
4. *Crop tool*
5. *Straighten tool*
6. *Red Eye Removal*
7. *Preferences dialog*
8. *Rotate image 90°CC*
9. *Rotate image 90°C*
10. *Toggle Mark for Delete*
11. *Preview*
12. *Toggle Full Screen*

Toolbar

Like the image adjustment tabs on the right of the ACR dialog, the contents of the program's toolbar are different depending on if you are working on files inside Photoshop Elements or Photoshop/ Bridge. Elements users have the following tools at their disposal (left to right):

Zoom tool (shortcut key = Z) – The Zoom tool is useful for looking closely at the image for problems with focus and execution – slow shutter speed, lack of stabilization, incorrect aperture setting. At 25% an image may appear to be quite impressive, yet when examining it at 100% often a bit of movement and/or lack of focus appear.

Hand tool (H) – When the preview image is enlarged you can use the Hand tool to easily move around the screen.

White Balance tool (I) – The White Balance tool is very powerful. Clicking this tool on a picture portion that is meant to be neutral (even amounts of red, green and blue) removes any color casts and adjusts the hue of the entire image in one fell swoop.

Crop tool (C) – Use the Crop tool to remove unwanted areas around your photo or to reshape the format of the image to fit a specific paper type. The tool can be click-dragged around the area to keep or a specific cropping format can be selected from the drop-down menu accessed via the small downward-facing arrow in the bottom right of the tool button.

Straighten tool (A) – The Straighten tool can automatically rotate a picture taken with the horizon slightly crooked. Simply drag the tool along the line in the image that is meant to be level and ACR will automatically rotate and crop the photo to realign the horizon. The Straighten and Crop tools don't actually remove parts of the Raw image, in fact it is just previewing the crop or horizon line that is going to be opened in the Editor, but is not actually cropping the Raw file.

Red Eye Removal (E) – Use the Red Eye Removal tool to recolor the pupil area of photos taken with flash. Either click onto the red pupil or click-drag a marquee around the problem area. The Pupil Size and Darken sliders can be used to adjust the quality of the results.

Open Preference dialog (Ctrl + K) – Displays the Camera Raw Preferences dialog.

Rotate image 90° counter-clockwise (L) – Rotates the selected photo to the left.

Rotate image 90° clockwise (R) – Rotates the selected photo to the right.

Toggle Mark for Delete – Use this tool carefully to delete files that you don't want to keep in the catalog.

Preview (P) – Switches the preview of current image adjustments settings on and off.

Toggle Full Screen (F) – Switches the display mode of the dialog from a floating window to full screen.

Output options

Now to the business end of the conversion task – outputting the file. At this stage in the process ACR provides several options that will govern how the file is handled from this point onwards. In previous versions of the dialog the lower right-hand corner house all the output options, now they are spread along the bottom of the window. The options include Save Image, Cancel, Open Image, Done and Help, and a further three: Save Image (without the options dialog), Reset and Open Copy, when the Alt button is pushed.

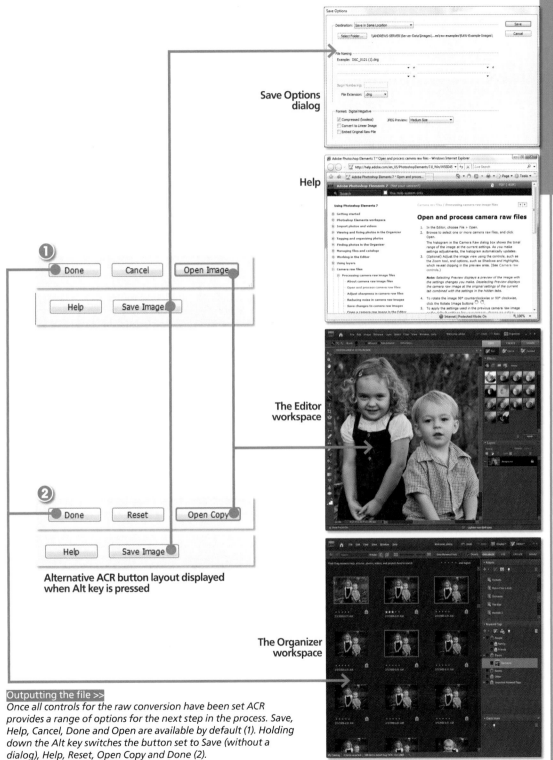

Save Options dialog

Help

① Done | Cancel | Open Image
Help | Save Image

The Editor workspace

② Done | Reset | Open Copy
Help | Save Image

Alternative ACR button layout displayed when Alt key is pressed

The Organizer workspace

Outputting the file >>
Once all controls for the raw conversion have been set ACR provides a range of options for the next step in the process. Save, Help, Cancel, Done and Open are available by default (1). Holding down the Alt key switches the button set to Save (without a dialog), Help, Reset, Open Copy and Done (2).

Help: Opens the Photoshop Elements help system with raw processing topics already displayed.

Cancel: This option closes the ACR dialog not saving any of the settings to the file that was open.

Save Image: The normal Save Image button, which includes several dots (...) after the label, displays the Save Options dialog. Here you can save the raw file, with your settings applied, in Adobe's own DNG format. The dialog includes options for inputting the location where the file will be saved, the ability to add in a new name as well as DNG file-specific settings such as compression, conversion to linear image and/or embed the original raw file in the new DNG document. It is a good idea to Select Save in Different Location in the Destination drop-down at the top to separate processed files from archive originals. Clearly the benefits of a compressed DNG file are going to help out in the storage issue arena and compression is a big advantage with DNG. Embedding the original raw file in the saved DNG file begs the questions of how much room you have in the designated storage device and whether you really want to have the original raw file here.

Save Image (without save options): Holding down the Alt key when clicking the Save button skips the Save Options dialog and saves the file in DNG format using the default save settings.

Options for saving >>
The Save Options dialog is displayed when the Save Image ... button is pressed. To skip this dialog and still save the processed file in DNG format hold down the Alt/Option key whilst clicking the Save Image button.

Open Image: If you click on the Open button Elements applies the conversion options that you set in ACR and opens the file inside the Editor workspace. At this point, the file is no longer in a raw format so when it comes to saving the photo from the Editor workspace Elements automatically selects the Photoshop PSD format for saving.

Open Copy: The Open Copy option differs from Open Image in that it applies the development settings to a duplicate of the file which is then opened into the Elements Editor workspace.

Reset: The Reset option resets the ACR dialog's settings back to their defaults. This feature is useful if you want to ensure that all settings and enhancement changes made in the current session have been removed. To access the Reset button click the Cancel button while holding down the Alt key.

Done or Update: The Done button applies the current settings to the photo and the dialog is then closed. The thumbnail preview in the PhotoBrowser workspace will also be updated to reflect the changes. In previous versions of the dialog clicking the Open button in conjunction with the Alt/Option key (the Update button) will update the raw conversion settings for the open image in the same way.

 Pro's tip: If the thumbnail doesn't update automatically, select the picture and then choose Edit > Update Thumbnail in the PhotoBrowser workspace.

Skip: In previous versions of Adobe Camera Raw holding down the Shift key whilst clicking the Open button will not apply the currently selected changes and just close the dialog. In this way it is similar to the Cancel button.

Camera Calibration >>
The Camera Calibration tab is new for the version of Adobe Camera Raw that ships with Photoshop Elements. The section contains a single drop down menu where you can select the camera profile that is used to interpret the colors, tones and white balance of your raw images. For many camera models there will be several options available with the highest numbered ACR entry representing the most recent profile (1). Adobe has also released a very new set of profiles titled Adobe Standard (2) which don't ship with Elements but can be downloaded and installed.

3.05 The new Camera Calibration tab
Suitable for Elements – 7.0 | Difficulty level – Advanced

The Camera Calibration pane contains a drop down menu of the camera profiles that ship with Adobe Camera Raw. These profiles tell ACR how to interpret the colors in an image. They are specific to individual manufacturers and camera models and the default selection will suit most users' needs straight out of the box. Depending on the camera you are using there may be several profiles available for use with your images. The default profile displayed will either be the most recent version available for your camera for new pictures, or for images you have already enhanced in ACR it will be the profile that was used for making these changes.

It is easy to switch from one profile to another by selecting and alternative entry from the drop-down menu. Because each profile renders colors differently, switching profiles will change the way that the colors appear in you photo which may in turn require a little tweaking of tones and colors in order to account for the different rendering. Keep in mind that the highest numbered entry will be the most recent profile available for your camera.

New Camera Profiles >>
At the time of writing the new camera profiles as well as the DNG Profile Editor utility are available in beta format from the labs.adobe.com website.

New Camera Profiles

For most users the general profiles supplied by Adobe are more than sufficient for their needs, but there may be occasions when difficult lighting, or the wayward characteristics of a specific camera, could benefit from some fine-tuning of how the raw data is interpreted by ACR. For this reason Adobe has released a new set of profiles along with a special editor utility designed to allow users to tweak how colors are rendered in their images. At the time of writing these are both in beta form (a special testing format before general release) and are available as a free download from labs.adobe.com. The formal name for the editing utility is the DNG Profile Editor.

Multiple Profiles >>
As the DNG Profile Editor provides the ability to quickly and easily create new profiles for a camera, installing the new camera profiles will display a variety of entries in the drop down menu. In this example the user has the option of selecting a way of rendering the colors, tones and white balance in a image from a list of 12.

Adding Adobe's new camera profiles

The new camera profiles can be downloaded from the beta website and when installed will automatically be available for use in the Camera Calibration tab of Adobe Camera Raw the next time you open it. You will find at least one new general profile available for all cameras supported by ACR. This is titled the Adobe Standard Beta. For some manufacturers and camera models there will also be a variety of other profiles available. These include profiles customized for different looks and styles. There are some suitable for landscape imagery, others that work well with portraits, as well as options for creating more vivid colors or a more subtle rendition of hues. Once installed you can quickly flip through each of the camera profiles to see which works best with your particular image.

Note: If you only see the Adobe Standard profile entry then there are currently no extra custom profiles available for you camera. For this reason it is a good idea to check adobe.com regularly to see which new camera profiles are available for download.

DNG Profile Editor >>
The DNG Profile Editor provides a set of controls for creating custom Camera Profiles.

Tweak colors   Tweak tones   Tweak White Balance   Profile options   Chart based adjustments

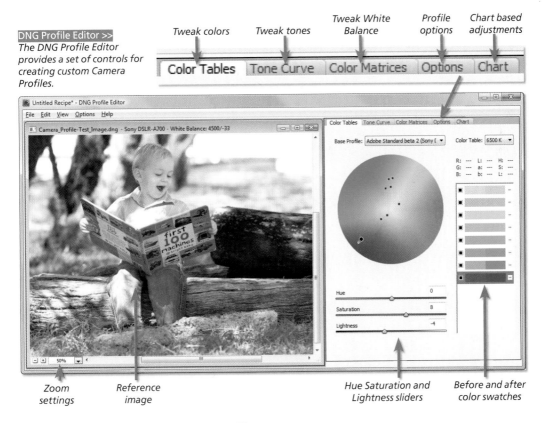

Zoom settings   Reference image   Hue Saturation and Lightness sliders   Before and after color swatches

Creating your own custom camera profiles

Now for those of you who really like to 'tinker under the hood', Adobe also provides an editor utility that can be used to create your own camera profiles. Called the DNG Profile Editor, at the time of writing the program is available from labs.adobe.com as a free beta download.

With this tool it is possible to fundamentally change how the hues that are recorded by the camera are translated into colors in the photo; for this reason, I must provide a cautionary note here. This an advanced technique and accompanying this level of color rendering power, comes the ability to really screw up how your photos appear. Thankfully creating and using a crazy profile with your photo won't permanently change your picture. To revert the image back to its original settings all you need to do is select one of the Adobe created profiles from the Camera Profile menu.

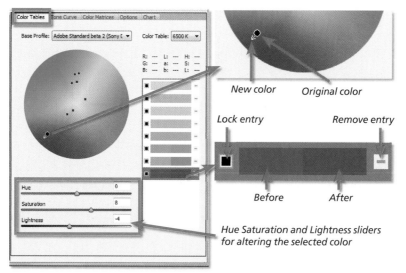

Customizing profiles >>
The Color Tables (pictured), Tone Curve, and Color Matrices sections in the DNG Profile Editor contain tools for adjusting the colors, tones and white balance.

The DNG Profile Editor can be used in two different ways.

1. Firstly, you can use the controls in the editor to tweak the colors of a reference photo. It is possible to change the hue, saturation and lightness of any color, alter the way that the tones in the image are distributed and change the base white balance settings. These alterations means that you can build a range of camera profiles that render colors, tones and white balance in different ways. For instance you may create a profile that emphasizes blues and greens and use this in conjunction with landscape photos. In contrast you may build a portrait profile that uses less saturation for skin tone colors than the other hues in the scene.

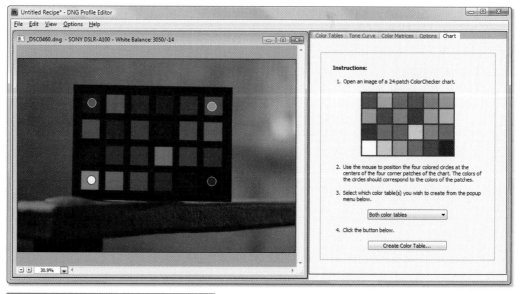

Creating camera profiles for specific lighting >>
The Chart section of the DNG Profile Editor is specifically designed to be used with the X-Rite ColorChecker to create accurate color rendition under difficult lighting or mixed light sources.

2. Secondly, the DNG Profile Editor can be used together with a color calibration target calibrate your camera's response to color under different light sources. The utility is designed to use the ColorChecker that is available from X-Rite (previously Gretagmacbeth). The process involves shooting the color checker using representative lighting for the scene. This image is then opened in the DNG Profile Editor and processed via the tools in the Chart section of the utility. The editor compares the colors of each swatch in the photo with the known values of these hues and then creates a 'recipe' of adjustments to correct any casts present in the photo. The recipe settings can then be exported as a new camera profile and used in Adobe Camera Raw. This is not a task that you would undertake for all images; instead, it is a calibration activity that you perform when encountering a difficult shooting scenario such as capturing under mixed lighting.

Note: In order to open photos in the DNG Profile Editor they must first be saved in or converted to Adobe's DNG or digital negative format. The easiest way for Elements users to do this is to open the raw file in Adobe Camera Raw and then use the Save Image .... (yes the one with the dots) with DNG selected as the file format.

3.06 The raw conversion process
Suitable for Elements – 7.0, 6.0, 5.0, 4.0, 3.0, 2.0, 1.0 | Difficulty level – Basic

Okay, now that we have a good understanding of the features and controls within the Adobe Camera Raw dialog let's move on and look at a typical conversion workflow.

1. Opening the raw file in the Editor workspace *Once you have downloaded your raw files from camera to computer you can start the task of processing. Keep in mind that in its present state the raw file is not in the full color RGB format that we are used to, so the first part of all processing is to open the picture into Adobe Camera Raw. Selecting File > Open from inside Elements will automatically display the photo in this.*

2. Starting with the PhotoBrowser *Starting in the PhotoBrowser or Organizer workspace simply right-click on the thumbnail of the raw file and select Full Edit or Go to Standard Edit from the pop-up menu to transfer the file to the Elements version of ACR in the Editor workspace.*

3. Rotate right (90 CW) or left (90 CCW) *Once the raw photo is open in ACR you can rotate the image using either of the two Rotate buttons at the top of the dialog. If you are the lucky owner of a recent camera model then chances are the picture will automatically rotate to its correct orientation. This is thanks to a small piece of metadata supplied by the camera and stored in the picture file that indicates which way is up.*

4. Preset changes *As we have seen you can opt to stay with the settings used at the time of shooting ('As Shot') or select from a range of light-source-specific settings in the White Balance drop-down menu of ACR. For best results, try to match the setting used with the type of lighting that was present in the scene at the time of capture. Or choose the Auto option from the drop-down White Balance menu to get ACR to determine a setting based on the individual image currently displayed.*

5. Manual adjustments *If none of the preset white balance options perfectly matches the lighting in your photo then you will need to fine-tune your results with the Temperature and Tint sliders (located just below the Presets drop-down menu). The Temperature slider settings equate to the color of light in degrees Kelvin – so daylight will be 5500 and tungsten light 2800. It is a blue to yellow scale, so moving the slider to the left will make the image cooler (more blue) and to the right warmer (more yellow). In contrast the Tint slider is a green to magenta scale. Moving the slider left will add more green to the image and to the right more magenta.*

6. The White Balance tool *Another quick way to balance the light in your picture is to choose the White Balance tool and then click on a part of the picture that is meant to be neutral gray.*
ACR will automatically set the Temperature and Tint sliders so that this picture part becomes a neutral gray and in the process the rest of the image will be balanced. For best results when selecting lighter tones with the tool ensure that the area contains detail and is not a blown or specular highlight.

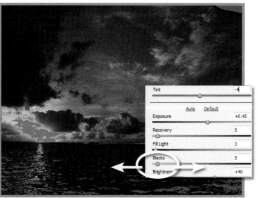

7. Setting the white areas *To start, adjust the brightness with the Exposure slider. Moving the slider to the right lightens the photo and to the left darkens it. The settings for the slider are in f-stop increments, with a +1.00 setting being equivalent to increasing exposure by 1 f-stop. Use this slider to peg or set the white tones. Your aim is to lighten the highlights in the photo without clipping (converting the pixels to pure white) them. To do this, hold down Alt/Option whilst moving the slider. This action previews the photo with the pixels being clipped against a black background. Move the slider back and forth until no clipped pixels appear but the highlights are as white as possible.*

8. Adjusting the shadows (blacks) *The Blacks or Shadows slider performs a similar function with the shadow areas of the image. Again the aim is to darken these tones but not to convert (or clip) delicate details to pure black. Just as with the Exposure slider, the Alt/Option key can be pressed whilst making Shadows adjustments to preview the pixels being clipped. Alternatively the Shadow and Highlights Clipping Warning features (top left and right corners of the histogram) can be used to provide instant clipping feedback on the preview image. Shadow pixels that are being clipped are displayed in blue and clipped highlight tones in red.*

9. Brightness changes *The next control, moving from top to bottom of the ACR dialog, is the Brightness slider. At first the changes you make with this feature may appear to be very similar to those produced with the Exposure slider but there is an important difference. Yes, it is true that moving the slider to the right lightens the whole image, but rather than adjusting all pixels the same amount the feature makes major changes in the midtone areas and smaller jumps in the highlights. In so doing the Brightness slider is less likely to clip the highlights (or shadows) as the feature compresses the highlights as it lightens the photo. This is why it is important to set white and black points first with the Exposure and Shadows sliders before fine-tuning the image with the Brightness control.*

10. Recovering highlights and shadow detail *If the highlights are still being clipped then use the Recovery slider to recreate detail in the problem area. Likewise if the shadow areas are too dark then drag the Fill Light slider to the right to lighten these tones in the photo. Be careful with over-application of either of these controls as it can make the image look low in contrast.*

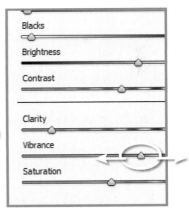

11. Increasing/decreasing contrast *The last tonal control in the dialog, and the last to be applied to the photo, is the Contrast slider. The feature concentrates on the midtones in the photo with movements of the slider to the right increasing the midtone contrast and to the left producing a lower contrast image. Like the Brightness slider, Contrast changes are best applied after setting the white and black points of the image with the Exposure and Blacks sliders.*

12. Local contrast control *The Clarity slider is used to alter the local contrast or the contrast of details within the photo. It works well with photos that have been photographed with diffused light or on a cloudy day. Use Clarity and Contrast sliders together. You can now also apply negative Clarity values to soften details or provide a diffused look to your images.*

13. Vibrance adjustment *Unlike the Saturation slider, which increases the strength of all colors in the photo irrespective of their strength in the first place, Vibrance targets its changes to just those colors that are desaturated. Use this control to boost the strength of colors in the photo with less risk of posterized results.*

14. Saturation control *The strength or vibrancy of the colors in the photo can be adjusted using the Saturation slider. Moving the slider to the right increases saturation, with a value of +100 being a doubling of the color strength found at a setting of 0. Saturation can be reduced by moving the slider to the left, with a value of -100 producing a monochrome image. Some photographers use this option as a quick way to convert their photos to black and white but most prefer to make this change in Photoshop Elements proper, where more control can be gained over the conversion process with features such as the Convert to Black & White.*

15. To sharpen or not to sharpen *The latest version of ACR contains four separate sharpening controls. Use the Amount slider to determine the overall strength of the sharpening effect. The Radius is used to control the number of pixels from an edge that will be changed in the sharpening process.*
The Detail and Masking sliders are both designed to help target the sharpening at the parts of the image that most need it (edges) and restrict the sharpening effects from being applied to areas that don't (skin tone and smooth graded areas). Moving the Detail slider to the right increases the local contrast surrounding edge areas and therefore enhances the appearance of details. Moving the slider to the left decreases the effect and also reduces the appearance of halos.
The Masking control interactively applies an edge locating mask to the sharpening process. A setting of 0 applies no mask and therefore all detail in the photo is sharpened. Moving the slider to the right gradually isolates the edges within the photo until, at a setting of 100, sharpening is only being applied to the most contrasty or dominant edges in the picture.

16. Reducing noise *ACR contains two different Noise Reduction controls. The Luminance Smoothing slider is designed to reduce the appearance of grayscale noise in a photo. This is particularly useful for improving the look of images that appear grainy.*
The second type of noise is the random colored pixels that typically appear in photos taken with a high ISO setting or a long shutter speed. This is generally referred to as chroma noise and is reduced using the Color Noise Reduction slider in ACR.
The noise reduction effect of both features is increased as the sliders are moved to the right.

17. Color depth *The section below the main preview window in ACR contains the output options settings. Here you can adjust the color depth (8 or 16 bits per channel) of the processed file. Earlier versions of Photoshop Elements were unable to handle 16 bits per channel images but the last two releases have contained the ability to read, open, save and make a few changes to these high color files.*

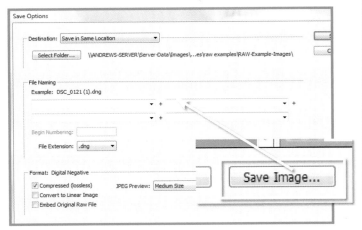

18. Opening the processed file in Photoshop Elements *The most basic option is to process the raw file according to the settings selected in the ACR dialog and then open the picture into the Editor workspace of Photoshop Elements. To do this simply select the Open Image button. Select this route if you intend to edit or enhance the image beyond the changes made during the conversion.*

19. Saving the processed raw file *Users also have the ability to save converted raw files from inside the ACR dialog via the Save Image button. This action opens the Save Options dialog which contains settings for inputting the file name as well as file type-specific characteristics such as compression. Use the Save option over the Open command if you want to process photos quickly without bringing them into the editing space.*

Pro's tip: *Holding down the Alt key whilst clicking the Save button allows you to store the file (with the raw processing settings applied) without actually going through the Save Options dialog*

20. Applying the raw conversion settings *There is also an option for applying the current settings to the raw photo without opening the picture. By Clicking the Done button (or Alt-clicking the OK button – holding down Alt key changes the button to the Update button in previous versions of the dialog), you can apply the changes to the original file and close the ACR dialog in one step.*
The great thing about working this way is that the settings are applied to the file losslessly. No changes are made to

the underlying pixels, only to the instructions that are used to process the raw file.
When next the file is opened, the applied settings will show up in the ACR dialog ready for fine-tuning, or even changing completely.

3.07 Keeping ACR up to date

Suitable for Elements – 7.0, 6.0, 5.0, 4.0, 3.0, 2.0, 1.0 | Difficulty level – Basic

The Adobe Camera Raw feature is installed as a plug-in inside Photoshop Elements when you first install the program. Periodically Adobe updates the feature releasing a new version that can be freely downloaded and installed. Typically the updates contain support for the latest digital camera models and occasionally new features and tools are included as well.

To download the latest ACR update point your browser to **www.adobe.com** (specifically http://www.adobe.com/products/photoshop/cameraRaw.html) and then look for the Adobe Camera Raw update page. Next download the latest version of the utility and install using these steps:

1. If Photoshop Elements is open exit the program.

2. Open the system drive (usually C:).

3. Locate the following directory:

   Program Files\Adobe\Photoshop Elements 7\ Plug-Ins\File Formats

4. Find the Adobe Camera Raw.8bi file in this folder.

5. Move the plug-in to another folder and note down its new location just in case you want to restore the original settings.

6. Drag the new version of the Adobe Camera Raw plug-in, the Adobe Camera Raw.8bi file (that you downloaded), to the same directory as in Step 3.

7. Restart Photoshop Elements.

3.08 Other Raw plug-ins

Suitable for Elements – 7.0, 6.0, 5.0, 4.0, 3.0, 2.0, 1.0 | Difficulty level – Basic

Often when installing the support software that was supplied with your digital camera an extra Raw utility is installed on your computer. This can mean that after installing the camera drivers you find that you no longer have access to Adobe Camera Raw and that instead the camera-based plug-in keeps appearing when you are attempting to open Raw files. If this occurs and you want to restore ACR as the default Raw utility then you will need to remove the camera-based plug-in from the plug-ins\Adobe Photoshop Elements 7\File Formats folder in Elements and add in the Adobe Camera Raw.8bi instead.

This is a problem that is often seen with Nikon users as the NEF.8bi plug-in designed to display and adjust Nikon Raw or NEF files takes precedence over the ACR utility.

4

Photo Organization and Management

Organizing your photos with Photoshop Elements

With no film or processing costs to think about each time we take a picture, it seems that many of us are pressing the shutter more frequently than we did when film was king. The results of such collective shooting frenzies are hard drives all over the country full of photos. Which is great for photography but what happens when you want to track down that once in a lifetime shot that just happens to be one of thousands stored on your machine? Well, believe it or not, being able to locate your files quickly and easily is more a task in organization, naming and camera set up than browsing through loads of thumbnails.

4.01 Add picture details in-camera

Suitable for Elements – 7.0, 6.0, 5.0, 4.0, 3.0, 2.0, 1.0 | Difficulty level – Basic
Related techniques – 4.02, 4.03, 4.04, 4.05

Getting those pesky picture files in order starts with your camera set up. Most models and makes have options for adjusting the numbering sequence that is used for the pictures you take. Generally you will have a choice between an ongoing sequence, where no two photos will have the same number, and one that resets each time you change memory cards or download all the pictures. In addition, many models provide an option for adding the current date to the file name, with some including customized comments (such as shoot location or photographer's name) in the naming sequence or as part of the metadata stored with the file.

In-camera labelling >> *Most cameras provide options for selecting the way in which files are numbered. The continuous option ensures that a new number is used for each picture even if memory cards are changed in the middle of a shoot.*

To adjust the settings on your camera search through the Set Up section of the camera's menu system for headings such as File Numbering and Custom Comments to locate and change the options. Ensure that number sequencing and date inclusion options are switched on and, where available, add these comments along with the photographer's name and copyright statement to the metadata stored within the picture file.

4.02 Organize photos while downloading

Suitable for Elements – 7.0, 6.0, 5.0, 4.0, 3.0 | Difficulty level – Basic | Related techniques – 4.01, 4.03, 4.04, 4.05

As we saw in the last chapter Photoshop Elements includes the Adobe Photo Downloader utility that moves pictures from your camera or memory card to the computer. As part of the download process, the user gets to select the location of the files and the way that the files are to be named and numbered, and automatically stack, tag and apply metadata to the photos.

It is at this point in the process that you need to be careful about the type of folder or directory structure that you use. Most photographers group their images by date, subject, location or client, but the approach that you employ is up to you. Once you have selected a folder structure though, try to stick with it. Consistency is the byword of photo organization.

If your camera doesn't provide enough Automatic Naming and metadata options to satisfy your needs then use the Elements Photo Downloader feature to enhance your ability to distinguish the current images with those that already exist on your hard drive by setting the location and filename of the picture files as you transfer them.

Naming via the downloader >> *Use the options in the Photo Downloader to thoughtfully locate (1) and name (2), your digital photos.*

 Nominate and create a new directory for each session of downloaded photos. Add extra metadata captions, keywords, photographer and copyright details using the tagging options in Elements.

You can select from a range of different naming schemes in the Rename drop-down menu.

A variety of names for any subfolders that are created for the downloaded photos can also be selected. Choosing the Custom Groups (Advanced) option redisplays the thumbnails in groups based on setting of the Slider control.

Automatically add files to a Photoshop Elements Album using the new Import to Album option.

Organize as you download >> *The Adobe Photo Downloader allows the user to automatically apply naming changes, metadata, group tags, suggest photo stacks and determine the location where transferred files will be saved. The downloader features provide five different ways to organize your pictures: (1) Locating existing, or creating new, folders for downloading. (2) Renaming pictures with meaningful titles. (3) Suggesting Photo Stack groupings. (4) Applying Group Custom Name as a Tag. (5) Adding custom metadata to the picture file which can be used as search criteria inside the Organizer workspace. New for Photoshop Elements 7.0 is the ability to add photos to an Album as they are being downloaded.*

Organizing using Photo Browser

The Photo Browser mode in the Organizer workspace not only provides thumbnail previews of your photos but the images can be categorized with different Keyword Tags, Notes and Caption entries, split in different Albums (previously Collections) and then searched based on the Keyword Tags, shot date and Metadata associated with each photo. Unlike a traditional browser system, which is folder based (i.e. it displays thumbnails of the images that are physically stored in the folder), the Elements Photo Browser creates a catalog version of the pictures and uses these as the basis for searches and organization. With this approach it is possible for one picture to be a member of many different collections and to contain a variety of different keywords.

Adding captions to several photos >>
After multi-selecting pictures in the Photo Browser workspace press the Change Caption option located in the Properties palette and then add the new caption in the dialog that is displayed. These captions can be added to or used to replace existing captions.

4.03 Captioning

Suitable for Elements – 6, 5.0, 4.0, 3.0 | Difficulty level – Basic | Related techniques – 4.01, 4.02, 4.04, 4.05

Captions are another way to 'title' your photos beyond the standard file name. Adding a meaningful caption provides yet another avenue for searching for individual photos as the Find > Find by Caption or Note feature targets the entries you make here. Captions can also be used, printed or displayed in Photo Projects (but need to be added before starting the creation process) and Online Galleries as well as on contact sheets. In Photoshop Elements 6.0 captions can be added and used in a range of different ways.

Adding a single caption – Captions can be added in the Single Photo View of the Photo Browser, the Properties pane (General tab), via the Add Caption command or in the Caption field in the Date View.

Adding multiple captions – Multi-select the images to be captioned and press the Change Caption button in the Properties palette, add in the caption details and click OK.

4.04 Naming and renaming

Suitable for Elements – 6, 5.0, 4.0, 3.0 | Difficulty level – Basic | Related techniques – 4.02, 4.03, 4.04, 4.05

Along with captioning, adding logical file names to photos is probably the most popular way that photographers organize their pictures. If the downloading utility that you use doesn't provide the opportunity to rename on-the-fly, the file titles can be changed either individually, via the Name section of the Properties palette, or as a group, using the Editor: File > Rename feature or as a group in the Editor using the File Renaming section of Process Multiple Files (File > Process Multiple Files). Be sure to use a unique name for your photos and preferably one that will help you locate them later.

Changing names >> *Rename a file by selecting its thumbnail in the Photo Browser workspace and then clicking on the General tab in the Properties palette. Type in the new title for the file in the Name section of the dialog that is displayed.*

Pro's Tip: Renaming as you download

As we saw in the previous section Elements ships with a specialised transfer utility called the Adobe Photo Downloader. Designed to make the process of transferring photos from your camera, or memory card reader, more efficient, this utility also contains options for renaming of files as they are being downloaded. Here we will take a closer look at the renaming feature and, in particular, the different naming schemes that are possible.

The download contains the option of two dialogs – Standard and Advanced dialog. Both contain a drop down Rename Files menu. The renaming options revolve around three key pieces of data – the current date, the shot date, a custom name and a sub-folder name. Each menu entry uses a different combination or sequence of these details. Elements users have the choice of 21 different naming schema. Unfortunately APD doesn't include the option to create your own customized naming schema, or Template, as is available in Lightroom's own transfer utility.

It is good to see that when dates are part of the renaming process that Adobe has thought to include both US and UK based date formats. It is also very handy to have the option to include the original filename stored in the XMP data associated with the photo. XMP data is searchable via the new Search option in the Organizer's shortcuts bar.

Renaming via the downloader >> *Elements users can retitle photos as they are downloading them via the Rename Files setting in the Adobe Photo Downloader utility.*

Step-by-step APD renaming:

Using a the Subfolder name

1. To create some consistency across your naming scheme some photographers will use the same title for both the download folder and the images contained within it. To do this start by selecting the Custom Name option in the Create Subfolder drop down menu.

2. Next input the title you wish to use in the text box directly below the Custom Name entry. This action sets the name of the folder that will be created on your hard drive and used to store the transferred photos.

3. Now select the Same as Subfolder Name entry from the options in the Rename Files drop down menu. APD will automatically insert the Subfolder custom name in the Rename Files text box. You still have the option to choose a different starting value for the sequential number by inputting this number in the box to the right of the text.

4. Finally, double check that the naming scheme provides the results that you expect by looking at the Example entry at the bottom of the Rename Files area. This text should display the subfolder custom name, the sequential number and the file extension.

Renaming Option	Action	Original Name	After Renaming
Do not rename files	Keeps the name allocated by the camera set up	DSC_0269.NEF	DSC_0269.NEF
Today's Date (yyyymmdd)	Substitutes the computer's date	DSC_0269.NEF	20070812_001.NEF
Shot Date (yyyymmdd)	Substitutes the shot date as determined by the camera	DSC_0269.NEF	20070810_001.NEF
Shot Date (yyddmm)	Substitutes shot date with the year noted in two digits	DSC_0269.NEF	070810_001.NEF
Shot Date (ddmmyy)	Substitutes shot date in UK date format	DSC_0269.NEF	100807_001.NEF
Shot Date (ddmm)	Substitutes shot date with only day and month recorded	DSC_0269.NEF	1008_001.NEF
Shot Date (yyyyddmmm)	Substitutes shot date with four digit year, two digit date and a three letter month	DSC_0269.NEF	200710Aug_001.NEF
Shot Date (ddmmmyyyy)	Substitutes shot date with the same details above but using the UK Date format	DSC_0269.NEF	10Aug2007_001.NEF
Custom Name	Changes the file name to one that the user has entered	DSC_0269.NEF	Jills_Birthday_001.NEF

Example renaming settings >> *With 21 different ways to change the names of your photos when download-ing it can be hard to know where to start. Here are some examples of the type of changes possible.*

Using a Custom name

1. To substitute a custom name for the one al-located by the camera choose the Custom Name option from the Rename Files drop down menu.

2. Next input the title you wish to use in the text box directly below the Custom Name entry. At

this point you can also add a starting number for the numbering sequence that will be used if more than one image is to be renamed. Here the value is set to 58.

3. Double check that the naming scheme provides the results that you expect by looking at the Example entry at the bottom of the Rename Files area. This text should display the custom name, the sequential number and the file extension.

4.05 Tagging your photos

Suitable for Elements – 7.0, 6.0, 5.0, 4.0, 3.0 | Difficulty level – Basic | Related techniques – 4.01, 4.02, 4.03, 4.05

In Elements descriptive words can be added to your photos in the form of Keyword Tags. The Keyword Tags panel stores the entries, provides an easy drag and drop approach to adding tags to selected photos and sits on the right of the Photo Browser workspace. The panel is grouped together with the Albums (previously Collections), Quick Share and Properties panels in the new Organize pane. Tags are applied to a picture by selecting and dragging them from the pane onto the thumbnail or alternatively the thumbnail can be dragged directly onto the Tags pane. Multiple Tags can be attached to a single picture by multi-selecting the Tags first and then dragging them to the appropriate thumbnail.

FEATURE SUMMARY

1. To add a Tag to a single image click-drag the tag entry from the Keyword Tags panel to the thumbnail image in the browser (Organizer) workspace.

2. To add a single Tag to multiple thumbnails, multi-select the thumbnails in the workspace and then drag the Tag entry from the pane onto one of the selected thumbnails.

Creating new Keyword Tags

New Keyword Tags are created and added to the pane by selecting the New Keyword Tag option from the menu displayed after pressing the New button (+ icon) at the top left of the pane. Next, fill out the details of the new entry in the Create Keyword Tag dialog, select a suitable icon for the Keyword Tag label and click OK. The first picture that you drag to the new tag determines the thumbnail you see on the Tag. This is the quickest way to add an image to the Tag icon.

Keyword Tags and Albums >> *Keyword Tags and Albums (Collections) are used to organize the pictures in the Organizer workspace. One photo can belong to many different Albums and contain multiple Keyword Tags.*

Book resources and video tutorials can be found at **www.photoshopelements.net**

PHOTO ORGANIZATION
AND MANAGEMENT

1. To create a new Keyword Tag, select the New
    Tag option from the New Button (+ icon)
    menu at the top of the Tags pane.

2. In the Create Keyword Tag dialog that is
    displayed, select a category for the Tag, add in
    a name and include any explanatory notes.

3. Next press the Edit Icon button and import for
    a picture to include the Tag label before sizing
    and cropping the photo in the Edit Tag Icon
    dialog.

4. Click OK to close both dialogs and add the
    new entry to the Keyword Tag list.

Make a new Tag >> *You can add to the
existing set of Tags using the New Tag
option. There is even an option to add your
own pictures as the Tag icon.*

4.06 Auto Face Tagging

Suitable for Elements – 7.0, 6.0, 5.0, 4.0, 3.0 | Difficulty level – Basic | Related techniques – 4.05

First introduced in version 5.0 was the ability to search through a group of photos and automatically select those that contain faces. Using this feature makes it much easier to locate and tag
photos of family and friends in the batches of pictures that you import. Start by selecting a group
of photos from inside the Organizer workspace. Next, click the Find Faces for Tagging button in
the Tags pane. The faces identified will be displayed in a new dialog box which also includes the
Tags pane. From here your Keyword Tags can be quickly dragged onto individual or groups of
selected face photos.

1. Multi-select a group of images from inside the Organizer workspace.

2. Either choose Find > Find Faces for Tagging or press the Find Faces for Tagging button
    at the top of the Keyword Tags pane.

3. Drag Tags onto the pictures that are displayed in the Face Tagging dialog. Click Done to
    return to the Photo Browser workspace.

Tagging by faces >>
*The Face Tagging option
in Elements 6 quickly
scans a group of
selected photos and
identifies those pictures
that contain faces then
displays these in a
separate dialog ready
for tagging.
(1) Organizer pane.*

4.07 Albums and how to group photos

Suitable for Elements – 7.0, 6.0, 5.0, 4.0, 3.0 | Difficulty level – Basic | Related techniques – 4.11, 4.12

Apart from tagging, Photoshop Elements also uses Albums (previously called Collections) as a way to organize your photos. Albums allow you to group images of a similar theme together in the one place making it easier to locate these images at a later date. After creating an Album in the Albums pane, photos can be dragged from the Photo Browser workspace to the Album heading to be added to the group, or alternatively the Album entry can be dragged to the photo to produce the same result. The Albums feature allows you to allocate the same image to several different groups. Unlike in the old days, this doesn't mean that the same file is duplicated and stored multiple times in different folders. Instead the picture is only stored or saved once and a series of Album associations is used to indicate its membership in different groups.

When you want to display the contents of an Album just click the entry in the pane and the program searches through its database of collection keywords and only shows those images that meet your search criteria. The Albums pane is the pivot point for all your grouping activities. Here you can view, create, rename and delete Albums. Albums are part of the Organize pane, which you can show by choosing Window > Show Task Pane then clicking the blue Organize tab. Alternatively, the Task Pane can be hidden or shown by clicking on the vertical resize bar on the left edge of the pane.

In Elements 7.0 Albums can be synchronized/backed up online via an active Photoshop.com account.

Grouping with Albums >> *Sort your pictures into groups of the same subject or theme using the Elements' Albums feature. (1) Album Pane.*

Adding photos to an Album

To start using Albums make a new Album entry first and then add your photos to it.

1. Start making a new Album by clicking on the New button (+ icon) in the Albums pane and select the New Album menu item. In the Create Album dialog choose the group that the new album will belong to, add the name and include any explanation details for the group. Click OK.

2. Select the photos to be included in the album in the Photo Browser and drag them to the Album heading in the Albums pane.

3. To view all the pictures contained in an album double-click on the Album heading or click near the album's thumbnail. A Binoculars icon will appear.

4. Single photos or even groups of pictures can be added to more than one album at a time by multi-selecting the album names first (use Ctrl–click to multi-select Albums without displaying their contents) before dragging the images to the pane.

Using Album groups

Different albums (and the photos they contain) can also be organized into groups that have a common interest or theme. For instance, albums that contain pictures of the kids, family vacations, birthday parties and mother- and father's-days events can all be collated under a single 'Family' Album Group heading.

Create an Album group by selecting the New Album Group option from the New menu (+ icon) in the Album Pane. Next, click-drag existing album entries listed in the pane to the Album Group heading. Alternatively, create the Album Group entry first and then create new albums selecting the new Album Group in the Create Album dialog. This will automatically add the new Album under the group heading in the Album pane.

The Album Advantage

The advantage of using an album over just viewing tagged files in the Photo Browser is that files in an album can be reordered by dragging them. Each member image of the Album is displayed with a small sequence number in the upper left of the thumbnail indicating the position in the Album order. The image sequence arranged in an Album is respected when the photos are used in the production of Elements' creation projects such as Photo Books, Online Albums and Slide Shows. Files in the Photo Browser window cannot be reordered in this way.

Sequencing with Albums >>
Placing images in an Album has the advantage that the photos can be arranged in a set sequence. The power of this ability is that the order is respected when the photos are incorporated into Elements projects.

Pro's Tip: Add photos to Albums as you download

Many photographers see the task of organizing their photos with features such as keywords and albums as tasks that just detract from the real work of editing and enhancing the images. It's true that that image management is not nearly as exciting as creating, editing and printing photos but you will quickly find that a little time spent arranging your photos will reap rewards later when you are trying to locate the best of your images.

For this reason, I always rejoice when Adobe adds an auto option to Elements that makes my management tasks less painful. New for Photoshop Elements is the ability to add photos to Albums as they are transferred from camera card to computer. This is terrific as, used

Auto Album addition >> *Use the new Import into Album option available in the Advanced dialog of the Adobe Photo Downloader to add the files you transfer to specific Elements Albums.*

correctly, this new feature can save you loads of time that you would use to manually add images to albums. The new Import to Album feature is located in the Advanced dialog of the Adobe Photo Downloader and is used in the following way:

1. After selecting the Import Into Album option in the Advanced dialog of the Adobe Photo Downloader, press the Settings button to display the Select an Album window.

2. Here you can choose which Album to add the photos to. The window also contains buttons to add new tags, edit the name of tags and delete tags. The edit and delete options are only available when selecting empty Albums that have been added in the window.

3. After setting up a new Album for the download, clicking OK will close the Settings window and Get Photos will download the pictures and add them to the new Album.

4. If you only want a selection of all the images stored in the camera, or located on the memory card, to be added to a specific album, then use the checkbox at the bottom right of each thumbnail to include or exclude the photo from both download and being added to the album.

4.08 Using Smart Albums

Suitable for Elements – 7.0, 6.0, 5.0, 4.0, 3.0 | Difficulty level – Basic | Related techniques – 4.06, 4.07

Adobe introduced a new album type in Photoshop Elements 6.0 called Smart Albums. Images are included in a Smart Album based on one or more search criteria established at the time that the album is created. Each time the Smart Album entry is selected Elements automatically adds any new photos that meet the criteria to the group. Smart Albums are a great way to keep important collections of images up to date without the need to manually find and add images to the album.

You can create Smart Albums either via the New Smart Album entry in the new album pop-up menu (click the '+' button at the top of the panel to display), or by executing a search using the Find > By Details (Metadata) feature. Both avenues provide the user with the chance to choose the search criteria used for the basis of the Smart Album. With the Find > By Details option, it is necessary to select the Save this Search Criteria as Smart Album setting at the bottom of the dialog before starting the search.

Establishing search criteria

The idea of setting up specific search criteria as the basis of creating a Smart Album may seem a little daunting, but the range of possibilities included in the search dialog, either New Smart Album, or the Find by Details, makes the process as simple as selecting options from several drop-down menus. With the dialog open, start by choosing if the photos need to contain any, or all, of the search criteria to be included in the album. Obviously for single criteria searches this isn't an issue, but the dialog allows the user to add several criteria (click the '+' button at the right end of the criteria entry) for searching. Next, create the basis for the search by selecting the criteria.

There are no less than 30 different criteria that can be used for the search. These include most camera settings (sometimes called EXIF data) such as lens, ISO, F-stop and Shutter Speed, individual photo details including file size, pixel dimensions and filename as well as Elements-specific criteria like keyword tags, project name, version set, project type or even map location. Once you are comfortable with creating search criteria the whole Smart Album system provides a very powerful and efficient way to locate and manage groups of images in your catalog.

Smart Album creation >> *To set up the search criteria used for a Smart Album pick the matching option first (1) and then the criteria from the drop-down menus (2).*

Creating a new Smart Album

There are three ways to create Smart Albums in Elements. The first is via the options in the Album panel.

1. Start by selecting the New Smart Album entry from the menu displayed by clicking on the '+' button in the Albums panel.

2. Next, add in a name for the album in the text box at the top of the New Smart Album dialog.

3. Choose how the files will match the criteria. You can select between matching **any** of the criteria or **all** of the criteria.

4. Now start with the drop-down menu on the left of the dialog and select the criteria group to use for the search, i.e. Filename, Project Name, Keyword Tags, Camera Model, etc.

5. Depending which entry you choose in the first menu the number of menus (and their content) on the right will change accordingly. The entries in these menus are designed to refine the search. For instance, if you choose the Project Type as your main search criteria then you will have a second menu containing Gallery, Photo Book and Slideshow.

6. With one criteria established you can add other criteria by clicking the '+' button on the right of the Search entry. This displays a new search criteria menu set.

Using Find to make Smart Albums

The second way to create Smart Albums in Elements is to use the search abilities in the Find > By Details (Metadata).

FEATURE SUMMARY

1. Select the By Metadata entry from the Find menu to display the Find by Details dialog. Input the match option and search criteria in the same way as outlined in steps 3–6 above.

2. Next, select the Save this Search Criteria as Smart Album option at the bottom of the dialog. This makes the Name text box active. Add a title for the New Smart Album here.

The best way that you choose to make use of the Keyword Tagging and Album features in Elements will depend a great deal on the way that you work, the pictures you take and the type of content that they include, but here a few different proven methods that you can use as a starting point.

Subject:

Photos are broken down into subject groups using headings such as family, friends, holidays, work, summer, night shots, trip to Paris, etc. This is the most popular and most applicable approach for most readers and should be the method to try first.

Time line:

Images are sorted and stored based on their capture date (when the picture was photographed), the day they were downloaded or the date that they were imported into the organizational package. This way of working links well with the auto file naming functions available with most digital cameras but can be problematic if you can't remember the approximate dates that important events

occurred. Try using the date approach as a sub-category for subjects headings, e.g. Bill's Birthday > 2005.

File type:

Image groups are divided into different file type groups. Although this approach may not seem that applicable at first glance it is a good way to work if you are in the habit of shooting RAW files which are then processed into PSD files before use.

Project:

This organizational method works well for the photographer who likes to shoot to a theme over an extended period of time. All the project images, despite their age and file type, are collated in the one spot making for ease of access.

Client or Job:

Many working pros prefer to base their filing system around the way that their business works, keeping separate groups for each client and each job undertaken for each client.

Naming, Album and Tagging strategies

Smart Albums via the new Search feature

The Adobe guys decided to include a new Search feature in the shortcuts bar at the top of the Organizer workspace. Like other such features typically found in computer operating systems this dedicated search box provides a speedy way to locate images based on a text entries associated with an image. This information may be stored in the filename, as a keyword or as part of the EXIF data for the photo.

Elements refines the results of the search as you type. Locating pictures in this way has the added bonus that the search term that you employed can be used to create a new Smart Album.

1 Start by typing the search term into the new text box located on the left of the Shortcuts bar. You may need to try a range of different search terms.

Search results become Albums >> Use the criteria for the new search feature as the basis of a new Smart Album.

2　Once the correct photos are displayed in the Organizer workspace choose the Save Search Criteria As Smart Album entry from the Options menu,

Converting Keyword Tags to Smart Albums

The last way to create Smart Albums is to use existing Keyword Tags as the basis for creating a new Smart Album.

1　After clicking the Keyword Tag entry to display the images containing the tag, choose the Save Search Criteria As Smart Album entry from the Options menu at the top left of the workspace.

FEATURE SUMMARY

Keywords become Albums >> Click onto the Keyword Tag entry to display the pictures with the associated keyword then choose the Save Search Criteria As Smart Album entry from the Options menu.

4.09 Synchronizing and Backing Up Albums

Suitable for Elements – 7.0 | Difficulty level – Medium | Related techniques – 4.07, 4.08

In Photoshop Elements 7.0, Adobe introduces a new option for synchronizing the albums you create in the Organizer workspace with copies stored at Photoshop.com. This feature means that not only can you share your Elements pictures via the web using the Online Albums, but you also have a secure backup of your photos as well. Now before we start, it is important to realize a couple of facts about working with synchronized albums:

* You need to have an active Photoshop.com account before being able to backup/synchronize your photos,

* Smart Albums cannot be synchronized,

* The Web Galleries feature found in previous versions of Elements has been replaced by 'Online Albums' which is part of the new synchronized album feature, and

* You need a good internet connect if you are wanting to sync more than just a few pictures.

Signing up for a Photoshop.com account is an easy process and can be initiated from either the Photoshop Elements 7.0 Welcome Screen or by visiting Photoshop.com. There are two levels of membership, Standard, which provides the user with webspace, a dedicated web address (URL), tutorials and access to the features of the website and online links from inside Photoshop Elements, and Plus, which gives the user more storage space for photos and albums and extra tutorials, artwork and themes for use with Elements' projects. Once you have signed up, you can log in at the home screen each time you start Elements, which in turn will give you access to all the features of the Photoshop.com website.

Synchronizing Photoshop.com and Photoshop Elements >> New for version 7.0 is the ability to synchronize/backup Elements' albums to Photoshop.com. In the screenshots above you can see the Album list from Elements (1) duplicated in the Photoshop.com account (2). Synchronized Albums can be created in Elements or online.

Rather than synchronizing your whole Photoshop Elements Catalog, the new synchronization system uses Albums which are common to both Photoshop.com and the Organizer. The Welcome screen in version 7.0 contains a series of new online options that are available to registered Elements users. One of these options is titled Backup Settings. Clicking this entry will display the Backup/Synchronization section of the Elements' Preferences dialog. This window can also be displayed by selecting the Preferences entry from the Edit screen in the Organizer workspace or by clicking the Backup/Synchronization preferences button at the top of the Albums pane.

The settings contained here allow you to turn the synchronization feature on and off, choose for all new albums to synchronized online by default, options for resolving synchronization conflicts and scenarios when you delete photos online as well as maximum size files included in the synchronization process. The dialog also provides a visual summary of the albums that are currently stored in both locations and whether they are synchronized, a space usage meter and the option to upgrade your membership to access more backup space and exclusive Elements tips and techniques.

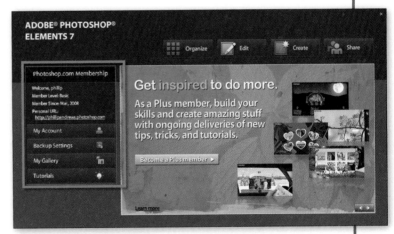

Sign In at the Home Screen >> You can sign up and sign in to use the new online options available in version 7.0 of Photoshop Elements at the Home screen that is displayed when first starting the program. Here you have options for adjusting you account and backup (synchronization) settings as well as quick links to any web galleries you are hosting at Photoshop.com. The last option available at the Home screen is a link to the new Inspirational Browser where authors like myself post video and step by step tutorials about how to get the most out of Elements.

Creating a Synchronized Album

1. Start by selecting the New Album entry from the menu displayed by clicking on the '+' button in the Albums panel.

2. Next, add in a name for the album in the text box at the top of the New Album dialog.

3. Select the Backup/Synchronize option.

4. Complete the rest of the dialog settings, drag images from the Photo Browser workspace to the Items area and click the Done button to finish.

5. Alternatively, click the Share button to create a styled web gallery from the images in the new album.

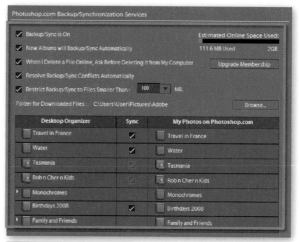

Synchronization settings >> The options for the new backup feature are grouped together in the Backup/Synchronization Services section of the Photoshop Elements Preferences.

When the backup/synchronization feature is active on your computer a new icon is added to your system tray. Called the Sync Monitor, right-clicking on the icon will display several options which indicate the current status of the feature. If the Pause or Stop entries are shown, then the sync system is currently active. Choosing the Backup/Sync only when Idle option restricts update activity (which occurs via an active internet connection) to times when the connection is not being used by other programs such as a web browser or email program. There is also another version of the Sync Monitor located in the bottom left of the Organizer workspace. Here there are options for viewing backup, not backed files as well as those that are waiting ('pending') to be backup.

4.10 Changing your view

*Suitable for Elements – 7.0, 6.0, 5.0, 4.0, 3.0 | Difficulty level – Basic
Related techniques – 4.11*

Your photos can be viewed in a range of different ways in the Organizer or Photo Browser workspace. The standard view (**Photo Browser View**) displays the pictures as a series of thumbnails in a 'rows and columns' format. You can sort the sequence of the photos according to date and import batch or folder location using the drop-down menu at the bottom left of the workspace. It is also possible to display only those images with a specific associated Tag or belonging to a particular collection by double-clicking on the entry in Keyword Tags or Albums or clicking on the column on the left of the palette.

Selecting the View >> Choosing one of the options from the drop-down Display menu at the end of the Photo Browser options bar, determines how the pictures are presented in the workspace.

Another option is to view the photos in **Date View** mode. Here the images are also grouped and displayed based on the date they were taken, but they are shown in a calendar format. You can choose a year-, month- or day-based calendar with each view containing a slide show feature that will automatically flick through all the photos taken on a specific date. Pictures displayed in Date View can be edited, printed, shared and included in Photo Creation projects by clicking one of the shortcut buttons at the top of the screen.

Photo Browser View >>

The **View Photos in Full Screen** option provides an instant slide show of the files that you have currently displayed in the Photo Browser. Seeing the photos full size on your machine is a good way to edit the shots you want to keep from those that should be placed in the 'I will remember not to do that next time' bin. With the provided menu you can play, pause, or advance to next or last photos, using the VCR-like controls. You can enlarge or reduce the size that the picture appears on screen with the Magnification slider (Zoom Level control). For quick magnification changes there are also 'Fit to Window' and 'Actual Pixels' buttons. But the real bonus of the feature is the list of actions that you can perform to pictures you review. You can automatically enhance, add and remove tags, mark the file for printing and add the file to a chosen collection using the choices listed under the Action menu. Specific picture properties such as Tag, History, and Metadata are available by hitting the Alt + Enter keys to display the properties window. As well as showing all the photos currently in the browser you can also multi-select the images to include in the review session before starting the feature, or even limit those pictures displayed to a particular collection. The Full Screen View options can be set when the feature is first opened or accessed via the last item on the Action menu.

Date View >>

View Photos in Full Screen mode >>

Closely linked to the View Photos in Full Screen feature detailed above is the **Compare Photos Side by Side** option which allows users to display two similar pictures side by side. This is a great way to choose

Compare Photos Side by Side mode >>

between several images taken at the same time to ensure that the best one is used for printing or passed on to the Editor for enhancement. To select the images to display click onto one of the compare workspaces and then click on a thumbnail. Now select the other workspace and click the comparison image thumbnail. Pressing the X key switches the photos in the display so that you can always keep the best images on the left of the screen as you flip through other photos on the right. All the same Full Screen adjustment and organizational controls are available in the Compare Photos feature, including the Zoom Control which provides the ability to examine candidate files more closely.

Locate by filename >> *When choosing the Date Range, Caption or Note, Filename (see above), History, and Details find options Elements displays a new dialog into which your search criteria can be entered.*

Find options >> *The Find menu in the Photo Browser workspace lists the many different ways to locate images within Elements.*

4.11 Locating files

Suitable for Elements – 7.0, 6.0, 5.0, 4.0, 3.0 | Difficulty level – Basic | Related techniques – 4.08

One of the great benefits of organizing your pictures in the Photo Browser workspace is the huge range of search options that then become available to you. In fact there are so many search options that Adobe created a new menu heading 'Find' specifically to hold all the choices. Here you will be able to search for your photos based on a selected date range, filename, caption, media type (video, photo, audio or creation), history (when an item was emailed, printed, received, imported, used in a creation project or even shared on-line) and even by the predominant color in the photo. After selecting one of the Find menu options Elements either displays files that meet the search criteria in a new view of the same window (Find by Version Sets, Media Type, Untagged Items) or opens a new dialog where the user must enter specific details (dates, filenames, details, captions) which will be used to base the search.

Locate tagged photos >> *To display all images tagged with a specific entry, click the Tag name in the Tags pane. Return the view to the whole collection by clicking the Show All photos button (1).*

Finding tagged photos or those contained in an Album

As well as the search options located in the Organizer: Find menu, you can make use of the Keyword Tags and Albums features to quickly locate and display sets of photos from your catalog.

To find tagged photos: Click the Keyword Tag entry in the Keyword Tags pane.

To display all the images in a collection: Click on the Album entry in the Albums pane or click on the column on the left of the pane. This will display the Binoculars icon.

To return the browser back to the original catalog of thumbnails: Click on the Show All Photos button at the top of the thumbnail group.

Finding Albums >> *To show all the photos in an album click the Album name in the Album Pane. Again, press the Show All Photos button to return to the catalog (1).*

Find by details or metadata

Version 6.0 of Elements also contains a Find option that is designed to allow users to search the details or metadata that is attached to their picture files. Most digital cameras automatically store shooting details from the time of capture within the photo document itself. Called metadata, you can view this information by clicking the Metadata button inside the Properties palette.

The Find > By Details (Metadata) option displays a sophisticated Search dialog that allows you to nominate specific criteria to use when looking within the metadata portion of the picture file. The dialog provides a section to input the text to search for as well as two drop-down menus where you can set where to look (Filename, Camera Make, Camera Model, Capture Date, etc.) and how to match the search text (Starts with, Ends with, Contains, etc.).

Beyond camera-based metadata you can also use this dialog to search for any Captions, Notes, Keyword Tags or Albums that you have applied to your pictures.

1. Select Find > By Details (Metadata) from the Photo Browser workspace.
2. Choose the type of details that you are looking for – Filename, Camera Make, Camera Model, etc. from the drop-down list in the Find by Details dialog.
3. Enter the text you want to search for (if needed).
4. Enter how the search text should appear in the located files (contained, not contained, etc.)

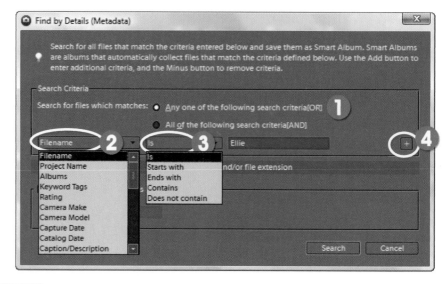

Find using details >> *The Find by Details feature allows you to customize the search options used via settings within the dialog. Choosing the type of detail to look for from the drop-down list (1) determines the contents of the rest of the dialog. In this instance selecting 'Filename' displays a second list (2) describing how to match the text you input (3). Extra search criteria can be added or removed by pressing the Plus or Minus buttons to the right of the dialog (4).*

Protecting your assets

Ensuring that you keep up-to-date duplicates of all your important pictures is one of the smartest work habits that the digital photographer can learn. Ask yourself 'What images can't I afford to lose – either emotionally or financially?' The photos you include in your answer are those that are in the most need of backing up. If you are like most image-makers then every picture you have ever taken (good and bad) has special meaning and therefore is worthy of inclusion. So let's assume that you want to secure all the photos you have accumulated.

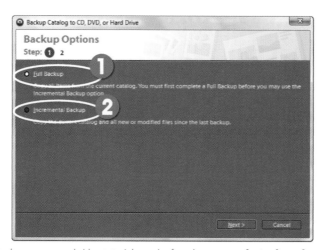

Backup files >>
The first screen of the Elements' Backup feature contains the choice of two different actions:

(1) Full Backup – This option is for first time use. It will create an archive for the full catalog.

(2) Incremental Backup – Once you have created a full backup then it is only necessary to copy changed or new files to the backup in order to keep the archive current. The incremental option is designed specifically for this purpose.

4.12 Creating a backup

Suitable for Elements – 7.0, 6.0, 5.0, 4.0, 3.0 | Difficulty level – Basic | Related techniques – 4.09

Gone are the days when creating a backup of your work involved costly tape hardware and complex server software. Now you can archive your pictures from inside the very software that you use to enhance them – Photoshop Elements.

The Backup feature (Organizer: File > Backup Catalog to CD, DVD or Hard Drive) is designed for copying your pictures (and catalog files) onto DVD, CD or an external hard drive for archiving purposes. To secure your work simply follow the steps in the wizard. The feature includes the option to backup all the photos you currently have cataloged in the Photo Browser and then just copy changed files for successive backups.

1. To start the backup process select File > Backup Catalog to CD, DVD or Hard Drive from the Photo Browser workspace.

2. At the next screen choose **Full Backup** for first time archiving or **Incremental Backup** for all backups after the first one. Click Next.

3. And finally select the place where you want the backup to be stored. This may be on a series of CDs or DVDs, an internal or external drive. Then click Done to backup your files.

Backup glossary

Multi-disk archive – A process, often called spanning, by which chunks of data that are larger than one disk can be split up and saved to multiple CD-ROMs or DVDs using spanning software. The files can be recompiled later using utility software supplied by the same company that wrote the disks.

Full backup – Duplicates all files even if they haven't changed since the last time an archive was produced.

Incremental – Backs up only those files that have changed since the last archive was produced. This makes for faster backups but means that it takes longer to restore files as the program must look for the latest version of files before restoring them.

Restore – Reinstates files from a backup archive to their original state on your hard drive.

CD-ROM or DVD writer – This option is very economical when coupled with writing software that is capable of writing large numbers of files over multiple disks. The sets of archive disks can easily be stored off site insuring you against theft and fire problems but the backup and restore process of this approach can be long and tedious.

Internal hard drive – Adding an extra hard drive inside your computer that can be used for backing up provides a fast and efficient way to archive your files but won't secure them against theft, fire or even some electrical breakdowns such as power surges.

External hard drive – Connect via USB or Firewire, these external self-contained units are both fast and efficient and can also be stored off site providing good all-round protection. Some, like the Maxtor One Touch models, are shipped with their own backup software. Keep in mind that these devices are still mechanical drives and that care should be taken when transporting them.

Backup hardware

Backup regularly

There is no point having duplicate versions of your data if they are out of date. Base the interval between backups on the amount of work you do. In heavy periods when you are downloading, editing and enhancing many images at a time backup more often; in the quieter moments you won't need to duplicate files as frequently. Most professionals backup on a daily basis or at the conclusion of a work session.

Store the duplicates securely

In ensuring the security of your images you will not only need to protect you photos from the possibility of a hard drive crash but also from such dramatic events as burglary and fire. Do this by storing one copy of your files securely at home and an extra copy of your archive disks or external backup drives somewhere other than your home or office. I know that this may sound a little extreme but swapping archive disks with a friend who is just as passionate about protecting their images will prove to be less painful than losing all your hard work.

Multi-disk and multi-session backups

From version 5.0 the Backup Catalog feature was enhanced so that it was possible to archive your catalog over a series of CD or DVD disks. In previous versions, the Backup feature only allowed writing to a single disk and even with the growing use of DVD-ROMs for archive scenarios, many digital photographers have a catalog of photos that far exceeds the space available on a single disk. The feature can estimate the space required for creating the backup copy of the catalog and, after selecting the drive that will be used for archiving, the feature also determines the number of disks required to complete the action. During the writing process the feature displays instruction windows at the end of writing each disk and when you need to insert a new disk. All disks need to be written for the backup to be complete. To restore a catalog from a set of backup disks use the File > Restore Catalog from CD, DVD or Hard Drive option in the Organizer workspace.

The backup feature also allows multi-session recording of archives. Multi-session DVD or CD-ROM recording means that you can add extra backup files to disks that you have already recorded to. Most Elements users will find this useful when performing incremental backups.

The online archive option that was included with version 5.0, called Online Backup; is no longer available. In its place is the much more sophisticated Synchronized/Backup Albums features found in Photoshop Elements 7.0.

Adobe Photoshop Elements

ⓘ Please insert Disc 2 to continue.

[Burn Disc 2]   [Cancel]

4.13 Versioning your edits

Suitable for Elements – 7.0, 6.0, 5.0, 4.0, 3.0 | Difficulty level – Basic | Related techniques – 4.07, 4.12

Creating a good archival system goes a long way to making sure that the images you create are well protected, but what about the situation where the original photo is accidentally overwritten as part of the editing process? Embarrassing as it is, even I have to admit that sometimes I can get so involved in a series of complex edits that I inadvertently save the edited version of my picture over the top of the original. For most tasks this is not a drama as the edits I make are generally non-destructive (applied with adjustment layers and the like) and so I can extract the original file from inside the enhanced document but sometimes, because of the changes I have made, there is no way of going back. The end result of saving over the original untouched digital photo is equivalent to destroying the negative back in the days when film was king. Yep, photographic sacrilege!

So you can imagine my relief to find that in the last few versions of Photoshop Elements Adobe have included a technology that protects the original file and tracks the changes made to the picture in a series of successively saved photos. The technology is called Versioning as the software allows you to store different versions of the picture as your editing progresses. What's more, the feature provides options for viewing and using any of the versions that you have previously saved. Let's see how this file protection technology works in practice.

Versions and Photoshop Elements

Versioning extends the idea of Elements image stacks by storing the edited version of pictures together with the original photo in a special Version Set. All photos enhanced in the Photo Browser space using a tool like Auto Smart Fix are automatically included in a Version Set. Those images saved in the Quick, Guided and Full Edit workspaces with the Save As command can also be added to a Version Set by making sure that the Save in Version Set with Original option is ticked before pressing the Save button in the dialog.

Saving in this way means that edited files are not saved over the top of the original; instead a new version of the image is saved in a Version Set with the original. It is appended with a file name that has the suffix '_edited' attached to the original name. This way you will always be able to identify the original and edited files. The two files are 'stacked' together in the Photo Browser with the most recent file displayed on top.

Save a version from Editor >> *To create a Version Set when saving an edited file from inside the Quick Fix or Full Edit workspace make sure that the 'Save a Version Set with Original' option is selected.*

Version Set icon >> *The Bundled photos icon at the top right of the thumbnail shows that the photo is part of a version set.*

Displaying Version Set photos >> *Selecting the Version Set > Expand Items in Version Set option from the right-click menu (context menu) displays the various pictures that have been bundled together in the set. Alternatively you can click the Expand/Collapse arrow on the right of the version set.*

When a photo is part of a Version Set, there is a small icon displayed in the top right of the Photo Browser thumbnail. The icon shows a pile of photos and a paint brush. To see the other images in the Version Stack simply right-click the thumbnail image and select Version Set > Expand Items in Version Set or click on the Expand/Collapse arrow button on the right of the version set thumbnail.

Using the other options available in the right-click pop-up menu the sets can be expanded or collapsed, the current version reverted back to its original form or all versions flattened into one picture. Version Set options are also available via the Photo Browser Edit menu. Unlike Stacks, you cannot add other images to a Version Set as the set only contains edits of the same image.

Elements' Image Stacks >> *To group alike photos into an Image Stack, multi-select the pictures in the Photo Browser workspace before choosing Stack > Stack Selected Photos from the right-click menu. To display stacked photos either click the sideways arrow on the right of the thumbnail or choose Expand Photos in the Stack from the Stack heading in the right-click menu.*

4.14 Creating Image Stacks

Suitable for Elements – 7.0, 6.0, 5.0, 4.0, 3.0 | Difficulty level – Basic | Related techniques – 4.07, 4.11

An Image Stack is slightly different from a Version Set as it is a set of pictures that have been grouped together into a single place in the Organizer workspace. Most often Stacks are used to group pictures that have a common subject or theme and the feature is one way that Elements users can sort and manage their pictures. To create a Version Stack, multi-select a series of thumbnails in the workspace then right-click on one of the selected images to show the menu and from here select the Stack > Stack Selected Photos option. The thumbnail you right-click on will be the top photo in the stack. You can identify stacked image groups by the small icon in the top right of the thumbnail.

Image Stacks icon >> *Image Stacks use a Layered Photos icon in the top right of the thumbnail to indicate that the picture is one of several images that have been grouped.*

Auto photo stacking

The idea of grouping together like photos in a single stack was introduced in version 3.0 of the program. Version 5.0 introduced the ability to auto stack images as they are downloaded from camera, imported into Elements from folders or even when displayed in the Organizer workspace. The feature searches for similar images, either visually similar, or multiple photos taken within a short period of time, and then assembles these in groups in the 'automatically suggest photo stacks' window. From here you can choose to remove selected photos from a group or even remove a group all together from the window. Once you have fine-tuned which photos to include, clicking the Stack All Groups button will create Photo Stacks from all the groups in the window.

To auto stack pictures that are already in your catalog select a group of thumbnails first and then choose Automatically Suggest Photo Stacks from either the Edit > Stack or the right-click pop-up menus. Alternatively, to stack when importing pictures from a folder, camera or card reader choose the Automatically Suggest Photo Stacks option in the Get Photos or Adobe Photo Downloader dialog.

Auto stack whilst downloading >>
The Advanced dialog of the Adobe Photo Downloader contains the Automatically Suggest Photo Stacks option so you can group alike images as you transfer your files from camera to computer.

Either of these two options will then display a new window with alike pictures pre-grouped.
Choosing the Stack All Groups button converts the groups to stacks. The Remove Group or
Remove Selected Photos buttons prevent individual images or group of pictures being made into
a stack.

Stacking cataloged photos >> *To employ the Auto Stacking feature with photos that you have already
cataloged, start by multi-selecting several images in the Photo Browser workspace. Next right-click one of the
pictures and choose Stack > Automatically Suggest Photo Stacks from the pop-up menu. Elements will then
display a window containing groups of photos that are suitable for converting into Photo Stacks. You can
remove images from groups by selecting the photo and then pressing the Remove Selected Photos button at
the bottom left of the dialog. Stop specific groups from being converted to a Photo Stack by clicking on the
Remove Group button at the top right of each group section. Finally, press the Stack All Groups button to
convert the groups to Photo Stacks and show these in the Photo Browser. You can edit the groups by click-
dragging photos between different groups or within the same group. The left-most thumbnail will be the top
photo in that stack.*

5

Pathways to Editing in Elements

In earlier editions of Photoshop Elements all editing and enhancement actions were centered around the tools and features in the Full Edit workspace. More recently Elements has provided the photographer with several different levels of editing to choose from. In the last edition we were introduced to a new option, the Guided Edit, which combines both instructions and tools in a single panel. All editing approaches have their own strengths and challenges and in this chapter I will overview each option in turn. In addition I will introduce the advanced concept of 'non-destructive editing' using some of Elements most powerful tools and a couple of features that we sneakily borrow from Photoshop. So let's get started!

Editing Options

The options can be grouped around five different approaches to the task:

- Automatic,
- Semi-automatic,
- Manual,
- Guided edits,
- Non-destructive and
- Photoshop assisted.

Automatic editing

The simplest tools are almost always fully automatic with the user having little control over the final results. These are the types of color, contrast, brightness and sharpness controls that are available in the Photo Browser either via option in the Edit menu, from the right-click pop-up menu or displayed in the new Fix panel on the right of the Organizer workspace. These options provide a great place to start if you are new to digital photography and want good results quickly and easily, but experienced users will find the lack of control frustrating.

Auto editing summary

- Simple control using Auto Smart Fix, Auto Color, Auto Levels, Auto Contrast, Auto Sharpen and Auto Red Eye Fix
- Rotate left or right options
- Manual cropping
- Changes applied automatically
- New users start here for good, quick results
- Automatic control of: contrast, color, shadow and highlight detail and sharpness.

Automatic editing options

Right-click menu

Photo Browser workspace

Auto-editing options >> *The range of auto enhance options in versions 6.0 and 7.0 of Photoshop Elements includes Auto Color, Auto Levels, Auto Contrast and Auto Sharpen options as well as Auto Smart Fix and Auto Red Eye Fix features found in the previous version. The features are grouped in the new Fix panel and include Rotate buttons and a new Crop option.*

5.01 Auto Smart Fix

Suitable for Elements – 7.0, 6.0, 5.0, 4.0, 3.0 | Difficulty level – Basic
Related techniques – 5.02, 5.03

The Auto Smart Fix feature enhances both the lighting and color in your picture automatically. The command is used to balance the picture hues and improve the overall shadow and highlight detail. Most images are changed drastically using this tool. In some cases the changes can be too extreme. If this occurs, the effect should be reversed using the Edit > Undo command and the more controllable version of the tool – Adjust Smart Fix – used instead. Adjust Smart Fix is located in the Editor workspace.

Auto Smart Fix >> *The Auto Smart Fix feature enhances color, brightness, shadow and highlight detail automatically.*

5.02 Auto Red Eye Fix

Suitable for Elements – 7.0, 6.0, 5.0, 4.0 | Difficulty level – Basic
Related techniques – 5.01, 5.03

One of the possible side effects of using the inbuilt flash on your compact digital camera is the appearance of red eyes in the subject. Elements has always had great options for correcting this problem and the current release is no different containing a specific Red Eye Removal tool. First introduced in Elements 5.0 was the ability to automatically detect the presence of red eye in a photo and then correct the problem. The feature cleverly checks out the metadata attached to the photo to see if flash was used to record the image before searching for the problem eyes and automatically correcting the red hue. This feature can also be applied when transferring images from camera to computer by selecting the Automatically Fix Red Eyes option in the Photo Downloader.

Auto Red Eye Fix >> *The Auto Red Eye Fix feature searches for and corrects the red eyes caused by on-camera flash.*

5.03 Other auto options

Suitable for Elements – 7.0, 6.0
Difficulty level – Basic | Related techniques – 5.01, 5.02

In Photoshop Elements 6.0 and 7.0 four auto enhance options that were previously only available in the Enhance menu of the Edit workspace, have been added to the new Fix pane in the Organizer. Unlike the Auto Smart Fix option which enhances several different image characteristics in the one action, features like Auto Levels, Auto Contrast, Auto Sharpen, and Auto Color Correction generally concentrate on adjusting just one aspect of the photo, providing more specific and controllable changes to your photo.

Quick guide to the Fix panel's auto enhance features	
Correction needed	**Feature to use**
Low contrast problem	Auto Contrast
High contrast problem	Auto Contrast
Color cast problem	Auto Color Correction or Auto Levels
Color cast and contrast problem	Auto Levels
Sharpness or clarity problem	Auto Sharpen

Auto Contrast is designed to correct images that are either too contrasty (black and white) or too flat (dull and lifeless). Unlike the Auto Levels feature, Auto Contrast ensures that the brightest and darkest pixels in the picture (irrespective of their colors) are converted to pure white and black. In doing so all the tones in between are expanded or contracted to fit.

Auto Color concentrates on correcting the color in the midtones of the picture and adjusting the contrast by reassigning the brightest and darkest pixels to white and black.

Auto Levels is similar to Auto Contrast in that it maps the brightest and darkest parts of the image to white and black but differs in that each individual color channel is treated separately. In the process of mapping the tones (adjusting the contrast) in the red, green and blue channels, dominant color casts can be neutralized.

Auto Sharpen applies a set amount of sharpening to the photo. Most photographers prefer to be able to adjust the degree of sharpening that is applied to their images and so would avoid using this auto feature in favor of a more manual approach involving the Editor: Enhance > Adjust Sharpness filter.

Sometimes such automatic fixes do not produce the results that you expect. In these scenarios use the Undo (Edit > Undo) command to reverse the changes and try one of the manual correction tools detailed in the next section.

Auto options also found in Edit >> *The Fix panel's auto features can also be found in the Enhance menu of the Full Edit or Quick Fix workspaces.*

Auto options examples >>
(a) Original uncorrected image.
(b) After applying Auto Levels.
(c) After applying Auto Contrast.
(d) After applying Auto Color Correction.
(e) After Auto Color and Auto Sharpen

Automating editing of several pictures at once

It's true that shooting digital has meant that many photographers have saved the time that they used to spend in the darkroom processing their images. The flip side to this coin is that now we while away the hours in on-screen production instead. Surely with all the power of the modern computer and flexibility of Elements there must be quicker ways to process files. Well yes there is!

5.04 Processing multiple files

Suitable for Elements – 7.0, 6.0, 5.0, 4.0, 3.0 | Difficulty level – Basic
Related techniques – 5.05, 5.06

Photoshop Elements users are able to automate a variety of editing functions with the Process Multiple Files feature located in the File menu of the Full Edit workspace. The feature is like a dedicated batch processing tool that can name, size, enhance, label and save in a specific file format a group of photos stored in a folder or selected via the file browser or Open Files.

The dialog's options include:

Source – Files to be processed can be stored in a single folder, the files currently open in the workspace, pictures in the Project Bin or images multi-selected in the file browser.

Destination – Sets the location where processed files will be saved.

File naming – Options for naming or renaming of selected files including a range of preset naming styles.

Image Size – Specify size and resolution changes after choosing the unit of measure to work with from the drop-down menu. Proportions can be constrained.

File type – Select the file format that processed files will be saved or converted to.

Quick Fix enhancement – Use the options here to apply automatic enhancement of the files being processed.

Add Labels – Add caption or file name labels to each of the processed files. Also contains an option for watermarking the pictures.

After setting the options for each of the sections in the dialog press the OK button to process the pictures.

Batch processing of files >> *Elements users can automate the application of basic enhancement and editing features to a group of files using the Process Multiple Files feature located in the Full Edit workspace.*

5.05 Multi-selection editing

Suitable for Elements – 7.0, 6.0, 5.0, 4.0, 3.0 | Difficulty level – Basic | Related techniques – 5.04, 5.06

Another method of applying automatic changes to several photos at once is to multi-select photos in the Photo Browser workspace then choose an editing option from the right-click pop-up menu or the new Fix panel. There are a multitude of options available using this approach, all of which provide quick editing changes to the selected photos. For best results always apply critical edits and enhancements manually, but multi-select edits are particularly useful if you want to process a bunch of files quickly. The added bonus is that the edited versions of the pictures are not saved over the original file, but rather they are kept in a Version Set, so that it is always possible to extract the original file, or reverse the enhancement changes, if need be.

Keystrokes for fast edits of multi-selected photos

Rotate Photos 90° Left – Ctrl + Left   **Auto Smart Fix** – Ctrl + Alt + M

Rotate Photos 90° Right – Ctrl + Right   **Auto Red Eye Fix** – Ctrl + R

Auto enhance several files >>
The editing and enhancement options located on the right-click menu or the new Fix panel in the Photo Browser workspace can be just as easily applied to several photos that have been multi-selected as to a single picture.

This method is a quick and easy means of making automatic changes to a group of photos.

5.06 Bulk Red Eye fixing

Suitable for Elements – 6, 5.0, 4.0 | Difficulty level – Basic
Related techniques – 5.04, 5.05

As well as being able to apply the Auto Red Eye Fix feature to individual photos this correction option is also available in the Adobe Photo Downloader dialog. So now it is possible to download pictures from your camera, or import them from a folder, and at the same time be searching the images for red eye and correcting it when it is present. This is a great time saver if you regularly photograph with on-camera flash but as always for the absolute best results apply the Red Eye Fix yourself manually.

Auto Red Eye Fix >> *The Auto Red Eye fix option is also available in dialogs that are used to import or download pictures onto your computer. Selecting this option instructs Elements to search and correct any occurrence of red eye in the photos you are loading into the Organizer workspace.*

Book resources and video tutorials can be found at **www.photoshopelements.net**

Semi-automatic editing

The second level of features sits in the middle ground between total user control and total program control over the editing results. The tools in this group are primarily available in the Quick Fix editor but also encompass some of the more automatic or easy-to-use controls available in the Full Edit workspace. Move to these tools once you feel more confident with the digital photography process as a whole (downloading, making some changes, saving and then printing) and find yourself wanting to do more with your pictures. Again, for the advanced user the tools listed here will provide a degree of frustration as the amount of control over the results is still limited.

5.07 Using the Quick Fix Editor

Suitable for Elements – 7.0, 6.0, 5.0, 4.0, 3.0 | Difficulty level – Basic
Related techniques – 5.08, 5.09

The Quick Fix Editor contains a reduced tool and feature set designed to facilitate the fast application of the most frequent of all enhancement activities undertaken by the digital photographer.

The Zoom, Hand, Crop tools and the Quick Selection Tool and Selection Brush are located in a small toolbar to the left of the screen and are available for standard image editing changes; the fixed Palette Bin, to the right, contains the necessary features to alter and correct the lighting, color and sharpness of your pictures. Rotate buttons are located at the bottom of the dialog. Three new retouch tools have been added to the red eye removal brush and positioned at the bottom of the pane on the right side of the workspace.

You can choose to apply each image change automatically, via the Auto button, or manually using the supplied sliders. This approach provides both convenience and speed when needed, with the option of a manual override for those difficult editing tasks.

The adjustment features are arranged in a fashion that provides a model enhancement workflow to follow – simply move from the top to the bottom of the tools starting with smart fixing, working through lighting and color alterations, applying sharpening and, lastly, paint on retouching to specific areas of the photo.

There is no doubt that for making speedy adjustments of your favorite images with the option of some override control, the Quick Fix editor is a great place to start. And the best thing of all is you can see the before and after results of your changes on screen via the zoomable preview windows.

- Middle-level control using the features in the Quick Fix and Full Edit workspaces
- Some changes applied automatically, others via a user controlled slider
- New users progress here with experience and understanding
- Control of: cropping, rotation, contrast, color, saturation, hue, temperature, tint, shadow and highlight detail, red eye, midtone contrast and sharpening.

Semi-auto editing summary

Smart Fix control

Red Eye Fix

Lighting control for changes to levels, contrast, shadows and highlights

Color control for changes to saturation, hue, color temperature and tint

Sharpening control

Retouch Tools

Zoom, Move, Crop, Quick Selection Brush and Selection Brush tools

Rotate image buttons

After preview

Before preview

The Quick Fix Editor >> *The Quick Fix editor combines the major automatic enhancing tools with manual override slider controls, great before and after preview pictures and now three new retouch tools in addition to the red eye removal tool.*

Adjust Smart Fix >> *The Adjust Smart Fix option provides a slider control for the auto enhancement effects applied by the feature.*

5.08 Adjust Smart Fix

Suitable for Elements – 7.0, 6.0, 5.0, 4.0, 3.0 | Difficulty level – Basic
Related techniques – 5.01, 5.03

The Adjust Smart Fix (Editor: Enhance > Adjust Smart Fix) version of the Auto Smart Fix feature provides the same control over color, shadow and highlight detail but with the addition of a slider control that determines the strength of the enhancement changes. Moving the slider from left to right will gradually increase the amount of correction applied to your picture. This approach provides much more control over the enhancement process and is a preferable way to work with all but the most general photos.

The Auto button, also located in the dialog, automatically applies a fix amount of 100% and provides a similar result to selecting Enhance > Auto Smart Fix.

Manual editing

The next approach to editing includes tools and features designed to give the user professional control over their editing and enhancement tasks. Many of the features detailed here are very similar to, and in some cases exactly the same as, those found in the Photoshop itself. These tools provide the best quality changes available with Elements, but they do require a greater level of understanding and knowledge to use effectively.

The extra editing and enhancement power of these tools comes at a cost of the user bearing all responsibility for the end results. Whereas the automatic nature of many of the features found in the other two groups means that bad results are rare, misusing or over-applying the tools found here can actually make your picture worse. This shouldn't stop you from venturing into these waters, but it does mean that it is a good idea to apply these tools cautiously rather than with a heavy hand. In fact once most users develop a good level of understanding and skill with the manual tools and features in the Full Edit workspace they seldom return to using automatic enhancement options, preferring to remain in complete control over the pixels in their pictures.

5.09 The Full Edit workspace

Suitable for Elements – 7.0, 6.0, 5.0, 4.0, 3.0, 2.0, 1.0 | Difficulty level – Basic Related techniques – 5.07

The Full Edit contains the features and tools used for the most sophisticated of the three different editing pathways provided in Elements. The groups of tools included in this workspace are designed to give the user professional control over all their editing and enhancement tasks.

Manual options >> *The manual versions of many automatic or semi-automatic enhancement features are located in the lower part of the Enhance menu.*

Manual editing summary

- Sophisticated control using the features in the Full Edit workspace
- Most editing changes applied manually via settings input by the user
- Great for complex editing and enhancement tasks performed by more experienced users
- The most control of all the major editing and enhancing of your digital photographs.

As well as providing manual versions of all the automatic enhancement options that we have looked at so far, the Full Edit workspace also includes tools that enable the user to isolate where and how the editing changes are applied to photos. For this reason most advanced techniques detailed in the ensuing chapters of this book make use of the extensive tool and feature set provided in this Editor workspace.

Toolbar   Menu bar   Options bar   Jump to Organizer

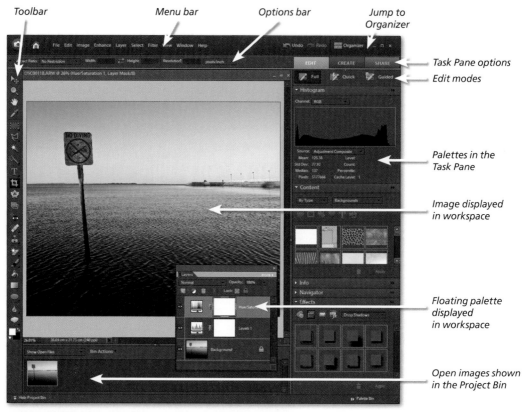

Task Pane options

Edit modes

Palettes in the Task Pane

Image displayed in workspace

Floating palette displayed in workspace

Open images shown in the Project Bin

The Full Edit >> *Advanced editing and enhancement techniques are generally applied in the Full Edit workspace.*

Auto/manual feature equivalents

Automatic feature	Manual equivalent
Auto Levels	Levels or Shadows/Highlights or Brightness/Contrast or Adjust Color Curves
Auto Color Correction	Remove Color Cast or Color Variations or Adjust Color For Skin Tones
Auto Contrast	Levels or Shadows/Highlights or Brightness/Contrast or Adjust Color Curves
Auto Red Eye Fix	Red Eye Removal Tool
Auto Smart Fix	Levels or Shadows/Highlights or Brightness/Contrast or Adjust Color Curves together with Remove Color Cast or Color Variations or Adjust Color For Skin Tones
Auto Sharpen	Unsharp Mask or Adjust Sharpness

Manual pathway choices >> *Photoshop Elements provides manual alternatives for all its automatic and semi-automatic editing options. This table summarizes the specific manual features that can be used as alternatives.*

Three Editing Modes in Elements plus one Online

The Guided Edit workspace was introduced into Elements in version 6. This mode combines the step-by-step instructions that used to be found in the How To feature with the direct enhancement control of the Quick Fix edit space. As part of the interface changes that also occured in Photoshop Elements 6, the guys at Adobe grouped features, tools and options into several task headings. The Task Pane and the associated headings are displayed on the right of the Element's workspaces with different options available in each. In the Edit workspace these include Edit, Create and Share, where as in the Organizer the choices include Organize, Fix, Create and Share. With all the management, editing, enhancement, and production options now available in Elements the inclusion of these task based headings helps the user navigate through the various phases of photographic workflow.

Edit task pane button

Three edit options >> In version 6.0 the Guided edit mode was added to help users with their enhancement activities.

Full Edit workspace

Quick Fix workspace

Guided Edit workspace

In the Edit workspace, Elements users have the luxury of three different ways of conducting their enhancement activities. Once you have selected the Edit heading you can then choose between Full Edit, Quick Fix and Guided Edit workspaces. New for Photoshop Elements 7.0 is the ability to perform simple editing tasks online via the tools and function available at Photoshop.com. Though these 'web' tools do not provide the level of manual control available in the Full edit workspace, they do provide a very usable alternative to many of the enhancement options available in Quick and Guided edit modes. When linked with Online Albums any changes made in the webspace are reflected in the duplicated photos stored in the Organizer..

We have already looked at the Full Edit and Quick Fix workspaces so let's now turn our attention to the newly created Guided Edit option.

5.10 Guided Edits

Suitable for Elements – 7.0, 6.0 | Difficulty level – Basic

Selecting the Guided tab from the Edit task pane displays a list of the tutorials that ship with Elements. Clicking a tutorial heading will reveal subheadings for specific topics. Selecting a heading topic will display a set of instructions together with associated buttons and controls. For instance, in the example on the next page, two Rotate buttons (rotate left and rotate right) are displayed in the panel. Clicking either of these buttons will perform the same action as selecting the same options from the Image > Rotate menu.

Guided edit is best used for learning how to use new tools and techniques or, as is the case with the new Photomerge Faces and Group Shot options, as a way to step through complex techniques.

The Guided Activities > Guide for Editing a Photo entry contains a collection of guided edits that are useful when correcting images. These include crop, lighten, darken, touch up and sharpen.

Guided Edits >> *The Guided edit workspace combines step-by-step instruction with embedded enhancement or edit controls.*

5.11 Enhancing via Photoshop.com

Suitable for Elements – 7.0 | Difficulty level – Basic

The partnership between Photoshop Elements and Photoshop.com goes way beyond merely providing a space on the web to view the pictures that you process in Elements. Because Photoshop.com grew out of Photoshop Express the site also contains simple editing features such as the ability to crop, resize, auto correct, alter white balance, adjust highlights, boost color, tint and distort photos.

To adjust an image online, click onto the My Photos heading first and then navigate to the photo. You can look for the photos visually by selecting an Album entry or Library heading on the left of the screen and then scrolling through the thumbnails in the main workspace. Alternatively, you can locate the photo by typing a search term into the Search box at the top right of the workspace and then hitting the Enter key. Photoshop.com tries to match the search term with album and file names, tags associated with the photos and picture captions.

Once you have located the photo, clicking on the picture's thumbnail switches the workspace to the edit mode and displays the photo as large as possible within the window. All the adjustments that can be applied to the photo, are grouped under three headings Basics, Tuning and Effects on the left.

For most options, when an adjustment is selected from the list, a series of thumbnails displaying varying degrees of application for the adjustment are displayed above the image. Clicking a thumbnail will preview a change to the photo. With some adjustments a slider control is also provided below the thumbnails for finer control. One thumbnail of the group will be displayed with a curved yellow arrow. Click this entry to reset the photo to the way it was before selecting the current adjustment. Click the green tick (top right) to save the current adjustment changes and click the red cross to cancel the alterations.

Despite the preview being updated to reflect the changes that you have made, the adjustments are not actually applied to the image until they are saved upon exiting the Editing mode. This way of working allows you to revert the photo to its original state by clicking the Reset All button at the bottom of the window. Also contained at the bottom of the editing window is the View Original image which allows you to see how the photo looked before your adjustments. Hold down the button to see the before image, let go of the button to return the picture to its current state.

Enhancing at Photoshop.com >> All image adjustments performed in Photoshop.com are undertaken in the Editing mode pictured to the left.

Synchronized Updating >> *For photos that you have edited, and are part of a synchronized album, clicking the Save button updates the image at Photoshop.com (1) and in your Photoshop Elements catalog (2).*

Some enhancement options, such as Red-Eye Removal and Touchup, require the user to interact directly with the image. With these tools you will need to click on or paint over the parts of the photo that you want to change. The Touchup tool in particular is very useful as it provides a way to remove small dust marks and spots from your photo. Once selected, you simply click and drag a circle around the dust mark and then let the mouse button go. Automatically the dust spot is removed. If the result didn't work as you expected, just click the circular orange arrow icon at the top right of the window. This is the Reset button and pressing it will remove all your retouching changes, allowing you to start again.

Once you are satisfied with your changes, you can saved the altered photo by clicking the blue Save button at the bottom of the editing window. This action will update the photo in the Photoshop.com library and will also update the picture in your Photoshop Elements Catalog if the picture belongs to an Album that is set for Backup/Synchronization.

Non-destructive editing, the professional's choice

Though not strictly an editing mode in itself, the idea of making changes to your images in a non-destructive fashion is key to all professional workflows. For this reason I feel that it is appropriate to introduce the idea here. When digital photography was in its infancy, all changes made to the photo were applied directly to the original pixels captured by the camera or scanner. At the time, the abilities of the software and hardware allowed frustratingly few alternatives to this destructive way of working.

For me, as a photographer who trained when film was king, I found the idea of changing my captured image rather distressing, as I would never have altered, cut, or intentionally marked my negatives, so why should I have to work this way when opting for a digital workflow. This would lead me to make countless copies of my original images to ensure that I had at least one copy of the primary capture file to refer to at all times.

Book resources and video tutorials can be found at **www.photoshopelements.net**

Thankfully times have changed and digital photography is now well out of 'short trousers' and software and hardware has developed to a stage where many of the editing activities we regularly carry out in Photoshop Elements can be executed non-destructively, that is, without altering the pixels of the captured file.

Throughout the rest of the text I will use non-destructive editing and enhancement techniques wherever possible, but to get you up to speed, here I introduce a selection of tools, techniques and features that can be employed to enhance your images non-destructively.

5.12 Adjustment Layers

Suitable for Elements – 7.0, 6.0, 5.0, 4.0, 3.0, 2.0, 1.0 | Difficulty level – Basic

These special layers alter the look of the layers that are arranged below them in the layers stack. They act as a filter through which the lower layers are viewed. You can use adjustment layers to perform many of the enhancement tasks that you would normally apply directly to an image layer without changing the image itself. When you choose to use an Adjustment Layer rather than applying the enhancement change directly to the image you are choosing to work non-destructively.

Creating an adjustment layer adds a new entry to the layers palette just above the active layer. The adjustment layer entry contains two thumbnails – the Layer Thumbnail on the left and the Layer Mask thumbnail on the right. Double clicking the Layer Thumbnail will display the adjustment layer's dialog. For instance, in the case of a Levels adjustment layer, double clicking the thumbnail will display the Levels dialog. This provides the user with the ability to make adjustments to existing settings, or even rest the dialog, at any time. The Layer Mask is used to customize where and how the adjustment layer's changes are applied. See Technique 5.15 for more details.

Elements contains eight different types of adjustment layers which are grouped together with the fill layers under the Create Adjustment Layer button in the Layers palette. The same options can also be found in the Layer > New Adjustment Layer menu. They are:

Levels – Adjusts the tones in the picture.

Brightness/Contrast – Lightens, darkens and controls contrast.

Hue/Saturation – Changes the color and strength of color in photos.

Gradient Map – Changes the photo so that all the tones are mapped to the values of a selected gradient.

Adjustment Layers >> *Photoshop Elements contains eight different adjustment layers.*

Adjustments applied downwards >> *Adjustment layers alter the look of the image layers that are positioned below them in the layers palette.*

Photo Filter – Reproduces the color changes of traditional photo filters.

Invert – Reverses all the tones in a picture, producing a negative effect.

Threshold – Converts the picture to pure black and white with no grays present at all.

Posterize – Reduces the total number of colors in a picture and creates a flat paint (or poster)-like effect.

Placing an adjustment layer at the top of a stack of layers will ensure that the editing changes will be applied to the content of all the layers beneath. If instead of changing all the lower layers you want to restrict the effects of the adjustment layer to a single layer then after selecting the adjustment layer, pick the Group with Previous option from the Layer menu. This will indent the adjustment layer in the palette and, more importantly, 'group' the adjustment with the layer immediately below it. This technique is an important one as it changes the way that adjustment layers work and allows their non-destructive editing powers to be applied to individual image layers only.

Gradient Map adjustment layer being applied to both image layers

Gradient Map adjustment layer grouped with Layer 1 so that the convert to gray change only occurs in one layer only

Restricting adjustments to a single layer >> *To link the changes made via an adjustment layer to a single layer only, make sure that the adjustment layer is directly above the image layer to be changed and then with the adjustment layer active, choose Layer > Group with Previous, or Ctrl + G.*
Pro Tip: *Alt-click on the border between a layer and the one below it to Group With Previous.*

5.13 Select and adjust in one stroke

Suitable for Elements – 7.0 | Difficulty level – Basic

One of the major changes introduced in Photoshop Elements 7.0 is the ability to select and make changes with the one tool. The new Smart Brush tool brings a whole new level of ease to the process of changing specific areas of your photo. By combining the selecting abilities of the Quick Selection tool and the enhancement options available via adjustment layers, the Adobe engineers have created a new way to change the look of your photos.

Book resources and video tutorials can be found at **www.photoshopelements.net**

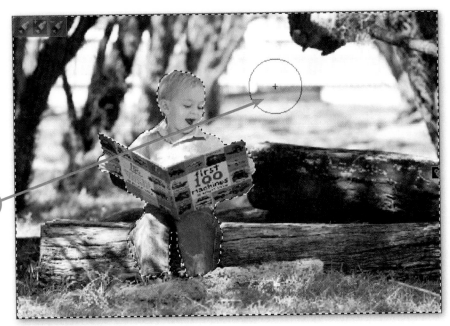

Smart Brush Tool >> After selecting the enhancement type, here I used one of the convert to black and white options, all you need to do is paint over the parts of the photo that you want to change. If the tool selects too much of the photo, switch to the Subtract from Selection mode (hold down the Alt key) and paint over the unwanted change to remove it.

Unlike the traditional way of applying adjustments where the user must first make a selection and then apply the adjustment, the Smart Brush Tool creates the selection and applies the adjustment as the user paints over the image. You can select the type of adjustment that will be applied with the tool from a list of over 65 that ships with Elements. These presets are grouped under general headings in the Preset Chooser located in the options bar. Here you will find options for altering image characteristics such as color, tone and saturation as well as subject based enhancements such as brightening teeth or making a dull sky bluer and, of course, a bunch of special effects changes. Preset entries can be displayed in a list or thumbnail form by selecting one of the options displayed when pressing the double sideways arrows in the top left of the Presets window.

The Smart Brush Tool is only available in Full editor workspace.

1 With the Smart Brush tool active, go to the Options Bar and select the type of enhancement from the Preset Chooser pop-up menu.

2 Now paint over the areas that you wish to select and enhance.

3 After the first selection area is drawn, the tool's mode automatically changes to Add to Selection so that you can include extra areas in the selection.

4 Subtract from the selection by painting over new areas after switching to the Subtract from Selection mode using the buttons in the Options Bar or the floating palette at the top right of the photo.

FEATURE SUMMARY

Book resources and video tutorials can be found at **www.photoshopelements.net**

Fine-tuning Smart Brush Tool effects >> *With some Smart Brush Tool entries the actual settings used for making the image adjustments can be edited. In this example, double-clicking on the thumbnail on the left of the entry displays the Brightness/Contrast dialog. In the dialog you can change the settings used for the adjustment.*

When you paint on a photo with the Smart Brush Tool, Elements creates a new Adjustment Layer and adds it to the layer stack with a mask based on the painted selection. Cool! We get the power of masked adjustment layers without any of the pain of creating them manually, but how do we alter Smart Brush Tool effects once they are added?

To alter the strength of a Smart Brush Effect: Changing the strength of the effect is a simple matter of selecting the Smart Brush Tool entry in the layers palette and then adjusting the Opacity slider at the top right of the palette. The lower the opacity number the more subtle the effect.

To change how the effect combines with the picture: Photoshop Elements controls how the contents of two layers are mixed together via the Blend Mode setting. Elements uses this setting to adjust how the Smart Brush Tool layer interacts with the background or image layer. To change Blend Modes just select a new entry from the drop down list at the top left of the layers palette.

To change the settings of the effect itself: As all Smart Brush Tool effects are based on masked adjustment layers, to change the style of the effects, it should be possible to double-click on the layer thumbnail and simply change the settings in the dialog that appears. For most Smart Brush Tool adjustments this is true (check out the Lighting options) as they are built upon Elements Adjustment Layers, but this is not always the case as some effects are based on features that are only available in Photoshop itself. If you try to adjust these you will get a warning notice saying that it is not possible to tweak the settings.

5.14 'All Layers' tool options

Suitable for Elements – 7.0, 6.0, 5.0, 4.0, 3.0, 2.0, 1.0 | Difficulty level – Basic

Removing dust and scratches is a regular correction activity for digital photographers, irrespective of if they are working on scanned historical photos, or recently captured portraits, where the client wants slight skin blemishes disguised. These changes are often performed with Elements' features such as the Clone Stamp tool, Spot Healing and Healing Brushes on the main or background layer. Working this way changes the original pixels forever. A non-destructive work around that provides the same results, makes use of the 'All Layers' options of these tools to keep the changes in a separate retouching layer that sits above the background.

Book resources and video tutorials can be found at **www.photoshopelements.net**

ND retouching >> *By using the All Layers option available with tools like the Clone Stamp and Spot Healing brush it is possible to remove dust and scratches from images without changing the original pixels.*

To use this technique start by creating a new layer above the background layer. Rename this layer Retouching. Next select the layer to make sure that it is active and choose the desired tool from the Elements' toolbar. Before commencing the repair work, select the All Layers option in the tool's options bar. Now proceed to use the tool normally. The retouching changes though stored in a separate layer are seamlessly blended with the background. For specific restoration and retouching techniques turn to Chapters 8 and 9.

5.15 Blend Modes
Suitable for Elements – 7.0, 6.0, 5.0, 4.0, 3.0, 2.0, 1.0 | Difficulty level – Basic

As we have seen with the Smart Brush Tool the way that individual layers interact with other layers in the stack is determined by the blending mode setting. By default the layer's mode is set to Normal, which causes the picture content on the upper layer to obscure the picture parts beneath, but Photoshop Elements has many other ways (modes) to control how these pixels interact.

Called 'blend modes', the different options provide a variety of ways to control the mixing, blending and general interaction of the layer content. The modes are grouped into several different categories based on the type of changes that they make. The layer blend modes are located in the drop-down menu at the top left of the Layers palette. Blend modes can also be applied to the painting and drawing tools via a drop-down menu in the tool's options bar. For a complete list of the Blend Modes available in Photoshop Elements go to the Appendix at the end of this book.

So how can blend modes help us when it comes to altering out images non-destructively? By providing us with a range of ways to mix the image content from two layers, Blend Modes increase our ability to edit and enhance without changing original pixels. Let's take the example of coloring a grayscale image to simulate the look of a hand colored photo of old. You may first think that the task is a simple one, select the color, choose the Brush tool and then paint over the grayscale background layer. Do this and you will get a paint stroke of solid color, that obscures all the detail of the original image. Not the look that we are wanting! However, if you change the Brush's Blend Mode (using the drop-down menu in the tool's option bar) to Color then the tool magically applies color in direct proportion as tone of the background image. All detail is retained in the underlying image, but this detail is colored the hue of the foreground swatch. This is the magic of the Color Blend Mode.

Blend Modes in action >> *By painting into a separate layer whose Blend Mode has been changed to Color you have the ability to tint the grayscale image while still retaining the original capture in the background layer.*
Note: *Keep in mind that the grayscale image needs to be in RGB Color mode to be tintable.*

That said, in applying the coloring directly to the background layer we are destructively altering the primary pixels. So let's rework the technique so that it still uses the Blend Mode but protects the original image. Start by creating a new layer to house the color changes. Next change the Blend Mode of the layer to Color. Select the foreground color and then the Brush tool. Make sure that the Blend Mode of the Brush is back to the default setting (Normal). With the new color changes layer selected, paint over the image. Notice that the same coloring effect is produced but this time the Blend Mode change is applied to the layer not the Brush.

5.16 Layer Masking
Suitable for Elements – 7.0, 6.0, 5.0, 4.0, 3.0, 2.0, 1.0 | Difficulty level – Basic

As we have already seen each time you add a fill or adjustment layer to an image two thumbnails are created in the Layers palette. The one on the left controls the settings for the adjustment layer. The thumbnail on the right represents the layer's mask that controls how the adjustment is applied to the picture.

The mask is a grayscale image. When it's colored white no part of the adjustment layer's effects are masked or held back from the picture below. The full changes are applied to the image. Conversely if the mask thumbnail is totally black then none of the layer's effects are applied to the picture. Shades of gray equate to various levels of transparency. In this way, the enhancement changes produced via an adjustment, or fill layer, can be selectively applied, or merged, with the layers beneath by painting (in black and white and gray) onto the layer mask.

Book resources and video tutorials can be found at **www.photoshopelements.net**

Masking >> *Modifying the mask associated with adjustment layers provides the option to customize where the effects of the layer are applied to the image layer. Using varying levels of gray will also change the strength of the enhancement effect. A darker gray will produce less noticeable changes whereas a light gray will allow more of the adjustment layer's effects to be seen.*

By default the layer mask is set to white so that the adjustment effect is fully applied. To customize the application of the effect, click onto the Layer Mask thumbnail (so that there is a second line border surround in the thumbnail), select the Brush tool and choose black, white or gray as the foreground color. Now paint over the surface of the image. Notice that the adjustment layer effect is reduced or eliminated in the areas where you paint with gray or black. Also notice that the mask thumbnail now displays the painted strokes. It is also worth noting that preselecting an area before creating the adjustment layer will result in a Mask the shape and size of the selection.

Many professionals use masks on a regular basis to help customize the application of adjustment layer changes and also for governing how the picture parts in separate image layers interact. Though Photoshop Elements doesn't contain all the masking power that its bigger brother Photoshop does, customizing adjustment layers is no problem and, with a simple 'work around' (see Technique 5.14), it is also possible to provide more masking functionality than is generally available to the Elements user.

5.17 Duplicate layers
Suitable for Elements – 7.0, 6.0, 5.0, 4.0, 3.0, 2.0, 1.0 | Difficulty level – Basic

In situations where none of the above techniques can be used to edit non-destructively it will be necessary to use other means to preserve the integrity of the original file. A clear example of this is when it comes time to add some sharpening to your photos. Now by design, applying a sharpening filter will pretty much change all the pixels in your photo in order to increase the clarity of the picture, which makes the action very destructive and one that should be avoided. So what other route can we take to provide the same results?

Well the simplest way is to duplicate the image layer, and then apply the sharpening filter to the copy, rather than the original layer. This way the primary pixels (in the original image layer) are

Editing layer copies >> *When there is no other option than apply editing changes directly to the image layer then the best way to ensure that your original pixels are protected is to duplicate the image layer and execute the changes on the copy (a). With multi-layer documents use the Copy Merge command to duplicate the contents of all layers first before applying the editing changes to the merge layer (b).*

protected and displaying the sharpened result is a simple matter of ensuring that it resides at the top of the layer stack. Alternatively the original can be hidden from view (click the 'eye' icon on the left of the layer entry).

In the case of a document that contains multiple image layers or a combination of image and adjustment layers some photographers would merge all the image layers before copying the resultant layer and applying the sharpen filter. The act of merging means that you will lose the ability to change the settings in the adjustment layers or edit any of the image layers independently. So forget the Layer > Merge Layers command, instead select the whole document using the Select > Select All command and then copy the contents of all the layers to memory by choosing the Copy Merged option from the Edit menu. Next select the uppermost layer in the layer stack and select Edit > Paste. This action inserts a new layer at the top of the stack that is the combination of all the layers in the document. This layer can then be filtered without fear of damaging the original photo.

Secret Pro's Tip: Instead of doing the select all, copy merged, paste to top of stack steps, pros simply add a new empty layer at the top of the stack and then do Shift-Alt-Control + E which is a undocumented Stamp Visible command that unfortunately has no menu equivalent.

Giving Elements a helping hand

It is true that Photoshop Elements contains a dazzling array of editing and enhancement tools. In fact, many would say that if you can't find a tool to perform the changes you desire, then you are not really trying. But as we have seen, just having the right tool to hand is not the whole story, it is also important to ensure that you are able to use the tools in a way that preserves the pixels first captured, and produces the best quality enhancements possible. This often means using the tools we have in ways that perhaps were not envisaged when the features were first designed. The next few techniques extend the editing abilities of Photoshop Elements beyond the standard workflow approaches advocated in most texts. These options may not need to be used with every photo, but they will certainly come in handy with specific enhancement tasks and will become an important technique in your editing kit bag.

Photoshop features in Elements >> *Users can add to the functionality of Elements by opening Photoshop documents (a) containing Photoshop only adjustment layers (e.g. Curves, Selective Color, Black and White and Color Balance) and then dragging these layers to their Element documents (b). The adjustment layer's enhancements will be applied to the document, but the settings for these layers can not be altered in Elements.*

5.18 Borrowing Photoshop features
Suitable for Elements – 7.0, 6.0, 5.0, 4.0, 3.0, 2.0, 1.0 | Difficulty level – Basic

Because of the professional nature of Photoshop, it contains a range of high level features and tools that are not available in Elements. This said, both Photoshop and Elements contain a range of tools and features and technology in common and much of the nuts and bolts that sit behind the scenes are shared by both programs. This cross over leads to an interesting situation where some features that are Photoshop only can be borrow to be used, in a limited way, in Elements.

We have been talking about the importance of Adjustment Layers as a way of non-destructive enhancing and, as you would expect, Photoshop contains more adjustment layer options than Elements. Of interest to us particularly are the Curves, Color Balance, Selective Color and the new Black and White adjustment layers. Though these features can't be invoked or Adjusted in Elements, a Photoshop document containing the layers can be opened in the program. The Adjustment layers can be seen as separate entries in the layers palette, but for the most part, the settings can't be adjusted, Black and White is an exception, but more on this later. When this scenario is coupled with the fact that Photoshop adjustment layers can be dragged from one document to another, users end up with the ability to apply non Elements based adjustment layers to Elements documents. Cool!

In practice, I created several documents in Photoshop containing Adjustment Layers with a variety of settings, but no image data. I then open these files in Elements and drag the required adjustment layer from the Photoshop document to the Elements file and hey presto, the enhancement is applied. Now that is fine for me, as I have both Photoshop and Elements on my machine, but I know that most readers do not have this luxury, so for this reason I have created several different Photoshop documents that are available from the book's website that you can use for your own projects.

Photoshop donor documents >> *The book's website contains several documents created in Photoshop that can be used to donate Photoshop only adjustment layers to your Elements document.*
(a) Photoshop-Selective-Color.psd
(b) Photoshop-Convert-to-gray.psd
(c) Photoshop-Curves.psd
(d) Photoshop-Split-Tones.psd

Photoshop donor documents

The book's website contains four key Photoshop donor documents (the files containing adjustment layers which can be dragged to Elements documents) designed to be used for specific enhancement activities. Each document includes multiple layers for a single adjustment feature. The settings for each layer differ providing a bunch of preset enhancement options that can be applied to Elements documents by simply dragging and dropping the layer to the Elements files. The donor documents include:

Photoshop-Selective-Color.psd – For boosting or reducing specific colors using the Selective Color Adjustment layer.

Photoshop-Convert-to-Gray.psd – Monochrome conversions using the Black and White feature.

Photoshop-Curves.psd – Curves based adjustment of the tones in your photos.

Photoshop-Split-Tones.psd – Sophisticated split toning effects using Photoshop's Color Balance adjustment layer to separately tone highlights and shadows.

5.19 Advanced layer masks

Suitable for Elements – 7.0, 6.0, 5.0, 4.0, 3.0, 2.0, 1.0 | Difficulty level – Basic

Along with extra adjustment layers Photoshop also contains advanced masking options that are not available in Elements. We have already see how it is possible to use the masks associated with Adjustment Layers to customize where the layer's effects are applied, well, Photoshop allows users to

Image layer masks >> *Though not designed for this purpose it is possible to use the Layer Masks associated with adjustment layers to mask image layers. In the example above the sky from the upper image layer is HomeSite with the foreground detail from the layer below using the layer mask in the Levels adjustment layer. For this to occur the adjustment layer needs to be created with no settings and then the upper image layer is Grouped with the adjustment layer.*

use masks with image layers to provide the same level of customization when montaging. When a mask is attached to an image layer, it can be used to adjust which parts of the upper layer are visible, and which parts are hidden from view allowing the contents of the layer beneath to show through. This is a very handy function as it is provides non-destructive montage abilities. Elements users can access such masking abilities by highjacking the mask associated with an adjustment layer and use it with an image layer.

The process involves adding an adjustment layer, with no settings applied, to the layers stack in between the two image layers to be montaged. Next the upper image layer is grouped with the no-settings adjustment layer. This action essentially links the image layer with the mask of the adjustment layer. As the mask by default is white, the upper image layer is displayed in full, but paint onto the layer mask with a black (or gray) brush and details of the lower layer will be revealed. By using black, white and gray paint strokes on the mask it is possible to non-destructively mix the contents of the two image layers. Look for examples of this technique throughout the next chapters.

6

Image Changes – Beyond the Basics

Advanced selection techniques

Many great image editing techniques are based on the 'selection' prowess of the photographer. Being able to manipulate the selection tools to isolate the precise pixels that you wish to edit is a key skill that we all should possess. The following techniques will help you build on your existing selection skills.

6.01 Adding to and subtracting from selections

Suitable for Elements – 7.0, 6.0, 5.0, 4.0, 3.0, 2.0, 1.0 | Difficulty level – Basic
Related techniques – 6.02, 6.03, 6.04, 6.05 | Tools used – Magic Wand, Lasso, Marquee

Only on a very rare occasion will you be able to create the perfect selection with a single tool applied once. Most editing jobs require the building of selections using multiple tools, creating new selections that are either added to, or subtracted from, existing selections. Photoshop Elements provides a range of features that are designed for just this purpose.

When a selection tool is in use four selection modes are available in the options bar. By switching between these modes while making additional selections you can:

- Create a **new** selection each time the tool is applied,
- **Add** to an existing selection,
- **Subtract** from an existing selection, or
- Make a selection from the **intersection** of the new and old selections.

The modes are available for all selection tools the exception being that the Intersect mode can not be used with the Quick Selection Tool or the Selection Brush tools. The New Selection option is

Adding to selections >> *Modify your selections by switching selection modes using the buttons found in the Options menu. (a) New selection. (b) Add to selection. (c) Subtract from selection. (d) Make new selection from the intersection.*

the default. Complex areas of a picture can be isolated by making a series of selections choosing the necessary tool (Lasso, Marquee, Magic Wand, Selection Brush or Quick Selection Tool) and mode (new, add to, subtract from, intersection of) as you go. The mode of the current tool can also be changed using a keyboard shortcut whilst selecting. Hold down the Shift key to add to a selection or the Alt key to take away or subtract from a selection.

6.02 Using the Selection Brush

Suitable for Elements – 7.0, 6.0, 5.0, 4.0, 3.0, 2.0 | Difficulty level – Intermediate | Resources – Web image 602
Related techniques – 6.01, 6.03, 6.04, 6.05 | Tools used – Selection tools | Menus used – Select

Responding to photographers' demands for even more options for making selections, Adobe included the Selection Brush for the first time in version 2.0 of Elements. The tool lets you paint a selection onto your image. The size, shape and edge softness of the selection are based on the brush properties you currently have set. These can be altered in the Brush Presets pop-up palette located in the options bar.

The tool can be used in two modes – Selection and Mask:

• The **Selection mode** is used to paint over the area you wish to select.

• The **Mask mode** is particularly well suited for showing the soft or feathered edge selections made when painting with a soft-edged brush or when making detailed edits to the selection. The Mask mode works by reverse painting in the areas you want to 'mask from the selection'.

Holding down the Alt (Windows) or Option (Mac) keys whilst dragging the brush switches the tool from adding to the selection to taking away from the area.

Painting selections >> *The Selection Brush tool allows the user to create selections by painting directly onto the picture surface.*

Selection Brush modes >> *The Selection Brush can work in either selection or mask modes.*

6.03 The Quick Selection Tool

Suitable for Elements – 7.0, 6.0 , 5.0, 4.0, 3.0, 2.0 | Difficulty level – Intermediate | Resources – Web image 6.02
Related techniques – 6.01, 6.03, 6.04, 6.05 | Tools used – Selection tools | Menus used – Select

Along with the Selection Brush tool, the new Quick Selection tool (previously the Magic Selection Brush) provides Elements users with a unique approach to creating and modifying selections. As we have seen, when using the Selection Brush the user must paint over the area to be encompassed by the selection. The accuracy of this painting step determines the accuracy of the final selection. For example, accidentally painting over an edge will result in the creation of a selection that goes beyond this picture part.

Quick 'magical' selections >> *The Quick Selection tool is coupled with the Selection Brush in the tool bar.*

The Quick Selection tool provides a quicker, easier and, in most cases, more accurate way to make selections by combining both the drawing and color selection approaches of the other tools we have covered. To make a selection choose the tool from the tool bar. If it is hidden from view click the small arrow at the bottom right of the Selection Brush button to reveal the tool. The Quick Selection tool doesn't require you to scribble or place some dots on the picture parts that you want to select as was the case with the Magic Selection Brush. Instead Elements creates the selection as you paint over specific picture areas. You don't have to be too careful with your initial painting as the program registers the color, tone and texture of the picture parts and then intelligently searches for other similar pixels to include in the selection.

Elements does the selection work >>
As you are drawing with the Quick Selection tool Elements automatically generates a selection of all the adjacent areas in the picture that have similar color, texture or tone.

Fine-tuning the areas selected with Quick Selection tool

Although this tool does a pretty good job of selecting alike areas, there will always be occasions when either too much or too little of the picture has been included. Just like the other tools we have looked at, the Quick Selection tool allows you to easily modify the selections it makes.

To include other areas in the selection, click the Add to Selection button in the tool's options bar (the cursor will change to include a small +) and paint over a new picture part. This step will cause Elements to regenerate the selection to include your changes. To remove an area from the selection, click on the Subtract from Selection button (cursor changes to the brush tip and a small - sign), and paint over the part to eliminate. Again, Elements will regenerate the selection to account for the changes. The Shift and Alt keys can be used whilst drawing to change modes on the fly and add to or subtract from the selection.

Add to Selection

Subtract from Selection

Adding to or subtracting from quick selections >> *The options bar of the Quick Selection tool contains several modes that can be used for altering or refining the selection created by the tool. You can add other picture parts to a selection by clicking on the Add to Selection button and then painting over the new area. Parts already selected can be removed by changing to the Subtract from Selection mode and painting on these areas.*

6.04 Advanced refining of selection edges

Suitable for Elements – 7.0, 6.0, 5.0, 4.0, 3.0, 2.0 | Difficulty level – Intermediate | Resources – Web image 602
Related techniques – 6.01, 6.03, 6.04, 6.05 | Tools used – Selection tools | Menus used – Select

Photoshop Elements also contains a way to modify the edges of the selections you create. Called the Refine Edge feature it is accessed either via the button now present in all the selection tools' options bars, or via the Select > Refine Edge menu entry. The feature brings together three different controls for adjusting the edges of the selection with two selection edge preview options. The edge controls previously existed as separate entries in either the Select or Select > Modify menu. Bringing them together in the one dialog, and then providing live preview options as well, means that the refining activity will be a lot more accurate, as you will be able to see the results of the changes made to any of the controls reflected in the image itself.

The feature's dialog contains a Preview toggle, and Zoom and Move tools which can be used for navigating around enlarged images to check the properties of the selection edge. The edge controls themselves come in the form of the following three sliders:

Smooth – This option removes stepped or jagged selection edges.

Feather – Softens the edge of the selection by a given pixel value. You can use this setting to provide a gradual transition between selected and non-selected areas.

Contract/Expand – Increase or decrease the size of the area outlined by the selection by the percentage value selected.

Preview Modes >> *The Quick Selection tool contains two preview modes. The standard option (left) shows the traditional marching ants outlining the selected area and the Mask view (right) displays a colored mask over the non-selected areas.*

The Preview modes buttons at the bottom of the dialog provide a range of different ways to view the selection on your picture. The left button displays a standard selection edge superimposed on the photo. The edge is outlined using the familiar 'marching ants' line.

The other button previews the selection as a mask, with the selected area displayed clear of color and the non-selected area colored with a specific color overlay. The color and transparency of the mask overlay can be altered by double-clicking the preview button.

Selecting the Mask option provides a much better way of viewing the quality of the selection edge as it is possible to preview the sharpness of the edge as well as how transparent the overlap is between selected and non-selected areas (feathering). For best results, use the Mask option in conjunction with the Zoom and Move tools to inspect an enlarged preview

Refine Edges dialog >> *The Refine Edge dialog brings together all the controls used for altering the characteristics of the selection's edge into a single dialog. The feature also includes two edge preview options.*

of the selection edge, as you make changes to the dialog's slider controls.

Press the 'P' key to turn off the preview of the current Refine Edge settings and the 'X' key to temporarily display the Full Image view.

Overlay options >> *By double-clicking the Mask Preview option you can alter the color and opacity of the mask.*

6.05 Saving and loading selections

*Suitable for Elements – 7.0, 6.0, 5.0, 4.0, 3.0, 2.0, 1.0 | Difficulty level – Intermediate | Resources – Web image 6.04
Related techniques – 6.01, 6.03, 6.04, 6.05 | Tools used – Selection tools | Menus used – Select*

Photoshop Elements thankfully gives you the option to save all your hard selecting work so that it can be used again later. With your selection active choose the Save Selection option from the Select menu. Your selection will now be saved as part of the file when you save in PSD, TIFF, PDF or JPEG 2000 formats. When you open the file later you can retrieve the selection by choosing Load Selection from the same menu. This feature is particularly useful when making sophisticated multi-step selections, as you can make sequential saves, marking your progress and ensuring that you never lose your work. The Save Selection dialog also provides you with another way to modify your selections. Here you will find the option to save a newly created selection in any of the four selection modes we looked at earlier. This provides you with an alternative method for building complex selections which is based on making a selection and then saving it as an addition. In this way you can create a sophisticated selection one step at a time.

Save Selection dialog >> *You can also choose to modify your selection via the modes in the Save Selection dialog.*

Step 1 >> *Use your favorite tool to make your first selection.*

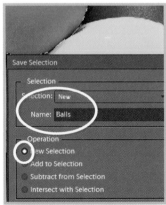

Step 2 >> *Save this as a new selection using the Select > Save Selection feature. Deselect (Ctrl + D).*

Step 3 >> *Make a new selection and then save it using the Add to Selection mode in the Save dialog.*

6.06 Modifying selections

Suitable for Elements – 7.0, 6.0, 5.0, 4.0, 3.0, 2.0, 1.0 | Difficulty level – Intermediate | Resources – Web image 6.04
Related techniques – 6.01, 6.02, 6.04 | Tools used – Selection tools | Menus used – Select

Apart from adding to and subtracting from selections, Photoshop Elements also offers several other ways to modify your selections. We have already seen some of these options in the Refine Edge feature. Here we look at them individually. Nested under the Select menu, most of these options change the positioning or character of the selection's edge. They can provide quick ways to adjust your selections. Use Refine Edge if you want to preview the changes to the selection before application.

- **Select > Feather** adjusts the smoothness of the transition between selected and non-selected areas. Low values are used for sharp-edged selections and higher values for softer ones.

- **Select > Modify > Border** creates a border of a specific pixel width at the selection's edge. Add color to this border using the Edit>Fill command. This option only creates soft edge borders. Use Edit>Stroke to create hard-edged lines around a selection.

- **Select > Modify > Smooth** searches for unselected pixels within the nominated radius. If these areas are surrounded by selected pixels then they will be included in the selection; if the surrounding areas are not selected then they will be removed from the selection.

- **Select > Modify > Expand** increases the size of the selection evenly by the pixel amount selected.

- **Select > Modify > Contract** decreases the selection size by the pixel amount selected.

- **Select > Grow** selects pixels adjacent to the selection that are within the tolerance range of the Magic Wand settings.

- **Select > Similar** chooses all pixels throughout the picture that fall within the Magic Wand tolerance settings.

Feather >> *Use this option to create graduated edges to your selections.*

Border >> *This option creates a soft-edged border, a specific number of pixels wide.*

Smooth >> *Use this option to include random unselected pixels in an otherwise selected area.*

Expand >> *Increase a selection's size by a given number of pixels with this command.*

Contract >> *Reduce the size of the selection by a given number of pixels with this setting.*

Grow >> *Use this option to select all adjacent pixels that fall within the current Magic Wand settings.*

Similar >> *This command selects all other pixels in the whole image that fall within the Magic Wand settings.*

6.07 Transforming a selection

Suitable for Elements – 7.0, 6.0, 5.0, 4.0, 3.0, 2.0, 1.0 | Difficulty level – Intermediate | Resources – Web image 606
Related techniques – 6.01, 6.02, 6.03, 6.05 | Tools used – Selection tools | Menus used – Image

By combining the abilities of the transformation tools that Photoshop Elements provides with several selection techniques you have the power to seamlessly change the way that your pictures look. The features grouped under the Transform heading include tools that can alter the scale and rotation of your picture as well as those that can be used to skew, distort or apply perspective to the image. These changes can be made to the photograph as a whole, to the contents of a layer, to a selection or to a shape that you have drawn. Not all transformation options are available in all situations. For example, the Distort & Perspective options cannot be applied to the contents of a text layer.

Select, copy and paste >>
By manipulating selected parts of your picture you can change a straight image into something that on the one hand is obviously not real, but because it has been so seamlessly altered, it has an aspect of believability. Here the eyes and mouth of the subject have been selected, copied and enlarged before being blended back into the original picture.

Transform >>
The Free Transform tool provides a fast and effective way to manipulate the size and shape of your pictures.

When a transformation tool is active the image area will be surrounded by a 'bounding box' containing several adjustment handles at its corners and sides. By dragging these handles you will be able to manipulate the picture. Most experienced image editors use the Free Transform tool (Image > Transform > Free Transform) for all their transformation changes. With this one feature and a few different keyboard combinations you can perform all your image adjustments without selecting another feature. Use the guide below to help you use the Free Transform tool:

- **To scale** – drag on one of the corner handles of the bounding box.
- **To scale from the center** – press the Alt key whilst dragging a corner handle.
- **To maintain aspect ratio whilst scaling** – hold down the Shift key whilst dragging.
- **To rotate** – move the cursor outside the bounding box until it changes to a curved two-ended arrow, then click and drag to rotate the picture or drag the Rotate handle at the bottom of the bounding box.
- **To distort** – hold down the Ctrl key whilst dragging any handle.
- **To skew** – hold down the Ctrl + Shift keys whilst dragging a side handle.
- **To apply a perspective change** – hold down Ctrl + Alt + Shift whilst dragging a corner handle.
- **To commit changes** – double-click inside the bounding box or hit Enter, or click the Commit icon (green tick) at the bottom of the marquee.

In the example the exaggerated eyes and mouth were created by firstly selecting the face parts, feathering the edge of the selection (Select > Feather) and then copying (Edit > Copy) and pasting (Edit > Paste) each part onto a new layer. With the appropriate layer selected the parts were then enlarged using the Free Transform feature (Image > Transform > Free Transform) and distorted a little (Image > Transform > Distort) to suit the rest of the face. As a final step a soft-edged eraser was used to remove sections of the face parts that didn't match the picture below. This step helped to blend changes into the original image.

Step 1 >> *Copy and paste onto new layers parts of the picture that were selected using a feather.*

Step 2 >> *Change the size of the face parts and apply some distortion using the Free Transform tool. Double-click inside the bounding box to commit your changes.*

Step 3 >> *Carefully erase the edge of the transformed face parts to blend them with the rest of the original image below.*

6.08 Precise control of selection size

Suitable for Elements – 7.0, 6.0, 5.0, 4.0, 3.0, 2.0, 1.0 | Difficulty level –
Intermediate | Related techniques – 6.01, 6.02, 6.03, 6.04
Tools used – Marquee | Menus used – Window, Edit, View

There will be times when you will need to know the precise
size of the selections you make. You can get this information
from the Info palette (Window > Info) where Elements
reports the width and height of your selection in the units
selected in the Units preferences (Edit > Preferences > Units
and Rulers). This dialog also shows the exact position of the
cursor. This can be helpful when you need to start and end a
selection at a set screen reference.

Info >> *The Info palette shows
the position of the cursor (a) as
well as the size of the selection
(b).*

Fixed Size selections >> *Make precise selections by inserting
the dimensions directly into the Marquee's option bar.*

If instead of just viewing the dimensions of the selection you actually want to specify the size, you
can input these values into the options bar of the Marquee tool. After selecting the tool, choose Fixed
Size from the Style drop-down menu in the Options bar. You can then enter the value for width
and height into the fields in the bar. Now when you click on the canvas with the Marquee tool, a
selection of the precise dimensions you input will appear on the picture. As with the Info dialog
the measurement units used here are
controlled by the settings in the Units
and Rulers preferences.

Another way to precisely control
the size of your selections is to use
the Elements Grid system as a guide.
Simply display the Grid over your
picture (View >Snap To > Grid) and
switch on the Snap to Grid option
(View > Snap to Grid). Now as you
are drawing a selection the cursor
will align itself with the grid lines or
intersections. The interval of the grid
lines and spacings can be altered via
the Grid preferences (Edit > Preferences
> Grid).

Grid as guide >> *Use the Elements Grid option to help make
precise selection. Image courtesy of www.darranleal.com.au.*

Understanding layers

In a lot of ways traditional film-based shooting is very similar to digital photography. After all, apart from a few useful additions such as a preview screen on the back and a slot for my memory card, my digital camera is not unlike my film camera (in fact they even share the same lenses). But thinking that these similarities extend to the pictures themselves can mean that you are missing out on some of the more powerful capabilities of your digital pictures.

Digital pictures are not always flat

The traditional photograph contains all the picture elements in a single plane. Digital images captured by a camera or sourced from a scanner are also flat files. And for a lot of new digital photographers this is how their files remain – flat. All editing and enhancing work is conducted on the original picture, but things can be different.

Most image editing packages contain the ability to use layers with your pictures. This feature releases your images from having to keep all their information in a flat file. Different image parts, added text and certain enhancement tasks can all be kept on separate layers. The layers are kept in a stack and the image you see on screen in the work area is a composite of all the layers.

Sound confusing? Well try imagining for example that each of the image parts of a simple portrait photograph are stored on separate plastic sheets. These are your layers. The background sits at the bottom. The portrait is laid on top of the background and the text is placed on top. When viewed from above the solid part of each layer obscures the picture beneath. Whilst the picture parts are based on separate layers they can be moved, edited or enhanced independently of each other. If they are saved using a file format like Photoshop's PSD file (which is layer friendly) all the layers will be preserved and present next time the file is opened.

Types of layers

Image layers: This is the most basic and common layer type, containing any picture parts or image details. Background is a special type of image layer.

Text layers: Designed solely for text, these layers allow the user to edit and enhance the text after the layer has been made.

Fill layers: Users can also apply a Solid Color, Gradient or Pattern to an image as a separate layer.

Adjustment layers: These layers alter the layers that are arranged below them in the stack. They act as a filter through which the lower layers are viewed. You can use adjustment layers to perform many of the enhancement tasks that you would normally apply directly to an image layer without changing the image itself. Adjustment layers are added automatically when using the Smart Brush Tool.

Layers >> *A digital picture is often composed of many parts, each stored on a separate layer.* Image courtesy of www.ablestock.com © 2005.

Shape layers: Drawing with any of the shape tools creates a new vector-based Shape layer. The layer contains a thumbnail for the shape as well as the color of the layer.

Frame layers: From Elements 5.0 Adobe has included a new layer type to coincide with its Photo Layout and Photo Book projects. Called the Frame layer, its role is to store both the frame and the picture that sits within it. Both the component parts remain as separate individual images despite being stored as one layer. What does this mean in day-to-day editing? Well it means that you can do things like change the size, shape and orientation of either the frame and picture combination, or the picture, independently of each other.

Background layers: An image can only have one background layer. It is the bottom-most layer in the stack. No other layers can be moved beneath this layer. You cannot adjust this layer's opacity or its blending mode. You can convert background layers to standard image layer's by double-clicking the layer in the Layers palette, setting your desired layer options in the dialog provided and then clicking OK.

The magic of Frame layers

Adobe introduced Frame layers as part of its revamp of Photo Project creation in version 5.0. For most Elements users, frame layers are seen as a way to add decorative edges to their photos when creating albums or scrapbooking pages, but their quiet power goes beyond mere framing. Frame layers are built on a Photoshop Technology called Smart Objects.

Professionals in the know use Smart Objects as a way of protecting their photos from the damage associated with resizing, rotating and distorting image layers. A smart object keeps the pixels safe by applying the changes made to the layer to a copy of the pixels rather than the original photo.

It may not be immediately apparent when you are first playing with your images in this way, but each time you make a change to the size or orientation of your photo the pixels are resampled. This means that the original pixels are being changed with each adjustment, and you know how I feel about that! Perform enough of these changes and gradually the image becomes less and less defined. See the example images on the right. How can

Non-destructive resizing with Frame layers >> *To give you an example of how destructive seemingly small changes to our image layers are I resized a standard image layer up and down three times. It is easy to see how blurry the photo has become (a). Next I added the same picture to a frame layer and performed exactly the same resizing activity. The result is an image as sharp as the original (b).*

we avoid this degradation? Well, one way to ensure that your files remain as crisp as the day that they were taken is to add the image to a frame layer before messing around with size and rotation. Don't want a frame around the photo? No problem just add the 'No Frame' frame layer to your document and then drag the picture from the project bin to the No Frame area in the composition. You can also simply drag a photo from the project bin onto an open document; it is added automatically as a Frame layer. Alternatively, you can right-click on a framed photo and choose Clear Frame from the context menu.

Now you can free transform to your heart's content without the fear of resampling, and therefore damaging, the pixels.

No Frame frame layer >> To gain the abilities of a frame layer without the frame, select the No Frame option from the Frames section of the Content palette.

Layer types >> (a) Text or type layer, (b) image layer with chequered transparent area, (c) background layer, (d) Layers palette, (e) preview window with separate layers viewed as a composite image.

Adding layers

When a picture is first downloaded from your digital camera or imported into Photoshop Elements it usually contains a single layer. It is a 'flat file'. By default the program classifies the picture as a background layer. You can add extra 'empty' layers to your picture by clicking the New Layer button at the bottom of the Layers palette or choosing the Layer option from the New sub-menu in the Layer menu (Layer > New > Layer). The new layer is positioned above your currently selected layer. Some actions, such as adding text with the Type tool, automatically create a new layer for the content. This is true when adding adjustment and fill layers to your image. When selecting, copying and pasting image parts, Photoshop also creates a new layer for the copied portion of the picture. Also when you use the Background eraser or the Magic Eraser, a new layer will automatically be created.

Viewing layers

Photoshop Elements's Layers palette displays all your layers and their
settings in the one palette. If the palette isn't already on screen when
opening the program, it may be hidden in the Palette Bin or you
may have to choose the option from the Window menu (Window >
Layers). The individual layers are displayed, one on top of the other,
in a 'layer stack'. The image is viewed from the top down through the
layers. When looking at the picture on screen we see a preview of how
the image looks when all the layers are combined. Each layer is

*Visible layers >> When the Eye icon
is present the layer is visible. Clicking
on the eye turns the icon off,
removing the layer from the preview
window.*

represented by a thumbnail on the left and a name on the right. The size of the thumbnail can be
changed, as can the name of the layer. By default each new layer is named sequentially (layer 1, layer
2, layer 3). This is fine when your image contains a few different picture parts, but for more complex
illustrations it is helpful to rename the layers with titles that help to remind you of their content (portrait,
sky, tree).

You can edit or enhance only one layer at a time. To select the layer that you want to change you need
to click on the layer. At this point the layer will change to a different color from the rest in the stack. This
layer is now the selected layer and can be edited in isolation from the others that make up the picture.
Layers can be turned off by clicking the eye symbol on the far left of the layer so that it is no longer showing. This action removes the layer from view but not from the stack. You can turn the layer back on again
by clicking the space where the eye symbol was. Holding down the Alt key whilst clicking on a layer's eye
symbol will turn off or hide all layers other than the one that you are clicking.

Manipulating layers

Layers can be moved up and down the layer stack by click-dragging. Moving a layer upwards will mean
that its picture content may obscure more of the details in the layers below. Moving downwards progressively positions the layer's details further behind the picture parts of the layers above.

You can reposition the content of any layers (except background layers) using the Move tool. Two or
more layers can be linked together so that when the content of one layer is moved the other details follow
precisely. Simply multi-select the layers in the Layers palette and then click on the Chain icon (Link
Layers button) at the top of the palette. The chain will be added to all the linked layers on the right of the
thumbnail. Unwanted layers can be deleted by click-dragging them to the Dustbin icon at the top of the
Layers palette.

Layer styles

In early image editing programs creating a drop shadow edge to a picture was a process that involved
many steps. Thankfully Elements includes this as one of the many built-in styles that can be quickly
and easily applied to your layers. Users can add effects by clicking on the Effects palette tab in the
Palettes pane and selecting a layer style from those listed in the Layer Styles section. You can edit
the style settings by double-clicking on the small 'fx' icon on the right of the thumbnail in the Layers
palette.

Blending modes >> *Changing the blending mode of upper layers will cause them to interact differently with the layers beneath. The example above shows how altering the blending mode of the text layer changes the way that it interacts with the image and background layers.*
(a) Normal mode.
(b) Color Burn mode.
(c) Difference mode.
(d) Overlay mode.
(e) Luminosity mode.
(f) Color Dodge mode.
(g) Exclusion mode.
(h) Hue mode.

Blending modes and opacity

As well as layer styles, or effects, the opacity (how transparent a layer is) of each layer can be altered by dragging the Opacity slider down from 100% to the desired level of translucency. The lower the number the more detail will show through from the layers below. The Opacity slider is located at the top of the Layers palette and changes the selected layer only. On the left of the Opacity control is a drop-down menu containing a range of blending modes. The default selection is 'normal', which means that the detail in upper layers obscures the layers beneath. Switching to a different blending mode will alter the way in which the layers interact. For more details see the full blending mode example in the Appendix.

Layer shortcuts

- **To display Layers palette** – Choose Window>Layers
- **To access Layers options** – Click the More button in the upper right-hand corner of the Layers palette
- **To change the size of layer thumbnails** – Choose Palette options from the Layers Palette menu and select a thumbnail size
- **To make a new layer** – Choose Layer>New>Layer or click the New Layer button in the Layers palette
- **To create a new adjustment layer** – Choose Layer>New Adjustment Layer and select the layer type or click the New Adjustment Layer in the layers palette
- **To add a style or effect to a layer** – Select the layer and choose a style from those listed in the Layer Styles section of the Artwork and Effects palette.

Masking techniques

Masking in traditional photography is used to physically protect part of the picture from development or exposure. In black and white darkrooms this process often involved the positioning of specially cut 'ruby' red sheets over the photographic paper, which shielded this part of the picture from being exposed during the enlargement process.

The digital version of masking is also designed to restrict effects to only certain portions of an image. Photoshop Elements provides a variety of ways to employ a masking system when editing your pictures.

6.09 Painting masks with the Selection Brush

Suitable for Elements – 7.0, 6.0, 5.0, 4.0, 3.0, 2.0 | Difficulty level – Intermediate | Resources – Web image 609
Related techniques – 6.02, 6.03 | Tools used – Selection Brush

The Selection Brush was a welcome addition to the Photoshop Elements tools line up when it was added in revision 2.0 of the program and, although its primary purpose is to aid the creation of complex selections, it can also be used in a 'Rubylith' Mask mode. Activate the mode by selecting the Mask option from the mode drop-down menu in the Tools options bar. Now when the brush is dragged across the surface of a picture it will leave a red, semi-transparent mask behind it. The mask will protect these parts of the picture from the effects of filters, color changes and tonal correction.

The size and edge softness of the Selection Brush as well as the mask opacity (overlay opacity) and mask color can be altered in the options bar. Switching back to the Selection mode will turn off the mask and make a selection from the parts of the picture that weren't painted. Whilst in Mask mode painting with the brush will add to the mask. Applying the brush in the Selection mode will add to the selection, which effectively is removing masked areas. You can also save carefully painted masks using the Save Selection option in the Select menu and pre-saved selections can be converted into a mask by loading the selection and then switching back to Mask mode. A quick tip for powers users – Alt-clicking the Layer Mask thumbnail displays shows the rubylith mask, which is handy when making lots of adjustments to the selected area.

Step 1 >> *Choose the Selection Brush (under the Magic Selection Brush) from the tool box and switch the brush to Mask mode.*

Step 2 >> *Paint on the parts of the picture that you want to shield from the editing process.*

Step 3 >> *Apply the editing changes to the non-masked areas. Here we applied the Crystallize filter.*

6.10 Fill and adjustment layer masks

*Suitable for Elements – 7.0, 6.0, 5.0, 4.0, 3.0, 2.0, 1.0 | Difficulty level – Intermediate | Resources – Web image 6.09
Related techniques – 6.07, 6.11, 6.12 | Menus used – Layer*

Another form of masking is available to Elements users via the Fill and Adjustment Layers features.
Each time you add one of these layers to an image, two thumbnails are created in the Layers palette.
The one on the left controls the settings for the adjustment layer. Double-clicking this thumbnail
brings up the dialog box and the settings used for the fill or adjustment layer. The thumbnail on
the right represents the layer's mask which governs how and where the settings are applied to the
image.

Eraser >> *Erasing parts of the fill
layer reveals the picture beneath.*

Black paint >> *Painting the mask
with black paint has the same effect
as erasing.*

White paint >> *Painting with white
paint restores the mask and the
pattern.*

The mask is a grayscale image. In its default state it is colored white, meaning that no part of the
layer's effects are being masked or held back from the picture below. Conversely, if the thumbnail
is totally black then none of the layer's effects is applied to the picture. In this monochrome world
shades of gray equate to various levels of transparency. With this in mind we can control which
parts of the picture are altered by the fill or adjustment layer and which parts remain unchanged by
painting (in black and white and gray) and erasing directly on the layer mask.

To start editing a layer mask, firstly apply a fill layer such as Pattern to the image. Check to see that
the default colors (white and black) are selected for the Elements foreground and background colors.
Next select the Eraser tool, and with the fill layer selected in the Layers palette, proceed to remove
part of the layer. The pattern is removed and the picture beneath shows through and a black mark
now appears in the layer thumbnail corresponding to your erasing actions. Switch to the Paint
Brush tool and select black as your foreground color and paint onto the patterned surface. Again
this action masks the picture beneath from the effects of the fill layer and adds more black areas to
the thumbnail. Painting with white as your foreground color restores the mask and paints back the
pattern. You can experiment with transparent effects by painting on the mask with gray. The lighter
the gray the more the pattern will dominate, the darker the gray the less the pattern will be seen. A
similar semi-transparent effect can be achieved if the opacity of the eraser or brush is reduced.

6.11 Using selections with layer masks

*Suitable for Elements – 7.0, 6.0, 5.0, 4.0, 3.0, 2.0, 1.0 | Difficulty level –
Intermediate | Resources – Web image 6.08 | Related techniques – 6.09,
6.10, 6.12 | Tools used – Select*

In addition to employing painting and erasing tools to work
directly on the layer mask you can also use a selection in
conjunction with an adjustment or fill layer to restrict the area
of your image that is altered. Make a selection in the normal
way and then, with the selection still active, create a new adjustment or fill layer. The selection confines the changes made
by the new adjustment/fill layer. You will notice the selected
area is colored white in the Layer Mask thumbnail. A layer
mask made in this way can be edited using the same painting
techniques as discussed above.

Selection >> *By having a selection
active when you make a new adjustment or fill layer you immediately
restrict the effects of this layer to just
the confines of the selection.*

6.12 'Group with Previous' masks

*Suitable for Elements – 7.0, 6.0, 5.0, 4.0, 3.0, 2.0, 1.0 | Difficulty level – Intermediate
| Resources – Web image 609 | Related techniques – 6.09, 6.10, 6.110 | Menus used –
Layer*

The final masking technique that Photoshop Elements employs uses the
special Group with Previous command found in the Layer menu. This
command uses the transparency surrounding objects on a layer as a
mask for the content of any layers that are above it in the stack. In the
example the balloon image was placed above the test text layer. With
the balloon layer active the Group with Previous command (Layer >
Group with Previous) was selected. The example image now fills the text
shape but is masked from showing through the rest of the layer by the
transparency surrounding the type. This technique also works with
shapes and filled selections drawn on a separate layer surrounded by
transparency.

Step 1 >> *Create some bold text in a
new document with a white
background layer.*

Step 2 >> *Copy and paste a color
image in a layer above the text.*

Step 3 >> *Select the color layer and
choose the Group with Previous
command from the Layers menu.*

Step 1 >> *Select Image > Mode > Grayscale and then click on the OK button in the Discard Color warning box.*

Step 2 >> *Using the Levels control, map the dark pixels to black by dragging the black point slider to the right.*

Step 3 >> *Correct the highlights by dragging the white point slider to the left.*

Increase contrast >> *By moving the black and white input sliders towards the center of the dialog you can increase the contrast of your picture.*

Converting color to black and white

One of the real advantages of shooting digital is the ease with which you can convert color images to black and white. Gone are the days of having to carry two camera bodies, one loaded with color film the other with black and white. Now you simply shoot color all the time and then convert selected images to black and white using a few simple steps.

6.13 Changing the mode to grayscale

Suitable for Elements – 7.0, 6.0, 5.0, 4.0, 3.0, 2.0, 1.0 | Difficulty level – Basic | Resources – Web image 610 | Related techniques – 6.14, 6.15 | Menus used – Image, Enhance

The simplest way to lose the colors in your picture is to convert the image to a grayscale. This process changes the photograph from having three color channels (red, green and blue) to being constructed of a single channel that contains the picture's detail only. Often this conversion produces a flat and lacklustre photograph and so a little manipulation of the tones is in order. My first point of call to help solve this problem would always be the Levels dialog (Enhance > Adjust Lighting > Levels). Using this control you can make sure that your image tones are spread across the grayscale spectrum.

Most grayscale conversion pictures need a general contrast increase. You can achieve this by moving the black and white input sliders towards the center of the dialog. Holding the Alt key down whilst you are moving the slider will enable you to preview the pixels that are being converted to pure black or pure white. Your aim is to map the darkest pixels in the picture to black and the lightest ones to white. Work carefully here as a heavy handed approach will produce pictures where delicate shadow and highlight details are lost forever.

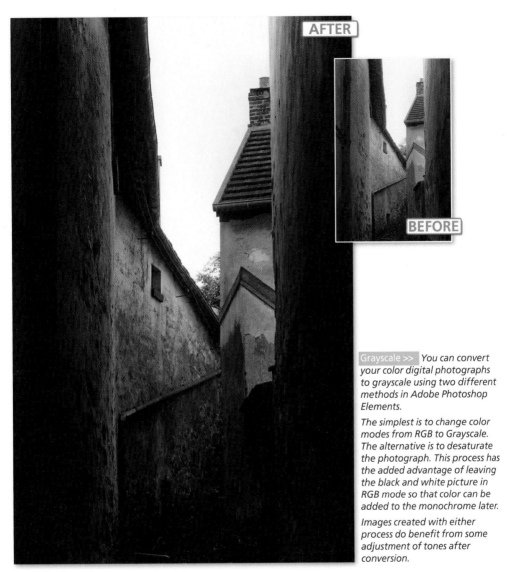

AFTER

BEFORE

Grayscale >> *You can convert your color digital photographs to grayscale using two different methods in Adobe Photoshop Elements.*

The simplest is to change color modes from RGB to Grayscale. The alternative is to desaturate the photograph. This process has the added advantage of leaving the black and white picture in RGB mode so that color can be added to the monochrome later.

Images created with either process do benefit from some adjustment of tones after conversion.

6.14 Desaturate the color file

Suitable for Elements – 7.0, 6.0, 5.0, 4.0, 3.0, 2.0, 1.0 | Difficulty level – Basic | Resources – Web image 611
Related techniques – 6.13, 6.15, 6.16 | Tools used – Dodge and Burn-in | Menus used – Image

Photoshop Elements uses the term 'saturation' to refer to the strength of the colors in a picture. Increasing saturation makes the colors in a picture more vivid, decreasing saturation makes the hues weaker. The program employs the Hue/Saturation (Enhance > Adjust Color > Hue Saturation) control to adjust the color's strength. If the Saturation slider is moved all the way to the left of the dialog (to a setting of –100) then all color is removed from the picture. You are effectively left with a grayscale or black and white photograph that is very similar to the 'convert to grayscale' version above but with one important difference – the picture is still an RGB file. This means that even though the photograph no longer contains any color, the color mode it is stored in is capable of supporting

Step 1 >> *Select the Hue/Saturation control from the Adjust Color heading in the Enhance menu.*

Step 2 >> *Move the Saturation slider completely to the left, removing all color from the picture.*

Step 3 >> *Use the Dodging and Burning-in tools to lighten and darken selected areas of the picture.*

color. So if you are wanting to try a little digital hand coloring, or experiment with pictures that contain monochrome as well as color components, then this is the technique for you. More details on these techniques can be found later in this book. Be warned though, once your picture is desaturated the color is lost for ever and so it is always a good idea to save a copy of the color version of the image before proceeding.

You can shortcut the desaturation process by selecting Enhance > Adjust Color > Remove Color, which provides the same results as using the Hue/Saturation control but in a single step.

Pro's Tip

Once the picture has been desaturated you may need to tweak the shadow, highlight and midtones using the Levels feature. Finally, add some drama to the picture by selectively lightening and darkening parts of the image using the Dodging and Burning-in tools. Used judiciously these devices can change the whole atmosphere of a photograph. In the example, I darkened the walls closest to the viewer and lightened those parts of the French alleyway that were in the background. These changes increased the sense of distance in the picture as well as helping to draw the viewer's eyes into the picture.

Desaturation shortcut >> *The Enhance > Adjust Color > Remove Color option is a shortcut that produces the same results as moving the Saturation slider to -100 in the Hue/ Saturation feature.*

Saturation control >> *By decreasing the saturation of the colors in a picture completely you convert the image to just black and white.*

6.15 A more sophisticated approach

Suitable for Elements – 7.0, 6.0, 5.0, 4.0, 3.0, 2.0, 1.0 | Difficulty level – Basic | Resources – Web image 612
Related techniques – 6.13, 6.14, 6.16 | Menus used – Layer

Despite the straightforward nature of the two conversion approaches detailed above, transforming a color photo to grayscale is not as simple as it first seems. Many converted images seem a little flat and lack the separation of tones that existed in the original photo. The trick with good conversions from color to grayscale is ensuring that the hues in the original picture are translated into distinct and different tones. For this reason no one conversion process will be suitable for all pictures.

Take for instance the example of a red flower photographed against the background of rich green foliage. When converted to grayscale by switching modes or desaturating there is a tendency for both the red of the flower and the green of the leaves to be converted to the same gray tone, making the monochrome picture much less vibrant and dynamic than the original. In order to restore some visual separation between flower and background it is necessary to convert these hues to different grays.

Just such a technique was developed by the Adobe evangelist, Russell Brown (www.russellbrown.com). The original method was designed for Photoshop but works just as well with Elements. It uses the Adjustment Layers technology in Photoshop Elements as a way to both convert the color image to black and white and also to control how the colors are represented in the grayscale. Like a lot of Russell's techniques it leaves the original image unchanged in the background. Hence this style of image enhancing is called non-destructive editing.

Step 1 >> *Make a new Hue/Saturation layer above your background. Don't make any changes to the default settings for this layer.*

Set the mode of the adjustment layer to Color. Label this layer 'Filter'.

Step 2 >> *Make a second Hue/Saturation adjustment layer above the Filter layer and alter the settings so Saturation is -100. Call this layer Black and White Film. The monochrome image now on screen is the standard result we would expect if we just desaturated the colored original.*

Step 3 >> *Next double-click on the layer thumbnail in the Filter layer and move the Hue slider. This changes the way that the color values are translated to black and white. Similarly, if you move the Saturation slider you can emphasize particular parts of the image.*

More control >> For more precise control of the separation of tones you can restrict your changes to a single color group (red, blue, green, cyan, magenta) by selecting it from the drop-down menu before manipulating the Hue and Saturation controls.

Gray conversion options >> Photoshop Elements provides a variety of options when you are wanting to convert color pictures to a grayscale or black and white photo.
(a) Original color photo.
(b) Change to grayscale mode.
(c) Desaturate the photo.
(d) The Russell Brown technique.

6.16 The Convert to Black and White feature

Suitable for Elements – 7.0, 6.0, 5.0 | Difficulty level – Basic Resources – Web image 613 | Related techniques – 6.13, 6.14, 6.15 | Menus used – Enhance

Taking this idea further in Elements 5 Adobe introduced a new Convert to Black and White feature (Editor: Enhance > Convert to Black and White). It provides the ability to customize the way that color areas are mapped to gray during the conversion process. The dialog consists of large before and after previews, a series of six conversion styles that are based on popular subject types or conversions and four slider control buttons for fine-tuning the results.

This feature provides the options for more sophisticated conversions by allowing the user to adjust which colors (red, green or blue) feature more prominently in the final result.

Convert to Black and White >> *From version 5.0 Photoshop Elements has contained a custom control for transforming color photos to grayscale. The Convert to Black and White feature allows you to control how the colors are mapped to gray.*
(a) Original color photo.
(b) Desaturate or Remove Color conversion.
(c) Convert to Black and White conversion emphasizing the blue areas in the original color photo.

Before preview

After preview

Feature tip and help link

Conversion style   *Adjustment sliders*

Convert to Black and White >> *The Convert to Black and White dialog contains a before and after preview, six different conversion styles or flavor presets as well as a set of adjustment buttons that can be used for customizing the way that particular colors are mapped to gray.*

This feature is great for situations where the color contrast of a scene isn't reflected in the monochrome conversion. Imagine the color contrast of a red rose against green foliage. Using a simple conversion feature such as Remove Color would result in both the rose and foliage being the same tone of gray. With Convert to Black and White the contrast of the original can be retained in the result by boosting or reducing the prominence of green or red parts of the picture.

Step 1 >> *With a suitable color image open in the Full Edit workspace select the Convert to Black and White feature from the Enhance menu. Click through the different conversion styles menu checking the After preview for a suitable result. Click OK to apply the conversion, Reset to remove current settings or Cancel to quit the feature.*

Step 2 >> *For a more customized conversion start by selecting a conversion style that is closest to your desired result and then fine-tune the results with one of the Adjustment Intensity sliders. The effects can be more dramatic by also applying the opposite adjustment in the other two color channels.*

Step 3 >> *In situations where the changes you make produce results that are undesirable you can return the after image back to its default state by clicking the Reset button in the top right of the dialog.*

Custom Black and White >> *You can create your own custom black and white style presets by editing the bwconvert.txt file (f) located in the \Program Files\Adobe\Photoshop Elements 7.0\Required folder (e). Alternatively, you can download and copy my own version of this file to the directory. It contains four custom conversion options Dark Skies (a), Moody (b), Separate Red Green (c) and White Skin (d). After restarting Elements the new options will appear in the Styles menu of the feature (g).*

6.17 Custom entries in Convert to Black and White

Suitable for Elements – 7.0, 6.0, 5.0 | Difficulty level – Basic | Resources – Web image 614 | Related techniques – 6.14, 6.15, 6.16 | Menus used – Enhance

The preset style entries in the Convert to Black and White feature are controlled by a simple text file located in the settings folders of the program. The features settings file is called 'bwconvert.txt' and is located in the *C:\Program Files\Adobe\Photoshop Elements 7.0\Required* folder. The file sets the values for the styles and can be easily edited if a user wants to have their own conversion preset values. Just make sure that you create a new line for each entry and follow the style of the other settings. You will also need to restart Elements for the new entries to take effect. Of course, I highly recommend backing up the installed version of the file so that you can easily restore the settings back to the default values.

If all this sounds too difficult then just download my customized version of the 'bwconvert.txt' file and copy it to the *C:\Program Files\Adobe\Photoshop Elements 7.0\Required* folder. My version contains four extra presets (Dark Skies, Moody, Separate Red Green and White Skin) designed to extend the styles in the feature further and provide some example conversions that you might find useful. As with all styles, to fully suit your images, apply the style first and then tweak the results with the sliders.

6.18 The Gradient Map conversions

Suitable for Elements – 7.0, 6.0, 5.0 | Difficulty level – Basic | Resources – Web image 615
Related techniques – 6.13, 6.14, 6.15 | Menus used – Enhance

Yet another way to convert a color image to grayscale is to employ the abilities of a Gradient Map Adjustment Layer. When set to a black to white gradient, this feature maps the tones and colors in an image so that they are evenly distributed along the gradient's tonal range. This creates a conversion with good overall contrast, as the darkest point of the photo is mapped to black and the lightest to white, but by playing with the gradient itself, you can also tweak the brightness of other tonal areas in the image as well. So with this technique you get to make the conversion, and adjust how shadows, midtones and highlights are mapped to gray. Cool!

Step 1 >> *To start let's make a simple Gradient Map grayscale conversion. Do this by adding a Gradient Map adjustment layer to the layers stack (Layer > New Adjustment Layer > Gradient Map). Next select a Black to White gradient from the drop-down menu. Click OK and the conversion is complete.*

Step 2 >> *To start to control how shadows midtones and highlights are mapped to gray we need to create a custom gradient In the Gradient Editor. Double-click on the Gradient Map thumbnail to open the feature's dialog. Next click onto the displayed gradient to open the Gradient Editor.*

Step 3 >> *At the moment the gradient has a color control (called Stops) at either end of the gradient – black and white. We want to add extra Stops for 25%, 50% and 75% brightness values. Do this by clicking just below the gradient. This adds a new Stop. Double-click the stop to open the Select Stop Color dialog. Type the gray value in the 'B' section for the HSB values. Click OK.*

Step 4 >> *Repeat the process adding in the other gray stops. Don't worry too much about their position along the gradient as we can alter this, just try to ensure that the 25% brightness value is left of center, 50% about center and 75% brightness is right of center. Once all the stops have been created add a name for the gradient in the Name area and click the New button to add the gradient to those listed in the palette. Don't click OK.*

Step 5 >> *To manipulate how the tones are mapped to gray click on a stop and drag it along the gradient in the Gradient Editor. In this example the shadows were lightened by dragging the 25% brightness stop to the left and midtones were darkened by dragging the 50% darkness to the right. The changes will be previewed in your image as long as the Preview option is ticked in the Gradient Map dialog.*

Step 6 >> *Finally to apply the conversion click the OK buttons in the Gradient Editor and the Gradient Map dialogs. The tones can be adjusted at a later date by double-clicking on the adjustment layer thumbnail and then clicking the gradient. This will display the Gradient Editor complete with your custom gradient containing the three additional brightness stops.*

6.19 Borrowing Photoshop's Black and White

Suitable for Elements – 7.0, 6.0, 5.0 | Difficulty level – Basic | Resources – Web image 6.16 | Related techniques –
6.13, 6.14, 6.15 | Menus used – Enhance

At the same time that Elements users were enjoying the monochrome mapping power of the
Convert to Black and White feature, Photoshop CS3 users were also given a specialized conversion feature called, Black and White. The new feature is available for use directly on an image or
via an Adjustment Layer. It contains six slider controls that adjust how specific color ranges are
mapped to gray. In addition, there is a toning option at the bottom of the dialog which provides
the ability to tint the converted monochrome.

Even though this is a Photoshop-only feature, we can make use of its color to gray mapping
abilities. Just drag an existing Black and White adjustment layer from a document created in
Photoshop, but opened into Elements, onto an Elements file. Just like magic the layer is added
to the Elements document and the conversion applied. Just in case you don't have Photoshop
handy I have created a special donor document called, *Photoshop-Convert-to-Gray.psd*, which
contains ten different conversion layers. For you to have the Photoshop feature working on your
documents just download the file from the book's website, open it into the edit workspace and
drag one of the layers to your Elements document.

Step 1 >> *Start by opening both the Photoshop donor
document (Photoshop-Convert-to-gray.psd) and the
Elements file that you want to enhance. Click onto the
Photoshop document and scroll through the list of
adjustment layers available in the document. Select a
layer and click-drag it onto the Elements document. The
enhancement change will be immediately previewed in
the workspace.*

Step 2 >> *Multiple Photoshop layers can be dragged
onto the Elements document and their effects hidden
or applied by clicking the 'eye' icon on the left of the
layer entry.*

Advanced dodging and burning-in

After years of my 'hit and miss' approach to dodging and burning in the darkroom I can still remember my reaction to seeing Photoshop Elements performing real-time lightening and darkening – 'You are kidding!'. Not only could I paint in light and dark areas on my picture using a soft-edged brush, I could also vary the strength of the effect and the size of the brush used for application. In addition, I could choose to alter shadow, midtones or highlights separately and 'undo' my actions with a single keystroke. All this flexibility and with the lights on as well!

I would think that most new users to Photoshop Elements would experience much of the same excitement as I did when they first discover the Dodge and Burn-in tools. For the majority of simple enhancement tasks a few quick strokes of these tools will provide plenty of control over your picture's tones, but there are occasions when you need a little more flexibility. I use the following techniques to provide a little more customization to my dodging and burning-in in my work.

Input and output sliders >>
(a) Black, midtone and white Input sliders.
(b) Black and white Output sliders.

6.20 Using selections to change tone

Suitable for Elements – 7.0, 6.0, 5.0, 4.0, 3.0, 2.0, 1.0 | Difficulty level – Intermediate | Resources – Web Image 617 Related Techniques – 6.18 | Tools used – Selection tools| Menus used – Select

You can evenly alter the tone of a large area of your picture quickly by making a feathered selection of the area first and then using the Levels control to darken or lighten the pixels. The amount you feather the selection will determine how soft the transition will be between dodged or burnt areas and the original picture. Using the Levels feature gives you great control over the brightness of shadow, mid- tone and highlight areas.

By manipulating the Input and Output sliders you can selectively alter specific tones in your image. You can also decrease or increase the contrast of the selection as well.

Use this table to help get you started.

Required image change	Action to take
To lighten the midtones of a selected area	Move the midpoint input triangle to the left
To darken the midtones of a selected area	Move the midpoint input triangle to the right
To lighten the midtones and highlights	Move the white point input triangle to the left
To darken the midtones and shadows	Move the black point input triangle to the right
To lighten the shadow tones	Move the black point output triangle to the right
To darken the highlight tones	Move the white point output triangle to the left
To decrease contrast	Move the white and black point Output sliders closer together
To increase contrast	Move the white and black point Input sliders closer together

Step 1 >> *Using one of the selection tools draw a rough selection around the area to dodge or burn-in.*

Step 2 >> *Feather and then inverse the selection. Use a large pixel amount for high-resolution pictures.*

Step 3 >> *With the selection still active manipulate the Levels Input and Output sliders to darken/lighten tones.*

Pro's Tip: Non-destructive dodging and burning-in

If you want to dodge and burn but not make any permanent changes to the picture you can use the same feathered selection technique, but apply the changes through an adjustment layer. Make the selection as before, feathering (Select > Feather or Refine Edge) the edge and inversing (Select > Inverse) the selection. With the selection still active, click onto the Create New Adjustment Layer button on the top of the Layers palette and choose Levels. If the Layers palette is not visible then you can perform the same action via the Layer menu (Layer > New Adjustment Layer). The Levels dialog appears and any changes made with the sliders alter the tones in the selected area of the picture just as before. The difference with this approach is that the dodging and burning-in takes place via an adjustment layer, leaving the original picture unchanged in the layer beneath. The selection is used as a basis to form a mask in the adjustment layer. We view the levels changes through the clear areas of this mask only. A second advantage to this approach is that the levels settings can be changed at a later date. Simply double-click the thumbnail on the left-hand side of the layer and alter the Levels settings.

Step 1 >> *With your feathered selection active click the New Adjustment Layer button.*

Step 2 >> *Select the Levels adjustment layer and adjust the dialog's settings to Dodge and Burn-in.*

A second non-destructive approach that was pioneered by Julianne Kost starts with you creating two empty layers above the background or image layer. Name them Dodge and Burn and set the blending mode for both of them to Soft Light. Using a Black brush at a low opacity (10–15%) paint on the burn layer to darken areas. Use a White brush at the same opacity on the dodge layer to lighten. This provides a non-destructive, subtle and artistic method for dodging and burning-in.

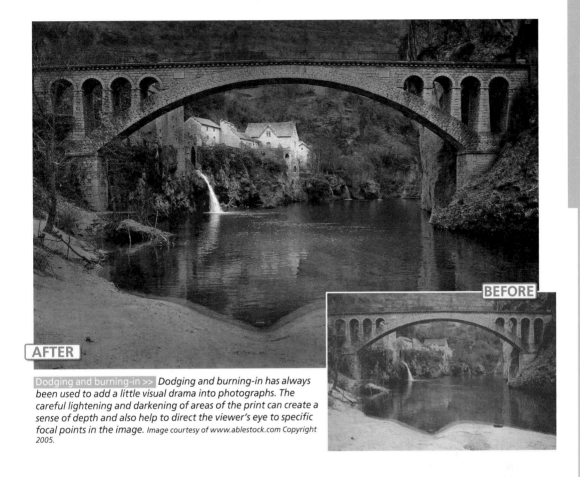

AFTER

BEFORE

Dodging and burning-in >> *Dodging and burning-in has always been used to add a little visual drama into photographs. The careful lightening and darkening of areas of the print can create a sense of depth and also help to direct the viewer's eye to specific focal points in the image.* Image courtesy of www.ablestock.com Copyright 2005.

6.21 Erase back through tonal layers

Suitable for Elements – 7.0, 6.0, 5.0, 4.0, 3.0, 2.0, 1.0 | Difficulty level – Intermediate | Resources – Web image 617 | Related Techniques – 6.16 | Tools used – Eraser Menus used – Enhance, Layer

A more artistic approach to dodging and burning-in can be found in a technique that involves making several different copies of the base picture. The background layer can be copied by either choosing Layer > Duplicate Layer or by dragging the layer to the Create New Layer button at the bottom of the Layers palette.

Each copy is stored on a separate layer and the overall tone of the duplicate image is changed using the Layers control. In the example I have created four layers, labelled them *light*, *midtone*, *dark* and *very dark*, and changed their tones accordingly. Next I selected the Eraser tool, set the mode to brush, the edge option to soft and the opacity to 20%. I then clicked on the Eye icon in both the light and midtone layers and selected the dark layer. Using the Eraser in overlapping strokes, I gradually removed sections of

Dodge and burn via erase >>
Make creative tonal changes using the Eraser tool and several adjusted layer copies.
(a) Light copy.
(b) Midtone/normal copy.
(c) Dark copy.
(d) Very dark copy.

the dark layer to reveal the very dark layer beneath. I then selected the midtone layer and performed the same action and finally I selected the light layer and erased sections to reveal the darker layers below. If this all sounds a little confusing, try thinking of the erasing action as actually painting the image darker, or burning the picture area in, and take my advice – make sure that you name your layers as you create them. This technique works particularly well if used with a graphics tablet as the opacity of the erasing stroke can be linked to the pressure on the stylus. Pressing harder with the stylus erases more of the layer and creates a greater change. Lighter strokes can be used to produce more subtle adjustments.

Step 1 >> *Make several copies of the basic image layer by dragging the layer to the Create New Layer button.*

Step 2 >> *Select each layer in turn and alter the overall brightness using the Levels dialog.*

Step 3 >> *Rename the layers by double-clicking the names in the Layers palette.*

Step 4 >> *Turn off the Eye icon for the light and midtone layers and select the dark layer.*

Step 5 >> *Using the Eraser tool remove parts of the dark layer to reveal the very dark picture below.*

Step 6 >> *Work your way through the other layers gradually removing unwanted areas to build up the picture.*

Book resources and video tutorials can be found at: **www.photoshopelements.net**

Masked based layers

To ensure the maximum ability to customize how the layers are applied you can make use of the mask in a No Settings adjustment layer to hide or reveal the detail for any particular layer. To work this way add No Settings adjustment layers below each of the top three image layers. Then use the Group with Previous command to link the image and adjustment layers.

Step 1 >> *Start by adding a No Settings adjustment layer below each of the image layers. Next Select the image layer and then Choose Layer > Group With Previous to view the layer detail through the adjustment layer mask.*

Step 2 >> *After selecting the Adjustment Layer Mask use a black Brush to paint in the areas of the layer that will be hidden from view (that will allow the detail from beneath to show through).*

6.22 Paint on dodging and burning-in

Suitable for Elements – 7.0, 6.0, 5.0, 4.0, 3.0, 2.0, 1.0
Difficulty level – Intermediate | Resources – Web image 618
Related Techniques – 6.20, 6.21 | Tools used – Brush Menus used – Layer

What if you want the flexibility of painting in your density changes (dodging and burning) but wanted to apply these changes non-destructively to your photo? Well, a solution can be found by combining aspects of the last technique with our understanding of adjustment layers and their associated layer masks.

Start by adding a Levels adjustment layer (Editor: Layer > New Adjustment Layer > Levels) to your photo. In the Levels dialog drag the Input midpoint slider to the right and the Output white point slider to the left. This will create an adjustment layer effect that darkens the whole image. Think of this change as how the image would look if you applied the Burn tool to the whole picture. Click OK to apply the change. Nothing new here you say. True, but what if we could selectively paint in this effect rather than apply it to the whole image? Well here is the trick. Click on the mask of the adjustment layer and fill it with black (Editor: Edit > Fill Layer). Remember black hides the adjustment layer effect so you should see the original tones of your photo restored in the preview window. With the mask still selected choose a soft-edged brush, lower the opacity slightly and make sure the paint colour is white.

Now paint onto the surface of the photo. The painted areas will darken. In reality you are not painting the photo but rather painting the mask and in so doing adding the adjustment layer effect in these areas.

BEFORE

AFTER

'Paint on' image changes >>
Use the mask of the Levels adjustment layer to paint burn and dodge effects non-destructively onto your photos.

Step 1 >> *Create a new Levels adjustment layer that darkens the photo.*

Step 2 >> *Select the layer mask of the adjustment layer in the Layers palette and fill with black.*

Step 3 >> *To burn non-destructively brush onto the photo with white whilst the layer mask is still selected.*

6.23 Blend mode Dodge and Burn

Suitable for Elements – 7.0, 6.0, 5.0, 4.0, 3.0, 2.0, 1.0 | Difficulty level – Intermediate | Resources – Web image 619 | Related Techniques – 6.20, 6.21 | Tools used – Brush | Menus used – Layer

One final technique for dodging and burning makes use of the Soft Light Blend Mode to change the brightness of different picture parts non-destructively. Start by adding a new layer above the background or main image layer. Next change the layer's Blend Mode setting to Soft Light. Now target the new layer and with a black soft-edged brush paint over the picture areas to be darkened. To lighten a portion of the image, switch to a white foreground color (click 'x' for a quick change between foreground and background colors) and paint over these areas. The Blending Mode applies the changes in brightness and the fact that the painting is stored in a separate layer makes the technique non-destructive.

Step 1 >> *Create a new layer and then change the Layer Blend Mode to Soft Light.*

Step 2 >> *Target the new layer and paint over the areas to be burned in with a black soft-edged brush.*

Step 3 >> *To lighten a picture part, switch the foreground color to white and paint again. Adjust the brushes opacity to fine tune the changes.*

Enhance your poorly exposed pictures

Good exposure is the cornerstone of great images. No matter how good your subject is, how well you have composed the image or how brilliantly you captured the scene, if your exposure is a little astray then you will be left with a less than perfect result. This is just as true for digital images as it was for traditional photographs. Overexposure leads to delicate highlight detail being recorded as pure white; underexposure on the other hand produces a picture with little detail in the shadow areas.

The best way to solve these problems is to re-shoot your picture using an aperture and shutter combination that will produce a well-exposed image but, as we all know, sometimes a 're-shoot' is just not possible. So how can Photoshop Elements help us enhance our poorly exposed pictures? I have found the following techniques particularly helpful when trying to enhance, or should that be disguise, images that are suffering from bad exposure.

6.24 Screening image layers to enhance tones

Suitable for Elements – 7.0, 6.0, 5.0, 5.0, 4.0, 3.0, 2.0, 1.0 | Difficulty level – Intermediate
Resources – Web image 620 | Related Techniques – 6.20 | Menus used – Layer, Enhance

The shadow and midtones of a picture are areas that suffer greatly when a photograph is underexposed. Valuable details are lost, the individual tones are too dark and the whole area is lacking in contrast. One way to help rectify this problem is to make an exact copy of the pictures and then combine the two images together in order to multiply the apparent detail and tone in the shadow areas. Photoshop Elements, via layers and blending modes, provides us with the tools necessary to perform these actions.

Step 1 >> *Copy the background layer by dragging it to the New Layer button in the Layers dialog.*

Step 2 >> *Select the copied layer and then change the blending mode to Screen.*

Step 3 >> *As a final touch insert a Levels Adjustment layer between the two layers. Peg the black and white points and lighten the midtones by dragging the midpoint to the left.*

Firstly, duplicate the background (image layer) by dragging it to the New Layer button at the bottom of the Layers dialog. Now, with the copy layer selected, change the layer blending mode to Screen. You should see an immediate brightening of the picture and the appearance of more detail in the shadow areas.

As a final tweaking of the image insert a Levels adjustment layer between the two layers. Do this by clicking on the bottom layer first and then selecting Levels from the drop-down list found when clicking the Create New Adjustment Layer button at the bottom of the Layers palette. Peg the highlights and shadows of the picture by moving the black and white points towards the center until they meet the first pixels in the histogram. Next, move the midtone to the left to increase the overall brightness of the image.

After duplicating image and changing the blending mode to Screen

BEFORE

Re-shot with exposure compensation

AFTER

Correcting underexposure >>
The best way to guarantee a great looking image where the tones are well distributed is to ensure that your exposure settings are correct before pushing the button. If, as is the case in this example, your camera meter is fooled by the scene then you can rescue an underexposed picture using a technique that involves duplicating the base image and then selecting the Screen option as the blending mode.

Those of you who are intimate with Elements will no doubt be asking 'Why not just use the Fill Flash or Shadows/Highlights feature to fix this underexposure problem?' and you are right to ask that question. The Fill Flash option is a great tool for lightening mid to dark tones that have plenty of details, but I have found that this 'duplication layers' technique provides a more pleasing result for underexposed images with little shadow information.

Solving exposure problems when shooting

The statue picture not only provides a great example for this technique but also demonstrates how such underexposure can occur. Set against a white overcast sky this dark statue was underexposed because the camera's meter was fooled by the bright sky behind the subject and therefore provided a shutter/aperture combination which was too dark. The thinking photographer would have predicted this problem and used the Exposure Compensation system on the camera to increase exposure by one to one-and-one-half stops to adjust for the back lighting. Most mid range digital cameras and above incorporate an Exposure Override system like this.

Exposure compensation >>
Use the camera's Exposure Compensation system to override your camera's settings.

To try this for yourself, the next time you encounter a back lit scene shoot two pictures – one with the camera set to auto and the other where you have added to the exposure. Compare the results later on the desktop, or better still, check your exposure in the field by examining the histogram graph of your image on you camera's monitor. This graph works exactly the same way as the graph in the Levels feature in Photoshop Elements. It displays the spread of tones of your image across a grayscale from black to white. Underexposure will result in a graph that bunches towards the black end of the spectrum whereas overexposure moves the pixels towards the white point. A simple check of this graph when shooting can indicate whether you need to adjust your camera and re-shoot to compensate for an exposure problem.

Step 1 >> *With the image at 100% magnification apply the Add Noise filter with Uniform/Monochrome settings.*

Step 2 >> *Select Burn-in tool, reduce exposure to 10% and choose mid-tone range. Set brush size and edge softness.*

Step 3 >> *Burn-in the white area using several overlapping strokes to build up the effect. Change to Shadow range and repeat if necessary.*

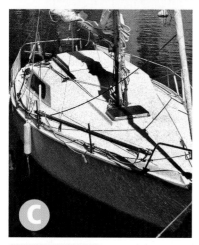

Texture burn-in >>

(a) Original image with blown highlights.
(b) Highlights burnt in using Burn-in tool.
(c) Highlights burnt in after adding a little texture.

6.25 Adding detail to highlights and shadows

Suitable for Elements – 7.0, 6.0, 5.0, 4.0, 3.0, 2.0, 1.0 | Difficulty level – Intermediate | Tools used – Dodging and Burning-in | Menus used – Filter

Sometimes, despite the utmost care on behalf of the photographer, digital images are captured with little or no shadow or highlight details. This scenario should ring true for any reader who has had the pleasure of photographing in very sunny countries. Along with the warmth, strong sun can provide a problem with contrast for the photographer. The deepest shadows and the brightest highlights are so far apart that even the best digital cameras have difficulty in recording all the tones. The result is a picture where either shadow or highlight detail (or in some extreme cases both) is not recorded. These parts of the picture are converted to pure black and white pixels in a process referred to as 'clipping'.

The same scenario can occur when using a scanner to convert slide or film originals into digital files. Incorrect scanner settings coupled with slides that are very dark or negatives that have been overdeveloped are the circumstances that most often produce 'clipped' files.

When presented with such pictures the experienced Elements user will attempt to restore detail in the highlight and shadow areas using the program's Dodging and Burning-in tools. But often such action only results in murky gray highlights and washed out shadow areas. The problem is that the program has no detail in these parts to actually lighten or darken. A solution to this scenario is to add a little (very little) texture to the image and then dodge and burn-in. The texture breaks up the pure white and pure black areas by filling these picture parts with random multi-tone (black, gray and white) pixels. This gives the tools some detail, albeit artificially created, to work on.

I use the Add Noise filter (Filter > Noise > Add Noise) to provide the texture and then select the Dodging tool set to midtones to work on the dark tones, or you could use the Burning-in tool also set to midtones to work on the highlights. A low exposure value of around 10% is coupled with repeated strokes over the offending area. To restrict the noise to just the highlight areas you could select these first using the Magic Wand and then apply the Noise filter.

This technique does have its down side. It doesn't recreate lost details and you will need to degrade your image by making it more noisy before you can dodge and burn. So it can't be considered a magic 'cure all' for problem pictures but it can help you get a little detail into that annoyingly white highlight or that equally frustrating blocked shadow area.

Tinted monochromes

One of the most enduring techniques utilized by photographers the world over is the practice of toning or changing the color of their black and white prints. The Sepia tone (brown) look has come to be linked with quality image production partly because it was a process that increased the longevity of black and white pictures and partly because only committed photographers would take their work through this extra processing step. Digital photographers have the tools at hand to not only 'tone' their black and white images but also to apply this same technique to their color ones.

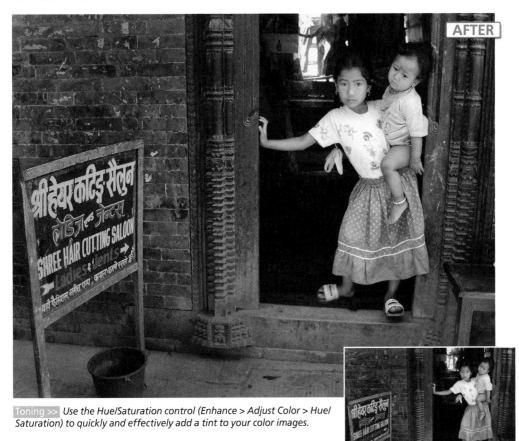

Toning >> *Use the Hue/Saturation control (Enhance > Adjust Color > Hue/Saturation) to quickly and effectively add a tint to your color images.*

6.26 Using Hue and Saturation to tone your pictures

Suitable for Elements – 6, 5.0, 4.0, 3.0, 2.0, 1.0 | Difficulty level – Intermediate | Resources – Web image 621
Related techniques – 6.27 | Menus used – Enhance

The simplest and fastest way to add color is to use the Hue/Saturation control (Enhance > Adjust > Color > Hue/Saturation). This can be applied directly to the whole image or as an adjustment layer (Layer > New Adjustment Layer > Hue Saturation). To change the feature into a toning tool click the Colorize option in the bottom right of the box. The picture will switch to a single color monochrome (one color plus white and black). The Hue slider now controls the color of your tone.

The sepia look in the example is a value of 30 on the Hue slider. The Saturation slider varies the strength of the color. The Saturation value used in the example was 25. The Lightness slider adjusts the brightness of the image but changes of this nature should be left for the Levels feature.

The predictability of this digital toning system means that you can achieve the same tint in each image for a whole series

Hue/Saturation toning >> *Check the Colorize option to convert the dialog to Toning mode.*

of pictures. The recipes for regularly used tones, or favorite colors, can easily be noted down for later use or if toning using an adjustment layer then the layer can be dragged from one image to another. You can even create a Toning palette like the example on the next page, which provides a range of tint options as well as hue strengths.

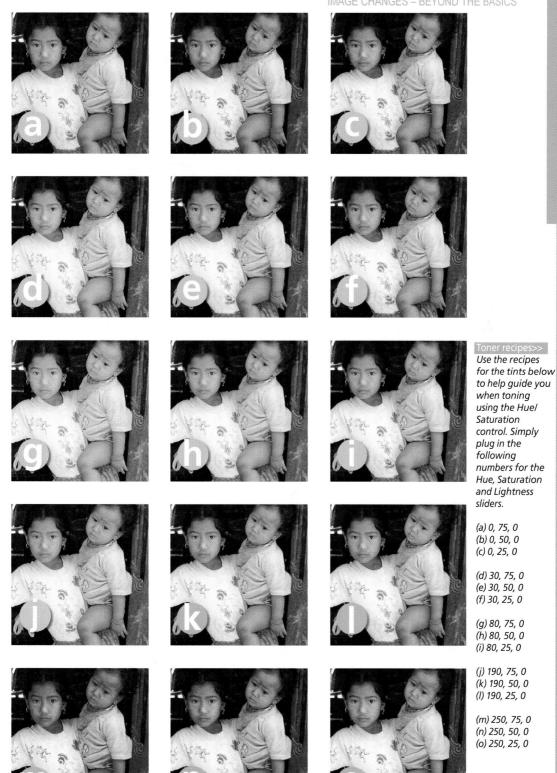

Toner recipes>>

Use the recipes for the tints below to help guide you when toning using the Hue/Saturation control. Simply plug in the following numbers for the Hue, Saturation and Lightness sliders.

(a) 0, 75, 0
(b) 0, 50, 0
(c) 0, 25, 0

(d) 30, 75, 0
(e) 30, 50, 0
(f) 30, 25, 0

(g) 80, 75, 0
(h) 80, 50, 0
(i) 80, 25, 0

(j) 190, 75, 0
(k) 190, 50, 0
(l) 190, 25, 0

(m) 250, 75, 0
(n) 250, 50, 0
(o) 250, 25, 0

6.27 Tinting borrowed from Photoshop

Suitable for Elements – 7.0, 6.0, 5.0, 4.0, 3.0, 2.0, 1.0
Difficulty level – Intermediate | Resources – Web image
621 | Related Techniques – 6.26, 6.28
Tools used – Brush | Menus used – Layer

We have already seen how we can borrow adjustment layers from Photoshop documents to handle our conversions to grayscale, but there is also the opportunity to tint your photos with the same Black and White feature. Nestled at the bottom of the dialog is a tint control that contains the same Hue and Saturation sliders that feature in the Hue Saturation adjustment layer.

After setting the conversion sliders, ticking the Tint options changes the image from a grayscale to a toned monochrome. The Hue slider determines the color of the tint and the Saturation slider the strength of the tint color.

To gain access to this Photoshop feature simply drag a Black and White adjustment layer from the donor document ('Photoshop-Convert-to-gray-tinting.psd') which is available from the book's website, to an open Elements file. There are several different tinting adjustment layers to choose from.

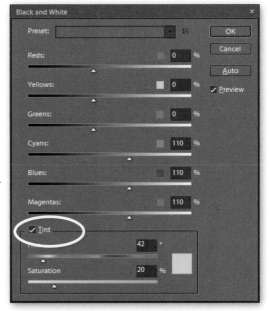

Photoshop's Black and White feature >> *After borrowing the Black and White adjustment layer, Elements users can open the feature's dialog by double-clicking the layer's thumbnail. At the base of the dialog is a Tint option that provides the opportunity for you to tone the images you convert to grayscale with the feature.*

Step 1 >> *Start by opening both the Photoshop donor document (Photoshop-Convert-to-gray-tinting.psd) and the Elements file that you want to enhance. Click onto the Photoshop document and scroll through the list of adjustment layers available in the document. Select a layer and click-drag it onto the Elements document. The enhancement change will be immediately previewed in the workspace.*

Step 2 >> *Multiple Photoshop layers can be dragged onto the Elements document and their effects hidden or applied by clicking the 'eye' icon on the left of the layer entry.*

Book resources and video tutorials can be found at: **www.photoshopelements.net**

Split toning

Once you have mastered the art of toning your pictures it is time to spread your 'tinting' wings a little. One of my favorite after-printing effects back in my darkroom days was split toning. This process involved passing a completed black and white print through two differently colored and separate toning baths. This resulted in the print containing a mixture of two different tints.

For example, when an image is split toned with sepia first and then blue toner the resultant picture has warm (brown) highlights and midtones, and cool (blue) shadows. Getting the right toning balance between the two solutions was difficult and then trying to repeat the process uniformly over a series of images was even harder. Thankfully I can replicate the results of split toning in my digital picture with a lot less trouble and a lot more predictability.

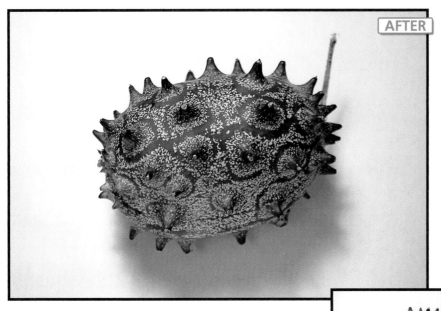

Split tone >> *With the aid of some tricky selection techniques it is possible to tint different tonal ranges of an image with alternative colors. This style of tinting is called split toning and traditionally is created by passing a photographic print through multiple toning baths.*

6.28 Select and tone

Suitable for Elements – 7.0, 6.0, 5.0, 4.0, 3.0, 2.0, 1.0 | Difficulty level – Intermediate| Resources – Web image 622 | Related techniques – 6.26 | Tools used – Magic Wand | Menus used – Select, Enhance

In order to tint a select range of tones such as midtones and shadows I must first select these areas of the image. The Magic Wand tool makes selections based on color and tone and so is perfectly suited for this type of selection. Normally we would use this tool with the Contiguous option turned on so that the selection comprises pixels that sit next to each other, but for this task turn this option off. The Tolerance value for the tool can range from 0 to 255. This setting determines how close to the selected pixel's tone the other pixels need to be before they too are included in the selection. The 0 setting is used to select other pixels in the image with exactly the same color and tone, whereas a setting of 20 will select other pixels that vary by as much as 20 tonal/color steps from the original.

Magic Wand settings >> *When using the Magic Wand to select a range of tones in an image be sure to turn off the Contiguous setting, increase the Tolerance value and then select your reference pixel.*

With this in mind we can easily employ this tool to select just the shadow and midtones of an image by setting the tolerance to a value of about 120 and then selecting the darkest part of the image (which we will assume has a value of 0 and therefore is black). The Magic Wand will then search the picture for pixels with a tonal value between 0 and 120. The resultant selection will include both shadows and midtones. It is then a simple matter of using the Hue/Saturation control to colorize these tones. To tint the rest of the pixels in the picture in an alternative color you must first invert the selection (Select>Inverse) and then repeat the Hue/Saturation toning procedure.

To soften the transition at the split of the two colors apply a feather of 1 or 2 pixels (Select > Feather) after your initial selection.

Step 1 >> Select the Magic Wand tool, adjust the Tolerance value and deselect the Contiguous option.

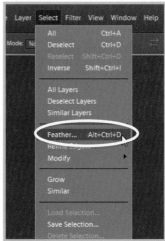

Step 2 >> Feather the selection by a value of 1 or 2 pixels to soften the split between toning colors.

Step 3 >> Tone the selected areas using the Hue/Saturation control.

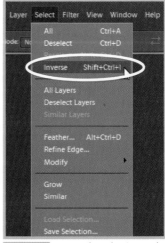

Step 4 >> Inverse the selection and tone the remaining pixels using an alternative color.

6.29 Two-layer erase

*Suitable for Elements – 7.0, 6.0, 5.0, 4.0, 3.0, 2.0, 1.0 | Difficulty level – Intermediate | Resources – Web image 623
Related Techniques – 6.28 | Tools used – Eraser | Menus used – Layer, Enhance*

You can extend the split toning idea beyond its darkroom origins by using this technique to create an image where one part of the picture is toned one color whilst the rest is colored in an alternative hue. To achieve this effect duplicate the image layer and then select and tone each layer in turn. Then use the mask from a No Settings adjustment layer to remove parts of the upper layer to reveal the color of the layer beneath.

Erasing toned layers>> *By duplicating the image layer and then toning the two layers it is possible to use a No Settings adjustment layer mask to erase the upper layer to reveal the alternate colored layer below.*

Step 1 >> *Duplicate the base image layer by dragging it to the New Layer button at the bottom of the Layers dialog.*

Step 2 >> *Select each layer in turn and tone using the Hue/Saturation control set to Colorize. Select the lower layer and add a new Levels Adjustment Layer with no settings applied between the layers.*

Step 3 >> *Select the uppermost layer and select Layer > Group with Previous. Now select the layer mask and a black soft brush and paint the details from the layer beneath.*

6.30 Color Variations based split toning

Suitable for Elements – 7.0, 6.0, 5.0, 4.0, 3.0, 2.0, 1.0 | Difficulty level – Intermediate | Resources – Web image 624 | Related Techniques – 6.28, 6.29 | Tools used – Brush | Menus used – Layer

The Color Balance feature in Photoshop provides a unique way of creating split tones. As the feature contains the ability to not only tint a grayscale image (that is in RGB Color mode), but also limit this tinting to one of three tonal ranges, shadows, midtones or highlights, it is the perfect tool for creating great split tones. The feature is also available as an Adjustment Layer meaning that split tones can be applied in Photoshop non-destructively.

Thankfully the Enhance > Adjust Color > Color Variations feature offers the same tinting abilities that are customized for specific tonal ranges. To start the toning process use the Convert to Black and White feature to change the color image to grayscale but still retain the RGB Color mode. Next open the Color Variations feature and target the Shadows, click onto one of the colored thumbnails a couple of times to add a tint to the shadows. Next choose the highlight setting and add a different color here. Hey presto! A split-toned print.

Step 1 >> *Start by converting the color original to gray using the Convert to Black and White feature. This removes the color but maintains the RGB Color mode of the file allowing for the split toning later.*

Step 2 >> *Next open the Color Variations feature and target the Shadow areas. Click onto one of the color thumbnails a couple of times to tint the shadows.*

Step 3 >> *While the Color Variations dialog is still open, switch to the Highlight tonal range and tint these values a different color.*

6.31 Photoshop's Color Balance split toning in Elements

Suitable for Elements – 7.0, 6.0, 5.0, 4.0, 3.0, 2.0, 1.0 | Difficulty level – Intermediate | Resources – Web image 625 | Related Techniques – 6.16, 6.17 | Tools used – Brush | Menus used – Layer

For elements users who want to employ a non-destructive workflow, the Color Balance adjustment layer from Photoshop can be dragged and dropped from a Photoshop document onto an Elements file. To keep the whole technique non-destructive a Photoshop Black and White adjustment layer should be used first to convert the image to grayscale. To help with this process I have created a

AFTER

BEFORE

Split toning >>
*Borrowing Color Balance
and Black and White
adjustment layers from
Photoshop documents
provides a way for
Elements users to split
tone non-destructively.*

Photoshop file containing a convert to gray layer and a range of split-tone options. To use,
download the Photoshop-Split-Tones.psd file from the book's website and open the document
into Elements. Drag the Convert-to-Gray layer to the Elements file first and then add a split tone
layer. Adjust the opacity of the split tone layer to control the strength of the split-tone colors.

Step 1 >> *Start by opening the
Photoshop-Split-tone.psd file into
the Elements editing workspace.
Drag the Convert-to-Gray layer from
the Photoshop document to an open
Elements file.*

Step 2 >> *Now drag a split tone
layer to the Elements document. If
need be adjust the opacity of the
layer to reduce the strength of the
tinting colors.*

AFTER

BEFORE

Color and black and white >>
By combining your selection skills, Elements' masking options and the features of the Gradient Map adjustment layers you can create an image where black and white and color happily coexist.

Black and white and color

The same 'two-layer erase back' technique can be used for creating photographs which contain both color and black and white elements, but I prefer to use a different method based around Elements' masking options.

6.32 Layer mask and gradient map

Suitable for Elements – 7.0, 6.0, 5.0, 4.0, 3.0, 2.0, 1.0 | Difficulty level – Intermediate | Resources – Web image 626 | Related Techniques – 6.18 | Tools used – Selection tools | Menus used – Select, Layer

With the color image open make a selection of the objects that will not be converted to black and white. In the example I used a combination of the Magnetic Lasso and the standard Lasso tools to select the three map pins, but you could also use the Magic Selection Brush to achieve the same results. Next, feather the selection (Select > Feather) slightly with a setting of 1 pixel to soften the edge of the effect. Invert the selection (Select > Inverse) so that the background (everything other than the map pins) is now selected. Then, with the selection still active, create a new Gradient Map adjustment layer (Layer > New Adjustment Layer > Gradient Map). When the Gradient Map dialog appears select the map with a smooth transition from black to white and click OK. Elements uses your selection to mask out the adjustment layer effects and restrict them from being applied to the originally selected map pins. You can create a multitude of other effects using the same process but different gradient maps or adjustment layers.

More effects >> *You can create other effects using the same masking technique with the Threshold (a), Posterize (b) and Invert (c) Adjustment Layers options.*

Make sure that you save your selections (Select > Save Selection) as you make them. This way you can always reload them later if you need to.

Step 1 >> *Make a selection of the parts of the image that you want to remain in color.*

Step 2 >> *Feather the selection by 1 pixel and then Inverse the selection.*

Step 3 >> *With the selection still active create a new Gradient Map adjustment layer.*

Border techniques

Creating a great border is one of those finishing touches that can really make your images stand apart from the crowd. Using Photoshop Elements you can easily create and apply a variety of different border styles to your photographs.

6.33 Simple borders

Suitable for Elements – 7.0, 6.0, 5.0, 4.0, 3.0, 2.0, 1.0 | Difficulty level – Intermediate | Resources – Web image 627 | Related Techniques – 6.34 | Tools used – Marquee | Menus used – Select, Window, Edit

A basic line border can be created by selecting the whole image (Select > Select All) and then stroking (Edit > Stroke) the selection on the inside with the foreground color. For fancier styles Elements provides a range of Frame and Edge treatments in its Artwork palette (Window > Effects). Some frames require you to make a selection first; others can be applied directly to the picture with no preliminary actions.

Stroked frame >> *Use the Eyedropper tool to select a suitable border color from the image. Select all the picture (Select > Select All). Stroke the selection (Edit > Stroke Selection) on the inside with the foreground color and a width of 10 pixels.*

Layer Effects >> *Display the Effects palette (Window > Effects) and then select the Special Effects > Photo Effects section. Choose frames from the drop-down list and then Drop Shadow from the thumb-nails. Press the Apply button.*

6.34 Sophisticated edges using grayscale masks

Suitable for Elements – 7.0, 6.0, 5.0, 4.0, 3.0, 2.0, 1.0 | Difficulty level – Intermediate | Resources – Web image 628 | Related techniques – 6.33 | Tools used – Paint Brush | Menus used – layer

You can create truly imaginative edges by using a grayscale mask to hide the edges of the picture. Start by using the Elements drawing tools to paint a black shape with rough edges on a white background. This is our grayscale mask. Ideally the dimensions of the painting should be the same as the picture to be framed. With both the picture and the mask open as separate documents, use the Move tool to drag the mask image on top of the picture. The mask will become a new layer. Use the Free Transform tool (Image > Transform > Free Transform) to scale the mask to fit the image precisely.

Grayscale mask borders >> *You can use a grayscale mask to produce a creative border effect by stacking the mask on top and then changing the layer mode to Screen.*

With the mask layer still active change the layer mode to Screen. This will cause the image from beneath to show through the black parts of the mask whilst the white areas of the mask hide the rest of the picture below.

This technique can also be used to create an image-filled border by inverting the mask before changing modes. This way the center of the picture is hidden by the white portion of the mask and the edges are filled with the image from below.

Search the web for pre-made grayscale masks that can be downloaded and used directly in Elements.

Pro's Tip

Step 1 >> *Create or download a grayscale mask. Open image and mask. Drag mask onto image as a new layer.*

Step 2 >> *With the mask layer selected use the Transformation tool (Image>Transform>Free Transform) to scale the mask to fit the image.*

Step 3 >> *Switch the mask layer's mode to Screen to create the edge effect. To invert the effect select Image > Adjustments > Invert before changing the mode.*

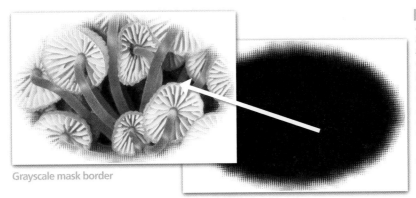

Grayscale mask border

Picture edges >>
More sophisticated masks of all manner of shapes, sizes and styles can be created using grayscale masks. By inverting the mask (Image > Adjustment > Invert) you can also create an edge filled with a picture rather than a picture surrounded by an edge.

Grayscale mask border inverted

6.35 Creating frames with Frame layers

Suitable for Elements – 7.0, 6.0, 5.0 | Difficulty level – Intermediate
Resources – Web image 629 | Related techniques – 6.34 Tools used – Paint
Brush Menus used – layer

Frame layers are brand new to Elements and have been introduced as part of the new system of creating multi-page themed documents (Photo or .PSE documents). Here, we will just take a quick look at the framing abilities of the new technology, but for a fuller description of how to create and edit PSE files go to Chapter 12.

Frame layers combine both the picture and the frame in a single layer. This a really cool aspect of this technology as it means that not only can the frame and layer combination be sized and rotated as a single composition, but the picture can also be manipulated independent of the frame. Photoshop Elements ships with a huge collection of frames that can be quickly and easily added to your pictures.

BEFORE

AFTER

Frame layers >> *Frame layers are a new way to dynamically add fancy borders to your photos.*

The various designs are collated in the Content palette (under the Frames option in the By Type section of the palette). To add a frame to a picture that is already open in the Full Edit workspace display the palette first (Window > Content) and then click on the left-side drop-down menu and select By Type. Next choose the Frames option from the right-hand drop-down menu. After locating the frame type you want to add to your photo click on its thumbnail and then press the Apply button at the bottom of the palette.

Elements automatically creates a new Frame layer, adds your photo to it and then provides a small adjustment palette at the top of the framed image containing controls for sizing, rotating and replacing your photo. Alternatively, extra positioning and sizing options are available from the right-click menu. Click on the photo and then click-drag the corner handles to resize the frame and image together or the rotate handle to pivot the combination. Double-click the Move tool on the photo to select just the picture and use the handles to alter the photo independently of the frame.

Step 1 >> *With a photo open in the editing space display the Frames section of the Content palette. Select the Frame Style thumbnail and click the Apply button.*

Step 2 >> *Elements automatically creates a new Frame layer and places your photo in the frame design. Adjust the size and orientation of the picture using the pop-up adjustment palette.*

Step 3 >> *More picture controls are available from the right-click menu. In most cases the Fit Frame To Photo option should be selected first and then any fine-tuning added later.*

Step 4 >> *Single-click the photo to select both frame and photo. Double-click to pick the photo only. Use the corner and rotate handles to fine-tune the size of picture and frame.*

Step 5 >> *To finish add a background to the composition by selecting the Background option from the right-hand menu. Next Choose the background and then click Apply.*

Adding texture

Texture is a traditional photographic visual element that is often overlooked when working digitally. All but the highest quality professional films have visible grain when they are printed. This is especially true when the print size goes beyond the standard 6 x 4 inches. In fact we are so familiar with the idea that grain is part of the photographic process that putting a little texture into an otherwise grainless digital picture can lend a traditional 'look and feel' to the image.

Many photographers add a little texture to their pictures as part of their regular image editing process. Some go beyond this and produce photographs with huge clumps of grain that resemble the results often seen with prints made from old style high ISO films.

6.36 Add Noise filter

Suitable for Elements – 7.0, 6.0, 5.0, 4.0, 3.0, 2.0, 1.0 | Difficulty level – Intermediate | Resources – Web image 6.30 | Related techniques – 6.37, 6.38 | Menus used – Filter

The simplest method for adding texture to your picture is to use the Add Noise filter (Filter > Noise > Add Noise). The feature is provided with a preview dialog which allows you to alter the 'Amount' of noise that is added to the photograph, the style of noise – Gaussian or Uniform – and whether the noise is random colored pixels or just monochrome. As with most filters it is important to use this feature carefully as once the filter is applied and the file saved you will not be able to undo its effects. For this reason, it pays to make a duplicate file of your picture which you can texturize without risk of destroying the original image.

Be sure to preview the image at least 100% when adding noise to ensure that the effect is not too strong. If in doubt, make a test print of sections of the picture with different Add Noise settings to preview the hard copy results.

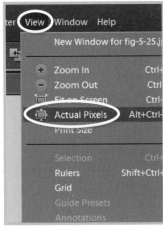

Step 1 >> *Zoom in so that the picture is at least at 100% view or the Actual Pixels entry.*

Step 2 >> *Select the Add Noise filter from the Filter menu.*

Step 3 >> *Adjust the Amount slider to change the strength of the effect and pick the noise type and color.*

6.37 Grain filter

Suitable for Elements – 7.0, 6.0, 5.0, 4.0, 3.0, 2.0, 1.0
Difficulty level – Intermediate | Resources – Web
image 630 | Related techniques – 6.36, 6.38
Menus used – Filter

As an alternative that provides a few more options than the technique above you can use the Grain filter (Filter > Texture > Grain) to add your choice of 10 different grain textures to your picture. Ranging from 'regular' through 'horizontal' to 'speckle' this filter produces a spectacular variety of texture effects. The feature's dialog also provides an Intensity slider to govern the strength of the texture and a Contrast control.

Adding grain >> *The Grain dialog provides a preview thumbnail, Intensity and Contrast sliders and a selection of 10 different grain types.*

The trick to creating good texture using this feature is the balancng of Intensity and Contrast settings. If the texture is too strong the shape and color of the original subject matter can be lost. If the contrast is too high then shadow and highlight details can be lost.

Texture options for the Grain filter >> *The Grain filter provides a range of unique texture options that can be applied to your picture. (a) Regular. (b) Sprinkles. (c) Clumped. (d) Enlarged. (e) Stippled. (f) Horizontal. (g) Speckle.*

Book resources and video tutorials can be found at: **www.photoshopelements.net**

6.38 Non-destructive textures

Suitable for Elements – 7.0, 6.0, 5.0, 4.0, 3.0, 2.0, 1.0 | Difficulty level – Intermediate | Resources – Web image 631 | Related techniques – 6.36, 6.37 | Menus used – Layer, Filter

As we have already seen adjustment layers are a great way to manipulate your pictures without actually altering the original image. This approach to image editing is referred to as 'non-destructive' as the integrity of the starting picture is always maintained. Mistakes or radical manipulations can always be reversed by switching off the adjustment layer leaving the untouched original below. Although there are no such things as Filter adjustment layers it would be handy to be able to use this same approach when making whole non-reversible image changes such as adding texture or noise to your pictures.

Such a technique was used in the following example. Despite the appearance of texture throughout the whole photograph the starting picture is still preserved at the bottom of the layer stack. To get the same results with your own pictures start by making a new layer (Layer > New > Layer) above the image. Next, fill this layer with 50% gray (Edit > Fill Layer) and Add Noise (Filter > Noise > Add Noise) to the layer. Change the mode of the gray textured layer to either Soft Light, Hard Light, Linear Light or Vivid Light. Notice how the texture is now applied to the picture. To soften the effect reduce the opacity of the texture layer.

Using this technique you not only preserve the integrity of the original picture but you can also alter the strength of the effect at any time. In addition, it is also a great way to apply the same amount and style of grain to several layers in a stack without having to individually select and filter each layer.

To apply the same texture settings to a series of images of the same size simply drag and drop the gray texture layer into each of the open documents.

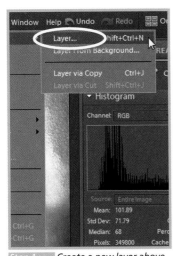

Step 1 >> *Create a new layer above the image layer or background.*

Step 2 >> *Fill the layer with 50% gray using the Edit > Fill layer command.*

Step 3 >> *Texture the layer with Add Noise and switch the layer mode to Vivid Light.*

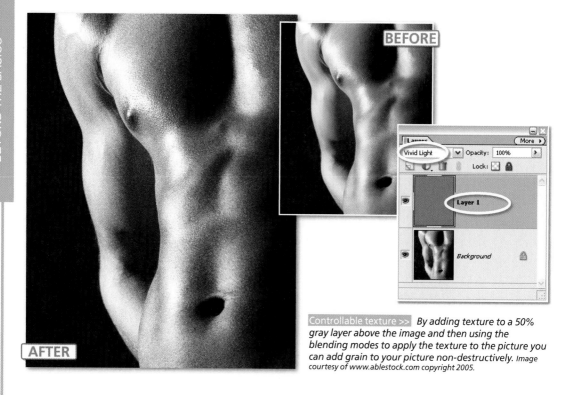

Controllable texture >> *By adding texture to a 50% gray layer above the image and then using the blending modes to apply the texture to the picture you can add grain to your picture non-destructively. Image courtesy of www.ablestock.com copyright 2005.*

Advanced sharpening secrets

To most of us sharpening is a way of improving the clarity of photos using a single-click option such as Enhance > Auto Sharpen in Elements, but why should we relinquish control when it comes to this final step in the editing process? Here we look a little deeper at some of the more customizable options that allow the user to more easily match the sharpening effect with the subject matter and output destination of their photos.

Sharpening – What are the options?

Photoshop Elements provides a variety of sharpening options designed to increase the clarity of digital photographs. In previous versions these options were listed in the Filter > Sharpen menu and include the Sharpen, Sharpen Edges, Sharpen More and Unsharp Mask filters. In version 5.0 the options were moved and are now grouped under the Enhance menu and include Auto Sharpen, Unsharp Mask and Adjust Sharpness filters.

Digital sharpening techniques are based on increasing the contrast between adjacent pixels in the image. When viewed

Sharpen options >> *Elements 5.0, 6.0 and 7 group the sharpening options under the Enhance menu. Unsharp Mask remains but the other filters have been replaced with the one-step Auto Sharpen and the sophisticated Adjust Sharpness options.*

from a distance, this change makes the picture appear sharper or more defined. So applying a sharpening filter does not, and will never, make a poorly focused picture suddenly appear as if it has been focused correctly. Instead these filters are designed to make your photos appear more sharply defined.

For many users selecting an option such as the Auto Sharpen is about as far as they go when it comes to thinking about how to sharpen their pictures, but this 'one-click' filter fail to take into account the content of the photo and the intended use for the image – two factors that should determine the amount of sharpening you apply. So for the ultimate control of your sharpening use the advanced features in the new Adjust Sharpness filter, or the tried and tested Unsharp Mask filter. Both these options contain controls that allow the user to manipulate the strength of the sharpening effect and adjust which parts of the picture the filters are applied. Let's look at each in turn.

6.39 Unsharp Masking to the rescue

Suitable for Elements – 7.0, 6.0, 5.0, 4.0, 3.0, 2.0, 1.0 | Difficulty level – Intermediate | Resources – Web image 632 | Related techniques – 6.40, 6.41 | Menus used – Enhance

Of the various sharpen filters that Photoshop Elements contains the Unsharp Mask provides some of the greatest control over the sharpening process by giving the user a range of sliders which, when adjusted, alter the way the effect is applied to pictures. Though a little confusing to start with, the Unsharp Mask filter is one of the best ways to make your scans or digital photographs clearer. However, to get the most out of the feature you must understand and control carefully each of the three sliders. So how does the feature work?

Step 1 >> *Make sure that your picture is zoomed in or magnified to at least 100% before selecting the Unsharp Mask option from the Enhance menu. Select the Preview option in the dialog to ensure that the sharpening effects are shown on the full image.*

Step 2 >> *Start with the radius set to 1 and the Threshold value adjusted to 0. Gradually move the Amount slider upwards watching the sharpening effect as you go. Stop when you find a setting where the picture appears clearer but contains no sharpening 'halos'.*

Step 3 >> *To restrict the effect from being applied to skin tones, blue skies or other areas of smooth tone gradually increase the Threshold slider until the sharpening is just being applied to the picture's edges.*

The **Amount** slider controls the strength of the sharpening effect. Larger numbers will produce more pronounced results whereas smaller values will create more subtle effects. Values of 50% to 100% are suitable for low-resolution pictures whereas settings between 150% and 200% can be used on images with a higher resolution.

The **Radius** slider value determines the number of pixels around the edge that are affected by the sharpening. A low value only sharpens edge pixels. High settings can produce noticeable halo effects around your picture so start with a low value first. Typically values between 1 and 2 are used for high-resolution images, settings of 1 or less for screen images.

The **Threshold** slider is used to determine how different the pixels must be before they are considered an edge and therefore sharpened. A value of 0 will sharpen all the pixels in an image whereas a setting of 10 will only apply the effect to those areas that are different by at least 10 levels or more from their surrounding pixels. To ensure that no sharpening occurs in sky or skin tone areas set this value to 8 or more.

Unsharp Mask Top Tip:

Be careful when you are using the Unsharp Mask filter with your pictures. A little sharpening will improve the look of your photographs but too much sharpening is really noticeable and almost impossible to repair once applied to your picture. If you are unsure of your settings, apply the effect to a copy of the image first.

Adding clarity >> *Careful sharpening can really add to the clarity of a digital photo, but like most enhancement techniques it is best to make such changes subtly. (a) No-sharpening. (b) After Unsharp Mask. (c) After Adjust Sharpness. (d) High Pass/Blend Light mode approach.*

6.40 Adjust Sharpness for the ultimate control

Suitable for Elements – 7.0, 6.0, 5.0 | Difficulty level – Intermediate | Resources – Web image 632
Related techniques – 6.39, 6.41 | Menus used – Enhance

Until the release of Photoshop Elements 5.0 the best way to take control of the sharpening in your photographs was to use the Unsharp Mask filter. But the most recent release has included a brand new sharpening tool that will easily steal this crown. The Adjust Sharpness filter (Enhance > Adjust Sharpness) provides all the control that we are familiar with in the Unsharp Mask dialog plus better edge detection abilities, which leads to less apparent sharpening halos. The Filter dialog contains a zoomable preview, sliders to control the sharpening plus a drop-down menu where you can choose the type of sharpening to apply. You can control the sharpening effect with the following settings:

Amount – Strength of sharpening effect.

Radius – Determines the extent of sharpening. Higher values equal more obvious edge effects.

Remove – Determines sharpening algorithm used. Gaussian Blur uses the same approach as the Unsharp Mask filter. Lens Blur concentrates on sharpening details and produces results with fewer halos. Motion Blur reduces the effects of blur caused by camera shake or subject movement.

Angle – Sets Motion Blur direction.

More Refined – Longer processing for better results.

Adjust Sharpness >> *The Adjust Sharpness feature introduced in Elements 5.0 extends the customized sharpening ability first started with the Unsharp Mask filter.*

Step 1 >> *Make sure that your picture is zoomed in or magnified to at least 100% and then select the Enhance > Adjust Sharpness filter. Select the Preview option in the dialogue to ensure that the sharpening effects are shown on the full image and also tick the More Refined option unless you are working with a large file or a slow computer.*

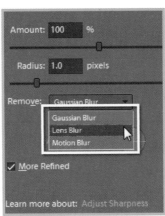

Step 2 >> *Choose the Lens Blur entry from the Remove menu. This option provides the best sharpening with least halo artifacts. Choose Gaussian Blur if you want to simulate Unsharp Mask results or Motion Blur if you are trying to get rid of the effects of camera shake.*

Step 3 >> *Start with the radius set to 1 and gradually move the Amount slider upwards watching the sharpening effect as you go. Stop when you find a setting where the picture appears clearer but contains no sharpening 'halos'.*

Adjust Sharpness Top Tip

One of the options for the new Adjust Sharpness filter is the Motion Blur entry in the Remove menu. The options listed in this menu determine the way in which sharpening is applied to the picture or more specifically, the algorithm used when filtering. The Motion Blur option is different to the other choices as it provides a

method of reducing the effects of blur in a photo due to the camera or subject moving during the exposure. When Motion Blur is selected you have the added option of inputting an angle for the blur reducing action. This can be achieved with the dial control by click-dragging the mouse or by inputting a specific angle.

6.41 Another approach

Suitable for Elements – 7.0, 6.0, 5.0, 4.0, 3.0, 2.0, 1.0 | Difficulty level – Intermediate | Resources – Web image 632 | Related techniques – 6.39, 6.40 | Menus used – Layer, Filter

There is no getting away from the fact that sharpening photos with filters alters them irreversibly and forever. For this reason many photographers duplicate their precious pictures multiple times and apply different sharpening options to the copies depending on their intended use. This is not a bad approach, especially if you have plenty of storage space to hand, but what if you could sharpen your photos without altering the original pixels? Well surprisingly the Blending Modes feature located in Photoshop Elements provides the key to just such a technique. In particular, we will use the Hard Light Blend Mode in conjunction with the High Pass filter to create a non-destructive sharpening effect. The High Pass filter provides the mechanism for controlling where the sharpening occurs by isolating the edges in a picture and then converting the rest of the image to mid gray. This is perfect for use with Hard Light blend mode as the mid gray areas will not be affected at all and the sharpening changes will only be applied to the edges of the photo.

Step 1 >> *Make a copy (Layer > Duplicate Layer) of the picture layer that you want to sharpen. Filter the copied layer with the High Pass filter (Filter > Other > High Pass) and press OK.*

Step 2 >> *With the filtered layer still selected switch the blend mode to Hard Light. This mode blends both the dark and light parts of the filtered layer with the picture layer, causing an increase in contrast.*

Step 3 >> *Adjust the opacity of this layer to govern the level of sharpening. Sharpening using this technique means that you can remove or adjust the strength of the effect later by manipulating the filtered layer.*

7

Darkroom Techniques on the Desktop

O nce you have mastered the basic editing and enhancement skills and techniques in Elements you will no doubt want to move on to some more challenging tasks that will extend and build upon what you already know. The group of techniques collected together here is loosely based on traditional photographic 'know how' that I have reworked in a digital fashion.

7.01 Diffusion printing

Suitable for Elements – 7.0, 6.0, 5.0, 4.0, 3.0, 2.0, 1.0 | Difficulty level – Intermediate | Resources – Web image 701 | Tools used – Eraser | Menus used – Filter, Layer

Even though as image-makers we spend thousands of dollars on equipment that ensures that we make sharp photographs, there is something enticing about a delicately softened picture. Especially when this lack of sharpness is contrasted against a well-focused section of the picture. Diffusion printing is one traditional printing technique that played with this idea. Parts of the image were purposely blurred whilst other areas remained sharp.

With non-digital photography, adding such an effect meant placing a 'mist' or 'fog' filter in front of the camera lens at the time of shooting. More recently, in an attempt to gain a little more control over the process, photographers have been placing diffusion filters below their enlarging lenses for part of the print's exposure time. This process gave a combination effect where sharpness and controlled blur happily coexisted in the final print.

Gaussian Blur filter >> The diffusion printing technique is based around the careful application of the Gaussian Blur filter.

Step 1 >> Duplicate the original picture by dragging it to the New Layer button or choosing the Layer>Duplicate Layer option.

Step 2 >> Apply the Gaussian Blur filter (Filter>Blur>Gaussian Blur) to the upper, duplicated, layer.

Step 3 >> Control the way that the blurred layer interacts with the one beneath by adjusting the blending mode and/or using a No Settings adjustment layer mask grouped with the upper layer to remove unwanted blurred areas.

AFTER

BEFORE

Diffusion printing >> *To control the style and position of the effect change the blending mode of the blurred layer and use the eraser to remove blurred areas to reveal the sharp original beneath. (a) Darken blending mode. (b) Lighten blending mode. (c) Normal blending mode.*

a

b

c

Creating this style of picture using digital processes offers the image-maker a lot more choice and control over the end results. The technique is based around the Gaussian Blur filter, which can be used to soften the sharp details of your photograph. A simple application of the filter to a base image produces a less than attractive result and one that doesn't combine the sharp and blurred imagery. Instead more control is possible if the filter is applied to a copy of the picture stored as a layer above the original image. This blurred layer is then combined with the original by either reducing the opacity of the blurred layer to allow the sharp original to show through, or by changing the blurred layer to a different blending mode such as Darken or Lighten.

Extending the technique

Blending mode or opacity changes provide control over the overall effect of the diffusion, but to fine-tune the results select the blur layer, add a No Settings adjustment layer below the blurred layer. Group the upper image layer with the adjustment layer and then use the mask of the adjustment layer to to gently remove parts of the top layer to reveal the sharpness beneath.

Polaroid transfer effect >> *The digital version of this traditional printing technique makes use of the two separate filters to construct the mottled image and the texturizer to create the paper effect before surrounding the whole picture with a frame scanned from a real Polaroid photograph.*

7.02 Instant film transfer effect

Suitable for Elements – 7.0, 6.0, 5.0 | Difficulty level – Advanced | Resources – Web images 702-1, 702-2, 702-3, Menus used – Filter, Layer, Enhance, Image

Most readers will probably be familiar with Polaroid instant picture products – you push the button and the print is ejected and develops right before your eyes. For many years professional image-makers have been using the unique features of this technology to create wonderfully textured images. The process involved substituting watercolor paper for the printing surface supplied by Polaroid. As a result the image is transferred onto the roughly surfaced paper and takes on a distinctly different look and feel to a standard Polaroid print.

Much acclaimed for its artistic appeal, the technique was not always predictable and, much to the frustration of photographers, it was often difficult to repeat the success of previous results. There were three main problems – dark areas of an image often didn't transfer to the new surface, colors and image detail would bleed unpredictably, and it was difficult to control how dark or light the final print would be. I know these problems intimately as it once took me 16 sheets of expensive instant film to produce a couple of acceptable prints.

A digital solution

This success ratio is not one that my budget or my temperament can afford. So I started to play with a digital version of the popular technique. I wanted to find a process that was more

predictable, controllable and repeatable. My first step was to list the characteristics of the
Polaroid transfer print so that I could simulate them digitally.

To me it seemed that there were four main elements: desaturated colors, mottled ink, distinct
paper texture and color, and the Polaroid film frame.

If I could duplicate these on my desktop then I would be able to make an image that captured the
essence of the Polaroid transfer process.

Step 1 >> *Desaturate the image tones slightly using the Hue/ Saturation feature.*

Step 2 >> *Duplicate the background layer by dragging it to the New Layers button at the top of the dialog.*

Step 3 >> *Apply both the Paint Daubs and Palette Knife filters to the upper layer (duplicate).*

Step 4 >> *Reduce the opacity of the filtered upper layer to allow some of the sharp details of the original image to show through.*

Step 5 >> *Check to see that the background color is set to white. Increase the size of the canvas to accommodate the Polaroid edge surround using the Canvas Size command with a setting of 120% for width and 140% for height. Copy Merge and paste the new layer.*

Step 6 >> *Either use one of the pre-installed textures available in the Texturizer filter or download and install the watercolor paper.psd file (web image 702-2) from this book's website. Use the filter to add the texture to the surround.*

Desaturate the image tones

The Polaroid technique requires the watercolor paper to be slightly wet at the time of transfer. The moisture, whilst helping the image movement from paper to paper, tends to desaturate the colors and cause fine detail to be lost. These characteristics are also the result of the coarse surface of the donor paper. So the first step of the digital version of the process is to desaturate the color of our example image. In Elements this can be achieved by using the Hue/Saturation control from the Adjust Color section of the Enhance menu. With the dialog open carefully move the Saturation slider to the left. This action will decrease the intensity of the colors in your image.

Mottle the ink

The distinct surface and image qualities of Polaroid transfer prints combine both sharpness and image break-up in the one picture. To reproduce this effect digitally, I copied the original image onto a second layer. My idea was to manipulate one version so that it displayed the mottled effect of the transfer print whilst leaving the second version untouched. Then, using the blending modes or opacity features of Elements' layers I could adjust how much sharpness or mottle was contained in the final result.

In practice, I started by duplicating the image layer. This can be achieved by selecting the layer to be copied and then using the Duplicate Layer command located under the Layer menu. Alternatively you drag the layer to the Create New Layer button at the top of the Layers palette. With the upper layer selected, I then needed to find a method to simulate the mottle of the transfer print. Though not exactly right, I found that by combining the effects of the Paint Daubs and Palette Knife filters I could produce reasonable results. When using these filters yourself

Step 7 >> *In the Levels feature select the blue and red channels separately, dragging in the white Output slider towards the center.*

Step 8 >> *Open the edge file as a separate document, apply a 'No Frame' frame to the photo and drag it onto the original picture.*

Step 9 >> *Switch the mode of the edge layer to Multiply and use the Scale command to adjust its frame or the edge to fit the picture below.*

keep in mind that the settings used will vary with the style and size of your image. This part of the process is not an exact science. Play and experimentation is the name of the game. You might also want to try other options in the Artistic, Sketch or Texture selections of the Filter menu. The last step in this stage is to combine the characteristics of the two layers. This can be achieved by either changing the Blending mode of the uppermost layer or by adjusting its opacity, or both. For the example image a simple opacity change was all that was needed, but don't be afraid to try a few different blend/opacity combinations with your own work.

Apply a paper texture and color

The paper color and texture is a critical part of the appeal of the transfer print. These two characteristics extend throughout the image itself and into the area that surrounds the picture. For this to occur in a digital facsimile it is necessary to provide some space around the image using Elements' Canvas Size feature. Unlike the Image Size command, this option allows the user to increase the size of the canvas without changing the image size (and all its associated layers). In the example the canvas width was increased by 120% and the height by 140%. To add the texture to both image and surround I copied and merged all of the document and then pasted the combined image to a new layer. Next, I photographed a section of watercolor paper to use as a customized texture with the Texturizer filter. You can download and use this very file from the book's website (*www.photoshopelements.net*). With the texture complete, I played with the overall color of the image using the Levels feature. I adjusted the blue and red channels independently and concentrated on the lighter tones of the image so that rather than the paper being a stark white it took on a creamy appearance.

Add the Polaroid frame

The last part of the process involves combining the final image with a photograph of a Polaroid film edge. The edge picture is nothing more complex than a scanned Polaroid print with the image removed. But rather than go to the trouble of making your own, you can download the edge I used for the example directly from the website (web image 702-3). Next, open the file as a separate Photoshop Elements document. Drag the No Frame frame from the Contents palette onto the Edge picture. Use the Fit Frame to Photo option from the right-click menu to adjust the frame to the edge. Click onto the edge frame layer and drag it onto your picture. The edge will automatically become a new layer on top of the existing image layer.

With the edge layer selected change the layer's mode to Multiply. Notice that the white areas of the layer are now transparent, allowing the picture beneath to show through. Finally, use the Scale or Free Transform command to adjust the size of the edge to fit the image. Remember that because the edge is sitting in a frame layer you click the picture once to adjust the frame and photo together and twice to change just the photo inside the frame. Though not an exact copy of the Polaroid transfer print, the digital version displays much of the character of the original and can be achieved for less cost and with more control.

7.03 Using the Unsharp Mask filter to add contrast

*Suitable for Elements – 7.0, 6.0, 5.0, 4.0, 3.0, 2.0, 1.0 | Difficulty level – Basic | Resources – Web image 703
Tools used – Burning-in | Menus used – Enhance*

USM local contrast settings >> *Instead of using the modest radius settings that we normally associate with the Unsharp Mask filter this technique requires the radius to be set to a high value.*

Most digital photographers have used the Unsharp Mask filter as a way to add some crispness to pictures that are a little soft. In another application this feature can be used to add some local contrast to flat images in much the same way that multi-contrast printing provides a boost to black and white prints.

The trick with this technique is to forget the way that you have been using the feature. Instead of selecting a high amount and low radius setting you do the opposite. You drag the amount downwards and the radius upwards. This produces a change in local contrast rather than a sharpening of individual pixels. To use the technique as part of your standard enhancement process you would adjust highlight and shadow points to set the contrast of the whole picture first, then employ the Unsharp Mask filter to increase the local contrast and then use the filter a second time, with different settings, to increase the photograph's sharpness.

The new Adjust Sharpness filter also contains Amount and Radius sliders which can be employed to produce similar contrast changing effects.

Step 1 >> *To change local contrast open the Unsharp Mask filter and select a low Amount value and a high Radius value.*

Step 2 >> *After adjusting the contrast sharpen the image using the Unsharp Mask filter in the normal fashion.*

Step 3 >> *The final step in the example image was to darken some of the tones around the door opening with the Burn tool.*

Book resources and video tutorials can be found at: **www.photoshopelements.net**

AFTER

BEFORE

a

USM contrast change >> *Until now most of us have used the Unsharp Mask filter for the sharpening of pictures, but with this technique you can use the feature to increase the local contrast of an image as well.*

The Adjust Sharpness alternative >> *The Adjust Sharpness filter can also be used to provide similar local contrast changes.*

b **c** **d** **e**

f **g** **h** **i**

Recipes for USM contrast changes >> *(a) Original image, no contrast change. (b) Amount 30, Radius 80, Threshold 0. (c) Amount 60, Radius 80, Threshold 0. (d) Amount 90, Radius 80, Threshold 0. (e) Amount 120, Radius 80, Threshold 0. (f) Amount 30, Radius 20, Threshold 0. (g) Amount 60, Radius 20, Threshold 0. (h) Amount 90, Radius 20, Threshold 0. (i) Amount 120, Radius 20, Threshold 0.*

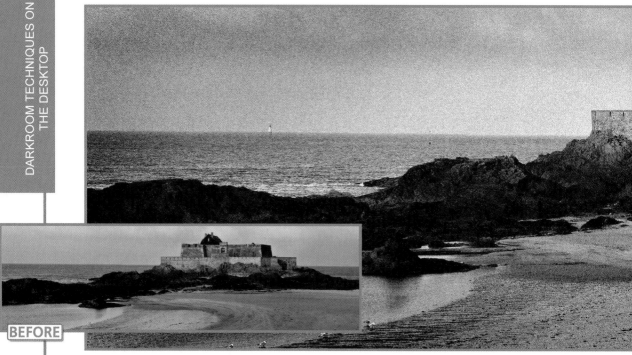

BEFORE

7.04 Lith printing technique

*Suitable for Elements – 7.0, 6.0, 5.0, 4.0, 3.0, 2.0, 1.0 | Difficulty level – Basic | Resources – Web image 704
Tools used – Dodging, Burning-in | Menus used – Enhance, Image, Filter*

Just a few short years prior to the massive uptake of digital photography many professional and amateur image-makers alike were discovering the beauty of a whole range of craft printing processes. There was a resurgence in the techniques involved in the production of high quality black and white pictures and a growing interest in 'alternative' processes that could create stunningly different monochromes.

One such process was lith printing. The process involves the massive overexposure of chloro-bromide-based papers coupled with development in a weak solution of lith chemistry. The resultant images are distinctly textured and richly colored and their origins are unmistakable. But rather than head back to the darkroom in pursuit of your first lith print you can use the following steps to recreate the results digitally.

Most lith prints have strong, distinctive and quite atmospheric grain that is coupled with colors that are seldom seen in a black and white print. They range from a deep chocolate, through warm browns, to oranges and sometimes even pink tones. If our digital version is to seem convincing then the final print will need to contain all of these elements.

Select a picture where the composition is strong. It should contain a full range of tones, especially in the highlights and shadows and good contrast will help make a more striking print. The first task is to lose the color. We want to achieve this change whilst still keeping the

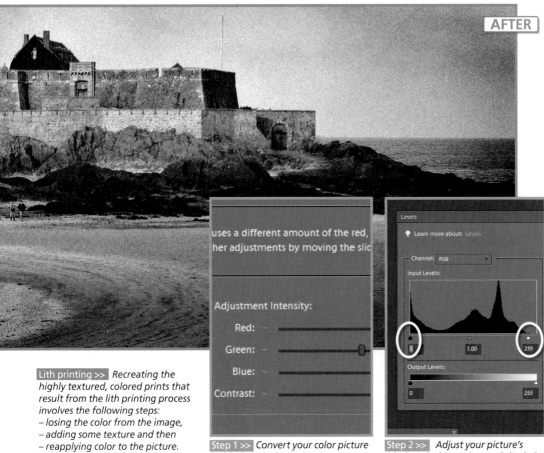

AFTER

Lith printing >> *Recreating the highly textured, colored prints that result from the lith printing process involves the following steps:*
– losing the color from the image,
– adding some texture and then
– reapplying color to the picture.

uses a different amount of the red,
her adjustments by moving the slic

Adjustment Intensity:

Red:
Green:
Blue:
Contrast:

Step 1 >> *Convert your color picture to black and white with the Convert to Black and White feature.*

Levels

Learn more about: Levels

Channel: RGB
Input Levels:

0   1.00   239

Output Levels:
0   255

Step 2 >> *Adjust your picture's black and white points and check the spread of tones using the Levels feature.*

Step 3 >> *Use the Dodging and Burning-in tools to add drama to specific areas of the picture.*

Add Noise

OK
Cancel
✓ Preview

100%

Amount 6.37 %

Distribution
● Uniform
○ Gaussian
✓ Monochromatic

Step 4 >> *Add some texture to the image using the Add Noise filter set to Gaussian and Monochrome.*

Hue/Saturation

Learn more about: Hue/Saturation

Edit: Master

Hue: 27
Saturation: 17
Lightness: 0

Step 5 >> *Apply some color using the Hue slider and Colorize option in the Hue/Saturation feature .*

picture in a color mode (RGB Color). This way later on we can add color back to the picture. If the original is a color picture use the Convert to Black and White feature (Enhance > Convert to Black and White) to lose the color. If you are starting the project with a grayscale picture change the color mode to RGB Color (Image > Mode > RGB Color).

Perform all your tonal enhancement steps now. Use the Levels feature (Enhance > Adjust Lighting > Levels) to ensure a good spread of tones and the Burning and Dodging-in tools to enhance specific parts of the picture. Add some texture to the image using the Add Noise filter (Filter > Noise > Add Noise) with the Gaussian and Monochrome options set. The final step is to add some color back to the picture. We can achieve this effect by selecting the Colorize option in the Hue/Saturation feature and then adjusting the Hue slider to select the color of the tint and the Saturation slider to alter the strength.

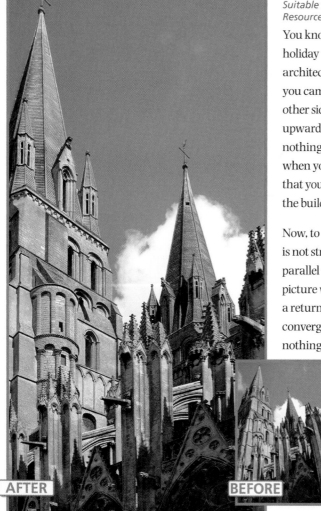

AFTER

BEFORE

7.05 Correcting perspective problems

*Suitable for Elements – 7.0, 6.0, 5.0 | Difficulty level – Basic
Resources – Web image 705 | Menus used – Filter*

You know the story: you're visiting a wonderful city on holiday wanting to capture as much of the local scenes and architecture as possible. You enter the local square and point you camera towards an impressive three-spired building on the other side of the road only to find that you must tilt your camera upwards to get the peaks into the picture. At the time you think nothing of it and you move on to the next location. It is only when you are back at home about to print your photograph that you realize that the innocent 'tilt' has caused the edges of the building to lean inwards.

Now, to a certain extent this isn't a problem; even though it is not strictly accurate, we all know that most buildings have parallel walls and the majority of people who look at you picture will take this into account – won't they? Apart from a return trip and a re-shoot is there any way to correct these converging verticals? Well, I'm glad you asked. Armed with nothing except Elements 5.0, 6.0 or 7.0, the Correct Camera Distortion filter and the steps detailed here, you can now straighten all those leaning architectural shots without the cost of the return journey.

Correcting perspective >> *When shooting upwards with a wide angle lens the sides of buildings converge inwards rather than remain parallel. You can correct this problem using the new Correct Camera Distortion filter from Elements 5.0.*

With the offending image open in the Full Edit workspace select Filter > Correct Camera Distortion. Ensure that the Grid option is switched on via the checkbox at the bottom of the dialog before starting to correct the photo. The dialog contains a variety of controls designed for correcting barrel and pincushion distortion, vertical and horizontal perspective, crooked horizons and the vignetting or the darkening of the corners of the picture frame. The key to using the feature is being able to identify the type of distortion that is present in the photo and then choosing the control to deal with the problem. The presence of a preview window means that you can see the results of the corrections as you apply them. Use the grid to guide your changes.

Step 1 >> *With the example image open in the Full Edit space of Elements select Filter > Correct Camera Distortion. Ensure that the Show Grid option at the bottom of the dialog is checked.*

Step 2 >> *The main problem with the example image is converging verticals which can be corrected by moving the Vertical Perspective control to the left. Unlike the correction techniques in earlier versions of Elements this slider also adjusts the height of the building as well.*

Step 3 >> *To complete the corrections straighten the photo with the Angle control and scale the results so that they fit within the original canvas area. Click OK to apply the changes and close the dialog – then use the Crop tool to remove unwanted areas of the photo.*

Hand tool

Zoom or
Magnify tool

Correct barrel and
pincushion distortion

Correct vignetting or
corner darkening

Alter vertical
perspective

Alter horizontal
perspective

Rotate picture

Scale altered image
inside the canvas area

Lens correction >>
The new Correct Camera Distortion filter provides a variety of controls for correcting the distortion that results from tilting the camera or using a wide angle lens.

Desaturate/saturate >> *Direct your viewer's gaze by increasing
the saturation of important parts of the picture whilst reducing
the color vibrancy of the rest of the image.*

7.06 Add emphasis with saturation

*Suitable for Elements – 7.0, 6.0, 5.0, 4.0, 3.0, 2.0, 1.0 | Difficulty level – Basic | Resources – Web image 706
Tools used – Selection tools | Menus used – Enhance, Select*

This technique, unlike the ones that we have looked at previously in this chapter, does not draw
easy parallels from the world of traditional photography. Until digital came along it was not
possible, at least not without a lot of professional smoke and mirrors, to change the vibrancy
of the color in one part of the picture whilst maintaining or even boosting it in another part. It
certainly wasn't an easy job to combine both black and white and full color in a single picture.

The Hue/Saturation feature has removed such limitations forever. When this tool is combined
with a carefully created (and feathered) selection it is possible to desaturate one part of the
picture and then, using an inverted selection, increase the saturation of the rest. Like dodging
and burning this technique can direct the viewer's interest to a part of the picture that the
photographer deems important. In fact it is when these two techniques, dodging and burning
and saturation/desaturation, are used in tandem that the desktop photographer can really start
to create some dramatic pictures.

In the example image the clown's head was selected using a combination of the Magnetic and
standard Lasso tools. Once completed the selection was feathered slightly (1–2 pixels) (Select
> Feather) to soften the transition of the effect and saved (Select > Save Selection). With the

selection still active the Hue/Saturation feature was opened and the color vibrancy of the clown increased by moving the Saturation slider to the right. To add more contrast, the selection was then inverted (Select > Inverse) and the saturation of the background was decreased almost to the point of just being black and white. An alternative way of working this technique is to create masked Hue/Saturation adjustment layers using the saved selection. This would allow you to readjust the amount of saturation and desaturation at any point later in time and would keep the original picture intact.

Non-destructive version >>
Use masked Hue/Saturation layers to produce the same results with fine-tuning options.

Step 1 >> *Carefully select the area to saturate/desaturate using your favorite selection tools.*

Step 2 >> *Feather the edge of the selection slightly so that the transition will be smoother.*

Step 3 >> *Save the selection so that you can use it or edit it later.*

Step 4 >> *With the selection still active use the Hue/Saturation feature to increase the saturation of the clown's face.*

Step 5 >> *Inverse the selection so that the rest of the picture is now selected.*

Step 6 >> *Use the Hue/Saturation slider to decrease the saturation and provide color contrast between the two picture parts.*

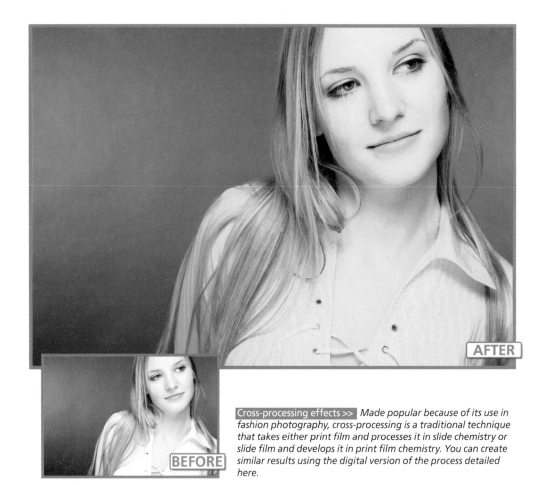

AFTER

BEFORE

Cross-processing effects >> *Made popular because of its use in fashion photography, cross-processing is a traditional technique that takes either print film and processes it in slide chemistry or slide film and develops it in print film chemistry. You can create similar results using the digital version of the process detailed here.*

7.08 Cross-processing effects

Suitable for Elements – 7.0, 6.0, 5.0, 4.0, 3.0, 2.0, 1.0 | Difficulty level – Intermediate | Resources – Web image 708 | Menus used – Enhance

Processing your film in the wrong chemistry sounds like an action that will guarantee disaster, but this is precisely the basis of the cross-processing technique. Print film is developed using slide chemistry or alternatively slide film is processed using print film chemistry. Whichever method you use the process results in distinctly recognizable images that have found their way into many fashion magazines in the last few years. As with many of these alternative techniques the process can be a little unpredictable, with strange color shifts and massive under- and overexposure problems, reducing the number of usable pictures resulting from any shooting session.

Four adjustment layers >>
This technique relies on the application of four different adjustment layers being stacked upon the original image.

Martin Evening of 'Adobe Photoshop for Photographers' Focal Press fame created a digital version of this process that uses a series of curve changes to create images that have a similar look and feel to those produced with the chemical cross-processing effect. Here I present an Elements-friendly version of the technique that provides equally impressive results without using the Photoshop curves feature. In addition, as the technique uses a series of adjustment layers to create the effect, the original picture remains unaltered throughout and the settings for each of the layers can be altered at any time to tweak the final result.

To recreate the look of cross-processing (print film developed in slide chemistry) we must change the image so that it contains creamy highlights, cyan shadows and is generally reduced in contrast. Start with a standard color image. Create a Levels adjustment layer and select the blue channel. Move the white Output slider to the left to flatten the highlights and color them yellow. Create a second

Step 1 >> *To start the process open a color image and create a Levels adjustment layer.*

Step 2 >> *To make the yellow highlights select the blue channel in the Levels feature and drag down the white Output slider. This adds some yellow to the highlights.*

Step 3 >> *Create another Levels adjustment layer, select the red channel and drag down the white input layer. This adds some warmth to the highlights.*

Step 4 >> *To add cyan to the shadow areas create another Levels adjustment layer, select the red channel and move the midtone Input slider to the right.*

Levels adjustment layer and with the red channel selected move the white Output slider to the left as well. This adds some warmth. Next create another Levels adjustment layer and select the red channel again. This time you need to move the mid point Input slider to the right to make the shadows and midtones cyan. With the Levels feature still open, and the red channel still selected, move the white and black Input sliders until they meet the first group of pixels in the histogram. To fine-tune the overall tones you can add yet another Levels adjustment layer and with the composite of all channels selected (RGB), alter contrast and brightness of the whole picture.

Hand coloring >> *Digital hand coloring works by applying painted sections of the image to the black and white original using the Color blending mode. This technique preserves the detail of the monochrome picture and tints the surface with the color of the upper layer in much the same way as oil paint was used to tint black and white prints of old.*

7.09 Digital hand coloring

*Suitable for Elements – 7.0, 6.0, 5.0, 4.0, 3.0, 2.0, 1.0 | Difficulty level – Basic | Resources – Web image 709
Tools used – Brush | Menus used – Layer*

Before the advent of color film the only way to add a hue to a picture was to apply water- or oil-based paints over the top of a black and white print. Most of us will have old photographs of family weddings that are delicately colored in this way. There is a simplicity and subtlety about this approach that is worth recapturing in the digital age.

If you look at the old images you will notice that the detail of the black and white picture shows through the colored paint. The combination of these details and the applied color creates the hand colored effect. To simulate this technique digitally we can use the Color blending mode in Elements. The color is applied to a separate layer using the paint brush and then the mode of the layer is changed to Color. This allows the details of the image beneath to show through the color above. Using the paint brush in the Normal mode will create large flat areas of color that hide the detail beneath.

Step 1 >> *Open a black and white picture and make sure that it is in RGB color mode. Make a new layer in the document.*

Step 2 >> *Select the layer and change its Blending mode to Color.*

Step 3 >> *Select the paint brush from the tool box and then select a foreground color to paint with from the Swatches palette.*

The color can be removed from any part of the picture with the eraser tool and the vibrancy of the hues can be altered by changing the opacity of the color layer.

For the ultimate control each individual color can be added via a new layer. This approach means that the various colors that make up the picture can be edited individually.

Step 4 >> *Paint over the area of the image that you want to hand color. Switch foreground colors and continue to paint.*

Step 5 >> *Make sure that the colors are being applied to the newly created layer. The strength of the coloring can be altered by adjusting the opacity of the layer.*

Hand coloring >> *Changing the opacity of the color layer will alter the strength of the hand coloring effect. (a) 0% opacity. (b) 25% opacity. (c) 50% opacity. (d) 75% opacity. (e) 100% opacity.*

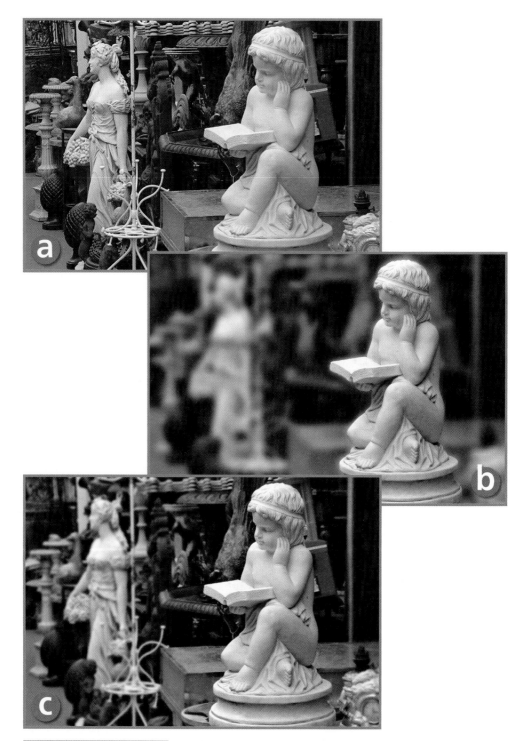

Artificial depth of field effects >>
It is possible to create realistic depth of field effects by making and blurring a series of selections that gradually increase in size. (a) Straight print. (b) Simple selection with Gaussian Blur. (c) Multiple selections with increasing Gaussian Blur values.

7.10 Realistic depth of field effects

Suitable for Elements – 7.0, 6.0, 5.0, 4.0, 3.0, 2.0, 1.0 | Difficulty level – Advanced
Resources – Web image 710 | Tools used – Selection tools | Menus used – Filter, Select

The shallow depth of field effect that is created when you select a small F-stop number (use a long lens or get in very close to your subject) controls the way that a viewer sees your picture. The eye is naturally drawn to the sharpest part of the image and shallow depth of field restricts the sharpness in a photograph to often only a single subject. The Gaussian Blur filter can be used in a similar way to produce results that help to direct the viewer's gaze. Areas of an image can be selected and blurred so that our eyes will be redirected to the sharp part of the print. In a way, by blurring parts of an otherwise sharp picture, this process is creating artificial depth of field.

When the potential of the Blur filter is first discovered many enthusiastic digital photographers take to the task of creating shallow DOF pictures from their sharp originals with gusto. The process they use is simple – select and blur. The results certainly provide a contrast in sharpness, but the pictures lack the sense of realism that is needed for the effect to be truly convincing.

To recreate shallow depth of field more effectively there needs to be a gradual decrease in sharpness as you move in front of, or behind, the main point of focus. Making a single selection doesn't provide the gradual change that is needed. In its place we need to use a series of overlapping selections that gradually move further away from the point of focus. Each selection is feathered to smooth the transition of the effect and then the selected area is blurred using the Gaussian Blur filter. The amount of blur is increased as the selection gets more distant from the point of focus.

Multiple selections >>
Convincing depth of field effects are based on the sequential blurring of multiple overlapping selections.

(a) First selection.
(b) Second selection.
(c) Third selection.
(d) Fourth selection.

DARKROOM TECHNIQUES ON THE DESKTOP

This simulates lens-based depth of field by surrounding the point of focus with the area of least blur and then gradually increasing the out of focus effect as the eye moves further from this part of the picture.

Start the process by creating a selection of the subject area that you want to remain sharp. Feather (Select > Feather) the edge slightly to ensure that the transition between blurred and sharp picture parts is less obvious. Inverse (Select > Inverse) the selection so that the rest of the picture is selected. Apply the Gaussian Blur filter (Filter > Blur > Gaussian Blur) to the selection

Step 1 >> *Carefully select the part of the picture that is to be your point of focus – the area that will remain sharp. Here I used the new Quick Selection tool.*

Step 2 >> *Feather (1 or 2 pixels) and then save the selection.*

Step 3 >> *Use the Inverse command to select the rest of the picture.*

Step 4 >> *Apply a small Gaussian Blur to this initial selection. Here I have used a radius of 1.0 pixels. Inverse the selection again.*

Step 5 >> *Increase the area that is selected by picking the Expand command from the Select > Modify menu. Inverse the selection again.*

Step 6 >> *Feather the new selection by a greater amount. Here I have used 10 pixels. Save the selection.*

using a low Radius value of 1 pixel. Now to recede the selection away from the point of focus. Here I have used the Contract command (Select > Modify > Contract) but you could just as easily draw another selection that is further away from the statue. The edge is feathered again, this time by a larger amount, and the whole thing blurred with a larger radius.

This process – contract, feather blur – is repeated as many times as is needed to ensure that the picture's background details are suitably unsharp. In the example image I used four selections to get the shallow depth of field effect.

Step 7 >> *Apply a larger Gaussian Blur (2 pixels) to this new section of the picture. Inverse the selection.*

Step 8 >> *Create a new larger selection around the statue using the Expand command set to 100 pixels. Inverse the selection.*

Step 9 >> *Feather and save the new selection. Here I have used a radius of 30 pixels.*

Step 10 >> *Blur the new selection with a higher Gaussian Blur setting. Inverse the selection again.*

Step 11 >> *Expand the selection by 100 pixels and then again by another 100 pixels before feathering the edge by 60 pixels and saving the selection.*

Step 12 >> *Inverse the selection and then apply the final Gaussian Blur to the selection using a radius of 4 pixels.*

AFTER

BEFORE

Creating realistic shadows >> *Simple shadows can be applied to any layer using the Drop Shadow options in the Elements Styles palette. More complex shadows, like the one in the example that looks like it is falling on the ground, can be created by making a shadow layer beneath the image.* Image courtesy of www.ablestock.com. Copyright © 2003 Hamera and its licensors. All rights reserved.

Elements' drop shadow styles >> *Elements provides a range of ready-made drop shadow styles that can be applied directly to any layer. (a) High. (b) Low. (c) Noisy. (d) Hard edge. (e) Soft edge. (f) Outline. (g) Fill/outline. (h) Neon.*

a   b   c   d

7.11 Beyond the humble drop shadow

*Suitable for Elements – 7.0, 6.0, 5.0, 4.0, 3.0, 2.0, 1.0 | Difficulty level – Advanced | Resources – Web image 711
Tools used – Selection tools | Menus used – Edit, Filter, Image*

The drop shadow effect has become very popular in the last few years as a way of making an image or some text stand out from the background. To coincide with this popularity Adobe created a series of drop shadow styles that can be applied directly to any layer. These options are suitable for many applications and Elements users can even customize the look of the effect by altering variables like the direction of the light and the shadow distance using the Style Settings dialog (Layer > Layer Style > Style Settings).

Drop shadow style settings >> *Alter the look of your drop shadows by changing the value of the options in the Style Settings dialog.*

But what if you want a more sophisticated shadow than these preset choices allow? Well then you will need to create your own shadows. Using the example image let's make a shadow that lies upon the ground that the model is standing on. To do so, we will need to revisit the steps that I used to use to create even the simplest drop shadow before the days of layer styles.

First select the subject with one of your favorite selection tools and copy it to memory (Edit > Copy). Next paste the picture (Edit > Paste) twice to form two new layers. Fill the background layer with white. Next fill the second image layer with black making sure that the Preserve Transparency option is turned on. This creates a silhouette exactly the same size and shape as the main picture. To allow for the shadow we will need to create some more space on the right-hand side of the picture. Use the Canvas Size feature for this (Image > Resize > Canvas Size). Here I have anchored the canvas on the left side and set the option to percent and then increased the width to 150%.

With the shadow layer still selected I used the Distort feature (Image > Transform > Distort) to push the shadow downwards and to the right. Keep in mind that for this type of shadow to be convincing it must be consistent with the lighting in the image generally. In the example the main light is coming from the left and so the shadow should be projected to the right. Also make sure that the shadow is positioned so that it grows from where the subject touches the ground. In the example it is the feet. If need be, use the Move tool and even the Rotate feature (Image > Rotate > Free Rotate Layer) to orientate the shadow so that it meets the shoes.

Next we need to blur the edges of the shadow and adjust its transparency to complete the illusion. With the shadow layer still selected use the Gaussian Blur filter (Filter > Blur > Gaussian Blur) to make the edges of the shadow less sharp. There are no hard and fast rules about the amount of blur to apply. It is a matter of trying a few settings with the Preview option switched on in the Filter dialog until you are happy with the results. To make the shadow a little brighter and more transparent I changed the blending mode from Normal to Multiply and dragged down the opacity of the whole layer.

Although not immediately obvious here, changing the blending mode to Multiply will give a more realistic shadow effect when laid over other picture areas. When used in conjunction with the layer's Opacity slider the density of the shadow can be adjusted to allow the detail from the picture beneath to show through.

Multiply shadows >> Switching the Blending mode of the shadow layer to Multiply will allow the detail of the layer below to show through, producing a more realistic effect.

Step 1 >> *Carefully select the main subject using your favorite selection tools. Here it was easier to select the uniform background and adjust the selection around the hair region rather than selecting the model.*

Step 2 >> *Change the selection from the background to the model by inversing the selection.*

Step 3 >> *Copy the selected area to the computer memory and then paste the contents twice to form two new image layers containing the copied model picture.*

Step 4 >> *Select the background layer and fill it with white.*

Step 5 >> *Select the lower of the two new layers and fill this layer with black, this time making sure that the Preserve Transparency option is turned on.*

Step 6 >> *Increase the size of the canvas to accommodate the shadow by anchoring the image on the left side and increasing the width by 150%.*

Step 7 >> *With the shadow layer still selected use the Distort tool to squash the shadow into the newly created space on the right side of the model.*

Step 8 >> *Blur the edge of the shadow using the Gaussian Blur filter.*

Step 9 >> *Switch the mode of the shadow layer to Multiply and adjust the opacity of the shadow until the desired brightness is shown.*

AFTER

BEFORE

Ring flash shadow >> *You can extend the technique detailed above to allow you to create shadows similar to those created when using a ring flash that surrounds the camera's lens. Image courtesy of www.ablestock.com. Copyright © 2003 Hamera and its licensors. All rights reserved.*

7.12 Ring flash shadow

Suitable for Elements – 7.0, 6.0, 5.0, 4.0, 3.0, 2.0, 1.0 | Difficulty level – Advanced | Resources – Web image 712
Tools used – Selection tools | Menus used – Edit, Filter, Image

You can extend the technique detailed above to create a shadow that is similar to those found in pictures created with a ring flash attached to the camera lens. These pictures are characterized by the model having a shadow projected onto the wall behind. As the light is coming from the same position as the camera the shadow is larger but directly behind the subject.

The first few steps are the same as those found in the previous technique. Start by selecting the main subject and copy and pasting it twice to form two new layers. Next fill the background with white. Select the lower image layer and fill it with black, making sure that the Preserve Transparency option is selected. Blur the shadow using the Gaussian Blur filter (Filter > Blur > Gaussian Blur). With the Preview option selected in the Filter dialog, adjust the Blur Radius so that the edge of the shadow is visible as a halo around the top image layer.

With the shadow layer still selected use the Move tool to shift its location upwards by a few pixels. For accuracy you can use the arrow keys instead of the mouse. Each arrow key press moves the shadow one pixel. To finalize the technique change the blending mode of the shadow to Multiply and reduce its opacity.

Step 1 >> *Select, copy and paste the model twice to create two image layers. Fill the background with white.*

Step 2 >> *Select the lower image layer and fill the image area with black. Make sure that the Preserve Transparency option is selected.*

Step 3 >> *Use the Gaussian Blur filter to blur the shadow so that it shows as a halo around the top image layer.*

Step 4 >> *Use the arrow keys to move the shadow gradually upwards so that it shows to the left, right and above but not below the model. Change the Blending mode to Multiply and adjust the opacity.*

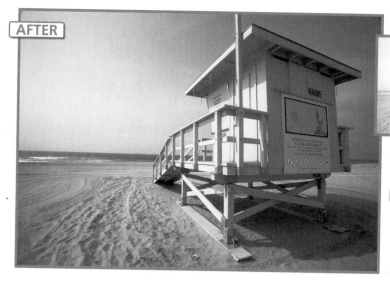

AFTER

BEFORE

Altering specific tones >>
Images with bright highlights often need a little curve tweak to darken these tones without changing the white and black points of the picture.

7.13 Elements' Curves features

Suitable for Elements – 5.0 | Difficulty level – Intermediate | Resources – Web image 713 | Menu used – Enhance

One of the regular complaints from Photoshop enthusiasts trying to put Elements users in their place is that the program 'doesn't contain curves' and so can't really be considered as a serious photo enhancement package. For the first four versions of the program this was indeed true, but in 5.0 Adobe included an easy-to-use version of Photoshop's famous Curves feature. This is great news as the Curves feature in Photoshop does offer a great deal of flexibility and creativity over manipulating the tones in your image. In particular, curves provide a great way to lighten shadow areas and darken highlights and it is precisely these two tasks that I use Curves for most. In version 6.0 curves was revamped and now has a simpler interface.

Adjust Color Curves feature

The Adjust Color Curves feature contains two different ways to manipulate the tones in your photo. The first is a series of enhancement presets, called Styles, that apply specific curve tweaks to your photos. These adjustments include the options to **Increase Midtones**, **Lighten Shadows**, **Increase Contrast**, **Darken Highlights**, create a **Solarize** effect and compensate for **Backlight** in a photo. Selecting one of these options adds the selected adjustment to the photo. Choosing a second option replaces the first tonal tweak with the second curves adjustment.

The second way to alter the tones in your photo when using the new Adjust Color Curves feature is via a set of four slider controls coupled with a graphical curves display located in the Adjust section. The sliders controls include **Adjust Highlights**, **Midtone Brightness**, **Midtone Contrast** and **Adjust Shadows** options. Moving any of the sliders directly alters the way that the tones are distributed in your photo and changes the shape of the curve. Using these controls you can fine-tune specific areas of your photo.

Darken highlights	Adjust Highlights:	Lighten highlights
Darken midtones	Midtone Brightness:	Lighten midtones
Reduce midtone contrast	Midtone Contrast:	Increase midtone contrast
Darken shadows	Adjust Shadows:	Lighten shadows

Advanced Options slider controls >> *Moving the position of the sliders in the Advanced Options section of the Adjust Color Curves dialog produces the changes listed above to specific tonal ranges in a photo.*

The Reset button removes all curves changes, both thumbnail selections and slider movements, and restores the feature back to the default setting, which does not apply any changes to image. Note that in the version 5.0 the Reset button switches the control to the Increase Midtones sample.

The easiest and most effective way to use this new Elements' Curves control is to use the Styles menu to select the general correction to apply to the photo first and then use the sliders to fine-tune the results.

Adjust Color Curves >> *The new Adjust Color Curves feature provides two different ways to tweak the tones in your photo. You can use each set of controls independently but the best results are obtained when the global changes are set by clicking a Styles entry and small fine-tuning to specific tonal ranges added next via the Slider controls.*

(a) Adjust Sliders section containing Slider controls for specific tonal ranges.

(b) The Styles presets which apply a set adjustment to the picture when clicked.

(c) Changes in the shape of the curve based on clicking the Sample thumbnails. Left to right: Increase Midtones, Lighten Shadows, Backlight, Increase Contrast, Darken Highlights and Solarize.

Fill Flash effects >> *The Shadows/Highlights option introduced in version 3.0 of Elements also easily lightens the shadows of contrasty photos without affecting the mid and highlight tones in the picture.*

Like the Adjust Color Curves feature, Shadows/Highlights is useful for lightening the shadows in backlit images such as this beach example.

Both options provide a Fill Flash effect which takes its name from the technique of using an on-camera flash in daylight to lighten the shadows caused by direct sunlight. This way of working is popular with photojournalists who in their haste to capture hard news images have little time to modify the lighting on their subjects.

Curves like control via the Shadows/Highlights feature

The Shadow/Highlights tool can also be used to alter specific tonal ranges in your photos. It contains three sliders – the upper one is for lightening shadows, which replaces the old Fill Flash tool (included up to version 2.0), the control in the middle darkens highlights and is a substitute for the old Adjust Backlighting tool (included up to version 2.0) and the final slider adjusts midtone Contrast. Moving the Shadows control to the right lightens all the tones that are spread between the middle values and black.

Sliding the Darken Highlights control to the right darkens those tones between middle values and white. The beauty of this feature is that unlike the Brightness/Contrast tool, these changes are made without altering other parts of the picture. To fine-tune the tonal changes a third slider is also included in the dialog. Moving this Midtone control to the right increases the contrast of the middle values and movements to the left decrease the contrast making the image 'flatter'.

7.14 Using Photoshop's Curves in Elements

Suitable for Elements – 7.0, 6.0, 5.0 | Difficulty level – Intermediate | Resources – Web image 713 | Menu used – Enhance

Though Photoshop's curves feature is not supported in Elements it is possible to make use of Curves Adjustment Layers in Elements documents. Like other Photoshop Adjustment Layer features, it is possible to create a series of Curves layers in Photoshop and save them to a donor PSD document. When this document is opened into Elements the adjustment layers are present and they still enhance the layers below them in the stack. It is not possible to change the settings of each layer but they can be dragged to an Elements document and be used to change the tones in that image.

As most Elements users will not have access to Photoshop, I have created a document with multiple Curves adjustment layers (Photoshop-Curves.psd). To use simply download the file from the website, open in Elements and drag the appropriate layer to your Elements file.

Photoshop Curves layers >> *The Photoshop-Curves.psd document available from the book's website contains a variety of Curves Adjustment layers that you can use with your Elements files.*

Step 1 >> *Download and open the Photoshop-Curves.psd from the website. Make sure that the layers palette is also visible.*

Step 2 >> *Open your Elements file and drag a suitable Curves layer from the layers palette onto the photo.*

Step 3 >> *Fine tune the effects of the curve by adjusting the opacity of the adjustment layer.*

7.15 Combining images seamlessly

Suitable for Elements – 7.0, 6.0, 5.0, 4.0, 3.0, 2.0, 1.0 | Difficulty level – Intermediate
Resources – Web images 715-1, 715-2 | Tools used – Selection tools | Menus used – Select, Layer

One of the most basic yet critical skills for any digital photographer to learn is the art of careful selection of image parts. Whether you need to isolate a portion of a picture so that it is not affected by a filter, or use a selection as a prelude to copying an image section from one photograph to another, being able to manipulate your program's selection tools is a very important skill.

The success of a simple task such as creating a montage from two separate pictures is largely dependent on how well the image parts are isolated and copied. As an example I will add an extra ornament from a separate picture to an existing shadow box image and in the process demonstrate some basic selection and montaging steps that will help you to increase your image editing skills.

With both images open in Elements check to see that they are similar in size (and resolution) by viewing both the images at the same magnification. Make image size adjustments using the Scale feature. This step can also be performed after copying and pasting have occurred. Using the Lasso tool carefully work your way around the edge of the subject to be copied, in this example it is an angel, being sure to pick out as much edge detail as possible. In scenarios where there is more contrast between the edge and the background the Magnetic Lasso could be used instead.

Most selections are not perfect first time round, but rather than scrapping the initial selection try using the modifying keys to adjust your results. To take away part of the selection hold down the Alt key and draw around the area. Increase the image magnification to ensure accuracy around areas or detail. To add to the selection hold down the Shift key and draw around the image part to be included. These keys work with all selection tools and can be used repeatedly to build up a perfect result. Keep in mind that you can switch between any of the selection tools during the modification process; this includes the Quick Selection Tool (Magic Selection Brush in PSE6).

Montaging picture parts >> *Selecting, copying and pasting picture parts from one image to another is a basic skill that most digital photographers should learn. Seamless integration is based on careful selection techniques so it is on developing these skills that you should spend your time.*

At this point a lot of digital photographers would copy the angel and paste it onto the shadow box image, but such an action can produce a very sharp edge to the selection, which is a dead give-away in the final montage. The best approach is to apply a little feathering (Select > Feather) to the edge of the selection before copying. In most cases a value of between 1 and 3 pixels will give a realistic result.

With the feather applied copy (Edit > Copy) the selected portion of the image. This action stores the copy in the computer's memory ready for the Paste command. Switch to the shadow box image and paste the copied angel onto the picture. At this point you should see the object sitting on top of the shadow box picture. Any problems with the relative sizes of the two images will now become obvious. To make small changes in size you can use the Image > Transform > Free Transform tool. When the angel picture was pasted onto the shadow box image a new layer was created. Keeping these two image parts on separate layers means that they can be altered, edited and moved independently of each other; just keep in mind that the changes will only be made to the layer that is selected. Using the Move tool the angel picture is placed in the spare box space in the shadow box. As a final touch of realism a small drop shadow is applied to the angel using the Layer Styles > Drop Shadow options (via the Layer Style menu in the Special Effects section of the Artwork and Effects palette). The direction and size (shadow distance) of the shadow can be altered via the Layer > Layer Styles > Style Settings dialog box. The shadow helps integrate the new picture element with the other ornaments already in the box.

Typically, as your skills increase you will attempt more and more complex selection tasks, some of which may take many minutes to complete. For this reason Adobe has included in version 2.0 of Elements a Save Selection (Select > Save Selection) feature that will allow you to store a copy of your carefully created selection with your image file, ready for later use. Input a name for the selection in the Save Selection dialog. It is good practice to save progress on complex selections as you go. This way if at any point you lose the work you have done you can simply reload the lost selection. Reinstating a saved selection is as simple as selecting the Load Selection option from the Select menu (Select > Load Selection) and choosing the particular selection name from the drop-down menu.

Edit>Paste >> *When part of a picture is selected, copied and pasted into a different document, Elements automatically creates a new layer to hold the pasted part. Having the element stored separately means that you can easily move, scale, change brightness or even add texture without altering the background image. In the example I added a drop shadow to the separate layer to help unify the new subject with the background.*

Step 1 >> *Open both images into the Elements workspace. Check their relative sizes by displaying them at the same magnification rate.*

Step 2 >> *Carefully select the subject to be copied using your favorite selection tool. Zoom in closer to ensure accuracy.*

Step 3 >> *Feather the selection slightly (1–2 pixels) to ensure that the edge of the copied part is not too crisp to appear real.*

Step 4 >> *Copy the selected picture part. This places the part into the computer's memory.*

Step 5 >> *Click onto the background document to make it active and paste the copied part. Use the Move tool to position it and, if need be, use the Free Transform tool to adjust its size to suit.*

Step 6 >> *To complete the illusion add a drop shadow to the object. Make sure that the size and direction of the shadow are consistent with the others in the background.*

7.16 Believable montages – a step further

Suitable for Elements – 7.0, 6.0, 5.0, 4.0, 3.0, 2.0, 1.0 | Difficulty level – Intermediate
Resources – Web images 716-1 to 716-5 | Tools used – Selection tools, Eraser, Clone Stamp
Menus used – Select, Layer, Filter, Enhance

Against the background of the basic montaging skills developed in the last technique let's really test out your abilities to combine disparate images by stepping through the following project that brings together five very different source pictures and with the aid of Photoshop Elements creates a single and hopefully convincing final illustration.

The project has two parts. The first involves creating a background street scene from three different pictures and then unifying the composition by applying a lighting effect. In the second phase of the project a car and bus are added, the street lights are turned on and a little blur is mixed in to create a sense of speed and motion.

Step 1 >> *Open the background images. Be careful to choose pictures with similar pixel dimensions and try to pick photographs with a consistent perspective. Create a new document (File > New) large enough to encompass all three photos and then click-drag the open pictures onto the canvas of the new document.*

Step 2 >> *To match the picture parts select the most different photo and adjust the brightness using the Levels feature. Next alter the color using the Color Variations feature. Finally, make a copy of the right background layer (Layer > Duplicate Layer). This will be used later in the process.*

Step 3 >> *Using the background as the base match the perspective, size and shape of the other background pieces to fit. Do this by reducing the opacity of the layer to be changed and then using the Free Transform feature to resize, rotate and change layer position. To alter perspective hold down the Ctrl key whilst dragging a corner or side handle.*

Step 4 >> *Use the Eraser tool set to Brush mode, low opacity and soft edge to carefully remove the sharp edges of the upper layers to allow them to blend with the lower ones. Alternatively, you can use a mask from a No Settings Adjustment Layer to hide parts of each layer.*

Step 5 >> *Complete the background by selecting the duplicate layer (Step 2) and flipping it horizontally (Image > Rotate > Flip Horizontal). Use this copy to form the left side of the composition. Size, shape and rotate the layer before blending it into the existing background.*

Step 6 >> *Make a flat version of the background by selecting all of the document (Select > All) and then choosing the Copy Merged command (Edit > Copy Merged). The merged copy is then pasted (Edit > Paste) as a new layer.*

Creating convincing montages:

1. When using a selection tool to cut out an object that will be pasted onto another background always apply a 1-pixel feather to the selection before cutting.

2. Try to ensure that all source images have similar lighting direction and quality.

3. Match the color, contrast and brightness of all picture parts before starting to merge them together.

4. Make sure that all source images are the same (or very similar) size and resolution.

5. Label all layers as you create them as this will help you keep track of the many

layers that often make up a complex montage.

7. Don't flatten all the layers and masks that you have used for editing – instead Select > All, then Edit > Copy Merged and finally Edit > Paste a composite of all the detail as a new layer.

Step 7 >> *Use the Clone Stamp to even out the textures and tones and the Burn and Dodge tools to darken or lighten areas. Next select white sky area with the Magic Wand tool and fill (Edit > Fill) with black. Use the Lighting Effects filter (Filter > Render > Lighting Effects) to add a yellow hotspot in the center of the picture, fading the edges of the buildings into the newly created black sky.*

Step 8 >> *Drag the car and bus images onto the background. Flip the bus horizontally (Image > Rotate > Flip Horizontal) and select the bus destination display and flip it back. Using the Free Transform tool (Image > Transform > Free Transform) both the car and bus images are resized and their perspective adjusted to suit the scene.*

Step 9 >> *Use a low opacity soft-edged eraser to remove the unwanted areas around the car and bus. Next darken the side of the bus and add a shadow underneath using the Burn-in tool. Apply similar burning-in changes to the car including shadows and darkening the front and windscreen areas. Use the Sponge tool to desaturate vivid color areas that can appear after burning-in.*

AFTER

BEFORE

All images courtesy of www.istockphoto.com © 2005.

Step 10 >> *Next select the Lens Flare filter (Filter > Render > Lens Flare) and add glows to the headlights of the car and bus and to most of the bigger street lamps using the filter. Because the filter preview window is so small, it is more difficult to apply the changes to the more distant lamp posts. Instead add these with a soft-edged, slightly transparent brush that is colored white.*

Step 11 >> *One of the side effects of the Lens Flare filter is a general lightening of shadow areas in the picture. For this reason use the Burn tool to restore some of the depth of tone to the shadow areas. Selecting Midtone or Shadows as the target range ensures that the highlights remain bright during the changes.*

Step 12 >> *Make a copy of the merged layer of the work to date using the technique outlined in Step 6 and then apply the Radial Blur filter (Filter > Blur > Radial Blur), set to zoom and with the center positioned over the car, to the copy. Reduce the opacity of the blurred layer to restore a little detail and then use a soft-edged eraser or No Settings mask to remove layer parts to reveal the detail beneath.*

7.17 Producing high-key pictures

Suitable for Elements – 7.0, 6.0, 5.0, 4.0, 3.0, 2.0, 1.0 | Difficulty level – Intermediate
Resources – Web image 717
Tools used – Selection tools
Menus used – Select, Layer

When, as a student, I was asked to produce a high-key portrait I can remember the extreme lengths that I went to making sure that my lighting was just right, my exposure perfect and my printing spot on. So finicky was the process that many photographers veer away from making many of these stylized portraits. There is no doubting the beauty of a well-produced high-key portrait. The skin tones become almost white, but still manage to retain just a hint of detail, whilst the shadows keep their depth and the detail throughout remains crisp.

AFTER

BEFORE

With digital now dominant, what new spin can this technology offer to this old technique? Well I'm glad you asked. This technique takes a standard portrait and with a few basic changes in Photoshop Elements creates a new high-key version. Just like the original technique the digital approach concentrates on lightening the subject's skin tones whilst still retaining depth in the shadows.

Step 1 >> *With the image open in Photoshop Elements, the first task is to create a Gradient Map adjustment layer. Do this by selecting the option from the Adjustment Layer button at the top of the Layers palette.*

Step 2 >> *Double-click in the gradient area in the dialog to display the Gradient editor. Now to change the tones that make up the start and end points of the gradient. Start with the left end of the gradient – double-click on the Color Stop box.*

Step 3 >> *The Color Picker dialog will open. Select a light gray and click OK. This sets this color as the left end of the gradient. Now double-click the color stop on the right end and select white as the gradient end point.*

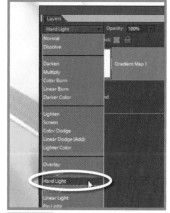

Step 4 >> *Select the adjustment layer and change the blending mode to Hard Light. This will produce a much lighter color image but still hold most of your highlight details.*

Step 5 >> *Now add a Levels adjustment layer so that it sits at the top of the Layer Stack. Adjust the Midtone slider to control the brightness of the subject's skin tones.*

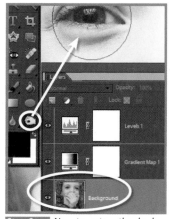

Step 6 >> *Now to restore the shadow detail. Select the image layer at the bottom of the stack and with the Burn-in tool set to shadow and an exposure of 10% enhance the shadow areas using light overlapping strokes.*

Gradient map?

This feature switches the colors in your picture with tones from a gradient. This option is often used to convert color images to black and white by using a black-to-white gradient map. The colors in your picture are mapped to the grays in the gradient. The feature works just as easily with colors and complex rainbow gradients as well. Try it yourself.

7.18 Correcting lens problems

Suitable for Elements – 7.0, 6.0, 5.0, 4.0, 3.0, 2.0, 1.0 | Difficulty level – Intermediate | Resources – Web images 718-1, 718-2 | Menus used – Filter, Image

The following techniques are designed to correct two of the most common lens problems:

- **Barrel distortion** and
- **Pincushion distortion**.

As we have already seen in technique 7.05 the new Correct Camera Distortion filter that ships with Photoshop Elements 6.0 and 7.0 can quickly and easily correct perspective problems in your photos, but this isn't the end of the feature's abilities. The Remove Distortion slider is designed specifically for removing the barrel distortion or pin cushioning effects common with some lenses. For best results this slider can be used in conjunction with the Rotate, Perspective and Vignetting controls to fine-tune the look of your photo. This feature can also be used to intentionally add the effects of each of these lens problems in order to produced bloated or pinched photos.

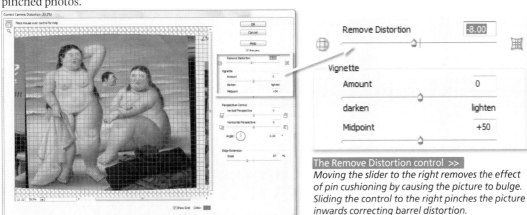

The Remove Distortion control >>
Moving the slider to the right removes the effect of pin cushioning by causing the picture to bulge. Sliding the control to the right pinches the picture inwards correcting barrel distortion.

Before Correct Camera Distortion filter (for previous Elements versions)

In previous versions of Photoshop Elements you could use the Spherize filter (Filter > Distort > Spherize) to help correct the distortion problems in your photos. It contains a preview thumbnail and a slider control that adjusts the degree of barrel or pin cushion correction that is applied to the picture. Moving the slider to the right balloons the picture and therefore counteracts the effects of pin cushioning. Sliding the control to the left contracts the image and reduces barrel distortion. But simply applying this filter to the problem picture will cause some parts of the photo to be left unchanged (corners) whilst the rest of the image is 'spherized'. To overcome this problem and apply the changes to all the picture, you will need to add some space around the image before applying the filter. Use the steps below to correct the photos you have in your collection that suffer from lens distortion.

Step 1 >> *Open the example image. Next select the Crop tool and click-drag the marquee so that it covers the whole of the picture. Now click on the marquee corner handles in the top left and bottom right and drag these outwards beyond the edge of the picture. Double-click in the center of the marquee to add the new canvas space.*

Step 2 >> *Open the Spherize filter (Filter > Distort > Spherize) and adjust the magnification of the thumbnail so that all the image can be seen. Drag the Amount slider to the left to remove the barrel distortion. Continue the adjustment until the ballooning effect is no longer evident. Click OK to apply.*

Step 3 >> *Next choose View > Grid and then select Image > Transform > Free Transform. Click-drag the top corner handles outwards until the building parts that should be vertical are aligned to a grid line. Drag the top handle upwards to counteract the squashing action and then double-click to transform. Use the Crop tool to remove edges.*

Step 1 >> *Open the example image and as before select the Crop tool and click-drag the marquee so that it covers the whole of the picture. Now click on the marquee corner handles in the top left and bottom right and drag these outwards beyond the edge of the picture. Double-click in the center of the marquee to add the new canvas space.*

Step 2 >> *Open the Spherize filter (Filter > Distort > Spherize) and adjust the magnification of the thumbnail so that all the image can be seen. Drag the Amount slider to the right to remove the pin cushion distortion. Continue the adjustment until the edges of the card are no longer bent. Click OK to apply.*

Step 3 >> *Select the Crop tool and after drawing the crop marquee around the picture click outside the marquee and drag to rotate the marquee until the edges of the marquee are parallel to the card's sides. Double-click in the centre of the marquee to crop and rotate the photo.*

AFTER

BEFORE

7.19 Change to old

Suitable for Elements – 7.0, 6.0, 5.0, 4.0, 3.0, 2.0, 1.0 | Difficulty level – Intermediate | Resources – Web images 719-1, 719-2 | Tools used – Selection tools, Free Transform | Menus used – Select, Layer, Enhance, Filter, Edit

Most people would say that old photographs have a certain look and feel about them that can almost be described as magical. It is hard to pin down exactly why we can be so fascinated by these aged images; it may be nostalgia pure and simple, or the knowledge that you are holding a piece of captured history in your hands or it may even be the fact that they look so different from their modern, dare I say it, digital, counterparts. But such is the fascination with old images that many contemporary shooters use a range of digital techniques to recapture this 'look and feel' in their pixel-based photographs. In this section we will gracefully add years of age to a straight portrait with the help of some of the features in Photoshop Elements.

Sepia toned vignettes with old background

In this technique we will take a modern portrait that uses a classic pose, give it an old time treatment and then add it to an original antique background. Such picture surrounds can be easily located at car boot sales or, as with my example, a French brocante shop. The state of the photograph itself is not all that important; it is the surround that we are interested in. The circular cutout won't suit the oval vignette of the example picture so some quick copy, paste and transform steps modify the original to fit our modern portrait. The last part of the process adds some texture and a little unsharpness to the original to ensure that it matches its new (or is that old?) surround.

To see how to create similar results using the new Frame layer technology included in Photoshop Elements go to Chapter 12.

Step 1 >> *Start by making an oval selection using the Elliptical selection tool from the Elements tool box. Feather the selection (Select > Feather or the Feather option in the Refine Edge dialog) to make the transition between the selected and non-selected areas more gradual. Inverse the selection (Select > Inverse) and then press the Delete key to remove the background of the portrait.*

Step 2 >> *A digital simulation of sepia toning can be obtained by opening the Hue/Saturation feature (Enhance > Adjust Color > Hue/ Saturation), ticking the Colorize option and then moving the Hue slider to a value of about 30. The strength of the color can be changed by sliding the Saturation slider.*

Step 3 >> *Open the photo-frame picture. This example was photographed using window light directed from the top of the picture. Change the circular cutout to suit the oval picture by making a feather selection of the oval and Edit > Copy and Edit > Paste the selection. Next use the Free Transform tool to make the circle taller. Double-click to apply the transformation.*

Step 4 >> *Flatten the picture (Layer > Flatten Image) and carefully select the inside of the cutout using one of the Lasso tools. Feather the selection by 1 pixel. Save the selection (Select > Save Selection) just in case you lose it during the next couple of steps. Switch back to the sepia-toned portrait and select (Select > All) and copy (Edit > Copy) the whole picture to memory. Click onto the background document and make sure that the cutout selection is still active. Now select the Paste Into Selection option from the Edit menu (not the Paste option).*

Step 5 >> *Straight after you paste the portrait into the surround select the Free Transform feature using the short-cut key – Ctrl T. This will place the familiar transformation handles around the pasted picture allowing you to manipulate the size of the portrait to suit the cutout. Check that the Constrain Proportions option is checked in the Options bar. This will help guarantee that the portrait remains in proportion when resizing. Double-click to apply the transformation.*

Step 6 >> *Although the picture now fits the surround well there is an obvious difference between the texture of the two parts. To help match these areas, select a portion of the picture surround and then copy and paste this into a new Elements document. Save the texture as a PSD file. Reload the original selection made for the cutout (Select > Load Selection). Now apply the saved copied texture to the portrait area using the Load Texture option in the Texturizer filter (Filter > Texture > Texturizer).*

7.20 Painterly photos

Suitable for Elements – 7.0, 6.0, 5.0, 4.0, 3.0, 2.0, 1.0
Difficulty level – Intermediate | Resources – Web image 720
Menus used – Filter

Before photography was even invented or digital became the way to take and make pictures, artists had been creating great pictures for centuries using such diverse materials as chalk, pastel, pen and ink, and, of course, paint. Now you can emulate the look of these old masterpieces by using your very own photographs as the starting point and adding the artistic 'look and feel' with a few well-chosen, but simple, digital embellishments. Here we will recreate four distinct artistic illustrations from a single humble photographic beginning using several enhancement steps and the filters contained in Elements.

BEFORE

a

Changing to a pen and ink drawing (See a)

Using the Graphic Pen filter it is possible to simulate the effect of making a drawing of a photograph with a thin graphic arts pen. Close overlapping strokes are used for the shadow areas; midtones are represented by balancing strokes with the paper color showing through; and highlight details are drawn with a few sparse strokes.

AFTER

Step 1 >> *Set the foreground colors to default by clicking the small black and white squares in the bottom left of the toolbar. The Graphic Pen filter uses the foreground color as the 'ink' color and the background color as the 'paper' color. Select the filter from the Sketch menu. Using the preview as a guide adjust the Stroke Length, Light/ Dark Balance and Stroke Direction controls. Click OK.*

Step 2 >> *To add a little more color to your Graphic Pen 'drawings' select colors other than black and white for the foreground and background values. Double-click each swatch to open the Color Swatch palette where you can select the new color. Here I changed the pen color to brown and the paper color to light cream.*

AFTER

b

Switching photographic tones with pastel strokes (See b)

As well as the pen and ink approach used above, another favorite with artists is the use of pastels or chalks on a roughly textured paper surface. The tones of the picture are layered upon the paper's texture so that the image detail gradually emerges from the background as a combination of stroke, color and texture.

Step 1 >> *To create this effect we make use of the Rough Pastel filter. The feature contains two distinct control sections. The upper two sliders, Stroke Length and Stroke Detail, are used to adjust the way that the photographic tone is converted to pastel strokes. With the preview window zoomed in to 100% move both sliders until you are happy with the mix of detail and tone.*

Step 2 >> *When drawing with pastels artists often use a heavily textured paper as a base for the picture. The lower section in the Filter dialog is used to apply such a surface texture to your pastel image. Here you can select the texture type (canvas, burlap, sandstone), the size of the texture (scaling), the strength of the texture effect (relief) and the direction of the light that provides shadow for the surface. After making your texture selections, check the preview and readjust the stroke length and detail if necessary before clicking OK to complete.*

AFTER

Creating a watercolor painting (See c)

If you want to create the feeling of a painted surface rather than a drawn one then the Watercolor filter in Photoshop Elements is a good place to start. With this feature the tone and hue of the original photograph is converted to daubs of semi-transparent color with the larger areas surrounded by a darker border edge. To make the effect even more convincing I have applied a texture to the picture after the watercolor conversion.

Step 1 >> *Start by opening the Watercolor filter from the Artistic option of the Filter menu. Next, with the preview set to 100%, adjust the Brush Detail and Shadow Intensity sliders to suit the picture. The third slider, Texture, is used to control the break-up of the painted areas rather than any simulated paper texture. This comes in the next step. Click OK to filter.*

Step 2 >> *Now to add a surface treatment to the picture that will really make the conversion to a watercolor painting complete. For this task we will use the Texturizer (Filter > Texture > Texturizer) filter which has the same controls and options that we looked at in the Rough Pastel filter. We can choose the type, scale, relief and light direction that will be used for the texture. Be sure to preview the effect of the settings at 100% before clicking OK to apply.*

AFTER d

Pop art posters (See d)

Andy Warhol made the technique famous in the sixties and now you can recreate his posterized effect using your own pictures. Warhol's images were extremely graphic and constructed of very few colors, which were then applied in broad flat areas of the picture. Others like Roy Lichtenstein added a cartoon-like feeling to the pop art pictures by including a black line around colored areas. Here we will use the Cutout and Poster Edges filters to recreate this image style.

Step 1 >> *To start we will use the Cutout filter (Filter > Artistic > Cutout) to reduce the colors in the picture and to simplify the photographs detail. The feature contains three sliders. The first , No. of Levels, determines the number of colors that will be present in the final picture. Smaller values mean less colors. The Edge Simplicity and Fidelity sliders are used to determine the amount of detail that is retained in the picture. Try several settings to ensure that you have a good balance of detail and flat tone. Click OK to filter.*

Step 2 >> *The final step in the pop art transformation is to add a black surround to the flat areas of color. For this job we will use the Poster Edges filter (Filter > Artistic > Poster Edges). The Edge Thickness slider adjusts the width of the line drawn around the picture parts, the Edge Intensity slider controls the darkness of the line and the Posterization setting is a further color reduction control. Check how the results of your settings appear when previewed at 100% and then click OK to complete.*

Book resources and video tutorials can be found at: **www.photoshopelements.net**

8

Professional Retouching

ADVANCED PHOTOSHOP ELEMENTS 7 FOR DIGITAL PHOTOGRAPHERS

When it comes to retouching, Photoshop Elements and Photoshop are definitely the royalty amongst image-editors. The programs jointly contain hosts of tools, filters and adjustment options that can help turn ordinary looking portraits into something that is truly dazzling.

The shear power and dominance of the programs in this area is not difficult to see as most glossy magazine covers, family scrapbooks and wedding albums contain a plethora of photos that have been 'shopped' in one way or another. The results, in most cases, are amazing and in a few instances, even a little scary. But for the average photographer (judging by the requests from readers) the interest is not about wanting to recreate the plastic look of celebrity stardom but

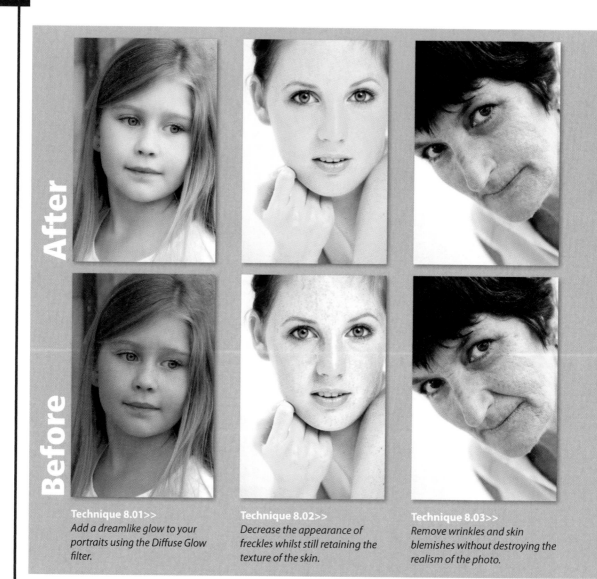

After

Before

Technique 8.01>>
Add a dreamlike glow to your portraits using the Diffuse Glow filter.

Technique 8.02>>
Decrease the appearance of freckles whilst still retaining the texture of the skin.

Technique 8.03>>
Remove wrinkles and skin blemishes without destroying the realism of the photo.

Book resources and video tutorials can be found at: **www.photoshopelements.net**

rather it centers around the gentle art of photo enhancement. And in truth, I feel that this is the best use of the retouching power of programs like Elements.

Visual surgery without a hint of anything plastic

So with this in mind, I present here a few of the basic techniques that are used by portrait photographers on a daily basis. Most work with, rather than paint over, the basic structure and texture of the model's face and in so doing they carefully enhance what already exists rather than replace it with something that is manufactured.

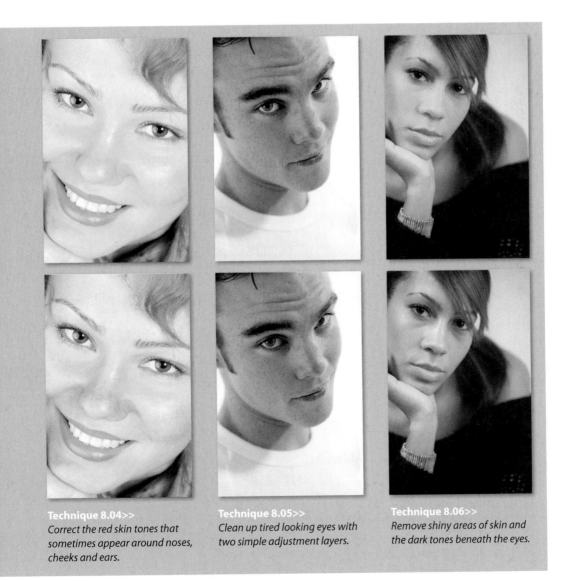

Technique 8.04>>
Correct the red skin tones that sometimes appear around noses, cheeks and ears.

Technique 8.05>>
Clean up tired looking eyes with two simple adjustment layers.

Technique 8.06>>
Remove shiny areas of skin and the dark tones beneath the eyes.

The Diffuse Glow filter adds a glamorous touch to standard portrait images.

8.01 Adding a dreamy effect

Suitable for Elements – 7.0, 6.0, 5.0, 4.0, 3.0, 2.0, 1.0 | Difficulty level – Basic Menus used – Filter | Resources – Web image 801

The Diffuse Glow filter is one of the Distort group of filters that can be found in Photoshop Elements. The feature creates a high-key (very light), glamorous and slightly grainy glowing version of your picture. The filter is great for smoothing out surface marks on the skin of your subject and is often used to add a Hollywood feel to portraits. Try low settings to start with, keeping an eye on the changes in the filter's preview window to ensure that you are not losing important picture detail in the surface glow.

The Filter dialog contains three sliders and a preview window. The Graininess control alters the dominance of the noise that will be added to the picture. The Glow Amount slider changes the strength of white glow in the picture (and how much detail is lost to it). The Clear Amount slider acts as a counter balance to the Glow Amount restoring detail in the glowing areas of the picture.

As it is often difficult to determine how well the filter will work, apply the changes to a copy of the image layer first and then, with this filtered layer above the original, change its opacity to vary the strength of the final effect.

Step 1 >> *Make sure that the default foreground and background colors are selected and then with your picture open select the Diffuse Glow filter from the Distort group in the Filter menu. Alternatively you can also choose the feature from the Effects palette (Filters > Distort).*

Step 2 >> *With the Filter dialog open make sure that the Preview option is clicked and that the preview window is set to 100%. Adjust the three sliders in turn carefully previewing the results. If necessary, drag the visible area in the preview window to examine more closely the changes in other areas of the picture. Click OK.*

Step 3 >> *As a finishing touch for this example I decided to apply a little sharpening to the eyes to ensure that they stood out from the rest of the scene. Using the Filter > Sharpen > Unsharp Mask feature increase the Levels value to restrict the changes to the areas of the picture with the greatest contrast. Click OK to complete.*

8.02 Softening freckles

Suitable for Elements – 7.0, 6.0, 5.0, 4.0, 3.0, 2.0, 1.0 | Difficulty level – Intermediate Tools – Brush | Resources – Web image 802

So many good retouching techniques are not about totally removing or changing the basic structure or make-up of the model's face. Instead, the aim should be to gently enhance the existing skin tones and textures. There is nothing worse, nor more obvious, than an overworked portrait where the skin's original texture and tone are replaced with a flat (or sometimes even shiny) surface that has more in common with plastic appliances than anyone I know.

The Brush tool in Lighten blend mode is used here to reduce the dominance of the model's freckles.

The example image is typical of the sort of photograph that is normally overworked. In an attempt to smooth out the appearance of the model's freckly skin most photographer's completely remove this skin characteristic with the result that the final portrait resembles a computer-generated model rather than an actual living and breathing person. This technique aims to reduce the dominance of the freckles rather than removing them totally. In this way the underlying structure of the face shines through and is complemented with, rather than over-ridden by, just a hint of the freckles.

Step 1 >> *Select the Eyedropper tool and then check to see that the Sample Size (in the options bar) is set to average 3 × 3 or 5 × 5 pixels. Next select a flesh color from the portrait that represents a midtone of the range available across the face surface.*
Pro's Tip: *The tone you select at this point in the process will determine which freckles are lightened. Choosing a darker skin tone will change only a few of the darkest freckles whereas a lighter tone selection will alter both midtone and dark freckles.*

Step 2 >> *With the skin tone selected the next step is to select the Brush tool and then switch the tool's blend mode to Lighten. Do this by selecting the Lighten option from the drop-down mode list in the tool's option bar. When the brush is in the Lighten mode Elements compares the paint color with the pixels being painted over. If the pixels are darker then they are replaced with the paint color, effectively lightening the area.*

Step 3 >> *The next step is to adjust the opacity of the Brush. Turn again to the options bar and this time reduce the opacity to about 40%. An opacity setting of 100% would produce a result that was too smooth. Reducing the opacity has the effect of allowing a little of the old freckle texture to show through – maintaining the feeling of realism whilst reducing the freckle's dominance. Now paint away, being careful not to paint over details like eyelashes as you go.*

8.03 Eliminating blemishes

Suitable for Elements – 7.0, 6.0, 5.0, 4.0, 3.0, 2.0, 1.0 | Difficulty level – Intermediate
Tools – Spot Healing Brush, Healing Brush, Clone Stamp | Resources – Web image 803

Ethical issues aside, Photoshop Elements is a great tool for removing, or at least making less pronounced, a variety of unwanted photo elements. Despite the fact that skin blemishes and wrinkles are a normal everyday occurrence for most of us, photographers are constantly asked to retouch these sections of portrait photos. Like all other techniques discussed here, the secret behind successful retouching of these areas is not to remove them completely but rather to reduce their appearance.

With this in mind let's look at the three tools that Elements offers for blemish removal and then set these tools to work on a typical portrait image.

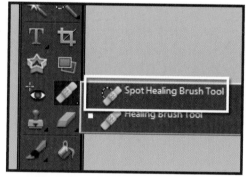

Clone Stamp tool

The most basic of all the retouching tools is called the Clone Stamp tool (or sometimes the Rubber Stamp tool). The feature selects and samples an area of your picture and then uses these pixels to paint over the offending marks. It takes a little getting used to, but as your confidence grows, so too will the quality of the repairs and changes you make.

There are several ways to use the tool. For starters, it acts like a brush, so changing the tip size allows cloning from just one pixel wide to hundreds across. You can also change the opacity in order to produce a range of subtle clone effects. It can be used in conjunction with any one of the options from the Blend menu and, most importantly, there's a choice between Cloning aligned or non-aligned with the sample area.

Select Aligned and the sample cursor will follow the destination cursor around keeping a constant distance between the two. When the Aligned option is unchecked the sample cursor starts where you left off with all ensuing paint strokes. Both choices have their advantages.

Healing Brush tool

The Healing Brush is designed to work in a similar way to the Clone Stamp tool; the user selects the area (Alt-click) to be sampled and then proceeds to drag the brush tip over the area to be repaired. The tool achieves great results by merging background and source area details as you paint. Just as with the Clone Stamp tool, the size and edge hardness of the current brush determines the characteristics of the Healing Brush tool tip. One of the best ways to demonstrate the sheer power of the Healing Brush is to remove the wrinkles from an aged face. In the step-by-step example image we used here, the deep crevices of the model's face have been easily removed with the tool.

The texture, color and tone of the face remain even after the 'healing' work is completed because the tool merges the new areas with the detail of the picture beneath.

Note: Sometimes the best source for sampling can be found in a different photo. With these both the Clone Stamp and Healing Brush tools, you can Alt-click in any open photo and sample from it.

BEFORE

AFTER

By carefully using any of the three retouching tools in Photoshop Elements it is possible to gently remove skin blemishes and signs of age like wrinkles and cracks.

Spot Healing Brush

In recognition of just how tricky it can be to get seamless dust removal with the Clone Stamp tool, Adobe decided to include the Spot Healing Brush in Photoshop Elements.

After selecting the new tool you adjust the size of the brush tip using the options in the tool's option bar and then click on the dust spots and small marks in your pictures.

The Spot Healing Brush uses the texture that surrounds the mark as a guide to how the program should 'paint over' the area. In this way, Elements tries to match color, texture and tone whilst eliminating the dust mark.

But don't just use this tool for spots, scratches too can get the treatment by click-dragging the tool's tip across the mark. The results are terrific and this tool should be the one that you reach for first when there is dust to remove from your photographs.

Clone Stamp tool step-by-step

Step 1 >> The Clone Stamp tool works by sampling a selected area and pasting the characteristics of this area over the blemish, so the first step in the process is to identify the areas in your picture that need repair. Then make sure that the image layer you want to repair is selected. Some photographers create a new layer and then apply their cloning to this layer. If this is your approach then also ensure that the Sample All Layers option is selected.

Step 2 >> Next, locate areas in the photograph that are a similar tone, texture and color to the picture parts that need fixing. It is these sampled areas that the Clone Stamp tool will copy and then use to paint over the model's wrinkles. At this point you can also alter the transparency of the cloning action by adjusting the Opacity slider in the tool's options bar. Values less than 100% will let some of the original texture through the clones areas.

Step 3 >> Now select the area to be sampled, or the 'Sample Point'. Do this by holding down the Alt key and clicking the left mouse button when the cursor (now changed to cross hairs) is over a part of the image that suits the area to be repaired.

Step 4 >> With the sample point selected you can now move the cursor to the area to be fixed. Click on the blemish and a copy of the sample point area is pasted over the mark. Depending on how well you chose the sample area, the blemish will now be blended into the background seamlessly. Continue to click and drag to repair more areas.

Step 5 >> You may need to reselect your sample point if you find that the color, texture or tone doesn't match the surrounds of the blemish. You can also change the brush size and hardness to alter the characteristics of both the sample and stamp areas. A softer edge helps blend the edge areas of the newly painted parts of the picture with the original image. Simply select a different brush tip from the Brush Preset drop- down palette.

Step 6 >> Switching between aligned and non-aligned (when the Aligned option is not selected) can really help when you are rebuilding missing parts of your restoration project. 'Aligned' sets the sample point so that it remains the same distance from the stamped area no matter where on the picture you start to click, and 'Non-aligned' repositions the sample point back to the original sample spot each time the mouse is moved and then clicked.

Healing Brush tool step-by-step

Step 1 >> *The Healing Brush is also a two-step process. After selecting the tool hold down the Alt/Option key and click a clear skin area to use as the sample for the healing. This action is the same as you would take when using the Clone Stamp tool to select a sample point.*

Step 2 >> *Now move to the area to be repaired and click-drag the cursor over the blemish. The Healing Brush will use the tones, textures and color of the sampled area to paint over the blemish but unlike the Clone Stamp tool, the Brush takes into account the general tone of the repair area and does a great job of seamlessly merging the new detail with the old.*

Step 3 >> *Like the Clone Stamp tool the Healing Brush contains a Sample All Layers option enabling photographers to perform non-destructive editing of their photos by painting the retouched areas onto a separate layer. Using a retouching layer also means that you can interactively adjust the strength of the changes via the layer's Opacity settings.*

Spot Healing Brush tool step-by-step

Step 1 >> *The Spot version of the Healing Brush removes the sampling step from the process. To use the brush you simply select the feature, adjust the brush tip size and harness and then click onto the blemish. Almost magically the Brush will analyse the surrounding texture, color and tones and use this as a basis for painting over the problem area.*

Step 2 >> *The Spot Healing Brush can also be used for removing marks, hairs, streaks or cracks by click-dragging the tool across the offending blemish.*
Pro's tip: *If unwanted detail is used to cover the repaired area undo the changes and then draw around the area to be healed with the Lasso tool and apply the brush again. This restricts the area around the blemish that the tool uses to heal.*

Step 3 >> *Like both of the previous tools the Spot Healing Brush also contains a Sample All Layers option enabling photographers to perform non-destructive editing of their photos by painting the retouched areas onto a separate layer. Using a retouching layer also means that you can interactively adjust the strength of the changes via the layer's Opacity settings.*

8.04 Removing the Red

Suitable for Elements – 7.0, 6.0, 5.0, 4.0, 3.0, 2.0, 1.0 | Difficulty level – Intermediate | Tools – Lasso | Resources – Web image 804

In this example the model's bright red (or is that orange?) hair is coloring the light that is reflected back onto the skin tones making them quite warm. This is particularly noticeable in the shadow areas of the face and around the hands. Add to this the fact that there is an obvious magenta tinge to the areas around the nose and chin and you can see that we need to do some color correction to the portrait.

Your initial thoughts might be to reach for the Auto Color Correct and Color Variations feature and use these to reduce the warmth in the photo but this action has the effect of reducing the vibrancy of the hair color at the same time as neutralizing the skin tones. This is not a desired scenario as the hair color is one of the strongest aspects of the image. So instead of making global (all over) changes to the picture this technique uses the Eyedropper tool to sample an area of neutral skin and then employs the Brush tool in Color mode to paint out the overly warm tones. This technique can be used to neutralize 'red ears' or the 'red nose' that is a sure sign of too much indulgence of the wine variety.

The way that color applied with the Brush tool interacts with the pixels being painted over is determined by the blend mode selected at the time of painting.

By default the Brush tool's mode is set to normal which causes the paint to obscure the pixels beneath, but Photoshop has many other ways to control how these pixels interact.

Called blend modes, these different options provide a variety of ways to control the mixing, blending and general interaction of the paint and the content beneath.

Blend modes can also be applied to the drawing tools via a drop-down menu in the tool's options bar as well as individual layers via the drop-down menu located at the top left of the Layers palette.

The retouching technique outlined here makes use of the Color blend mode to neutralize the red or magenta tinges that sometimes appear in portraits.

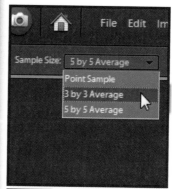

Step 1 >> *Start by ensuring that the Eyedropper tool's Sample Size is set to an average of either '3 × 3' or '5 × 5' pixels and not the Point Sample setting. To do this select the tool and then choose a different option from the drop-down list on the tool's options bar. This change will make sure that when you use the tool that you sample an average of the pixel tones and colors rather than just a single pixel's value.*

Step 2 >> *Next locate a portion of skin tone that is free from red or magenta casts and click on it with the Eyedropper tool. You will notice that the foreground color in the toolbox now contains the color you sampled. Check to see that the color is not too dark or light and that the hue is free from any strange casts. If this isn't the case, then resample a different areas of skin until you are happy with the color.*

AFTER

BEFORE

Even out skin tones by sampling and using the model's own skin color to remove unwanted areas of red and magenta.

Step 3 >> *With the skin color set as the foreground color select the Brush tool and change the Blend mode from Normal to Color (towards the bottom of the drop-down list in the Brush tool's options bar).*

Step 4 >> *The last step in the process is to apply the skin colored paint over the red/magenta areas in the photo. Notice that because the brush is in the Color mode that the paint is laid down in such a way that the details of the photo beneath are retained and only the color is altered.*

Step 5 >> *A non-destructive version of this technique starts with creating a new empty layer above the original photo. Next change the Blend mode of the new layer to Color using the drop-down list at the top of the Layers palette. Select the skin tone with the Eyedropper tool and then switch to the Brush tool. Make sure it is set to the Normal mode and then brush this color onto the new layer. With this approach the colorization of the skin is handled by the layer's blend mode.*

Book resources and video tutorials can be found at: **www.photoshopelements.net**

8.05 Brighten Eyes

Suitable for Elements – 7.0, 6.0, 5.0, 4.0, 3.0, 2.0, 1.0 Difficulty level – Intermediate
Tools – Lasso | | Resources – Web image 805

No amount of clever photography or tricky lighting can cover the traces of lack of sleep or overindulgence in the eyes of your model. A set of 'sore red eyes' staring back at you can easily ruin an otherwise well-produced photo. Elements certainly has the tools to add back the sparkle and life, but over enhancing can easily lead to sci-fi-like results. This technique uses a selection with a couple of adjustment layers for its effect, allowing changes and fine-tuning to the strength of the effect at a later date.

Step 1 >> *Use the Lasso tool to make a careful selection around the main part of the eye. Soften the edge by choosing Select > Feather. Here I used a value of 5 pixels but the setting you use will be determined by the pixel dimensions of your photo. Photos with more pixels will need a larger feather, those with less a smaller amount.*

Step 2 >> *With the Eyes selections still active, create a new Levels adjustment layer by choosing Layer > New Adjustment Layer > Levels. Notice that because of the active selection, a mask has been automatically added to the adjustment layer.*

Step 3 >> *The addition of a mask means that the changes made in the Levels dialog will be restricted to the clear part of the mask (the eyes). Add a simple brightening and contrast adjustment by dragging the black and white. Click the OK button to apply the changes. Re-select the eye areas by Ctrl/Command clicking the mask section of the adjustment layer.*

Step 4 >> *Now add a Hue/Saturation adjustment layer. Again the changes will be limited to the eyes via the mask. Select Red in the drop-down Edit menu at the top of the dialog and then pull down the Saturation slider and push up the Lighten setting. This will help to lessen the red veins in the eyes. Click OK to apply.*

Book resources and video tutorials can be found at: **www.photoshopelements.net**

8.06 Tone down skin highlights and shadows

Suitable for Elements – 7.0, 6.0, 5.0, 4.0, 3.0, 2.0, 1.0 | Difficulty level – Intermediate Tools – Brush | Resources – Web image 806

The example image has all the attributes of a great portrait but as with a lot of photos of this type there are a couple of places where the model's skin is a little shiny and the area under her eyes is a little dark. Gentle lightening of the dark areas and darkening of the light area are two techniques that, when mastered, you will use often when enhancing your portrait images.

This technique makes use of the Brush tool in both Lighten and Darken blending modes, along with the model's own skin color, to reduce the appearance of these areas in the final image.

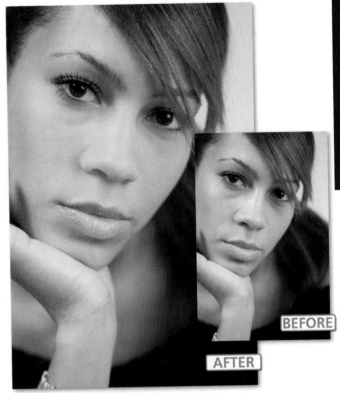

Remove shiny skin areas and bags under the eyes using the Brush in Lighten/Darken modes.

Step 1 >> *Start by selecting the Brush tool from the tool bar. Next go to the tool's options bar and select Darken as the Brush mode. At the same time I also adjust the opacity of the tool so that a little of the original texture remains after retouching.*
Then select a flesh tone that is slightly darker than the highlight areas whilst still using the brush by holding down the Alt key and clicking on the skin color.

Step 2 >> *Next gently brush over the shiny areas on the model's nose, forehead and cheek regions. When brushing using the Darken mode, only the pixels that are lighter than the sampled color will be adjusted. For the best results keep selecting different sample colors as you brush.*
Pro's tip: *For even more control apply the enhancement changes to a separate layer. The strength of the changes can then be adjusted via the layer's Opacity setting.*

Step 3 >> *The same technique can also be used to lighten the dark areas under the model's eyes. This time select the Lighten mode before sampling a flesh tone that is slightly lighter than the dark areas you want to fix. Again make sure that you choose a range of sample tones whilst brushing to ensure that the results are not too uniform and plastic looking. If you applied the changes to a separate layer, adjust the opacity of the layer to bring back some of the underlying face structure.*

8.07 Retouching non-destructively

Suitable for Elements – 7.0, 6.0, 5.0, 4.0, 3.0 | Difficulty level – Intermediate

When first starting to retouch your portrait photos it seems logical to apply the changes directly to the photograph or image layer itself, but this is not the way that most professional photographers work. For them the original picture is like the negatives of old and should be carefully maintained and not changed in any way. For this reason you will often hear them talking about employing non-destructive editing techniques as an alternative method for retouching their photos. We have already touched on some of these techniques but they are so important let's take a look at them again in the context of enhancing portraits. Remember these techniques produce the same results as editing the original image but employ some advanced Elements options that leave these 'virgin' pixels untouched.

Sample all layers

Step 1 >> *Retouching features such as the Clone Stamp, Spot Healing Brush and Healing Brush tools all contain an All Layers setting on their options bar. Designed to allow the tools to retouch the contents of several layers this option can also be used to protect your original photo pixels.*

Step 2 >> *To make use of this option for non-destructive retouching firstly create a new blank layer above the image layer. Make this the active layer and then select the retouching tool and choose the Sample All Layers option. Now when you retouch the changes will be stored on the newly created layer.*

Use Adjustment layers

Step 1 >> *Many of the editing or enhancement changes that are possible via the options in the Enhance menu can also be applied via Adjustment Layers. Wherever possible use an Adjustment Layer to make a change rather than applying the alteration directly to the image.*

Retouch duplicate layer

Step 1 >> *If the technique you are using can't be applied non-destructively then make a duplicate of the image layer and make the changes to the copied image instead of the original. This also gives you the chance to adjust the strength of the changes with the layer's Opacity slider.*

Mask editing adjustments

Step 1 >> *Keep in mind that you can mask the effects of adjustment layers by selecting the layer mask in the Layers palette and then painting onto the image with black to hide the effect and white to apply the change.*

Step 2 >> *You can also selectively apply the effects of a duplicate image layer by grouping this layer with a blank (no settings applied) Levels adjustment layer. Once grouped painting onto the Levels layer mask will either hide or apply the changes made in the duplicate layer.*

Book resources and video tutorials can be found at: **www.photoshopelements.net**

9

Dust and Scratches tricks

Photo Restoration

As a digital photography author one of the areas that I am often asked about is photo restoration. As photographers, it is an editing activity that most of us will attempt at least once during our life time. After all, many of the memories of important family events and history are associated with images of the time and, even with the right care and attention, lots of these photos end up a little worse for wear. In this chapter I thought that I would present you

with a variety of techniques that you can use to restore, or repair, those images most precious to you. Rather than detailing the techniques in isolation, where sometimes they lose significance, I have chosen to apply them as part of a process of restoring 'real life' photos.

As you will discover, most retouching projects require the application of a variety of techniques in multiple steps to coax the

Before

Restoration basics

Dust and Scratches tricks

Uncovering the faded

Correcting wayward colors

After

aged photo back to its best. So even though the example photos presented here have quite different problems (and associated solutions) they also contain some degree of overlap in areas such as removing of dust and scratches. These techniques are by no way an exhaustive list of all that are possible, but they will provide you with a good basis to start your restoration work.

Below and opposite >> *The example images here are shown with the before versions above and the after results below. The main restoration tasks involved with each photo are listed in the headings and all the techniques used to produce the results displayed here are contained on the following pages.*

Restoring old slides   *Adjusting shadow tones*   *Recreating missing content*   *Removing stains*

9.01 Restoration basics

Suitable for Elements – 7.0, 6.0, 5.0, 4.0, 3.0, 2.0, 1.0 | Difficulty level – Intermediate | Resources – Web image 901

In the last chapter we looked at how the retouching tools in Photoshop Elements can be used to remove unwanted marks and skin details in portraits. In this chapter the same tools are used for critical restoration and surgery work and with some photos, they are even called upon, to recreate detail that has been lost.

Though the application is different, the basic functionality of features such as the Clone Stamp Tool, Spot Healing Brush and Healing Brush, remains the same. Let's look at how a feature like the Clone Stamp can be used in the world of Photo Restoration.

Step 1 >> *The Clone Stamp tool works by sampling a selected area and pasting the characteristics of this area over the blemish, so the first step in the process is to identify the areas in your picture that need repair. Make sure that the image layer you want to sample is selected. NB: To work non-destructively, create a new blank layer above the background and select All Layers in the options bar.*

Step 2 >> *Next locate areas in the photograph that are a similar tone, texture and color as the areas needing to be fixed. Use these areas to paint over the dust and scratches marks. Select the area to be sampled by holding down the Alt key and clicking the mouse button when the cursor (now changed to cross hairs) is over a part of the image that suits the area to be repaired.*

Step 3 >> *With the sample point selected you can now move the cursor to the area to be fixed. Click on the blemish and a copy of the sample point area is pasted over the mark. Depending on how well you chose the sample area, the blemish will now be blended into the background seamlessly. Continue to click repairing more blemishes as you go.*

AFTER

The Clone Stamp tool is handy for removing dust and scratches but can also be used for recreating the detail lost in areas such as cracks or tears.

Step 4 >> *You may need to reselect your sample point if you find that the color, texture or tone doesn't match the surrounds of the blemish. It may also be necessary to change brush size to suit different repair tasks. Changing the brush size will alter the size of both the sample and stamp areas.*

Step 5 >> *For difficult repair jobs where you need to recreate picture elements select a similar part from the photograph as your sample point. Here the seam in the dress above the scratch is sampled to repair the damaged area. The same process is used to recreate the folds in the fabric and the texture of the glove.*

Step 6 >> *Switching between aligned and non-aligned options can really help you rebuild picture parts. Aligned – sets the sample point so that it remains the same distance from the stamped area no matter where on the picture you start to click, and Non-aligned – repositions the sample point back to the original sample spot each time the mouse is moved and then clicked.*

PHOTO RESTORATION

Removing dust automatically >> *One of the most tedious jobs for the digital photographer is the removal of dust and scratch marks from a badly damaged slide or print. Using the Clone Stamp tool to patch each individual mark can take considerable time and effort. A more automated approach that doesn't soften the detail in an image is detailed here. It uses the much besmirched Dust and Scratches filter in conjunction with the Layer blending modes to restrict changes to just the areas where it is needed.*

9.02 Dust and scratches be gone

*Suitable for Elements – 7.0, 6.0, 5.0, 4.0, 3.0, 2.0, 1.0 | Difficulty level – Intermediate
Resources – Web image 902 | Menus used – Layer, Filter*

The enticingly named Dust and Scratches filter (Filter > Noise > Dust and Scratches) teases us with the promise of a simple solution to repairing the dust and scratches in our scanned pictures. Nearly always the results of using the filter are disappointingly soft or the tones flattened. It is not that the filter doesn't obscure or disguise the problem marks, it is just that in doing so the rest of the image is also filtered. In areas where there is no dust this causes a deterioration of the picture. If only we could restrict the application of the filter to just the areas where the dust marks appear the results would be more usable.

Pro's Tips for using the Dust and Scratches filter:

1. Always start with both sliders set to 0.

2. Move the Radius slider first until the marks disappear.

3. Next move the Threshold slider until the texture of the image returns. Do not move this slider so far that the marks start to reappear.

The Lighten and Darken blending modes in Elements can be used for just this purpose. By applying the Dust and Scratches filter to a copy of the background and then blending this filtered layer using the Darken mode, the layer will only change the light dust marks of the original image and will leave the rest of the image unaffected. Similarly a second copy layer also filtered for dust and scratches could also be applied to the original image using the Lighten blending mode to remove the black marks from the picture. If we control where the effects are applied with a layer mask then it is possible to restrict the changes made by the Dust and Scratches filter to just the areas where it is needed most.

Step 1 >> *Start the technique by copying the base layer by dragging the background to the New Layer button at the bottom of the Layers palette. Label the new layer Darken Light Spots.*

Step 2 >> *With the new layer selected apply the Dust and Scratches filter. Start with both sliders set on 0. Move the Radius slider first until you see the dust spots disappear. Next gradually move the Threshold slider to the right until the texture returns to the picture – not so far that you start to see the spots again.*

Step 3 >> *With the Darken Light Spots layer still selected change the mode of the layer to Darken. This will only apply the dust and scratches changes to the areas where this original layer is lighter – the white dust spots.*

Step 4 >> *Add a Levels adjustment layer with no changes to the default settings above the background layer. Select the Darken White Spots layer and the choose Layers > Group with Previous.*

Step 5 >> *Select the layer mask of the Levels adjustment layer and then choose the Edit > Fill Layer option to fill the mask with black. This action hides the upper layer and reveals the unretouched layer beneath.*

Step 6 >> *With the layer mask still selected choose white as the foreground color and proceed to paint onto the canvas over the white marks in the photo. The white strokes will reveal the results of the upper layer.*

Step 7 >> *Create a copy of the background layer and label it Lighten Dark Spots. Apply the Dust and Scratches filter to remove the black marks and change the mode of this layer to Lighten.*

Step 8 >> *Create a blank Levels adjustment layer and then group it with the Lighten Dark Spots layer. Fill the Levels layer mask with black to hide the filtered results.*

Step 9 >> *With white set as the foreground color and the mask still selected paint over the dark marks on the picture with the Brush tool.*

Book resources and video tutorials can be found at: **www.photoshopelements.net**

9.03 Uncovering the faded

Suitable for Elements – 7.0, 6.0, 5.0, 4.0, 3.0, 2.0, 1.0 | Difficulty level – Intermediate | Resources – Web image 903 | Menus used – Layer, Enhance

Unfortunately this treasured family photo is well and truly past its prime. Poor storage and exposure to bright light has caused the image to almost fade completely. Though complete restoration is almost impossible due to the extent of the fading it is worth noting the techniques that are used here to conjure hidden detail from the vintage photo.

Step 1 >> *Using the Levels feature (Layer > New Adjustment Layer > Levels) in Photoshop Elements you can adjust black and white points of the photo. To set the shadow tones, hold down the Alt key and then drag the black point input slider to the right until the first pixels are revealed in the preview. Now move the slider slightly to the left until no clipped pixels are shown.*

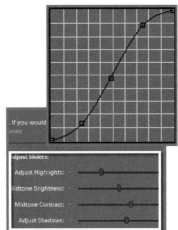

Step 2 >> *Next we will set the highlight tones. With the Alt key still pressed, drag the white point slider towards the left until you see the first clipped pixels displayed in the preview, then move the slider slightly to the right until no pixels are shown.*

Step 3 >> *With the white and black points set, it is time to encourage hitherto hidden detail from the rest of the photo. We can do this with some careful adjustment with Adjust Color Curves control, but this feature can not be used as an Adjustment Layer so the first step is to Select > All the document and the Edit > Copy Merge to store a composite of all the visible layers in memory. Final Edit > Paste to create a new layer based on the merged details.*

Step 4 >> *Now we can alter this layer with the Adjust Color Curves option. Here I selected the Increase Contrast Style first and then customized the enhancement by moving the Adjust Sliders until the Curve diagram resembled the classic steep 'S' shape. This adjustment spreads the tones and provides more contrast overall.*

Step 5 >> *In the process of removing the red cast and converting the picture to grayscale it is also possible to emphasize other hidden detail using the Convert to Black and White feature (Enhance > Convert to Black and White). Adjusting the red and blue color range changes how these hues are mapped to gray provided more opportunity to reveal details hidden by the cast.*

Step 6 >> *To remove marks, spots and scratches a new blank layer is added to the layers palette above the picture merged layer. Target the new layer and then use the Spot Healing Brush with the Sample All Layers option selected to repair the damaged areas.*

Step 7 >> *The final step is to add some definition to flat or faded sections of the photo. Do this by adding a new blank layer (Layer > New > Layer) at the very top of the layers stack. Change the Blend Mode to Soft Light and then use a black soft-edged brush to burn-in detail, or a soft-edged white brush to lighten sections.*

9.04 Levels based color restoration

Suitable for Elements – 7.0, 6.0, 5.0, 4.0, 3.0, 2.0, 1.0 | Difficulty level – Intermediate
Resources – Web image 904 | Menus used – Enhance

Old images, whether they be captured on color films, negatives or slides, are prone to fading and color changes as the dyes they are constructed of break down. It is a source of concern for all photographers who have big collections of images stored away in attics, cupboards or under the bed. After all, many of these photographs, though not valuable in the commercial sense, are irreplaceable as they hold glimpses of a family's history and echoes of days gone by.

Recently a loyal reader and avid Elements user emailed me with exactly this problem. Tom Edwards asked me if I had a solution for restoring the color to the hundreds of fading slides that he had taken in the Orient in the early 70s as they now all appear to be turning red.

The first step in any such restoration work is diagnosing the problem that is causing the color shift and fading. To get a good understanding of the cause I always turn to the Levels feature (Enhance > Adjust Lighting > Levels) for help. It contains a descriptive display of the spread pixels in the image and also includes the tools needed to coax the picture back to life.

When the Levels feature is first opened it displays a graph of the combined red, green and blue pixels. This is signified by the RGB label in the Channels drop-down menu. To really see what is happening to the tones in your picture select and view the graph for each of the individual color channels. The graphs for each channel of Tom's example image can be seen to the right. Notice how the green and blue channels are fairly similar but the red channel has all the signs of being overexposed, that is, all the tones being pushed to the right end of the graph. This is where our problem lies.

Restoring faded slides >>
When you look at the histogram for each of the red, green and blue channels separately it is easy to see why the faded slide appears so warm.

(a) Red channel.
(b) Green channel.
(c) Blue channel.

To help restore the original color and brightness of the photograph the tones of each of the color channels have to be adjusted individually. Starting with the red channel, drag the black input triangle towards the center of the graph until it meets the first major group of pixels. Do the same for the green and blue channels, but with these also adjust the white point Input slider in the same way.

To restore the color in the image work on each channel separately, dragging the white and black points in to meet the first major group of pixels.

This action will help to restore the color and contrast of the picture and will give good results for all but the most faded slides or prints. Final adjustments to tone and the removal of any slight color casts that remain can be achieved using levels on the combined RGB channel setting and the Color Variations features.

This will balance the distribution of the tones in each of the channels and restore the slide's color and contrast.

Fading slides >> *Over time traditional color photographs, slides and negatives can show signs of fading and take on a dominant color cast. Using the color correction and tonal change tools in Elements might not be aggressive, or selective enough, to correct these problems. Instead use the steps detailed here to rebalance the tones and colors in your picture. Image courtesy of Tom Edwards © 1972.*

Step 1 >> *Open the Levels feature from the Enhance > Adjust Lighting or Layer > New Adjustment Layer menus.*

Step 2 >> *Start with the red channel and drag the black input triangle to meet the first group of pixels.*

Step 3 >> *Next select the green channel and move both the white and black input sliders to the first group of pixels.*

Step 4 >> *Make the same black and white point adjustments for the blue channel as well. Click OK and then Select All, Copy Merge and Paste.*

Step 5 >> *With the image now balanced, target the Copy Merged layer and use Color Variations to remove any color casts that remain.*

Step 6 >> *As a final check of the tones open the Levels feature again and adjust white, middle and black points for the composite channel (RGB).*

9.05 Working with a scanned print

Suitable for Elements – 7.0, 6.0, 5.0, 4.0, 3.0, 2.0, 1.0
Difficulty level – Intermediate
Resources – Web image 905
Menus used – Enhance

Okay with these basics under our belt let's look at how to restore a scanned print rather than a scanned slide. Unlike their traditional black and white counterparts, color photographic prints often suffer from dramatic fading, or color changes, after only a few years of viewing. In this example, as was the case with the previous slide, the image has become very red. Apart from the removal of dust marks and the lightening of the photo, restoration will involve the reorientation of the photo and the correction of the dominant color.

Step 1 >> *Like many a scanned image, this photo ended up being a 'little' crooked when it opened in Elements. So the first step is to straighten the photo. To do this select the Straighten tool from the toolbar and click-drag a measurement line a along the top edge of the photo.*

Step 2 >> *To remove the excess background automatically, select the Magic Wand tool and select the background. Now Inverse the selection and choose the image > Crop command. Hit the Ctrl D keys to deselect.*

Step 3 >> *To remove the dominant red cast, start by adding a new Levels adjustment layer. In the Levels dialog, select the Red channel from the drop-down menu and drag the black and white input sliders inwards. Hold down the Alt key while you do this to ensure that no pixels are clipped.*

Step 4 >> *Repeat this process for both the Green and Blue channels in the Levels dialog before clicking the OK button. Now fine-tune the brightness and contrast of the picture with the addition of a Brightness/Contrast adjustment layer. Make any final color changes with a Color Variations feature to a Copy Merged layer.*

Step 5 >> *Now let's turn our attention to the marks and scratches on the photo. A new layer is added above the copy merged layer. Using the Spot Healing Brush and with the new blank layer targeted in the Layers palette. The Sample All Layers setting is selected in the tool's options bar and the small marks removed.*

Step 6 >> *Targeting the same layer, the Spot Healing Brush is switched to the Clone Stamp tool. The Current and Below setting is selected in the Sample drop-down menu of the tool's options bar before cloning away marks and scratches not able to be corrected with the Spot Healing Brush.*

Step 7 >> *When cloning skin detail it is often a good idea to reduce the opacity of the tool and build up the repair areas slowly with repeated strokes. It also pays to move the sample point regularly to reduce the repetition of cloning content. Many photographers use a graphics tablet and stylus setup for this type of editing.*

Step 8 >> *With the simple marks and scratches removed it is now time to tackle the larger damaged areas in the photo. Here the missing detail must be reconstructed from other areas in the photo. Here I created a soft-edged selection of the boy's hair and then copied and pasted the detail as a new layer.*

Step 9 >> *I then duplicated this new layer. To quickly create a copy of a layer hold down the Alt key and click-drag a new copy to a different position in the document. Next each of the new 'hair' layers was selected in turn and the Free Transform tool (Ctrl T) used to deform the content to cover the damaged area.*

Step 10 >> *After creating, and targeting, a new blank layer above the copied hair layers, the Clone Stamp tool is then used to sample existing hair detail, color and tone and carefully blend the pasted detail with the background. Again the opacity of the tool was reduced and detail was built gradually with different sample points.*

Step 11 >> *A similar approach was used when reconstructing the missing portions of the faces in the photo. This time a soft-edge selection of the cheek and eye was created, copied and pasted into position on the opposite side of the face. Next this layer was flipped (Image > Rotate > Flip Horizontal) and the content rotated to fit.*

Step 12 >> *Flipping the copied face content meant that the cheek details were correctly position but left the eyes looking 'cross eyed'. To correct this problem a second feathered selection was created of just the eye area. The eye was then copied, pasted and flipped horizontally before the Move and Free Transform tools were used to massage the detail into place.*

Step 13 >> *The Clone Stamp tool and Spot Healing brush were then used to help blend the edges of the newly pasted content with the background details. This same process was used to reconstruct the other damaged areas in the photo.*

Step 14 >> *When making small adjustments or edits on highly magnified sections of the photo it is a good idea to use the View > New Window for... option to display a second 100% view of the document being corrected. This provides a great way to check your work up close and at a distance at the same time.*

PHOTO RESTORATION

9.06 Extra correction help

Suitable for Elements – 7.0, 6.0, 5.0, 4.0, 3.0, 2.0, 1.0 | Difficulty level – Intermediate | Resources – Web image 906 | Menus used – Enhance

In the previous techniques we looked at how to balance the color of a photo with a dominant cast. With some images the Levels correction method still doesn't provide completely cast-free results.

An alternative method for achieving good results is to employ a specialist plug-in for the task. ASF (Applied Science Fiction) now owned by Kodak produces some specialist plug-ins for Photoshop Elements that work well with restoration projects. The Digital ROC (Recreation Of Color) plug-in automatically analyzes corrects, balances and restores the color in problematic images. To give you an idea of how the plug-in performs we used it to correct the cast in the picture from the previous technique and it produced the results you see here.

The plug-in contains two display windows. By default the left window previews the file after changes and the one on the right as a navigator panel and displays a before version of the photo. When first opened the plug-in analyzes the color problems with the image and then automatically displays, what it considers, a 'best correction'. You can modify the results with the color and brightness sliders on the right of the dialog.

Some contrast changes can also be applied using the slipping adjustments at the bottom of the dialog. For best results, though, alter contrast with features such as Levels or Curves back in Photoshop. The contrast and brightness controls are only included in the professional version of the plug-in.

For more details about Digital ROC or any of the other ASF plug-ins or to download a trial version go to www. asf.com.

The Digital ROC plug-in quickly restores the color to a problematic image like this one.

Step 1 >> *When first opened the plug-in automatically analyzes the color in the photo and then displays a corrected version of the picture. You can switch between before and after versions of the file with the settings under the main preview window. Use the three color slider controls to fine-tune the correction. Moving the slider towards a color will add the color to the photo and remove its opposite.*

Step 2 >> *As a final step, in the Pro version of the plug-in, you can also adjust the brightness and contrast of the photo. If these options are not available then these changes can be made when the photo is back in Elements. Click the OK button to apply the changes, close the plug-in and return the corrected image to Elements. Complete the restoration by removing dust and scratches using the techniques described in the previous pages.*

AFTER

BEFORE

9.07 Adjusting shadow tones

*Suitable for Elements – 7.0, 6.0, 5.0, 4.0, 3.0, 2.0, 1.0 |
Difficulty level – Intermediate | Resources – Web
image 907 | Menus used – Enhance*

Some family heirloom images survive the
ravages of time pretty much intact. This is the
case with the example portrait we see here.
Of course, there are a few marks, scratches,
creases and a slight stain on the left to remove,
but in addition to these enhancements, a good
restoration job would also include the revealing
of shadow details lost because of print overexposure or incorrect scanner settings.

Step 1 >> *The first step is for us to
'peg' the white and black points.
Using a Levels Adjustment layer, the
black and white point input sliders
are dragged in towards the middle of
the histogram while holding down
the Alt key. Move the sliders until the
point just before you start to see
clipped pixels in the preview.*

Step 2 >> *Now that the black and
white points are set, let's reveal some
of the hidden shadow details. Start
by selecting all (Select > Select All),
Edit > Cop Merged and then pasting
(Edit > Paste) the content as a new
layer. Then using the Adjust Color
Curves feature select the Lighten
Shadows Style from the menu.*

Step 3 >> *Now to fine-tune the
preset enhancment. First we will
concentrate on the shadow areas.
Move the Adjust Shadows slider to
the right of the dialog. This will
lighten and add contrast and
separation to the shadow areas.*

Step 4 >> *This change will also
slightly affect the midtones and
highlights in the photo. To control
these tones separately use the
Midtone Brightness and Midtone
Contrast sliders. Here I pushed the
brightness slider to the right to
lighten the midtones and the
contrast slider to the left to reduce
the contrast slightly.*

Step 5 >> *With the tones adjusted, the
next task is to remove spots, creases
and marks. A new layer is added (and
targeted) above the copy merged
layer. The Spot Healing Brush in the
Sample All Layers mode is then used to
non-destructively retouch these
problem areas.*

Step 6 >> *To remove the noise that
pervades the shadow area, a new
copy merge layer was created and
pasted above the other layers. This
later was filtered with the Reduce
Noise filter targeting the shadow
noise. A No Settings Levels
adjustment layer was then grouped
with the filtered layer, the mask filled
with black and a white brush used to
paint in the noise reduction to the
areas that need it.*

BEFORE   AFTER

9.08 Recreating missing content

Suitable for Elements – 7.0, 6.0, 5.0, 4.0, 3.0, 2.0, 1.0 | Difficulty level – Intermediate | Resources – Web image 908 | Menus used – Enhance

The stylish surround of this vintage French portrait is suffering from a little neglect. To restore the photo to its former glory the corners and edge of the presentation card need to be recreated and the tones of the photo itself need a little tweaking.

Step 1 >> *Before commencing any corrective work we will adjust the tones in the picture section of the document. So that these changes are applied to the photo only and not the textured background use the new Quick Selection Tool to isolate the circular shaped image.*

Step 2 >> *Next with the selection still active, a Levels adjustment layer is added to the document. Automatically a mask, the shape and size of the selection, is attached to the layer so that the changes are only applied to the selected area. Set the black and white points first and then drag the middle input slider to the left to lighten.*

Step 3 >> *In the process of lightening and adding contrast, the strength of the vignetting effect has been diminished. Add a new layer above the adjustment layer and change the Blend mode to Soft Light. To rectify this Ctrl click the Levels mask to load the original selection. Now select a soft-edged black brush and paint around the selection's edge to create a new vignette.*

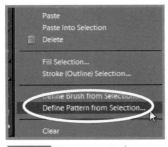

Step 4 >> *Now to recreate the corner content. Start by targeting the background layer and then selecting an unblemished section of the card surround with the Rectangular Marquee tool. Now choose Edit > Define Pattern. Enter a name in the Define Pattern dialog that appears and click OK. This pattern will be used for the repair work in the next two steps.*

Step 5 >> *To recreate the missing corners make a 1 pixel feathered selection in the same shape as the top left-hand corner but positioned at the bottom right of the card. This selection will confine our pattern filling activities and rebuild the corner of the photo frame.*

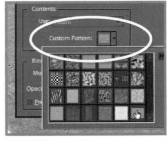

Step 6 >> *Now fill the selection (Edit > Fill) with the newly created pattern (select Pattern in the Use menu). Create another selection in the opposite corner and fill it also. Now Lasso the torn side sections, add a 1 pixel feather and pattern fill this selection also. Next use the Healing Brush in Pattern mode with the new pattern selected as the source to disguise the new areas and repair the other wrinkles.*

9.09 Removing stains

Suitable for Elements – 7.0, 6.0, 5.0, 4.0, 3.0, 2.0, 1.0
Difficulty level – Intermediate | Resources – Web
image 909 | Menus used – Enhance

In this example, the repair work centered around the removal of a yellowish stain running through the middle of the photo. There was also the need to try to restore some details in the highlights sections of the photo.

BEFORE   AFTER

Step 1 >> *Some of the highlight areas in the example file are clipped. The Recovery slider in Adobe Camera Raw 4 is able to reconstruct details in some blown highlights by referencing the details in the other channels. So the first step is to rebuild as much lost detail as possible using this control. NB: ACR 4 also works with TIFF and JPEG files as well as RAW formats. See side panel.*

Step 2 >> *Next the file is opened into Elements from Adobe Camera Raw. To remove the yellow stain a Black and White Adjustment layer was dragged from a Photoshop donor document and added above the image layer. Double-click the layer thumbnail to open the feature. By adjusting the Yellow slider it is possible to hide the stain in the grayscale conversion process.*

Step 3 >> *To minimize the blue pen scribble on the subject's nose, adjust the Blue and Cyan sliders. Variation in density of the stain or scribble may cause some or only part of the stain to disappear. This is the case here so we will have to resort to another process for the final touch up of these problems.*

Step 4 >> *To retouch residual stains and other marks. Create a new layer above the background image layer but under the Black and White adjustment layer. Select the new layer and then choose the Spot Healing Brush. Change the brush settings to Sample All Layers in the options bar and proceed to retouch problem areas.*

ACR and JPEG/TIFF files

The version of Adobe Camera Raw that ships with Photoshop Elements 6.0 and 7.0 is also capable of enhancing JPEG and TIFF files. Use the steps below to open your non-raw files in ACR:

Step 1 >> *Display the Elements Full Edit workspace. Next Select the File > Open As option. This enables the user to open specific documents as if they were created in a different format. In this scenario, we will use the option to open a TIFF or JPEG file as if it were a Raw file.*

Step 2 >> *Next navigate to the file in the file browser window and single click the entry. Choose the Camera Raw option from the Open As menu at the bottom of the Dialog. Click OK and the file will appear in the Adobe Camera Raw dialog. Process as you would normally and then select Open to transfer the converted file in to the Full Edit workspace with the enhancements applied.*

Step 5 >> *After removing dust marks and scratches add another blank layer at the top of the layers stack. Change the Blend Mode of the layer to Soft Light and choose a black soft-edged brush. This set up works like the Burn tool but the changes are made non-destructively. Carefully add some depth to the areas of the image that appear flat because of the harsh, direct, flash lighting.*

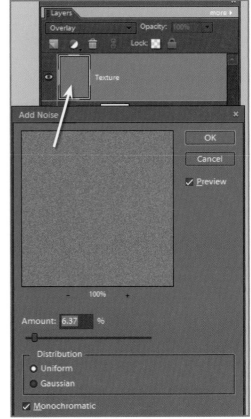

Step 6 >> *The last part of the restoration process is to add a very small amount of texture to the photo to provide detail in the blown-out areas. Add a new blank layer and change the mode to Overlay. Next fill the layer with 50% gray and filter the layer with the Add Noise filter. Make sure that you view the photo at 100% in order to properly gauge the appearance of the texture.*

Making Better Panoramas

When Adobe Photoshop Elements was first released one of the real bonuses of the program was the inclusion of the Photomerge technology. Designed to stitch together a series of overlapping images to form a wide vista print this feature really sets hearts racing amongst those of us with a secret passion for panoramas. There is just something about a long thin photograph that screams special to me. I have often dreamt of owning a camera capable of capturing such beauties, but alas the bank balance always seems to be missing the required amount that would be needed to make such a purchase.

And to be honest, the pragmatist in me also has to admit that the comparatively few shots that I would take in this format would not warrant the expense. It was in the midst of such thoughts a couple of years ago that I was first introduced to Photomerge, which has proven to be a solution to my 'wide vista' problems that suited both my budget and my infrequent production.

The feature combines several overlapping images to form a new wide angle photograph. Once in this form the panorama can be treated like any other Elements document, providing photographers with the ability to create truly stunning and interesting, wide and thin compositions. Elements now offers even more possibilities when it comes to creating wide angle photos. Photomerge was completely revamped for the last release and now the utility not only works more efficiently than before but many images can be stitched automatically with no input needed from the user. Great!

Photomerge in action >>
In this example two separate pictures were joined using Photomerge and the result dodged and burnt before being toned using the Hue and Saturation control.

Producing your panorama

In last couple of versions of Photoshop Elements the panorama option of Photomerge has been completely revamped to include several new auto modes as well as the manual method for stitching photos. Now when selecting the Photomerge Panorama option from inside the Editor workspace you are presented with an enhanced dialog that not only contains Browse/Open, Remove and Add Open Files options, which prompt the user to nominate the picture files that will be used to make up the panorama, but also a list of stitching approaches (on the left of the dialog).

Photomerge dialog >>
As well as the source files list (a) that was present in the previous version of Photomerge the dialog now includes five different Layout modes (b). The first four stitch the source images automatically and the fifth option transfers the pictures to the Photomerge workspace where the pictures can be manually placed.

Photomerge Panorama stitching modes

The five different Photomerge Panorama Stitching and Blending or Layout options in Photoshop Elements are:

Auto – aligns and blends source files automatically.

Perspective – deforms source files according to the perspective of the scene. This is a good option for panoramas containing 2–3 source files.

Cylindrical – designed for panoramas that cover a wide angle of view. This option automatically maps the results back to a cylindrical format rather than the bow tie shape that is typical of the Perspective option.

Reposition Only – aligns the source files without distorting the pictures.

Interactive Layout – transfers the files to the Photomerge workspace (which was the only option available in previous releases of Elements) where individual source pictures can be manually adjusted within the Photomerge composition. This is the only non-auto option.

Layout options >>
The auto Layout options in the revised Photomerge dialog use different approaches when producing the final panoramic photo.
(a) Auto and Perspective.
(b) Cylindrical.
(c) Reposition Only.

In most circumstances one of the auto options will easily position and stitch your pictures, but there will be occasions where one or more images will not stitch correctly. In these circumstances use the Interactive Layout option. This displays the Photomerge workspace where individual pieces of the panorama can be moved or rotated using the tools from the toolbar on the left-hand side of the dialog. Reposition Only and Perspective options are set using the controls on the right. Photoshop Elements constructs the panorama when the OK button is clicked.

From the Organizer >> *From the Organizer, select the files you want to use for the stitching process (a), then click Add Open Files in the Photomerge dialog box (b). The source photos will then be listed in the dialog (c).*

You can also start the creation of a panorama from source images that you have multi-selected in the Organizer workspace. Simply Shift-click the thumbnails to include and then choose File > New > Photomerge Panorama and then click the Add Open Files option to insert these photos in the Photomerge Panorama Source Files dialog. If the files are not loaded automatically just click the Add Open Files button. The Browse option allows the user to locate suitable files which are then listed in the Source Files section of the box. Any of the files listed here can be removed if incorrectly added by highlighting the file name and clicking the Remove button. With the Layout mode selected, clicking OK exits the dialog and starts the initial opening and arranging steps in Photomerge Panorama.

The auto workflow

If you have selected one of the auto Layout options then Photomerge will take care of the rest. The utility will open all images, combine them as separate layers into a single Photoshop Elements document and then align and blend the source photos. The final result will be the completed panorama.

Press Alt+Cancel to reset the dialog and send all images back to Light box.

Navigator preview

Zoom slider

Reposition only option

Perspective settings

Snap match source images

Interactive layout >>
The main Photomerge Panorama dialog allows you to edit and adjust the layout of your panorama.

Select Image, Rotate Image, Set Vanishing Point, Zoom and Move tools — *Scroll bar* — *Layout area and panorama preview* — *Unmatched pictures* — *Light box area*

The manual workflow

If you have selected the Interactive Layout option in the Photomerge dialog then the Photomerge dialog will display and you will see the utility load, match and stitch the source images together. If the pictures are stored in raw, or 16-bit form, they must be converted to 8-bit mode before being used in Photomerge.

For the most part, Photomerge Panorama will be able to correctly identify overlapping sequential images and will place them side by side in the editing workspace. In some instances, a few of the source files might not be able to be automatically placed and Elements will display a pop-up dialog telling you this has occurred. Don't be concerned about this as a little fine-tuning is needed even with the best panoramic projects, and the pictures that haven't been placed can be manually moved into position in the main Photomerge Panorama workspace.

Interactive Layout Step-by-Step

1. Select Photomerge Panorama from the File > New menu to start a new panorama.

2. Click the Browse button in the dialog box.

3. Search through the thumbnails of your files to locate the pictures for your panorama.

4. Click the Open button to add files to the Source Files section of the dialog.

5. Choose the Interactive Layout option at the base of the list.

6. Select OK to open the Photomerge Panorama main workspace. Edit the layout of your source images.

7. To change the view of the images use the Move View tool or change the scale and the position of the whole composition with the Navigator.

8. Images can be dragged to and from the Light box to the work area with the Select Image tool.

9. With the Snap to Image function turned on, Photomerge Panorama will match like details of different images when they are dragged over each other.

10. Ticking the Perspective box will instruct Elements to use the first image placed into the layout area as the base for the composition of the whole panorama. Images placed into the composition later will be adjusted to fit the perspective of the base picture.

11. To align the images without distorting the photos to fit select the Reposition Only option.

12. The final panorama file is produced by clicking the OK button.

When moving the cursor over the photos in the preview area, hold down the Alt key to see which image is active. This is useful when you are changing the vanishing point of your images.

Manual adjustment >>
You can move source images (in the Interactive Layout mode) to and from the Light box and Layout areas by clicking and dragging them.

Photomerge Stitching Summary

	Version 5.0 workflow	Version 7/6 workflow
Starting a new panorama	Select Photomerge from the File menu (Editor: File > New > Photomerge Panorama) to start a new panorama or select images in the Photo Browser and choose File > New > Photomerge Panorama.	
	Click the Browse button in the dialog box. If the images are opened already then they will automatically be added to the Photomerge Source Files list.	
	Search through the thumbnails of your files to locate the pictures for your panorama.	
	Click the Open button to add files to the Source files section of the dialog.	
	Select OK to open the Photomerge dialog box. Edit the layout of your source images.	Choose the Layout type from the options listed on the left of the dialog. All but the Interactive Layout option stitch the images automatically.
		Select OK to start the Photomerge process. If the Interactive layout option is selected then the Photomerge dialog will open. Edit the layout of your source images.
		Interactive Layout option selected. / All other 'Auto' layout options.
Editing in Photomerge	To change the view of the images use the Move View tool or change the scale and the position of the whole composition with the Navigator.	The files are stitched automatically using two steps; aligning and blending.
	Images can be dragged to and from the Light box to the work area with the Select Image tool.	
	With the Snap to Image function turned on, Photomerge will match like details of different images when they are dragged over each other.	
	Ticking the Use Perspective box will instruct Elements to use the first image placed into the layout area as the base for the composition of the whole panorama. Images placed into the composition later will be adjusted to fit the perspective of the base picture.	
	The Cylindrical Mapping option adjusts a perspective corrected image so that it is more rectangular in shape.	The Reposition Only setting overlaps the images without distorting them to fit. This is useful for stitching items such as maps or scanned documents.
	The Advanced Blending option will try to smooth out uneven exposure or tonal differences between stitched pictures.	
	The effects of Cylindrical Mapping as well as Advanced Blending can be viewed by clicking the Preview button.	
	If the source images do not quite line up using the automatic 'Snap to' setting you can manually drag to reposition or rotate any picture by clicking on the Rotate Image and Select Image tools from the toolbar and then clicking on the image to adjust.	
Producing the panorama	The final panorama file is produced by clicking the OK button. In version 5.0, you need to select the Keep as Layers option to get a multi-layered file. Otherwise, the result is a flattened file. All layout options in Elements 6.0 and 7.0 result in layered documents	

Photomerge basics>>

For those readers who are new to the feature, use the workflow in the table above to guide you through making your first Photomerge panorama.

Once you are confident with creating simple wide vista images using the feature, work through the advanced techniques discussed in the rest of the chapter to refine your panoramic prowess.

The technology behind the 'Image Stitching' idea is simple. Shoot a range of images whilst gradually rotating a standard camera so that each photograph overlaps the next. Next, import the pictures into Elements and then Photomerge and proceed to stitch the images together to form a wide, no make that very wide, panoramic picture.

From here the photo could be printed, or if the original series of images covered the full 360° of the scene with the first and last pictures overlapping, a special 'wrap-around view', called virtual reality (VR) panorama, could be produced. Programs like Apple's QuickTime use these 360° panoramas and allow the viewer to stand in the middle of the action and spin the image around. It is like you are actually there.

Despite the comparative ease with which Photomerge stitches images together the best quality panoramas are made when attention is paid to every step of the capture, stitch and print process. The following techniques go beyond the basic steps needed to create a panorama and will help you produce the best pictures possible with the Photomerge system.

Tips for great panoramas:

1. Panoramas are first and foremost a photographic exercise. Composition, lighting and point of view are all critical, although they have to be dealt with differently to traditional photography.

2. Elements is your friend. Use it to fix problem areas in your finished panorama.

3. If possible use a special panorama head to capture your pictures. If you can't afford a commercial model search the net for plans of a DIY version for your camera and lens combination.

Advanced shooting techniques

When producing panoramas the importance of the photographic step in the process cannot be underestimated. It is here that much of the final quality of your VR scene is determined. A few extra minutes taken in the setting up and shooting phases will save a lot of time later sitting in front of the computer screen fixing problems.

10.01 Positioning the camera

Suitable for Elements – 7.0, 6.0, 5.0, 4.0, 3.0, 2.0, 2.0 | Difficulty level – Basic
Related techniques – 10.02

Photographers have long prided themselves in their ability to compose the various elements of a scene so that the resultant picture is dynamic, dramatic and balanced. These aims are no less important when creating panoramic images, but the fact that these pictures are constructed of several separate photographs means that a little more thought needs to be given to the positioning of the camera in the scene. For the best results the photographer needs to try and pre-visualize how the final picture will appear once the single images are combined and then select the camera's position.

Rule of thirds >> *The same ideas of composition should be followed when making decisions about where to position the camera to capture a panorama sequence of pictures. To ensure that the resultant wide vista picture contains all the drama of a traditional photograph you should ensure that the foreground, mid ground and background details are all present in the final stitched picture.*

One common mistake is to move to the center of the environment, set up the equipment and create a sequence of images with most of the subject detail in the mid or background of the picture. This type of panorama provides a good overview of the whole scene but will have little of the drama and compositional sophistication that a traditional picture with good interaction of foreground, mid ground and background details contains.

When deciding on where to position your camera sweep the area whilst looking through the viewfinder. Ensure that the arc of proposed images contains objects that are close to the camera, contrasted against those subjects that are further into the frame.

Camera positioning >> *Unlike traditional photography the panoramic image-maker must pre-visualize how the stitched picture will appear when considering where to position the camera.*

Extend this compositional idea further by intentionally positioning the nearest and most dramatic objects in the scene one-third (or two-thirds) of the way into the sequence of images. This will provide balance to the photograph by positioning this point of focus according to the 'rule of thirds' in the final panorama.

10.02 Camera support

Suitable for Elements – 7.0, 6.0, 5.0, 4.0, 3.0, 2.0, 1.0 | Difficulty level – Intermediate | Related techniques – 10.01, 10.09

Though not essential for shooting the odd sequence of images, most panoramic professionals insist on using a tripod coupled with a special panoramic head to capture their pictures. The tripod provides a stable and level base for the camera; the panoramic head positions the camera and lens precisely over the pivot point of the tripod and also contains regular click stops to indicate points in the spin to capture a photograph. Each stop is designed to provide optimum coverage for each frame, taking into account the required edge overlap.

This set up increases the effectiveness of your stitching software's ability to accurately blend the edges of your images. Companies like Kaidan (www.kaidan.com), Manfrotto (www.manfrotto.com) and Peace River Studios (www.peaceriverstudios.com) manufacture VR equipment specifically for particular cameras and lenses. You can purchase a tripod head designed specifically for your camera or choose a head that can be adjusted to suit any camera.

Why all this bother with specialized equipment? Photomerge's main task is to seamlessly blend the edges of overlapping images. This is best achieved when the edge details of the two pictures are as similar as possible. Slight changes in the relationship of the objects in the scene will cause problems when stitching, often resulting in 'ghosting' of the objects in the final panorama. Now, for the occasional Photomerge user this is not too big a deal as a little deft work with your Elements editing tools and the picture is repaired (see

Panoramic tripod heads >> *Specialized panoramic or VR (virtual reality) tripod heads are perfect for ensuring that the lens' nodal point is over the pivot point of the tripod. This precision pays dividends at stitching time as Photomerge will produce much better results when the edges of sequential images can be exactly matched. (a) Adjustable Manfrotto VR head suitable for a range of cameras. (b) Camera-specific Kaidan head suitable for a single camera body only.*

technique 5.09), but frequent panorama producers will want to use a technique that produces better results faster. Using a special VR (virtual reality) or panoramic tripod head produces such results by positioning the 'nodal point' of the lens over the pivot point of the tripod. Images shot with this set up will have edges that match more evenly, which means that Photomerge can blend these overlapping images more successfully and accurately.

Finding the nodal point

If you have a VR head designed specifically for your camera and lens then the hard work is already complete. Simply set up the equipment according to the manufacturer's instruction and you will be taking 'nodal point correct' pictures in no time. If, however, you are using a fully adjustable VR head or you just want to find the nodal point for a specific camera and lens combination you can use the following techniques as a guide.

Some camera or lens manufacturers provide details about the nodal points of their products but, on the whole, this type of data is hard to find and it is up to the shooter to determine the nodal point of his or her own equipment. For this the main method is usually referred to as the 'lamp post' test and is based on a two-step process. With the camera set up and levelled on a panoramic head use the step-by-step guide to find the nodal point.

If the lens' nodal point is rotating over the tripod pivot point then the visual distance (gap) will remain the same throughout the movement. If the distance changes then the lens is not positioned correctly and needs to be moved either forwards or backwards to compensate.

With a little trial and error you should be able to locate the exact nodal point for each of your lenses, cameras and lens zoom points. VR tripod heads, like those made by Manfrotto, excel in this area. The fine-tuning controls and set up scales enable the user to accurately locate and note

Left to right adjustment >>
The lens and tripod should be viewed from the front and the lens position adjusted from left to right until it sits vertically above the tripod's pivot point.
You can check your positioning skills by turning the camera 90° down (so that the lens faces the tripod pivot) and confirming that the pivot point is located centrally in the LCD Preview screen. This is the easy part.

Front to back adjustment >>
Move the camera back and forward to find the nodal point of the lens. Set camera and tripod up so that there is a vertical object such as a lamp post or sign very near the camera and a similar vertical object in the distance. The closer the foreground object the more accurate the results of the test will be. Watching the LCD Preview screen (or looking through the viewfinder in an SLR camera) rotate the camera and compare the distance between the foreground and background objects.

the position of the nodal points for a variety of lenses and/or cameras. With the tests complete the results should be recorded and used whenever the same camera set up is required again.

Pro's Tip

If you don't have a special panoramic head try rotating the camera around the lens rather than pivoting around your body. Also, if you are shooting 'hand-held' use longer focal lengths rather than wide angle lenses; this will help with stitching later.

Handy Guide to Nodal Point Corrections

Use these rules to help you correct nodal point errors:

1. Moving the lens backwards: if rotating the camera away from the foreground object, increases the visual gap, or

2. Moving the lens forwards: if rotating the camera away from the foreground object, decreases the visual gap.

Nodal point errors >> *Many stitching errors are the result of source images being shot with the camera and lens not being centered over the nodal point.*

Some mid to high range compact digital cameras now include a panorama assist mode that ghosts the previously taken photo so that the next image in the sequence can be easily aligned. This approach helps ensure that sequential source photos are correctly spaced and positioned.

(a) Area of the scene being framed.

(b) Ghosted section of previous photo to be lined up with current scene.

(c) Current scene in the LCD viewfinder.

Other capture methods

Camera assisted hand-held

Unless you are a committed panoramic shooter you probably won't have a specialized tripod head handy the next time you want to capture a series of source images. This generally leads to a situation where you attempt to photograph the pictures by simply spinning the camera in your hands. Photomerge in version 6.0 and 7.0 of Elements will be able to blend pictures captured in this way but the inaccuracy of the photography process may lead to more editing work back at the desktop.

To improve the accuracy of hand-held capture several of the bigger camera companies such as Nikon and Canon include a special 'panorama assist' shooting mode in their mid to high range compact cameras. The mode ghosts the previous shot in the LCD screen so that you can line up the next picture accurately. This saves you from the expense of purchasing a professional panoramic tripod head whilst still ensuring accurate overlap and positioning of the series of photos.

As well as helping with correct alignment and positioning these special shooting modes also lock in focus, aperture, contrast and white balance at the beginning of the shooting sequence. This action helps to provide source photos that are more consistent and therefore more easily blended.

10.03 Exposure

Suitable for Elements – 7.0, 6.0, 5.0, 4.0, 3.0, 2.0, 1.0 |
Difficulty level – Basic | Related techniques – 2.03, 10.11

As the lighting conditions can change dramatically whilst capturing the sequence of images you need to make up a panorama, it is important that the camera's exposure be set manually. Leaving the camera set to auto exposure (Program, Aperture priority or Shutter speed priority) will result in changes in brightness of sequential images, especially if you are capturing pictures throughout a full 360° sweep of the scene.

Manual exposure >> *Set your camera to manual exposure to ensure consistency across the sequence of images.*

Take readings from both the shadow and highlight areas in several sections of the environment before selecting an average exposure setting, or one that preserves important highlight or shadow detail. Lock this shutter speed and aperture combination into your camera and use the same settings for all the source images. If the scene contains massive changes in brightness this will mean that some parts of the picture are rendered pure white or pure black (with no details); so you may want to consider using the steps in technique 10.11 as a way of capturing more details in these areas. To ensure that you have sufficient picture data to complete the technique capture two or three complete sequences with varying exposures. The exposure for one sequence should be adjusted to record highlights; one for shadows and if required a third can be used to capture midtones.

Pro's Tip
Use your camera's exposure bracketing system to shoot the over-, mid and underexposures automatically.

🌓 1/60th ⚫ f 16

Average exposure>>
To help ensure that your exposure setting is suitable for all the source images take several readings from all over the scene and then change your camera to the average of these results.

🌓 1/60th ⚫ f 1.8

🌓 1/60th ⚫ f 5.6

10.04 Focus and zoom

Suitable for Elements – 7.0, 6.0, 5.0, 4.0, 3.0, 2.0, 1.0 | Difficulty level – Basic | Related techniques – 10.05

A similar problem of differences from image to image can occur when your camera is set to auto-focus. Objects at different distances from the camera in the scene will cause the focus to change from shot to shot, altering the appearance of overlapping images and creating an uneven look in your final panorama. Switching to manual focus will mean that you can keep the point of focus consistent throughout the capture of the source images. In addition to general focus changes, the zoom setting (digital or optical) for the camera should not be changed throughout the shooting sequence either.

 When setting your focus also consider the depth of field that you desire for the image.

Manual focus>> Switch your camera to manual focus and then set the distance to encompass the subjects in the scene taking into account 'depth of field' effects as well.

10.05 Depth of field

Suitable for Elements – 7.0, 6.0, 5.0, 4.0, 3.0, 2.0, 1.0 Difficulty level – Basic | Related techniques – 10.04

Despite the fact that cameras can only focus on one part of a scene at a time (focus point) most of us have seen wonderful landscape images that look sharp from the nearest point in the picture right through to the horizon. Employing a contrasting technique, many contemporary food books are filled with highly polished pictures where little of the shot is sharp. I'm sure that you have seen images where only one tiny basil leaf is defined whilst the rest of the food and indeed the plate is out of focus. Clearly focusing doesn't tell the whole sharpness story.

This phenomenon of changing degrees of sharpness in a picture is referred to as the 'depth of field of acceptable sharpness' or 'DOF'. When shooting panoramas it is important to know the factors that control this range of sharpness and, more importantly, how to control them.

Focus and DOF >> Ensure that you consider focus and depth of field at the same time, as both these variables will affect the subject sharpness in your source images.
(a) Sharp foreground detail.
(b) Background unsharp due to shallow DOF.

DOF is controlled by three distinct photographic variables:

Aperture – Changing the aperture, or F-Stop number, is the most popular technique for controlling depth of field. When a high aperture number like F32 or F22 is used, the picture will contain a large depth of field – this means that objects in the foreground, mid ground and background of the image all appear sharp. If, instead, a low aperture number is selected (F1.8 or F2), then only a small section of the image will appear focused, producing a shallow DOF effect.

Focal length – The focal length of the lens that you use to photograph also determines the extent of the depth of field in an image. The longer the focal length (more than 50 mm on a 35 mm camera) the smaller the depth of field will be, the shorter the focal length (less than 50 mm on a 35 mm camera) the greater DOF effect.

Distance from the subject – The distance the camera is from the subject is also an important depth of field factor. Close-up, or macro photos, have very shallow DOF, whereas landscape shots where the main parts of the image are further away have a greater DOF. In other words the closer you are to the subject, despite the aperture or lens you select, the shallower the DOF will be in the photographs you take.

Aperture and DOF >> *Most photographers turn to their aperture control first when they want to change the depth of field of sharpness in their images. (a) A small aperture number produces pictures with a shallow depth of field. (b) Selecting a large aperture number produces a larger depth of field.*

As most panoramic pictures require sharp details in the foreground, mid and background you should practise setting up your camera for the largest depth of field possible. This means selecting a high aperture number, wide angle lenses and increased camera-to-subject distances wherever possible. It is also good practice to take a couple of test shots of sections of the scene and review these on the LCD monitor on the back of the camera (using the magnification option) to ensure that you have sharpness in the areas of the picture that you desire.

Use the table below as a quick guide for setting up your camera for either shallow or large depth of field effects.

Depth of field effect required	Aperture number	Focal length	Subject to camera distance
Shallow	Low (e.g. F 2.0, 2.8)	Longer than standard (e.g. 120 mm)	Close
Large	High (e.g. F 22, 32)	Wider than standard (e.g. 24 mm)	Distant

10.06 White balance

Suitable for Elements – 7.0, 6.0, 5.0, 4.0, 3.0, 2.0, 1.0 | Difficulty level – Basic
Related techniques – 2.07

As we have already seen in Chapter 2 the White Balance feature assesses not the amount of light entering the camera, but the color, in order to automatically rid your images of color casts that result from mixed light sources. Leaving this feature set to 'auto' can mean drastic color shifts from one frame to the next as the camera attempts to produce the most neutral result. Switching to manual will produce images that are more consistent but you must assess the scene carefully to ensure that you base your white balance settings on the most prominent light source in the environment.

For instance if you are photographing an indoors scene that combines both daylight through a window and domestic lights hanging from the ceiling then the Auto White Balance feature will alter the color of the captured images throughout the sequence. Switching to manual will allow you to set the balance to match either of the two light sources or even a combination of both using the preset feature (see technique 2.07 in Chapter 2).

White balance errors >>
Shooting with your camera set to the auto white balance setting can cause inconsistent color between sequential source images. Switching your camera to a mode that suits the dominant light source for the scene will produce more even results.

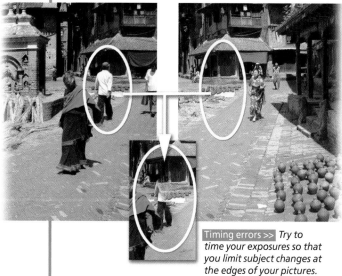

Timing errors >> *Try to time your exposures so that you limit subject changes at the edges of your pictures.*

10.07 Timing

Suitable for Elements – 7.0, 6.0, 5.0, 4.0, 3.0, 2.0, 1.0
Difficulty level – Basic
Related techniques – 10.09

Though not strictly a photographic technique, timing is very important when photographing your sequence of images. Objects that move in the frame or are positioned at the edges of one picture and not the next cause stitching problems when Photomerge tries to blend the edges. The best approach to solving this problem is to wait until the subjects have moved through the frame before capturing the image. A similar solution can be used when photographing in changing lighting conditions. For instance, if you start to capture a sequence of images in full sunshine only to find that halfway through a rogue cloud shadows the scene, then it is best to wait until the sun is shining again before recommencing the capture.

Even though I present some editing techniques later in the chapter that will help you rectify these types of problems the best solution is always to try and capture the most accurate and error-free sequence of source images. In this situation 'prevention is better than cure' and definitely more time efficient as well.

10.08 Ensuring consistent overlap

Suitable for Elements – 7.0, 6.0, 5.0, 4.0, 3.0, 2.0, 1.0
Difficulty level – Basic

As you are capturing, ensure that the edges of sequential images are overlapping by between 15 and 40%. The exact number of images needed to complete the sweep of the vista or the full circle will depend on the angle of view of the lens as well as the amount of overlap that you have used.

A quick way of calculating the pictures needed for 30% overlap is to count the number of images required to complete a full 360° rotation with no overlap and then multiply this value by 3. Or, alternatively, you can use the recommendations detailed in the table below as a starting point for the number of overlap portrait images required to construct a 360° panorama.

Professional VR heads ensure overlap consistency by placing 'click-stops' at regular points on the circumference of the head. On many models this is a variable feature that allows the photographer to change the interval to suit different lenses and/or overlapping amounts. Those on a more modest budget can mark regular intervals on their tripod head using a protractor or use the grid within the camera's viewfinder as a guide.

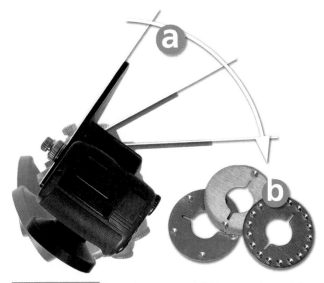

Click-stop heads >> *To evenly space sequential image capture points and ensure consistent overlap some companies like Kaidan (www.kaidan.com) produce panorama tripod heads with a built-in 'click-stop' system. The number of stop points is dependent on the angle of view of the lens used to capture the source pictures.*
(a) Rotating the camera and stopping to capture picture.
(b) A variety of click-stop disks designed for use with different camera lenses or zoom settings.

Pro's Tip Some cameras now provide a special Panorama mode that ghosts the previous shot in the LCD screen so that you can line up or overlap the next picture accurately.

Focal length in mm (35 mm equivalent)	Number of images required for 360° panorama
14	12
18	12
20	12
24	18
28	18
35	20
42	24
50	28

Number of images for 360° >> *Use the table above to calculate the number of overlapping pictures you will need to capture to create a 360° panorama.*

10.09 Dealing with the moving subject

Suitable for Elements – 7.0, 6.0, 5.0, 4.0, 3.0, 2.0, 1.0 | Difficulty level – Intermediate
Related techniques – 10.07 | Tools used – Clone Stamp, Selection tools | Menus used – Filter, Edit

One of the banes of the panoramic photographer's life is the subject that moves during a shooting sequence. These may be people, cars or even clouds but no matter how good your nodal point selection or stitching is, these moving subjects cause very noticeable errors in panoramas. The stitched picture often features half a person, or object, as a result of Photomerge trying to match the edges of dissimilar pictures. These problems can be fixed in one of two ways – either remove or repair the problem area.

(a) Remove – To remove the problem you can use the Clone Stamp tool to sample background parts of the scene and paint over stitching errors. The success of this type of work is largely based on how well you can select suitable areas to sample. Color, texture and tone need to be matched carefully if the changes are to be disguised in the final panorama.

Be careful though as repeated application of the Clone Stamp tool can cause noticeable patterns or smoothing in the final picture. These problems can be disguised by adding a little noise (Filter>Noise>Add Noise) to the image.

(b) Repair – In some instances it is easier to select, copy and paste the damaged subject from the original source image into the flattened panorama picture. This

Step 1 >> *Using the Clone Stamp tool (or Healing Brush tool), sample the background around the moving subject and paint over the offending area.*

Step 2 >> *As repeated stamping can produce a noticeable smoothing of the treated area, disguise the effects by adding a little texture back to the picture with the Add Noise filter.*

Step 1 >> *Using one of the selection tools, outline the problem area in the original source image.*

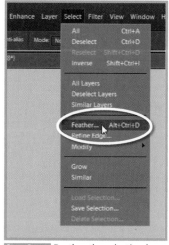

Step 2 >> *Feather the selection by a couple of pixels. This will help blend the selected area when it is added to the panorama.*

approach covers the half blended subject with one that is still complete. If you have used the Perspective option in Photomerge or have resized the panorama then you will need to adjust the pasted subject to fit the background. Use the Elements transformation tools such as Rotate, Perspective and Scale to help with this task.

Step 3 >> *Copy the selected area (Edit > Copy), click onto the panorama document and paste (Edit > Paste) the selection. Use the Move tool to move the copy into position.*

Step 4 >> *Use the Eraser tool set to a soft edge and low opacity to help blend the edges of the pasted selection into the background.*

Adjusting the opacity of the pasted subject while you are transforming will help you match its details with those beneath. When the editing is complete, then the opacity is changed back to 100%.

Finishing touches can be applied to the edges of the pasted images to ensure precise blending with the background with the Eraser tool.

Apply a slight feather (Select>Feather) to the selection before copying and pasting. This will help disguise the sharp crisp edge that is the tell-tale sign of so many repair jobs. A setting of 1 or 2 pixels at the most will be sufficient.

Ghosted image repair in Photoshop Elements 6.0 and 7.0 >> *Despite the increased power and effectiveness of the Photoshop Elements 6.0 and 7.0 versions of Photomerge, you may still find some ghosting of areas where the subject has moved or the details in areas of overlap has changed. Thankfully the revamped Photomerge feature now has more editing abilities and provides users with two different ways of correcting these problems. This example displays the problem well. The rider and cycle are half seen because they happened to be captured on the edge of one source file and then don't appear in the next.*

Erase then stitch >> *One way of correcting this situation is to erase the problem parts from the overlapping portions of the source photos before stitching them.*

10.10 Advanced panorama editing in Photoshop Elements 7/6

*Suitable for Elements – 7.0, 6.0 | Difficulty level – advanced
Related techniques – 10.09 | Tools used – Clone Stamp,
Selection tools | Menus used – Filter, Edit*

Though the latest version of Photomerge does an admirable job of blending overlapping photos together, as we have seen in the previous technique there may be some areas in the finished panorama that have ghosted details or parts of a subject missing. Thankfully the Photomerge file preserves the original source images in separate layers, distorts the photos and then applies blending via a series of masks. Some of the ghosting problems can be corrected by editing these layer masks directly. Others, can be fixed by erasing the problem areas first before stitching.

Edit the blend masks >> *Another solution is to edit the blend masks that are attached to the image layers that make up the panorama.*

For example, the front wheel of the bike in the center of the picture is missing. To paint this detail back in, locate the bike layer and then hide the layer beneath it (click on the eye icon in the layers palette). This approach works best if the source images have been captured with fixed exposure and white balance settings. When source images vary widely in brightness or color, balance these factors first, before stitching and mask editing. Next click onto the bike layer mask. Select the brush tool and set the foreground color to white (white reveals the image/black hides the image). Paint onto the image to reveal the wheel. Now show the under layer. Notice that the wheel has now obscured the parking sign and the girl just behind it. Switch the foreground color to black and with the bike layer mask still selected, paint back in the parking sign and the girl. In reality, painting with black means that you are hiding the parts of the wheel that are obscuring the girl and sign.

If this mask editing solution still doesn't provide good results, try erasing the problem areas such as the gent behind the bicycle and the girl in front of it, before sending the files to Photomerge. Doing so will force Photomerge to use the pixel information in the other source image to fill the erased area. Keep in mind that for this technique to work, the erased areas must be transparent. So the first step is to convert the background layer to a standard image layer, before using the Eraser tool to remove the unwanted areas. It is important that you only perform this editing on copies of the original files and only on the parts of the image that overlap the next source file.

Step 1 >> *Start by locating the specific layer containing the detail that is missing. It can be helpful to click on the eye icon to turn layers on an off when searching for a specific source photo.*

Step 2 >> *Now select the mask for the layer and choose a soft-edged white brush. Paint onto the image to reveal the masked or missing areas. Change the size and shape of the brush tip to paint in smaller details.*

Step 3 >> *If you accidently paint too much detail back, switch to a black foreground colour and paint over the image again to hide the detail.*

Step 1 >> *Perform a text stitch so that you can identify problem areas in the panorama. Next, locate the subject that is causing the ghosting problem in the source images. Identify the areas on the source image that are overlapping and common to both pictures.*

Step 2 >> *Double click on Background layer of one of the source photos to display the New Layer dialog. Add in name for the Layer and click OK.*

Step 3 >> *Finally erase the problem areas in the source images before using Photomerge to stitch the photos. With these picture parts no longer present Photomerge blends detail from other photos to fill the gap. Be sure to only erase detail that is contained in the overlapping sections of the source photos.*

Misalignment >> *When capturing source images by hand, or using a standard tripod, slight changes in perspective and position result in Photomerge having difficulty in matching the edges of sequential pictures. The misaligned picture parts need to be edited and rebuilt using technique 10.11.*

10.11 Fixing misaligned picture parts

Suitable for Elements – 7.0, 6.0, 5.0, 4.0, 3.0, 2.0, 1.0 | Difficulty level – Intermediate
Related techniques – 10.09 | Tools used – Clone Stamp

Shooting your source sequence by hand may be your only option when you have forgotten your tripod or you are purposely travelling light, but the inaccuracies of this method can produce panoramas with serious problems. One such problem is ghosting or misalignment. It is a phenomenon that occurs when edge elements of consecutive source pictures don't quite match. When Photomerge tries to merge the unmatched areas of one frame into another the mismatched sections are left as semi-transparent, ghosted or misaligned.

The affected areas can be repaired using the clone stamp techniques but by far the best solution, and certainly the most time, efficient one, is to ensure that the camera and lens nodal points are situated over the pivot of the tripod at the time of capture. A little extra time spent in setting up will save many minutes editing later.

Too much contrast >> *When the contrast range of a scene exceeds the abilities of the camera's sensors, some of the details at the highlight and shadow end of the spectrum are lost. These details are converted to pure white and black. Panoramic pictures that encompass a wide angle of view often suffer from this problem. (a) Range of brightness and detail in the scene. (b) Brightness range of the scene is reduced (clipped) as it is recorded by the sensor. (c) Reduced range of detail and brightness as it is stored in the digital file.*

10.12 Coping with extremes of brightness

Suitable for Elements – 6, 5.0, 4.0, 3.0, 2.0, 1.0 | Difficulty level – Intermediate | Resources – Web images 1012-1, 1012-2, 1012-3 | Related techniques – 10.03 | Menus used – Layer

Digital cameras have a limit to the range of brightness that they can capture before details in shadow and highlight areas are lost. For most shooting scenarios the abilities of the average sensor or film is up to the job but in certain extreme circumstances, such as when a panorama encompasses both a view of a sunlit outdoor scene as well as a dimly lit interior, the range of tones is beyond the abilities of these devices.

Rather than accept blown highlights or clogged shadows, the clever panorama photographer can combine several exposures of the same scene to extend the range of brightnesses depicted in the image. The process involves shooting three (or two for less brightness difference) images of the one scene using different exposures. Each exposure is designed to capture either highlight, midtone or shadow details. The difference in exposure should be great enough to encompass the contrast in the scene. These exposures can be captured automatically using the exposure bracketing technology that can now be found in most medium to high range digital cameras.

Combining the three images: With the three separate image documents open in Elements, hold down the Shift key and drag the background layers of two of the images onto the canvas of the third. Holding down the Shift key will make sure that the new layers are kept in register with the existing background. With the Layers palette open, rename and rearrange the layers so that they are ordered top to bottom – underexposed, normal and overexposed.

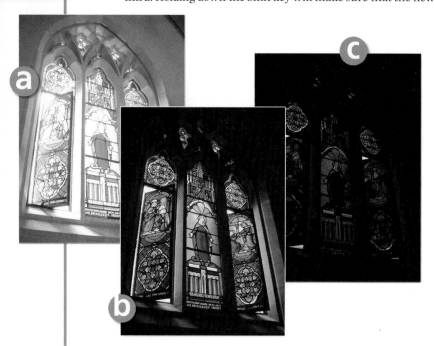

Changing the overexposed layer: To blend the overexposed image, firstly turn off the topmost layer (underexposed), then change the normal layer's blending mode to Screen. Now select the overexposed layer and choose the Levels function from the Enhance>Adjust Brightness/ Contrast menu. Drag the white Output slider towards the middle of the control, watching the results preview on screen. When the shadow details are visible and you are satisfied with the effect, click OK.

Capturing all the detail >> *With your camera fixed to a tripod, shoot three separate images adjusting the exposure settings to: (a) two stops over indicated exposure, (b) indicated exposure and (c) two stops under the settings indicated by your camera.*

Changing the underexposed layer: To blend the underexposed image, select its layer and change the blend mode to Multiply. With the layer still selected choose the Levels function and drag the shadow Output slider towards the center of the dialog. When the highlight and shadow details are visible and you are satisfied with the effect click OK. Save a layered version of this image as the original and a flattened (no layers) copy which can be imported into Photomerge as a source image for your stitch.

Step 1 >> *Open the images with different exposures. Tile the documents so that all pictures can be seen (Window > Images > Tile).*

Step 2 >> *Drag two of the pictures onto the third with the Move tool whilst holding down the Shift key.*

Step 3 >> *Arrange the layers so that from top to bottom they are positioned underexposed, normal and overexposed. Name the layers.*

Step 4 >> *Hide the top layer by clicking the Eye icon. Change the normal layer's mode to Screen. With the overexposed layer selected, choose the Levels function. Drag the white point Output slider towards the center of the dialog.*

Step 5 >> *Change the mode of the underexposed layer to Multiply. Select the Levels feature and move the black point Output slider towards the center of the dialog.*

Step 6 >> *To fine-tune the process, apply a Levels adjustment layer (Layer > New Adjustment Layer > Levels) to the stack, being sure not to clip newly created highlight and shadows detail.*

Pro's Tip

This technique can be applied non-destructively to the layered image by using Levels adjustment layers to change the tonal values of the under- and overexposed layers.

To ensure that the levels adjustment is only applied to a single layer start by inserting the adjustment layer above the layer to be changed.

Next make the tonal alterations and then group the adjustment layer with the changed layer using the Editor: Layer > Group with Previous command.

10.13 Creating artificially increased DOF

Suitable for Elements – 7.0, 6.0, 5.0, 4.0, 3.0, 2.0, 1.0 | Difficulty level – Intermediate
Related techniques – 10.06 | Tools used – Selection tools, Eraser | Menus used – Edit

In some environments it may not be possible to gain enough depth of field to extend the sharpness from the foreground details into the background of the picture. In these circumstances you can still simulate this large depth of field by shooting two different sets of source images – one with focus set for the foreground objects and a second set for the background details. Later, at the desktop, the sharp detail from the foreground can be cut out and pasted over the background pictures. As we have seen with other cut and paste techniques, a little feather applied to the selection before cutting helps to ensure a convincing result at the pasting stage.

Artificially increasing depth of field >> *Increase the amount of your panorama that appears sharp by cutting and pasting between two separately focused and shot sequences. (a) Sharp details. (b) Unsharp details.*

Step 1 >> *Open the two source files. Carefully select the foreground detail using your favorite selection tool. Feather the selection by 1 pixel.*

Step 2 >> *Copy and paste the selection onto the background, using the Move tool to position. Clean up with the Eraser tool if needed.*

10.14 Correcting exposure differences

Suitable for Elements – 7.0, 6.0, 5.0, 4.0, 3.0, 2.0, 1.0 | Difficulty level – Intermediate
Related techniques – 10.03, 10.14 | Tools used – Eyedropper | Menus used – Image, Window

Changes in density from one source image to the next can occur for a variety of reasons – the sun went behind a cloud during your capture sequence or the camera was left on auto exposure and changed settings to suit the 'through the lens' reading. The images that result vary in density. When these images are blended the change in tone can be visible at the stitch point in large areas of similar color and detail such as sky or road surface. This is less of an issue with the current release of Photomerge as it handles these sort of changes more effectively than previous releases, but if you are still having problems then here are a couple of correction options.

Auto Fixes – In Elements 5.0 Photomerge contained an 'Advanced Blending' feature that tries to account for slight changes in overall density from one frame to the next by extending the graduation between one source image and the next. This 'auto' technique will disguise small variations in exposure and generally produce a balanced panorama, but for situations with large density discrepancies the source images may need to be edited individually.

Advanced Blending >> *In the last release the Advanced Blending option needed to be selected to disguise slight differences in contrast, brightness and color. In versions 6.0 and 7.0 this option is used automatically.*

Manual Fixes – The simple approach to balancing the density of your source images is to open two or more of the pictures and visually adjust contrast and brightness using tools like the Levels feature. For a more precise approach it would be useful to know the exact values of the same section of two overlapping images. The Info palette in Elements displays the RGB values of a specific area in a picture. When used in conjunction with the Levels feature it is also possible to

Info palette >> *With the aid of the Info palette you can easily determine differences in color, brightness and contrast between sequential source images.*

display the values before and after density changes. Knowing the RGB values of the first image, you can alter the values in the second to match, thus ensuring a seamless stitch.

This process is time-consuming and is a 'work around' for what is essentially a flaw in your shooting technique. So if your source images continually need this level of adjustment revisit the process you use to capture your pictures and ensure that:

- You have your camera set to manual exposure, and
- You are capturing all the source images under the same lighting conditions.

Density correction >>
Fixing brightness or contrast differences before stitching will produce a far better result than expecting Photomerge to hide these problems.
(a) Before. (b) After.

Step 1 >> *Open a picture with good brightness and contrast as well as the picture that needs adjusting. At the same time display the Info palette (Window > Info).*

Step 2 >> *Click onto several matching points on both pictures taking note of the red (R), green (G), blue (B) and grayscale (K) settings for each.*

Step 3 >> *Make contrast and brightness adjustments to the problem image checking the changed readings in the Info palette as you go until both pictures display similar values.*

10.15 Adjusting for changes in color balance

Suitable for Elements – 7.0, 6.0, 5.0, 4.0, 3.0, 2.0, 1.0 | Difficulty level – Intermediate
Related techniques – 10.13 | Tools used – Eyedropper tool | Menus used – Image, Window

Slight changes in the color balance of sequentially shot images can result from using the Auto White Balance feature to rid images of casts resulting from mixed light sources. As the color of each frame is assessed and corrected independently, changing subject matter can cause such color shifts. More uniform results are obtained if the white balance is set based on the primary light source in the scene and then kept constant for the rest of the shooting sequence.

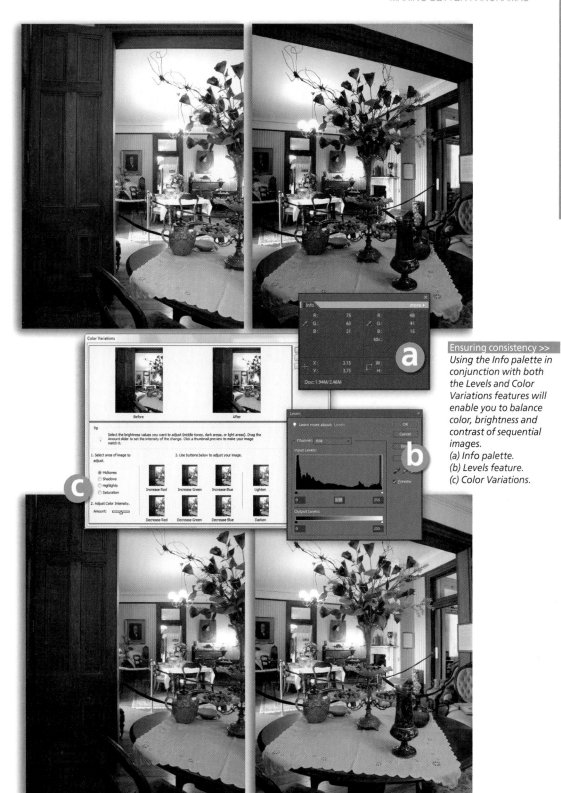

Ensuring consistency >>
Using the Info palette in conjunction with both the Levels and Color Variations features will enable you to balance color, brightness and contrast of sequential images.
(a) Info palette.
(b) Levels feature.
(c) Color Variations.

MAKING BETTER PANORAMAS

For slight discrepancies in color, tools such as the Auto Color Correction (Enhance>Auto Color Correction) feature will be able to automatically even out some of the changes, but for big changes in color a frame-by-frame correction technique similar to the one outlined for exposure differences can be used. This time instead of using Levels to make your adjustments you can employ a color control feature such as Color Variations (Enhance>Color Variations), to match different color values in sequential images.

10.16 Vertical panoramas

Suitable for Elements – 7.0, 6.0, 5.0, 4.0, 3.0, 2.0, 1.0
Difficulty level – Basic | Related techniques – 10.16

For most of the time you will probably use Photomerge to make horizontal panoramas of wide vistas, but occasionally you may come across a situation where you can make use of the stitching technology to create vertical panoramas rather than horizontal

Vertical stitching >> *Don't restrict yourself to only stitching horizontal pictures. Why not also use Photomerge to stitch those very tall shots that you just can't capture in a single photograph?*

ones. When capturing the vertical source images be sure to follow the same guidelines used for standard panoramas, i.e. check exposure, focus, white balance, focal length and shooting position.

Step 1 >> *Add your pictures to Photomerge as you would for a horizontal composition.*

Step 2 >> *For most panoramas, Photomerge will be able to stitch the photos effectively. If this isn't the case with your vertical panorama then go to the next step.*

Step 3 >> *Restart the Photomerge process and choose the Interactive Layout option so that you can manually drag the unplaced pictures into position.*

10.17 High-resolution mosaics

Suitable for Elements – 7.0, 6.0, 5.0, 4.0, 3.0, 2.0, 1.0
Difficulty level – Basic | Related techniques – 10.15

Another not so familiar use of the Photomerge technology is the production of high-resolution picture mosaics. In this application, the photographer captures a series of overlapping images, both vertically and horizontally, of the same scene. These images are then stitched together to form a photograph that is both wider and taller and contains more pixels than your camera would normally be capable of.

This approach is particularly suitable for those scenes where you just don't have a lens wide enough to encompass the whole vista, or situations where detail is critical. The higher resolution of the final stitched result also provides the extra digital information necessary to print big pictures (A3, A3+ or even A2) with little or no loss of quality or detail.

Unlike when you are capturing the source pictures for panorama production, high-resolution stitches require pictures that overlap on all sides that are to be stitched. This means that at the time of shooting you need to pay particular attention to edges of the frame and ensure a 20 to 40% consistent overlap.

Pro's Tip: If your camera contains a grid feature that can be displayed in the viewfinder, position the grid line closest to the edge of the frame on a subject that will be present in the overlap. Next turn the camera and make sure that the same subject is present in the frame on the grid line at the opposite side of the viewfinder.

Mosaic stitches >> *Create very high-resolution wide angle pictures that contain stunning detail and quality by capturing a series of overlapping pictures and stitching them with the Photomerge feature. (a) Mosaic source images that overlap on all stitching sides. (b) Add the files to the Photomerge dialog and then select the Auto Layout option in Photomerge. (c) Use the Cropping tool to trim away the ragged edges that are the result of the perspective deformation. (d) The final mosaic picture is higher resolution and covers more of the scene than would have been possible with a single camera shot.*

10.18 Panoramic printing

Suitable for Elements – 7.0, 6.0, 5.0, 4.0, 3.0, 2.0, 1.0 | Difficulty level – Intermediate | Menus used – Edit

Given the format of most wide vista photographs, printing on standard inkjet paper will result in much of the printing surface being left unused. Printer companies like Epson now produce pre-cut panoramic paper in a photographic finish. These sheets are convenient to use and their proportions are stored as one of the default paper settings on all the latest model printers.

Another approach is to use the roll paper format that is now available as an option on several different models. This option provides the ability to print both long, thin and standard picture formats on the same paper, reducing the need for multiple paper types. Using these special roll holders the printer can output different image formats back to back and edge to edge, providing cutting guidelines between pictures if needed.

For those of you with just the occasional need to print panoramas, another approach is to cut standard printing papers lengthways. This action produces very usable wide thin stock that is half the usable dimensions of the standard sheet. See the table below for the different paper types and the panorama print sizes that can be output on each.

With the paper organized it is now necessary to set up the printer for the new sizes. If you are using the pre-cut sheet or roll paper, then these options should be available in the drop-down paper menu of the latest printer driver for your machine. If the options are not present, or you are using panorama paper that you have cut yourself, then you will need to set up a custom paper size to suit your needs. On Epson machines you can do this by opening the printer driver, selecting the Paper tab and choosing the User Defined option. The dialog that is displayed will allow you to create, label and save your own paper size. These newly created paper size options will then be available for you to choose when you next open the Elements print dialog.

Basic Paper Type	Possible Panorama Print Size
A4	105 x 287 mm (1/2 full sheet)
A3	148 x 420 mm (1/2 full sheet)
A2	210 x 594 mm (1/2 full sheet)
A4 Roll	210 mm x 10 m
100 mm wide Roll	100 mm x 8 m
Panoramic Paper	210 x 594 mm (pre-cut sheet)

Step 1 >> *Select the Paper tab from the Epson printer driver and choose User Defined from the drop-down Paper Size menu. Input the paper size in the width and height boxes and then save the settings. Click OK.*

Step 2 >> *Once saved the new paper sizes can be found as extra options under the Paper Size menu.*

Step 3 >> *When it comes time to print a panoramic picture you can now select one of your pre-defined paper sizes and Elements will preview the photograph positioned against the background of the new paper format.*

Panoramic print options >> *Because of the wide thin nature of most panoramic photographs, printer companies like Epson have developed special settings for their hardware as well as a range of paper sizes to accommodate the unusual format. (a) Roll paper can be customized to suit both standard print formats as well as wide panoramic prints. (b) Special pre-cut papers in 'photo print' finishes are also available. (c) Panoramas can be printed on standard paper sizes, but much of the sheet is left blank.*

10.19 Spinning panorama movies

Suitable for Elements – 7.0, 6.0, 5.0, 4.0, 3.0, 2.0, 1.0 | Difficulty level – Intermediate | Resources – Web links

Many wide vista photographers choose to present their work in an interactive spinning format rather than as a print. This way of looking at images is often called Virtual Reality (VR) and is used extensively on the internet to give viewers the feeling that they are actually standing in the environment they are seeing on screen. Holiday destinations and real estate previews come to life via this technology. When the VR panorama opens you can navigate around the scene looking left and right with nothing more than simple mouse movements.

Although the ability to output your flat panoramic pictures in a VR format is not an integrated function of the Elements Photomerge feature there are several options for those who want to get their wide vista pictures spinning.

Moving panoramas >> *Photomerge users can take their panorama pictures beyond the static print by converting their stitched images to spinning vistas that can be navigated on screen and distributed via the web. For a complete 360° spin overlapping images need to be captured for the whole scene.*

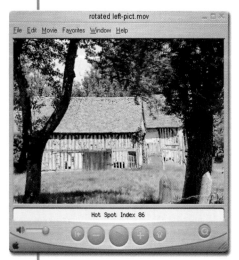

Apple QuickTime Viewer >> *The QuickTime plug-in is the most well known of all the VR viewers.*

Converting flat pictures to spinning movies

The process of getting your flat Photomerge panoramas to spin on screen involves two essential steps:

- Converting the panoramic photograph to a format that is suitable to be displayed, and
- Linking the converted file to a viewer or presentation utility which actually controls the on-screen display.

The standard QuickTime web plug-in, that can be freely downloaded from Apple and installed, is the most well known of all VR viewers. Along with being able to show movies, play sound and display a variety of still picture files the plug-in can also show panoramic movies that are saved in the QuickTime movie format. The viewer includes buttons to zoom in ('+') and zoom out ('-') of the panorama and the viewer navigates the scene by click-dragging the cursor side to side or up and down in the display window.

There are many commercial, shareware and even freeware utilities that will help you convert your flat Photomerge Panorama files to the QuickTime VR movie format (QTVR). Most of the commercial programs contain their own stitching utilities (like Photomerge) and the Conversion to VR movies feature is just one of the many output options offered. As Photomerge users don't need the stitching component of these programs the QuickTime utilities included here and detailed below only handle the conversion process. Once converted to the QTVR format the files can be viewed using the QuickTime plug-in.

There is also a range of non-QuickTime viewers and conversion utilities. Most of these use a small Java script-based program to provide similar display features to those found with QTVR. Again, most utilities used for creating these non-QuickTime movies are included with stitching features in a fuller program, but the options detailed below use stand-alone software to create spinable movies from basic JPEG panorama picture files.

OPTION 1: Converting Photomerge output to the QuickTime movie format

Elements users can convert their Photomerge output to Apple's QuickTime VR movie format using a free utility available from the Apple website. Both Windows and Macintosh versions of the software are available. Simply save the stitched image as a Macintosh PICT file, rotate it to the left (so that it is tall and thin) and then convert the picture using the Make Panorama utility. The resultant file can be viewed (and navigated) with any QuickTime player and has the added bonus of being able to be uploaded to the web and viewed on-line.

Free convert to QuickTime VR utilities:

Go to http://developer. apple.com/samplecode/ VRMakePano/index.html and download the VRMakePano utility.

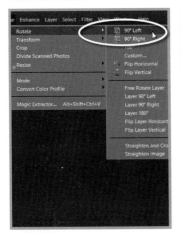

Step 1 >> *Rotate the completed Photo-merge file to the Left (Image > Rotate > 90° Left before saving as a PICT file (File > Save As).*

Step 2 >> *Start the VRMakePano utility and open the PICT file via the Test > Make Movie menu. Follow the on-screen prompts and specify image, tile and movie files in the dialogs provided.*

Step 3 >> *In a new dialog you will be prompted to export the results to a movie file. Here you can adjust the quality and size of the final panorama using the options on this screen.*

OPTION 2: Using Pano2Exe

Windows users can make similar spinning panoramas to those destined for displaying in a QuickTime viewer using a small economical utility called Pano2Exe (http://www.change7.com/pano2exe/). The program converts JPEG output from Photomerge to a self-contained EXE file, which is a single easily distributable file that contains the image itself as well as a built-in viewer.

Step 1 >> *Save completed Photomerge file as a JPEG file (File>Save As or File> Save for Web).*

Step 2 >> *Open picture into Pano2Exe program (File > Open Panoramic Image) and set width and height of navigation window.*

Step 3 >> *Save the spinning panorama as an executable file (.EXE) ready for distribution.*

Pano2Exe >> *The Pano2Exe utility provides a convenient and economical way to convert your Photomerge vistas to distributable navigable panoramas. See www.change7.com for details.*

OPTION 3: Making web pages with a Java Applet-based viewer

For those readers with a good understanding of how to create web pages you can also add your Photomerge panoramas to your website with the aid of a small piece of viewer code. In most cases this code is supplied in the form of a Java Applet. Civic-minded developers like Karl Maloszek at www.panorado.com supply their own applet for free when used on private websites.

The web panorama page is built of three components:

• The HTML page,
• The panorama image file (saved as a JPEG), and
• The viewer applet.

These three files must be present in order for the page to display properly.

To create a panorama page you will need to download the Panorado applet and save the Java archive (Panorado.jar) to your destination folder. Next create a blank web page and insert the HTML code, that controls the viewer and links your panorama photo to the viewer, into the code of the page. To make this process a little easier, example HTML code can be cut and pasted from the Panorado website directly into your page.

Java applet >> www.Panorado.com provides Java Applet viewer that can be used free of charge for non-commercial websites.

The viewer can be positioned in a scalable pop-up window which also contains HTML-based control buttons or in the middle of a document page (normally in a smaller rectangle or frame).

 Creating web pages using a Java-based viewer is not as automated as the other two approaches detailed previously. The process requires that the user understands the basics of HTML coding and how to correctly set parameters in that code.

www.panorado.com >>
Karl Maloszek at Panorado produces a non-QuickTime viewer that can be used to create interactive panorama web pages. Along with his applet and viewer software his site also contains a variety of example panoramas that display how this technology works. Images courtesy of www.panorado.com © 2005.

10.20 Panorama workflow

If the 'proof of the pudding is in the eating' then the success of all your careful shooting, stitching and editing work is in the viewing (of the final panorama). Logical planning and execution is the key to high quality wide vista photographs.

In this chapter I have introduced a range of techniques that will help you make great panoramas, but remembering the techniques and order that they should be used can be difficult. Use the steps in the workflow table (aside) to help you sequence your setting up, shooting, stitching, editing and producing activities.

Recommended Panoramic Workflow

Setting up	Choose camera position to ensure good foreground, mid ground and background distribution of subject	
	Sweep the scene looking through the viewfinder to position points of focus using the rule of thirds layout	
	Use camera hand-held	Mount camera on VR tripod head
		Adjust camera position to ensure nodal point pivot
		Adjust 'click-stop' setting to suit overlap and lens
Shooting	Select Manual Exposure mode	Select Manual Exposure mode
		Meter for both highlight and shadow detail
	Turn off Auto White Balance feature	Turn off Auto White Balance feature
		Select the White Balance setting that best suits the dominant light source in the scene
	Select Manual Focus mode	Select Manual Focus mode
		Preview depth of field to ensure foreground and background objects are sharp
	Don't alter zoom settings	
	Shoot source sequence ensuring 20–50% overlap	Shoot 2 or 3 source sequences ensuring 20–50% overlap with different exposure settings for highlights, shadows and mid-tones.
		Shoot close-up details to use for artificial depth of field effects
Stitching and editing	Download and stitch source images using Photomerge	Combine multi-exposure source images
		Make adjustments for exposure differences
		Make adjustments for color differences
		Import corrected source images and stitch using Photomerge
	Edit misaligned areas	
	Edit moving subject areas	
	–	Add artificial depth of field foreground elements
Produce panorama	Print panorama or produce spinning VR image	
Image quality	Good	Best

11

Extending Your Web Abilities

I'm old enough to still remember the ubiquitous 'black' folio case. In fact I think my chiropractor remembers it as well; I have been a regular client ever since. It wasn't just the weight of 30–40 matted prints that made the task difficult; it was the unwieldy size of the case that made touting the folder from office to office a daunting task.

I'm happy to say that there is a new set of image-makers (professionals and amateurs alike) who have no knowledge of my folio-carrying woes. The notion of the folio still exists and remains the stable marketing device of most creative professions, but the black case may be gone forever. In its place is a cyberspace folio, accessible any time, any place, for potential clients or admirers, armed with nothing but a common web browser.

Open 24/7

The web is a 'godsend' for photographers who are eager to display their pictures. An on-line gallery space which contains biographical and résumé details, as well as a folio full of examples of past work, is like having a personal promotions manager on hand 24 hours a day, 7 days a week. Never before has it been possible to share your photographs with such ease or obtain this much exposure of your talent and abilities for such little cost.

Gone are the days where you have to send your precious images to far-flung parts of the country in order to share that precious moment of little Johnnie's first step. A few simple clicks from anywhere in the world and Johnnie's agility and prowess can be admired by all.

Photo site styles

Photo sites come in all shapes and sizes and no matter whether you are part of a multinational imaging company or a weekend shooter who wants a few images on a page, a little design thought early on will

Photo website styles

The style of the site you make will depend on the nature of your work and the content that you wish to share with the world.

Thumbnail and gallery >>

Prolific image-makers who want to keep an archive of their work on-line will need to use a design that allows many images to be previewed before selecting a single picture to look at in higher resolution. Usually referred to as a 'thumbnail and gallery' design, this is by far the most popular form of photo website on the net today.

Used by photographers, galleries and stock agencies, this design is a great way to provide quick access to a lot of pictures. Because of the size of the thumbnails they download quickly and placing a single image on individual gallery pages also speeds up their display time. The format has proved so popular that packages like Photoshop Elements include automated wizards for creating these type of photo sites.

On-line résumé >>

Professional image-makers saw the potential of the web as a marketing tool very early in the life of the net. They frequently use it to hold CV or résumé information including lists of past and present clients, contact details and, of course, a few of their images. In fact, most shooters who make a living from their pictures probably have a site that is a combination of the thumbnail/gallery type introduced above and the on-line résumé we see here. This type of web presence is now a necessity rather than a nicety for most photographic businesses.

Slide show >>

In an interesting variation of the thumbnail/gallery folio site, some image-makers have dragged the automated slide show presentation idea of old squarely into the 21st century. Using interactive technologies like the Adobe Flash format and the new animated web templates in Elements, these photographers have created on-line slide shows that display a changing sequence of their best images.

All on one page >>

The simplest approach to making your own website is to combine your images and text on the one page. Doing so means that there is no need to worry about making and linking extra pages. This approach is handy for those who want to give their audience a taste of their work and then provide contact details for further information, or for the photographer who wants to establish a web presence quickly, before finally linking the thumbnails to a range of gallery pages.

make for a better site. Just as there are various styles of digital imaging magazines there are also different forms of the humble photo website.

A little time spent surfing will have you easily identifying different types of sites made by photographers. There are those that are full of shooting information – facts and figures, others that display a design-based approach, and the most popular – the virtual gallery. Time spent on the web will also provide you with the opportunity to see what works and what needs to be avoided when creating your own site. Using what you learn from your on-line roaming make some decisions about the style of site you want. Are the pages full of information about you, your history and your past work, is the site a sales point for your images or is your web presence designed to 'wow' your friends and family with the vibrancy and energy of your imaging and/ or design skills?

Building websites – the basics

All websites are constructed of several different components or elements. With Flash-based sites these separate parts are incorporated into a single design. In contrast standard or HTML-based sites work quite differently. The separate website pieces, which include text, images, buttons and headings are arranged, or laid out, in groups on individual pages. When viewed on screen these pages appear as a single document, much the same as a word-processed page. But unlike a typical printed page the components that make up a website remain separately saved files and the web page document itself simply acts as a series of pointers that indicate where elements are to be found and how they look and where they are placed on the page.

You can view the source code or HTML text of any page by selecting the View > Source option in your browser. What you will see is a series of instructions for the location and layout of the page parts and their files. When a viewer looks at the page, the browser software recreates the

Website styles >> *Most photographers' websites are based around a gallery idea and consist of:*
(a) a front or home page,
(b) an index of thumbnails, and
(c) a series of individual gallery pages.
www.brittan.demon.co.uk.
Courtesy of Philip J Brittan © 2007, UK.

Website assets

The various components that are used to make up a web page or site can be broken into several main categories:

Images >>

Images form the backbone of any photo site. Creating image assets is a process where the picture is optimized in size and quality so that it can be transmitted quickly over the net. For a photo gallery site both thumbnail and gallery images need to be created.

Headings >>

Headings that are present on every page are usually created and saved as a picture rather than text. For this reason the same optimization process involved in the production of pictures for the net is used to create headings for the site.

Buttons >>

Buttons come in a variety of formats, both still and 'roll-over' or animated. The face of the button is created with an illustration or picture using an image editing package. The Button function, moving the viewer to another page on the site for instance, is controlled by a small piece of code added later in the layout package.

Text >>

Text can be typed directly into position using the layout software or compiled in a word processing package and then imported. In the example site the photographer's information and details may be able to be taken from an already prepared CV or résumé.

Animation, sound and movies >>

Animation, Sound and Movie assets are usually created in third-party dedicated production packages and added to the site in the layout part of the process.

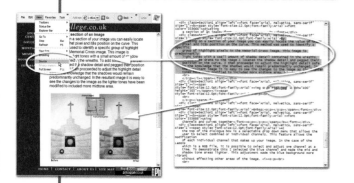

HTML code >> *Web pages are constructed of several different parts including text, images, buttons and headings. The position of each of these components is controlled by the HTML code that sits behind the page. The page parts are brought together using these coded settings when you look at the page in your browser.*

document, finding the component files and laying them out as instructed by the HTML code. As you start to make your own pages this is an important concept to remember, as you will need to keep track of all the various files that are used throughout the site and ensure that they are available when requested by the browser.

Creating web pages without writing HTML or knowing Flash

Until recently, creating your own web pages required budding net designers to have a good working knowledge of HTML or the code used to tie all the pieces together.

If you wanted to create a more dynamic site, that contained a little animation, or interactivity, then you had to be proficient at using Adobe Flash. Thankfully there are now many software programs on the market including Elements that allow you to create a web page or site without ever having to resort to creating HTML coding or using Flash.

Two approaches to site creation

There are essentially two approaches. You can:

- Choose to use a package designed specifically for web page production such as Microsoft FrontPage and use Elements to optimize your pictures and create other assets, or
- Employ some of the great automated web production features bundled as extras in Elements.

Either way you get to concentrate on the design not the code. Thank goodness! In this chapter we will look at both approaches by firstly creating a muti-page website using the newly revised Elements' Online Album feature and then go on to create some key assets for a second site that will eventually be laid out using a third-party program.

11.01 Elements' Online Album websites

Suitable for Elements – 7.0, 6.0, 5.0 | Difficulty level – Basic | Related techniques – 10.02, 10.03 | Menu used – File

The Elements Online Album tool (previously called Online Gallery and HTML Online gallery tool) is a purpose-built feature designed to take a selection of images and produce a multi-page fully linked gallery site in a matter of a few minutes. The updates of the feature over the last few editions of Elements mean that users now have even more choice and control over the way their site looks and works. You now can choose between basic thumbnail and gallery type sites or animated or interactive designs. All sites produced by the feature use Adobe Flash technology and so the pages load quickly and the animated components in the productions work smoothly. The feature's settings are contained in several panels located in the new Task pane area on the right of the Organizer workspace. Using these controls you can select the style of the site and then customize both the look of the pages as well as the information presented.

In most site styles the viewers navigate round the site, from image to image or back to the front page via a series of arrow buttons or, with some designs, the images automatically change in a slide show format. Once completed the finished site can then be shared with the world. In Elements 5.0 and 6.0 the program handled the often confusing task of uploading to an ISP or web server. In version 7.0 the link through to Photoshop.com provides an even easier mechanism for getting your photos on the web. So with as little as five mouse clicks it is possible to select, create and upload your very own professionally designed web gallery.

Choose the images

In the latest versions of Elements you can multi-select the images to include in the gallery from the Organizer workspace before opening the Online Albums feature. Don't panic if you forget an image though as you can also choose to add or remove photos from inside the feature's first dialog. Select your images and then choose the Online Album entry from the new Share task pane.

As no edit or enhancing options are available inside the Website Production feature make sure that the photos that you want to include are already enhanced before starting the process.

Auto website creation >>
The quickest and easiest way to create a website is to use the in-built Online Album feature in Elements. With a few clicks you will have a fully functioning 'thumbnail and gallery' website.

Select a website style

The Online Album feature contains several wizard-based panels. The first lists the images selected in the Organizer workspace and provides options for adding extra images or removing existing photos from the group. If you have sourced the photos from an Elements' Album (collection) then the sequence of images is preserved during import, otherwise the images are listed top to bottom in the same order that they were selected (left to right) in the Photo Browser. The order can also be adjusted once the files are in the pane by click-dragging individual thumbnails around the group. Clicking the Share button builds a preview of the website displaying it on the left of the workspace. You have the option of changing the design of the site by clicking on the Change Template button. This action displays another panel and is used for selecting and alternative design.

In version 7.0 the template galleries have been arranged thematically and include the following groups: Classic, Family, Fun, Occasions, Seasons and Travel. Theses options are presented with the Template drop down menu and a list of representative thumbnails. The choice you make here will alter the template design thumbnails displayed in the rest of the pane. Each thumbnail represents an individual design with differences ranging from simple color changes to completely different looks and feel to the website. Select a thumbnail and then click Next to move to the following panel.

The template menu also includes a Show All entry to display all available templates as well as a Photoshop.com option for listing the templates available from the website. In the top right of the pane is a double-sideways arrow button that allows you to set the content for the template pane. The choices are:

- Only Show Photoshop.com Content
- Only Show Local Content
- Show All Content

Online Album >> *All the main options for your website creation are contained in several panels. The first screen is for selecting the images to include in the album and titling the entry (a), next you can either change the template design or go straight to sharing the album (b), the Change Template pane provides options for choosing a new design for the website (c), the settings and title details for the site are contained in the next pane (d) and finally the share settings are grouped in the final pane (e).*

Step 1 >> *Multi-select the images to include in the site from those in the Organizer workspace. To pre-order a group of pictures, add them to an Album first and then click-drag them into your chosen sequence.*

Step 2 >> *Start the feature by choosing the Online Album entry from the Share Task Pane. Add in an Album name and select an Album Group for the entry.*

Step 3 >> *With the first open, click-drag photos to alter the order that they will be used. Add new photos to the list or remove existing images using the add (+) or remove (-) buttons.*

Step 4 >> *Clicking the Share button creates a preview of the album using a default design. If you are happy with this look then pick the way that you want to share the site and click Next.*

Step 5 >> *To alter the design, click on the Change Template button. Next pick a new album template group and then select a design thumbnail from those displayed. Click Next.*

Step 6 >> *Add in the Title and Subtitle for the Album pages in the next pane. Alter any other site settings available. Click Refresh to see the changes and Next to continue.*

Step 7 >> *When choosing Photoshop. com as the mechanism for sharing, the next pane will contain options for displaying the album publicly or with a select group of invited friends. Click Share to publish the site.*

Step 8 >> *Alternatively you can choose the Export to CD/DVD option if you want to distribute the website via disk. Click the Export button to write the files to the disk.*

Step 9 >> *To upload to an existing web space, pick Export to FTP option. Add your ISP settings to the pane (these are available from your ISP provider) and click the Export button to upload the pages to your site.*

Adjusting the website settings

The next panel contains custom settings for the site. The number and type of customization options will depend on the website template that you have selected. For all templates you can add in a site title and contact details for the photographer, however when selecting the Standard category websites you will find that you have many more customization options. With this set of templates you can also adjust site colors, border and button opacity, connection speed optimization, slide show settings, and caption and file name inclusion.

Previewing your site

A functioning preview of the completed site will also be displayed on the left of the workspace. After making any changes to design or when you have switched templates you can display the alterations by clicking the Refresh button.

Sharing the site

The only job left now is to share your masterpiece of web design with the world. This used to be a tricky task involving complicated procedures and extra bits of utility software but since version 5.0 it has become a much easier and more streamlined process. The Online Album feature includes three quick ways to share your website. The choices are listed in the Share To area at the bottom of the dialog and include:

Photoshop.com – Upload to a free on-line sharing area provided by Adobe Photoshop Services.

Export to FTP – Transfer to your own ISP or net space provider.

Export to CD/DVD – An option for burning the gallery directly to disk.

Share To options >> *After completing the design part of the process you can then elect to share your website in a variety of ways. The easiest option is the direct link with Photoshop.com.*

Online Gallery versus Online Album

In version 7.0 the Online Album option replaces the Online Gallery feature that was available in the previous release. Both features are designed to help you quickly and easily create a presentation that displays your photos on the internet, but Online Albums uses a workflow that duplicates the Albums found in the Organizer space of Photoshop Elements and places the copy online at Photoshop. com. This means that not only are your Online Albums a means of displaying your photos but they also become way to archive your photos.

An Online Album provides both a way to view your images on the web and also an automatic backup of your photos.

Another approach to publishing to the web

As we have already seen, the Online Albums feature is linked to the general Album options found in the Photoshop Elements' Organizer workspace. Given this link then it will come as no surprise that it is also possible for you to publish your pictures online via the settings in the Albums Pane. There are a couple of ways that you can create a gallery of images using this approach so let's look at each in turn.

Share a new Album

The first starts with the creation of a new Album. You might not have noticed that Share is one of the options that is available when creating a new Album. The Share button sits between the Done and Cancel buttons at the bottom of the Album Details pane that is used to create a new Album entry. Selecting this option at the time of Album creation, transfers the album images straight to the Online Album wizard. With a couple more clicks of your mouse (to move through the wizard steps) the photos are published. In one easy sequence you have created an Album and published the contents online. Good job!

Now if you are an experienced Elements user then you probably have developed a workflow for publishing web galleries that involves:

1. creating an album,
2. adding selected images to the album,
3. adjusting the sequence of the pictures,
4. selecting the photos from the album that you want to use,
5. create the web gallery, and then
6. publish the gallery on line.

Sharing at time of Album creation >>
Clicking the Share button in the New Album pane takes you directly to the Online Album wizard, fast tracking the web publishing process.

As you can see, in Photoshop Elements 7.0 this process is much simplified. Now you can fast-track your gallery production right from the Album pane. It may take a little time to get used to this way of working, but it is certainly faster than the old method. It also has the added bonus that if you select the Backup/Synchronize settings, located in the same pane, you will instruct Elements to automatically back up the contents of this album.

Online Album viewing options >> *Users can switch between album styles by pressing the display buttons located in the top right of the slideshow screen at Photoshop.com. Buttons for the three default styles are always available (a) but the themed button (b) is only present for albums which have been created with the Elements' Online Album wizard.*

Slideshows at Photoshop.com

As we saw earlier in the chapter, the Online Albums, or slideshows as they are called in Photoshop.com, that you create in Elements can be uploaded to the website and viewed either by the general public or by a select group of fiends or family members. Using the Online Album feature in Elements to create these slideshows provides the user with the most control over the look of the final web gallery. Apart from being able to select from a range of designs or templates for the website, you also have the chance to adjust colors and titles for most designs.

However, this is not the only way to view your images on Photoshop.com. The website has several built-in slideshow styles that can be automatically applied to albums that are stored on the site. There are three main styles to choose from: Filmstrip, Grid and Ring. Each presents the Album's photos in a different animated style, allowing the user to select specific images which then snap into enlarged view.

To view an Album as a slideshow, select its entry in the My Photos workspace and then click onto the Album Slideshow option at the bottom of the screen. To switch between slideshow styles click on one of the Display buttons at the top right of the slideshow window. If a Themed slideshow has been created for the Album then this will be the default slideshow view for the Album. You can still switch to the other styles using the display buttons, returning to the themed presentation if you wish, by clicking on the fourth, themed button. This extra display button is only available when a themed slideshow has been created for an online album.

Creating individual web assets using Photoshop Elements

Now that you have seen how to create pages and their assets automatically using the Web Gallery let's take a little more control of the process by manually creating each of the major assets using Elements. We will then lay out the results of our labor in a web production package to create our final site.

11.02 Optimizing photos for the web

Suitable for Elements – 7.0, 6.0, 5.0, 4.0, 3.0, 2.0, 1.0 | Difficulty level – Basic
Related techniques – 10.01 | Menus used – File

The skill of making a highly visual site that downloads quickly is largely based on how well you optimize the pictures contained on the pages of the site. The process of shrinking your pictures for web use involves two steps:

- Firstly, the pixel dimensions of the image need to be reduced so that the image can be viewed without scrolling on a standard screen. This usually means ensuring that the image will fit within a 640 x 480 or 800 x 600 pixel space.

- Secondly, the picture is compressed and saved in a web-ready file format. There are two main choices here – GIF and JPEG.

The best way to optimize your pictures for web use is via the Save for Web (Editor: File > Save for Web) option in Elements. This feature provides before and after previews of the compression process as well as options for reducing the size of your pictures, all in the one dialog. Using this feature you can select the file format, adjust compression settings, examine the predicted file size and preview the results live on screen.

Before preview / After compression preview / Compression type and associated settings / Original pixel dimensions

Zoom level / Original name and file size / File size and predicted download time after compression / Preview in browser / Animation settings for GIF format / New pixel size settings

To create a typical 'thumbnail and gallery' site you will need two different versions of your images – full screen size images suitable for use as gallery pictures and small thumbnails that can be laid out together on an index page. To make these resources you will need to size and compress each image twice and then save the finished files into two separate folders titled 'thumbnails' and 'gallery'. Make sure that the gallery images are no bigger than one full screen and that the thumbnails are small enough to fit several on the page at the one time.

Save for Web >> *The best way to ensure that you are using the best balance between file size and image quality is to preview your compression and file type choices in the Save for Web feature.*

File formats for images on the web

The standard PSD or Photoshop Elements file format is not suitable for web use; instead several different picture types have been developed especially for on-line work. The two most common are JPEG and GIF.

1. **JPEG**, or JPG, or Joint Photographic Experts Group, is a file format specially developed for photographic web images. It uses a lossy compression technique to reduce files to as little as 5% of their original size. In the process some of the detail from the original picture is lost and 'tell-tale' artifacts, or visual errors, are introduced into the picture. The degree of compression and the amount of artifacts can be varied so that a balance of file size and image quality can be achieved. More compression means smaller file sizes, which in turn means poorer image quality. On the other hand less compression gives larger files of better quality JPEG images that can contain millions of colors rather than the comparative few available when using GIF. The format has massive support on the net and is the main way that photographers display their web pictures.

2. **GIF**, or the Graphics Interchange Format, has had a long (in internet terms) history with web use. It has the ability to compress images mainly by reducing the numbers of colors they contain. For this reason it is great for headings, logos and any other artwork with limited colors and tonal graduation. It can also display pictures that contain areas of transparency and can be used for simple 'cell-'based animation. This format is not suitable for most photographic images.

How big is too big?

When you are producing your first web pages there is always the temptation to keep as much image quality in your pictures as possible, resulting in large file sizes and a long wait for your site visitors. Use the table aside to help you predict how long a web picture will take to download to your recipient's computer.

Balancing Compression and Image Quality >>

Photographers wanting to display their images on the net are caught between the two opposing forces of image quality and image file size. When Adobe created Elements they were well aware of these difficulties and, to this end, they have included sophisticated compression features that give the user a range of controls over the process.

The Save for Web feature contains a Preview option that allows you to view the original image after the compression and conversion to web format has taken place. In addition, the dialog also displays predicted compressed image sizes that will allow you to ensure that your web files are not too cumbersome and slow to download.

File size	Download Speed			
	14.4 Kbps (modem)	28.8 Kbps (modem)	56.6 Kbps (modem)	128 Kbps (Cable)
30KB	24 secs	12 secs	6 secs	3 secs
100KB	76 secs	38 secs	19 secs	9 secs
300KB	216 secs	108 secs	54 secs	27 secs
1000KB (1MB)	720 secs	360 secs	180 secs	90 secs

Step 1 >> *Open the original image and select the File >Save for Web feature. Input the image size into the New Size section, being sure to keep the pixel dimensions less than 640 x 480. Click Apply. Set previews to 100%.*

Step 2 >> *Try different file format, compression setting or numbers of colors. Determine the best balance of file size and image quality. Check the download times. Click Save to store the image.*

Step 3 >> *After creating the gallery images you can repeat the process using smaller pixel dimensions to generate the thumbnail versions of the pictures. Thumbnails should be between 60 x 60 or 100 x 100 pixels.*

Generally, a delay of 10–15 seconds for large gallery images is acceptable, but download times longer than this may cause your audience to surf elsewhere.

Pro's Tips for good image compression

• Always use the Save for Web compression tool to preview the side-by-side images of the original and compressed picture.

• For GIF images try reducing the number of colors to gain extra compression.

• Always view the compressed image at 100% or greater so that you can see any artifacts.

• For JPEG images carefully adjust the Quality slider downwards to reduce file size.

• Do not sharpen the photos to be compressed. Non-sharpened pictures compress to smaller sizes.

• Take notice of the predicted file size and predicted download time when compressing images.

11.03 Making seamless backgrounds

Suitable for Elements – 7.0, 6.0, 5.0, 4.0, 3.0, 2.0, 1.0 | Difficulty level – Intermediate | Tools used – Selection tools, Clone Stamp Menus used – Filter, File

The HTML language has a specific feature designed for including backgrounds with your pages. As you can imagine, using a full size image for a background would greatly increase the file size and therefore the download time of your pages, so in their wisdom, the early web engineers included the ability to tile a small graphic pattern over the whole of the background of each page. Using this method, a small, highly optimized picture can be repeated in a grid over the expanse of the whole screen, giving the appearance of a seamless background with little download time cost. Using the Offset filter (Filter>Other>Offset) in Elements you can create a special background graphic containing matched edges that will seamlessly tile across a whole web page. Select a section of a suitable image. Copy and paste the selection as a new document. Apply the filter using offset settings that are exactly 50% of the dimensions of the image and choose the Wrap Around option. This displays the edges of the tile in a cross in the center of the image. Use the Clone Stamp tool to disguise the joins by merging similar areas and textures together. To finish save the file in JPEG format using the Save for Web feature. With the tile made you can now select it as the background image in your web layout program.

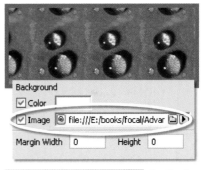

Repeating background tiles >> *The tiles that you make using the Elements Offset filter can be used to create repeating backgrounds by selecting them as the background image in your web layout program. The GoLive dialog above shows how the tile image can be used for creating seamless web backgrounds.*

Step 1 >> *Select an area of an image to use as a base for the tile. Copy and paste the selection into a new document.*

Step 2 >> *Select the Offset filter and input width and height values that are 50% of the image size. Select the Wrap Around option.*

Step 3 >> *Use the Clone Stamp or Spot Healing Brush tools to disguise the joins in the picture. Save as a JPEG using the Save for Web feature.*

11.04 Using background matting

Suitable for Elements – 7.0, 6.0, 5.0, 4.0, 3.0, 2.0, 1.0 | Difficulty level – Basic | Menus used – File

Most photos that are optimized for use on the internet are saved in the JPEG format. As part of the construction process of a web page, the pictures are placed on top of a colored background. The JPEG format does not contain a transparency option and so when an irregularly shaped graphic is saved as a JPEG and placed onto a web page it is surrounded by a plain colored box, usually white. Background matting is a technique for adding the web page color to the background of the object at the time of web optimization. When the matted object is then used to create the web page, it appears to be sitting on the background as if it was surrounded by transparency. The transparent pixels surrounding the object are replaced with the matte color and the semi-transparent pixels are blended. The Matte option is located in the settings area of the Editor: File > Save for Web feature.

Step 1 >> *Choose the web page color by double-clicking the foreground swatch to show the Color Picker and then selecting the Only Web Colors option. Next create a picture with a transparent background.*

Step 2 >> *Choose Editor: File > Save for Web feature and the JPEG option. Select the same color for the Matte by double-clicking the swatch and selecting from the Color Picker. Click OK to save.*

Step 3 >> *Now construct the web page with the same color in the background and add in the new matted graphic. When the page is displayed the object will seamlessly merge with the page color.*

12

Free Form Photo Collages

Photoshop Elements 5.0 heralded a major change in the way that photographers created free form layouts and multi-page books. Versions 6.0 and 7.0 continue the revolution with the refining of both these features, now called Photo Book and Photo Collage, and a complete revamp of the Photo Bin, now called the Project Bin, so that rather than just being a place to view open images it becomes a multi-purpose 'go to' area for your project actions. I believe that these features provide photographers with new and powerful ways to use their images to generate create projects in ways that even Photoshop users can only dream of. So to get started let's look at some of the technology that underpins this new way of working.

Adobe has created a new layer type, **Frame layers**, a new file format, the Photo Project or **PSE**, a new design system that uses special matched frames and backgrounds sets called **Themes**, created an updated version of the Photo Bin, called the **Project Bin**, a set of **Photo Projects** that makes use of all this new technology and, finally, a new **Task Mode** based layout workflow.

Sound confusing? Well some of the features are new and some are continuations of technology from version 5.0, but once you begin to play with Photo Collages, the process seems so logical and familiar that it isn't long before you will start to feel at home with the new workflow. So to get you started this chapter will look at the basic techniques that are involved in the layout workflow.

Create Task Pane

Create Photo Book

Create Photo Collage

Choose paper size

Select a Theme (the theme can be replaced after creation)

Multi-select images to include in the Photo Project

Organizer workspace

Before you start – edit then layout

The production of Photo Collages, or any of the other Photo Projects, in Photoshop Elements is essentially a presentation exercise for photos that have already been enhanced. For this reason it is a good idea to complete any preliminary editing work such as color and tonal correction, spotting and retouching changes and the application of sharpening before including the picture in a new Photo Collage.

This is especially true when working with the special framed picture elements of a Photo Collage as these visual components are stored in a special Frame layer which has to be simplified before it can be edited. The act of simplification, which is also called rasterization, converts the Frame layer to a standard image layer and in the process removes the layer's ability to scale, rotate and distort repeatedly without image quality loss.

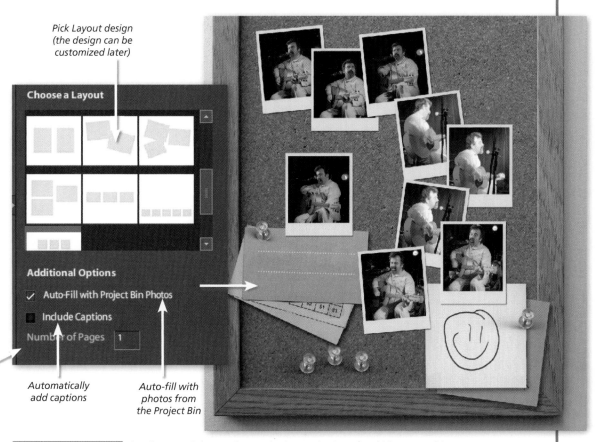

Pick Layout design
(the design can be
customized later)

Automatically
add captions

Auto-fill with
photos from
the Project Bin

Great layouts quickly >> *The Photo Book feature fast tracks the production of multi-image, multi-page projects in Photoshop Elements. The Photo Collage option on the other hand is used for creating single page montages of multiple pictures. To use either simply select the images to include in the Organizer space and pick either the Photo Book, or Photo Collage, entry from the new Create Task pane. The Editor workspace then opens and the selected images are displayed in the Project Bin. Next style the layout with the theme and/or layout options in the Create Task Pane and then click the OK button to produce the layout in Full Edit space.*

12.01 Basic steps for layout creation

*Suitable for Elements – 7.0, 6.0, 5.0 | Difficulty level – Basic | Resources – Web image 1201-1, 1201-2, 1201-3
Related techniques – 12.02, 12.03, 12.04*

Using the Photo Collage feature, one of the Photo Project options in Elements, is a simple multi-step process with the creation options centered around the new Create Task pane.

Step 1 >> *The process of creating a Photo Collage will generally start in the Organizer workspace. Here you can multi-select the photos that will be used in the layout. To choose a series of images click on the first thumbnail and then hold down the Shift key and click the last picture in the series.*

Step 2 >> *To pick non-sequential photos, select the first and then hold down the Control key whilst clicking on other thumbnails to be included in the selection. With the images highlighted the next step is to choose the Photo Collage option from the Create Task pane.*

Step 3 >> *Using an Elements' Album (collection) as a starting point you can alter the order or sequence that the photos appear in the multi-page document. After rearranging the position of photos in the Album, multi-select those to be included in the layout.*

Step 4 >> *Alternatively a blank document can be created by selecting the Photo option in Create Task pane in either the Editor or Organizer spaces. Photos that are already open can then be dragged into the blank document from the Project Bin area of the Editor. Non-opened pictures can be added by clicking onto the Click Here to Add Photo section of the newly created frames. Album images can also be displayed in the Project Bin by choosing the Album entry from the Bin's menu.*

Step 5 >> *Next choose the Photo Collage option from the Create Task Pane. The selected images are transferred to the Project Bin and the Projects panel is displayed in the Create Task Pane. You can select the size of the photo collage document from those contained in the drop-down list at the top of the panel.*

Step 6 >> *The next step is to choose the Theme for the collage. The Theme options provide the chance to refine the way that the layout looks. Here you can choose matched background and frame treatments. The Layout settings control the number and general position of the pictures on the document pages. The last section provides the Additional Options of auto filling the pages created with selected photos, adding caption details and altering the total number of pages created.*

Step 7 >> *Extra pages and images can be added or removed after the Photo Collage has been created from inside the Full Edit workspace. The frames, backgrounds and themes can also be changed by applying an alternative design from those listed in the Content panel situated in the Artwork section of the Create pane.*

Step 8 >> *Once the Photo Collage characteristics are set then clicking the Done button at the bottom of the pane will instruct Elements to create the free form multi-page document. This process can take a little while as the program creates the pages and then sources, sizes and inserts the pictures into the new Photo Collage.*

Step 9 >> *Each photo is stored on a separate Frame layer which is indicated by a small plus icon in the bottom right of the layer's thumbnail. The Layers palette can be displayed (along with other editing tools) when selecting the Edit option in the Task Pane area of the Editor workspace.*

Step 10 >> *Frame layers are unlike other image layers in that they contain both the photo as well as its surrounding frame. These picture parts are stored separately and remain editable even though they appear as a single layer. When the creation process is finished you can flip between pages (if you have created a multi-page document) by clicking on the next (or previous) page in the Project Bin or pressing the Forward and Back buttons in the Organizer space.*

Step 11 >> *Unlike the album pages in earlier versions of Elements, Photo Collage and the other Photo Project, and their contents, remain editable after they have been saved and reopened. To enable this new ability Adobe created a completely new file format for the multi-page editable documents. Called the Photo Project Format it has an extension of .PSE as opposed to the .PSD that is associated with standard Photoshop and Photoshop Elements documents.*

Step 12 >> *When saving a newly created Photo Collage the file format in the Save dialog automatically changes to .PSE. By default the Include in the Organizer option is also selected ensuring that the new document is cataloged and displayed in the Organizer space. A small Multi-page icon is displayed at the top right of the thumbnail of each Photo Collage document displayed in the Organizer.*

Quick change layouts using Themes >> *The Photo Collage and Photo Book features in Elements can be used to quickly create a series of photo album pages using photos selected in the Organizer workspace. A variety of layout designs are shipped with the program with other variations promised as downloads in the future. Changing a design (a specific background and frame) is as simple as Applying a new Theme from the Artwork > Content section of the Create pane.*

12.02 The new super Project Bin

Suitable for Elements – 7.0, 6.0, 5.0 | Difficulty level – Basic | Resources – Web image 1201-1, 1201-2, 1201-3 Related techniques – 12.02, 12.03, 12.04

Starting life as a humble place to store photos open in the Editor workspace the Photo Bin, now called the Project Bin, was upgraded for version 6 of Photoshop Elements. Sure, the bin still displays those images that are open in the workspace but this is only part of the story.

The Project Bin contains two drop down menus on the upper edge of the bin. The menu on the left provides a choice of which images are displayed in the bin. The options include:

Show Open Files – This option displays all images currently open in the editor workspace in a group in the project bin.

Show Files From Organizer – Use this choice to display any images currently selected in the Organizer workspace.

Show Albums – Though not a specific entry itself, the next group of options in the menu are headings for all the Albums that have been saved in the Organizer workspace. The number of entries listed here will be determined by the number of Albums you have created in the Organizer. Selecting an entry here will display all the images contained in the Album in the Project Bin.

Providing better control over the images that are displayed in the Project Bin helps users when they are constructing Photo Book pages or individual Photo Collages. It is no longer necessary to bounce back and forwards between Editor and Organizer workspaces, locating suitable photos to include in your compositions. Just group all the images into an Album and then proceed to the Editor workspace. Display the images in the Project Bin by choosing the Album entry from the drop-down list. Next select the Create Option from the Bin Actions menu and choose the Photo Book or Photo Collage option from the Create Task Pane.

By selecting the Auto Fill with Project Bin Photos option at the bottom of the Photo Book or Photo Collage pane, the pictures will be inserted into new frames and pages. Alternatively a blank multi-page document can be created by deselecting this option and then the pictures can be dragged to the blank frames from the Project Bin.

Project Bin actions

On the right of the 'show' drop-down menu there is a second menu containing special actions that can be performed directly from the Project Bin.

Auto-Fill >> The Auto-Fill with Project Bin Photos option inserts the images from the bin into the frames and onto the pages created in the multi-page document. Elements will create as many pages as is needed to place all of the images displayed in the bin.

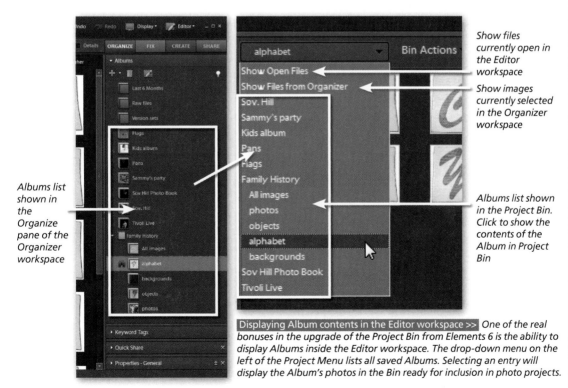

Albums list shown in the Organize pane of the Organizer workspace

Show files currently open in the Editor workspace

Show images currently selected in the Organizer workspace

Albums list shown in the Project Bin. Click to show the contents of the Album in Project Bin

Displaying Album contents in the Editor workspace >> One of the real bonuses in the upgrade of the Project Bin from Elements 6 is the ability to display Albums inside the Editor workspace. The drop-down menu on the left of the Project Menu lists all saved Albums. Selecting an entry will display the Album's photos in the Bin ready for inclusion in photo projects.

There are four possible Project Bin actions:

Create – Selecting this entry switches the Task Pane on the right of the editor workspace to the Create option providing easy access to the Photo Projects.

Share – The Share option displays the Share Task Pane on the right of the Editor workspace.

Print Bin Files – Select this entry to automatically add the images currently displayed in the Bin to the Print Photos dialog. This is a fast way to print all open files.

Save Bin as an Album – Use this option to save all files displayed in the Bin as a new Album. This provides a great way to group images that you have been working on in the Editor workspace so that you can return to them later.

Bin Actions >> *The Bin Actions menu is located beside the 'show' menu at the top edge of the Project Bin. The menu contains four different actions that can be performed from the bin.*

12.03 Editing existing Photo Collages

Suitable for Elements – 7.0, 6.0, 5.0 | Difficulty level – Basic | Related techniques – 12.01, 12.03, 12.04

As we have seen, the Photo Collage feature can create a multi-page document complete with photos in frames on a background. In producing this design Elements will make decisions about the size and position of the frames and the pictures within them. On many occasions you will probably want to use the pages the feature produces with no alterations, but there will be times when you will want to tweak the results. At these times use the following techniques to edit the automatically produced designs.

Basic adjustments >>
To move the picture and frame combination to a new position on the canvas just click and drag the combination.
The size and orientation of the Frame/Picture can be altered by clicking on the picture and frame first, to select it, and then using the corner, edge and rotate handles to scale or pivot.
Click on the Commit button (green tick) at the bottom of the selected picture to apply the changes. To disregard the changes click the Cancel button (red circle with diagonal line through it) instead.

Frame and picture combination changes summary

Other adjustment options are available via the right-click menu when the Move tool is selected. Selections in this menu allow you to:

Rotate 90° Right or Left – Pivot the frame and picture by a set amount.

Position Photo in Frame – Switch to Picture Select mode to allow scaling, rotating and moving the photo within the frame.

Fit Frame to Photo – Automatically adjust the frame size to accommodate the dimensions and format of the place photo. Use this option if you don't want to crop the photo with the edges of the frame.

Replace Photo – Displays a file dialog where you can select a new photo for the frame.

Clear Photo – Removes the photo but keeps the frame.

Clear Frame – Removes the frame but keeps the photo.

Bring to Front/Bring Forward – Moves the frame and photo up the layer stack.

Send to Back/Send Backward – Moves the frame and photo down the layer stack.

Edit Text – Switches text layers to the edit mode.

Altering the picture only >>

As well as being able to alter the characteristics of the frame by selecting the photo you can perform similar changes to the picture itself. Double-clicking with the Move tool or choosing the Position Photo in Frame option from the right-click menu selects the photo and displays a marquee around the picture. A small control panel is also displayed at the top of the marquee.

To move the position of the photo in the frame simply click and drag on the image, releasing the mouse button when the picture is correctly placed. You can alter the size of the photo within the frame by moving the Scale slider (in the control panel) or by dragging one of the handles of the marquee.

Moving a corner handle will scale the photo proportionately, whereas dragging a side handle will squish or stretch the image. The picture can be rotated in 90° increments (to the left) by clicking the Rotate button in the control panel. Alternatively, you can rotate the image to any angle using the rotate handle (middle of the bottom edge of the marquee) or by click-dragging the cursor outside the boundaries of the marquee.

The photo can be replaced with a new picture by clicking the Replace button in the control panel and then selecting the new picture from the file dialog that is displayed.

Altering the Picture Only summary

Extra image adjustment options are available from the right-click menu. The actions available are:

Free Transform – The default mode where dragging the corner of the marquee scales proportionately and dragging the edges squashes or stretches the picture. The following keys alter the action of dragging a handle when in this mode:

Shift + corner handle – Scales proportionately (this option is set by default when first scaling so it may not be necessary to hold down Shift unless you moved an edge handle),

Ctrl + any handle – Distorts the picture,

Ctrl + Shift + middle edge handle – Skews the picture, and

Ctrl + Alt + Shift + corner handle – Applies perspective.

Scale – Resizes in the same manner as the Free Transform mode.

Free Rotate Layer – Rotates the image when click-dragging outside of the marquee.

Skew – Skews the photo when dragging an edge handle.

Distort – Distorts the picture when moving any handle.

Perspective – Applies a perspective effect when dragging a corner handle.

12.04 Adding, removing and replacing photos

Suitable for Elements – 7.0, 6.0, 5.0 | Difficulty level – Basic | Related techniques – 12.01, 12.03, 12.04

Photo Collages do not become static documents once they are created. In the previous section we saw how it is possible to adjust the size, position and orientation of both the photo and frames that were added during the initial creation process, but the feature's flexibility doesn't end there. You can also add new photos, replace existing pictures with alternative choices and even remove images that you no longer want to keep. Here's how.

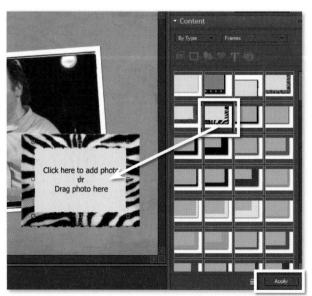

Adding new photos >>
All editing of Photo Projects occurs in the Full Editor workspace. So to add new photos to an existing layout you need to add a new blank frame to the composition. Do this by clicking on the selected frame in the Content section of the Artwork area of the Create pane and pressing the Apply button. A new frame will be created on the current page of the document.
To add a photo to the frame, click-drag one from the Project Bin to the frame or click the text in the empty frame and select a photo from the file browser that opens. Using this approach you can add a photo without it first having to be open in the Project Bin.
When moving the photo make sure that the frame is highlighted with a blue rectangle before releasing the mouse button to insert the picture.

Getting new photos to fit >>

The last part of the process is to fine-tune the picture by adjusting size, orientation and position within the frame. Use the techniques in the previous section to make these alterations.

A good starting place is to select the Fit Frame to Photo option from the right-click menu. After the image and frame are the same size you can then scale, rotate and move the combination.

Replace existing photos >>

It is just as easy to replace existing photos with different images whilst still retaining the frame. Select the frame first and then click-drag a picture from the Project Bin to the frame.
This action swaps the two pictures but you will need to have the replacement image already open in the Full Editor workspace beforehand. If this isn't the case, then an alternative is to select the Replace Photo entry from the right-click menu and choose a new picture via the file dialog that is displayed.

Switching photos >>

You can also switch photos between frames on a page by dragging the content of one frame over another. You will see a special Cursor icon when the image is in position and the content will be switched.

Removing photos >>

Pictures inserted into frames can be removed whilst still retaining the frame by selecting the Clear Photo option from the right-click menu. The frame will then revert to a blank state providing the opportunity to add a new image to the composition.
If you want to remove both the frame and the photo it contains then select the frame first and click the Delete key. A warning window will display asking you if you want to delete selected layers. Answer yes to remove the frame and picture from the composition.

12.05 Adding, moving and deleting pages

Suitable for Elements – 7.0, 6.0, 5.0 | Difficulty level – Basic | Related techniques – 12.01, 12.02, 12.03

If you selected the Auto Fill option when first creating your Photo Collage then Elements will have generated enough pages to insert the photos that were initially included. If you want to add images, some text or graphics later on then you will need to add some extra pages. The new Photo Project file format (.PSE) was developed especially to handle multi-page documents and to ensure that tasks such as adding, deleting and moving pages was as easy as possible.

All page management activities are centered around the PSE document in the Project Bin. The document can be displayed collapsed, where all the pages are grouped together on top of each other, or expanded, where each of the thumbnails representing a single page can be viewed separately.

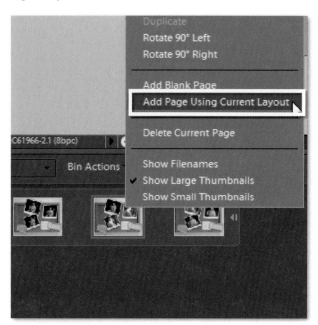

Adding Pages >>
All new pages in a PSE document are added after the current selected page. So start by expanding the multi-page document in the Project Bin and then selecting the thumbnail of the page before the position where the new page is to be created.
So to add a new page you choose either the Add Blank Page or Add Page Using Current Layout option from the Edit menu.
The new page is then added to the document and a new thumbnail is displayed in the Project Bin to the right of the selected page.
These Add Page options are also available from the right-click menu when you select a page in the Project Bin.

Adding pages options:

In Elements you have two options for creating new pages:

Add Blank Page – Use this option to add a white page with no frames, backgrounds or themes present. Once the page is created then text, graphics, shapes, frames, backgrounds and special effects can be added from the Artwork and Effects palette.

Add Page Using Current Layout – This feature duplicates the layout settings of the selected page when creating the new one. Use this option to add new pages to a group of pages that already contain a background and frames as it will help to keep the look of the whole document consistent.

Moving pages >>

The position of pages (from left to right) in the expanded view of a multi-page document in the Project Bin indicates the page's location in the production. The first page in the document is the one position furthest to the left, the second page is the next one along to the right and so on. Changing the position of the page thumbnail in the Project Bin preview alters the page's actual position in the document. Moving pages is a simple task – just click on the page to move and drag it to a new location in the document, release the mouse button and the page is relocated.

Deleting pages >>

Pages, and the frames and photos they contain, can be deleted from a multi-page document by selecting the page thumbnail in the Project Bin and then choosing Edit > Delete Current Page. Alternatively, the Delete Current Page entry can also be selected from the right-click menu.

Viewing pages >>

Navigate between the different pages of your PSE document by selecting the thumbnail of the page that you want to display from the Project Bin. Alternatively you can move from one page to the next using the Forward and Backward buttons located at the bottom of the document window.

PSE document shown collapsed

PSE documents in the Project Bin >>

Multi-page Photo Project (.PSE) documents are displayed in the Project Bin with a shaded background. The document can be expanded or collapsed via the sideways arrow button on the right of the last thumbnail on the right.

Single Photo Collage page   *Individual photo*

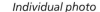

PSE document shown expanded   *Collapse/Expand button*

12.06 Using the Content and Effects panes

Suitable for Elements – 7.0, 6.0, 5.0 | Difficulty level – Basic | Related techniques – 12.01, 12.02, 12.03, 12.04

Photoshop Elements contains a variety of tools and options for customizing a Photo Book or Photo Collage project. Most changes are made via options in the Effects, Content, Favorite and Layers palettes. These palettes or panes as they are sometimes called can be accessed via the Edit or Create (Artwork section) Task panes.

> It is worth noting though that different options are available for Photo Books and Photo Collage features. Because Photo Books are designed for the creation of documents that contain between 20 and 80 pages it is important to keep the files as streamlined as possible. For this reason it is not possible to access the Edit Task pane options. This means that there is no access to the Layers Palette and that the options in the Effects palette are limited. Photo Collage documents are designed for fewer pages and so can access the full range of features.

Content Palette or Pane

So once a multi-page document is created the various components housed in the Content palette can be used to add to or alter the look and feel of your design. The palette was completely revamped in version 6 and contains a drop-down menu on the left for the way that the content is sorted (by type, activity, color, event, etc.) and the right for filtering the content so that only specific types are displayed (backgrounds, frames, graphics, etc.).

The content types include backgrounds, frames, graphics, shapes, text and themes. The themes area houses prebuilt and fully styled layout designs combining matched frame sets and backgrounds. Many of the frame and theme options featured in these sections are also available in the Photo Projects panes displayed when first producing the Photo Book or Photo Collage. The Text section contains a variety of one-click text effects that can be added quickly and easily to type. The Favorites group holds user selected favorites chosen from the other areas. To add a theme, frame, background or any other entry from the palette select the entry and then click the Add to Favorites button. To apply a theme or add artwork to a document select the Palette entry and click the Apply button. Extra palette options and preferences are available via the More button at the top of the palette.

Effects Palette

The Effects palette (previously called Special Effects) includes filters, layer styles, and photo effects options. In versions 6.0 and 7.0 these options have been given their own palette located under the Edit tab, rather than being grouped together in a single Artwork and Effects palette as was the case in Photoshop Elements 5. To apply an effect to a document select the item in the layout to change and then choose the Palette entry and click the Apply button. The effect can also be dragged and dropped over the frame or graphic to apply the change.

Multiple designs in seconds >>

You can change both frames and backgrounds of an existing layout with just two clicks – one to select the new theme (combination of frame and background) and two to apply it to the design. All the designs here were created in this way. If you drag the design from the palette and drop it on the document, then you can make the change with only one click. Cool!

Create > Artwork > Content section >>

The Content section of the Artwork area of the Create task pane contains backgrounds, picture frames, graphics, text, themes and shapes that can be added to your layouts. Backgrounds, graphics and shapes all create their own layers when added. Frames, on the other hand, are applied to existing layers. To add a piece of artwork click on the thumbnail in the palette and then press the Apply button. To add a picture to a frame drag the image from another open document to the frame.

All artwork except Backgrounds can be scaled and rotated via the corner, middle edge and rotate handles. Click the image layer to activate the handles.

Create > Artwork > Content > Text section >>

The Text section of the Content panel contains a variety of text effects that you can apply to the type in your Elements documents. The effects include bevels, drop shadows, glows and gradients, and only work with text layers. To add text to your composition click the thumbnail of the effect that you want to apply in the pane before finally clicking the Apply button.

With Photo Collage compositions the attributes of the text effects (size of drop shadow, color of stroke, etc.) can be adjusted via the Layer > Layer Style > Style Settings. Text effects can be removed by selecting the Layer > Layer Style > Clear Layer Style entry. These options are not available for Photo Book productions.

Create > Artwork > Effects section >>

The Effects section of the Artwork pane groups together filters, layer styles and photo effects. Note that not all of these options are available for use with Photo Books.

The Filters group contains many of the options that are listed under the Filter menu. To apply a filter select the layer to change, then the thumbnail in the palette and click Apply. Layers styles add effects such as drop shadows, outer glows and strokes to selected layers. These can be applied to text, image and shape layers and the characteristics of the styles can be customized via the Layer > Layer Style > Style Settings dialog. Photo effects alter your photos via a series of automatic editing steps. Options include convert to black and white, create a photo frame and add soft focus. Some Photo effects are applied to standard image layers, others only work with background layers. After selecting the effect to apply, a pop-up dialog will indicate if you are working with the wrong layer type. To correct, simply convert image layers to background, or vice versa, and apply the effect again.

Create > Artwork > Favorites section >>
The Favorites section of the Artwork pane lists all the artwork, effects, themes and styles that you have nominated as favorites.

This area is a great place to store the Artwork entries that you use time and time again. For instance when you find a layer style or filter that you particularly like, rather than have to search for it each time you want to use it, simply click the Add Favorites star at the bottom of the palette to store the style in the Favorites area.

Remove items from the Favorites by right-clicking on the thumbnail of the Favorites entry and selecting Remove from Favorites entry in the pop-up menu.

Create > Artwork > Content > Themes section >>
The Themes section lists a variety of pre-designed backgrounds and matched frame sets that can be applied to your Elements' document. A document page can only have one theme at a time so trying to apply a second theme will replace the existing background and frames. A multi-page document can have many differently themed pages though. Themes are a great place to start when you want to provide a consistent look and feel to your album or scrapbook pages. Commencing your project with themes doesn't mean that you can't add other frames, graphics, shapes or text later. Just choose and apply the selected frame style from the Artwork pane as you would normally.

You can also change the theme's background by picking and applying a new background. Different frame styles can be substituted by dragging the new style over the existing frame and letting go when the layer border turns blue.

Adjusting Style Settings in Photo Collages >> The attributes of the Text Effects or Layer Styles in Photo Collage designs can be adjusted using the Style Settings dialog which is displayed by double-clicking the 'fx' icon in the layer or by selecting Layer > Layer Style > Style Setting.

12.07 Align, arrange and distribute your frames

Suitable for Elements – 7.0, 6.0, 5.0 | Difficulty level – Basic | Related techniques – 12.01, 12.02, 12.03, 12.04

The Auto Fill option within the Photo Collage feature is a great way to get your photos into a layout quickly and easily. In the previous sections we have looked at how to adjust the pictures and the picture and frame combinations; now let's look at how to change the way that each of the picture elements relate to each other.

Photoshop Elements contains three specialist controls designed for this purpose. They are located on the options bar of the Move tool and are divided into Arrange, Align and Distribute headings. When clicked each shortcut button displays a variety of composition options in a drop-down menu.

Composition changes >>
The options grouped under the Align, Arrange and Distribute shortcut buttons provide quick ways to alter the composition of your framed photos.

Align >>
The Align option is one of three arrangement features designed to work with the contents of layers.

After multi-selecting several layers in the Layers palette, the picture content of these layers can be composed according to the options in the Align menu.

Top and **Bottom Edges** align the picture via the top or bottom extremities of layer content. The **Vertical Centers** option arranges the picture parts around a horizontal line or axis. **Left** and **Right Edges** move the picture content to either side aligning the edges of the detail. The **Horizontal Centers** feature arranges all the content of the selected layers around a vertical axis.

In the example, the three pictures are aligned using the top edge of the frame. Do this by selecting the layers first and then choosing Align > Top Edges.

BEFORE

AFTER

Arrange >>

The Arrange option is one of three new layer organization features contained on the Move tool's options bar. Unlike the Align and Distribute features, Arrange moves a selected layer (or group of layers) up or down the layer stack rather than moving the contents of these layers around the canvas area.

To use the feature select a layer, or layers, in the Layers palette and then choose one of the options in the drop-down Arrange menu in the Move tool options bar. In the example document the red pepper picture (top layer) was selected and then the Send Backward option chosen. This moved the layer one position down in the order of the stack changing the picture so that the red pepper now sits behind the lemon. The Arrange options include – **Bring Forward** and **Send Backward** which moves the layer up or down one position and **Send to Back** which pushes the layer to the bottom and **Bring to Front** which places the layer on the very top of the stack.

BEFORE

AFTER

Distribute >>

The Distribute option also arranges the content of layers within the canvas space. After multi-selecting several layers in the Layers palette, the picture content of these layers can be arranged according to the options in the Distribute drop-down menu. This feature can be used very successfully to evenly space picture parts within the canvas area.

The Distribute > **Horizontal** and **Vertical Centers** options arrange the picture parts so that the axes of the objects are evenly spaced. The **Top** and **Bottom Edges** base the spacings on the upper or bottom most part of the object. The **Left** or **Right Edges** option distributes the objects using the side boundaries as the reference point for the spacing.

In this example an even space was placed between the three photos by first selecting all three layers and then choosing the Distribute > Horizontal Centers option.

12.08 Printing your Photo Collages and Photo Books

Suitable for Elements – 7.0, 6.0, 5.0 | Difficulty level – Basic | Related techniques – 12.01, 12.02, 12.03, 12.04

As part of the technology behind the new Photo Collage feature the folk at Adobe created a new file format called the Photo Project Format. The files saved in this format differ from traditional Photoshop Elements files in that they can include multiple pages. The format has a file extension of .PSE. If a layout document consists of only one page then you can choose to save the file in either the Photoshop Elements format (.PSD) or the Photo Projects format, but once you have multiple pages in the layout then you can only save the document in the PSE file type.

This new file type also brings with it different possibilities when it comes to output. You can now choose to print any single page from the document, all pages from the layout, a contact sheet, picture package, or label set of the pages or even order a Kodak Photo Book of the complete project all from inside Photoshop Elements.

All printing options, except the on-line photo book ordering, are handled by either the Print (for single prints) or Print Photos (for multiple prints) dialogs. Print is accessed from inside the Full Edit space by selecting File > Print. The Print Photos dialog is displayed by either selecting File > Print Multiple Photos from the Full Edit space, Print Bin Files from the Bin Actions menu or File > Print from the Organizer (the Photo Project thumbnail must be selected first).

Bin Actions menu

Full Edit

Organizer

Printing PSE documents >>
Multi-page PSE, or Photo Project documents that are open in the Full Edit workspace, can be printed either a page at a time via the File > Print option or as a group of prints with the File > Print Multiple Photos. Also the new Print Bin Files option located in the Bin Actions menu can be used to output the files displayed as thumbnails in the bin space.
The Photo Project can also be printed directly from the Organizer space without the need to open the document by electing the project's thumbnail and then choosing the File Print option.

Print Preview

There is no need to display the individual page you want to print before moving to the Print
Preview screen as a pair of Navigation buttons now appear below the preview thumbnail in the
window. Use these to flip through the pages in your document to select the page to output. If
you decide that you want to print more than one page then click onto the Print Multiple Photos
button at the top of the dialog to display the Print Photos screen.

Print Photos

Once inside the Print Photos dialog you will notice that the pages of your Photo Project are listed
as individual prints on the left side of the screen. Here you can choose to remove any pages that
you don't want to print by clicking on the thumbnail and then choosing the Remove button at
the bottom of the screen. It is important to know that this action only removes the page from
the print list and doesn't make any changes to the Photo Project document itself. As well as the
Individual Print Type setting, the Print Photos dialog also provides the ability to output the
pages as a contact sheet, picture package or label set. See Chapter 13 for more details on
these options.

Order a Kodak Photo Book or Kodak Prints

You can also opt for getting your multi-page Photo Book produced as a Kodak Photo Book or a
series of Kodak Prints. This option might not be available in some locations. Simply select the
completed creation project thumbnail in the Organizer space and then choose the Order Prints
option from the Print On-line shortcut button. This will take you to the Kodak Print store where
you can select the size and finish of the prints and where to send them. Add in your payment
details and then the files are uploaded and the completed prints are delivered back in the post.

Ordering Prints of Photo Book pages >>
*Finished multi-page Photo Collage
documents can be produced as individual
prints via the File > Order Prints option.*

To produce a Kodak Photo Book select the Order button in the new floating options bar that appears alongside the preview of the photo book pages when open in the Full Edit workspace. This action will take you to the login screen for the online book production service. In most countries this service is provided by Kodak Easy Share gallery. If you have an account then you can proceed to the book ordering process otherwise you will need to undertake the free registration process before moving to the next screen. The process involves several steps including selecting the cover finish, adding in delivery and payment details and finally confirming the order. A few days later a professionally printed and bound book will arrive at your door.

Ordering Photo Books and Prints >>
Finished multi-page Photo Collage documents can be produced as bound books with the Order Kodak Photo Books option.

13

Finely Crafted Output

I t is one thing to be able to take great pictures with your digital camera and quite another to then produce fantastic photographic prints. In the old days of film most photographers passed on the responsibility of making a print to their local photo store. Most, that is, except for a few dedicated individuals who spent their hours in small darkrooms under stairs or in the attic.

Digital has changed all this. Now more shooters than ever before are creating their own prints. Gone are the dank and smelly darkrooms. Now the center of home or office print production sits squarely on the desk in the form of a table-top printer.

Printing basics

There are several different printer technologies that can turn your digital pictures into photographs. The most popular, at the moment, is the Ink Jet (or Bubble Jet) printer, followed by Dye Sublimation and Laser machines.

CMYK color >> *Most printing systems are based on breaking the full color picture (a) down into several color parts. Here the picture is separated into cyan (b), magenta (c), yellow (d) and black (e), which correspond to the inks of the printer.*

Creating millions of colors from as little as four

Each of the printing technologies creates the illusion of millions of colors in the photograph by separating the picture into four separate base colors (some systems use six or seven colors). In most cases, these colors are Cyan, Magenta, Yellow and Black. This type of separation is referred to as CMYK (where K stands for the black component), which has been the basis of newspaper and magazine printing for decades.

Once the picture is broken into these four colors, the printer lays down a series of tiny colored dots in a specific pattern on the paper. Looking at the picture from a distance, our eyes mix the dots together so that we see an illusion of many colors rather than just the four that the picture was created from.

Tones and colors made of dots

To create darker and lighter colors the printer produces the colored dots at varying sizes. The lighter tones are created by printing small dots so that more of the white paper base shows through. The darker tones of the photograph are made with larger dots leaving less paper showing. This system is called halftoning. In traditional printing, such as that used to create the book you are now reading, different dot sizes, and therefore tone, are created by 'screening' the photograph. In desktop digital printing different shades are created using 'simulated halftones'.

This process breaks each section of the image into minute grids. Then as part of the separation process, the printer's software will determine the tone of each image part and decide how to best balance the amount of white space and ink dots in the grid in order to simulate this tone. Sound confusing? Well let's use a simple example.

We are printing a black and white picture with a printer capable of five levels of tone:

• White,
• Light gray (25% gray),
• Mid gray (50% gray),
• Dark gray (75% gray) and
• Black (100% black).

We are using black ink only. Let's say that one part of the image is represented by a grid of two dots by two dots.

If this part of the picture was supposed to be white then the software would print no dots in the grid. If the area was light gray then one dot (out of a possible four) would be printed. If the image was a midtone then two dots would be printed. If the shade was a little darker then three dots would be laid down and finally if this part of the photograph was black then all parts of the grid (that is, all four dots) would be printed.

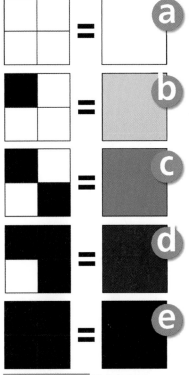

Simulated tones >> *Digital printers represent tones in a similar fashion using small grids containing areas of ink color and sections where the paper shows through. (a) White. (b) 25% gray. (c) 50% gray. (d) 75% gray. (e) Black.*

Keep in mind that modern photographic inkjet printers are capable of many more levels of tone
than the five used in our example. Also remember that different colored dots are being laid

Color from dots >>
The separate colors are laid down on the paper surface in the form of minute dots which, when seen at a distance, mix together to simulate all the other colors in the photograph.

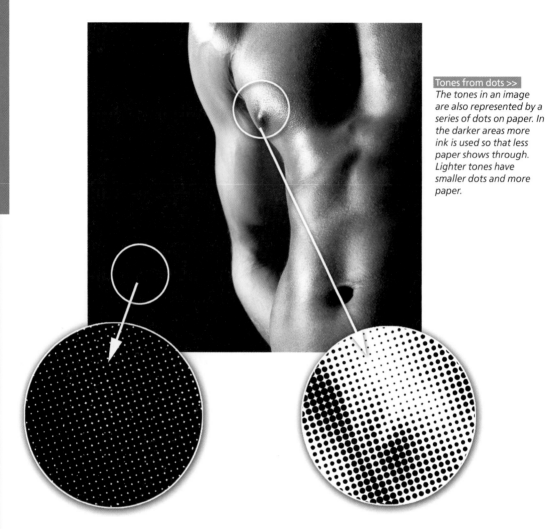

Tones from dots >>
The tones in an image are also represented by a series of dots on paper. In the darker areas more ink is used so that less paper shows through. Lighter tones have smaller dots and more paper.

down at the same time. In this way both simulated tone and color are created by drawing the picture with a series of dots using a small set of printing inks. The fact that all the current crop of desktop printers handle this type of separation and the creation and application of the dots with such precision and speed is nothing short of a technological miracle. Now let's look at the three main desktop printing technologies in turn.

The inkjet printer

Costing as little as US$60 the inkjet printer provides the cheapest way to enter the world of desktop printing. The ability of an inkjet printer to produce great photographs is based on the production of a combination of fineness of detail and seamless graduation of the color and tone. The machines contain a series of cartridges filled with liquid ink. The ink is forced through a set of tiny print nozzles using either heat or pressure. Different manufacturers have slightly different systems but all are capable of producing very small droplets of ink (some are four times smaller than the diameter of a human hair!). The printer head moves back and forth across the paper laying down color whilst the roller mechanism gradually feeds the print through the machine. Newer models have multiple sets of nozzles which operate in both directions (bi-directional) to give faster print speeds.

The most sophisticated printers from manufacturers such as Canon, Epson and Hewlett Packard also have the ability to produce ink droplets that vary in size. This feature helps create the fine detail in photographic prints. Most photographic quality printers have very high resolution approaching 6000 dots per inch, which equates to pictures being created with very small ink droplets. They also have 6, 7 or even 8 different ink colors enabling these machines to produce the highest quality prints. These printers are often more expensive than standard models but serious photographers will value the extra quality they are capable of.

Printers optimized for business applications are often capable of producing prints faster than the photographic models. They usually only have three colors and black, and so do not produce photographic images with as much subtlety in tonal change as the special photo models.

One of the real advantages of inkjet printing technologies for the digital photographer is the choice of papers available for printing. Different surfaces (gloss, semi-gloss, matt, iron-on transfer, metallic, magnetic and even plastic), textures (smooth, water color and canvas), thickness (from 80 gsm to 300 gsm) and sizes (A4, A3, 10 x 8 inch, 6 x 4 inch, Panorama and even roll) can all be fed through the printer. This is not the case with laser printing, where the choice is limited in surface and thickness, nor Dye Sublimation printing, where only the specialized paper supplied with the colored ribbons can be used.

Simulated tones >> *The best photographic printers contain the standard four colors plus light versions of black, cyan and magenta to help create truer colors and smoother graduation of tones.*
(a) Black. (b) Light or Photo black. (c) Cyan. (d) Light cyan. (e) Magenta. (f) Light magenta. (g) Yellow.

Laser

Although most laser printers you see are used for black and white business prints more and more are capable of producing good quality color output. These devices use a modified version of photocopier technology to produce their crisp hard-edged prints.

They work by drawing the image or text to be printed onto a photo-sensitive drum using either a laser or a series of LEDs (light emitting diodes). This process changes the electromagnetic charge on the drawn sections of the drum. The drum is then passed by a dispenser and the oppositely charged toner (the 'ink' used by laser printers) is attracted to the drum, which then is passed by electrostatically charged paper where the toner is deposited. Color laser printers use four different drums for each of the separation colors – cyan, magenta, yellow and black.

Laser printers >> *Laser printers use photocopier-type technology to produce crisp output. Some models can even produce full color prints.*

The strengths of laser printers are their speed, cost per printed page and the sharp-edged clarity of the prints they produce. For businesses that regularly produce short runs of color brochures a color laser may be a cost-effective alternative to printing outside, but for the dedicated digital photographer, inkjet printers provide a cheaper way to produce photographic quality prints.

Dye Sublimation

Where laser and inkjet technology printing prowess is based on the creation of tone and color via discrete dots, Dye Sublimation printers use a different approach. Often called a continuous tone printing system, 'Dye Sub' machines create prints by laying down a series of overlapping transparent dyes to build up the picture.

Expensive when the technology was first released, these printers have gained more popularity as newer models have dropped in price and increased in speed and image quality. Rather than using a set of inks, color is added to the picture using a heating element to transfer dye from cyan, magenta, yellow and, in some machines, black ribbons onto a specially treated paper.

Dye Sublimation printers >> *Dye Sublimation printers use a multi-colored donor ribbon which is heated to transfer the color to a special receiving paper.*

The dyes are absorbed into the paper surface leaving a slightly blurred edge which blends with adjacent colors and tones. This gives the image a continuous tone (non-dotty) appearance at relatively low resolutions (300 dpi) compared to inkjet technology equivalents.

The dyes are layered on a full paper size ribbon and each color is added in turn. With some machines a protective clear coating is also applied at the last stage in the process. Accurate registration is critical throughout the whole printing process.

Other printing processes

Though less well known, the following processes are also being used to produce photo images:

Thermal wax transfer – Initially designed for use in the graphic design and printing industries this technology uses very small heating elements to melt and transfer color wax from donor sheets onto the printing paper. These printers produce very strong and vibrant colors but sometimes struggle to create truly photographic prints.

Pictrography – Developed by Fuji, this system uses a three-color laser (red, green and blue) to draw the picture onto a donor paper at a resolution of about 400 dpi. The donor paper is then placed in contact with a printing paper and the image transferred using heated water. The final print is very similar to standard photographic paper.

Offset lithography – Used for printing newspapers and magazines. Typically a color image is separated into the standard four base colors (CMYK) and a halftone version of the image created at the same time. This produces four separate versions of the picture, one for each color, which are used to create four different printing plates. The color inks (called process colors) are applied to each plate and the printing paper is fed past each plate with the ink being laid down in registration.

Inkjet media >> *One advantage of creating your photographs with an inkjet machine is the large range of paper stocks available for printing.*

Image resolution vs printer resolution

As we have already seen from our discussions in Chapter 2 the true dimensions of any digital file are measured in pixels, not inches or centimeters. These dimensions indicate the total number of samples that were made to form the file. It's only when an image's resolution is chosen that these dimensions will be translated into a print size that can be measured in inches or centimeters.

The image resolution determines how the digital information is spread over the print surface. If a setting of 100 dpi is chosen then the print will use 100 pixels for each inch that is printed. If the image is 800 pixels wide then this will result in a print that is 8 inches wide. If the image resolution is set to 200 dpi then the resultant print will only be 4 inches wide because twice as many pixels are used for every inch of the print. For this reason the same digital file can have many different printed sizes.

With this in mind, the following table shows the different print sizes possible when the same picture is printed at different resolutions:

Pixel dimensions:	Print size at 100 ppi:	Print size at 200 ppi:	Print size at 300 ppi:
640 x 480 pixels	6.4 x 4.8 inches	3.2 x 2.4 inches	2.1 x 1.6 inches
1440 x 960 pixels	14.4 x 9.6 inches	7.2 x 4.8 inches	4.8 x 3.2 inches
1600 x 1200 pixels	16 x 12 inches	8.0 x 6.0 inches	5.3 x 4 inches
1920 x 1600 pixels	19.2 x 16 inches	9.6 x 8 inches	6.4 x 5.3 inches
2304 x 1536 pixels	23 x 15.4 inches	11.5 x 7.7 inches	7.6 x 5.1 inches
2560 x 1920 pixels	25.6 x 19.2 inches	12.8 x 9.6 inches	8.5 x 6.4 inches
3000 x 2000 pixels	30 x 20 inches	15 x 10 inches	10 x 6.6 inches

Printer resolution refers to the number of ink droplets placed on the page per inch of paper. Most modern printers are capable of up to 5600 dots per inch. This value does not relate to the image resolution discussed above. It is a measure of the machine's performance not the spread of picture pixels.

Keep in mind that different printing technologies have different optimum resolutions. For example, perfectly acceptable photographic images are produced on Dye Sublimation machines with a printing resolution as small as 300 dpi, whereas the same appearance of photographic quality may require a setting of 1440 dpi on an inkjet machine.

Step 1 >> *With your image open in Elements select Print from the File menu.*

Step 2 >> *Select the printer that you want to use from the drop-down list displayed in the Print dialog or via Page Setup and Printer buttons.*

Step 3 >> *Choose the media type and Quality mode from the main section of the printer driver.*

13.01 Basic steps

Suitable for Elements – 7.0, 6.0 5.0, 4.0, 3.0, 2.0, 1.0 | Difficulty level – Basic | Related techniques – 13.04– 13.08 | Menus used – File

Let's revisit the basic steps used in printing from Elements before introducing some advanced techniques that will really help you to produce top quality images from your desktop printer.

Make sure that your printer is turned on and your image is open in Elements. Select the Print option from the File menu (File > Print). If your print was too big for the page in earlier versions of the program then a Clipping Warning will appear indicating that part of your image will be truncated if you proceed. You could choose to squeeze the picture onto the paper by checking the Scale to Fit Media box, click preview

Step 4 >> *Check that the paper size and source are correctly set in the Paper section of the printer driver. Click OK.*

Step 5 >> *As a final step adjust the size of the photo on the page using the corner handles in the preview. Be careful though as increasing the size of the photo here reduces image quality by printing at a lower resolution.*

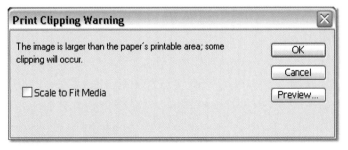

Print Clipping Warning >> *The Print Clipping Warning appears when your image is too big for the default paper size set for your printer.*

to take you directly to the Print Preview dialog or select OK to continue printing the trimmed image. This will open up the printer's control panel, often called the Printer Driver dialog. The type and style of dialog that you see will be determined by the printer manufacturer and model that you own. Here I have shown a dialog box or printer driver typical for Epson machines.

A little more sophistication

Thankfully in versions 5.0, 6.0 and 7.0 of Photoshop Elements the whole process has been simplified. Now choosing the File > Print option takes you directly to the Print Preview option. With this dialog you preview your picture as it will appear on the printed page. This thumbnail snapshot of picture on page means that problems with sizing and picture orientation are immediately obvious. You can choose to let the program adjust the picture size to suit the paper automatically by employing the Scale to Fit option or you can manually position and size the image. Simply deselect the Scale to Fit and Center Image options and choose the Show Bounding Box feature. Now you can drag the picture around the paper surface and scale the printed image using the corner handles in the thumbnail. To adjust paper size and orientation or change the printer you are using to output your image select the Page Setup button and input the values you require in the Page Setup dialog.

Print Preview >>
The Print Preview dialog provides a more comprehensive and visual approach to adjusting printing variables than what was available with the Print command in previous versions. (a) Preview image on paper. (b) Image position. (c) Image size. (d) Color Management selection. (e) Printer preferences. (f) Page Setup dialog. (g) Print Multiple Photos dialog.

The Print Preview feature also provides the option for users to better control the way that Elements communicates how the colors in the picture will output to the printer. The Color Management section which used to be displayed via the Show More button is now always on display. Here you can select the precise color profile to use when printing. Most photo-quality printers now include generic profiles that are copied to your system when you install your printer drivers. To ensure the best color reproduction from your printer select the precise profile for your model from the drop-down list. With the color management, paper size and orientation as well as image size and position set, pressing the Print button will start the output process.

Basic settings

All the basic printer settings are controlled via the Printer Driver dialog. This is different for each printer model but generally contains similar controls (even if they are named slightly differently). Check to see that the name of the printer is correctly listed in the Name box. If not, select the correct printer from the drop-down menu. Click on the Properties button and choose the 'Main Tab'. Select the media type that matches your paper, the Color option for photographic images and Automatic and Quality settings in the mode section. These options automatically select the highest quality print settings for the paper type you are using. Click OK.

Select the Paper tab to alter the paper size and its rotation. Also nominate if the paper is being loaded from the sheet feeder or via a roll. Click OK. Select the Main tab once more and input the number of copies you want to print. Click OK to start the print process. Depending on the size of your picture and the quality of the print this part of the process can take a few minutes before you will see any action from the printer.

PIM and EXIF Print ?

Epson printer users will find two extra options in the Print dialog (detailed above) when outputting their JPEG photos from the Photo Browser workspace. Called PIM (PRINT Image Matching) and Exif Print, enabling these options when printing will generally provide better results than when they are left unchecked.

Both these technologies aim to match the photo picture characteristics more closely with the printer's abilities. These print options are lost when photos are edited outside the Photo Browser in either the Standard or Quick Fix Editor workspaces.

Print command >> *The Print command located in previous versions of Elements provided a basic set of options that allow you to select your printer and adjust its settings (via the Properties button).*

When the File > Print option is selected in Photoshop Elements 6.0 and 7.0 the Print Preview dialog is displayed. (a) Printer selection. (b) Printer Properties dialog. (c) Media type (paper type). (d) Printing mode. (e) Number of prints.

13.02 Creating contact sheets

Suitable for Elements – 7.0, 6.0, 5.0, 4.0, 3.0
Difficulty level – Basic | Related techniques – 13.03
Menus used – File

With the one simple Contact Sheet command Elements can create a series of small thumbnail versions of photos in a catalog or those that were multi-selected before opening the tool. These small pictures are automatically arranged on pages and labelled with their file names. From there it is an easy task to print a series of contact sheets that can be kept as a permanent record of the folder's images. The job of selecting the best pictures to

Contact sheets >> *Create prints of thumbnail versions of your images using the Contact Print feature in Elements.*

manipulate and print can then be made with hard copies of your images, without having to spend the time and money to output every image to be considered. This is a real bonus for digital photographers as it provides a quick tactile record of their day's efforts.

Elements also contains a version of the feature that is part of the Print Multiple Photos dialog and is easier to use than the File > Contact Sheet II version that was found in earlier versions of the program.

Step 1 >> *From the Editor open the images to be printed, otherwise multi-select the pictures from inside the Photo Browser. Select File > Print and choose Contact Sheet from the Select Type of Print menu.*

Step 2 >> *Use the Add and Remove Photos buttons to adjust the list of pictures to be included. Select the printer from the drop-down list in section 1 of the dialog and adjust the hardware settings by clicking the Printer Preferences button.*

Step 3 >> *In the final section (3) choose the number of columns to use (and therefore the total number of thumbnails to place on a single sheet) and select the content of the label text to be included. Click Print to output the contact sheet.*

13.03 Multiple prints on a page

Suitable for Elements – 7.0, 6.0, 5.0, 4.0, 3.0, 2.0, 1.0
Difficulty level – Basic | Related techniques – 13.02
Menus used – File

The Picture Package option extends the contact
sheet idea by allowing you to select one of a series
of predestined multi-print layouts that have been
carefully created to fit many images neatly onto a
single sheet of standard paper. Previously located
in the Print Layouts section of the File menu where
the Contact Sheet command was also placed, the
revamped Picture Package has now been integrated
into the Print Multiple Photos dialog. Macintosh
users of Elements 6.0 can access the feature via the
File menu in the Editor or under the Automate menu
in the file browser.

There are designs that place multiples of the same
size pictures together and those that surround one
or two larger images with many smaller versions.
The feature provides a preview of the pictures in the
layout. You can also choose to repeat the same image
throughout the design by selecting the One Picture
per Page option. There is no option to add labels the
feature, but you can select a frame from one of the

Picture Package >> *As well as the Contact
Sheet feature the Picture Package option also
provides the ability to print multiple images of
different sizes on the one sheet of paper.*

many listed to surround the photos you print. Whichever layout and frame design you pick,
this feature should help you to keep both family members and football associates supplied with
enough visual memories to make sure they are happy.

Step 1 >> *Open images in the Editor
or multi-select pictures in the Photo
Browser. Select Editor: File > Print
Multiple Photos or Photo Browser:
File > Print and then Picture Package.
Use the Add and Remove Photos
buttons to adjust the list of pictures
to be included in the contact sheet.*

Step 2 >> *Drag the photos to alter
the layout. Add more pictures from
the film strip by dragging them to
the preview area. Select the printer
from the drop-down list. Click the
Printer Preferences button to adjust
the hardware settings.*

Step 3 >> *In the final section choose
the Layout and Frame design to be
included. To repeat a single image on
a page click the One Photo per Page
option. To add many different
pictures to the same page leave this
item unchecked. Click Print to output
the Picture Package pages.*

Ensuring color consistency between devices

One of the biggest problems faced by the digital photographer is matching the color and tone in the scene with what they see on screen and then with what is output as a print. This problem comes about because when working digitally we use several different devices to capture, manipulate and output color photographs – the camera, or scanner, the monitor or screen, and the printer. Each of these pieces of hardware sees and represents color in a different way. The camera converts a continuous scene to discrete digital tones/colors, the monitor displays a full color image on screen using phosphors or filtered LCDs and the printer creates a hard copy of the picture using inks on paper.

One of the earliest and most complex problems facing manufacturers was finding a way to produce consistent colors across all these devices. As many readers will attest too, often what we see through the camera is not the same as what appears on screen, which in turn is distinctly different to the picture that prints. These problems occur because each device can only work with a small subset of all the possible colors. This set is called the color gamut of the machine. As the gamut changes from device to device so too does the range of colors in the picture. For example, the range of tones and colors the camera recorded may not be visible on screen and the detail that can be plainly seen on the monitor may be outside the capabilities of the printer.

Color and digital devices >> *The devices used to capture, process and output color pictures all respond to color in a different way. Each piece of hardware is only capable of working with a subset of all possible hues. This range of colors is called the device's color gamut. (a) Camera gamut. (b) Screen gamut. (c) Printer gamut.* Graph images generated in ICCToolbox, courtesy of www.icctools.com.

Color gamut >> *The difference between the gamuts of different devices can lead to photographers not being able to match what they see on screen with printer output.*
(a) All visible colors.
(b) Screen colors.
(c) Printable colors.
Graph generated in ICCToolbox, courtesy of www.icctools.com.

Add to this scenario the fact that if I send the same image to three of my friends it will probably appear differently on each of their screens. On one it may be a little contrasty, on another too blue and on the last screen it could appear overexposed. Each of the monitors is interacting with the digital file in a slightly different way.

So with all these complexities are digital photographers condemned to poor color consistency? The answer is a resounding NO! Through the use of a color-managed system we can maintain predictable color throughout the editing process and from machine to machine.

Essentially color management is concerned with describing the characteristics of each device in the editing chain. This description, often called an ICC profile, is then used to translate image detail and color from one device to another. Pictures are tagged, when they are first created, with a profile and when downloaded to a computer, which has a profiled screen attached, the image is translated to suit the characteristics of the monitor. With the corrections complete the tagged file is then sent to the printer, where the picture is translated, again to suit the printer's profile.

A similar scenario occurs when viewing files on different machines. As the picture is passed around, the profile for each monitor translates and accounts for individual hardware and color changes. The result is a picture that appears very similar on all devices.

Pro's Tip: To ensure that you get the benefits of color management at home, be sure to turn on color management features for your camera, scanner, monitor, software and printer. Always tag your files as you capture them and then use this profile to help keep color consistency as you edit, output and share your work.

Color-managed workflows >> *When color management is not used the same digital photograph can display differently on different screens (a). When a tagged picture is displayed on several profiled monitors in a color-managed environment the image will appear similar despite the different characteristics of each computer and screen set up (b).*

Color management and printing

So how does color management impact on our printing workflow? Well as we have already seen when dealing with resolution, so much of how we start the digital process determines the quality of our outcomes. Color management is no different in this respect. It is a fact that the digital photographer who considers color management at the point of shooting (or scanning), and then again when editing, will output better quality (and more predictable) printed images than one who doesn't. So at each stage of the digital process – capture, manipulation (editing) and output – your pictures should be color managed.

CAPTURE

Color-managed capture – When shooting we should make sure that any color management or ICC profile settings in the camera are always turned on. This will ensure that the pictures captured will be tagged with a profile. Those readers shooting film and converting to digital with scanners should search through the preference menus of their scanners to locate, and activate, any inbuilt color management systems here as well. This way scanned pictures will be tagged as well.

EDIT & ENHANCE

Color-managed manipulation – When setting up Elements we should make sure that one of the color management options is selected in the Color Settings dialog of the program. This ensures that tagged pictures coming into the workspace are correctly interpreted and displayed ready for editing and enhancement. It also guarantees that when it comes time to print, Elements can correctly translate your on-screen masterpieces into a format that your printer can understand.

OUTPUT

Color-managed output – The final step in the process is the printer and it is critical, if all your hard work to this point is going to pay off, that you load and use the printer's profile in the Print Preview > Show More Options settings. This step means that the tagged file exiting Elements will be accurately translated into the colors and tones that the printer is capable of creating.

Think of the whole system as a chain. The strength of your color management and therefore the predictability of the process is based on both the integrity of the individual links and their relationship to each other. The ICC profiles are the basis of these relationships. They ensure that each device knows exactly how to represent the color and tones in an image.

13.04 Setting up a color-managed workflow

Suitable for Elements – 7.0, 6.0, 5.0, 4.0, 3.0, 2.0, 1.0 | Difficulty level – Intermediate
Related techniques – 13.05, 13.06, 13.07, 13.08 | Menus used – File

Now that I have convinced you that a color-managed system has distinct quality advantages over a 'hit and miss' non-managed approach, you will, no doubt, be eagerly wanting to make sure that you are working this way at home. So here are the steps that you will need to follow to put in place a full ICC profile color-managed system for capture, manipulation and print.

Scanners and cameras

Start by searching through the manuals for your digital camera and scanner to find references for 'Changing Color Spaces' or 'Tagging your Scanned File'. Most cameras automatically tag the images they make with the sRGB ICC profile. Even if there is no mention of attaching profiles to pictures in the camera documentation, don't assume that the file is being imported without a profile. It may be that this function is occurring in the background and that your particular camera does not offer the facility to change or manipulate the camera's color profile.

To check to see if your pictures are tagged, open the file in the Elements Editor and click the sideways arrow at the left of the status bar (at the bottom of the picture window) to reveal a fly-

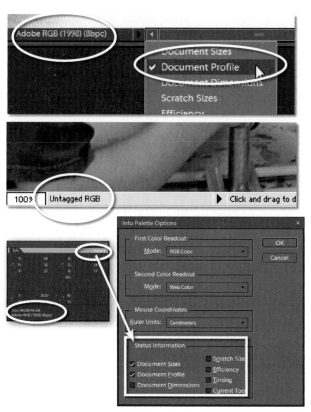

out menu. Choose the Document Profile option from the list. Now to the left of the arrow you will see the profile name attached to your file. If the picture is not tagged then it will be labelled 'Untagged RGB'. Alternatively, you can also display the profile as part of the Info palette (Editor: Window > Info) by selecting the setting from the More Options button.

Some more expensive cameras contain the ability to alter the default profile settings, allowing the user to select different color spaces. For the moment just make sure that the camera is attaching a profile to your images. We will discuss 'which profiles are best to use when' later in this chapter.

Do the same type of investigation for your scanner. Unfortunately you will probably find that most

Checking profiles in Elements >> *Use the Document Profile option in the Info palette on the document's status bar to check what profile is attached to your pictures.*

entry level scanners don't seem to have color profile options, but this situation is changing. Many more budget models are 'profile aware' so make sure you search the preferences part of your scanner driver carefully to ensure that all color management options are turned on.

Step 1 >> *The color settings, for cameras with this option, can usually be found in the Set Up or Preferences menu.*

Step 2 >> *For example, Nikon D100 users can access these settings via the Color Mode option located in the Shooting Menu.*

Step 3 >> *In this menu Nikon provides three options for attached color spaces.*

Step 1 >> *Look for the area of your scanner driver that contains the settings for attaching profiles to your scans.*

Step 2 >> *Once in the settings or preference area locate the Color Settings defaults.*

Step 3 >> *Activate the scanner's Color Management features and then select the profile to attach.*

Monitors and screens

Now let's turn our attention to our screen or monitor. Most manufacturers these days supply a general ICC profile for their monitors that installs with the driver software when you first set up your screen. The default profile is generally the sRGB color space. If you want to check what profile is set for your monitor then Windows users will need to view the options in the Advanced settings of the Display control panel. If you are working on a Mac computer using OSX then you will find a similar group of settings in the Color section of the Display control panel which is located in the System Preferences.

At this stage, simply ensure that there is a profile allocated for your screen. In the following techniques I will show you how to create specific profiles for your screen using either the monitor calibration utility that comes with Elements, Adobe Gamma, or using a hardware tool called a Spyder.

Checking monitor profiles >> *Windows users can check the profile that is being used for the monitor via the Settings > Color Management section of the Display control panel. Mac OSX users will locate the default monitor profile in the Color section of the Display control panel.*

Step 1 >> *Windows users should select the Control Panel option from the Start menu.*

Step 2 >> *Click on the Display icon from those listed.*

Step 3 >> *Select the Settings tab and then the Advanced settings. Click Add to install a new profile.*

Image editing program – Photoshop Elements

In previous versions of the program Elements offered three options for color management – *No color management, Limited color management* and *Full color management.* Users could nominate the option that they wished to use for an editing session by clicking on a Radio button in the Color Settings dialog (Edit > Color Settings). To use a fully managed workflow you needed

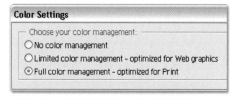

Checking Elements' color management >> *You can check the Color Management settings for Elements by selecting the Color Settings option from the Edit menu. Users of versions 1.0, 2.0 and 3.0 have three options.*

Book resources and video tutorials can be found at: **www.photoshopelements.net**

to pick the Full color management option as this is the only choice that made use of a complete ICC profile workflow.

From version 4.0 of Elements Adobe revamped the color management system to make it easier to understand and more logical to use. You now have four options to choose from in the Color Settings dialog. In addition to these settings you also have the ability to change the profile attached to your photo or even remove it totally.

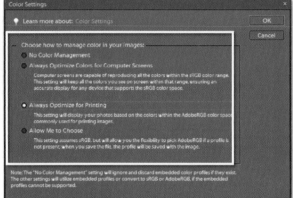

Color management options >> *Elements 4.0 introduced new color management options including clearer options in the Color Settings dialog and the ability to switch the profiles attached to photos.*

To ensure that Elements is operating with a color-managed workflow think about how you would normally view your work and then choose between Screen Optimized and Print Optimized options. If you need image-by-image control over what profile is used then select the Allow Me To Choose setting.

Options for Color Settings

No Color Management – This option leaves your image untagged, deletes attached profiles when opening images and doesn't add a profile when saving.

Always Optimize Colors For Computer Screens – Attaches sRGB to photos without a profile and uses sRGB as the working space but maintains any attached profiles when opening images.

Always Optimize For Printing – Attaches AdobeRGB to photos without a profile and uses AdobeRGB as the working space but maintains any attached profiles when opening images.

Allow Me To Choose – Maintains all attached profiles but allows the user to choose between sRGB and AdobeRGB when opening untagged files (Editor workspace only).

Missing Profile >> *When opening an untagged file after first having selected the Allow Me To Choose option in the Color Settings a new Missing Profile dialog is displayed. Here you can choose which profile is attached to the photo.*

Assigning rather than converting profiles

Selecting one of the options in the Image > Convert Color Profile menu will convert the picture's color to the selected color space. However, if you press Ctrl when selecting a new profile, it will apply the profile without converting. This gives the image the appearance that it has been converted but maintains the underlying colors of the original. This option is the same as Photoshop's Assign Profile command.

sRGB versus Adobe RGB

The two color space options available from Photoshop Elements 4.0 are widely used industry standards. AdobeRGB encompasses a range of colors (color gamut) that more closely matches the characteristics of both desktop and commercial printers, whereas sRGB is a profile that is very closely aligned with the gamut of the average computer screen. Choosing which profile to use as your standard will depend largely on what will be the final outcome of the majority of your work.

Printer

The photo quality of desktop printers is truly amazing. The fine detail and smooth graduation of vibrant colors produced is way beyond my dreams of even just a few short years ago. As the technology has developed, so too has the public's expectations. It is not enough to have colorful prints; now the digital photographer wants these hues to be closely matched with what is seen on screen. This is one of the reasons why a lot of printer manufacturers are now supplying generic, or 'canned', printer profiles. Using such profiles at the time of printing greatly increases the predictability of your output.

Step 1 >> *To set up the color management options for Elements choose Color Settings from the Edit menu.*

Step 2 >> *Choose Always Optimize for Printing from the options listed for a print-based ICC-managed workflow.*

To check that you have a printer profile installed on your system open the Color Management section of the printer driver and search the list of installed profiles for one that matches your machine. If one is not listed then check the manufacturer's website for the latest drivers or profile updates. The general nature of these profiles means that for most pictures, on most surfaces, you will get a good result, but for the best prints you will need a different set up for each paper stock that you use. Some manufacturers provide matched profiles for all the media they supply, which makes the job of choosing a suitable profile much easier. Later in this chapter I will show you how to customize your printer's output specifically for output on different speciality papers.

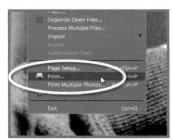

Step 1 >> *To check to see if you have a printer profile installed, open a picture in Elements and then select Print from the File menu.*

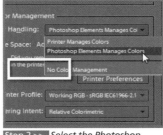

Step 2 >> *Select the Photoshop Elements Manages Color option in the Handling section of the dialog to display the printer profile settings.*

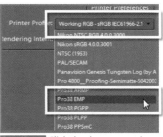

Step 3 >> *Click the down arrow in the Printer Profile section of the dialog and locate your printer profile.*

FINELY CRAFTED OUTPUT

13.05 Calibrating your screen – ColorVision Spyder

Suitable for Elements – 7.0, 6.0, 5.0, 4.0, 3.0, 2.0, 1.0 | Difficulty level – Intermediate
Related techniques – 13.04–13.08 | Tools used – ColorVision Spyder

The profile that is included with your screen drivers is based on the average characteristics of all the screens produced by the manufacturer. Individual screens will display slightly different characteristics even if they are from the same manufacturer and are the same model number. For this reason most professionals calibrate their screens with a combined hardware/software solution like the well-known Spyder from ColorVision (www.colorvision.com). Like the old Adobe Gamma utility that used to ship with Elements, the system will calibrate your screen so you can be sure that the images you are viewing on your monitor have accurate color, but unlike the Adobe Gamma this solution does not rely on your eyes for calibration accuracy.

Instead the ColorVision option uses a seven-filter colorimeter attached to the screen during the calibration process. This piece of hardware samples a range of known color and tone values that the software displays on screen. The sampled results are then compared to the known color values, the difference calculated and this information is then used to generate an accurate ICC profile for the screen. Unlike the Adobe Gamma approach this method does require the purchase of extra software and hardware but it does provide an objective way for the digital photographer to calibrate their screen. The ColorVision Spyder2 system works with both CRT (standard) and LCD (flat) screens.

Corrected monitor curves >> *ColorVision's Spyder2 provides a combined hardware and software solution that measures the inconsistency in a monitor's display and creates correction curves to account for it. (a) Uncalibrated curves. (b) Corrected red, green and blue curves.*

In previous versions of the program the calibration process contains two steps handled by two separate utilities:
1. *PreCAL*, which is used to set the white and black points of your screen as well as balance the red, green and blue components of the display, and
2. *OptiCAL*, designed to calibrate the screen and create a monitor profile that will ensure that colors and tones will be displayed accurately.
In the latest release these steps have been combined into a single step-by-step wizard.

Target settings for general digital photography:

Color temp. – 6500
Gamma – 2.2 (Windows)
Gamma – 1.8 (Mac)

Before you start...
1. Set the screen to 24-bit color and a resolution of at least 640 x 480 pixels or greater and ensure that the screen has warmed up for at least 30 minutes.
2. Make sure that you know how to change the Color, Contrast and Brightness settings of your monitor. This may be via dials or on-screen menus.
3. Ensure that no light source is shining on the screen during the calibration process.
4. Once the calibration process has started don't move the on-screen calibration window.

Step 1 >> *Start by selecting the display type that needs calibrating. Here I have chosen an LCD screen.*

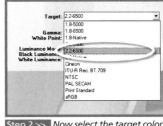

Step 2 >> *Now select the target color temperature and gamma from those listed in the drop-down menu.*

Step 3 >> *Choose the Luminance mode between Visual (single screen) and Measured (multiple screens).*

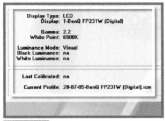

Step 4 >> *Review the Target Display settings to check that they are correct.*

Step 5 >> *Indicate which controls are present on the monitor.*

Step 6 >> *Return all settings to their factory default. Check with the monitor manual for instructions.*

Step 7 >> *Check that four separate white blocks can be seen in the scale. Adjust with the contrast control.*

Step 8 >> *Check that four separate black blocks can be seen in the scale. Adjust with the brightness control.*

Step 9 >> *Choose the way that the monitor adjusts color from the three options listed.*

Step 10 >> *Attach the Spyder and check to see that it is set up correctly for your screen type.*

Step 11 >> *Attach the Spyder to the monitor ensuring no other light sources are reflecting on screen.*

Step 12 >> *The sensor will initialize and then several colors will be displayed and tested.*

Step 13 >> *Adjust the individual Red, Green and Blue controls to balance the screen color.*

Step 14 >> *Press the Continue button and let the Spyder read the color and tone swatches displayed.*

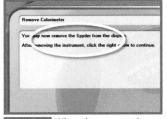

Step 15 >> *When the program is finished, save the new profile.*

Getting intimate with your printer

With the screen now well and truly calibrated and our scanner, camera and printer all ICC profiled terrific prints should be certain to follow, and in most cases this is true. But despite the use of a fully profiled system there are still those annoying occasions where the print doesn't meet our expectations. As long as you keep to standard papers and paper surfaces these occasions won't be too frequent, but the more that you experiment with different paper types and finishes the more you will be presented with unexpected results.

The culprit is the generic print profile supplied with your machine. By definition it is designed to provide good results with average images, surfaces and paper types. For those of you who want a little more than 'average' results you can fine-tune your printer profile for different paper and surface types.

As was the case with screens, here too we have a couple of different approaches. The first makes use of the extra color controls hidden away in the printer driver to modify your output and the second uses another ColorVision hardware/software solution to create separate print profiles for each paper type and surface that you use.

13.06 Calibrating your printer – resolution, color, tone and sharpness tests

Suitable for Elements – 7.0, 6.0, 5.0, 4.0, 3.0, 2.0, 1.0 | Difficulty level – Intermediate
Resources – Web text images 13.06-1, 13.06-2 | Related techniques – 13.04–13.08

Good prints are made from good images and, as we know from previous chapters, digital image quality is based on high image resolution and high bit depth. Given this scenario, it would follow that if I desire to make the best prints possible, then I should at first create pictures with massive pixel dimensions and huge numbers of colors. The problem is that such files take up loads of disk space and, due to their size, they are very, very slow to work with, to the point of being practically impossible to edit on most desktop machines.

The solution is to find a balance between image quality and file size that still produces 'good prints'. For the purposes of this book 'good prints' are defined as those that appear photographic in quality and can be considered visually 'pixel-less'. As we have also seen the quality of all output is governed by a combination of the printer mechanism, the ink set used and the paper, or media, the image is printed on. To find the balance that works best for your printer set up and the various papers that you use, you will need to perform a couple of simple tests with your printer.

Quality printing >> *Quality printing is based on paper, ink and machine all working together. Changing any of these components can alter the color, shadow, highlight or midtone rendition of the print. For the best control different set ups or profiles are necessary for each of the paper/ink/printer combinations you work with.*

Testing tones

There are 256 levels of tones in each channel (red, green and blue) of a 24-bit digital image. A value of 0 is pure black and a value of 255 is pure white. Desktop inkjet machines do an admirable job of printing most of these tones but they do have trouble printing delicate highlight (values of between 230 and 255) and shadow (values between 0 and 40) details. The absorbency of the paper in combination with the inkset and the printer settings means that some machines will be able to print all 256 levels of tones whilst others will

Quality printing >> *When using some paper, ink and printer combinations delicate highlight and shadow details are lost. Being able to account for these output characteristics makes for better prints. (a) Lost highlights. (b) Lost shadows.*

only be able to output a smaller subset. Being able to predict and account for lost shadow and highlight tones will greatly improve your overall print quality.

To test your own printer/ink/paper set up make a stepped grayscale that contains separate tonal strips from 0 to 255 in approximately five-tone intervals. Alternatively, download the example grayscale from the book's website (www.photoshopelements.net). Print the grayscale using the best quality settings for the paper you are using. Examine the results. In particular, check to see at what point it becomes impossible to distinguish dark gray tones from pure black and light gray values from white. Note these values down for later use as they represent the range of tones printable by your printer/paper/ink combination.

Step 1 >> *Download and print the tone-test.jpg image using your favorite settings and paper type.*

Step 2 >> *Examine the print after 30 minutes drying time to locate the values where you cannot distinguish shadow and highlight detail.*

Step 3 >> *Input these values as the black and white output points in the Levels dialog when next printing with this paper, ink and printer combination.*

When you are next adjusting the levels of an image to be printed, move the Output sliders at the bottom of the dialog until black and white points are set to those you found in your test. The spread of tones in your image will now meet those that can be printed by your printer/paper/ink combination.

Step 1 >> *Create a high-resolution composite image and print the picture at several different image-resolution settings.*

Step 2 >> *When complete examine the prints carefully and decide which picture provides the best balance of quality and resolution.*

Step 3 >> *Use this image resolution as the basis of your prints using this ink, paper and printer combination.*

Testing resolution

Modern printers are capable of incredible resolution. Some are able to output discrete dots at a rate of almost 6000 per inch. Many users believe that to get the utmost detail in their prints they must match this printer resolution with the same image resolution. Although this seems logical, good results can be achieved where one pixel is printed with several printer dots. Thank goodness this is the case, because the result is lower resolution images and therefore more manageable, and smaller, file sizes. But the question still remains – exactly what image resolution should be used?

Again a simple test can help provide a practical answer. Create a high-resolution file with good sharp detail throughout. Using Image > Resize > Image Size make a series of 10 pictures from 1000 dpi to 100 dpi reducing in resolution by a factor of 100 each time. Alternatively download the resolution examples from the book's website. Now print each of these pictures at the optimum setting for your machine, ink and paper you normally use. Next examine each image carefully. Find the lowest resolution image where the picture still appears photographic. This is the minimum image resolution that you should use if you want your output to remain photographic quality. For my set up this setting varies from between 200 and 300 dpi. I know if I use these values I can be guaranteed good results without using massive file sizes.

Testing color

For the majority of output scenarios, using the ICC profile that came with your printer will provide good results. If you do happen to strike problems where images that appear neutral on screen continually print with a dominant cast then most printer drivers contain an area where individual colors can be changed to eliminate casts.

Step 1 >> *Print a full color test image using the Tonal and Resolution values derived in the two previous tests.*

Step 2 >> *Assess the color of the dominant cast and with the printer driver open, alter the color settings to remove the cast. Save the settings.*

Step 3 >> *Reprint the example image using the new color settings. Assess the results and make adjustments if necessary.*

Wayward color casts often occur when non-standard papers are used for printing. The cause can be the base color of the paper itself, the absorbency of the paper or the type of surface being printed upon. Eliminating all-over casts is possible using the Color Adjustment sliders found in the Printer dialog.

Determine the exact settings you need for a specific paper type by running a series of print tests, carefully adjusting the color settings until the resultant output is cast-free. Save the corrective settings for use whenever you want to output using the same paper, ink and printer combination.

Removing color casts with the printer driver >>
Use the following guide when customizing the output from your printer using the color sliders in your printer driver:

- *To subtract red from the print – add cyan*
- *To add red to a print – subtract cyan*
- *To add blue to a print – subtract yellow*
- *To subtract blue from a print – add yellow*
- *To add green to a print – subtract magenta*
- *To subtract green – add magenta*

Testing sharpness

Often overlooked but definitively just as important is the amount of sharpness that is applied to the photo. Unfortunately most image-makers apply a standard degree of sharpening to all their photos irrespective of the final printed size, subject matter and the stock that they will be reproduced upon. And just like other settings when it comes to sharpness, one size definitely does not fit all.

To find what works best for your set up, copy an indicative section of you image and duplicate it several times (at 100%) in a new document. Open the Adjust Sharpness filter selecting each duplicate in turn and filtering the picture part using successively more aggressive settings. Note down each of the settings for use later. Now print the test file using the same set up that you use for making final prints. Carefully examine the printed results using the same lighting conditions and viewing distance that will be used to display the print and select the best overall sharpness. This part of the process is pretty subjective but most viewers can pick over- and under-sharpened images when confronted with several versions of the same image sharpened to different degrees, making the task of selecting the best sharpness much easier. Now to apply the sharpness to the original print photo. Rather than applying the filter directly to the document it is best to sharpen a copy and save this duplicate with a name that includes it's intended outcome, i.e. 'portrait-A3-Epson2400-sharpened'.

13.07 Calibrating your printer – ColorVision PrintFIX

Suitable for Elements – 7.0, 6.0, 5.0, 4.0, 3.0, 2.0, 1.0 | Difficulty level – Intermediate
Related techniques – 13.04–13.08 | Tools used – ColorVision PrintFIX

Want to take your printer calibration one step further? The dream printing set up for most photographers is a situation where they have a profile created specifically for each of their paper, ink and printer combinations. Until recently this way of working has indeed been a dream, as the hardware and software system needed for creating high quality printer profiles could cost well over $1800. But ColorVision (www.colorvision.com) now produces a more economical option designed specifically for the digital photographer. Just like the Spyder, ColorVision's PrintFIX comprises a hardware and software solution that takes the guesswork out of calibrating your printer's output. The process involves three easy steps (illustrated below):

(a) Output a set of color test patches from your printer using the ink and paper you want to calibrate,
(b) Read the patches using a modified scanner supplied with the system, and
(c) Use the supplied calibration utility to generate an ICC printer profile based on the scanner output.

Using this system you can build a complete set of profiles for all the papers that you use regularly. The system saves you time and money by reducing the waste normally associated with getting the perfect print on varying paper stock.

PrintFIX print settings

Elements' Print dialog:
- *Source Space Document – Document*
- *Print Space Profile – the one you create with PrintFIX*
- *Print Space Intent – Saturation*

Printer Driver dialog:
- *Color – No Color Adjustment*
- *Paper – Enhanced Matte or Photo Quality Ink Jet*

Step 1 >> *Select the PrintFIX option from the Automation Tools section of the File menu.*

Step 2 >> *Choose the Load Calibration Chart option and then select the printer model in the PrintFIX dialog.*

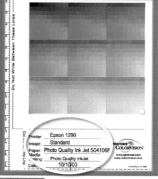

Step 3 >> *Input the details into the spaces provided on the test print image.*

Book resources and video tutorials can be found at: **www.photoshopelements.net**

Step 4 >> *In the Printer Profile menu choose a profile that is the same as the source profile.*

Step 5 >> *Proceed to the printer driver and choose Photo Quality Ink Jet paper.*

Step 6 >> *Select 'No Color Management' and choose the Print Quality required. Print the test.*

Step 1 >> *Wait 5 minutes for drying then cut out the test print, insert it in the plastic sleeve and preload it into the scanner.*

Step 2 >> *Select the PrintFIX option from the Import section of the File menu.*

Step 3 >> *Set scanner for Color, 400 dpi, 0% Brightness and Contrast, 2 Gamma, 255 Highlight and 0 Shadow. Click Read.*

Step 1 >> *Use the Cropping tool to isolate the color patches from the rest of the scan.*

Step 2 >> *Select PrintFIX from the Automation Tools options and select Build Profile.*

Step 3 >> *Save the finished ICC printer profile using a name that combines printer, paper and inkset.*

13.08 Making great black and white prints

Suitable for Elements – 7.0, 6.0, 5.0, 4.0, 3.0, 2.0, 1.0 | Difficulty level – Intermediate
Resources – Web image 13.08 | Menus used – File

Photography has had a long history of fine black and white print making. Practitioners like the famed Ansel Adams took the craft to dizzy heights, inventing the Zone system along the way. It wasn't too long ago that digital prints were judged not by their visual quality but by their ability to disguise their pixel origins. Thankfully, shooting and printing technology has improved to such an extent that we are now released from the 'guess if I'm digital' game to concentrate on more important things, like making great images. After all, this is the reason that most of us got into photography in the first place. But producing high quality black and white prints digitally, even with a fully color-managed system, does have its problems. In my experience making great monochrome prints relies heavily on choosing the right paper and inks to print with.

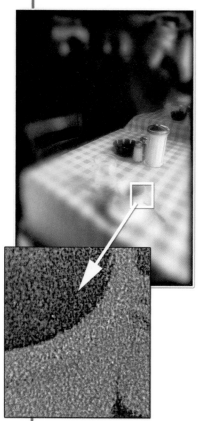

Black and white in color >>
When printing a black and white image using a standard inkjet printer many of the gray tones are produced using a combination of colored ink droplets.

Choosing paper and inks

There is now an incredible range of papers and inks that are suitable for use in desktop printers. The combination you choose will determine the 'look and feel' of your prints. One of the first things that screams quality is the type of stock that your images are printed on. Fiber-based papers have always held a special place within the photographic community. Images produced on this type of paper ooze quality and demand respect. Professionals and amateurs alike take a lot of time, and spend a lot of money, choosing the right paper for their photographs.

Selecting which paper to use when you are digital printing is no different. Surface, weight and base tint should all be carefully considered and tested before making your final decision. The papers supplied by your printer manufacturer provide the easiest way to obtain predictable and reliable quality output. The surfaces of these papers are often specially designed to work in conjunction with the inks themselves to ensure the best balance of archival stability and image quality. But this is not the limit of your choices; there is a myriad of other papers available from photographic companies such as Kodak and Ilford as well as paper manufacturers like Somerset. Often specialist suppliers will sell you a sample pack containing several paper types so that you can test the papers that work best for you.

There are also decisions to be made about the inks to use to make your prints. The cartridges supplied and recommended by your printer's manufacturer are specifically designed to work in conjunction with your machinery. These ink sets provide the quickest way to get great photo-realistic images. But along with standard four- or five-color inksets you now also have a choice of printers that make use of multiple

Yellow/green shadows

Blue/cyan highlights

CMYK ink set

Multi-black Neutral ink set

Neutral grays >> *Because many of the gray tones in a monochrome print are created with colored dyes it can be almost impossible to produce completely neutral tones throughout the whole of a grayscale when printing with standard ink sets. Neutral grays are possible, however, if the black and white print is produced using a dedicated multi-black ink set.*

blacks (black plus varying shades of gray) as well as cyan, magenta and yellow (CMY). The midtone and light gray inks are used to create the tones in monochrome pictures and replace the colored dots that have previously been employed for the same job. Using this approach, digital photographers can produce the rich and smoothly graduated monochrome output they have preciously created traditionally, without any of the problems of strange and unwanted color casts creeping into their black and white prints.

Why use monochrome inks?

Most photo-quality inkjets use the three colored inks as well as black to produce monochromes. Using the four inks (sometimes six – five colors plus black) provides the greatest range of tonal levels. With dot sizes now being so small it is only under the closest scrutiny that the multi-colored matrix that lies beneath our black and white prints is revealed. Balancing the different colors so that the final appearance is neutral is a very tricky task. Too many dots of one color and a gray will appear blue, too few and it will contain a yellow hue. For most users slight color variations are not a problem, but for image-makers with a monochrome heritage to protect, nothing less than perfection is acceptable.

Too often the black and white prints produced using a color ink set contain strange color casts. For the most part these errant hues are the consequence of mixing different ink types and paper products and can be rectified with a little tinkering of the printer driver's color settings or by using a custom-made profile. One paper I use, for instance, continually presents me with magenta-tinged black and white prints. But as the cast is consistent across the whole of the tonal range, I am able to rid the pictures of this tint by adjusting the Magenta/Green slider in the printer settings. I saved the set up that produced a neutral image and now use it each time I print to this surface.

ADVANCED PHOTOSHOP ELEMENTS 7 FOR DIGITAL PHOTOGRAPHERS

Paper types >>

There are many papers on the market that are suitable for inkjet printing. Most can be divided into two groups – 'coated' and 'uncoated'. The coating is a special ink receptive layer that increases the paper's ability to produce sharp 'photo-realistic' results with a wide color gamut and a rich maximum black (high D-max). Uncoated papers can still be used with most printing equipment but changes in the printing set up may be necessary to get good results.

Apart from coatings, paper surface is the other major factor that discriminates between paper types. The general categories of surface are:

Glossy Photographic – Designed for the production of the best quality photographic images. These papers are usually printed at the highest resolution that your printer is capable of and can produce either 'photo-realistic' or highly saturated colors.

Matt/Satin Photographic – Papers designed for photographic images but with surfaces other than gloss. Surfaces specially coated so that, like the gloss papers, they can retain the finest details and the best color rendition and often produce the best archival results.

Art Papers – Generally thicker based papers with a heavy tooth or texture. Some coated products in this grouping are capable of producing photographic quality images, but all have a distinct 'look and feel' that can add subtle interest to images with subject matter that is conducive. Unlike other groups this range of papers also contains examples that contain colored bases or tinted surfaces.

General Purpose – Papers that combine economy and good print quality and are designed for general usage. Different to standard office or copy papers as they have a specially treated surface designed for inkjet inks. Not recommended for final prints but offer proofing possibilities.

Specialty Papers – Either special in surface or function. This grouping contains papers that you might not use often but it's good to know that on the occasion that you do need them they are available. The range in this area is growing all the time and now includes such diverse products as magnetic paper, back light films and a selection of metallic sheets.

It is not these consistent casts that cause much concern amongst the critical desktop printing fraternity, rather it is the way that some printers produce a different cast for highlights and shadows. As we have seen already in this chapter, as part of my printer set up procedure I always output a grayscale to help me determine how the machine handles the spread of tones from highlights to shadows. The test prints remain fairly neutral when they are made with the manufacturer's recommended papers, but as soon as I start to use different stock, the gray tonal scale ceases to be so gray. For the occasional print, I can put up with the strange colors present in my black and white masterpiece, but for the dedicated monochrome producer it is enough to send them screaming back to the darkroom. Well almost!

Specialist ink sets – the solution for monochrome printing

With just this type of situation in mind several of the bigger printer manufacturers are now producing specialist machines that are much more suited to monochrome printing. The system they use is simple – rather than trying to create grays from three or more colors, these printers use extra gray inks for the task. So, in addition to the standard colors – CMY, the manufacturers have added in extra gray inks to create a seven- or even eight-color cartridge. All gray inks are derived from the same pigment base as the black, so prints made with these cartridges contain no strange color casts. That's right, no color casts! That's no overall magenta tint with my favorite paper, or strange color changes in the shadows and highlights of my grayscales.

Printing with a specialist monochrome printer is the closest thing to making finely-crafted fiber-based prints that the digital world has to offer. Not only are your images cast-free, they also display an amazing range of grays. With pictures that have been carefully adjusted to spread image tones and retain shadow and highlight details, the multi-black system produces unparalleled quality prints on a wide range of gloss, satin, matt and fine-art stock.

Not all inks are created equal. Different printers use different inks sets, which in turn have their own characteristics. They generally fall into two categories:

Dye-based Inks – Most standard cartridges use this type of ink. They are generally easy to use with fewer problems with streaking, long drying times and puddling than pigmented inks. Some varieties are also capable of a greater range of colors.

Pigment-based Inks – These products last longer than most dye-based inks. They are also more water resistant. But be warned, these ink sets can be more difficult to print with and some particular brands do not have the same color or density range as their dye-based equivalents.

13.09 What about permanence?

Suitable for Elements – 7.0, 6.0, 5.0, 4.0, 3.0, 2.0, 1.0
Difficulty level – Intermediate

So with the availability of such great products that produce fantastic images most photographers believe that we are living in Desktop Printing Nirvana. To some extent this is true. The tools for the creation of great looking prints are well within the reach of most of us, but the youth of the technology in conjunction with our haste to embrace all that is digital, has us forgetting, or at the very least overlooking, some of the lessons of the past. Many photographic enthusiasts still see the 1950s, 60s and 70s as golden years of print production. Then, just like now, countless image-makers were taking control of the print production process by setting up their own darkrooms and churning out high quality black and white prints.

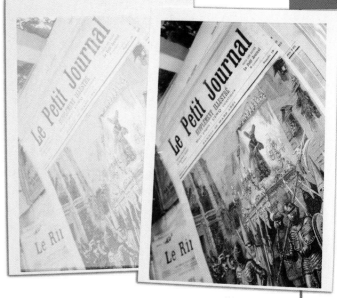

The print emerges from the machine crisp, clean and brilliantly colored but in as little as a few weeks of standard display the same image is no more than a faded ghost of its former self. Image permanence is the hidden quality factor to consider when choosing a print system.

The best crafted prints made during this period exhibit many of the characteristics we still value today. They are sharp, show good gradation and exhibit an exceptional range of gray tones, from deep blacks through to delicate highlights. In addition to the presence of these obvious image-quality characteristics, many of the prints made in this period also boast exceptional permanence characteristics. Put simply, if well cared for, these prints will last a long time, no make that a very long time, with little or no fading. Much time and effort was spent by companies and practitioners alike establishing archival print processing systems that would ensure that the images we created would last a lifetime. It was against this historical background that the first color print processes were introduced and, more recently, the first digital print systems invented.

New doesn't always mean better

In embracing these new printing possibilities it seems that sharpness, gradation and gamut were held up as the quality characteristics to be cherished and poor old permanence 'faded' into the background. For a few rocky years image-makers were teased with the release of new printer models that boasted better resolution, tonal gradation and color gamut, but these advances were coupled with permanence characteristics that were well short of expectations. Thankfully this is no longer the case. All the major printer companies have spent the last few years chipping away at the print permanence issue and now we are blessed with a range of machines that not only produce a great looking print but also one that will last.

Print systems are more than a sum of their parts

By combining specialist inksets with matched papers and customized print heads, companies like Epson and Hewlett Packard have been able to achieve substantial increases in the projected life of their prints, without sacrificing the other image qualities that we all hold so dear. This revolution started in the high end or pro range of printers but now has filtered down to entry level machines. Permanence ratings beyond four score years is now a regular occurrence, with several ink, paper, printer combinations breaking the 100 year barrier.

The extended print life is directly related to the interaction of the matched papers and inks. Despite what you read in advertising campaigns, or even on the packets of ink and paper produced by third-party vendors, not all inks and paper combinations will provide this same level of permanence. Sure, the print might look the same when it exits the machine with sharpness, color, tonal range and brightness all equivalent to a photo produced with OEM (Original Equipment Manufacturer) supplied materials, but it is only further down the track that the differences in permanence become apparent. So if the image quality is comparable for photos produced with a variety of inks and paper combinations (both OEM and third-party) how do we tell if a print is going to last the distance? By testing its permanence.

Testing permanence

Thankfully the major players in the world of inkjet printing markets, Epson, Hewlett Packard, Canon and Lexmark also uphold permanence as a key component of print quality. Over the last few years these companies have been instrumental in improving the longevity of their own print systems. In addition they have taken the permanence bull by the horns and have been testing the life of their products and publishing these results so the consumer can make informed decisions about their purchases.

But judging print permanence is a tricky proposal. After all how do you really know how long a print will last unless you are there to view it after the 100-year predicated life? Most industry-based tests are predictions based on light, humidity and temperature levels of an average display location. Rather than expose the print to these variables over a long period the photos are given a shorter exposure to a much brighter light source and the results then extrapolated back to the standard viewing conditions. With these results it is possible for manufacturers to predict the performance of individual printer, ink and paper combinations and for consumers to have confidence in the longevity of the prints they make.

Comparing 'apples with apples'

Most manufacturers have settled on average display light levels of between 450 or 500 lux per 12-hour day as the basis of their predicated permanence ratings. I say most because there are still some players in the third-party media and ink market who either don't publish their permanence findings at all or who use lower daily light exposure values to generate higher-

How long will my prints last?

Photo printers				
Epson PictureMate Personal Photo Lab	Inkjet	Pigment	PictureMate included with cartridge	104 years
Epson Stylus Photo R1800	Inkjet	Pigment	Epson matt paper heavyweight	>150 years
			Epson Glossy Photo paper	104 years
Epson Stylus Photo R800	Inkjet	Pigment	Epson matt paper heavyweight	>150 years
			Epson Glossy Photo paper	104 years
Epson Stylus Photo R300	Inkjet	Dye	Epson ColorLife Photo Paper	36 years
			Epson matt paper heavyweight	30 years
Epson Stylus Pro 9800	Inkjet	Pigment	Epson Premium Gloss Photo paper	85 years
			Epson Ultrasmooth Fine Art paper	108 years
Epson Stylus Pro 2100	Inkjet	Pigment	Epson Premium Gloss Photo paper	85 years
			Epson Ultrasmooth Fine Art paper	108 years
Epson Stylus Pro 2000p	Inkjet	Pigment	Epson Premium Semi-Gloss Photo Paper	>100 years
			Epson Enhanced (Archival) Matt Paper	>100 years
Hewlett Packard Photosmart 8750	Inkjet	Dye	HP Premium Plus Photo Paper High Gloss	108 years
			HP Premium Plus Photo Paper Soft Gloss	108 years
Hewlett Packard Designjet 130	Inkjet	Dye	HP Premium Plus Photo and Proofing Gloss	82 years
			HP Premium Plus Photo Paper Soft Gloss	82 years
HP Photosmart 325 and 375 Compact Photo Printers	Inkjet	Dye	HP Premium Plus	82 years
			HP Premium Photo High Gloss	82 years
Olympus p-10 Digital Photo Printer	Dye-sub	Dye-sub ribbon	Dye-sub paper	8 years
Canon S800 Photo Printer	Inkjet	Dye	Canon Photo Paper Pro	27 years
Kodak Edge Generations/Royal Generations papers	Traditional photo	Color couplers	Silver halide paper	19 years
Agfacolor Sensatis/Splendex Paper	Traditional photo	Color couplers	Silver halide paper	22 years
Fuji Crystal Archive type one paper	Traditional photo	Color couplers	Silver halide paper	40 years

*How were the tests conducted?

All print permanence ratings detailed here are drawn from data provided by the Wilhelm Imaging Research. The full articles and information sheets from which the information is extracted can be accessed via the company's website – www. wilhelm-research.com. These ratings are based on accelerated light stability tests conducted at 35 Klux with glass-filtered cool white fluorescent illumination with the air temperature maintained at 24°C and 60% humidity. Data was extrapolated to a display condition of 450 lux for 12 hours per day using the Wilhelm Imaging Research 'Visually Weighted End Point Criteria' and represents years of display for easily noticeable fading, changes in color balance and/or staining to occur.

FINELY CRAFTED OUTPUT

predicted print life figures. As you can expect, this leads to much confusion when it comes time to purchase media and inks, with claims and counter claims of predicted print life featuring prominently on packaging of competing products.

To solve this problem many companies submit their products for testing and evaluation to Wilhelm Imaging Research, a well-respected independent testing company, to provide comparative results produced under the same stringent conditions. This process has worked quite successfully for the last few years with consumers 'in the know' seeking out the valuable testing results that are freely published on the company's website – www.wilhelm-research.com. The information is then used to inform print system purchasing decisions or provide data about predicted life expectancy of specific printer, ink and paper combinations.

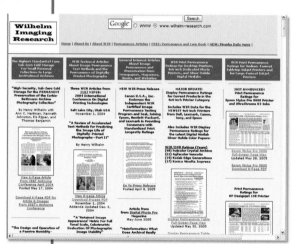

Testing print life >> *Wilhelm Imaging Research, Inc. (www. wilhelm-research.com), conducts research on the stability and preservation of traditional and digital color photographs and motion pictures. The company publishes brand name-specific permanence data for desktop and large format inkjet printers and other digital printing devices.*

Henry Wilhelm is co-founder, President, and Director of Research at Wilhelm Imaging Research, Inc. and appears frequently as a speaker on inkjet printing technologies and print permanence at industry conferences, trade shows, and museum conservation meetings.

In 2005 Epson, Hewlett-Packard, Canon and Lexmark endorsed the Wilhelm Imaging Research independent permanence testing program which provides consumers with standardized print longevity ratings.

The WIR certification program

Taking the idea further, in 2005 the top four manufacturers of inkjet printers, inks, and inkjet photo papers worldwide – Epson, Hewlett-Packard, Canon and Lexmark – endorsed an independent image permanence testing program that includes a certified seal for print and ink packaging. With testing data supplied by the Wilhelm Imaging Research center the WIR certification program will provide customers with standardized print longevity ratings. The program has three components:

(1) *The WIR Certified Tests* – A comprehensive set of test methods developed by Wilhelm Imaging Research to evaluate image permanence,
(2) *WIR Test Data* – Permanence data generated with the WIR Certified Tests, and
(3) *The WIR Seal* – Signifies that the product has been tested by WIR, and that detailed image permanence data is available on the WIR website.

The standardized image permanence test methods and specifications undertaken by WIR provide consumers throughout the world with 'apples-to-apples' comparisons for a wide range of inks and photo papers. The testing program and associated seal will help us all differentiate between printer manufacturers' papers that have been optimized for that company's inks, and third-party and store-label 'universally compatible' papers that may use less demanding test methods or supply no image permanence information at all about this critical – but initially hidden – aspect of total product quality. For example, WIR gave one leading third-party inkjet paper a WIR Display Permanence Rating of 11 years when printed with an HP printer and the HP No. 57 inkjet cartridge. The paper's manufacturer rated the display life of the same paper at 162 years by using far less rigorous tests, with 120 lux UV-filtered illumination and measurements made at only a single density point rather than the two that is the standard with the WIR tests.

To qualify for use of the Seal, a product must have a minimum WIR Display Permanence Rating of 25 years and a WIR Album/Dark Storage Rating at least equal to the display rating. Complete results and details of WIR test methods are available at www.wilhelm-research.com. You will start to see the WIR seal appearing on the packaging of your favourite print products over the coming months but until then, for the latest information on print permanence, check out the WIR website.

13.10 Preparing your images for professional outsourcing
Suitable for Elements – 7.0, 6.0, 5.0, 4.0, 3.0, 2.0, 1.0 | Difficulty level – Intermediate

Professional lab services are now expanding into the production of large and very large prints using the latest inkjet and piezo technology as well as digital images on color photographic paper. Now that you are part of the digital fraternity you too have the choice of outputting your humble Photoshop Elements images on these 'big printing beasts'.

Outputting to color print paper via machines like the Lambda and Pegasus has quickly become the 'norm' for a lot of professional photographers. Adjusting of image files that print well on desktop inkjets so that they cater for the idiosyncrasies of these RA4 machines is a skill that most of us are continuing to learn. The re-education is definitely worth it – with image quality and archival permanence of our digitally generated imagery finally meeting that of traditional prints as well as the expectations of photographers and their clients. But just when you thought that you could become complacent with your new skills the wide format printing market has really started to take off.

With improved quality, speed and competition in the area, the big players like Epson, Kodak and Hewlett Packard are manufacturing units that are capable of producing images that are not only stunning, but also very, very big. Pictures up to 54 inches wide can be made on some of the latest machines, with larger images possible by splicing two or more panels together. You can now walk into a bureau with a CD containing a favorite image and walk out the same day with a spliced polyester poster printed with fade-resistant all-weather inks the size of a billboard. Not that everyone wants their output that big but the occasional poster print is now a very real option.

Getting the set up right is even more critical with large format printing than when you are outputting to a desktop machine. A small mistake here can cause serious problems to both your 48 x 36 inch masterpiece as well as your wallet, so before you even turn on your computer talk to a few local professionals. Most output bureaus are happy to help prospective customers with advice and usually supply a series of guidelines that will help you set up your images to suit their printers. These may be contained in a pack available with a calibration profile over the counter, or might be downloadable from the company's website. Some companies will check that your image meets their requirements before printing, others will dump the unopened file directly to the printer's RIP assuming that all is well. So make sure that you are aware of the way the bureau works before making your first print.

Outsourcing guidelines

The following guidelines have been compiled from the suggestions of several output bureaus. They constitute a good overview but cannot be seen as a substitute for talking to your own lab directly.

Ensure that the image is orientated correctly. Some printers are set up to work with a portrait or vertical image by default; trying to print a landscape picture on these devices will result in areas of white space above and below the picture and the edges being cropped.

Make sure the image is the same proportion as the paper stock. This is best achieved by making an image with the canvas the exact size required and then pasting your picture into this space.

Don't use crop marks. Most printers will automatically mark where the print is to be cropped. Some bureaus

will charge to remove your marks before printing.

Convert a layered image to a flat file before submission. Most output bureaus will not accept layered PSD (Photoshop Elements) files so make sure that you save a flattened copy of the completed image to pass on to the lab.

Use the resolution suggested by the lab. Most output devices work best with an optimal resolution. Large format inkjet printers are no different. The lab technician will be able to give you details of the best resolution to supply your images in. Using a higher or lower setting than this will alter the size that your file prints, so stick to what is recommended.

Use the file format recommended by the lab. The amount of time spent in setting up a file ready to print is a big factor in the cost of outsourced

printing. Supplying your file in the wrong format will either cost you more, as a lab technician will need to spend time converting the picture, or will have your print job rejected altogether.

Keep file sizes under the printer's maximum. The bigger the file, the longer it takes to print. Most bureaus base their costings on a maximum file size. You will need to pay extra if your image is bigger than this value.

Watch out for fancy fonts. Elements does not have 'preflight' features to ensure that all fonts associated with the document are included when submitted. So if you supply a PSD file to a printer and they do not have the same fonts on their system that you used in your picture they will get a message about updating fonts when the document is opened. To avoid this only supply flattened files in TIFF or JPEG formats.

13.11 Shoot small print big

Suitable for Elements – 7.0, 6.0, 5.0, 4.0, 3.0, 2.0, 1.0 | Difficulty level – Intermediate | Menus used – Image

You know the scenario. You hand over what in a lot of countries amounts to a year's salary for a snazzy new digital camera with all the bells and whistles and a modest three megapixel sensor only to be told by someone like me in the preceding chapters of this book that you can now print great photo-quality images – but only up to 10 x 8 inches. Wrong, Wrong, Wrong.

The thinking behind such a statement is sound. As we saw earlier in this chapter the recommended image resolution for most inkjet and professional digital output is between 200 and 400 dots per inch. So if we divide the pixel dimensions of the sensor the recommended resolution for inkjet output (200 dots per inch) we will get the maximum print size possible. For example, if we divide an image produced by a chip that is 2000 x 1600 pixels by a resolution of 200 dpi then the maximum print would be 10 x 8 inches. If a higher resolution of 400 dpi was used then the final print size would be reduced to a mere 5 x 4 inches. Right? Wrong!

In truth, this is still the way to achieve the absolute best quality from your digital files. But for the average camera owner the promise of superb image quality is no consolation if all you want is a bigger print. When faced with this problem those 'non-professional' shooters amongst us have been happily upscaling their images using the Resample option in the Image Size feature of Elements, whilst those of us who obviously 'know better' have been running around with small, but beautifully produced, prints. After all it is common knowledge that increasing the numbers of pixels in an image by resampling or 'interpolating' the original data can only lead to unsharp, and more importantly, unacceptable, albeit large, pictures. Right! Well, sort of!

What is interpolation anyway?

Interpolation is a process by which extra pixels are generated in a low-resolution image so that it can be printed at a larger size than its original dimensions would normally allow. Interpolation, or as it is sometimes called, Upsizing, can be implemented by increasing the number of pixels in the width and height fields of the Photoshop Elements Image > Resize > Image Size dialog.

This approach works by sampling a group of pixels (a 4 x 4 matrix in case of Bicubic interpolation) and using this information together with a special algorithm as a basis for generating the values for newly created pixels that will be added to the image.

The sophistication of the algorithm and the size of the sampling set determine the quality of the interpolated results.

The interpolated results are never as sharp or clear as an image made with the correct pixel dimensions to start with, but when you need a big print from a small file this is a great way to go.

Interpolated big prints >> *To create big prints images can be resized in Elements using the Image Size dialog (Image > Resize > Image Size). (a) Original test print 5.3 x 3.2 inches. (b) Interpolated print 32 x 24 inches.*

Quietly over the last few years and right under our very noses it seems, a small revolution in refinement has been happening in the area of interpolation technologies. The algorithms and processes used to apply them have been continuously increasing in quality until now they are at such a point that the old adages such as • *Sensor dimension / output resolution = maximum print size* don't always apply. With the Bicubic option set in the Image Size dialog it is now possible to take comparatively small files and produce truly large prints of great quality. This process, often called interpolation or upscaling, artificially increases the number of pixels in an image so that with more image data in hand, bigger prints can be made.

Upscaling techniques

So what are the steps involved in increasing the size of my pictures. Here I will demonstrate two approaches to upscaling. The first is the simplest and involves inputting new values into Image Size dialog (a) and the second, called Stair Interpolation (b), uses the same technique but increases the size of the picture incrementally rather than in one jump. Stair Interpolation is the preferred approach by many professionals, who believe that the process provides sharper end results. Both approaches use the Image Size dialog and are based on the Bicubic interpolation option.

From version 4.0 several changes were made in the Image Size dialog and its options:
1. The Resample Image option is NOT checked by default when you first open the dialog;
2. Bicubic Smoother (for upscaling) and Bicubic Sharper (for downscaling) options have been added to the drop-down menu of resampling methods;
3. A Scale Styles option has been included to automatically adjust any styles present in the picture in proportion to any size changes made.

The results

In the example, image skin tones and other areas of graduated color handled the upsizing operation the best. Sharp-edged elements evident in the lash areas of the eyes and the straight lines of the buildings tended to show the results of the interpolation more clearly. Though not unacceptable at normal viewing distances for big-sized prints, image-makers whose work contains a lot of hard-edged visual elements and who rely on ultimate sharpness in these areas for effect will need to 'test to see' if the results are suitable for their style of images. For portrait, landscape and general shooters upscaling using either of the two approaches listed here is bound to surprise and excite.

Interpolation via Image Size >> *With Resample Image ticked and Bicubic selected input the new values into the Width or Height sections of the dialog. (a) Original file size. (b) Original pixel dimensions. (c) Original print size and resolution. (d) Resample Image option – tick to interpolate. (e) Select Bicubic (in version 4.0 and later pick Bicubic Smoother for upscaling and Bicubic Sharper for when reducing picture size) for quality. (f) Interpolated file size. (g) Interpolated pixel dimensions. (h) Interpolated print size and resolution.*

I still cringe saying it, but it is now possible to break the 'I must never interpolate my images rule' in order to produce more print area for the pixels you have available.

I will provide some provisos though:

1. Images captured with the correct number of pixels for the required print job will always produce better results than those that have been interpolated.

2. The softening effect that results from high levels of interpolation is less noticeable in pictures with general content such as landscape or portrait images and more apparent in images with sharp-edged elements.

3. The more detail and pixels in the original file the better the interpolated results will be, and a well-exposed sharply focused original file that is saved in a lossless format such as TIFF is the best candidate image for upsizing.

The improved Bicubic Smoother resampling option found in version 4.0, 5.0, 6.0 and 7.0 of the program provides great upscaling results without the need for incremental resampling.

Step 1 >> *With the image open in Elements select Image > Resize > Image Size.*

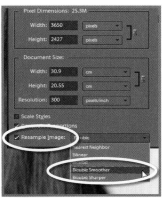

Step 2 >> *Tick Resample Image and choose the Bicubic Smoother option. Input the new values into the width and height areas.*

Step 1 >> *For Stair Interpolation start the process by opening the Image Size feature.*

Step 2 >> *This time select the percent option for Width and Height. Tick Resample Image and choose Bicubic.*

Step 3 >> *Input a value of 110% into the Width box and click OK. Open the Image Size dialog again.*

Step 4 >> *Input a value of 110% again and click OK. Continue this process until you reach your desired print size.*

13.12 Printing workflow

The key to producing good quality prints is knowing the characteristics of your printer. No printer is going to produce perfect results on all paper types with all images. Understanding the strengths and weaknesses of your machine will help you ensure predictable results more often. And the foundation of all such predication is a good color-management system.

Recommended Printing Workflow

Color-Management Set up	Use 'canned' screen profile supplied with monitor	Calibrate screen using ColorVision Spyder utility	
	Turn on Color Management in the Color Settings of Photoshop Elements and select between Screen or Print Optimized options		
	Activate camera color management		
	Activate scanner color management		
	Perform Resolution test to determine optimum image resolution needed to maintain photo-quality output		
	Load 'canned' printer profile that came with print driver	Use tone and color tests to modify 'canned' printer profile for all printer, ink and paper combinations	Use ColorVision PrintFIX to create ICC profile for all printer, ink and paper combinations
Printer Set up	Select correct media or paper type		
	Choose paper size and orientation		
	Select Quality Print setting	Select same settings used for printer tests	Select same settings that were used for ICC profile creation
	Check that 'canned' ICC profile is loaded		Load PrintFIX profile
Image Set up	Adjust image tones and colors to suit		
	Set image resolution to optimum determined from the Resolution test		
	Upscale small image if making big print (if necessary)		
	Apply Unsharp Mask filter		
Print Quality	Good	Better	Best

It may be implemented using the built-in features contained in your camera, scanner and printer controls in conjunction with the color-management system in Photoshop Elements or it may take a more sophisticated form relying on customized profiles generated with specialist products from companies like ColorVision.

Either way the important thing to remember is that you need to start thinking about image management right from the time that you shoot or scan.

If you want to enjoy all the rewards of high quality output then it is critical that you employ a holistic approach to color management.

Just as is the case with factors like resolution and bit depth, decisions about color management need to be made at the point of capture, not left until it comes time to print.

14

Extending
the Power
of Elements

Photoshop Elements and Photoshop Lightroom

It might seem a little strange talking about Photoshop Lightroom in a Photoshop Elements book, but the reality is that I have found more and more readers have started to use Lightroom as their image management, raw adjustment and output software and Elements as their editing tool of choice. Yes that is right, contrary to what you might have heard you can use Photoshop Elements as the 'linked' editor for Lightroom. For this reason it makes sense that Elements users who are wanting to stretch their imaging wings a little would see Lightroom as the next logical step.

Perfect partners >> *Many Photoshop Elements users see moving to Lightroom as a logical step in the progression of their editing skills, but such a move doesn't render Elements to the back room. Instead the program can be linked with Lightroom to perform the pixel editing tasks that are not possible in the Lightroom itself. All the editing skills built through time spent with Elements can then put to good use on Lightroom managed photos.*

Introducing Photoshop Lightroom – The ultimate in Raw control

It is true that Elements users can process raw files using the version of Adobe Camera Raw that ships with the program, but if you are a dedicated raw shooter, then you may find that you want a few more tools and features when processing your raw files. This is where Lightroom can help. Designed as a complete raw workflow product, the program is a deceptively simple product that feels like a well-designed and streamlined photographer's work tool.

The software is based around a workflow that includes the following modules:

Library – All image management starts with the Library module. Here you import your photos, arrange them in collections, add keywords, search your library or browse individual shots. All this activity is handled with the options in the left-hand panel, while in the workspace you can view your images in magnified Loupe mode, side-by-side Compare mode, the sorting Survey mode, or Grid mode.

Develop – The Develop module is the next step in the Lightroom workflow and is central to all enhancement changes that are applied to your photos. Just like when you are working in the Adobe Camera Raw dialog, the enhancement settings and controls are grouped in a panel on the right of the window and a preview of the interpolated raw file is also included.

Slideshow – The Slideshow module is where you can lay out a group of images and present them to clients or family and friends as a slideshow or produce them as a self-running PDF presentation.

Print – Here in the one dialog are all the controls you need to output contact sheets, picture packages as well as individual prints. Gone are the layer upon layer of settings dialogs, replaced with a single pane of settings with all the critical controls and settings up front.

Web – The Web module has the ability to create both traditional thumbnail and feature image HTML-based galleries, or the more interactive Flash-based sites complete with animation and simple navigation controls.

The whole workflow is lossless – read 'non-destructive'. Image enhancement and raw conversion settings are stored separately to the original image data and are then used to generate screen previews of the pictures, print output and the screen-based slideshows of the files.

Why Lightroom plus Elements

With this level of functionality you may well ask why Lightroom users need a dedicated editing program like Elements in addition to what seems to be a comprehensive imaging program. Well the short answer is that Lightroom's forté is global enhancement of images. That is, tweaking the tones, colors and sharpness contained in a single image. Even with the extra power resulting from the addition of the local correction tools introduced in version 2.0, Lightroom is designed to be used with a single image.

Now we know that this is not the case with Elements. Because of the layer structure used in the program, Elements users can montage picture parts from several different photos in a single composition.

In its most basic form this means that you can do things like swap skies in a landscape photo, or heads in a portrait image. These type of changes are generally referred to as pixel editing, and it is for these features that Lightroom users need Elements.

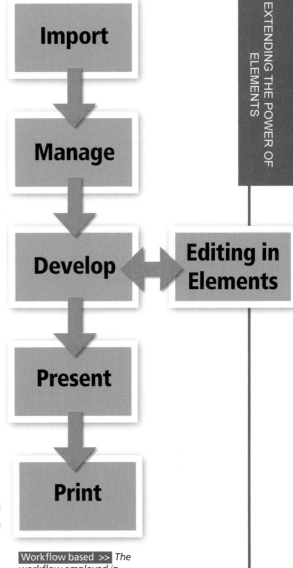

Workflow based >> *The workflow employed in Lightroom roughly follows a route that progresses from one module to another. Import and management functions are carried out in the **Library** module. Raw conversion settings are applied in the **Develop** module and output to screen or print processes are handled in the **Slideshow**, **Web** and **Print** modules. Elements can play an important role in this workflow by providing pixel based editing for images managed in Lightroom.*

So what does that mean in terms of workflow? Well, this way of working positions Lightroom as the program used for image management, raw processing, presenting and printing and Elements as the package used for 'nitty gritty' pixel based editing. This is great news for Elements' users who are migrating to Lightroom as all the editing skills that they have built can be applied to Lightroom managed photos. Cool!

With this 'modus operandi' in mind, I thought that it would be a good idea to use this chapter to introduce Lightroom to Elements users and then to describe how to employ Elements editing power with the package.

Enough talk, let's get to it!

Photoshop Lightroom is based on two core technologies: a relational database that stores all the details, settings and metadata relating to your images and the engine that drives Adobe Camera Raw. The database provides fast, reliable searching and cataloging options and the ACR engine supplies the tools needed for enhancing your pictures. The user accesses these technologies via an interface based around the five workflow modules that we briefly looked at earlier. Let's start with the interface.

Lightroom Interface
As a full workflow product Lightroom contains not just the tools and controls needed for the conversion of raw files, but also for their management and presentation. These functions are all contained in a slick interface with a workspace that can be broken down into the following sections:
1. left panel,
2. filmstrip,
3. preview area,
4. right panel,
5. module menu,
6. program menu, and
7. tools.

The workspace

The Lightroom workspace can be divided into several sections.

1. The **left panel's** role changes depending on which module or mode you are in. The example screen shot shows Lightroom in the Develop mode, which is primarily designed for enhancing the file. You will find settings here for controlling colors, tones and sharpness as well as tools for cropping, straightening, spot removal and local correction (dodge and burn, etc.). If you switch to the Library, Slideshow, Print or Web modules the contents change to display preset and saved options settings.

2. The **filmstrip** area is located at the bottom of the screen and displays all the images from the currently selected Collection, Folder or Find results. Individual pictures, or groups of images, can be selected from the filmstrip in any module.

3. In the default setting for the Library module, the main workspace displays a grid view of thumbnails. Double-clicking any thumbnail will display an enlarged **preview** in what is called Loupe view. A single mouse click on the preview image zooms the picture to and from a default 1:1 magnification setting. Images can be viewed in Grid (like a sorting area on a slide box), Loupe (enlarged to 1:1 or a range of other settings), Compare (side-by-side comparisons of multiple photos) or Survey (interactive review of multiple photos) modes. In Slideshow, Web and Print modes the workspace displays a preview of the images as they will appear on screen or on the printed page.

4. The **right-hand panel** holds the settings controls available for the current module. In Library mode it displays some quick development options. In the Develop module the panel contains the complete set of enhancement controls, and in the Slideshow, Web and Print modules it houses layout and output settings.

5. The **module** menu appears at the top of the screen and not only lists the options available but also highlights the one currently selected. There are five modules included in Lightroom (Library, Develop, Slideshow, Print, Web).

6. The **menu** bar provides access to standard menu commands, but like most screen elements in the Lightroom interface, this too can be hidden from view and restored when needed.

7. The small section beneath the histogram in the right panel of the Develop module houses the **tools** that can be used to crop, straighten, remove spots of red-eye and brush on adjustments. More tools or options are available in a section just below the preview space. These change according to the module selected. For instance, when Library is selected view mode buttons, rating settings, and zoom settings are just some of the options available here.

The Lightroom workflow modules

Adobe consulted far and wide when they were putting together Lightroom. Who did they talk to? The answer is photographers! They asked them to describe their workflows and to list the sort of enhancement controls they regularly used. From these discussions the Lightroom team created a simple modular-based workflow. Let's look at each module in turn.

Library module

Library left panel contents

As we have seen in the quick look at the interface on the previous pages, the contents of both right and left panels change according to which module is selected. The left panel of the Library contains the following options:

Navigator – The Navigator acts as another way to preview images in a slightly larger format than what is generally displayed with the filmstrip thumbnails. The options at the top of the Navigator provide various zoom modes for the Loupe view. Selecting any of these entries will automatically switch the preview space to the Loupe view and enlarge to the zoom setting. With settings greater than the Fit option, a rectangle is shown that indicates the extent of the area currently displayed. Click-dragging the rectangle around the Navigator will move the picture parts previewed.

Catalog – The Catalog section lists details of the status of the Lightroom database. Here you will find numbers relating to all the photographs in your Catalog, the images currently marked for inclusion in the Quick Collection and the amount of photos in the last import.

Folders – The Folders section mirrors the folder hierarchy of your hard drive and displays the folder where images currently included in the catalog are located. It is possible to move files from one folder to another by selecting the pictures in the grid view and dragging them to the new folder. Unlike many other management changes in Lightroom, moving files in this way forces a corresponding change at system level. The same is true for the changes made in the operating system file browser outside Lightroom. Folder structure and contents made in the OS file browser are reflected in the Folder display. Folders can be added or removed using the + or - buttons at the top of the section.

Collections – Collections are one way that Lightroom helps you organize your photos. Unlike folders, collections are virtual groupings of images. The same image can be a member of several different collections. This doesn't mean that the photo is duplicated and stored several times, rather that the

Library - Left panel

different collections reference the same image in its original folder. Elements users should think of Collections as being similar to Albums.

Import and Export buttons – The Import button at the bottom of the left-hand panel provides a shortcut to importing files or other Lightroom catalogs. More extensive import options are located in the File menu. The Export button displays the Export dialog which contains a range of options that can be used to output either single or groups of photos in specific formats.

Library right panel contents

Histogram – The Histogram appears in both the Library and Develop modules, but in slightly different forms. In the Library module the graph provides a visual representation of the spread of tones in the image from black (left) to white (right).

Quick Develop – The Quick Develop section provides the most used tone and color controls right inside the Library for easy and fast adjustments during the picture management phase. The controls are button driven rather than slider based. The single sideways arrow makes changes in small steps, whereas the double sideways arrow uses larger settings jumps.

Keyword List – Another approach to image management is to use keywords for searches and creating groups of similar photos. These descriptive words are added to the metadata either at the time of importing, or during the sorting process in the Library module. You can filter the images currently displayed in the grid view by selecting specific Keywords from those listed .

Metadata – The Metadata section is used to display groups of images based on the metadata entries associated with the photos. Selecting an entry from the list will sort through the photos and only display those images that contain the metadata entry. Much of the metadata or EXIF information associated with digital photos is recorded at time of capture and is inaccessible to the user, but there are groups of metadata details that can added, or changed, by the users.

Keywording – Unlike the Keyword List pane, which is used to filter the preview display based on keywords attached to images, the Keywording section is used for adding keywords to photos. You can attach a keyword to a selected photo by either typing it directly into the Keywording space (using commas to separate multiple keywords) or by clicking onto one of the keyword entries in the Keyword Set section of the panel. Click on the entry a second time to remove a keyword attached incorrectly.

Library - Right panel

Sync Settings and Sync Metadata buttons – The Sync Settings and Sync Metadata buttons are active when two or more images are selected in the grid view. The Sync Settings button copies the Develop settings from the reference image to the rest of the preselected photos. The Sync Metadata button copies the metadata to the selected photos.

Library tools

Several view options are grouped under the preview area. The specific entries listed here change according to the module currently selected. The following are options for the Library module, but the display can change depending on those entries selected in the Toolbar Content menu.

Views Modes – Used for setting how images are displayed in the preview area.

Sort order and direction – The order that thumbnails are displayed in the grid view can be adjusted with the drop-down menu option displayed in the toolbar.

Adding Ratings, Flags, Pick settings and Color Labels – Clicking any of the buttons will then place the Rating, Pick flag or Color Label on the selected image or images in the preview space.

Rotating photos – The Rotate buttons pivot the selected photo or photos in 90° increments either left or right.

Navigate and Slideshow options – There are two Navigation buttons available for display on the toolbar. The Select Next Photo or Select Previous Photo buttons move the selection from one photo to another. The Play button displays the images in a full screen slideshow using the current settings of the controls in the Slideshow module.

Zoom settings – The Thumbnail slider controls the size of the thumbnails in the Grid View of the preview area.

Information bar – When the filmstrip is displayed, an information bar is also shown just above the filmstrip area and below the preview space.

Develop module

Develop left panel contents

Navigator – The Navigator as displayed in the Develop module functions in the same way that it does in the Library module. For more details refer to the Library section of this chapter.

Presets –The Preset section stores groups of Develop settings. Some of these are supplied with the program as general defaults (Zeroed, Flat, Sepia, etc.)

Develop - Left panel

and are stored under the Lightroom Presets heading. Others are presets saved by the user.

Snapshots – Snapshots are saved history states. They can be used to revert a photo's development to a specific stage in its enhancement.

History – An entry is placed in the History panel for each editing or enhancement setting change. The values for specific controls are listed to the right of each entry. The entries are listed chronologically. This process of creating entries happens automatically, and the entries remain associated with the file until the Clear button, located at the top of the panel, is selected. Like the Snapshot entries, selecting an entry from the History list will adjust the image to the settings listed.

Copy and Paste buttons – The Copy and Paste buttons at the bottom of the left side panels are used for copying the Develop settings from one photo and applying them (Paste) to another photo.

Develop right panel contents

Histogram – The Histogram we see here contains the same full color graph of the spread of pixels in the image as was the case in the Library module but with a couple of differences – the graph can be directly manipulated with your mouse cursor (push and pulled around) and the top left and right corners contain the shadow and highlight clipping warning buttons and displays.

Basic – The contents of the Basic panel reflect those provided by ACR in the Photoshop Elements version of the utility. See Chapter 3 for more details on the raw enhancement controls found here.

Tone Curve – The Tone Curve option in Lightroom provides the user with the option of adjusting the shape of the curve, and therefore the tones in the photo, in four different ways:

- You can push/pull the curve directly by clicking onto the line of the curved and click-dragging with the mouse.

- Segments of the curve are broken into four tonal ranges called Highlights, Lights, Darks and Shadows. Beneath the curves dialog are slider controls for each of these tonal ranges.

- Yet another way to manipulate the curve in Lightroom is to select an entry from the Point Curve drop-down menu at the bottom of the dialog.

- The final curve control is again a unique feature in Lightroom as well as being one that is used for other controls. The Targeted Adjustment Tool (TAT) located at the top left-hand corner of the dialog is used to make changes by click-dragging on the image itself.

Develop - Right panel

HSL/Color/Grayscale – In the color modes (HSL and Color) the feature allows the independent adjustment of Hue, Saturation and/or Luminance of red, orange, yellow, green, aqua, blue, purple and magenta colors. Selecting the Grayscale option switches the concerns of the control to how the eight color groupings are mapped to gray tones. .

Split Toning – The Split Toning control allows for separate tinting of shadow and highlight areas and has both Hue and Saturation controls plus a Balance slider that controls the position of the split along the tonal scale.

Detail – Like the Basic panel the options available here are similar to those found in the Detail tab of Adobe Camera Raw. See Chapter 3 for more information.

Camera Calibration – The controls in the Camera Calibration panel allow for fine-tuning of the default color conversion options of specific camera models.

Previous and Reset buttons – Selecting the Previous button applies the Develop settings of the last selected photo to the newly selected image. Clicking the Reset button changes the Develop settings for the current image back to the Lightroom defaults.

Develop module toolbar >>
Lightroom contains five tools that you can use to alter the way that your photo appears.

Develop tools

The toolbar located below the histogram in the Develop module of Lightroom contains five key features used for editing your photos.

Crop Overlay – The Crop Overlay tool is used for removing unwanted edges and straightening photos.

Spot Removal – Designed to eliminate dust spots and unwanted subject marks, the tool works by sampling another part of the photo and using this detail, color and texture to paste over the problem spot.

Red Eye Correction – This tool allows you to non-destructively remove Red Eye from your flash photos.

Graduated Filter – This feature can be used to apply custom gradients across the full height or width of the photo. Once created, the size, position and rotation of the gradient remains editable along with the image characteristics that can be altered via the gradient.

Adjustment Brush – Like the Graduated Filter, the Adjustment Brush is used to apply image changes to specific areas of the photo. This means that you can brush on changes in exposure, brightness, contrast, saturation, clarity, sharpness and color to selected parts of your picture.

Slideshow module

Slideshow left panel contents

Preview – The Preview panel displays a thumbnail view of the current selected template. Moving over the template entries will switch the preview between different slideshow templates whilst viewing a preview of how your images will look with each layout.

Template Browser – Lists Lightroom default and user-created slideshow templates.

Export PDF and Export JPEG buttons – The Export PDF button produces the slideshow as a self-running PDF presentation. The Export JPEG option creates a series of JPEG screen shots of the current slideshow.

Slideshow right panel contents

Options – The options panel contains Stroke Border and Cast Shadow settings as well as the option to force photos to 'Zoom to Fill Frame'.

Layout – The four slider controls in the Layout panel control the margin spaces around the slideshow picture. Changing these values will alter the size and positioning of the photo in the slide frame.

Overlays – Choose what other content will be included on the slide along with the photo in this panel. You can include the Identity Plate, Rating settings and/or metadata or custom text.

Backdrop – Select the background color, or whether to include a color wash or a background image.

Titles – Customized intro and ending screens.

Playback – The Playback panel includes options for including an accompanying soundtrack, and settings for slide duration and transition timing and for systems with two screens, a choice on which screen the slideshow plays.

Preview and Play buttons – The production can be previewed in the central workspace by pressing one of the VCR-type Play buttons in the toolbar or the Preview button at the bottom of the right panel entries. Press the play button to present the slideshow full screen.

Slideshow tools

Navigation buttons – The First Slide button displays the initial image in the show. The Play and Stop buttons are used for previewing the show using the current settings.

Slideshow - Right panel

Add Text to Slide button – Selecting the Add Text button allows the user to input custom text, or choose from a list of metadata entries, to be displayed in the slide. Adding text automatically selects the Text Overlays option in the Overlays panel.

Print module

Print left panel contents

Preview – The Preview pane displays the layout of the print template that is currently selected. The images are not shown in the layout, just the spaces where these photos will be positioned.

Template Browser – The Template Browser contains a list of supplied print layouts along with any template designs saved by the users.

Print - Right panel

Page Setup button – Printer level control is also possible with the options accessed via the Page Setup button on the toolbar.

Print right panel contents

Layout Engine – Provides a choice between Contact Sheet/Grid for multiple images, and Picture package, for a single image repeated, layout styles.

Image Settings – The Image Settings panel houses placement controls such as Zoom to Fill Frame, Auto-Rotate to Fit, and Repeat One Photo per Page options along with border size and color settings.

Layout – The Margins, Grid and Cell options in the Layout panel control the image positioning and overall design of the print template.

Guides – Controls for displaying non-printing guides.

Overlays – Just as was the case for the Slideshow module, the settings in the Overlays panel determine what other details are printed alongside the images themselves.

Print Job –The Print Job settings group together the main output options of Resolution, Sharpening, and Color Management. Users can input their preferred pixels per inch (ppi) setting in the Print Resolution section.

Print One – This option bypasses the OS print dialog and uses the current settings to produce a print.

Print button – Pressing the Print button will also display the OS and printer dialogs to ensure proper setup before finally outputting the photo. Holding down the Alt/Opt key will bypass these dialogs and print the photo using the last settings.

Web module

Web left panel contents

Preview – The Preview panel displays a small version of the Web Gallery template currently selected in the Template Browser.

Template Browser – The Template Browser lists supplied and user-created templates. Applying a template to the current group of selected images is as easy as clicking on the entry in the template list.

Preview in Browser – The Preview in Browser button produces the website and then displays it in a new browser window. This process can take some time as Lightroom performs all of the web optimizing of the image files and the building of the pages and navigational structure. The progress of the action is detailed in the top left corner of the Lightroom workspace.

Web right panel contents

Engine – This section contains two gallery template options: Flash Gallery, for websites created with Flash technology, and HTML Gallery, for more traditional style web pages and sites.

Site Info – The contents of the Site Info panel may vary slightly depending on the gallery template selected and if the website is Flash or HTML based. In most cases, the site title, collection title, collection description, contact info and web or mail link can be added here.

Color Palette – The colors used in the template design can be adjusted or replaced with the controls in the Color Palette panel. The number of website components listed here will depend on the design of the template.

Appearance – Along with the Color Palette, the Appearance panel contains the main controls for changing the look and style of a web template. In this section the user can adjust characteristics such as drop shadows, selection borders, the number of images displayed in index or grid pages, displaying or hiding of cell numbers and the use of photo borders.

Image Info – The Image Info panel contains settings for the inclusion of extra text with each of the photos displayed. There are two areas where more details can be added – the Title and Caption areas.

Output Settings – The Output Settings for most templates include a Quality slider that governs the image quality of the larger gallery images, plus the option to display a watermark-based copyright on the larger images.

Web - Right panel

Upload Settings – Lightroom has the ability to upload the completed website directly to the web server where your pages are stored and displayed to the world. For this to occur the program uses an FTP, or file transfer protocol, utility that links the user's computer with the web server and then transfers the files. To make the connection, Lightroom uses details contained in the Custom Settings section of the Upload Settings panel.

Export and Upload buttons – The Export button at the bottom of the right panel provides the option to save the Lightroom website to disk in a format that can be viewed with a web browser. The Upload button uses the in-built FTP utility to transfer the files to your web server.

Web tools

Go to First Page – The Go to First Page button looks like a square box on the left side of the toolbar. Click this button to change the main preview window in the center of the screen to main or front page of the website.

Previous and Next photo – The right and left arrow buttons in the toolbar are the Previous Photo and Next Photo buttons. These controls move the focus between the selected photos in the filmstrip that are featured in the website.

Elements edits Lightroom files >> *Once Elements has been registered in Lightroom as an External Editing program it is possible to open Lightroom photos into the Full Edit workspace, make your adjustments and then save the files back to the Lightroom Library. The edited file is stored as a separate photo in an image stack.*

Using Elements to edit Lightroom managed images

When an Elements user switches to a Lightroom based workflow the features and tools described on the previous pages would largely be used instead of the image management, raw conversion and output functions found in Adobe Camera Raw and the Organizer workspace. It is the pixel based editing tools and features located in Elements' Full edit mode that are not present in Lightroom that will form the basis of the partnership between the two programs.

Selecting Elements as an External Editor >> *Use the settings in the External Editing section of Lightroom Preferences (Edit > Preferences) to select Elements as a linked program.*

Setting up Lightroom

In order to use Elements as a linked program you must first adjust the preferences for Lightroom. Start by going to the Edit > Preferences > External Editing dialog. If Photoshop is installed on the computer then it will automatically be selected as a editing program. To choose Elements, go the the Additional External Editing part of the dialog, click the Choose button and locate the PhotoshopElements.exe file. This program file is located in c:/Program Files/Adobe/Photoshop Elements 7.0/ folder.

You will also need to select the file format, color space, bit depth and resolution for the file that is transferred across to Elements. Selecting PSD as the file type will ensure that you can use the complete functionality of the Full Edit workspace. Bit depth, color space and resolution will be dependant on the end outcome for the file. For instance AdobeRGB is generally used for files that will be published, where as sRGB is employed for pictures destined for the web.

These settings can be saved as a preset by picking the Save Current Settings as a New Preset entry from the Preset menu. Creating a preset will automatically add an entry to the Photo > Edit In menu.

Editing in Elements >> *To edit a file in Elements you can select the Edit in Photoshop Elements option from the Edit In menu of the right-click menu.*

Passing photos to Photoshop Elements

There are two main ways to pass Lightroom managed pictures to Photoshop Elements:

1. **From the menu** – To edit a photo from your Lightroom Library in Photoshop Elements select the image in the Library or Develop module and then choose Photo > Edit in > Edit in Adobe Photoshop Elements. The shortcut key for this action is Ctrl/Cmd + Alt/Opt + E.

2. **Right-click access** – Alternatively you can right-click on a photo in the Library module (in Grid, Loupe, Compare, or Survey View) and select the Edit in > Edit in Adobe Photoshop Elements option from the pop-up menu. This option is also available in the Develop module.

Edit Photo options >> *Depending on if you are trying to pass a raw or tiff/jpeg/psd file to Elements you will have up to three different processing options. These include the ability to create copies of the original file with or without Lightroom adjustments applied and also the possibility of editing the original picture.*

Edit Photo dialog

Once the Edit in Adobe Photoshop Elements option is selected, Lightroom displays the Edit Photo with Adobe Photoshop Elements dialog. Here you can select from three possible options:

Edit a Copy with Lightroom Adjustments – Lightroom duplicates the raw file, applies the current set of development or conversion settings and then opens the new file into Photoshop Elements. The file format, color space and bit depth of the copy are determined by the settings in the Copy File Options section of the dialog. This is the only option available for raw or DNG files. The duplicated file is titled with the original filename plus '-Edit'.

Edit a Copy – Lightroom opens a copy of the file in Photoshop Elements. No Develop settings are applied to the copy. This option is only available with non- raw files (i.e. PSD, TIFF or JPEG). The format, color space and bit depth of the copy are controlled by the settings in the Copy File Options section of the dialog. The filename of the copy is automatically set to the original name plus '-Edit'.

Edit Original – Again this option is only available with non-raw files. Lightroom opens the original file into Photoshop Elements. All saved changes are applied to the original file.

Stacking edited versions in Lightroom

Selecting the 'Stack with original' option in the Edit Photo dialog saves the duplicate or copied photo that you edit in Elements alongside the original in the Lightroom library. Once you have completed your editing inside Photoshop Elements and you save the file (File > Save) automatically the new photo is stacked with the original inside the Lightroom Library.

Appendices

Blend modes

The way that layers interact with other layers in the stack is determined by the Blending mode of the upper layer.

By default the layer's mode is set to Normal, which causes the picture content on the upper layer to obscure the picture parts beneath, but Photoshop Elements has many other ways (modes) to control how these pixels interact.

Called Blend modes, the different options provide a variety of ways to control the mixing, blending and general interaction of the layer content.

In the following Blend mode examples the picture has two layers – 'Top' (1) and 'Bottom' (2). In each example the Blend mode of the top layer has been changed to illustrate how the two layers blend together.

Normal

The pixels in the top layer are opaque and therefore block the view of the bottom layer. Adjusting the opacity of the top layer will make it semi-transparent causing it to blend with the top layer.

Dissolve

Combines the top layer with the bottom using a pattern of pixels. There is no effect if the top layer is at 100% opacity. Reduce the opacity to see the effect. The example is set to 80% opacity.

Darken

Compares the color of the top and bottom layers and blends the pixels where the top layer is darker than the bottom.

Multiply

Multiplies the color of the bottom layer with the top layer producing an overall darker result. There is no image change where the top layer is white.

Color Burn

Darkens or 'burns' the image using the contents of the top layer. There is no image change where the top layer is white.

Linear Burn

Uses the same approach as the Color Burn mode but produces a stronger darkening effect. There is no image change where the top layer is white.

Lighten

Compares the color in the top and bottom layers and blends the pixels if the top layer is lighter than the bottom.

Screen

The opposite to the Multiply mode as it multiplies the inverse of the top layer with the bottom layer producing a much lighter image.

Color Dodge

Makes the picture lighter using the top layer to dodge the bottom layer. There is no effect where the top layer is black.

Linear Dodge

Similar to the Screen mode but produces a much stronger lightening effect. There is no effect where the top layer is black.

Overlay

Combines the effect of both the Multiply and Screen modes whilst blending the top layer with the bottom. There is no effect if the top layer is 50% gray.

The modes are grouped into several different categories based on the type of changes that they make (1).

The Layer Blend modes are located in the drop-down menu at the top left of the Layers palette (2). Blend modes can also be applied to the painting and drawing tools via a drop-down menu in the Tool's options bar (3).

Soft Light

Similar to the Overlay mode but produces a more subtle effect. There is no change where the top layer is 50% gray.

Hard Light

Uses the same approach as the Overlay mode but the change is more dramatic. Here the top layer is either Screened or Multiplied depending on its color. There is no effect where the top layer is 50% gray.

Vivid Light

Combines the effects of both Color Burn and Color Dodge modes and applies the blend based on the color of the top layer. There is no effect where the top layer is 50% gray.

Linear Light

Similar to the Vivid Light mode but produces a more dramatic result. There is no effect where the top layer is 50% gray.

Pin Light

Blends the light colors in the top layer using the Lighten mode and blends the dark colors using the Darken mode. There is no effect where the top layer is 50% gray.

Hard Mix

Creates a flat toned picture with limited colors and lots of posterization. The luminosity of the top layer is blended with the color of the bottom.

Difference

Displays the tonal difference between the contents of the two layers by subtracting the lighter pixels from either of the layers. This results in a dark and sometimes reversed image.

Exclusion

Similar to the Difference mode but produces less dramatic effects.

Hue

Combines the Hue (color) of the top layer with the Saturation (color vibrancy) and Luminance (tones) of the bottom layer.

Saturation

Combines the Saturation (color vibrancy) of the top layer with the Hue (color) and Luminance (tones) of the bottom layer.

Color

Combines the Hue (color) and Saturation (color vibrancy) of the top layer with the Luminance (tones) of the bottom layer.

Luminosity

Combines the Luminance (tones) of the top layer with the Saturation (color vibrancy) and Hue (color) of the bottom layer.

Faster Elements at no extra cost

Many dedicated Photoshop Elements users can get substantial speed gains from their existing, albeit modest, equipment by simply optimizing their computer and software so that it runs Elements more efficiently. So to make sure that you are getting the best from the bucks you have already spent, here is a collection of speed-enhancing tips for optimizing your machine.

Allocate a scratch disk >>

Photoshop Elements uses RAM memory to run itself, store picture information and to save undo and history state steps. Unless you are working with particularly small photo files it won't take too many editing changes before the RAM is completely used up. At this point Elements cleverly uses a portion of hard drive space as 'fake' RAM.

This is not a new idea. Most operating systems use the same approach (called Virtual Memory), to ensure that enough memory is available for running essential programs. Photoshop Elements calls this extra memory a 'Scratch Disk', and correctly setting up the disk will provide immediate speed and efficiency benefits.

To set your scratch disk, select Full Edit: Edit > Preferences > Performance. Then choose a drive that has the most free space from those listed in the pop-up menu. If you have other drives listed you can also allocate these as extra scratch drives.

Elements will make use of the drive listed first until it is full and then move to the next drive if even more memory is needed.

Most imaging professionals who regularly work with large files install a specific 'fast access' drive just to be used as a scratch disk by Photoshop Elements.

Set RAM percentage >>

Photoshop Elements shares the RAM on your computer with the Operating System (Windows or OSX) and any other programs running at the same time. The percentage designated in the Photoshop Elements Performance preferences determines the upper amount of RAM memory that can be used by Elements. Most new users push this setting as high as possible, some as much as 90%, thinking that this will speed up the processing of their files.

Unfortunately if this allocation is set too high the operating system, as well as Elements, may need to move information from the fast RAM memory to the slower hard drive memory whilst processing. This action is called page swapping as the data is moved back and forth between the different memory spaces, and results in Photoshop Elements actually running slower.

If you experience slower performance when raising the percentage of RAM allocated to Elements, try reducing the total amount to 50–60% for systems with up to 2Gb, and 70% for computers with 4Gb of RAM.

Remember that you have to restart Photoshop Elements after making any memory changes to ensure that these alterations will take effect.

Defragment your drives >>

As images and files are saved and resaved to disk they tend to become fragmented. This means that rather than the whole file being saved in one continuous space on the hard drive the information is broken into pieces and stored in several locations (wherever there is empty disk space). Later when the file is reopened the document is reconstructed from each of the individual pieces. This file fragmentation slows down the opening and saving of files, as well as the running of programs such as Photoshop Elements, if they were fragmented when initially installed. You can overcome this problem by regularly defragmenting the drives you use to store your images and load your programs.

To defragment a drive in Windows XP and Vista:

Click Start > All Programs > Accessories > System Tools > Disk Defragmenter. Choose the drive to be defragmented and then select the Defragment button.

To defragment a drive in Mac OSX:

Despite the fact that the latest version of Mac OSX contains automatic defragmentation of files smaller than 20Mb most Apple users prefer to defrag their drives with third-party utilities.

Minimize History states >>

The Photoshop Elements Undo History palette is a great feature especially if you make mistakes as often as I do. Each successive edit is recorded as a step in the palette, enabling you to step back through the changes, gradually reversing your edits as you go. But such a great feature does come at a cost. Each step uses memory resources and, when you make complex changes to large files, you can imagine how much memory is used to store a collection of steps.

Thankfully Adobe provides a setting in the Edit > Preferences > General dialog that can be used to alter the number of History States (or undo steps) stored by your system.

By default it is set to 20, but if you find that Elements is running slowly after making a few editing changes then try reducing the number. Less History States does mean less opportunity to reverse editing changes, but this action frees up memory resources and can bring new life back to a slow running machine.

Multi-page documents >>

When working with large PSE or multi-page projects you can increase the speed of working by creating the project and then immediately saving and closing the file. After reopening, the images in the Photo Bin are thumbnail versions of each page, but only page 1 is fully open in the Editor. Other pages will open when you click the thumbnail or navigate to them. In this way you can limit the number of open pages when working on large books.

Reduce the number of open files >>

It may seem like stating the obvious, but the more pictures you have open in Elements the more of the total resources of the machine is taken up, just maintaining each open file. When you add in the memory used to ensure undo or multiple History States for each file, it is not too hard to imagine that you will very quickly run out of RAM, forcing Photoshop Elements to use the much slower Scratch Disk space.

To speed up the processing, make sure that you only open (and keep open) files that are essential for your current editing task.

Scratch Disk versus Virtual Memory >>

Both Elements and the Windows XP operating system use hard drive space as extra 'fake' RAM. Adobe recommends that Elements Scratch Disks be positioned on a different drive to the one used by Windows for its Virtual Memory system. On most set ups the Windows swap file is stored on the start up or C drive.

To help with overall Elements and Windows performance, ensure that you don't position the Scratch Disk on the same drive. To set the location of your scratch disk select Full Edit: Edit > Preferences > Plug-Ins & Scratch Disks and choose the drive to use from the drop-down menu. Remember, don't select Startup or C drive unless you have no other choices.

Alter the Image Cache setting >>

Photoshop Elements uses a special image cache to help redraw high-resolution images quickly. Instead of displaying all the information contained in these big files, Elements creates lower resolution versions of the photo that are then used to update the screen quickly.

You can elect to store from 1–8 cached versions of the photo. A value of 1 disables the caching. Higher values store multiple versions of the file, which in turn produces faster screen redraws. The default setting is 4, but inputting higher numbers will help speed up the redraw process.

When a high cache number is set, it will take longer to open files as Elements creates the low-resolution versions of the photo at this point. To alter the Image Cache setting select Full Edit: Edit > Preferences > Image Cache and enter a value from 1 to 8 in the Cache Levels text box.

Run Elements by itself >>

A simple measure to speed up Elements is to make sure that no other programs are running at the same time. Seemingly simple utilities such as iTunes, Outlook and Word all chew up memory and processor resources that could be used to drive Elements more efficiently.

The golden rule is that if the program is not essential for the editing task then close the software.

Before

After

Plug-ins

Since the first version of Elements Adobe provided the opportunity for third-party developers to create small pieces of specialist software that could plug into the program. These extra features extend the capabilities of the program and some of them have become so popular that they find themselves added into the program proper in the next release of the software.

Most plug-ins register themselves as extra options in the Filter menu, where they can be accessed just like any other Elements feature.

The Delta100 filter (1) from www. silveroxide.com is a great example of plug-in technology. Designed to reproduce the look of particular types of black and white film stock, the installed filter can be selected from the Silver Oxide group (2) of products in the Filter menu.

Plug-in options

Flaming Pear – *Super Blade Pro*
Effect: This plug-in provides the most sophisticated control over surface and texture, characteristics of text and objects available.
OS: Mac, Windows   **Cost:** US$30.00
Website: www.flamingpear.com

Alien Skin – *Eye Candy*
Effect: Eye Candy 4000 is a collection of 23 different creative filters used for creating effects such as shadows, bevels, chrome, smoke, wood and even fur.
OS: Mac, Windows   **Cost:** US$169.00
Website: www.alienskin.com

Harry's – *Filters*
Effect: A free collection of filters that can be used for creating up to 69 different imaging effects. Also contains the option to encrypt your photos.
OS: Mac, Windows   **Cost:** FREE
Website: www.thepluginsite.com

PhotoTune – *20/20 Color MD*
Effect: Using a side-by-side comparison approach this PhotoTune plug-in takes the guesswork out of correcting the colors in your photos.
OS: Mac, Windows   **Cost:** US$49.95
Website: www.phototune.com

Extensis – *Intellihance Pro*
Effect: Capable of comparing and applying up to 25 different enhancement options at one time, Intellihance Pro is the master of the quick fix.
OS: Mac, Windows   **Cost:** US$199.00
Website: www.extensis.com

Digital Film – *Ozone*
Effect: Simulates the same tonal control available when using the film-based Zone system (created by Ansel Adams) with your digital photographs.
OS: Mac, Windows   **Cost:** US$50.00
Website: www.digitalfilmtools.com

Photowiz – *Color Washer*
Effect: The Color Washer plug-in is used for the correction and enhancement of colors in your pictures. Great for restoring faded colors in old photos.
OS: Windows   **Cost:** US$49.95
Website: www.thepluginsite.com

AutoFX – *Photo/Graphic Edges*
Effect: Photo/Graphic Edges provides 14 photographic effects that are used to create an astonishing array of edges and borders for your images.
OS: Mac, Windows   **Cost:** US$179.00
Website: www.autofx.com

Power Retouche – *Black & White Studio*

Effect: This plug-in replicates many of the effects of a traditional darkroom including specific film looks.
OS: Mac, Windows **Cost:** US$75.00/£45.00
Website: www.powerretouche.com

VanDerLee – *Old Movie*

Effect: Create the look and feel of an old photo or movie frame with this plug-in. Includes controls for film type, scratches, camera, dust, fat and hair.
OS: Windows **Cost:** US$19.95
Website: www.v-d-l.com

Andromeda – *Shadow Filter*

Effect: Billed as the 'most advanced shadowing plug-in available' this filter really lives up to the hype. Master the controls and any shadows are possible.
OS: Mac, Windows **Cost:** US$109.00
Website: www.andromeda.com

Richard Roseman – *Vignette Corrector*

Effect: The plug-in removes or adds the darkened edges that are produced by low quality wide angle lenses.
OS: Windows **Cost:** FREE
Website: www.richardroseman.com

Lokas – *Artistic Effects*

Effect: The Artistic Effects collection is a series of customized filters that add surface effects to text and shapes. The options include gel, ice, metal, smoke and snow.
OS: Windows **Cost:** US$59.95
Website: www.artistic-effects.com

NIK – *Sharpener Pro Inkjet*

Effect: The range of NIK sharpening plug-ins is designed to sharpen your pictures to clarify output to a variety of print devices.
OS: Mac, Windows **Cost:** US$79.95
Website: www.nikmultimedia.com

AV Bros – *Puzzle Pro*

Effect: Although at first this seems like a simple jigsaw-puzzle maker the ability to customize and add extra shapes really extends the options for this plug-in.
OS: Mac, Windows **Cost:** US$49.95
Website: www.avbros.com

ASF – *Digital GEM Airbrush*

Effect: Provides glamor photo-type results by automatically smoothing skin whilst retaining details in the areas like eyelashes and hair.
OS: Mac, Windows **Cost:** US$99.95
Website: www.asf.com

Digital Element – *Aurora*

Effect: The Aurora plug-in is an advanced world creator that produces highly sophisticated water, sky and lighting elements.
OS: Mac, Windows **Cost:** US$199.00
Website: www.digi-element.com

Andrew's Plugins – *V8*

Effect: There is plenty of creative choice here with nearly 20 different plug-in sets providing thousands of different effects and only costing $10.00 each.
OS: Mac, Windows **Cost:** US$10.00
Website: www.graphicxtras.com

The Imaging Factory – Convert to B&W

Effect: Powerful and customizable conversion plug-in designed for the dedicated monochrome enthusiast.
OS: Mac, Windows **Cost:** US$99.00
Website: www.theimagingfactory.com

PictureCode – *Noise Ninja*

Effect: Noise Ninja is a very sophisticated noise reduction plug-in that works extremely well with photographs taken using high ISO settings.
OS: Mac, Windows **Cost:** US$44.95
Website: www.picturecode.com

Jargon buster

A >>

Albums An album is another way that you can order and sort your photos in Elements.

Aliasing The jaggy edges that appear in bitmap images with curves or lines at any angle other than multiples of 90°.

Anti-Aliasing This feature smooths out the saw-tooth edges that appear on letters or shapes that have diagonal or circular sides. The anti-aliasing function in Elements softens around the edges of images to help make the problem less noticeable.

Aspect ratio This is usually found in dialog boxes concerned with changes of image size and refers to the relationship between width and height of a picture. The maintaining of an image's aspect ratio means that this relationship will remain the same even when the image is enlarged or reduced. Not maintaining the aspect ratio will result in the image being distorted – squished or stretched.

Automatically Tile Windows Automatically resizes open windows to fit the current work-space.

B >>

Background layer An image can only have one background layer. It is the bottom-most layer in the stack. No other layers can be moved or dragged beneath this layer. You cannot adjust this layer's opacity or its Blending mode.

Background printing A printing method that allows the user to continue working whilst an image or document is being printed.

Batch processing Refers to a function called Process Multiple Files. Batching applies a series of commands to several files at the one time. This function is useful for making the same changes to a folder full of images. In Elements this function is found under the File menu and is useful for converting groups of image files from one format to another.

Bit Stands for 'binary digit' and refers to the smallest part of information that makes up a digital file. It has a value of only 0 or 1. Eight of these bits make up one byte of data.

Bitmap or **'raster'** The form in which digital photographs are stored and is made up of a matrix of pixels.

Blend mode The way in which a color or a layer interacts with others. The most important after Normal are probably Multiply, which darkens everything, Screen, which adds to the colors to make everything lighter, Lighten, which lightens only colors darker than itself, and Darken, which darkens only colors lighter than itself. Both the latter therefore flatten contrast. Color maintains the shading of a color but alters the hue to the selected foreground color. Glows therefore are achieved using Screen mode, and Shadows using Multiply.

Brightness range The range of brightnesses between shadow and highlight areas of an image.

Burn tool Used to darken an image, can be targeted to affect just the Shadows, Midtones or Highlights. Opposite of the Dodge tool. Part of the toning trio, which also includes the Sponge.

Byte The standard unit of digital storage. One byte is made up of 8 bits and can have any value between 0 and 255. 1024 bytes are equal to 1 kilobyte. 1024 kilobytes are equal to 1 megabyte. 1024 megabytes are equal to 1 gigabyte.

C >>

Canvas Elements makes a distinction between

the canvas, upon which pictures and other content is placed, and the image content itself.

Caption Captions are another way to 'title' your photos beyond the standard file name and can be added using the Properties pane in Elements.

Catalog When you import pictures into the Photo Browser Elements creates a database of the images and their details. This database is called a catalog.

CCD or **Charge Coupled Device** Many of these devices placed in a grid format comprise the sensor of most modern digital cameras.

Clone Stamp or **Rubber Stamp tool** Allows a user to copy a part of an image to somewhere else. It is therefore ideal for repair work, e.g. unwanted spots or blemishes. Equivalent to Copy and Paste in a brush.

Color mode The way that an image represents the colors that it contains. Different color modes include Bitmap, RGB and Grayscale.

Compression Refers to a process where digital files are made smaller to save on storage space or transmission time. Compression is available in two types – lossy, where parts of the original image are lost at the compression stage, and lossless, where the integrity of the file is maintained during the compression process. JPEG and GIF use lossy compression whereas TIFF is a lossless format.

D >>
Defringe The defringe command removes the contrasting edge pixels from picture parts that have been cut or extracted from their backgrounds.

Digitize This is the process by which analog images or signals are sampled and changed into digital form.

Dodge tool For lightening areas in an image. See also Burn tool.

Downsample To reduce the size of a digital photo. Most methods for achieving this result remove unwanted pixels in the process.

DPI or **Dots per inch** A term used to indicate the resolution of a scanner or printer.

Dynamic range The measure of the range of brightness levels that can be recorded by a sensor.

E >>
Enhancement A term that refers to changes in brightness, color and contrast that are designed to improve the overall look of an image.

Export The Export feature in the Photo Browser is designed to provide a quick easy automated way to create and save copies of multi-selected pictures from inside the workspace.

F >>
Feather The Feather command softens the transition between selected and non-selected areas of a photo.

File format The way that a digital image is stored. Different formats have different characteristics. Some are cross-platform, others have inbuilt compression capabilities or a limited color range.

Filter In digital terms a filter is a way of applying a set of image characteristics to the whole or part of an image. Most image editing programs contain a range of filters that can be used for creating special effects.

Front page Sometimes called the Home or Index page, refers to the initial screen that the viewer sees when logging onto a website. Often the name and spelling of this page file is critical if it is to work on the web server. Consult your ISP staff for the precise name to be used with your site.

G >>

Gamma The contrast of the midtone areas of a digital image.

Gamut The range of colors or hues that can be printed or displayed by particular devices.

Gaussian Blur When applied to an image or a selection, this filter softens or blurs the image.

GIF or **Graphic Interchange Format** This is an indexed color mode format that contains a maximum of 256 colors that can be mapped to any palette of actual colors. It is extensively used for web graphics, buttons and logos, and small animated images.

Grayscale A monochrome image containing just monochrome tones ranging from white through a range of grays to black.

Group You can group photos with similar content into a single Image Stack in the Photo Browser workspace.

Grow The Select > Grow feature increases the size of an existing selection by incorporating pixels of similar color and tone to those already in the selection.

H >>

Histogram A graph that represents the tonal distribution of pixels within a digital image.

History Adobe's form of Multiple Undo.

Hot linked This term refers to a piece of text, graphic or picture that has been designed to act as a button on a web page. When the viewer clicks the hot linked item they are usually transported to another page or part of a website.

HTML The Hyper Text Mark Up language is the code used to create web pages. The characteristics of pages are stored in this language and when a page file is downloaded to your computer the machine lays out and displays the text, image and graphics according to what is stated in the HTML file.

Hue Refers to the color of the light and is separate from how light or dark it is.

I >>

Image layers Images in Elements can be made up of many layers. Each layer will contain part of the picture. When viewed together all layers appear to make up a single continuous image. Special effects and filters can be applied to layers individually.

Indexed color The Indexed Color mode can support up to 256 different colors and is the default Color mode for the GIF file format.

Interpolation This is the process used by image editing programs to increase the resolution of a digital image. Using fuzzy logic the program makes up the extra pixels that are placed between the original ones that were generated at the time of scanning.

ISP The Internet Service Provider is the company that hosts or stores web pages. If you access the web via a dial-up account then you will usually have a portion of free space allocated for use for your own site; others can obtain free (with a small banner advert attached) space from companies like www.tripod.com.

J >>

JPEG A file format designed by the Joint

Photographic Experts Group that has inbuilt lossy compression that enables a massive reduction in file sizes for digital images. Used extensively on the web and by press professionals for transmitting images back to newsdesks worldwide.

JPEG2000 The newest version of JPEG is called JPEG2000 and uses wavelet technology to produce smaller (by up to 20%) sharper files with less artifacts than traditional JPEG.

L >>

Layer opacity The opacity or transparency of each layer can be changed independently. Depending on the level of opacity the parts of the layer beneath will become visible. You can change the opacity of each layer by moving the Opacity slider in the Layers palette.

LCD or **Liquid Crystal Display** A display screen type used in preview screens on the back of digital cameras, in laptop computers and more and more as replacement desktop screens.

Liquify A tool that uses brushes to perform distortions upon selections or the whole of an image.

M >>

Marquee A rectangular selection made by click-dragging to an opposite corner.

Maximize mode The Maximize mode is one of the many ways that open pictures can be viewed in Photoshop Elements. Selecting the option from the Window > Images menu switches the view from Auto Tiled mode to a single image surrounded by the gray work area background.

Megapixel One million pixels. Used to describe the resolution of digital camera sensors.

Metadata Metadata is a variety of non-image

information about your picture that is attached to the photo file. Some of the detail is created at time of capture or creation and other parts are added as the file is edited or enhanced.

N >>

Navigator In Elements, a small scalable palette showing the entire image with the possibility of displaying a box representing the current image window frame. The frame's color can be altered; a new frame can be drawn (scaling the Image window with it) by holding the Command/Ctrl keys and making a new marquee. The frame can be dragged around the entire image with the Hand tool. The Zoom tools (Mountain icons) can be clicked, the slider can be dragged, or a figure can be entered as a percentage.

Noise Noise is the digital equivalent of the grain that appeared in photos taken with high ISO films. Noisy photos or those images that contain a lot of random speckled pixels instead of smooth tones generally result from long exposures times or the use of a high ISO or sensitivity setting. The Reduce Noise filter in Elements can be used to help correct this picture problem.

O >>

Optical resolution The resolution that a scanner uses to sample the original image. This is often different from the highest resolution quoted for the scanner as this is scaled up by interpolating the optically scanned file.

Optimization for Web The best way to optimize your photos for web use is via the Save for Web option. This feature provides before and after previews of the compression process as well as options for compression and reducing the dimensions of your pictures, all in the one dialog.

Options bar Long bar beneath the menu bar, which immediately displays the various settings for whichever tool is currently selected. Can be moved to other parts of the screen if preferred.

P >>

Palette A window that is used for the alteration of image characteristics: Options palette, Layers palette, Styles palette, Hints palette, File Browser, History, etc. These can be docked together vertically around the main image window or if used less frequently can be docked in the Palette Well at the top right of the screen (dark gray area).

Palette Bin The Palette Bin stores the Elements palettes and sits to the right of the main screen in the Editor workspace.

Photo Browser The Photo Browser or Organizer workspace is the main picture viewing, sorting and management area in Elements. Pictures can be imported into the Browser using the Get Photos command, viewed side by side with the Photo Compare command and seen as a slide show by selecting the Photo Review option.

Pixel Short for picture element, refers to the smallest image part of a digital photograph.

Q >>

Quantization Refers to the allocation of a numerical value to a sample of an analog image. Forms part of the digitizing process.

R >>

RGB All colors in the image are made up of a mixture of red, green and blue colors. This is the typical mode used for desktop scanners, painting programs and digital cameras.

S >>

Sponge tool Used for saturating or desaturating part of an image that is exaggerating or lessening the color component as opposed to the lightness or darkness.

Status bar Attached to the base of the window (Mac) or beneath the window (PC). Can be altered to display a series of items from Scratch Disk usage and file size to the time it took to carry out the last action or the name of the current tool.

Stock A printing term referring to the type of paper or card that the image or text is to be printed on.

Swatches In Elements, refers to a palette that can display and store specific individual colors for immediate or repeated use.

T >>

Thumbnail A low resolution preview version of larger image files used to check before opening the full version.

TIFF or **Tagged Image File Format** A file format that is widely used by imaging professionals. The format can be used across both Macintosh and PC platforms and has a lossless compression system built in.

W >>

Warp tool A means of creating differing distortions to pieces of text such as arcs and flag ripples.

Keyboard shortcuts

General >>

Action	*Windows*	*Macintosh*
Open a file	Ctrl + O	Command + O
Open file browser	–	Shift + Command + O
Close a file	Ctrl + W	Command + W
Save a file	Ctrl + S	Command + S
Step backward	Ctrl + Z	Command + Z
Step forward	Ctrl + Y	Command + Y
Free Transform	Ctrl + T	Command + T
Auto levels	Shift + Ctrl + L	Shift + Command + L
Auto contrast	Alt + Shift + Ctrl + L	Option + Shift + Command + L
Auto Color Correction	Shift + Ctrl + B	Shift + Command + B
Convert to Black and White	Alt + Ctrl + B	Option + Command + B
Hue/Saturation	Ctrl + U	Command + U
Levels	Ctrl + L	Command + L
Select All	Ctrl + A	Command + A
Apply last filter	Ctrl + F	Command + F
Show/Hide rulers	Shft + Ctrl + R	Command + R
Show/Hide selection	Ctrl + H	Command + H
Help	F1	Command + ?
Print Preview	Ctrl + P	Command + P
Exit Elements	Ctrl + Q	Command + Q
Deselect	Ctrl + D	Command + D
Feather a selection	Alt + Ctrl + D	Option + Command + D

Viewing >>

Action	Windows	Macintosh
Fit image on screen	Ctrl + 0	Command + 0
100% magnification	Alt + Ctrl + 0	Option + Command + 0
Zoom in	Ctrl + +	Command + +
Zoom out	Ctrl + -	Command + -
Scroll image with Hand tool	Spacebar + drag mouse pointer	Spacebar + drag mouse pointer
Scroll up or down 1 screen	Page Up or Page Down	Page Up or Page Down

Selection/Drawing tools >>

Action	Windows	Macintosh
Add to an existing selection	Shift + Selection tool	Shift + Selection tool
Subtract from an existing selection	Alt + Selection tool	Command + Selection tool
Constrain Marquee to square or circle	Shift + drag Selection tool	Shift + drag Selection tool
Draw Marquee from center	Alt + drag Selection tool	Option + drag Selection tool
Constrain Shape tool to square or circle	Shift + drag Shape tool	Shift + drag Shape tool
Draw Shape tool from center	Alt + drag Shape tool	Option + drag Shape tool
Exit Cropping tool	Esc	Esc
Enter Cropping tool selection	Enter	Return
Switch Magnetic Lasso to Lasso	Alt + drag tool	Option + drag tool
Switch Magnetic Lasso to Polygonal Lasso	Alt + drag tool	Option + drag tool
Switch from Selection to Move tool	Ctrl (except Hand tool is selected)	Command

Painting >>

Action	Windows	Macintosh
Change to Eyedropper	Alt + painting or Shape tool	Option + painting or Shape tool
Cycle through blending modes	Shift + + or -	Shift + + or -
Set exposure or opacity for painting	Painting tool + Number key (%= number key × 10)	Painting tool + Number key (%= number key × 10)
Display Fill dialog box	Shift + Backspace	Shift + Delete
Perform Fill with background color	Ctrl + Backspace	Command + Delete
Change Brush tip size	[to decrease size] to increase size	[to decrease size] to increase size
Change Brush tip hardness	Shift + [to decrease hardness Shift +] to increase hardness	Shift + [to decrease hardness Shift +] to increase hardness

Type editing >>

Action	Windows	Macintosh
Select word	Double-click	Double-click
Select line	Triple-click	Triple-click
Decrease font size by 2 points/pixels	Selected text + Shift + <	Selected text + Shift + <
Increase font size by 2 points/pixels	Selected text + Shift + >	Selected text + Shift + >

Elements/Photoshop feature equivalents

Activity	Elements	Photoshop
Lighten shadow areas in an image	Fill Flash feature (ver. 1.0/2.0), Shadows/Highlights (ver. 3.0 – 7.0) Adjust Color Curves (ver. 5.0 – 7.0)	Curves and Shadow/Highlight feature
Darken highlight areas in an image	Backlighting feature (ver. 1.0/2.0), Shadows/Highlights (ver. 3.0 – 7.0) Adjust Color Curves (ver. 5.0 – 7.0)	Curves and Shadow/Highlight feature
Transformation	Image > Transform	Edit > Transform
Rotate layer	Image > Rotate > Layer 90° left	Edit > Transform > Rotate 90° CCW
Rotate canvas	Image > Rotate > 90° left	Image > Rotate Canvas > 90° CW
Resize image	Image > Resize > Image Size	Image > Image Size
Resize canvas	Image > Resize > Canvas Size	Image > Canvas Size
Batch dialog	File > Batch Processing or File > Process Multiple Files	File > Automate > Batch
Web Photo Gallery	File > Create Web Photo Gallery or Create>HTML Photo Gallery	File > Automate > Web Photo Gallery
Contact Sheet	File > Print Layouts > Contact Sheet or File > Process Multiple Files	File > Automate > Contact Sheet II
Picture Package	File > Print Layouts > Picture Package or File > Process multiple Files	File > Automate > Picture Package
Auto Levels	Enhance > Auto Levels	Image > Adjustments > Auto Levels
Auto Contrast	Enhance > Auto Contrast	Image > Adjustments > Auto Contrast
Auto Color Correction	Enhance > Auto Color Correction	Image > Adjustments > Auto Color
Hue/Saturation	Enhance > Adjust Color > Hue/Saturation	Image > Adjustments > Hue/Saturation
Color Variations	Enhance > Adjust Color > Color Variations	Image > Adjustments > Variations
Brightness/Contrast	Enhance > Adjust Brightness/Contrast > Brightness/Contrast	Image > Adjustment > Brightness/Contrast
Levels	Enhance > Adjust Brightness/Contrast > Levels	Image > Adjustments > Levels

	Ctrl + O
...ser	Shift + Ctrl + O
	Ctrl + W
	Ctrl + S
...rd	Ctrl + Z
...d	Ctrl + Y
...orm	Ctrl + T
	Shift + Ctrl + L
	Alt + Shift + Ctrl + L
...rast	Shift + Ctrl + B
...or Correction	Ctrl + U
...uration	Ctrl + L
	Ctrl + A
...All	Ctrl + F
...last filter	Ctrl + R
.../Hide rulers	Ctrl + H
.../Hide selection	F1
	Ctrl + P
...t Preview	Ctrl + Q
...t Elements	Ctrl + D
...elect	Alt + Ctrl + D
...n selection	

Index